A

PLAIN INTRODUCTION

TO THE

CRITICISM OF THE NEW TESTAMENT.

Cambridge:
PRINTED BY C. J. CLAY, M.A.
AT THE UNIVERSITY PRESS.

A
PLAIN INTRODUCTION
TO THE
CRITICISM OF THE NEW TESTAMENT.

FOR THE USE OF BIBLICAL STUDENTS.

BY

FREDERICK HENRY SCRIVENER, M.A.

OF TRINITY COLLEGE, CAMBRIDGE.

RECTOR OF ST GERRANS, CORNWALL.

In templo Dei offert unusquisque quod potest: alii aurum, argentum, et lapides pretiosos: alii byssum et purpuram et coccum offerunt et hyacinthum. Nobiscum benè agitur, si obtulerimus pelles et caprarum pilos. Et tamen Apostolus contemtibiliora nostra magis necessaria judicat.—HIERONYMI *Prologus Galeatus.*

CAMBRIDGE:
DEIGHTON, BELL, AND CO.
LONDON: BELL AND DALDY.
1861.

ADVERTISEMENT.

The following pages are chiefly designed for the use of those who have no previous knowledge of the Textual Criticism of the New Testament; but since the Author has endeavoured to embody in them the results of very recent investigations, he hopes that they may prove of service to more advanced students. He asks the reader's indulgence for the annexed list of *Addenda et Corrigenda*, both by reason of the peculiar character of his work, and the remoteness of West Cornwall from Public Libraries. He might easily have suppressed the greater part of them, but that he has honestly tried to be accurate, and sees no cause to be ashamed of what Porson has well called "the common lot of authorship." He has only to add that he has not consciously borrowed from other writers without due acknowledgement, and to return his best thanks to the Rev. H. O. Coxe for important aid in the Bodleian, and to Henry Bradshaw Esq., Fellow of King's College, for valuable instruction respecting manuscripts in the University Library at Cambridge.

Falmouth, *September*, 1861.

ADDENDA ET CORRIGENDA.

Page 7, l. 31, *for* 16 *read* 20.

p. 12, last line but one, *for* Acts xiv. *read* Acts xvi.

p. 14, note, *add:* Yet Cod. Augiensis (F) reads $\overline{\kappa\rho\nu}$ 1 Cor. ix. 1.

p. 27, l. 17, *read* hieroglyphics.

pp. 27, 28, Cod. Friderico-August. is Plate I. No. 3, Cod. Alexandrin. Plate I. No. 2.

p. 29, n. 1, *phi* has the same lozenge shape in Cod. Bezae, p. 34, l. 13, and elsewhere.

p. 30, l. 25, and p. 35, l. 6, *for* p. 28 *read* p. 29.

p. 36, n. 2; p. 40 bis; p. 138, l. 8, *for* Sylvestre *read* Silvestre.

p. 37, l. 3, *for* Plate I. *read* Plate III.

p. 47, n.; p. 51, n. 2; p. 85, n. 2, *for* Horne II. *read* Horne IV.

p. 57, l. 21; p. 83, l. 39; p. 95, l. 1; p. 110, l. 5; p. 135, l. 30, *for* 1711 *read* 1710.

p. 85, n. 1, J. W. B. of the *Guardian* is now known to be the Rev. J. W. Burgon, M.A., Fellow of Oriel College, Oxford, whose delightful "*Letters to Home Friends*," are announced for republication. Mr Burgon has an unique and beautiful photograph of Act. i. 1—3? in Cod. B.

p. 90, n. 3, Mr Westcott kindly points out that Dr Dobbin is quoting Tregelles' *Lecture on the Historic Evidence of the N. T.*, p. 84.

p. 96, l. 34. Cod. Bezae is numbered Nn. II. 41 in the Catalogue of Manuscripts at Cambridge.

p. 99, l. 29. The letters in Cod. D, as a whole, are *larger* than in AB. Scrivener is engaged on a new edition of it, printed line for line in common Greek type, with Prolegomena, Notes and *fac-similes*, to be sold at a low price. He finds, by recent experience, that Kipling's accuracy is over-stated in pp. 98, 99.

p. 106, l. 33. *Add after* "canons": *τίτλοι* and the larger *κεφάλαια* in red (those of St John being lost): the church-notes seem *primâ manu*. Each member in the genealogy in Luke iii. forms a separate line, as in Cod. B, (*see* p. 87).

p. 110, l. 23: *add:* Another *facsimile* is given in Silvestre, No. 76. Cod. M contains Eusebius' letter to Carpianus, a note in Slavonic, and others in a contemporaneous cursive hand.

p. 115, ll. 16—24 is obviously the same fragment as N^b, p. 111, one of the most difficult to read I ever examined.

p. 121, l. 6, *for* less *read* greater.

p. 123, l. 14. I now observe that Hug (*Introd.* I. 283, Wait) divides the kindred Cod. G of St Paul into *στίχοι* on the same plan.

p. 126, l. 37. Cod. Zacynthius is just announced as ready (Sept. 1861). See also p. 347, l. 32.

p. 137, l. 40, *for* de *read* des.

p. 142. Cod. 1 was *formerly* numbered B. VI. 27 at Basle.

p. 149, l. 1. Elsewhere (except in p. 150, l. 5; p. 152, l. 3) more correctly called by its modern name the *University* Library.

p. 158, Cod. 124, *for* Nessel 118, *read* Nessel 188.

p. 170, Cod. 311, *for* Reg. 303, *read* Reg. 203.

p. 182, l. 20, *for* 187, *read* 181.

p. 185, l. 12, *for* Psaltery *read* Psalter.

p. 187, Act. 4. *Insert* X *between* B *and* 20.

p. 188, Act. 20. *Add:* 4°, the Pauline Epistles precede the Acts and Catholic Epp. (*see* p. 61). One leaf is lost in Hebr. (Casley) and the manuscript is quite illegible in parts.

p. 188, Act. 21. *Add* (Wetstein).

p. 192, l. 24, Act. 72. *For* 97 *read* 96.

p. 193, Act. 102. *See* p. 225 note, where the error is corrected.

p. 197, Act. 178 is now Middle Hill 1461, Apoc. m.^{scr}.

p. 203, Paul 119, *prefix an asterisk to this Codex.*

p. 206, Paul 213. From the reading (*τοῦ θεοῦ καὶ πατρὸς τοῦ χριστοῦ*) in Coloss. ii. 2 it is pretty clear that this is one of the 22 Barberini manuscripts mentioned in p. 157, Evan. 112.

p. 208. l. 34, Apoc. 41 *is* Alexandrino-Vat. 68, *not* 69.

p. 223, Apost. 2. *Add:* The lessons exactly correspond with those in our list (pp. 68—74): five of the Saints' day lessons are from the Catholic Epistles. This codex is written in a fine bold hand with red musical notes.

p. 224, Apost. 44, 45 are respectively BB and CC of Missy, but 1633, 1634 of his Sale Catalogue.

p. 272, l. 31. *Spell* Giorgi *to be uniform with* p. 116, l. 12, and p. 273, l. 7.

p. 274, l. 20. Dean Ellicott (*Philipp. &c.*) marks an Arian tinge in the rendering of Phil. ii. 6—8 in the Gothic, which he praises as usually accurate and faithful.

p. 278, l. 20, &c. Ellicott, speaking from personal experience, "cannot in any way agree" with Tregelles' estimate of the Æthiopic, adding "in St Paul's Epistles I have found it any thing but *the dreary paraphrase* which he terms it" (*Philipp.* &c. Preface, p. viii. n. 2). On this point I can only record the contradictory judgments of others.

p. 306, l. 11, Luke xix. 4: *add* E² *after* B.

p. 310, l. 39. I observe that Kuenen (*N. T. ad fidem Cod. Vatican.* Praef. p. li.) cites Æschyl. *Suppl.* 391 for κρῖμα, but adds "apud Nonnum a Stephano laudatum εἰς κρίμα δισσὸν ἔβην. Hinc sequitur scriptores N. T. omnes aequalium consuetudinem secutos κρίμα dixisse." But how was Nonnus [v] an *aequalis* of the sacred writers?

p. 319, l. 6. *Spell* Gerhard à Mästricht, *uniformly with* p. 152, l. 36.

p. 329, l. 2. *Read* and *facsimiles* of Manuscripts (twenty-nine in all), the whole being &c.

p. 330, l. 17, *for* Wilkin's *read* Wilkins'.

p. 340, l. 12. *Read* one of the most celebrated philologists.

p. 400, l. 39. *Insert* Since *before* Dean Alford.

p. 425, l. 18. *For* καὶ *read* και. The few stops are *inserted* for the reader's convenience.

p. 431, l. 23, *for* vv. 9—12 *read* vv. 9—20.

Postscript. We have not named in the body of this work the papyrus fragments of St Matthew and St James, said to have been unrolled by M. Simonides, and now in the possession of Mr Mayer of Liverpool, to which a marvellous date has been assigned. When *facsimiles* shall have been published and studied and compared with the originals, we shall be better able than at present to estimate their value.

I have reserved till this place the corrections to Dr Bloomfield's list of manuscripts, collated or inspected by him, which renewed examination has enabled me to make. My venerated friend has not distinguished in his Catalogue between the Harleian and Additional codices in the British Museum.

p. 186. Addl. 14774, *add:* A splendid copy, 4°, κεφ. *t* (red or gold), κεφ., τίτλοι, *Am.*, *Eus.* (often omitted), *men.*, *lect.*, with illuminations (cost £84).

Ibid. Addl. 15581, *add:* 12° neat, with leaves misbound. *Am.*, *Eus.* (mostly omitted), *lect.* secundâ manu, the Latin chapters later still.

Ibid. Addl. 16184, *add:* except the Apocalypse, in the usual *Greek* order (*see* p. 61), preceded by liturgical matter on paper and vellum, 37 or 38 lines on a small 4° page. The gospels have κεφ. *t.*, *prol.*, κεφ., τίτλοι (*rubro*, almost obliterated), *Am.* (not *Eus.*), *lect.*, the Epistles *prol.*, κεφ. *t*, Euthalian τίτλοι, *lect.*, with full *syn.*, and other matter at the end.

Ibid. Addl. 17469, 17741 are wrongly set down by Bloomfield as 17467, 17740 respectively.

p. 187. Addl. 18211, *add:* with 12 leaves *chart.* [xv] to fill up hiatus, κεφ. *t*, τίτλοι, *Am.* (not *Eus.*), some *lect.*, from Patmos. F. V. J. Arundell, British Chaplain at Smyrna (1834), describes this copy, given him by Mr Borrell, and a Lectionary sold to him at the same time, in his "*Discoveries in Asia Minor*," Vol. II. p. 268. He there compares it with the beautiful Cod. Ebnerianus (Evan. 105), which it does not resemble in the least, being larger and far less elegant.

Ibid. Addl. 19387, *add:* 4°, in the Museum Catalogue [xiv].

Ibid. Addl. 19389, *add:* τίτλοι, *Am.* (not *Eus.*), *lect.*, elegantly written by Cosmas, a monk; bought of Simonides, 1853.

p. 207, l. 3. Codd. 5540, 5742 are neither Harl., nor Addl. I cannot set right these false references.

Ibid. l. 4. Addl. 19389 must mean 19388 [xiii or xiv], 4°, small but very neat, bought of Simonides, 1853. Here again the Pauline Epp. precede the Catholic (begins 2 Cor. xi. 25, ends 1 Pet. iii. 15), the Acts being absent. *Prol.*, *lect.*, Euthalian κεφ.

pp. 218, 219. Evst. 151 and 152 were also inspected by Bloomfield.

p. 223, l. 9. Cod. 536 is neither Harl. nor Addl., and I cannot explain the error. *Dele* Codd. 1575, 1577. Addl. 5153 is [xii or xi], 4°, 2 vol., *mut.*, in bad condition, with red musical notes, and some leaves supplied on paper and vellum. We have omitted Bloomfield's 5684 (Harl., not Addl.) as being Evan. G (*see* p. 106).

Ibid. Addl. 18212 [xii] 4°, much *mut.* at the end, with red musical notes and an older leaf from the Old Testament prefixed.

Ibid. Addl. 19460 [xiii] 4° small, is very coarsely written, imperfect, and in bad condition.

Ibid. Addl. 19993 [xiv] 4° small, *chart.*, damaged, but in a bold hand. At the beginning is an *Avertissment*, signed *G. Alefson*, which ends literally thus: "*Je l'ai acheté seulement pour le sauver des mains barbares qui allait le destruire intierement au prix de sch.* 15 *a Chypre, A.D.* 1851."

p. 225, l. 35. From our totals we must strike off two codices of St Paul and three Evangelistaria, which we cannot recognise, but 19388 must be added to the list of the *Catholic* Epistles; thus our total of known cursives is 1456.

CONTENTS.

CHAPTER I.

PAGE

PRELIMINARY CONSIDERATIONS. . . . 1

Various readings in the text of Holy Scripture might be looked for beforehand, §§ 1—3, pp. 1—3. They actually exist, § 4, p. 3. Sources of information on this subject numerous, § 5, p. 3. *Textual criticism* usually inapplicable to modern books, § 6, p. 4. Importance of this study, § 7, p. 5. Not difficult, § 8, p. 5. Its results not precarious, nor tending to unsettle Scripture, § 9, p. 6. Various readings classified and their sources traced, §§ 10, 11, pp. 7—16. Their extent, § 12, p. 17. General divisions of this whole work, § 13, p. 17.

CHAPTER II.

ON THE GREEK MANUSCRIPTS OF THE NEW TESTAMENT.

SECTION I.

Their general character 19

Authorities named, § 1, p. 19. Materials for writing, §§ 2, 3, pp. 20—2. *Palimpsests*, § 4, p. 22. Ornaments, § 5, p. 23. Ink, § 6, p. 23. Pens, § 7, p. 24. Shape of manuscripts, § 8, p. 24. Style of writing: *uncial* and *cursive* characters, § 9, p. 25. Principles for determining the date of writing, illustrated by examples and *facsimiles*, §§ 10, 11, pp. 27—38. Use of ι ascript or subscript, § 12, p. 38. Breathings and accents in manuscripts, § 13, p. 39. Punctuation, § 14, p. 42. Abbreviations, § 15, p. 43. *Stichometry*, § 16, p. 44. Correction or revision of manuscripts, § 17, p. 46. Ancient divisions of the New Testament, § 18. (1) Vatican, p. 47. (2) Tatian's, p. 48. (3) Ammonian, Eusebian, p. 50. (4), (5) Euthalian, &c. pp. 53, 54. Subscriptions to the various books, § 19, p. 54. Foreign matter in manuscripts of the N. T. § 20, p. 56. Table of divisions, ancient and modern, § 21, pp. 57, 58. Modern divisions, § 22, p. 58. Contents of N. T. manuscripts, § 23, p. 60. Order of the sacred books, § 24, p. 61. *Lectionaries* or Greek Service-books, § 25, p. 62. Notation and classes of manuscripts, § 26, p. 65.

APPENDIX TO SECT. I.

PAGE

Synaxarion and Menology, or tables of lessons read in the Greek Church daily throughout the year &c. . 68—75

SECTION II.

Description of Uncial Manuscripts of the Greek Testament. 76

Codex Sinaiticus, p. 76. Cod. Alexandrinus, p. 79. Cod. Vaticanus, p. 84. Cod. Ephraemi, p. 94. Cod. Bezae, p. 96. *Of the Gospels:* Cod. E. p. 103. Cod. F, p. 104. Cod. F^a, p. 105. Codd. G, H, p. 106. Codd. I, K, p. 107. Cod. L, p. 108. Cod. M, p. 109. Cod. N, p. 110. Cod. N^b, p. 111. Codd. O, O^a, O^b, O^c, O^d, O^e, p. 112. Codd. P, Q, p. 113. Codd. R, p. 114. Cod. S, p. 115. Codd. T, T^s, p. 116. Codd. U, V, W^a, p. 117. Codd. W^b, W^c, X, p. 118. Codd. Y, Z, p. 119. Cod. Γ, p. 121. Cod. Δ, p. 122. Codd. Θ, Λ, p. 124. Cod. Ξ, p. 126. Codd. Tischendorfiani, p. 127. *Of the Acts,* &c.: Cod. E, p. 128. Codd. G, H, p. 129. Cod. K, p. 130. *Of St Paul:* Cod. D, p. 130. Cod. E, p. 132. Cod. F, p. 133, Cod. G, p. 135. Cod. H, p. 137. Cod. M, p. 138. Cod. N^c, p. 140. *Of the Apocalypse:* Cod. B, p. 140.

SECTION III.

List and brief description of the Cursive Manuscripts of the Greek Testament 142

SECTION IV.

List and brief description of the Lectionaries or Manuscript Service-books of the Greek Church . . . 211

N.B. Index I. pp. 465—477, has been constructed to facilitate reference to the Manuscripts described in Sections II, III, IV.

CHAPTER III.

ON THE ANCIENT VERSIONS OF THE NEW TESTAMENT IN VARIOUS LANGUAGES 226

Use in criticism and classification of versions, § 1, p. 226. Cautions respecting their employment, § 2, p. 227. Syriac versions, § 3: (1) Peshito, p. 229. (2) Curetonian, p. 236. (3) Philoxenian, p. 241. (4) Jerusalem, p. 245. (5), (6) Minor Syriac versions, p. 246. Specimens of each, p. 248. Latin versions, § 4: (1) Old Latin, p. 252. (2) Vulgate, p. 260. Specimens of each, p. 267. Egyptian versions, § 5, p. 270: (1) Memphitic, p. 271. (2) The-

PAGE

baic, p. 272. (3) Basmuric, p. 273. Gothic version, § 6, p. 274. Armenian, § 7, p. 276. Æthiopic, § 8, p. 277. Georgian, § 9, p. 279. Slavonic, § 10, p. 280. Anglo-Saxon, § 11, p. 280. Frankish, § 12, p. 280. Persic, § 13, p. 281. Arabic, § 14, p. 281.

CHAPTER IV.

ON THE CITATIONS FROM THE GREEK NEW TESTAMENT MADE BY EARLY ECCLESIASTICAL WRITERS . . . 283

Critical use of such quotations, § 1, p. 283. Obstacles to their application, § 2, p. 284. State of this branch of the subject, § 3, p. 285. Dated list of chief ecclesiastical writers, § 4, p. 286.

CHAPTER V.

ON THE EARLY PRINTED, AND LATER CRITICAL EDITIONS OF THE GREEK NEW TESTAMENT 288

First printed portions of N. T. p. 288. Complutensian Polyglott, § 1, p. 288. Erasmus' editions, § 2, p. 294. Aldus', &c. § 3, p. 298. Robert Stephens', § 4, p. 299. Early editions compared in St James' Epistle, p. 301. Beza's editions, § 5, p. 302. Elzevirs', § 6, p. 303. Full collation of Stephens 1550, Beza 1565, Elzevir 1624, &c. pp. 304—311. The London Polyglott, § 7, p. 312. Curcellaeus' and Bp. Fell's editions, § 8, p. 313. Mill's, § 9, p. 315. Kuster's, p. 318. Mästricht's N. T. § 10, p. 318. Bentley's projected edition, p. 319. Mace's, § 11, p. 321. Bengel's edition, p. 322. Wetstein's, § 12, p. 324. § 13, (1) Matthaei's, p. 327. (2) Alter's, p. 329. (3) Birch's edition, p. 330. Griesbach's, § 14, p. 332. Scholz's, § 15, p. 336. Lachmann's, § 16, p. 340. Tischendorf's, § 17, p. 344. Tregelles', § 18, p. 346. Postscript, p. 348.

Appendix to Chapter V.

Collation of the N. T. text in the Complutensian Polyglott 1514 *with that in Elzevir* 1624 349

CHAPTER VI.

ON THE LAWS OF INTERNAL EVIDENCE, AND THE LIMITS OF THEIR LEGITIMATE USE 369

Internal evidence distinguished from conjectural emendation, p. 369. Seven Canons discussed, pp. 371—7. In practice often opposed to each other, p. 377.

CHAPTER VII.

PAGE

ON THE HISTORY OF THE TEXT, INCLUDING A DISCUSSION OF RECENT VIEWS OF COMPARATIVE CRITICISM . . 379

Fate of the sacred autographs, § 1, p. 379. Heretical corruptions of Scripture, § 2, p. 381. Testimony of Irenaeus as to the state of the text, § 3, p. 382. That of Clement of Alexandria and of Origen, § 4, p. 384. Old Latin text and its corruptions, § 5, p. 385. State of the text in the fourth century —Eusebius, § 6, p. 387. Relation of the Codex Sinaiticus to Eusebius' and other ancient texts, § 7, p. 388. Testimony of Jerome, § 8, p. 389. Hug's theory of Recensions, § 9, p. 391. *Comparative Criticism* defined: its objects and true process, § 10, p. 393. The text of Scripture should be settled from the use of *all* available evidence, § 11, p. 396. Scheme of Tregelles, § 12, p. 396. Its advantages and defects: Dean Alford's view, § 13, p. 398. Various readings examined in Luke viii. 30—x. 25, § 14, p. 400. Results of their analysis, § 15, p. 403. Inferences, § 16, p. 404. Internal character of later codices, § 17, p. 406. Three practical rules stated, § 18, p. 408. Results of an analysis of the readings of Codd. R (PQ), § 19, p. 409. *Note on Cowper's edition of Cod. Alexandrinus*, p. 409.

CHAPTER VIII.

ON THE PECULIAR CHARACTER AND GRAMMATICAL FORM OF THE DIALECT OF THE NEW TESTAMENT . . . 412

Origin and character of this dialect, §§ 1—3, p. 412. The "attached" ν, § 4, p. 413. Orthography of Proper Names, § 5, p. 414. Peculiar grammatical forms, § 6, p. 415. Dialectic varieties, § 7, p. 417. Mere barbarisms inadmissible on any evidence, § 8, p. 418.

CHAPTER IX.

APPLICATION OF THE FOREGOING MATERIALS AND PRINCIPLES TO THE CRITICISM OF SELECT PASSAGES OF THE N. T. . 419

Explanation, p. 419. (1) Matthew i. 18...p. 419. (2) Matth. vi. 13...p. 421. (3) Matth. xix. 17...p. 422. (4) Matth. xx. 28...p. 425. (5) Matth. xxi. 28—31...p. 426. (6) Matth. xxvii. 35...p. 428. (7) Mark xvi. 9—20...p. 429. (8) Luke vi. 1...p. 433. (9) Luke xxii. 43—4...p. 434. (10) John i. 18... p. 436. (11) John v. 3, 4...p. 438. (12) John vii. 53—viii. 12...p. 439. (13) Acts viii. 37...p. 443. (14) Acts xv. 34...p. 444. (15) Acts xx. 28...p. 444. (16) Romans v. 1...p. 447. (17) 1 Corinth. xiii. 3...p. 448. (18) Philipp. ii. 1...p. 449. (19) Coloss. ii. 2...p. 450. (20) 1 Tim. iii. 16...p. 452. *Reading of Cod. Alex.* p. 453 n. (21) 1 Peter i. 23...p. 456. (22) 1 Peter iii. 15... p. 456. (23) 1 John ii. 23...p. 456. (24) 1 John v. 7, 8...p. 457. (25) Apoc. xiii. 10...p. 463. Conclusion, p. 464.

INDEX I.

PAGE

OF ALL GREEK MANUSCRIPTS OF THE NEW TESTAMENT, ARRANGED ACCORDING TO THE COUNTRIES WHEREIN THEY ARE NOW DEPOSITED 465

INDEX II.

OF THE PRINCIPAL PERSONS AND SUBJECTS REFERRED TO IN THIS VOLUME 478

INDEX III.

OF THE TEXTS OF THE NEW TESTAMENT ILLUSTRATED OR REFERRED TO IN THIS VOLUME 488

DESCRIPTION OF THE CONTENTS OF THE TWELVE LITHOGRAPHED PLATES.

N.B. The dates are given within brackets: thus [VI] means writing of the sixth century of the Christian aera. For abridgements in the ancient writing, *see* p. 43.

PLATE I. Three alphabets selected from (1) the ROSETTA STONE (*see* p. 27) [B.C. 196], (2) the COD. ALEXANDRINUS [V], (3) the COD. SINAITICUS [IV], with HN abridged at the end (*see* p. 78), from Tischendorf's *facsimile* of Luke xxiv.
[(2), (3) are wrongly numbered (3) (2), pp. 27, 28.]

PLATE II. Similar alphabets from (4) the COTTON FRAGMENT N (*see* p. 110), Titus C. xv [VI], and (5) from COD. NITRENSIS R (*see* p. 114), B. M. Add. 17211.

PLATE III. Similar alphabets from (6) COD. DUBLINENSIS Z (*see* p. 119), (7) COD. HARLEIAN. 5598 [*dated* 995], *see* p. 218. (8. c) COD. BURNEY 19 [wrongly assigned to Plate I. in p. 37, l. 3], *see* p. 179 [X]. Above *psi* in (7) stands the crosslike form of that letter in Apoc. Cod. B [VIII]: *see* p. 141.

PLATE IV. (9) Extract from HYPERIDES' Λόγος ἐπιτάφιος (Babington, 1858), dating from B.C. 100 to A.D. 100, on Egyptian papyrus, in a running hand (*see* p. 36). λ̊υντασ πνα των πο|λιτων ααικωσ δεο|μαι υμων και ετωι|και αντιβολωι κε|λευσαι καμε καλεσαι|τους συνερουντασ >: *see* pp. 38, 44. (10) Extract from PHILODEMUS περὶ κακιῶν (*Herculanensium voluminum quae supersunt*, fol., Vol. III. Col. xx. l. 6: *see* p. 29). ουτωσ πολυμαθεστατον προσ|αγορευομενον οιεται παντα|

δυνασθαι γινωσκειν και ποι|ειν ουχ οιον εαυτον οσ ενιοισ|ουδεν τι φωραται κατεχων | και ου συνορων οτι πολλα δει|ται τριβησαν και απο τησ αυ|τησ γινηται μεθοδου καθα|περ τα τησ ποιητικησ μερη και | διοτι περι τουσ πολυμαθεισ| (11. a) Cod. Friderico-August. [iv], 2 Sam. vii. 10, 11, Septuagint. *σεαυτον καθωσ αρ|χησ και αφ ημερω̄|ων εταξα κριτασ|επι τον λαον μου|ισ̄λ και εταπινω|σα απαντασ τους|εχθρουσ σου και|αυξησω σε και οι|*: *see* pp. 43, 44, 78. (11. b). Cod. Sinaiticus ℵ [iv] Luke xxiv. 33 *τη ωρα ὑπεστρε|ψαν εισ ἱερουσα|λημ και ευρον η|θροισμενουσ τουσ| ενδεκα και τουσ|συν αυτοισ λεγο̄|*: *see* pp. 28, 30 note. There are no large or capital letters in this Plate.

Plate V. (12) Cod. Alexandrin. A [v] Gen. i. 1—2, Septuagint. These four lines are in bright red, with breathings and accents: *see* pp. 39—40, 391 note. Henceforth capital letters begin to appear. *Ἐν ἀρχῆ ἐπόιησεν ὁ θ̄σ τὸν ὀυ|ρανὸν και τῆν γῆν ἡ δὲ γῆ ῆν ἀό|ρατοσ κὰι ἀκατασκεύαστοσ· | καὶ σκότοσ ἐπάνω τῆσ αβύσσου.|* (13) *Ibid.* Act. xx. 28, in common ink: *see* p. 447. *Προσεχετε εαυτοισ και παντι τω | ποιμνιω· εν ω ὑμασ το π̄ν̄α το | αγιον εθετο επισκοπουσ· | ποιμαινειν την εκκλησιαν| του κ̄ῡ ην περιεποιησατο δια|του αιματος του ιδιου·|* (14) Cod. Cotton. Titus C. xv. N of the Gospels [vi], *see* pp. 110, 111, and for the Ammonian section and Eusebian canon in the margin, p. 53. John xv. 20. *του λογου ου | εγω ειπον ὑ|μιν· ουκ εστιν| δουλοσ μιζω̄ | του κ̄ῡ αυτου.*

Plate VI. (15) Cod. Burney 21 [*dated* 1292], *see* pp. 37 and note 2, 180. John xxi. 17, 18. *πρόβατά μου· ἀμὴν ἀμὴν λέγω σοι· | ὅτε ῆσ νεώτεροσ, ἐζώννϋεσ ἑ|αυτὸν· καὶ περιεπάτησ ὅπου ἤθε|λεσ· ὅταν δὲ γηράσησ, ἐκτενεῖσ|* (16) Cod. Arundel 547, Evangelistar. [ix], *see* pp. 42, 220. The open work indicates stops and musical notes in red. John viii. 13. *Αυτω οἱ φαρισᾶι|οι + σὺ περὶ σὲαυτοῦ| μαρτυρεῖσ ἡ μαρ|τυρία σου· ὀυκ ἔσ|τιν ἀληθῆσ + ἀπε|* (17) Cod. Nitriensis, R of the Gospels, a palimpsest [vi]: *see* pp. 22, 114, and note 2. Luke v. 26. *ξαζον τον θ̄ν̄ | και επλησθη|σαν φοβου λε|γοντεσ οτι |.*

Plate VII. (18) Cod. Dublin, Z of the Gospels, a palimpsest [vi] from Barrett; *see* pp. 119—121. Matth. xx. 33, 34. *ανοιγωσιν οι οφθαλ|μοι ημων | Cπλαγχνισθεισ δε ο ῑσ̄ | ηψατο των ομματω̄ | αυτων και ευθεωσ|.* (19) Cod. Claromontanus, D of St Paul [vi], in a stichometrical form (*see* pp. 44—46), with the Greek and Latin in parallel columns (*see* p. 130), from Silvestre, *Paléographie Universelle*, No. 67. Tit. i. 8, 9. *μὴ ἀισχροκερδῆ | ἀλλὰ φιλόξενον | φιλαγαθον σώφρονα | δίκαιον ὅσιον | ἐνκρατῆ | ἀντεχόμενον ||* non turpilucrum | sed hospitalem | benignum sobrium | justum sanctum | continentem | adpectentem ||

Plate VIII. (20) Cod. Vatican. B [iv] Psalm i. 1—3, Septuagint, stichometrically arranged in two columns on the page (pp. 45, 86) from Silvestre, No. 60, a tolerable *facsimile*, but very inferior to the yet unpublished and unique photograph of Acts i. 1—3?, in the possession of the Rev. J. W. Burgon of Oriel. The numeral ᾱ in the upper margin may be *primâ manu*, the line above being thus found in the Herculanean rolls (*see* p. 43): for the bar, crosses, ornaments, and initial capital M see p. 87: the title (mis-spelt *ψααμοι*) is late, as may be seen from the shape of *μ*, which closely resembles those in Plate XI, No. 38. *μακάριοσ ἀνὴρ ὃσ ὀυκ ἐπορέυθη ἐν βουλῆ ἀσεβῶν | κὰι ἐν οδῶ ἀμαρτωλῶν ουκ έστη | κὰι ἐπι καθέδραν λοιμῶν ουκ ἐκαεισε̄ | ἀλλ ἡ ἐν τῶ νόμω κ̄ῡ τὸ εσλημα ἀυτῦ | κὰι ἐν τῶ νόμω ἀυτοῦ μελετήσε | ἡμέρας και νυκτὸσ | κὰι ἔσται ὡσ τὸ ξύλον τὸ πεφυτευ |* The breathings and accents are by a later hand (*see* p. 86), and most of the errors in spelling may fairly be imputed to Silvestre's artist. (21) COD. REGIUS 62 (L of the Gospels) [VIII], see pp. 108—109: retraced after Tregelles (*see* p. 37, note 1). John xii. 13, 14. + ὁ βασιλευσ τοῦ | ιη̅λ + | Ευρων δὲ ὁ ι̅σ̅· | ὀναριον εκαθει|σεν επ αυτο· κα|θωσ ἐστιν γεγρα | In the margin stand the greater κεφάλαιον ιδ (14, *see* p. 48), the Ammonian section ρα (101, *see* p. 50) and the Eusebian canon ζ (7, *see* p. 52). (22) COD. NANIANUS, U of the Gospels [IX or X], retraced after Tregelles. Mark vi. 18. Βάντοσ αυτου | ἐισ τὸ πλῶιō | παρεκάλει ἀυ|τὸν ὁ δαιμο|νισθεισ ἵνα |. For the margin see p. 117. (23) COD. BASIL. 1 of the Gospels [X], *see* pp. 37, 142, retraced after Tregelles. Matth. xv. 1, 2. Προσέρχονται αὐτῶι φαρισαῖοι καὶ γραμματεῖς | ἀπὸ ἱεροσολύμων. λέγοντεσ· διατί οἱ μαθη|ταί σου παραβαίνουσι τὴν παράδοσιν τῶν | πρεσβυτέρων· οὐ γὰρ νίπτονται τὰς χειρασ |.

PLATE IX. (24) COD. EPHRAEMI, C, a palimpsest [V] from Tischendorf's *facsimile: see* pp. 22, 94, 452. The upper writing [XII?] is τοῦ τὴν πληθῦν τῶν | ἐμῶν ἁμαρτημά || σομαι· οἶδα ὅτι μετὰ | τὴν γνῶσιν ἥμαρτον. translated from St Ephraem the Syrian. The earlier text is 1 Tim. iii. 15, 16. ωμα τησ αληθειασ· | Και ομολογουμενωσ μέγα ἐστιν το τησ ἐυσεβειασ μυ|'στηριον· θ̅σ̅ ἐφανερωθη εν σαρκι· εδικαιωθη ἐν πνῑ. For the accents &c. *see* p. 96. (25) COD. LAUD. 35, E of the Acts [VI] Latin *and* Greek, see pp. 128—129, in a sort of stichometry (p. 45). Act. xx. 28, regere | ecclesiam | domini || ποιμενειν | την εκκλησιαν | του κ̅υ̅ | Below are specimens of six letters taken from other parts of the manuscript.

(37) Matth. i. 1—3, Greek and Latin, from the Complutensian Polyglott, 1514: see pp. 288—294, especially p. 290.

PLATE X. (26) COD. BASIL., E of the Gospels [VIII] retraced after Tregelles, as are (27), (28), (29). See pp. 103—104, and for the stops p. 42. Luke xxii. 2, 3. Και ἐζήτουν οἱ ἀρχιέρεῖσ και οἱ | γραμματεῖσ, τὸ πῶσ ἀνέλω|σιν αὐτὸν, ἐφοβουντω γαρ | τὸν λαόν· εἰσῆλθεν δὲ σα | The Ammonian sections σξα, σξβ (261, 262) and Eusebian canon α (1) are in the margin. (27) COD. BOREELI, F of the Gospels [IX or X], *see* pp. 104, 105. Mark x. 13 (Ammonian section *only*, ρ̅ϛ̅ or 106). Καὶ προσέφερον | αὐτῶ παιδία | ἵν' ἅψηται ἀυ|τῶν· οἱ δὲ μαθη|τὰι ἐπετίμων |. (28) COD. HARLEIAN. 5684, G of the Gospels [X], *see* p. 106. Matth. v. 30, 31. βληθη· εισ γεεν|ναν· τε̂ τησ λ̅ε̅ [*see* p. 107]. | Ἐρρηθη δὲ· Ὅτι ὃσ | ἀν ἀπολυση την | γυναῖκα ἀυτοῦ· | ἀρ (ἀρχὴ) stands in the margin of the new lesson. (29) COD. CYPRIUS, K of the Gospels [IX], *see* pp. 107, 108. Luke xx. 9 (with the larger κεφάλαιον O or 70 in the margin). Γειν την παραβολην ταυτην ἀ̅ν̅ο̅σ̅ ἐφύτευ|σεν ἀμπελῶνα· καὶ ἐξέδοτο ἀυτὸν γεωργοῖσ· (8. b.) COD. BODLEIAN., Λ of the Gospels [X or IX], in *sloping* uncials, *see* pp. 36 note 1, 124. Luke xviii. 26, 27 and 30. σαντεσ· κὰι Τίσ, | δύναται σωθῆναι· | ὁ δὲ ι̅σ̅. εἶπεν· || τοῦτω· κὰι ἐν | τῶ ἀιῶνι τῶ ἐρ|χομένω ζωὴν |.

PLATE XI. (30) COD. WOLFII B, H of the Gospels [IX], *see* p. 106. John i. 38—40. τοὺσ ἀκολοθοῦντασ λέγει ἀυτοῖσ + τί ζη|τεῖτε + οἱ δε· εἶπον ἀυτῶ + ραββεί· ὃ λέγε|ται ἑρμηνευόμενον διδάσκαλε ποῦ μέ|νεισ + λέγει ἀυτοῖσ + ἐρχεσθε και ἴδετε + ἦλ |. Retraced after Tregelles, as is No. 31: in the originals of both codices the dark marks seen in our *facsimiles* are no doubt red musical notes. (31) COD. CAMPIANUS, M of the Gospels [IX], *see* pp. 109, 110. Matth. iii. 11. Ἐγῶ μὲν· βαπτίζω | ὑμᾶσ ἐν ὕδατι ἐισ | μετάνοιαν + ὁ δὲ ὀ | πίσω μου ἐρχόμε |. In the margin stand the Ammonian section ια (11), and the Eusebian canon α (1). (31. b)

COD. EMMAN. COLL. CANTAB. Act. 53, Paul. 30 [XII], *see* pp. 44, 191. This minute and elegant specimen, beginning Rom. v. 21, χ̅υ̅ τοῦ κ̅υ̅ ἡμων· and ending vi. 7, δεδικαίωται ἀ, is left to exercise the reader's skill. (38) COD. RUBER, M of St Paul [X], *see* pp. 138—140. 2 Cor. i. 3—5. παρακλήσεωσ· ὁ παρακαλων | ἡμᾶσ ἐπὶ πάση Τῆι θλίψει. ἐισ τὸ | δύνασθαι ἡμᾶσ παρακαλεῖν | τοὺσ ἐν πάση θλίψει διὰ τῆσ πα|ρακλήσεωσ ἧσ παρεκαλούμε|θα ἀυτοὶ ὑπὸ τοῦ θ̅ῡ. ὅτι καθὼσ|. (8. a) COD. BODLEIAN., Γ of the Gospels [IX], *see* pp. 36 note 1, 121—122. Mark viii. 33, πιστραφεὶσ καὶ ἰδὼν τουσ μα|θητὰσ ἀυτοῦ. ἐπετίμησεν τῷ | πέτρω λέγων. ὕπαγε ὀπίσω μȣ |.

PLATE XII. (32) PARHAM. 18 Evangelistarium [*dated* 980], *see* pp. 37 note 3, 220. Luke ix. 34. γοντοσ ἐγένετο νε|φέλη κὰι ἐπεσκίασεν | ἀυτοὺσ ἐφοβήθησᾱ. Annexed are six letters taken from other parts of the manuscript. (33) COD. MONACENSIS, X of the Gospels [IX], *see* pp. 118, 119: retraced after Tregelles, as also is (34). Luke vii. 25, 26. τίοισ ἠμφιεσμένον· ἴδου δι | ἐν ἱματισμῷ ἐνδόξω και τρυ|φῆ ὑπάρχοντεσ ἐν τοισ βασιλεί | οισ ἐισὶν· ἀλλα τί ἐξεληλυθα |. (34) COD. REGIUS 14, 33 of the Gospels, Paul. 17 [XI], *see* pp. 37, 145. Coloss. i. 24, 25. παθήμασιν ὑπερ ὑμῶν· καὶ ἀνταναπληρῶ τὰ 'ὑστερήματα των θλίψεων του χ̅υ̅ ἐν | τη σαρκί μου ὑπερ τοῦ σώματοσ ἀυτοῦ ὅ εστιν ἡ ἐκκλησία· ἧσ ἐγενόμηω ἐγὼ πᾶυλοσ διά |. (35) COD. LEICESTRENSIS, 69 of the Gospels, Paul. 37 [XIV], *see* pp. 24, 38, 151. 1 Tim. iii. 16. τῆς εὐσεβε(?)ίας μυστήρίον· ὁ θ̅ς̅ ἐφανερώθη ἐν σαρ|κί· ἐδικαιώθη ἐν πνεύματι· ὤφθη ἀγγέλοις· | ἐκηρύχθη ἐν ἔθνεσιν· ἐπις-εύθη ἐν κόσμω· ἀνελή— (36) COD. BURNEY 22, Evangelistar. [*dated* 1319], *see* pp. 38, 220. The Scripture text is Mark vii. 30. βεβλημέν ον ἐ|πὶ τὴν κλίνην κ̀ | τὸ δαιμόνιον ἐξε|λήλυθῶσ:—The subscription which follows is given at length in p. 38, note 1.

The reader will have observed throughout these specimens that the breathings and accents are usually attached to the *first* vowel of a diphthong.

INTRODUCTION TO THE CRITICISM

OF THE

TEXT OF THE NEW TESTAMENT.

CHAPTER I.

PRELIMINARY CONSIDERATIONS.

1. WHEN God was pleased to make known to man His purpose of redeeming us through the death of His Son, He employed for this end the general laws, and worked according to the ordinary course of His Providential government, so far as they were available for the furtherance of His merciful design. A revelation from heaven, in its very notion, implies supernatural interposition; yet neither in the first promulgation, nor in the subsequent propagation of Christ's religion, can we mark any *waste* of miracles. So far as they were needed for the assurance of honest seekers after truth, they were freely resorted to: whensoever the principles that move mankind in the affairs of common life were adequate to the exigences of the case, more unusual and (as we might have thought) more powerful means of producing conviction were withheld, as at once superfluous and ineffectual. Those who heard not Moses and the prophets would scarcely be persuaded, though one rose from the dead.

2. And as it was with respect to the *evidences* of our faith, so also with regard to the volume of Scripture. God willed that His Church should enjoy the benefit of His written word, at once as a rule of doctrine and as a guide unto holy living. For

this cause He so enlightened the minds of the Apostles and Evangelists by His Spirit, that they recorded what He had imprinted on their minds or brought to their remembrance, without the risk of error in anything essential to the verity of the Gospel. But this main point once secured, the rest was left, in a great measure, to themselves. The style, the tone, the language, perhaps the special occasion of writing, seem to have depended much on the taste and judgment of the several penmen. Thus in St Paul's Epistles we note the profound thinker, the great scholar, the consummate orator: St John pours forth the simple utterings of his gentle, untutored, affectionate soul: in St Peter's speeches and letters may be traced the impetuous earnestness of his noble yet not faultless character. Their individual tempers and faculties and intellectual habits are clearly discernible, even while they are speaking to us in the power and inspiration of the Holy Ghost.

3. Now this self-same parsimony in the employment of miracles which we observe with reference to Christian evidences and the inspiration of Scripture, we might look for beforehand, from the analogy of divine things, when we proceed to consider the methods by which Scripture has been preserved and handed down to us. God *might*, if He would, have stamped His revealed will visibly on the heavens, that all should read it there: He *might* have so completely filled the minds of His servants the Prophets and Evangelists, that they should have become mere passive instruments in the promulgation of His counsel, and the writings they have delivered to us have borne no traces whatever of their individual characters: but for certain causes that we can perceive, and doubtless for others beyond the reach of our capacities, He has chosen to do neither the one nor the other. And so again with the subject we propose to discuss in the present work; namely, the relation our existing text of the New Testament bears to that which originally came from the hands of the sacred penmen. Their autographs *might* have been preserved in the Church as the perfect standards by which all accidental variations of the numberless copies scattered throughout the world should be corrected to the end of time: but we know that these autographs perished utterly in the very infancy of Christian history. Or if it be too much to expect that the autographs of the inspired writers should escape the fate which has over-

taken that of every other known relique of ancient literature, God *might* have so guided the hand or fixed the devout attention of copyists during the long space of fourteen hundred years before the invention of printing, and of compositors and printers of the Bible for the last four centuries, that no jot or tittle should have been changed of all that was written therein. Such a course of Providential arrangement we must confess to be quite possible, but it could have been brought about and maintained by nothing short of a continuous, unceasing miracle: by making fallible men (nay, many such in every generation) for one purpose absolutely infallible. If the complete identity of all copies of Holy Scripture prove to be a fact, we must of course receive it as such, and refer it to its sole Author: yet we may confidently pronounce beforehand, that such a fact could not have been reasonably anticipated, and is not at all agreeable to the general tenour of God's dealings with us.

4. No one who has taken the trouble to examine any two editions of the Greek New Testament needs be told that this supposed complete resemblance of various copies of the holy books is *not* founded in fact. Even several impressions derived from the same standard edition, and professing to exhibit a text positively the same, differ from their archetype and from each other, in errors of the press which no amount of care or diligence has yet been able to get rid of. If we extend our researches to the manuscript copies of Scripture or of its versions which abound in every great library in Christendom, we see in the very best of them variations which we must at once impute to the fault of the scribe, together with many others of a graver and more perplexing nature, regarding which we can form no probable judgment, without calling to our aid the resources of critical learning. The more numerous and venerable the documents within our reach, the more extensive is the view we obtain of the variations (or VARIOUS READINGS as they are called) that prevail in manuscripts. If the number of these variations was rightly computed at thirty thousand in Mill's time, a century and a half ago, they must at present amount to at least fourfold that quantity.

5. As the New Testament far surpasses all other remains of antiquity in value and interest, so are the copies of it yet existing in manuscript and dating from the fourth century of our

æra downwards, far more numerous than those of the most celebrated writers of Greece or Rome. Such as have been already discovered and set down in catalogues are hardly fewer than two thousand; and many more must still linger unknown in the monastic libraries of the East. On the other hand, manuscripts of the most illustrious classic poets and philosophers are far rarer and comparatively modern. We have no complete copy of Homer himself prior to the thirteenth century, though some considerable fragments have been recently brought to light which may plausibly be assigned to the fifth century: while more than one work of high and deserved repute has been preserved to our times only in a single copy. Now the experience we gain from a critical examination of the few classical manuscripts that survive should make us thankful for the quality and abundance of those of the New Testament. These last present us with a vast and almost inexhaustible supply of materials for tracing the history, and upholding (at least within certain limits) the purity of the sacred text: every copy, if used diligently and with judgment, will contribute somewhat to these ends. So far is the copiousness of our stores from causing doubt or perplexity to the genuine student of Holy Scripture, that it leads him to recognise the more fully its general integrity in the midst of partial variation. What would the thoughtful reader of Æschylus give for the like guidance through the obscurities which vex his patience, and mar his enjoyment of that sublime poet?

6. In regard to modern works, it is fortunate that the art of printing has well nigh superseded the use of *verbal* or (as it has been termed) *Textual* criticism. When a book once issues from the press, its author's words are for the most part fixed, beyond all danger of change; graven as with an iron pen upon the rock for ever. Yet even in modern times, as in the case of Barrow's posthumous works and Lord Clarendon's History of the Rebellion, it has been occasionally found necessary to correct or enlarge the early editions, from the original autographs, where they have been preserved. The text of some of our older English writers (Beaumont and Fletcher's plays are a notable instance) would doubtless have been much improved by the same process, had it been possible; but the criticism of Shakespeare's dramas is perhaps the most delicate and difficult problem in the whole history of literature, since

that great genius was so strangely contemptuous of the praise of posterity, that even of the few plays that were published in his lifetime the text seems but a gathering from the scraps of their respective parts which had been negligently copied out for the use of the actors.

7. The design of the science of TEXTUAL CRITICISM, as applied to the Greek New Testament, will now be readily understood. By collecting and comparing and weighing the variations of the text to which we have access, it aims at bringing back that text, so far as may be, to the condition in which it stood in the sacred autographs; at removing all spurious additions, if such be found in our present printed copies; at restoring whatsoever may have been lost or corrupted or accidentally changed in the lapse of eighteen hundred years. We need spend no time in proving the importance of such a science, if it affords us a fair prospect of appreciable results, resting on grounds of satisfactory evidence. Those who believe the study of the Scriptures to be alike their duty and privilege, will surely grudge no pains when called upon to separate the pure gold of God's word from the dross which has mingled with it through the accretions of so many centuries. Though the criticism of the sacred volume is inferior to its right interpretation in point of dignity and practical results, yet it must take precedence in order of time: for how can we reasonably proceed to investigate the sense of holy writ, till we have done our utmost to ascertain its precise language?

8. The importance of the study of Textual criticism is sometimes freely admitted by those who deem its successful cultivation difficult, or its conclusions precarious; the rather as Biblical scholars of deserved repute are constantly putting forth their several recensions of the text, differing not a little from each other. Now on this point it is right to speak clearly and decidedly. There is certainly nothing in the nature of critical science which ought to be thought hard or abstruse, or even remarkably dry and repulsive. It is conversant with varied, curious, and interesting researches, which have given a certain serious pleasure to many intelligent minds; it patiently gathers and arranges those facts of *external* evidence on which alone it ventures to construct a revised text, and applies them according to rules or canons of *internal* evidence, whether sug-

gested by experience, or resting for their proof on the plain dictates of common sense. The more industry is brought to these studies, the greater the store of materials accumulated, so much the more fruitful and trustworthy the results have usually proved; although beyond question the true application even of the simplest principles calls for discretion, keenness of intellect, innate tact ripened by constant use, a sound and impartial judgment. No man ever attained eminence in this, or any other worthy accomplishment, without much labour and some natural aptitude for the pursuit; but the criticism of the Greek Testament is a field in whose culture the humblest student may contribute a little that shall be really serviceable; few branches of theology are able to promise even those who seek but a moderate acquaintance with it, so early and abundant reward for their pains.

9. Nor can Textual criticism be reasonably disparaged as tending to precarious conclusions, or helping to unsettle the text of Scripture. Even putting the matter on the lowest ground, critics have not *created* the variations they have discovered in manuscripts or versions. They have only taught us how to look ascertained phænomena in the face, and try to account for them; they would fain lead us to estimate the relative value of various readings, to decide upon their respective worth, and thus at length to eliminate them. While we confess that much remains to be done in this department of Biblical learning, we are yet bound to say that, chiefly by the exertions of scholars of the last and present generations, the debateable ground is gradually becoming narrower, not a few strong controversies have been decided beyond hope of reversal, and while new facts are daily coming to light, critics of very opposite sympathies are coming to agree better as to the right mode of classifying and applying them. But even were the progress of the science less hopeful than we believe it to be, one great truth is admitted on all hands;—the almost complete freedom of Holy Scripture from the bare suspicion of wilful corruption; the absolute identity of the testimony of every known copy in respect to doctrine, and spirit, and the main drift of every argument and every narrative through the entire volume of Inspiration. On a point of such vital moment I am glad to cite the well-known and powerful statement of the great

Bentley, at once the profoundest and the most daring of English critics: "The real text of the sacred writers does not now (since the originals have been so long lost) lie in any MS. or edition, but is dispersed in them all. 'Tis competently exact indeed in the worst MS. now extant; nor is one article of faith or moral precept either perverted or lost in them; choose as awkwardly as you will, choose the worst by design, out of the whole lump of readings." Or again: "Make your 30,000 [variations] as many more, if numbers of copies can ever reach that sum: all the better to a knowing and a serious reader, who is thereby more richly furnished to select what he sees genuine. But even put them into the hands of a knave or a fool, and yet with the most sinistrous and absurd choice, he shall not extinguish the light of any one chapter, nor so disguise Christianity, but that every feature of it will still be the same[1]." Thus hath God's Providence kept from harm the treasure of His written word, so far as is needful for the quiet assurance of His church and people.

10. It is now time for us to afford to the uninitiated reader some general notion of the nature and extent of the various readings met with in manuscripts and versions of the Greek Testament. We shall try to reduce them under a few distinct heads, reserving all formal discussion of their respective characters and of the authenticity of the texts we cite for a later portion of this volume (Chapter IX).

(1). To begin with variations of the gravest kind. In two, though happily in only two instances, the genuineness of whole passages of considerable extent, which are read in in our printed copies of the New Testament, has been brought into question. These are the weighty and characteristic paragraphs Mark xvi. 9—16 and John vii. 53—viii. 11. We shall hereafter defend these passages, the first without the slightest misgiving, the second to a high degree of probability, as entitled to be regarded authentic portions of the Gospels in which they stand.

(2). Akin to these omissions are several considerable interpolations, which though they have never obtained a place

[1] "Remarks upon a late Discourse of Free Thinking by Phileleutherus Lipsiensis," Part I. section 32.

in the printed text, nor been approved by any critical editor, are supported by authority too respectable to be set aside without some inquiry. One of the longest and best attested of these paragraphs has been appended to Matt. xx. 28, and has been largely borrowed from other passages in the Gospels (see below, class 9). It appears in several forms, slightly varying from each other, and is represented as follows in a document as old as the fifth century:

"But you, seek ye that from little things ye may become great, and not from great things may become little. Whenever ye are invited to the house of a supper, be not sitting down in the honoured place, lest should come he that is more honoured than thou, and to thee the Lord of the supper should say, Come near below, and thou be ashamed in the eyes of the guests. But if thou sit down in the little place, and he that is less than thee should come, and to thee the Lord of the supper shall say, Come near, and come up and sit down, thou also shalt have more glory in the eyes of the guests[1]."

(3). Again, a shorter passage or mere clause, whether inserted or not in our printed books, may have appeared originally in the form of a marginal note, and from the margin have crept into the text, through the wrong judgment or mere oversight of the scribe. Such we have reason to think is the history of 1 John v. 7, the verse relating to the three heavenly witnesses, once so earnestly maintained, but now pretty generally given up as spurious. Thus too Acts viii. 37 may have been derived from some Church Ordinal: the last clause of Rom. viii. 1 (*μὴ κατὰ σάρκα περιπατοῦσιν, ἀλλὰ κατὰ πνεῦμα*) is much like a gloss on *τοῖς ἐν Χριστῷ Ἰησοῦ*: *εἰκῇ* in Matt. v. 22 and *ἀναξίως* in 1 Cor. xi. 29 might have been inserted to modify statements that seemed too strong: *τῇ ἀληθείᾳ μὴ πείθεσθαι* Gal. iii. 1 is precisely such an addition as would help to round an abrupt sentence. Some critics would account in this way for the adoption of the doxology Matt. vi. 13; of the section relating to the bloody sweat Luke xxii. 43, 44; and of that remarkable verse, John v. 4: but we may well hesitate before we so far assent to their views.

[1] I cite from Canon Cureton's very literal translation in his "Remains of a very antient recension of the four Gospels in Syriac," in the Preface to which (pp. xxxv—xxxviii) is an elaborate discussion of the evidence for this passage.

(4). Or a genuine clause is lost by means of what is technically called Homœoteleuton (ὁμοιοτέλευτον), when the clause ends in the same word as closed the preceding sentence, and the transcriber's eye has wandered from the one to the other, to the entire omission of the whole passage lying between them. This source of error is familiar to all who are engaged in copying writing, and is far more serious than might be supposed, prior to experience. In 1 John ii. 23 ὁ ὁμολογῶν τὸν υἱὸν καὶ τὸν πατέρα ἔχει is omitted in many manuscripts, because τὸν πατέρα ἔχει had ended the preceding clause: it is not found in our commonly received Greek text, and even in the authorised English version is printed in italics. The whole verse Luke xvii. 36, though but slenderly supported, may possibly have been early lost through the same cause, since vv. 34, 35, 36 all end in ἀφεθήσεται. Thus perhaps we might defend in Matth. x. 23 the addition after φεύγετε εἰς τὴν ἄλλην of κἂν ἐν τῇ ἑτέρᾳ διώκωσιν ὑμᾶς, φεύγετε εἰς τὴν ἄλλην (ἑτέραν being substituted for the first ἄλλην), the eye having passed from the first φεύγετε εἰς τὴν to the second. The same effect is produced, though less frequently, when two or more sentences *begin* with the same words, as in Matth. xxiii. 14, 15, 16 (each of which commences with οὐαὶ ὑμῖν), one of the verses being lost in some manuscripts.

(5). Numerous variations occur in the order of words, the sense being slightly or not at all affected; on which account this species of various readings was at first much neglected by collators. Examples abound in every page: e.g. τὶ μέρος or μέρος τι Luke xi. 36; ὀνόματι Ἀνανίαν or Ἀνανίαν ὀνόματι Acts ix. 12; ψυχρὸς οὔτε ζεστὸς or ζεστὸς οὔτε ψυχρὸς Apoc. iii. 16. The order of the sacred names Ἰησοῦς Χριστὸς is perpetually changed.

(6). Sometimes the scribe has mistaken one word for another, which differs from it only in one or two letters. This happens chiefly in cases when the *uncial* or capital letters in which the oldest manuscripts are written resemble each other, except in some fine stroke which may have decayed through age. Hence in Mark v. 14 we find ΑΝΗΓΓЄΙΛΑΝ or ΑΠΗΓΓЄΙΛΑΝ; in Luke xvi. 20 ΗΛΚΩΜЄΝΟC or ЄΙΛΚΩΜЄΝΟC; so we read Δαυὶδ or Δαβὶδ indifferently, as, in the later or *cursive* character, β and υ have nearly the same shape. Akin to these errors of the eye are such transpositions as ЄΛΑΒΟΝ for ЄΒΑΛΟΝ or ЄΒΑΛΛΟΝ, Mark xiv. 65: omissions or insertions of the same or similar letters, as ЄΜΑϹϹΩΝΤΟ or ЄΜΑϹΩΝΤΟ Apoc. xvi. 10: ΑΓΑΛΛΙΑϹΘΗΝΑΙ or ΑΓΑΛΛΙΑ-ΘΗΝΑΙ John v. 35; ΠΡΟЄΛΘΩΝ or ΠΡΟϹЄΛΘΩΝ Matth. xxvi. 39; Mark xiv. 35: or the dropping or repetition of the same or a similar syllable, as ЄΚΒΑΛΛΟΝΤΑΔΑΙΜΟΝΙΑ or ЄΚΒΑΛΛΟΝΤΑΤΑΔΑΙΜΟΝΙΑ Luke ix. 49; ΟΥΔЄΔЄΔΟΞΑϹ-ΤΑΙ or ΟΥΔЄΔΟΞΑϹΤΑΙ 2 Cor. iii. 10; ΑΠΑΞЄΞЄΔЄΧЄΤΟ or ΑΠЄΞЄΔЄΧЄΤΟ 1 Peter iii. 20. It is easy to see how the ancient practice of writing uncial letters without leaving a space between the words must have increased the risk of such variations as the foregoing.

(7). Another source of error is described by some critics as proceeding *ex ore dictantis*, in consequence of the scribe writing from dictation, without having a copy before him. I am not, however, very willing to believe that manuscripts of the better class were executed on so slovenly and careless a plan. It seems more simple to account for the *itacisms*, or confusion of certain vowels and diphthongs having nearly the same sound, which exist more or less in manuscripts of every age, by assuming that a vicious pronunciation gradually led to a loose mode of orthography adapted to it. Certain it is that itacisms are much more plentiful in the original subscriptions and marginal notes of the writers of mediæval books, than in the text which they copied from older documents. Itacisms prevailed the most extensively from the eighth to the twelfth century, but not by any means during that period exclusively. In the most ancient manuscripts the principal changes are between ι and ει, αι and ε: in later times η ι and ει, η οι and υ, even ο and ω, η and ε are used almost promiscuously. Hence it arises that a very large portion of the various readings brought together by collators are of this description, and although in the vast majority of instances they serve but to illustrate the character of the manuscripts which exhibit them, or the fashion of the age in which they were written, they sometimes affect the grammatical form (e.g. ἔγειρε or ἔγειραι Mark iii. 3; Acts iii. 6; *passim:* ἴδετε or εἴδετε Phil. i. 30), or the construction (e.g. ἰάσωμαι or ἰάσομαι Matth. xiii. 15: οὐ μὴ τιμήσῃ or οὐ μὴ τιμήσει Matth. xv. 5: ἵνα καυθήσωμαι or ἵνα καυθήσομαι 1 Cor. xiii. 3, compare 1 Peter iii. 1), or even the sense (e.g. ἑταίροις or ἑτέροις Matth. xi. 16; μετὰ διωγμῶν or, as in a few copies, μετὰ διωγμὸν Mark x. 30; καυχᾶσθαι δὴ οὐ συμφέρει or καυχᾶσθαι δεῖ· οὐ συμφέρ. 2 Cor. xii. 1: ὅτι χρηστὸς ὁ Κύριος or ὅτι χριστὸς ὁ Κύριος 1 Peter ii. 3). To this cause we may refer the perpetual interchange of ἡμεῖς and ὑμεῖς, with their oblique cases, throughout the whole Greek Testament: e.g. in the single epistle 1 Peter i. 3; 12; ii. 21 *bis;* iii. 18; 21; v. 10.

(8). Introductory clauses or Proper Names are frequently interpolated at the commencement of Church-lessons (περικοπαὶ), whether from the margin of ordinary manuscripts of the Greek Testament (where they are usually placed for the convenience of the reader), or from the Lectionaries or proper Service Books, especially those of the Gospels (Evangelistaria). Thus in our English Book of Common Prayer the name of Jesus is introduced into the Gospels for the 14th, 16th, 17th and 18th Sundays after Trinity; and whole clauses into those for the 3rd and 4th Sundays after Easter, and the 6th and 24th after Trinity. To this cause is due the prefix εἶπε δὲ ὁ Κύριος Luke vii. 31; and καὶ στραφεὶς πρὸς τοὺς μαθητὰς εἶπε Luke x. 22; and such appellations as ἀδελφοὶ or τέκνον τιμόθεε (after σὺ δὲ in 2 Tim. iv. 5) in some copies of the Epistles. Hence the frequent interpolation (e.g. Matth. iv. 18; viii. 5; xiv. 22) or changed position (John i. 44) of Ἰησοῦς.

(9). A more extensive and perplexing species of various readings arises from bringing into the text of one (chiefly of the three earlier) Evangelists expressions or whole sentences which of right belong not to him, but to one or both the others. This natural tendency to assimilate the several Gospels must have been aggravated by the laudable efforts of Biblical scholars (beginning with Tatian's Διὰ τεσσάρων in the second century) to construct a satisfactory Harmony of them all. Some of these variations also may possibly have been mere marginal notes in the first instance. As examples of this class we will name εἰς μετάνοιαν interpolated from Luke v. 32 into Matth. ix. 13; Mark ii. 17: the prophetic citation Matth. xxvii. 35 ἵνα πληρωθῇ κ.τ.λ. to the end of the verse, unquestionably borrowed from John xix. 24: Mark xiii. 14 τὸ ῥηθὲν ὑπὸ Δανιὴλ τοῦ προφήτου, probably taken from Matth. xxiv. 15: Luke v. 38 καὶ ἀμφότεροι συντηροῦνται from Matth. ix. 17 (where ἀμφότεροι is the true reading): the whole verse Mark xv. 28 seems spurious, being received from Luke xxii. 37. Even in the same book we observe an anxiety to harmonise two separate narratives of the same event, as in Acts ix. 5, 6 compared with xxvi. 14, 15.

(10). In like manner transcribers sometimes quote passages from the Old Testament more fully than the writers of the New Testament had judged necessary for their purpose. Thus *ἐγγίζει μοι...τῷ στόματι αὐτῶν καὶ* Matth. xv. 8: *ἰάσασθαι τοὺς συντετριμμένους τὴν καρδίαν* Luke iv. 18: *αὐτοῦ ἀκούσεσθε* Acts vii. 37: *οὐ ψευδομαρτυρήσεις* Rom. xiii. 9: *καὶ κατέστησας αὐτὸν ἐπὶ τὰ ἔργα τῶν χειρῶν σου* Hebr. ii. 7: *ἢ βολίδι κατατοξευθήσεται* Hebr. xii. 20, are all open to suspicion as being genuine portions of the Old Testament text, but not also of the New.

(11). Synonymous words are often interchanged, and so form various readings, the sense undergoing some slight and refined modification, or else being quite unaltered. Thus *ἔφη* should be preferred to *εἶπεν* Matth. xxii. 37, where *εἶπεν* of the common text is supported only by one known manuscript, that at Leicester. Thus also *ὀμμάτων* is put for *ὀφθαλμῶν* Matth. ix. 29 by the Codex Bezæ at Cambridge. In Matth. xxv. 16 the evidence is almost evenly balanced between *ἐποίησεν* and *ἐκέρδησεν* (cf. *v.* 17). Where simple verbs are interchanged with their compounds (e.g. *μετρηθήσεται* with *ἀντιμετρηθήσεται* Matth. vii. 2; *ἐτέλεσεν* with *συνετέλεσεν ibid. v.* 28; *καίεται* with *κατακαίεται* xiii. 40), or different tenses of the same verb (e.g. *εἰληφὼς* with *λαβὼν* Acts xvi. 24; *ἀνθέστηκε* with *ἀντέστη* 2 Tim. iv. 15) there is usually some *internal* reason why one should be chosen rather than the other, if the *external* evidence on the other side does not greatly preponderate. When one of two terms is employed in a sense peculiar to the New Testament dialect, the easier synonym may be suspected of having originated in a gloss or marginal interpretation. Hence *cæteris paribus* we should adopt *δικαιοσύνην* rather than *ἐλεημοσύνην* in Matth. vi. 1; *ἐσκυλμένοι* rather than *ἐκλελυμένοι* ix. 36; *ἀθῶον* rather than *δίκαιον* xxvii. 4.

(12). An irregular, obscure, or incomplete construction will often be *explained* or *supplied* in the margin by words that are subsequently brought into the text. Of this character is *ἐμέμψαντο* Mark vii. 2; *δέξασθαι ἡμᾶς* 2 Cor. viii. 4; *γράφω* xiii. 2. Or an elegant Greek idiom may be transformed into simpler language, as Acts xiv. 3, *ᾔδεισαν γὰρ πάντες ὅτι Ἕλλην ὁ πατὴρ* αὐτοῦ ὑπῆρχεν for ᾔδεισαν γὰρ ἅπαντες τὸν πατέρα αὐτοῦ ὅτι Ἕλλην ὑπῆρχεν....On the other hand a Hebraism may be softened by transcribers, as in Matth. xxi. 23, where for ἐλθόντι αὐτῷ many MSS. prefer the easier ἐλθόντος αὐτοῦ before προσῆλθεν αὐτῷ διδάσκοντι: and in Matth. xv. 5; Mark vii. 12 (to which perhaps we may add Luke v. 35), where καὶ is dropped in some copies to facilitate the sense. This perpetual correction of harsh, ungrammatical, or Oriental constructions characterises the printed text of the Apocalypse and the recent MSS. on which it is founded (e.g. τὴν γυναῖκα Ἰεζαβὴλ τὴν λέγουσαν ii. 20, for ἡ λέγουσα).

(13). Hence too arises the habit of changing ancient dialectic forms into those in vogue in the transcriber's age. The whole subject will be more fitly discussed at length hereafter (Chapter VIII); we will here merely note a few peculiarities of this kind adopted by recent critics from the most venerable manuscripts, but which have gradually though not entirely disappeared in copies of lower date. Thus in the latest editions Καφαρναούμ, Μαθθαῖος, τέσσερες, ἕνατος are substituted for Καπερναούμ, Ματθαῖος, τέσσαρες, ἔννατος of the common text; οὕτως (not οὕτω) is used even before a consonant; ἤλθαμεν, ἤλθατε, ἦλθαν, γενάμενος are preferred to ἤλθομεν, ἤλθετε, ἦλθον, γενόμενος; ἐκαθερίσθη, συνζητεῖν, λήμψομαι to ἐκαθαρίσθη, συζητεῖν, λήψομαι; and ν ἐφελκυστικὸν as it is called is appended to the usual third persons of verbs, even though a consonant follow. On the other hand the more Attic περιπεπατήκει ought not to be converted into περιεπεπατήκει in Acts xiv. 8.

(14). Trifling variations in spelling, though very proper to be noted by a faithful collator, are obviously of little consequence. Such is the choice between καὶ ἐγὼ and κἀγώ, ἐὰν and ἄν, εὐθέως and εὐθύς, Μωυσῆς and Μωσῆς, or even πράττουσι and πράσσουσι, εὐδόκησα, εὐκαίρουν and ηὐδόκησα, ηὐκαίρουν. To this head may be referred the question whether ἀλλά, γε, δέ, τε, μετά, παρά &c. should have their final vowel elided or not when the next word begins with a vowel.

(15). A large portion of our various readings arises from the omission or insertion of such words as cause little appreciable difference in the sense. To this class belong the pronouns αὐτοῦ, αὐτῷ, αὐτῶν, αὐτοῖς, the particles οὖν, δέ, τε, and the interchange of οὐδὲ and οὔτε, as also of καὶ and δὲ at the opening of a sentence.

(16). Manuscripts greatly fluctuate in adding and rejecting the Greek article, and the sense is often seriously influenced by these variations, though they seem so minute. In Mark ii. 26 *ἐπὶ Ἀβιάθαρ ἀρχιέρεως* "in the time that Abiathar was high priest" would be historically incorrect, while *ἐπὶ Ἀβιάθαρ τοῦ ἀρχιέρεως* "in the days of Abiathar the high priest" is suitable enough. The article will often impart vividness and reality to an expression, where its presence is not indispensable: e.g. Luke xii. 54 *τὴν νεφέλην* is the peculiar cloud spoken of in 1 Kings xviii. 44 as portending rain. Bishop Middleton's monograph ("Doctrine of the Greek Article applied to the Criticism and Illustration of the New Testament"), even if its philological groundwork be thought a little precarious, will always be regarded as the text-book on this interesting subject, and is a lasting monument of intellectual acuteness and exact learning.

(17). Not a few various readings may be imputed to the peculiarities of the style of writing adopted in the oldest manuscripts. Thus ΠΡΟϹΤЄΤΑΓΜЄΝΟΥϹΚΑΙΡΟΥϹ Acts xvii. 26 may be divided into two words or three; ΚΑΙΤΑΠΑΝΤΑ *ibid.* *v.* 25, by a slight change, has degenerated into *κατὰ πάντα.* The habitual abridgement of such words as Θεὸς or Κύριος sometimes leads to a corruption of the text. Hence probably comes the grave variation ΟϹ for $\overline{\text{ΘϹ}}$ 1 Tim. iii. 16, and the singular reading *τῷ καιρῷ δουλεύοντες* Rom. xii. 11, where the true word *Κυρίῳ* was first shortened into $\overline{\text{ΚΡω}}$[1], and then read as ΚͅΡω, Κͅ being employed to indicate ΚΑΙ in very early times. Or a large initial letter, which the scribe usually reserved for a subsequent revision, may have been altogether neglected: whence we have *τι* for *Οτι* before *στενὴ* Matth. vii. 14. Or —, placed over a letter (especially at the end of a line) to denote *ν*, may have been lost sight of; e.g. *λίθον μέγα* Matth. xxvii. 60 in several copies, for ΜЄΓ$\overline{\text{Α}}$. It will be seen hereafter that as the earliest manuscripts have few marks of punctuation, breathing or accent, these points (often far from indifferent) must be left in a great measure to an editor's taste and judgment.

[1] Tischendorf indeed (Nov. Test. 1859) says, "ΚΥΡΙω omnino scribi solet $\overline{\text{Κω}}$," and this no doubt is the usual form, even in MSS. which have $\overline{χρω}$ $\overline{ιηυ}$, as well as $\overline{χω}$ $\overline{ιυ}$, for *χριστῷ ἰησοῦ*.

(18). Slips of the pen, whereby words are manifestly lost or repeated, mis-spelt or half-finished, though of no service to the critic, must yet be noted by a faithful collator, as they will occasionally throw light on the history of some particular copy in connection with others, and always indicate the degree of care or skill employed by the scribe, and consequently the weight due to his general testimony.

The great mass of various readings we have hitherto attempted to classify (to our *first* and *second* heads we will recur presently) are manifestly due to mere inadvertence or human frailty, and certainly cannot be imputed to any deliberate intention of transcribers to tamper with the text of Scripture. We must give a different account of a few passages (we are glad they are only a few) which yet remain to be noticed.

(19). The copyist may be tempted to forsake his proper function for that of a reviser, or critical corrector. He may simply omit what he does not understand (e. g. τὸ μαρτύριον 1 Tim. ii. 6), or may attempt to get over a difficulty by inversions and other changes. Thus the μυστήριον spoken of by St Paul 1 Cor. xv. 51, which rightly stands in the received text πάντες μὲν οὐ κοιμηθησόμεθα, πάντες δὲ ἀλλαγησόμεθα was easily varied into πάντες κοιμηθησόμεθα, οὐ π. δὲ ἀλ., as if in mere perplexity. From this source must arise the omission in a few manuscripts of υἱοῦ Βαραχίου in Matth. xxiii. 35; of Ἱερεμίου in Matth. xxvii. 9; the substitution of τοῖς προφήταις for Ἡσαΐᾳ τῷ προφήτῃ in Mark i. 2; perhaps of οὔπω ἀναβαίνω for οὐκ ἀναβαίνω in John vii. 8, and certainly of τρίτῃ for ἕκτῃ John xix. 14. The variations between Γεργεσηνῶν and Γαδαρηνῶν Matth. viii. 28, and between Βηθαβαρᾶ and Βηθανίᾳ John i. 28, have been attributed, we should hope unjustly, to the misplaced conjectures of Origen.

Some would impute such readings as ἔχωμεν for ἔχομεν Rom. v. 1; φορέσωμεν for φορέσομεν 1 Cor. xv. 49, to a desire on the part of copyists to *improve* an assertion into an ethical exhortation, especially in the Apostolical Epistles; but it is at once safer and more simple to regard them with Canon Wordsworth (N. T. 1 Cor. xv. 49) as instances of *itacism:* see class (7) above.

(20). Finally, whatever conclusion we arrive at respecting the true reading in the following passages, the discrepancy could hardly have arisen except from doctrinal preconceptions. Matth. xix. 17 *Τί με λέγεις ἀγαθόν; οὐδεὶς ἀγαθὸς εἰ μὴ εἷς, ὁ θεός·* or *Τί με ἐρωτᾷς περὶ τοῦ ἀγαθοῦ; εἷς ἐστὶν ὁ ἀγαθός*: John i. 18 *ὁ μονογενὴς υἱὸς* or *ὁ μονογενὴς θεός*: Acts xvi. 7 *τὸ πνεῦμα* with or without the addition of *Ἰησοῦ*: Acts xx. 28 *τὴν ἐκκλησίαν τοῦ Θεοῦ* or *τὴν ἐκκλησίαν τοῦ Κυρίου*: perhaps also Jude *v.* 4 *δεσπότην* with or without *Θεόν*. I do not mention Mark xiii. 32 *οὐδὲ ὁ υἱός*, as there is hardly any authority for its rejection now extant; nor Luke ii. 22, where *τοῦ καθαρισμοῦ αὐτῆς* of the Complutensian Polyglott and most of our common editions is supported by almost no evidence whatever.

11. It is very possible that some scattered readings cannot be reduced to any of the above-named classes, but enough has been said to afford the student some general notion of the nature and extent of the subject[1]. It may be reasonably thought that a portion of these variations, and those among the most considerable, had their origin in a cause which must have operated at least as much in ancient as in modern times, the changes gradually introduced after publication by the authors themselves into the various copies yet within their reach. Such revised copies would circulate independently of those issued previously, and now beyond the writer's control; and thus becoming the parents of a new family of copies, would originate and keep up diversities from the first edition, without any fault on the part of transcribers[2]. It is thus perhaps we may best account for the omission or insertion of whole paragraphs or verses in manuscripts of a certain class [see above (1), (2), (3)]; or, in cases where the work was in much request, for those minute touches and trifling improvements in words, in construction, in tone, or in the mere colouring of the style [(5), (11), (12)] which few authors can help attempting, when engaged on revising their favourite compositions.

[1] Dr Tregelles, to whose persevering labours in sacred criticism I am anxious, once for all, to express my deepest obligations, ranges various readings under three general heads:—*substitutions; additions; omissions.* I do not find, however, that an arrangement seemingly so simple enables the student to gain more distinct views of this complicated subject.

[2] This source of variations, though not easily discriminated from others, must have suggested itself to many minds, and is well touched upon by Isaac Taylor in his "History of the Transmission of Antient Books to modern times," 1827, p. 24.

12. The fullest critical edition of the Greek Testament hitherto published contains but a comparatively small portion of the whole mass of variations already known; as a rule the editors neglect, and rightly neglect, mere errors of transcription. Such things must be recorded for several reasons, but neither they, nor real various readings that are slenderly supported, can produce any effect in the task of amending or restoring the sacred text. Those who wish to see for themselves how far the common printed editions of what is called the "textus receptus" differ from the judgment of the most recent critics, may refer if they please to the small Greek Testament lately published in the series of "Cambridge Greek and Latin Texts[1]," which exhibits in a thicker type all words and clauses wherein Robert Stephens' edition of 1550 (which is taken as a convenient standard) differs from the other chief modifications of the *textus receptus* (viz. Beza's 1565 and Elzevirs' 1624), as also from the revised texts of Lachmann 1842—50, of Tischendorf 1859, and of Tregelles 1844, 1857. The student will thus be enabled to estimate for himself the limits within which the text of the Greek Testament may be regarded as still open to discussion, and to take a general survey of the questions on which the theologian is bound to form an intelligent opinion.

13. The work that lies before us naturally divides itself into three distinct parts.

I. A description of the sources from which various readings are derived (or of their EXTERNAL EVIDENCE), comprising

(*a*) Manuscripts of the Greek New Testament or of portions thereof (Chapter II).

(*b*) Ancient versions of the New Testament in various languages (Chapter III).

(*c*) Citations from the Greek Testament or its versions made by early ecclesiastical writers, especially by the Fathers of the Christian Church (Chapter IV).

(*d*) Early printed or later critical editions of the Greek Testament (Chapter V).

[1] "Novum Testamentum Textûs Stephanici A.D. 1550...curante F. H. Scrivener. Cantabr. 1860," 12mo.

2

II. A discussion of the principles on which external evidence should be applied to the recension of the sacred volume, embracing

(*a*) The laws of INTERNAL EVIDENCE, and the limits of their legitimate use (Chapter VI).

(*b*) The history of the text and of the principal schemes which have been proposed for restoring it to its primitive state, including recent views of Comparative Criticism (Chapter VII).

(*c*) Considerations derived from the peculiar character and grammatical form of the dialect of the Greek Testament (Chapter VIII).

III. The application of the foregoing materials and principles to the investigation of the true reading in the chief passages of the New Testament, on which authorities are at variance (Chapter IX).

It will be found desirable to read the following pages in the order wherein they stand, although the last two sections of Chap. II. and some portions elsewhere (indicated by being printed like them in smaller type) are obviously intended chiefly for reference.

CHAPTER II.

ON THE GREEK MANUSCRIPTS OF THE NEW TESTAMENT.

AS the extant Greek manuscripts of the New Testament supply both the most copious and the purest sources of Textual Criticism, we propose to present to the reader some account of their peculiarities in regard to material, form, style of writing, date and contents, before we enter into details respecting individual copies, under the several subdivisions to which it is usual to refer them.

SECTION I.

On the general character of Manuscripts of the Greek Testament.

1. The subject of the present section has been systematically discussed in the "Palaeographia Graeca" (Paris, 1708, folio) of Bernard de Montfaucon [1655—1741[1]], the most illustrious member of the learned Society of the Benedictines of St Maur. This truly great work, although its materials are rather too exclusively drawn from manuscripts deposited in French libraries, and its many illustrative *facsimiles* somewhat rudely engraved, still remains our best authority on all points relating to Greek Manuscripts, even after more recent discoveries, especially among the papyri of Egypt and Herculaneum, have necessarily modified not a few of its statements. The four splendid volumes of M. J. B. Silvestre's "Paléographie Universelle" (Paris, 1839,

[1] In this manner we propose to indicate the dates of the birth and death of the person whose name immediately precedes.

&c. folio) afford us no less than forty-one coloured specimens of the Greek writing of various ages, sumptuously executed; though the accompanying letter-press descriptions, by F. and A. Champollion Fils, seem in this branch of the subject a little disappointing; nor are the valuable notes appended to his translation of their work by Sir Frederick Madden (London, 2 vol. 1850, 8vo) sufficiently numerous or elaborate to supply the Champollions' defects. Much, however, may also be learnt from the "Herculanensium voluminum quæ supersunt" (Naples, 10 tom. 1793—1850, fol.); from Mr Babington's three volumes of papyrus fragments of Hyperides, respectively published in 1850, 1853 and 1858; and especially from the Prolegomena to Tischendorf's editions of the Codices Ephraemi (1843), Friderico-Augustanus (1846), Claromontanus (1852), and those other like publications (e.g. Monumenta sacra inedita 1846, 1855 &c. and Anecdota sacra et profana 1855) which have rendered his name the very highest among living scholars in this department of sacred literature. What I have been able to add from my own observation, has been gathered from the study of Biblical manuscripts now in *England*.

2. Stone, wood, tablets covered with wax, the bark of trees, the dressed skins of animals, the reed papyrus, paper made of cotton or linen, are the chief *materials* on which writing has been impressed at different periods and stages of civilisation. The most ancient manuscripts of the New Testament now existing are composed of vellum or parchment (*membrana*), the term vellum being strictly applied to the delicate skins of very young calves; and parchment (which seems to be a corruption of *charta pergamena*, a name first given to skins prepared by some improved process for Eumenes, king of Pergamus, about B.C. 150) to the integuments of sheep or goats. In judging of the date of a manuscript written on skins, attention must be paid to the quality of the material, the oldest being almost invariably described on the thinnest and whitest vellum that could be procured; while manuscripts of later ages, being usually composed of parchment, are thick, discoloured, and coarsely grained. Thus the Codex Friderico-Augustanus of the fourth century is made of the finest skins of antelopes, the leaves being so large, that a single animal would furnish only

two (Tischendorf, Prolegomena, § 1). Its contemporary, the far-famed Codex Vaticanus, challenges universal admiration for the beauty of its vellum: every visitor at the British Museum can observe the excellence of that of the Codex Alexandrinus of the fifth century: that of the Codex Claromontanus of the sixth century is no less remarkable: the material of those purple-dyed fragments of the Gospels which Tischendorf denominates N, also of the sixth century, is so subtle and delicate, that some persons have mistaken the leaves preserved in England (Brit. Mus. Cotton, Titus C xv) for Egyptian papyrus. Paper made of cotton (*charta bombycina*, called also *charta Damascena* from its place of manufacture) may have been fabricated in the ninth[1] or tenth century, and linen paper (*charta* proper) as early as the twelth; but they were seldom used for Biblical manuscripts earlier than the thirteenth, and had not entirely displaced parchment at the æra of the invention of printing, about A.D. 1450. Cotton paper is for the most part easily distinguished from linen by its roughness and coarse fibre; some of the early linen paper, both glazed and unglazed, is of a very fine texture, though perhaps a little too stout and crisp for convenient use. Lost portions of parchment or vellum manuscripts are often supplied in paper by some later hand; and the Codex Leicestrensis of the fourteenth century is unique in this respect, being composed of a mixture of inferior vellum and worse paper, regularly arranged in the proportion of two parchment to three paper leaves, recurring alternately throughout the whole volume.

3. Although parchment was in occasional, if not familiar, use at the period when the New Testament was written (*τὰ βιβλία, μάλιστα τὰς μεμβράνας*, 2 Tim. iv. 13), yet the cheaper and more perishable papyrus of Egypt was chiefly employed for ordinary purposes, and was probably what is meant by *χάρτης* in 2 John *v.* 12. This vegetable production had been long used for literary purposes in the time of Herodotus (B.C. 440), and that not only in Egypt (Herod. Hist. II. 100) but elsewhere, for

[1] Tischendorf (Notitia Codicis Sinaitici, p. 54) has recently taken to St Petersburg a fragment of a Lectionary, which cannot well be assigned to a later date than the ninth century, among whose parchment leaves are inserted two of cotton paper, manifestly written on by the original scribe.

he expressly states that the Ionians, for lack of byblus[1], had been compelled to have recourse to the skins of goats and sheep (v. 58). We find a minute, if not a very clear, description of the mode of preparing the papyrus for the scribe in the works of the elder Pliny (Hist. Nat. l. XIII. c. 11, 12). Its frail and brittle quality has no doubt caused us the loss of some of the choicest treasures of ancient literature; the papyri which yet survive in the museums of Europe owe their preservation to the accidental circumstance of having been buried in the tombs of the Thebais, or beneath the wreck of Herculaneum. As we before intimated, no existing manuscript of the New Testament is written on papyrus, nor can the earliest we possess on vellum be dated higher than the middle of the fourth century.

4. We have some grounds for suspecting that papyrus was not over plentiful even in the best times of the Roman dominion; and it may be readily imagined that vellum (especially that fine sort by praiseworthy custom required for copies of Holy Scripture) could never have been otherwise than scarce and dear. Hence arose, at a very early period of the Christian æra, the practice and almost the necessity of erasing ancient writing from skins, in order to make room for works in which the living generation felt more interest. This process of destruction, however, was seldom so fully carried out, but that the strokes of the elder hand might still be traced, more or less completely, under the more modern writing. Such manuscripts are called *codices rescripti* or palimpsests (παλίμψηστα), and several of the most precious monuments of sacred learning are of this description. The Codex Ephraemi at Paris contains large fragments both of the Old and New Testament under the later Greek works of St Ephraem the Syrian: and the Codex Nitriensis, recently disinterred from a monastery in the Egyptian desert and brought to the British Museum, comprises a portion of St Luke's Gospel, nearly obliterated, and covered over by a Syriac treatise of Severus of Antioch against Grammaticus, comparatively of no value whatever. It will be easily believed that the collating or transcribing of palimpsests has cost much toil and patience to

[1] Herodotus calls the whole plant *byblus* (II. 92), but Theophrastus (Hist. Plant. IV. 9) *papyrus*, reserving the term βίβλος for the *liber*, the inner rind, from which alone the writing material was fabricated.

those whose loving zeal has led them to the attempt: and after all their true readings will be sometimes (not often) rather uncertain, even though chemical mixtures (such as prussiate of potash or the *tinctura Giobertina*) have recently been applied, with much success, to restore the faded lines and letters of these venerable records.

5. We need say but little of a practice which St Jerome[1] and others speak of as prevalent towards the end of the fourth century, that of dyeing the vellum purple, and of stamping rather than writing the letters in silver and gold. The Cotton fragment of the Gospels, mentioned above (p. 21), is one of the few remaining copies of this kind, and it is not unlikely that the great Dublin palimpsest of St Matthew owes its present wretched discolouration to some such dye. But, as Davidson sensibly observes, "the value of a Manuscript does not depend on such things" (Biblical Criticism, vol. II. p. 264). We care for them only as they serve to indicate the reverence paid to the Scriptures by men of old. The style, however, of the pictures, illustrations, arabesques and initial ornaments that prevail in later copies from the eighth century downwards, whose colours and gilding are sometimes as fresh and bright as if laid on but yesterday, will not only interest the student by tending to throw light on mediæval art and habits and modes of thought, but will often fix the date of the books which contain them with a precision otherwise quite beyond our reach.

6. The ink used in the most ancient Manuscripts has unfortunately for the most part turned red or brown, or very pale, or peeled off, or eaten through the vellum; so that in many cases (as in the Codex Vaticanus itself) a later hand has ruthlessly retraced the letters, and given a false semblance of coarseness or carelessness to the original writing. In such instances a few passages will usually remain untouched, just as the first scribe left them, and from the study of these a right notion can be formed of the primitive condition of the rest: see, for example, the two facsimile plates (63, 64) of the Coislin MS. (H) of St Paul's Epistles in Silvestre's Paléographie Universelle.

[1] "Habeant qui volunt veteres libros, vel in membranis purpureis auro argentoque descriptos." Præf. in Job.

From the seventh century downwards it is said that the ingredients of ink have but little changed. The base has been soot, or lamp-black made of burnt shavings of ivory, mixed with wine-lees or gum, and subsequently sepia or alum. Vitriol and gall-nuts are now added, the mineral serving to fix the vegetable ingredients. In many manuscripts of about the twelfth century (e.g. Gonville and Caius MS., 59 of the Gospels) we observe what seems to be, and very well may be, the Indian ink of commerce, still preserving a beautiful jet black on the inner and smoother side of the parchment, and washed out rather than erased, whenever corrections were desired. The coloured inks (red, green, blue or purple) are often quite brilliant to this day: the four red lines which stand at the head of each column of the first page of the Codex Alexandrinus are far more legible than the portions in black ink below them, yet are undoubtedly written by the same hand.

7. While papyrus (*χάρτης*) remained in common use, the chief instrument employed was probably a reed (*κάλαμος*, 3 John *v.* 13), such as are common in the East at present: a few existing manuscripts (e. g. the Codd. Leicestrensis and Lambeth 1350) appear to have been thus written. Yet the firmness and regularity of the strokes, which often remain impressed on the vellum or paper after the ink has utterly gone, prove that in the great majority of cases a metal pen (*stylus*) was preferred. We must add to our list of writing materials a bodkin or needle (*acus*), by means of which and a ruler the blank leaf was carefully divided into columns and lines, whose regularity much enhances the beauty of our best copies. The vestiges of such points and marks may yet be seen deeply indented on the surface of nearly all manuscripts, those on one side of each leaf being usually sufficiently visible to guide the scribe when he came to write on the reverse.

8. Little needs be said respecting the *form* of manuscripts, which in this particular much resemble printed books. A few are in large folio; the greater part in small folio or quarto, the prevailing shape being a quarto, whose height but little exceeds its breadth; some are octavo, an inconsiderable number smaller still. In some copies the sheets have marks in the lower margin of their first or last pages, like the *signatures* of a modern volume, the

folio at intervals of four, the quarto at intervals of eight leaves[1], as in the Codex Augiensis of St Paul's Epistles (F). Not to speak at present of those manuscripts which have a Latin translation in a column parallel to the Greek, as the Codex Bezae, the Codex Laudianus of the Acts, and the Codices Claromontanus and Augiensis of St Paul, many copies of every age have two Greek columns on each page; of these the Codex Alexandrinus is the oldest: the Codex Vaticanus has three columns on a page, the Codex Friderico-Augustanus four. The unique arrangement[2] of these last two has been urged as an argument for their higher antiquity, as if they were designed to imitate *rolled* books, whose several skins or leaves were fastened together lengthwise, so that their contents always appeared in parallel columns; they were kept in scrolls which were unrolled at one end for reading, and when read rolled up at the other. This fashion prevails in the papyrus fragments yet remaining, and in the most venerated copies of the Old Testament preserved in Jewish synagogues.

9. We now approach a more important question, the *style* of writing adopted in manuscripts, and the shapes of the several letters. These varied widely in different ages, and form the simplest and surest criteria for approximating to the date of the documents themselves. It will prove convenient to abide by the usual division of Greek characters into *uncial*[3] and *cursive;*

[1] Eusebius sent to Constantine's new city (Euseb. Vit. Const. Lib. IV.) *πεντήκοντα σωμάτια ἐν διφθέραις* (c. 36)...*ἐν πολυτελῶς ἠσκημένοις τεύχεσι τρισσὰ καὶ τετρασσὰ* (c. 37): on which last words Valesius notes, "Codices enim membranacei ferè per quaterniones digerebantur, hoc est quatuor folia simul compacta, ut terniones tria sunt folia simul compacta. Et quaterniones quidem sedecim habebant paginas, terniones vero duodenas."

[2] The manuscript in four columns is quite unique, but besides the Cod. Vaticanus, the Vatican Dio Cassius and two copies of the Samaritan Pentateuch at Nablous are stated by Tischendorf (Cod. Frid-Aug. Proleg. § 11) to be arranged in *three* columns. He has more recently discovered a similar arrangement in two palimpsest leaves of Religious Meditations from which he gives extracts (Not. Cod. Sinait. p. 49); in a Latin fragment of the Pentateuch; in a Greek Evangelistarium of the eighth century; and a Patristic manuscript at Patmos of the ninth (*ibid.* p. 10); so that the argument drawn from the *triple* columns must not be pressed too far.

[3] "Uncialibus, ut vulgo aiunt, literis, onera magis exarata, quam codices" Hieronymi Præf. in Job. From this passage the term *uncial* seems to be derived, *uncia* (an inch) referring to the size of the characters. The conjectural reading

uncial manuscripts being written in what have since been regarded as capital letters, formed separately, having no connection with each other, and (in the earlier specimens) without any space between the words, the marks of punctuation being few: the *cursive* or running hand comprising letters more easily and rapidly made, those in the same word being usually joined together, with a complete system of punctuation not widely removed from that of printed books. Speaking generally, and limiting our statement to Greek manuscripts of the New Testament, uncial letters prevailed from the fourth to the tenth, or (in the case of liturgical books) as late as the eleventh century; cursive letters were employed as early as the ninth or tenth century, and continued in use until the invention of printing superseded the humble labours of the scribe.

But besides the broad and palpable distinction between uncial and cursive letters, persons who have had much experience in the study of manuscripts are able to distinguish those of each class from one another in respect of style and character; so that the exact period at which each was written can be determined within certain inconsiderable limits. After the tenth century many manuscripts bear dates, and such become standards to which we can refer others resembling them that are undated. But since the earliest dated Biblical manuscript yet discovered (Vatican. 354 or S of the Gospels) was written A.D. 949; we must resort to other means for estimating the age of more venerable, and therefore more important, copies. By studying the style and shape of the letters on Greek inscriptions, Montfaucon was led to conclude that the more simple, upright, and regular the form of uncial letters; the less flourish or ornament they exhibit; the nearer their breadth is equal to their height; so much the more ancient they ought to be considered. These results have been signally confirmed by the subsequent discovery of Greek papyri in Egyptian tombs, which vary in age from the third century before the Christian æra to the third century after that epoch; and yet further from numerous fragments of Philodemus, of Epicurus, and other philosophers, which were buried in the ruins of Herculaneum A.D. 79. The evidence of these papyri, indeed, is even more weighty than that of inscriptions, inasmuch as

"*initialibus*" will most approve itself to those who are familiar with the small Latin writing of the middle ages, in which *i* is undotted, and *c* much like *t*.

workers in stone were often compelled to prefer straight lines, as better adapted to the hardness of their material, where writings on papyrus or vellum would naturally flow into curves.

10. While we freely grant that a certain tact, the fruit of study and minute observation, can alone make us capable of forming a trustworthy opinion on the age of manuscripts; it is worth while to point out the *principles* on which a true judgment must be grounded, and to submit to the reader a few leading facts, which his own research may hereafter enable him to apply and even to extend.

The first three plates at the end of this volume represent the Greek alphabet, as found in the seven following monuments:

(1). The celebrated Rosetta stone, discovered near that place during the French occupation in 1799, and now in the British Museum. This most important inscription, which in the hands of Young and Champollion has proved the key to the mysteries of Egyptian hieroglyhics, records events of no intrinsic consequence that occurred B.C. 196, in the reign of Ptolemy V. Epiphanes. It is written in the three forms of hieroglyphics, of the demotic or common character of the country, and of Greek uncials, which last may represent the *lapidary* style of the second century before our æra. The words are undivided, without breathings, accents, or marks of punctuation, and the uncial letters (excepting ⌶ for Zeta) approach very nearly to our modern capital type. In shape they are simple, perhaps a little rude; rather square than oblong; and as the carver on this hard black stone was obliged to avoid curve lines whenever he could, the forms of E, Ξ and Σ differ considerably from the specimens we shall produce from documents described on soft materials.

(2). The Codex Friderico-Augustanus of the fourth century, published in lithographed facsimile in 1846, contains on 43 leaves fragments of the Septuagint version, chiefly from 1 Chronicles and Jeremiah, with Nehemiah and Esther complete, in oblong folio, with four columns on each page. It is so carefully executed that the very form of the ancient letters and the colour of the ink are represented to us by Tischendorf, who discovered it in the East. Two years ago the same indefatigable scholar brought to Europe the remainder of this manuscript, which seems as old as the fourth century and perhaps anterior to the Codex Vaticanus itself, and purposes to publish it, in facsimile type cast for the purpose, 4 tom., with twenty pages lithographed or photographed, in 1862, at the expense of the Emperor of Russia, to whom the original belongs. This book, which Tischendorf now calls Codex Sinaiticus, contains, besides much more of the Septuagint, *the whole New Testament* with Barnabas' Epistle and Hermas' Shepherd annexed. As a kind of *avant-courier* to his great work he has put forth a tract entitled, "Notitia Editionis Codicis Bibliorum Sinaitici Auspiciis Imperatoris Alexandri II. susceptæ" (Leipsic, 1860), from which we have derived the account of the manuscript given in the opening of the next section of this chapter, under the appellation of *Aleph* (א), assigned to it by Tischendorf, in the exercise of his right as its discoverer.

(3). Codex Alexandrinus of the fifth century (A).

(4). Codex Purpureus Cotton: N of the Gospels. } of the

(5). Codex Nitriensis Rescriptus, R of the Gospels } sixth

(6). Codex Dublinensis Rescriptus, Z of the Gospels } century.

(7). Evangelistarium Harleian. 5598, *dated* A.D. 995.

These manuscripts will be more fully described in the succeeding sections of the chapter. At present we wish to compare them with each other for the purpose of tracing, as closely as we may, the different styles and fashions of uncial letters which prevailed from the fourth to the tenth or eleventh century of the Christian æra. The varying fashions of cursive manuscripts cannot so well be seen by exhibiting their alphabets, for since each letter is for the most part joined to the others in the same word, *connected* passages will alone afford us a correct notion of their character and general features. For the moment we are considering the uncials alone.

If the Rosetta stone, by its necessary avoiding of curve lines, so far fails to give us a correct notion of the manner adopted in common writing, it resembles our earliest uncials at least in one respect, that the letters, being as broad as they are high, are all capable of being included within circumscribed squares. Indeed, yet earlier inscriptions are found almost totally destitute of curves, even O and Θ being represented by simple squares, with or without a bisecting horizontal line (*see theta, p.* 32)[1]. The Herculanean papyri, however, (a specimen of which we have given in *facsimile* 10, Plate IV), is much better suited than inscriptions can be for comparison with our earliest copies of Scripture[2]. Nothing can well be conceived more elegant than these simply-formed graceful little letters (somewhat diminished in size perhaps by the effects of heat) running across the volume, 39 lines in a column, without capitals or breaks between the words. There are scarcely any stops, no breathings, accents, or marks of any kind; only that >, < or ▷ are now and then found at the end of a line, to fill up the space, or to join a word or syllable with what follows. A very few abbreviations occur, such as ΠΡ in the first line of our specimen, taken from Philodemus *περὶ κακιῶν* (Hercul. Volum. Tom. III. Col. XX. ll. 6—15), the very treatise to which Tischendorf compared his Cod. Frederico-Augustanus (Proleg. § 11). The papyri, buried for so many ages from A.D. 79 downwards, may probably be a century older still, since Philodemus the Epicurean was the contemporary and almost the friend of Cicero[3]. Hence from three to four hundred years must have elapsed betwixt the writing of the Herculanean rolls and of our earliest Biblical manuscripts; yet the fashion of writing changed but little during the interval, far less in every respect than in the four centuries which next followed; wherein the plain, firm, upright and square uncials were giving place to the compressed, oblong, ornamented or even sloping forms which predominate from the seventh or eighth century downwards. While advising the reader to exercise his skill on facsimiles of *entire passages*, especially in contrasting the lines from Philodemus (No. 10), with those

[1] The Cotton fragment of the book of Genesis of the fifth century, whose poor shrivelled remains from the fire of 1731 are still preserved in the British Museum, while in common with all other *manuscripts* it exhibits the round shapes of O and Θ, substitutes a lozenge ◊ for the circle in *phi*, after the older fashion (Φ).

[2] Our facsimile is borrowed from the Neapolitan volumes, but Plate 57 in the Paléographie Universelle *φιλοδημου περι μουσικη* has the advantage of *colours* for giving a lively idea of the present charred appearance of these papyri.

[3] Cicero de Finibus, Lib. II. c. 35. The same person is apparently meant in Orat. in Pisonem, cc. 28, 29.

from the oldest uncials of the New Testament (Nos. 11—14; 17—20; 24); we purpose to examine the several alphabets (Nos. 1—7) letter by letter, pointing out to the student those variations in shape which palæographers have judged the safest criteria of their relative ages. *Alpha*, *delta*, *theta*, *xi*, *pi*, *omega* are among the best tests for this purpose.

Alpha is not often found in its present familiar shape, except in inscriptions, where the cross line is sometimes broken into an angle with the vertex downwards (A): even on the Rosetta stone the left limb leans against the upper part of the right limb, but does not form an angle with its extremity, while the cross line, springing not far from the bottom of the left limb, *ascends* to meet the right about half way down. Modifications of this form may be seen in the Herculanean rolls, only that the cross line more nearly approaches the horizontal, and sometimes is almost entirely so. The Cod. Frid-August.[1] does not vary much from this form, but the three generating lines are often somewhat curved. In other books while the right limb is quite straight, the left and cross line form a kind of loop or curve, as is very observable in the Nitrian fragment R, and often in Codd. Alex., Ephraemi, Bezae, and in the Vatican more frequently still, in all which *alpha* often approximates to the shape of our English *a*. *And this curve may be regarded as a proof of antiquity.* Cod. N (which is more recent than those named above) makes the two lines on the left form a sharp angle, as do the Cotton fragment of Genesis (see p. 28, note 1) and Cod. Claromontanus No. 19, only that the lines which form the angle in this last are very fine. In later times, as the letters grew tall and narrow, the modern type of A became more marked, as in the first letter of Arundel 547 (No. 16), of about the 10th century, though the form and thickness seen in the Cod. Claromontanus continued much in vogue to the last. Yet *alpha* even in Cod. Claromontanus and Cotton Genesis occasionally passes from the angle into the loop, though not so often as in Cod. A and its companions. Cod. Borgianus (T), early in the fifth century, exaggerated this loop into a large ellipse, if Giorgi's facsimile may be trusted. In Cod. Laudianus E of the Acts and Cureton's palimpsest Homer too the loop is very decided, the Greek and Latin *a* in Laud. (No. 25) being alike. Mark also its form in the papyrus scrawl No. 9 (from one of the orations of Hyperides edited by Mr Babington), which *may* be as old as the Rosetta stone. The angular shape adopted in Cod. Z (Nos. 6, 18) is ugly enough, and (I believe) unique.

Beta varies less than *Alpha*. Originally it consisted of a tall perpendicular line, on the right side of which four straight lines are

[1] We prefer citing Cod. Frid-August., because our examples have been actually taken from its exquisitely lithographed pages; but the *facsimile* of part of a page from Luke xxiv. represented in the Notitia Cod. Sinaitici, from which we have borrowed six lines (No. 11 b), will be seen to resemble exactly the portion published in 1846.

so placed as to form two triangles, whereof the vertical line forms the bases, but a small portion of the vertical line entirely separates the triangles (ꞵ). This ungraceful figure was modified very early, even in inscriptions. On the Rosetta stone (No. 1) the triangles are rounded off into semicircles, and the lower end of the vertical curved. Yet the shape in manuscripts is not quite so elegant. The lower curve is usually the larger, and the curves rarely touch each other. Such are Codd. ANRZ and the Cotton Genesis. In the Herculanean rolls the letter comes near the common cursive β, in some others its shape is quite like the modern B. When oblong letters became common, the top (e.g. Cod. Bezae) and bottom extremities of the curve ran into straight lines, by way of return into the primitive shape (see No. 32, *dated* 980). In the very early papyrus fragment of Hyperides it looks like the English R standing on a base (No. 9, l. 4). But this specimen rather belongs to the semi-cursive hand of common life, than to that of books.

Gamma in its simplest form consists of two lines of equal thickness, the shorter so placed upon the longer, which is vertical, as to make one right angle with it on the right side. Thus we find it in the Rosetta stone, the papyrus of Hyperides, the Herculanean rolls and very often in Cod. A. The next step was to make the horizontal line very thin, and to strengthen its extremity by a point, or knob, as in Codd. Ephraemi, RZ: or the point was thus strengthened without thinning the line, e.g. Codd. Vatican., N and most later copies, such as Harl. 5598 (No. 7) or its contemporary Parham 18 (No. 32). In Cod. Bezae *gamma* much resembles the Latin r.

Delta should be closely scrutinized. Its most ancient shape is an equilateral triangle, the sides being all of the same thickness (Δ). Cod. Claromontanus, though of the sixth century, is in this instance as simple as any: the Herculanean rolls, Codd. Frid-August., Vatican., and the very old copy of the Pentateuch at Paris (Colbert) and Leyden, much resemble it, only that sometimes the Herculanean sides are slightly curved, and the right descending stroke of Cod. Vatican. is thickened. In Cod. A a tendency begins to appear to prolong the base on one or both sides, and to strengthen the ends by points; we see a little more of this in the palimpsest Homer of the fifth century, published by Cureton. The habit increases and becomes confirmed in Codd. Ephraem, the Vatican Dio Cassius of the 5th or 6th century, in Cod. R, and particularly in N and E of the Acts (Nos. 4, 14, 25). In the oblong later uncials it becomes quite elaborate, e. g. Cod. B of the Apocalypse, or Nos. 7, 21, 32. On the Rosetta stone and in the Cod. Bezae the right side is produced beyond the triangle, and is produced and slightly curved in Hyperides; curved and strongly pointed in Cod. Z.

Epsilon has its ordinary angular form on the Rosetta marble and other inscriptions; in the oldest manuscripts it consists of a semicircle, from whose centre to the right of it a horizontal radius is drawn to the concave circumference. Thus it appears in the Herculaneum rolls (only that here the radius is usually broken off before it meets the circle), in Codd. Frid-August., Vatican., the two *Paris* Pentateuchs (Colbert-Leyden 4th cent., Coislin. 6th) and the Cotton Genesis. In Cod. Alex. a slight trace is found of the more recent practice of strengthening each of the three extremities with knobs; the custom increases in Codd. Ephraemi, Bezae and still more in Codd. NRZ, wherein the curve becomes greater than a semicircle. In Hyperides (and in a slighter degree in Cod. Claromon. No. 19) the shape almost resembles the Latin *e*. The form of this and the other round letters was afterwards much affected in the narrow oblong uncials: see Nos. 7, 16, 32.

Zeta on the Rosetta stone maintains its old form (⌶), which is indeed but the next letter reversed. In manuscripts it receives its usual modern shape (Z), the ends being pointed decidedly, slightly, or not at all, much after the manner described for *epsilon*. In old copies the lower horizontal line is a trifle curved (Cod. R. No. 5), or even both the extreme lines (Cod. Z, No. 6), and Cod. Augiensis of St Paul. In such late books as Parham 18 (A.D. 980, *facsim.* No. 32) *Zeta* is so large as to run far below the line, ending in a kind of tail.

Eta does not depart from its normal shape (H) except that in Cod. Ephraemi and some narrow and late uncials (e.g. Nos. 7, 32) the cross line is often more than half way up the letter. In a few later uncials the cross line passes *outside* the two perpendiculars, as in the Cod. Augiensis, 26 times on the photographed page of Scrivener's edition.

Theta deserves close attention. In some early inscriptions it is found as a square, bisected horizontally (⊟). On the Rosetta stone and most others (but only in such monuments) it is a circle, with a strong central *point*. On the Herculanean rolls the central point is spread into a short horizontal line, yet not reaching the circumference (No. 10, l. 8). Then in our uncials from the fourth to the sixth century the line becomes a horizontal diameter to a true circle (Codd. Frid-August. Vatican. Codd. ANRZ, Ephraemi, Claromont. and Cureton's Homer). In the 7th century the diameter began to pass out of the circle on both sides: thence the circle came to be compressed into an ellipse (sometimes very narrow) and the ends of the minor axes to be ornamented with knobs, as in Cod. B of the Apocalypse (8th cent.), Cod. Augiensis (9th cent.), LX of the Gospels, after the manner of the 10th century (Nos. 7, 16, 21, 32, 33).

Iota would need no remark but for the custom of placing over it and *upsilon*, when they commence a syllable, either a very short straight line, or one or two dots. After the papyrus rolls, no copy is quite without them, from the Codex Alexandrinus, the Cotton Genesis and Paris-Leyden Pentateuch, to the more recent cursives; although in some manuscripts they are much rarer than in others. By far the most usual practice is to put two points, but Cod. Ephraemi, in its *New* Testament portion, stands alone in exhibiting the straight line; Codd. Borgianus (T) and Claromont. have but one point; Cod. N has two for *iota*, one for *upsilon*.

Kappa deserves notice chiefly because the vertex of the angle formed by the two inclined lines very frequently does not meet the perpendicular line, but falls short of it a little to the right: we observe this in Codd. ANR, Ephraemi, and later books. The copies that have strong points at the end of *epsilon* &c., (e.g. Codd. NR and AZ partly) have the same at the extremity of the thin, or upper limb of *Kappa*.

Lambda much resembles *alpha*, but is less complicated. All our models (except Harl. 5598, No. 7) from the Rosetta stone downwards, have the right limb longer than the left, which thus leans against its side, but the length of the projection varies even in the same passage (e.g. No. 10). In most copies later than the Herculanean rolls and Cod. Frid-August. the shorter line is much the thinner, and the longer slightly curved. In Cod. Z (Nos. 6, 18) the projection is curved elegantly at the end, as we saw in *delta*.

Mu varies as much as most letters. Its normal shape, resembling the English M, is retained in the Rosetta stone and most inscriptions, but at an early period there was a tendency to make the letter broader and not to bring the re-entering or middle angle so low as in English (e.g. Codd. Frid-August. Vatican.). In Cod. Ephraemi this central angle is sometimes a little rounded: in Codd. Alex. and Parham 18 the lines forming the angles do not always spring from the top of the vertical lines: in Arund. 547 (No. 16) they spring almost from their foot, forming a thick inelegant loop below the line, the letter being rather narrow: Harl. 5598 (No. 7) somewhat resembles this last, only that the loop is higher up. In the Herculanean rolls (and to a less extent in the Cotton Genesis) the two outer lines cease to be perpendicular, and lean outwards until the letter looks much like an inverted W (No. 10). In the papyrus Hyperides (No. 9) these outer lines are low curves, and the central lines rise in a kind of flourish above them. This form is so much exaggerated in some examples, that by discarding the outer curves, we obtain the shape seen in Cod. Z (Nos. 6, 18), and one or two others (e.g. Paul M. in Harl. 5613), almost exactly resembling an inverted *pi*.

Nu is easier, the only change (besides the universal transition from the square to the oblong in the later uncials) being that in a few cases the thin cross line does not pass from the top of the left to the bottom of the right vertical line as in English (N), but only halfway or two-thirds down in the Cotton Genesis, Cod. A, Harl. 5598, and others; in Codd. ℵNR Parham 18 it often neither springs from the top of one, nor reaches the foot of the other (Nos. 4, 5, 11b, 12, 32); while in Cod. Claromont. (No. 19) it is here and there not far from horizontal. In a few *cursives* (e.g. 440 Evan. at Cambridge, and Tischendorf's lo[tl] of the Acts), H and N almost interchange their shapes.

Xi in the Rosetta stone and Herculanean rolls consists of three parallel straight lines, the middle one being the shortest, as in modern printed Greek: but all our Biblical manuscripts exhibit modifications of the small printed ξ, which must be closely inspected, but cannot easily be described. In the Cotton Genesis this *Xi* is narrow and smaller than its fellows, much like an old English ʒ resting on a horizontal base which curves downwards: while in late uncials, as B of the Apocalypse, Cod. Augiensis (l. 13 *of photographed page*), and especially in Parham 18 (No. 32) the letter and its flourished finial are continued far below the line. For the rest we must refer to our *facsimile* alphabets, &c. The figures in Cod. Frid-August. (Nos. 3, 11, ll. 3, 8) look particularly awkward.

Omicron is unchanged, excepting that in the latest uncials (No. 16, 32) the circle is mostly compressed, like *theta*, into a very eccentric ellipse.

Pi requires attention. Its original shape was doubtless two vertical straight lines joined at top by another horizontal, thinner perhaps but not much shorter than they. Thus we meet with it on the Rosetta stone, Codd. R Frid-August., Vatican., Ephraem., Claromontanus, Laud. of the Acts, the two Pentateuchs, Cureton's Homer, and sometimes Cod. Alexand. (No. 12). The fine vertical line is, however, slightly produced on both sides in such early documents as the papyri of Hyperides and Herculaneum, and the Cotton Genesis, as well as in Cod. Alexand. occasionally. Both extremities of this line are fortified by strong points in Cod. N and mostly in Cod. A, but the left side only in Cod. Z, which in Cod. Bezae becomes a sort of hooked curve. The later oblong *pi* was usually very plain, with thick vertical lines and a very fine horizontal, in Arund. 547 (No. 16) not at all produced; in Harl. 5598 (No. 7) slightly produced on both sides; in Parham 18 (No. 32) only on the left.

Rho is otherwise simple, but in all our authorities except inscriptions is produced below the line of writing, least perhaps in the papyri and Cod. Claromont., considerably in Cod. AX (Nos. 12, 33), most in Parham 18 (No. 32): Cod. N and many later copies have the lower extremity boldly *bevelled*.

Sigma retains its angular shape (Ϲ or Σ) only on inscriptions, as at Rosetta, and that long after the square shapes of *omicron* and *theta* were discarded. The semicircular form, however, arose early, and to this letter must be applied all that was said of *epsilon* as regards terminal points, and its cramped shape in later ages.

Tau in its oldest form consists of two straight lines of like thickness, the horizontal being bisected by the lower and vertical one. As early as in Cod. Frid-August. the horizontal line is made thin, and strengthened on the left side *only* by a point or small knob (Nos. 3, 11): thus we find it in Cod. Laudian. of the Acts sometimes. In Cod. Alex. *both* ends are slightly pointed, in Cod. Ephraem. and others much more. In Cod. Bezae the horizontal is curved and flourished; in the late uncials the vertical is very thick, the horizontal fine, and the ends formed into heavy triangles (e.g. No. 16).

Upsilon on the Rosetta stone and Herculanean rolls is like our Y, all the strokes being of equal thickness and not running below the line: nor do they in Codd. XZ Augiensis or Hyperides, which have the upper lines neatly curved (Nos. 6, 9, 18, 33). The right limb of many of the rest is sometimes, but not always curved; the vertical line in Codd. Frid-August. and Vatic. drops slightly below the line; in Codd. Alexand., Ephraem., Cotton Genesis, Cureton's Homer and Laud. of the Acts somewhat more; in others (as Codd. Bezae RN) considerably. In later uncials (Nos. 7, 32) it becomes a long or awkward Y, or even degenerates into a long V (No. 16); or, in copies written by Latin scribes, into Y reversed. We have described under *iota* the custom of placing dots &c. over *upsilon*.

Phi is a remarkable letter. In most copies it is the largest in the alphabet, quite disproportionately large in Codd. ZL (Paris 62) and others, and to some extent in Codd. AR Eph. Clar. The circle (which in the Cotton Genesis is *sometimes* still a lozenge, see above, p. 28 note), though large and in some copies even too broad (e.g. No. 18), is usually in the line of the other letters, the vertical line being produced *far* upwards (Cod. Augiens. and Nos. 16, 19), or downwards (No. 10), or both (No. 32). On the Rosetta stone the circle is very small and the straight line short.

Chi is a simple transverse cross (X) and never goes above or below the line. The limb that inclines from left to right is for the most part thick, the other thin (with final points according to the practice stated for *epsilon*), and this limb or both a little curved.

Psi is a rare but trying letter. Its oldest form resembled an English V with a straight line running up bisecting its interior angle. On the Rosetta stone it had already changed into its present form (Ψ), the curve being a small semicircle, the vertical rising and falling a little below the line. In the Cotton Genesis *psi* is a little taller than the rest, but the vertical line does not rise above the level of the circle. In Codd. ANR the under line is prolonged: in R the two limbs are straight lines making an angle of about 45° with the vertical, while oftentimes in Hyperides and Cod. Augiensis. (*photogr.* ll. 18, 23) they curve *downwards;* the limbs both in N and R being strongly pointed at the ends, and the bottom of the vertical bevelled as usual. In Cod. B of the Apocalypse the limbs (strongly pointed) fall into a straight line and the figure becomes a large cross (No. 7).

Omega took the form Ω, even when *omicron* and *theta* were square; thus it appears on the Rosetta stone, but in the Hyperides and Herculanean rolls is a single curve, much like the w of English writing, only that the central part is sometimes only a low double curve (No. 10, l. 6). In the Cotton Genesis, Codd. Frid-August., Vatican., Alex., Ephraem., Bezae, Claromont., Nitriens. there is little difference in shape, though sometimes Cod. Vatic. comes near the Herculanean rolls, and Cod. A. next to it: elsewhere their strokes (especially those in the centre) are fuller and more laboured. Yet in Cod. N it often is but a plain semicircle, bisected by a perpendicular radius, with the ends of the curve bent inwards (No. 14, l. 2). In the late uncials (Nos. 7, 16) it almost degenerates into an ungraceful W, while in Cod. Augiensis (*photogr. l.* 18) the first limb is occasionally a complete circle.

These details might be indefinitely added to by references to other codices and monuments of antiquity, but we have employed most of the principal copies of the Greek Testament, and have indicated to the student the chief points to which his attention should be drawn. Two leading principles have perhaps been sufficiently established by the foregoing examples:

First, that the upright square uncials are more ancient than those which are narrow, oblong, or *leaning*[1].

Secondly, that the simpler and less elaborate the style of writing, the more remote is its probable date.

Copies of a later age occasionally aim at imitating the fashion of an earlier period, or possibly the style of the older book from which their text is drawn. But this anachronism of fashion may be detected, as well by other circumstances we are soon to mention, as from the air of constraint which pervades the whole manuscript: the rather as the scribe will now and then fall into the more familiar manner of his contemporaries; especially when writing those small letters which our Biblical manuscripts of all dates (even the most venerable) perpetually crowd into the ends of lines, in order to save space.

11. We do not intend to dwell much on the cursive handwriting. No books of the Greek Scriptures earlier than the tenth century in that style are now extant[2], though it was prevalent long before in the intercourse of business or common life. The papyri of Hyperides (e.g. No. 9) and the Herculanean rolls, in a few places, shew that the process had even then commenced, for the letters of each word are often joined, and their shapes prove that swiftness of execution was more aimed at than distinctness. This is seen even more clearly in a petition to Ptolemy Philometor (B.C. 164) represented in the Paléographie Universelle (No. 56); the same great work contains (No. 66) two really cursive charters of the Emperors Maurice (A.D. 600) and Heraclius (A.D. 616); yet the earliest *books* known to be written in cursive letters are the Bodleian Euclid (dated A.D. 888) and the twenty-four dialogues of Plato in the same Library (dated A.D. 895)[3]. There is reason to believe, from the compa-

[1] Codd. B of Apocalypse, Θ Λ (No. 8b) of the Gospels, and Silvestre's No. 68, all of about the 8th century, slope more or less to the right: Cod. Γ (No. 8a) of the 9th century, a very little to the left.

[2] The earliest cursive Biblical manuscript we can mention is Sylvestre, No. 78, Paris 70, Wetstein's 14 of the Gospels, subscribed *ἐγράφη νικηφόρου βασιλεύοντος ἰνδ. ζ´*, which can only be A.D. 964, and the sovereign Nicephorus II: the years neither of the first emperor of that name (802—811), nor of the third (1078—81) will suit the indiction. Cod. 429 of the Gospels is dated 978, Cod. 148 of the Acts 984, Cod. 5[pe] 994. The date (835) assigned to Cod. 461 by Scholz seems quite improbable, though the Indiction (13) is correct.

[3] At the end of the Euclid we read *εγραφη χειρι στεφανου κληρικου μηνι σεπτεμβριωι ινδ. ζ̄ ετει κοσμου ϛτϟζ εκτησαμην αρεθας πατρευς την παρουσαν βιβλιον*: of

ratively unformed character of the writing in them all, that Burney 19 in the British Museum (from which we have extracted the alphabet No. 8c, Plate I.), and the minute, beautiful and important Codex 1 of the Gospels at Basle (of which see a *facsimile* No. 23)[1] are but little later than the Oxford books, and may be referred to the tenth century. Books copied after the cursive hand had become regularly formed, in the eleventh, twelfth and thirteenth centuries, are hard to be distinguished by the mere handwriting, though they are often dated, or their age fixed by the material (see p. 21), or the style of their illuminations. Colbert. 2844, or 33 of the Gospels, "the Queen of the cursives" as it has been called, from its critical value (*facsim.* No. 34), is attributed to the eleventh century. Our next specimen, Burney 21 (*facsimile* No. 15) is dated A.D. 1292, and affords a good example of the style usual with the religious persons who were the official scribes (*καλλίγραφοι*)[2] of their respective convents, and copied the Holy Scriptures for sale. *Beta* (l. 1 letter 4) *when joined to other letters*, is barely distinguishable from *upsilon*[3]; *nu* is even nearer to *mu;* the tall forms of *eta* and

the Plato, *εγραφη χειρι ιω καλλιγραφου· ευτυχως αρεθη διακονωι πατρει· νομισματων βυζαντϊεων δεκα και τριων· μηνι νοεμβριωι ινδικτιωνος ιδ· ετει κοσμου ςυδ βασιλειας λεοντος του φιλοχυ υιου βασιλειου του αειμνιστου.* It should be stated that these very curious books, both written by monks, and *all the dated manuscripts of the Greek Testament we have seen* except Canonici 34 in the Bodleian (which reckons from the Christian æra, A.D. 1515—6), calculate from the Greek æra of the Creation, September 1, B.C. 5508. To obtain the year A.D., therefore, from January 1 to August 31 in any year, subtract 5508 from the given year; from September 1 to December 31 subtract 5509. The indiction which usually accompanies this date is a useful check in case of any corruption or want of legibility in the letters employed as numerals.

[1] For the facsimiles of Codd. EFGHKLMUX 1. 33, we are indebted to the liberality and kindness of Dr Tregelles, who permitted an artist to copy them from tracings of one whole page of every manuscript he has collated which he took with his own hand, and will, it may be hoped, at some time make public.

[2] The writer of Burney 21 (r^{scr}), *ὁ ταπεινος Θεοδωρος ἁγιωπετριτης ταχα και καλλίγραφος* as he calls himself (that is, I suppose, monk of the Convent of Sancta Petra at Constantinople, short-hand and fair writer), was the scribe of at least *five* more copies of Scripture now extant: Birch's Havn. 1, A.D. 1278 [Scholz Evan. 234]; Wetstein's Evan. 90, A.D. 1293; q^{scr} A.D. 1295; Scholz's Evan. 412, A.D. 1301; Wetstein's Evan. 74, *undated.*

[3] Hence in the later uncials, some of which must therefore have been copied from earlier cursives, B and Υ (which might seem to have no resemblance) are confounded: e.g. in Parham 18 (A.D. 980), *υ* for *β*, Luke vi. 34; *β* for *υ*, John x. 1.

epsilon are very graceful, and the whole style elegant and, after a little practice, easily read. Burney 22 (*facsimile* No. 36) is dated about the same time, A.D. 1319, and the four Biblical lines much resemble Burney 21, but the lines below, containing the date (which yet on the whole seem to be *primâ manu*) are so full of flourishes and contractions, that they cannot easily be deciphered at a first glance[1]. In the fourteenth century a careless style came into fashion, of which Cod. Leicestr. (No. 35) is an exaggerated instance, and during this century and the next our manuscripts, though not devoid of a certain beauty of appearance, are too full of arbitrary and elaborate contractions to be conveniently read. The formidable lists of abbreviations and ligatures represented in Donaldson's Greek Grammar (p. 20, 2nd ed.) originated at this period in the perverse ingenuity of the Greek emigrants in the West of Europe, who subsisted by their skill as copyists; and these pretty puzzles (for such they now are to many a fair classical scholar), by being introduced into early printed books[2], have largely helped to withdraw them from use in modern times.

12. We have now to describe the practice of Biblical manuscripts as regards the insertion of *ι* forming a diphthong with the long vowels *eta* and *omega*, whether by being *ascript*, i.e. written by their side, or *subscript*, i.e. written under them. In the earliest inscriptions and in the papyri of Thebes *ι ascript* (the *iota* not smaller than the other letters) is invariably found. In the petition to Ptolemy Philometor (*above*, p. 36) it occurs four times in the first line, three times in the third: in the fragments of Hyperides it is perpetually though not always read, even where (especially with verbs) it has no rightful place, e.g. ετωι και αντιβολωι (*facsim.* No. 9, ll. 3, 4) for *αἰτῶ καὶ ἀντιβολῶ*. A little before the Christian æra it began to grow obsolete, probably from its being lost in pronunciation. In the Herculaneum Philodemus (the possible limits of whose

[1] The full signature is *ἐτελειώθη τὸ παρὸν ἅγιον εὐαγγέλιον κατὰ τὴν κ̄ζ̄ τοῦ ἰαννουαρίου μηνὸς τῆς ω̄κ̄ζ ἐγχρονίας*. Presuming that ϛ̄ is suppressed before ω̄κ̄ζ, this is 6827 of the Greeks, A.D. 1319.

[2] Thus the type cast for the Royal Printing Office at Paris, and used by Robert Stephens, is said to have been modelled on the style of the calligrapher Angelus Vergecius, from whose skill arose the expression "he writes like an angel." Codd. 296 of the Gospels, 124 of the Acts, 151 of St Paul are in his hand.

date is from B.C. 50 to A.D. 79) it is often dropped, though more usually written. In Cod. Frid-August. it is very rare, and from this period it almost disappears from Biblical uncials[1]; in Cureton's Homer of the fifth or perhaps of the sixth century ι *ascript* is sometimes neglected, but usually inserted; sometimes also ι is placed *above* Η or Ω, an arrangement neither neat nor convenient. With the cursive character ι *ascript* came in again, as may be seen from the subscriptions in the Bodleian Euclid and Plato (page 36, *note* 3). The *semi-cursive* fragment of St Paul's Epistles in red letters, used for the binding of Harleian 5613, contains ι *ascript* twice, but I have tried in vain to verify Griesbach's statement (*Symbol. Crit.* II. p. 166) that it has ι *subscript* "bis tantum aut ter." I can find *no* such instance in these leaves. The cursive manuscripts, speaking generally, either entirely omit both forms, or, if they give either, far more often neglect than insert them. Cod. 1 of the Gospels (*facsim.* No. 23, l. 1) exhibits the *ascript* ι. Of 43 codices now in England which have been examined with a view to this matter, twelve have no vestige of either fashion, fifteen represent the *ascript* use, nine the *subscript* exclusively, while the few that remain have both indifferently. The earliest cursive copy ascertained to exhibit ι *subscript* (and that but a few times) is the Cod. Ephesius or Wetstein's 71, dated A.D. 1160. The *subscript* ι came much in vogue during the 15th century, and thus was adopted in printed books.

13. Breathings and accents present more difficulty, by reason of a practice that prevailed about the 7th or 8th centuries of inserting them in older manuscripts, where they were absent *primâ manu.* That such was done in many instances (e.g. in Codd. Vatican. and Coislin. 202 or H of St Paul) appears clearly from the fact that the passages which the scribe who retouched the old letters (p. 23) for any cause left unaltered, are destitute of these marks, though they appear in all other places. The case of Cod. Alexandrinus is less easy. Though the rest of the book has neither spirits (except a few here and there) nor accents, the first four lines of *each* column of the book of Genesis (see *facsimile* No. 12), which are written in red, are fully furnished

[1] Yet Tischendorf (N. T. 1859, Proleg. p. cxxxiii) cites ηιδισαν from Cod. Bezae (Mark i. 34), ξυλωι (Luke xxiii. 31) from Cod. Cyprius, ωι from Cod. U (Matth. xxv. 15), Cod. Λ (Luke vii. 4).

with them. These marks Baber, who edited the Old Testament portion of Cod. A, pronounced to be by a second hand (Notae, p. 1); Sir Frederick Madden, a more competent judge, declares them the work of the original scribe (Madden's Sylvestre, Vol. I. p. 194 note), and after repeated examination we know not how to dissent from his view. The Cureton palimpsest of Homer also has them, though they are occasionally obliterated, and some few are evidently inserted by a corrector; the case is nearly so with the Milan Homer edited by Mai; and the same must be stated of the Vienna Dioscorides (Sylvestre No. 62), whose date is fixed by internal evidence to about A.D. 500. These facts, and others like these, may make us hesitate to adopt the notion generally received among scholars on the authority of Montfaucon (*Palaeogr. Graec.* p. 33), that breathings and accents were not introduced *primâ manu* before the 7th or 8th century; though even at that period, no doubt, they were placed very incorrectly, and often omitted altogether. The breathings are much the more ancient and important of the two. The *spiritus lenis* indeed may be a mere invention of the Alexandrian grammarians of the second or third century before Christ, but the *spiritus asper* is in fact the substitute for a real letter (H) which appears on the oldest inscriptions; its original shape being the first half of the H (|–), of which the second half was subsequently adopted for the *lenis* (–|). This form is sometimes found in manuscripts of about the eleventh century (e.g. Lebanon, B.M. Addit. 11300 or k[scr], and usually in Lambeth 1178 or d[scr]), but even in the Cod. Alexandrinus the comma and inverted comma are several times substituted to represent the *lenis* and *asper* respectively (*facsim.* No. 12): and at a later period this last was the ordinary, though not quite the invariable mode of expressing the breathings. Aristophanes of Byzantium (keeper of the famous Library at Alexandria under Ptolemy Euergetes, about B.C. 240) though probably not the inventor of the Greek accents, was the first to arrange them into a system. Accentuation must have been a welcome aid to those who employed Greek as a learned, though not as their vernacular tongue, and is so convenient and suggestive that no modern scholar can afford to dispense with its familiar use: yet not being, like the rough breathing, an essential portion of the language, it was but slowly brought into general vogue. It would seem that in Augustine's age [354—430], the distinction between the smooth and rough breathing in manuscripts was just such a point as a careful reader would mark, a hasty one overlook[1]. Hence it is not surprising that though these marks are entirely absent both from the Theban and Herculaneum papyri, a few breathings appear by the first hand in Cod. Borgianus or T (Tischendorf, N.T. 1859, Proleg. p. cxxxi). Such as appear, together with some accents in the Coislin Octateuch of the 6th or 7th century, may not the less be *primâ manu* because many pages are destitute of them; those of Cod. Claromontanus, which were once deemed original, are now pronounced by its editor Tischendorf to be a later addition. Cod. N, the purple fragment so often spoken of already, exhibits *primâ manu* over some vowels a kind of smooth breathing or slight acute accent, sometimes little larger than a point, but on no intelligible principle, so far as we can see, and far oftener omits them entirely: all copies of Scripture which have not been specified, down to the end of the 7th century, are quite destitute of them. The chief manuscript of the 8th century, Cod. L or Paris 62 of the Gospels, has them for the most part, but not always; though often in the wrong place, and at times in utter defiance of all grammatical rules. Cod. B of the Apocalypse, however, though of the same age, has breathings and accents as constantly and correctly as most. Codices of the ninth century, with the exception of three written in the West of Europe (Codd. Augiensis or Paul F, Sangallensis or Δ of the Gospels and Boernerianus or Paul G, which will be particularly described in the next section), are all accompanied with these marks in full, though set often down without any precise rule, so far as our experience has enabled us to observe. The uncial Evangelistaria (e.g. Arundel 547; Parham 18; Harleian. 5598), especially, are much addicted to prefixing the *spiritus asper* improperly; chiefly, perhaps, to words beginning with H, so that documents of that age are but poor authorities on such points. Of the cursives the

[1] He is speaking (Quæstion. super Genes. clxii.) of the difference between *ῥάβδου αὐτοῦ* and *ῥάβδου αὑτοῦ*, Gen. xlvii. 31. "Fallit enim eos verbum Græcum, quod eisdem literis scribitur, sive *ejus*, sive *suæ*: sed accentus [he must mean the breathings] dispares sunt, et ab eis, qui ista noverunt, in codicibus non contemnuntur." (Opera, Tom. IV. p. 53, ed. 1586, Lugdun.) adding that "suæ" *might* be expressed by *ἑαυτοῦ*.

general tendency is to be more and more accurate as regards the accentuation, the later the date: but this is only a general rule, as some that are early are as careful, and certain of the latest as negligent as can well be imagined. All of them are partial to placing accents or breathings over both parts of a word compounded with a preposition (e. g. *ἐπὶσυνάξαι*), and on the other hand often drop them between a preposition and its case (e. g. *ἐπάροτρον*).

14. The punctuation in early times was very simple. In the papyri of Hyperides there are no stops at all; in the Herculanean rolls exceeding few: Codd. Frid-August. and Vaticanus (the latter very rarely by the first hand) have a single point here and there on a level with the top of the letters, and occasionally a very small break in the continuous uncials, with or without the point, to denote a pause in the sense. Codd. A N have the same point a little oftener; in Codd. C, W[a] (Paris 314) Z the single point stands indiscriminately at the head, middle or foot of the letters, while in E (Basil. K. IV. 35) of the Gospels and B of the Apocalypse this change in the position of the point indicates a full-stop, half-stop, or comma respectively. In Cod. L of the same date as these two, besides the full point we have the comma (::.) and semicolon (::), with a cross also for a stop. In Codd. Y Θ (of about the eighth century) the single point has its various powers as in Cod. E, &c., but besides this are double, treble, and in Cod. Y quadruple, points with different powers. In late uncials, especially Evangelistaria, the chief stop is a cross, often in red (e.g. Arund. 547); while in Harleian. 5598 ⁝ seems to be the note of interrogation. When the continuous writing came to be broken up into separate words (of which Cod. Augiensis in the ninth century affords the earliest example) the single point was intended to be placed after the last letter of each word, on a level with the middle of the letters. But even in this copy they are often omitted in parts, and in Codd. Δ G, written on the same plan, more frequently still. Our statements refer only to the *Greek* portions of these copies; the Latin semicolon (;) and note of interrogation (?) occur in the Latin versions. The Greek interrogation (;) first occurs about the ninth century, and (,) used as a stop a little

later. In the earliest cursive the system of punctuation is much the same as that of printed books: the English colon (:) not being used, but the upper single point in its stead. In a few cursives (e. g. Gonville or 59 of the Gospels), this upper point, set in a larger space, stands also for a full stop: indeed (·) is the only stop found in Tischendorf's lo[ti] of the Acts (Brit. Mus. Add. 20,003): while (;) and (·) are often confused in 440 of the Gospels (Cantab. Mm. 6. 9). The English comma, placed above a letter, is used for the apostrophus, which occurs in the very oldest uncials, especially at the end of proper names, or to separate compounds (e. g. *απ' ορφανισθεντες* in Cod. Clarom.), or when the word ends in *ρ* (e. g. *θυγατηρ'* in Codd. Sinait. and A, *χειρ'* in Cod. A, *ὥσπερ'* Dioscorides, A.D. 500), or even to divide syllables (e.g. *συριγ'γας* in Cod. Frid-August., *πολ'λα*, *κατεστραμ'μενη*, *αναγ'γελι* in Cod. Sinaiticus). This mark is more rare in Cod. Ephraemi than in some others, but is used more or less by all, and is found after *εξ*, or *ουχ*, and a few like words, even in the most recent cursives.

15. Abbreviated words are stated to be least met with in Cod. Vatican., though we scarcely know that copy intimately enough to speak on such a minute point: but even it has $\overline{θσ}$, $\overline{κσ}$, $\overline{ισ}$, $\overline{χσ}$ for *θεός*, *κύριος*, &c. and their cases. Besides these Codd. Frid-August., Alex., Ephraem. and the rest supply $\overline{ανοσ}$, $\overline{ουνοσ}$, $\overline{πνα}$ ($\overline{πνε}^{υ}$ Cod. L), $\overline{πηρ}$, $\overline{μηρ}$, $\overline{ιλημ}$ or $\overline{ιηλμ}$ or $\overline{ιημ}$, $\overline{ιηλ}$ or $\overline{ισλ}$ or $\overline{ιηλ}$, $\overline{δαδ}$, and some of them $\overline{σηρ}$ for *σώτηρ*, $\overline{υσ}$ for *υἱός*, $\overset{θ}{\overline{παρνοσ}}$ for *παρθενος*. Cod. Bezae abridges the sacred names into $\overline{χρσ}$, $\overline{ιησ}$[1] &c. and their cases, as very frequently, but by no means invariably, do the kindred Codd. Augiens., Sangall., and Boerner. A few dots sometimes supply the place of the line denoting abbreviation (e. g. $\dot{θ}\dot{σ}$ Cotton Genesis, $\ddot{α}\ddot{ν}\ddot{ο}\ddot{σ}$ Colbert. Pentateuch). A straight line over the last letter of a line indicates N (or also M in the Latin of Codd. Bezae and Claromont.) in all the Biblical uncials, but is simply placed over numerals in the Herculanean rolls: ϗ, τ\, and less often θ\ for *καί*, *-ται*, *-θαι* are met with in Cod. Frid-August. and all later: ȣ for *ου*

[1] Even Codex Sinaiticus has $\overline{ιηυ}$ and $\overline{ιυ}$ in consecutive lines (Apoc. xxii. 20, 21).

chiefly in Codd. L, Augiensis and the more recent uncials. Such *compendia scribendi* as [symbol] in the Herculanean rolls (above p. 29) occur mostly at the end of lines: that form, $\mathrm{M}^{o}\Upsilon$ (No. 11a, l. 4), and a few more even in the Cod. Frid-August.; in Cureton's Homer we have Π^{s} for *πους*, C^{s} for *-σας* and such like. In later books they are more numerous and complicated, particularly in cursive writing: the terminations ° for *ος*, ¯ for *ν*, \` for *ον*, ~ for *ως*, ^{s} for *ης*, ^{v} for *ου* are familiar; besides others, peculiar to one or a few copies; e. g. h for *αυ*, b for *ερ*, ¯ for *α*, ⊐ for *αρ* in the Emmanuel College copy of the Epistles (Paul 30), and : for *α*, ʳ for *αν*, √ for *ας* in Parham 17 of the Apocalypse. The mark > is not only met with in the Herculanean rolls, but in the Hyperides (*facsim.* 9, l. 6) in Codd. Frid-August., the two Pentateuchs, Codd. Augiensis, Sangall. and Boernerianus, and seems merely designed to fill up vacant space, like the flourishes in a legal instrument. Capital letters at the beginning of clauses, &c. are freely met with in all documents excepting in the oldest papyri, the Herculanean rolls, Codd. Frid-August., Vatican., the Colbert Pentateuch and one or two fragments besides. Their absence is a proof of high antiquity. All however are apt to crowd small letters into the end of a line to save room, and if these small letters preserve the form of the larger, it is natural to conclude that the scribe is writing in a natural hand, not an assumed one, and the argument for the antiquity of such a document, derived from the shape of its letters, thus becomes all the stronger. The continuous form of writing separate words must have prevailed in manuscripts long after it was obsolete in common life: Cod. Claromont., which is continuous even in its Latin version, divides the words in the inscriptions and subscriptions to the several books.

16. The stichometry of the sacred books has next to be considered. The term *στίχοι*, like the Latin *versus*, originally referring whether to rows of trees, or of the oars in a trireme (Virg. *Æn.* v. 119), would naturally come to be applied to lines of poetry, and in this sense it is used by Pindar (*ἐπέων στίχες Pyth.* IV. 100) and also by Theocritus (*γράψον καὶ τόδε γράμμα, τό σοι στίχοισι χαράξω Idyl.* XXIII. 46), if the common reading be correct. Both Epiphanius [d. 403] and Chrysostom (*vid. Suicer.*

Thesaur. Eccles. Tom. II. p. 1033) inform us that the book of Psalms was in their time divided into στίχοι, as in fact we may see for ourselves in Codd. Sinaiticus and Vatican. (*facsimile* No. 20), wherein, according to the true principles of Hebrew poetry, the verses do not correspond in metre or quantity of syllables, but in the parallelism or relationship subsisting between the several members of the same sentence or stanza[1]. It seems to have occurred to Euthalius, a deacon of Alexandria, as it did long afterwards to Bishop Jebb when he wrote his "Sacred Literature," that a large portion of the New Testament might be divided into στίχοι on the same principles: and that even where that distribution should prove but artificial, it would guide the public reader in the management of his voice, and remove the necessity for an elaborate system of punctuation. Such, therefore, we conceive to be the use and design of stichometry, as applied to the Greek Testament by Euthalius, whose edition of St Paul's Epistles thus divided was published A.D. 458, that of the Acts and Epistles A.D. 490. Who arranged the στίχοι of the Gospels (which are in truth better suited for such a process than the Epistles) has not appeared. Although but few manuscripts now exist that are written στοιχηδόν (a plan that consumed too much vellum to become general), we read in many copies at the end of each of the books of the New Testament, a calculation of the number of στίχοι it contained, sufficiently unlike to shew that the arrangement was not the same in all codices, yet near enough to prove that they were divided on the same principle (*for these numbers see below*, p. 57)[2]. In the few documents that remain written στιχηρῶς, the length of the clauses is very unequal; some (e.g. Cod. Bezae, *see* sect. II. *of this chapter and the specimen pages*) containing as much in a line as might be conveniently read aloud in a breath, others (e.g. Cod. Laud. of the Acts) having only one or two words

1 That we have rightly understood Epiphanius' notion of the στίχοι is evident from his own language respecting Psalm cxli. 1, wherein he prefers the addition made by the Septuagint to the second clause, because by so doing its authors ἀχώλωτον ἐποίησαν τὸν στίχον: so that the passage should run "O Lord, I cry unto Thee, make haste unto me || Give hear to the voice of my request," τῆς δεήσεώς μου to complete the rhythm.

2 At the end of 2 Thess., in a hand which Tischendorf states to be very ancient, but not that of the original scribe, the Codex Sinaiticus has στιχων ρπ [180; the usual number is 106]: at the end of 2 Cor. there is no such note.

in a line. The Cod. Claromontanus (*facsim.* No. 19) in this respect lies between those extremes, and the fourth great example of this class (Cod. Coislin. 202, H of St Paul) of the sixth century, has one of its few surviving pages (of 16 lines each) arranged *literatim* as follows (1 Cor. x. 22, &c.): *εσμεν* | *παντα μοι εξεστιν* | *αλλ ου παντα συμφερει* | *παντα μοι εξεστιν* | *αλλ ου παντα οικοδομει* | *μηδεισ το εαυτου ζη|τειτω* (*ob necessitatem spatii*) | *αλλα το του ετερου* | *παν το εν μακελλω πω* | *λουμενον* (*ob necessitatem*) | *εσθιετε μηδενα ανα* | *κρινωντεσ δια πην* | *συνειδηοινι* | *του γαρ κ̅ν̅ η γη καμοπλη* | *ορωμα αυτησ* (*ob necessit.*) | *ιδετιοααλθιυμαοιτō.* | Other manuscripts written *στιχηρῶς* are Matthaei's V of the 8th century, Bengel's Uffenbach 3 of St John (Wetstein's 101), Alter's Forlos. 29 (26 of the Apocalypse), and, as it would seem, the Cod. Sangallensis Δ. In Cod. Claromont. there are scarcely any stops (the middle point being chiefly reserved to follow abridgements or numerals), the stichometry being of itself an elaborate scheme of punctuation, but the longer *στίχοι* of Cod. Bezae are often divided by a single point.

17. In using manuscripts of the Greek Testament, we must carefully note whether a reading is *primâ manu* or by some subsequent corrector. It will often happen that these last are utterly valueless, having been inserted even from printed copies by a modern owner (like some marginal variations of the Cod. Leicestrensis), and such as these really ought not to have been extracted by collators at all; while others by the second hand are almost as weighty, for age and goodness, as the text itself. All these points are explained by critical editors for each document separately; in fact to discriminate the different corrections in regard to their antiquity and importance is often the most difficult portion of such editor's task (e. g. in Cod. Claromontanus), and one on which he often feels it hard to satisfy his own judgment. Corrections by the original scribe, or a contemporary reviser, where they can be satisfactorily distinguished, must be regarded as a portion of the testimony of the manuscript itself, inasmuch as every carefully prepared copy was reviewed and compared (*ἀντεβλήθη*), if not by the writer himself, by a skilful person appointed for the task (*ὁ διορθῶν, ὁ διορθωτής*), whose duty it was to amend manifest errors, sometimes also to insert ornamented capitals in places which had been reserved for them;

in later times (and as some believe at a very early period) to set in stops, breathings and accents: in copies destined for ecclesiastical use to place the musical notes that were to guide the intonation of the reader.' These notices of revision are sometimes met with at the end of the best manuscripts. Such is the note in Cod. H of St Paul *εγραψα και εξεθεμην προσ το εν Καισαρια αντιγραφον τησ βιβλιοθηκησ του ἁγιου Παμφιλου*, the same library of the Martyr Pamphilus to which the scribe of the Cod. Frid-August. resorted for his model[1]; and that in Birch's most valuable Urbino-Vatican. 2 (157 of the Gospels), written for the Emperor John II (1118—1143), wherein at the end of the first Gospel we read *κατὰ Ματθαῖον ἐγράφη καὶ ἀντεβλήθη ἐκ τῶν ἐν ἱεροσολύμοις παλαιῶν ἀντιγράφων τῶν ἐν ἁγίω ὄρει* [Athos] *ἀποκειμένων*: similar subscriptions are appended to the other Gospels. See also Evan. Λ. 20. 164. 262. 300. 376; Act. 15. 83, in the third section of this chapter.

18. We have next to give some account of ancient divisions of the text, as found in manuscripts of the New Testament, which must be carefully noted by the student, as few copies are without one or more of them.

(1). So far as we know at present, the oldest still extant are those of the Codex Vaticanus, which are printed from its margin in Mai's second edition. These sections seem to have been formed for the purpose of reference, and a new one always commences where there is some break in the sense. Many, however, at least in the Gospels, consist of but one of our modern verses, and they are so unequal in length as to be rather inconvenient for actual use. St Matthew contains 170 of these divisions, St Mark 62, St Luke 152, St John 80. In the Acts of the Apostles are two sets of sections, 36 longer and in an older hand, 69 smaller and

[1] The following subscription to the book of Ezra (and a very similar one follows Esther) in the Cod. Frid-August. (fol. 13. 1) will show the care bestowed on the most ancient copies even of the Septuagint. *Αντεβληθη προσ παλαιωτατον λιαν αντιγραφον δεδιορθωμενον χειρι του αγιου μαρτυροσ Παμφιλου· ὁπερ αντιγραφον προσ τω τελει ὑποσημειωσισ τισ ἰδιοχειροσ αυτου ὑπεκειτο εχουσα ουτωσ· μετελημφθη και διορθωθη προσ τα εξαπλα ωριγενουσ· Αντωνινοσ αντεβαλεν· Παμφιλοσ διορθωσα.* Tregelles suggests that the work of the *διορθώτης* or *corrector* was probably of a critical character, the office of the *ἀντιβάλλων* or *comparer* rather to eliminate mere clerical errors (Treg. Horne, II. p. 85).

more recent. Each of these also begins after a break in the sense, but they are quite independent of each other, as a larger section will sometimes commence in the middle of a smaller, the latter being in no wise a subdivision of the former. Thus the greater Γ opens Acts ii. 1, in the middle of the lesser β, which extends from Acts i. 15 to ii. 4. As in most manuscripts, so in this, the Catholic Epistles follow the Acts, and in them and in St Paul's Epistles there are also two sets of sections, only that in the Epistles the older sections are the more numerous. The Pauline Epistles are reckoned throughout as one book in the elder notation, with however this remarkable peculiarity, that though in the Vatican itself the Epistle to the Hebrews stands next after the second to the Thessalonians, *and on the same leaf with it*, the sections are arranged as if it stood between the Epistles to the Galatians and Ephesians; for whereas that to the Galatians ends with § 58, that to the Ephesians begins with § 70, and the numbers proceed regularly down to § 93, with which the second to the Thessalonians ends. The Epistle to the Hebrews which then follows opens with § 59; the last section extant opens Hebr. ix. 11, and the manuscript ends abruptly at *καθα v.* 14. It plainly appears, then, that the sections of the Codex Vaticanus must have been copied from some yet older document, in which the Epistle to the Hebrews preceded that to the Ephesians. For a list of the more modern divisions in the Epistles see the Table in p. 58 below. The Vatican sections of the Gospels have been recently observed by Tregelles in *one* other copy, the palimpsest Codex Zacynthius of St Luke (Ξ), which he is preparing for publication.

(2). Hardly less ancient, and indeed ascribed by some to Tatian the Harmonist, the disciple of Justin Martyr, is the division of the Gospels into larger chapters (*κεφάλαια majora*, called in the Latin copies *breves*), or titles (*τίτλοι*), which latter name they bear from the circumstance that not only is the sacred narrative distributed by them into sections, but the title, or general summary of contents, is appended to the numeral, either in a separate table preceding each Gospel, or at the top and bottom of the pages, or (what is usual enough) in both ways in the same manuscript. It is strange that in none of the four Gospels does the first section stand at its commencement. In St Matthew section A begins at chap. ii. verse 1, and has for its title *περὶ τῶν μάγων*: in St Mark at chap. i. *v.* 23, *περὶ τοῦ δαιμονιζομένου*: in St Luke at ch. ii. *v.* 1, *περὶ τῆς ἀπογραφῆς*: in St John at ch. ii. *v.* 1, *περὶ τοῦ ἐν Κανᾶ γάμου.* Mill accounts for this circumstance by supposing that in the first copies the titles at the head of each Gospel were reserved till last for more splendid illumination, and thus eventually forgotten (Proleg. N. T. § 355); Griesbach holds, that the general inscriptions of each Gospel, *Κατὰ Ματθαῖον*, *Κατὰ Μάρκον*, &c. were regarded as the special titles of the first sections also. On either supposition, however, it is hard to explain how what was really the second section came to be *numbered* as the first; and it is worth notice that the same arrangement takes place in the *κεφάλαια* (though these are of a later date) of all the other books of the New Testament except the Acts, 2 Corinth., Ephes., 1 Thess., Hebrews, James, 1, 2 Peter, 1 John, and the Apocalypse: e.g. the first section of the Epistle to the Romans opens ch. i. *v.* 18, *Πρῶτον μετὰ τὸ προοίμιον, περὶ κρίσεως τῆς κατὰ ἐθνῶν τῶν οὐ φυλασσόντων τὰ φυσικά.*

The *τίτλοι* in St Matthew amount to 68, in St Mark to 48, in St Luke to 83, in St John to 18. This mode of division is found in the Codices Alexandrinus and Ephraemi of the fifth century, and in the Codex Nitriensis of the sixth; each of which have tables of them prefixed to the several Gospels: but the Codices Alexandrinus and Dublinensis of St Matthew, and that portion of the purple Cotton fragment which is in the Vatican, exhibit them in their usual position, at the top and bottom of the pages. Thus it appears that even if no trace of these *τίτλοι* be extant in the Sinai manuscript (on which point Tischendorf is silent), they were too generally diffused in the fifth century, not to have originated at an earlier period; although we must concede that the *κεφάλαιον* spoken of by Clement of Alexandria (*Stromat.* I.) when quoting Dan. xii. 12, or by Athanasius (*c. Arium*) on Act. ii., and the *Capitulum* mentioned by Tertullian (*Ad Uxorem* II. 2) in reference to 1 Cor. vii. 12, contain no certain allusions to any specific divisions of the sacred text, but only to the particular paragraphs or passages in which their citations stand. But that the contrary habit has grown inveterate[1], it

[1] And this too in spite of the lexicographer Suidas: Τίτλος διαφέρει κεφαλαίου· καὶ ὁ μὲν Ματθαῖος τίτλους ἔχει ξη', κεφάλαια δὲ τνέ.

were much to be desired that the term *τίτλοι* should be applied to these longer divisions, at least in the Gospels, and that of *κεφάλαια* reserved for the smaller sections (*κεφάλαια minora,* as they are sometimes called) which we now proceed to explain.

(3). The Ammonian sections, or *κεφάλαια* proper, were not constructed, as the Vatican divisions and the *τίτλοι*, for the purpose of easy reference, or distributed like them according to the breaks in the sense, but for a wholly different purpose. So far as we can ascertain, the design of Tatian's Harmony was simply to present to Christian readers a single connected history of our Lord, by taking from the four Evangelists indifferently whatsoever best suited his purpose[1]. As this plan could scarcely be executed without *omitting* some portions of the sacred text, it is not surprising that Tatian, without any evil intention, should have incurred the grave charge of mutilating Holy Scripture[2]. A more scholar-like and useful attempt was subsequently made by Ammonius of Alexandria, in the third century, who, by the side of St Matthew's Gospel which he selected as his standard, arranged in parallel columns, as it would seem, the corresponding passages of the other three Evangelists, so as to exhibit them all at once to the reader's eye; St Matthew in his proper order, the rest as the necessity of abiding by St Matthew's order prescribed. This, at least, is the account given by the celebrated Eusebius, Bishop of Cæsarea, the Church historian, who in the fourth century, in his letter to Carpianus, describes his own most ingenious system of Harmony, as founded on the labours of Ammonius[3]. It has been generally thought that the *κεφάλαια*, of

[1] *Ὁ Τατιανὸς, συνάφειάν τινα καὶ συναγωγὴν οὐκ οἶδ' ὅπως τῶν εὐαγγελίων συνθεὶς, τὸ διὰ τεσσάρων τοῦτο προσωνόμασεν· ὃ καὶ παρά τισιν εἰσέτι νῦν φέρεται.* Euseb. Hist. Eccl. IV. 29.

[2] Ambros. in Procem. Luc. seems to aim at Tatian when he says "Plerique etiam ex quatuor Evangelii libris in unum ea quæ venenatis putaverunt assertionibus convenientia referserunt." Eusebius H. E. IV. 29 charges him on report with *improving* not the Gospels, but the Epistles: *τοῦ δὲ ἀποστόλου φασὶ τολμῆσαι τινὰς αὐτὸν μεταφράσαι φωνάς, ὡς ἐπιδιορθούμενον αὐτῶν τὴν τῆς φράσεως σύνταξιν.*

[3] *Ἀμμώνιος μὲν ὁ Ἀλεξανδρεύς, πολλήν, ὡς εἰκός, φιλοπονίαν καὶ σπουδὴν εἰσαγηοχώς, τὸ διὰ τεσσάρων ἡμῖν καταλέλοιπεν εὐαγγέλιον, τῷ κατὰ Ματθαῖον τὰς ὁμοφώνους τῶν λοιπῶν εὐαγγελιστῶν περικοπὰς παραθεὶς, ὡς ἐξ ἀνάγκης συμβῆναι τὸν τῆς ἀκολουθίας εἱρμὸν τῶν τριῶν διαφθαρῆναι, ὅσον ἐπὶ τῷ ὕφει τῆς ἀναγνώσεως.* Epist. ad Carpian.

which St Matthew contains 355, St Mark 236, St Luke 342, St John 232, were made by Ammonius for the purpose of his work, and they have commonly received the name of the Ammonian sections: but this opinion has been called in question by Bp Lloyd (*Nov. Test. Oxon.* 1827, *Monitum pp.* viii—xi), who strongly urges that, in his Epistle to Carpianus, Eusebius not only refrains from ascribing these numerical divisions to Ammonius, but almost implies that they had their origin at the same time with his own ten canons, with which they are so intimately connected[1]. That they were essential to Eusebius' scheme is plain enough: their place in Ammonius' parallel Harmony is not easily understood, unless indeed (what is nowhere stated, but rather the contrary), he did not set the passages from the other Gospels at full length by the side of St Matthew's, but only these numerical references to them[2].

There is, however, one ground for hesitation before we ascribe the sections, as well as the canons, to Eusebius; viz. that not a few ancient manuscripts (e.g. Codd. FHY) contain the former, while they omit the latter. Of palimpsests indeed it may be said with reason, that the rough process which so nearly obliterated the ink of the older writing, would completely remove the coloured paint (*κιννάβαρις*, *vermilion*, prescribed by Eusebius, though blue or green is occasionally found) in which the canons were invariably noted; hence we need not wonder at their absence from the Codices Ephraemi, Nitriensis, Dublinensis, Codd. IW[b] of Tischendorf, and the Wolfenbüttel fragments (P, Q), in all which the sections are yet legible in ink. The Codex Sinaiticus contains both; but Tischendorf decidedly pronounces them to be

[1] I subjoin Eusebius' own words (Epist. ad Carpian.) from which no one would infer that the *sections* were not his, as well as the *canons*. *Αὕτη μὲν οὖν ἡ τῶν ὑποτεταγμένων κανόνων ὑπόθεσις· ἡ δὲ σαφὴς αὐτῶν διήγησις, ἔστιν ἥδε. Ἐφ' ἑκάστῳ τῶν τεσσάρων εὐαγγελίων ἀριθμός τις πρόκειται κατὰ μέρος, ἀρχόμενος ἀπὸ τοῦ πρώτου, εἶτα δευτέρου, καὶ τρίτου, καὶ καθεξῆς προϊὼν δι' ὅλου μέχρι τοῦ τέλους τοῦ βιβλίου* [the sections]. *Καθ' ἕκαστον δὲ ἀριθμὸν ὑποσημείωσις διὰ κινναβάρεως πρόκειται* [the canons], *δηλοῦσα ἐν ποίῳ τῶν δέκα κανόνων κείμενος ὁ ἀριθμὸς τυγχάνει.*

[2] Something of this kind, however, must be the plan adopted in Codex E of the Gospels, as described by Tregelles, who himself collated it. "[It has] the Ammonian sections; but instead of the Eusebian canons there is a kind of harmony of the Gospels noted at the foot of each page, by a reference to the parallel sections of the other Evangelists." Horne's Introd. Vol. II. p. 200. Yet the canons *also* stand in this copy under the Ammonian sections: only the *table* of Eusebian canons is wanting.

in a later hand. In the Codex Bezae too, as well as the Codex Cyprius (K), even the Ammonian sections, without the canons, are by a later hand, though the latter has prefixed the list or table of the canons. Of the oldest copies the Codex Alexandrinus, Tischendorf's Codd. W^a Θ, and the Cotton fragment (N) alone contain both the sections and canons. Even in more modern cursive books the latter are often deficient, though the others are present. This we have observed in Burney 23, in the British Museum, of the twelfth century, although the Epistle to Carpianus stands at the beginning; in a rather remarkable copy of about the twelfth century, in the Cambridge University Library (Mm. 6. 9, Scholz Evan. 440), which, however, the table of canons but not the Epistle to Carpianus precedes; in the Gonville and Caius Gospels of the 12th century (Evan. 59), and in a manuscript of about the thirteenth century at Trinity College, Cambridge (B. x. 17)[1]. These facts certainly indicate that in the judgment of critics and transcribers, whatever that judgment may be deemed worth, the Ammonian sections had a previous existence to the Eusebian canons, as well as served for an independent purpose.

In his letter to Carpianus, their inventor clearly yet briefly describes the purpose of his canons, ten in number. The first contains a list of 71 places in which all the four Evangelists have a narrative, discourse, or saying in common: the second of 111 places in which the three Matthew, Mark, Luke agree: the third of 22 places common to Matthew, Luke, John: the fourth of 26 passages common to Matthew, Mark, John: the fifth of 82 places in which the two Matthew, Luke coincide: the sixth of 47 places wherein Matthew, Mark agree: the seventh of 7 places common to Matthew and John: the eighth of 14 places common to Luke and Mark: the ninth of 21 places in which Luke and John agree: the tenth of 62 passages of Matthew, 21 of Mark, 71 of Luke and 97 of John which have no parallels, but are peculiar to a single Evangelist. Under each of the 1165 Ammonian sections, in its proper place in the margin of a manuscript, is put in coloured ink the number of that Eusebian canon to which it refers; on searching for that Ammonian

[1] To this list of manuscripts of the Gospels which have the Ammonian sections without the Eusebian canons add Codd. 54, 60, 68 (to be described in the third section of this chapter), and probably some others (e.g. Cod. 263).

section in the proper table or canon, there will also be found the parallel place or places in the other Gospels, each indicated by its proper numeral, and so readily searched out. A single example will serve to explain our meaning. In the facsimile of the Cotton fragment (Plate v. No. 14), in the margin of the passage (John xv. 20) we see $\frac{\overline{\mathrm{P}\Lambda\Theta}}{\Gamma}$, where ΡΛΘ (139) is the proper section of St John, Γ (3) the number of the canon. On searching the third Eusebian table we read MT. ϛ Λ. $\overline{\nu\eta}$ ΙΩ. $\overline{\rho\lambda\theta}$, and thus we learn that the first clause of John xv. 20 is parallel in sense to the 90th (ϛ) section of St Matthew (x. 24), and to the 58th ($\overline{\nu\eta}$) of St Luke (vi. 40). The advantage of such a system of parallels to the exact study of the Gospels is too evident to need insisting on.

(4). The Acts of the Apostles and the Epistles are also divided into *chapters* (κεφάλαια) in design precisely the same as the τίτλοι of the Gospel, and nearly resembling them in length. Since there is no trace of these chapters in the two great Codices Alexandrinus and Ephraemi, of the fifth century (which yet exhibit the τίτλοι and Ammonian sections), it seems reasonable to assume that they are of later date. They are sometimes connected with the name of Euthalius, deacon of Alexandria, and afterwards Bishop of Sulci[1], whom we have already spoken of, as the reputed author of Scriptural stichometry (*above*, p. 45). We learn, however, from Euthalius' own Prologue to his edition of St Paul's Epistles (A.D. 458), that the "summary of the chapters," and consequently the numbers of the chapters themselves, was taken from the work of "one of our wisest and pious fathers[2]," i.e. some Bishop that he does not wish to particularise, whom Mill (Proleg. N. T. § 907) conjectures to be Theodore of Mopsuestia, who lay under the censure of the Church. Soon after[3] the publication of St Paul's Epistles, on

[1] Sulci in Sardinia is the only Bishop's see of the name I can find in Carol. a Sancto Paulo's Geographia Sacra (1703), or in Bingham's Antiquities, Bk. IX, Chapp. II, VII. Horne and even Tregelles speak of Sulca in Egypt, but I have searched in vain for any such town or see.

[2] καθ' ἑκάστην ἐπιστολὴν προτάξομεν τὴν τῶν κεφαλαίων ἔκθεσιν, ἑνὶ τῶν σοφωτάτων τινὶ καὶ φιλοχρίστων πατέρων ἡμῶν πεπονημένην.

[3] Αὐτίκα δῆτα is his own expression.

the suggestion of one Athanasius, then a priest and afterwards Patriarch of Alexandria, Euthalius put forth a similar edition of the Acts and Catholic Epistles, also divided into chapters, with a summary of contents at the head of each chapter, though even these he is thought to have derived (at least in the Acts) from the manuscript of Pamphilus the Martyr [d. A.D. 308], to whom the very same chapters are ascribed in a document published by Montfaucon (Bibliotheca Coislin. p. 78); the rather as Euthalius fairly professes to have compared his book in the Acts and Catholic Epistles "with the copies in the library at Cæsarea" which once belonged to "Eusebius the friend of Pamphilus." The Apocalypse still remained to be divided, about the end of the fifth century, by Andreas, Archbishop of the Cappadocian Cæsarea, into twenty-four *paragraphs* (λόγοι), corresponding to the number of the elders about the throne (Apoc. iv. 4); each paragraph being subdivided into three *chapters* (κεφάλαια). The summaries which Andreas wrote of his seventy-two chapters are still reprinted in Mill's and other large editions of the Greek Testament.

(5). To Euthalius has been also referred a division of the Acts into sixteen lessons (ἀναγνώσεις or ἀναγνώσματα) and of the Pauline Epistles into thirty-one; but these lessons are quite different from the much shorter ones adopted by the Greek Church. He is also said to have numbered the quotations from the Old Testament in each Epistle of St Paul, which are still noted in many of our manuscripts, and to have been the author of that reckoning of the στίχοι which is annexed in most copies to the Gospels, as well as to the Acts and Epistles. Besides the division of the text into στίχοι or *lines* (*above*, p. 44) we find in the Gospels alone another division into ῥήματα or ῥήσεις "sentences," differing but little from the στίχοι in number. Of these last the precise numbers vary in different copies, though not considerably: whether that variation arose from the circumstance that ancient numbers were represented by letters and so easily corrupted, or from a different mode of arranging the στίχοι adopted by the various scribes.

19. It is proper to state that the *subscriptions* (ὑπογραφαὶ) appended to St Paul's Epistles in many manuscripts, and retained

even in the Authorised English version of the New Testament, are also said to be the composition of Euthalius. In the best copies they are somewhat shorter in form, but in any shape they do no credit to the care or skill of their author, whoever he may be. "Six of these subscriptions," writes Paley in that masterpiece of acute reasoning, the Horæ Paulinæ, "are false or improbable;" that is they are either absolutely contradicted by the contents of the epistle [e.g. 1 Cor. Galat. 1 Tim.], or are difficult to be reconciled with them [e.g. 1, 2 Thess. Tit.] (Hor. Paul. Ch. xv).

The *subscriptions* to the Gospels have not, we believe, been assigned to any particular author, and being seldom found in printed copies of the Greek Testament or in modern versions, are little known to the general reader. In the earliest manuscripts the subscriptions, as well as the *titles* of the books, were of the simplest character. Κατὰ Μαθθαῖον, κατὰ Μάρκον, &c. is all that the Codex Vaticanus (and apparently Cod. Sinaiticus also) has, whether at the beginning or the end. Εὐαγγέλιον κατὰ Ματθαῖον is the subscription to the first Gospel in the Codex Alexandrinus; εὐαγγέλιον κατὰ Μάρκον is placed at the beginning of the second Gospel in the same manuscript, and the self-same words at the end of it by Codices Alex. and Ephraem: in the Codex Bezae (in which St John stands second in order) we merely read εὐαγγέλιον κατὰ Μαθθαῖον ἐτελέσθη, ἄρχεται εὐαγγέλιον κατὰ Ἰωάννην. The same is the case throughout the New Testament. After a while the titles become more elaborate, and the subscriptions afford more information, the truth of which it would hardly be safe to vouch for. The earliest worth notice are found in the Codex Cyprius of the eighth or ninth century, which, together with those of several other copies, are given in Scholz's Prolegomena N. T. Vol. I. pp. xxix, xxx. *Ad fin. Matthæi:* Τὸ κατὰ Ματθαῖον εὐαγγέλιον ἐξεδόθη ὑπ' αὐτοῦ ἐν ἱεροσολύμοις μετὰ χρόνους η̄ [ὀκτὼ] τῆς τοῦ Χριστοῦ ἀναλήψεως. *Ad fin. Marci:* Τὸ κατὰ Μάρκον εὐαγγέλιον ἐξεδόθη μετὰ χρόνους δέκα τῆς τοῦ Χριστοῦ ἀναλήψεως. Those to the other two Gospels exactly resemble St Mark's, that of St Luke however being dated 15, that of St John 32 years after our Lord's Ascension, periods in all probability too early to be correct.

20. The foreign matter so often inserted in later manuscripts has more value for the antiquarian than the critic. That splendid copy of the Gospels Lambeth 1178, of the 10th or 11th century, has more such matter than is often found, set off by fine illuminations. At the end of each of the first three Gospels (but not of the fourth) are several pages relating to them extracted from Cosmas Indicopleustes, who made the voyage which procured him his cognomen about A.D. 522; also some iambic verses of no great excellence, as may well be supposed. In golden letters we read: *ad fin. Matth.* *ἰστέον ὅτι τὸ κατὰ ματθαῖον εὐαγγέλιον ἑβραΐδι διαλέκτωι γραφὲν ὑπ' αὐτοῦ· ἐν ἱερουσαλὴμ ἐξεδόθη· ἑρμηνεύθη δὲ ὑπὸ ἰωάννου· ἐξηγεῖται δὲ τὴν κατὰ ἄνθρωπον τοῦ χῦ γένεσιν, καί ἐστιν ἀνθρωπόμορφον τοῦτο τὸ εὐαγγέλιον.* The last clause alludes to Apoc. iv. 7, wherein the four living creatures were currently believed to be typical of the four Gospels[1]. *Ad fin. Marc.* *ἰστέον ὅτι τὸ κατὰ μάρκον εὐαγγέλιον ὑπηγορεύθη ὑπὸ πέτρου ἐν ῥώμηι· ἐποιήσατο δὲ τὴν ἀρχὴν ἀπὸ τοῦ προφητικοῦ λόγου τοῦ ἐξ ὕψους ἐπιόντος τοῦ ἡσαΐου· τὴν πτερωτικὴν εἰκόνα τοῦ εὐαγγελίου δεικνύς.* *Ad fin. Luc.* *ἰστέον ὅτι τὸ κατὰ λουκᾶν εὐαγγέλιον ὑπηγορεύθη ὑπὸ πέτρου ἐν ῥώμηι· ἅτε δὲ ἱερατικοῦ χαρακτῆρος ὑπάρχοντος ἀπὸ ζαχαρίου τοῦ ἱερέως θυμιῶντος ἤρξατο.* The reader will desire no more of this. The oldest manuscript known to be accompanied by a *catena* (or continuous commentary by different authors) is the palimpsest Codex Zacynthius (Ξ of Tregelles), an uncial of the eighth century. Such books are not very common, but there is a very full commentary in minute letters, surrounding the large text in a noble copy of the Gospels, of the 12th century, now belonging to Sir Thomas Phillipps (Middle Hill 13975), yet uncollated; another of St Paul's Epistles (No. 27) belongs to the Public Library at Cambridge (Ff. 1.30); and the Apocalypse is often attended with the exposition of Andreas (p. 54), or Arethas, also Archbishop of the Cappadocian Cæsarea in the

[1] The whole mystery is thus unfolded (appareutly by Cosmas) in Lamb. 1178, p. 159. *Καὶ γὰρ τὰ Χερουβὶμ τετραπρόσωπα· καὶ τὰ πρόσωπα αὐτῶν εἰκόνες τῆς πραγματείας τοῦ υἱοῦ τοῦ θεοῦ· τὸ γὰρ ὅμοιον λέοντι, τὸ ἔμπρακτον καὶ βασιλικὸν καὶ ἡγεμονικὸν* [John i. 1—3] *χαρακτηρίζει· τὸ δὲ ὅμοιον μόσχωι, τὴν ἱερουργικὴν καὶ ἱερατικὴν* [Luke i. 8] *ἐμφανίζει· τὸ δὲ ἀνθρωποειδές, τὴν σάρκωσιν* [Matth. i. 18] *διαγράφει· τὸ δὲ ὅμοιον ἀετῶι, τὴν ἐπιφοίτησιν τοῦ ἁγίου πνεύματος* [Mark i. 2] *ἐμφανίζει.*

tenth century, or (what is more usual) with a sort of epitome of them (e. g. Parham No. 17), above, below and in the margin beside the text, in much smaller characters. In *cursive* manuscripts only the Subject (ὑπόθεσις), especially that written by Œcumenius in the tenth century, sometimes stands as a Prologue before each book, but not so often before the Gospels or Apocalypse as the Acts and Epistles. Before the Acts we occasionally meet with Euthalius' Chronology of St Paul's Travels, or another Ἀποδημία Παύλου. The Leicester manuscript contains between the Pauline Epistles and the Acts (1) An Exposition of the Creed, and statement of the errors condemned by the seven general Councils, ending with the second at Nice. (2) Lives of the Apostles, followed by an exact description of the limits of the five Patriarchates. Similar treatises may be more frequent in manuscripts of the Greek Testament than we are at present aware of.

21. We have not thought it needful to insert in this place either a list of the τίτλοι of the Gospels, or of the κεφάλαια of the rest of the New Testament, or the tables of the Eusebian canons, inasmuch as they are all accessible in such ordinary books as Stephens' Greek Testament 1550 and Mill's of 1707, 1711. The Eusebian canons are given in Bishop Lloyd's Oxford Greek Test. of 1827 &c. and in Tischendorf's of 1859. We subjoin, however, for the sake of comparison, a tabular view of ancient and modern divisions: the numbers of the ῥήματα and στίχοι in the Gospels are derived from the most approved sources, but a synopsis of the variations of manuscripts in this respect has been drawn up by Scholz, Prolegomena N. T. Vol. I. Cap. V. pp. xxviii, xxix.[1]

[1] The numbers of the Gospel στίχοι in our table are taken from the uncial copies Codd. GS and 27 cursives named by Scholz: those of the ῥήματα from Codd. 9. 13. 124 and 7 others. In the ῥήματα he cites no other variation than that Cod. 339 has 2822 for St Matthew: but Mill states that Cod. 48 (Bodl. 7) has 1676 for Mark, 2507 for Luke (N. T. Proleg. §. 1429).

In the στίχοι, a few straggling manuscripts fluctuate between 3397? and 1474 for Matthew; 2006 and 1000 for Mark; 3827 and 2000 for Luke; 2300 and 1300 for John. But the great mass of authorities stand as we have represented.

TABLE OF ANCIENT AND MODERN DIVISIONS OF THE NEW TESTAMENT.

	Vatican MS. older sections.	Vatican MS. later sections.	τίτλοι	κεφάλαια Ammon.	στίχοι	ῥήματα	Modern chapters	Modern verses.
Matthew	170	—	68	355	2560	2522	28	1071
Mark	62	—	48	236	1616	1675	16	678
Luke	152	—	83	342	2740	3803	24	1151
John	80	—	18	232	2024	1938	21	880
			Euthal. κεφάλ.			ἀναγνώσματα		
Acts	36	69	40	N.B. The στίχοι of the Acts and all the Epistles except Hebr. are taken from the Codex Passionei (G and J), an uncial of the ninth century.	2524	16	28	1007
James	9	5	6		242		5	108
1 Peter	8	3	8		236		5	105
2 Peter	desunt	2	4		154		3	61
1 John	14	3	7		274		5	105
2 John	1	2	1		30		1	13
3 John	1	desunt	1		32		1	15
Jude	2	desunt	4		68		1	25
Romans	93 sections in Rom. 1, 2 Corinth. Gal. Eph. Coloss. 1, 2 Thess. to Hebr. ix. 14.	8	19		920	5	16	433
1 Corinth.		19 (1, 2 Corinth.)	9		870	5	16	437
2 Corinth.			10		590	4	13	256
Galat.		3	12		293	2	6	149
Ephes.		3	10		312	2	6	155
Philipp.		2	7		208	2	4	104
Coloss.		3	10		208	2	4	95
1 Thess.		2	7		193	1	5	89
2 Thess.		2	6		106	1	3	47
1 Tim.		—	18		230	1	6	113
2 Tim.		—	9		172	1	4	83
Titus		—	6		98	1	3	46
Philem.		—	2		38	1	1	25
Hebrews		5 to ix. 11	22		703	3	13	303
Apocalypse	24 λόγοι, 72 κεφάλαια, 1800 στίχοι.						22	405

22. On the divisions into chapters and verses prevailing i our modern Bibles we need not dwell long. For many centurie the Latin Church used the Greek *τίτλοι* (which they calle *breves*) and Euthalian *κεφάλαια*, and some of their copies eve retained the calculation by *στίχοι*: but about A.D. 1248 Ca dinal Hugo de Santo Caro, while preparing a Concordance, c

index of declinable words, for the *whole Bible*, divided it into its present chapters, subdividing *them* in turn into several parts by placing the letters A, B, C, D &c. in the margin, at equal distances from each other, as we still see in many old printed books, e.g. Stephens' N. T. of 1550. Cardinal Hugo's divisions (unless indeed he merely adopted them from Lanfranc or some other scholar) soon took possession of copies of the Latin Vulgate; they gradually obtained a place in later Greek manuscripts, especially those written in the West of Europe, and are found in the earliest printed and all later editions of the Greek Testament, though still unknown to the Eastern Church. They certainly possess no strong claim on our preference, although they cannot now be superseded. The chapters are inconveniently and capriciously unequal in length; occasionally too they are distributed with much lack of judgment. Thus Matth. xv. 39 belongs to ch. xvi, and perhaps ch. xix. 30 to ch. xx; Mark v. 1 and ix. 1 properly appertain to the preceding chapters; Luke xxi. 1—4 had better be united with ch. xx, as in Mark xii. 41—44; Acts v. might as well commence with Acts iv. 32; Acts viii. 1 (or at least its first clause) should not have been separated from ch. vii; Acts xxi. concludes with strange abruptness. Bp. Terrot (on Ernesti's Institutes, Vol. II. p. xxi.) rightly affixes 1 Cor. iv. 1—5 to ch. iii; 1 Cor. xi. 1 belongs to ch. x; Col. iv. 1 must clearly go with ch. iii.

In commendation of the modern verses still less can be said. As they are stated to have been constructed after the model of the ancient στίχοι (called "*versus*" in the Latin manuscripts) we have placed in the Table the exact number of each for every book in the New Testament. Of the στίχοι we reckon 19241 in all, of the modern verses 7959[1], so that on the average (for we have seen that the manuscript variations in the number of στίχοι are but inconsiderable) we may calculate about five στίχοι to every two modern verses. The fact is that some such division is simply *indispensable* to every accurate reader of Scripture; and Cardinal Hugo's divisions by letters of the alphabet, as well as those adopted by Sanctes Pagninus in his Latin version of the whole Bible (1528), having proved inconveniently large, Robert Stephens, the justly celebrated printer and editor of the Greek

[1] Our English version, by dividing 2 Cor. xiii. 12 into two, contains 7960 verses.

Testament, undertook to form a system of verse-divisions, taking for his model the short verses into which the Hebrew Bible had already been divided, as it would seem by Rabbi Nathan, in the preceding century. We are told by Henry Stephens (Præf. N. T. 1576) that his father Robert executed this design on a journey from Paris to Lyons "*inter equitandum;*" that is, we presume, while resting at the inns on the road. Certain it is, that although every such division must be in some measure arbitrary, a very little care would have spared us many of the disadvantages attending that which Robert Stephens first published at Geneva in his Greek Testament of 1551, from which it was introduced into the Geneva English Testament of 1557, into Beza's Greek Testament of 1565, and thence into all subsequent editions. It is now too late to correct the errors of the verse-divisions, but they can be neutralised, at least in a great degree, by the plan adopted by modern critics, of banishing both the verses and the chapters into the margin, and breaking the text into paragraphs, better suited to the sense. The *pericopæ* or sections of Bengel[1] (whose labours will be described in their proper place) have been received with general approbation, and adopted, with some modification, by several recent editors.

23. We now come to the *contents* of manuscripts of the Greek Testament, and must distinguish regular copies of the sacred volume or of parts of it, from Lectionaries, or Church-lesson books, containing only extracts, arranged in the order of Divine Service daily throughout the year. The latter we will consider presently: with regard to the former it is right to bear in mind, that comparatively few copies of the whole New Testament remain; the usual practice being to write the four Gospels in one volume, the Acts and Epistles in another: manuscripts of the Apocalypse, which was little used for public worship, being much rarer than those of the other books. Occasionally the Gospels, Acts and Epistles form a single volume; sometimes the Apocalypse is added to other books; as to the Pauline Epistles in Lambeth 1186, or even to the Gospels, in a later hand (e. g. Cambridge Publ. Libr. Dd. 9. 69: Gospels No. 60,

[1] Novum Testamentum Græcum. Edente Jo. Alberto Bengelio. Tubingæ 1734. 4to.

dated A.D. 1297). The Apocalypse, being a short work, is often found bound up in volumes containing very miscellaneous matter, (e. g. Vatican. 2066 or B; Harleian. 5678, No. 31; and Barocc. 48, No. 28). The Codex Sinaiticus of Tischendorf is the more precious, that it happily exhibits the whole New Testament complete: so would the Codices Alexandrinus and Ephraemi, but that they are sadly mutilated: no other uncial copies have this advantage, and very few cursives. In England only four such are known, the great Codex Leicestrensis, which is imperfect at the beginning and end; Butler 2 (Additional 11837), dated A.D. 1357, and Additional 17469, both in the British Museum; and Canonici 34 in the Bodleian, dated A.D. 1515—16. The Apocalypse in the well-known Codex Montfortianus at Dublin is usually considered to be by a later hand. Besides these Scholz enumerates only nineteen foreign copies of the whole New Testament[1]; but twenty-seven in all out of the vast mass of extant documents.

24. Whether copies contain the whole or a part of the sacred volume, the general *order* of the books is the following: Gospels, Acts, Catholic Epistles, Pauline Epistles, Apocalypse. A solitary manuscript of the fifteenth century (Venet. 10, Evan. 209) places the Gospels between the Pauline Epistles and the Apocalypse[2]; in the Codices Sinaiticus, Leicestrensis, Fabri (Evan. 90), and Montfortianus, as in Bodleian Canonici 34, the Pauline Epistles *precede* the Acts; the Codex Basiliensis (No. 4 of the Epistles) and Lambeth 1182, 1183 have the Pauline Epistles immediately after the Acts and before the Catholic Epistles, as in our present Bibles; Scholz's Evan. 368 stands thus, St John's Gospel, Apocalypse, then all the Epistles; in

[1] Coislin. 199, Evan. 35; Vatic. 2080, Evan. 175; Palat. Vat. 171, Evan. 149; Lambecc. 1 at Vienna, Evan. 218; Vatic. 1160, Evan. 141; Venet. 5, Evan. 205; its alleged duplicate Venet. 10, Evan. 209; Matthaei k, Evan. 241; Moscow Synod. 280, Evan. 242; Paris, Reg. 47, Evan. 18; Reg. 61, Evan. 263; Vatic. 360, Evan. 131; Vat. Ottob. 66, Evan. 386; Vat. Ottob. 381, Evan. 390; Taurin. 302, Evan. 339; Richard. 84, Evan. 368; S. Saba, 10 and 20, Evan. 462 and 466: perhaps he ought to have added Venet. 6, Evan. 206, which he states to contain the whole New Testament, Proleg. N. T. Vol. I. p. lxxii. In Evan. 180 all except the Gospels are by a later hand.

[2] I presume that the same order is found in Evan. 393, where Scholz states "sec. XVI, continet epist. cath. paul. ev." Proleg. N. T. Vol. I. p. xc.

Havniens. 1 No. 234 of the Gospels (A.D. 1278) the order appears to be Acts, Paul. Ep., Cath. Ep., Gospels; in Basil. B. VI. 27 or Cod. 1, the Gospels now follow the Acts and Epistles; while in Evan. 175 the Apocalypse stands between the Acts and Catholic Epistles; in Evan. 51 the *binder* has set the Gospels last: these, however, are mere accidental exceptions to the prevailing rule[1]. The four Gospels are almost invariably found in their familiar order, although in the Codex Bezae (as we partly saw above, p. 55) they stand Matthew, John, Luke, Mark; in the Codex Monacensis (X) John, Luke, Mark, Matthew (but two leaves of Matthew *also* stand before John); in Cod. 90 (Fabri) John, Luke, Matthew, Mark; in the Curetonian Syriac version Matthew, Mark, John, Luke. In the Pauline Epistles that to the Hebrews precedes the four Pastoral Epistles and immediately follows the second to the Thessalonians in the four great Codices Sinaiticus, Alexandrinus, Vaticanus and Ephraem[2]: in the copy from which the Cod. Vatican. was taken the Hebrews followed the Galatians (*above, p.* 48). The Codex Claromontanus, the document next in importance to these four, sets the Colossians appropriately enough next to its kindred and contemporaneous Epistle to the Ephesians, but postpones that to the Hebrews to Philemon, as in our present Bibles; an arrangement which at first, no doubt, originated in the early scruples prevailing in the *western* Church, with respect to the authorship and canonical authority of that divine epistle.

25. We must now describe the *Lectionaries* or Service-books of the Greek Church, in which the portions of Scripture publicly read throughout the year are set down in chronological order, without regard to their actual places in the sacred volume. In

[1] Mr Horne in the second volume of his own Introduction (a very different book from Dr Tregelles', and not a worse one) tells us that in some of the few manuscripts which contain the whole of the New Testament the books are arranged thus: Gospels, Acts, Catholic Epistles, Apocalypse, Pauline Epistles (p. 92 ed. 1834). This statement may be true of some of the foreign MSS. named in note 3, but of the English it can refer to none except perhaps Wake 2, No 27 of Apocalypse, which seems to conclude with a fragment of the Gospels.

[2] Tischendorf cites the following copies in which the Epistle to the Hebrews stands in the same order as in ℵABC, "H [Coislin. 202] 17. 23. 47. 57. 71. 73 *aliique.*" Add 77. 189. 196. Epiphanius (*adv. Hær.* I. 42) says: ἄλλα δὲ ἀντίγραφα ἔχει τὴν πρὸς ἑβραίους δεκάτην, πρὸ τῶν δύο τῶν πρὸς Τιμόθεον καὶ Τίτον.

length and general arrangement they resemble not so much the Lessons as the Epistles and Gospels in our English Book of Common Prayer, only that *every* day in the year has its own proper portion, and the numerous Saints' days independent services of their own. These Lectionaries consist either of lessons from the Gospels, and are then called *Evangelaria* or *Evangelistaria* (εὐαγγελιστάρια); or from the Acts and Epistles, termed *Praxapostolos* (πραξαπόστολοι); the general name of Lectionary is often, though incorrectly, confined to the latter class. A few books (called ἀποστολοευαγγέλια in Matthæi's ξ and Burney 18) have lessons taken both from the Gospels and the Apostolic writings. The peculiar arrangement of Lectionaries renders them very unfit for the hasty, partial, cursory collation which has befallen too many manuscripts of the other class, and this circumstance, joined with the irksomeness of using service-books never familiar to the habits even of scholars in this part of Europe, has caused these documents to be so little consulted, that the contents of the very best and oldest among them have until recently been little known. Matthaei, of whose elaborate and important edition of of the Greek Testament (12 tom. Riga 1782—88) we shall give an account hereafter (Chap. v.), has done excellent service in this department; two of his best copies, the uncials B and H, being Evangelistaria. The present writer also has collated three noble uncials of the same kind, Arundel 547 being of the ninth century, Parham 18 bearing date A.D. 980, Harleian. 5598, A.D. 995. Not a few other uncial Lectionaries remain quite neglected, for though none of them perhaps are older than the eighth century, the ancient character was retained for these costly and splendid service-books till about the eleventh century (Montfauc. Palaeogr. Graec. p. 260), before which time the cursive hand was generally used in other Biblical manuscripts. There is, of course, no place in a lectionary for divisions by κεφάλαια, for the Ammonian sections or canons of Eusebius.

The division of the New Testament into Church-lessons was, however, of far more remote antiquity than the employment of separate volumes to contain them. Towards the end of the fourth century, that golden age of Patristic theology, Chrysostom recognises some stated order of the lessons as familiar to all his hearers, for he exhorts them to peruse and mark before-hand the passages (περικοπαὶ) of the Gospels which were to be publicly read to them the ensuing Sunday or Saturday[1]. All the information we can gather favours the notion that there was no great difference between the calendar of Church-lessons in earlier and later ages. Not only do they correspond in all cases where such agreement is natural, as in the proper services for the great feasts and fasts, but in such purely arbitrary arrangements as the reading of the book of Genesis, instead of the Gospels, on the *week* days of Lent; of the Acts all the time between Easter and Pentecost[2]; or the selection of St Matthew's history of the Passion *alone* at the Liturgy on Good Friday[3]. The earliest formal Synaxarion, or Table of proper lessons, now extant is prefixed to the Codex Cyprius (K) of the eighth or ninth century; another is found in the Codex Campensis (M), which is perhaps a little later; they are more frequently found than the contrary in later manuscripts of every kind; while there are comparatively few copies that have not been accommodated to ecclesiastical use either by their original scribe or a later hand, by means of noting the proper days for each lesson (often in red ink) at the top or bottom or in the margin of the several pages. In the text itself are perpetually interpolated, especially in vermillion or red ink, the beginning (ἀρχὴ or αρχ) and ending (τέλος or τελ) of each lesson, and the several words to be inserted or substituted in order to suit the purpose of public reading; from which source (as we have stated above, p. 11) various readings have almost unavoidably sprung: e. g. in Acts iii. 11, τοῦ ἰαθέντος χωλοῦ of the Lectionaries ultimately displaced αὐτοῦ from the text itself.

We propose to annex to this section a table of lessons throughout the year, according to the use laid down in Synaxaria and Lectionaries, as well to enable the student to compare the proper lessons of the Greek Church with our own, as to facilitate reference to the manuscripts themselves, which are now

[1] Chrysost. in Joan. Hom. x κατὰ μίαν σαββάτων ἢ καὶ κατὰ σάββατον. I cite these words for the benefit of any one whom Dr Davidson (Bibl. Crit. Vol. II. p. 19) may have persuaded that σάββατον in the primitive Church meant *Sunday*.

[2] See the passages from Augustin Tract. VI. in Joan.; and Chrysost. Hom. VII. ad Antioch.; Hom. LXIII, XLVII. in Act. in Bingham's Antiquities, Book XIV, Chap. III. Sect. 3. Chrysostom even calls the arrangement τῶν πατέρων ὁ νόμος.

[3] August. Serm. CXLIII. de Tempore. The few verses Luke xxiii. 39—43, John xix. 31—37 are merely wrought into one narrative with Matth. xxvii. each in its proper place.

placed almost out of the reach of the inexperienced. On comparing the manner in which the terms are used by different scribes and authors, we conceive that *Synaxarion* (συναξάριον) is a general name applied to any catalogue of Church-lessons; that tables of daily lessons are entitled *Eclogadia*, "Selections" (ἐκλογάδιον τῶν δ' εὐαγγελιστῶν, or τοῦ ἀποστόλου), and that these have varied but slightly in the course of many ages throughout the whole Eastern Church; that tables of Saints' day lessons, called *Menologia* (μηνολόγιον), distributed in order of the months from September (when the new year and the indiction began) to August, differed widely from each other, both in respect to the lessons read and the days kept holy[1]. While the great feasts remained entirely the same, different generations and provinces and even dioceses had their favorite worthies, whose memory they specially cherished; so that the character of the menology (which sometimes formed a larger, sometimes but a small portion of a Lectionary) will often guide us to the country and district in which the volume itself was written. The Parham Evangelistarium 18 affords us a conspicuous example of this fact: coming from a region of which we know but little (Ciscissa in Cappadocia Prima), its menology in many particulars but little resembles those usually met with.

26. It only remains to say a few words about the *notation* adopted to indicate the several classes of manuscripts of the Greek Testament. These classes are six in number; that containing the Gospels, or the Acts and Catholic Epistles, or the Pauline Epistles, or the Apocalypse, or Lectionaries of the Gospels, or those of the Acts and Epistles. When one manuscript (as often occurs) belongs to more than one of these classes, its distinct parts are numbered separately, so that a copy of the *whole* New Testament will appear in four lists, and be reckoned four times over. In this way we calculate that there are little short of one thousand manuscripts proper or Lectionaries of the

[1] Thus συναξάριον will include Scholz's definition "indices lectionum ita exhibet, ut anni ecclesiastici et uniuscujusque evangelii ratio habeatur" (N. T. Vol. I. p. 454), as exemplified by his Codex Cyprius (K) &c.; and also Suicer's "vitae sanctorum et martyrum in compendium redactae, et succincta expositio solennitatis de quâ agitur" (Thes. Ecc. Tom. II. 1108), as we find the word used in Lambeth 1178, Burney 18 &c.

Gospels, and about another thousand of all the other books put together; whereof those of St Paul are more numerous, those of the Apocalypse fewer than those of the Acts and Catholic Epistles. All critics are agreed in distinguishing the documents written in the uncial character by capital letters; the custom having originated in the accidental circumstance that the Codex Alexandrinus was designated as Cod. A in the lower margin of Walton's Polyglott. These uncials are few: in the Gospels indeed they amount to thirty-four, but far the greater part of these are fragments, most of them of inconsiderable length; in the Acts they are ten; in the Catholic Epistles six; in the Pauline Epistles fourteen (many of them fragments); in the Apocalypse only four: Lectionaries in uncial letters are not marked by capitals, but by Arabic numerals, like cursive manuscripts of all classes. Michaelis judges that the use of these numerals, which were first introduced by Wetstein (N. T. 1751—52), is likely to lead to confusion and faults of the press: one can only say in reply that Mill's mode of citing copies by abridgments of their names (e. g. *Alex. Cant. Mont.* &c.) is more cumbersome, and has been found just as liable to error. A more serious cause of complaint is the facility with which documents have been admitted to crowd a list, when they have not been subjected to a thorough collation; many without being examined even cursorily. Such a practice, commenced by Wetstein, too much countenanced even by Griesbach (N. T. 1796—1806), conscientious labourer though he was in this field of critical study, was carried to its height by Scholz (N. T. 1830—36), who professes to have collated entire no more than *twenty-two* of the six hundred and seven manuscripts which his edition added to previous catalogues. On this point we shall enter more into detail hereafter (Chap. v.); the result, however, has been to convey to the inexperienced reader a totally false notion of our actual acquaintance with the contents of the cursive or later copies. Hence, while we owe a large debt of gratitude to those who have done so much for the uncial manuscripts of the Greek Testament, and freely accord the highest praise to Tischendorf and Tregelles for their indefatigable exertions in making them known to us, we are bound to state that the long list of the cursives is at present but a snare and a delusion; "a splendid wretchedness," as it has been called by one who knows its nature well. Even the catalogue itself of the later manuscripts is full of mis-statements, of repetitions and loose descriptions, which we have tried to remedy and supply, so far as our means of information extend. In describing the uncials (as we purpose to do in the next section) our course is tolerably plain; but the lists that comprise the third and fourth sections of this chapter, and which respectively detail the cursive manuscripts and Lectionaries of the Greek Testament, must be regarded only as a kind of first approximation to what such an enumeration ought to be, though much pains and time have been spent upon them: the comparatively few copies which seem to be sufficiently known are distinguished by an asterisk from their less fortunate kindred. Meanwhile the student is warned against the practice of Scholz, and not of Scholz only, who habitually alleges in defence of readings of the received text for which we know of almost no *specific* authority whatever, "*rec. cum multis recentibus familiæ constant. codicibus*[1]," "*rec. cum plerisque codicibus*," and such like expressions, which will be found on enquiry to prove nothing, save the writer's profound ignorance of what the mass of copies contains. Indeed the whole system of representing and of citing the cursive manuscripts is so radically unsound, that Tischendorf in his last edition (N. T. 1859) has chosen to add nothing to Scholz's numerical list, preferring to indicate the materials which have lately accrued by some other notation which he judges more convenient; such as lo^{ti} for the important copy of the Acts he discovered and sold to the British Museum (Addit. 20,003); 1^{pe}, 2^{pe}, &c. for the eleven which Edward de Muralt collated at St Petersburg for his New Test. 1848; and a^{scr}, b^{scr}, &c. for those derived from "A collation of about twenty manuscripts of the Holy Gospels...by F. H. Scrivener, 1853."

[1] The precise words of Scholz in speaking of ὅτι Matth. xviii. 28, for which it is believed that y^{scr}, an Evangelistarium unknown to Scholz, is the *sole* authority. Tregelles indeed in his N. T. 1857 cites the margin of the Codex Leicestrensis (69); but this, together with many other of its marginal notes, was inserted from a printed book by Wm. Chark, who owned the manuscript in Queen Elizabeth's reign.

APPENDIX TO SECTION I.

SYNAXARION AND ECLOGADION OF THE GOSPELS AND APOSTOLIC WRITINGS DAILY THROUGHOUT THE YEAR.

[Gathered chiefly from Evangelist. Arund. 547, Parham 18, Harl. 5598, Burney 22, and Christ's Coll. Camb.]

Ἐκ τοῦ κατὰ Ἰωάννην [Arundel, 547]

Τῇ ἁγίᾳ καὶ μεγάλῃ κυριακῇ τοῦ πάσχα.

Easter-day	John i. 1–17.	Acts i. 1–8.
2nd day of Easter week (τῆς διακινησίμου)	18–28.	12–26.
3rd	Luke xxiv. 12–35.	ii. 14–21.
4th	John i. 35–52.	38–43.
5th	iii. 1–15.	iii. 1–8.
6th (παρασκευῇ)	ii. 12–22.	ii. 22–36.
7th (σαββάτῳ)	iii. 22–33.	iii. 11–16.
Ἀντίπασχα or 1st Sunday after Easter	xx. 19–31.	v. 12–20.
2nd day of 2nd week	ii. 1–11.	iii. 19–26.
3rd	iii. 16–21.	iv. 1–10.
4th	v. 17–24.	13–22.
5th	24–30.	23–31.
6th (παρασκευῇ)	v. 30–vi. 2.	v. 1–11.
7th (σαββάτῳ)	vi. 14–27.	21–32.
Κυριακῇ γ′ or 2nd after Easter	Mark xv. 43–xvi. 8.	vi. 1–7.
2nd day of 3rd week	John iv. 46–54.	8–vii. 60.
3rd	vi. 27–33.	viii. 5–17.
4th	48–54.	18–25.
5th	40–44.	26–39.
6th (παρασκευῇ)	35–39.	40–ix. 19.
7th (σαββάτῳ)	xv. 17–xvi. 1.	19–31.

Κυριακῇ δ′ or 3rd Sunday after Easter	John v. 1–15.	ix. 32–42.
2nd day of 4th week	vi. 56–69.	x. 1–16.
3rd	vii. 1–13.	21–33.
4th	14–30.	xiv. 6–18.
5th	viii. 12–20.	x. 34–43.
6th (παρασκευῇ)	21–30.	44–xi. 10.
7th (σαββάτῳ)	31–42.	xii. 1–11.
Κυριακῇ ε′ or 4th Sunday after Easter	iv. 5–42.	xi. 19–30.
2nd day of 5th week	viii. 42–51.	xii. 12–17.
3rd	51–59.	25–xiii. 12.
4th	vi. 5–14.	xiii. 13–24.
5th	ix. 39–x. 9.	xiv. 20–27.
6th (παρασκευῇ)	x. 17–28.	xv. 5–12.
7th (σαββάτῳ)	27–38.	35–41.
Κυριακῇ ς′ or 5th Sunday after Easter	ix. 1–38.	xvi. 16–34.
2nd day of 6th week	xi. 47–54.	xvii. 1–9.
3rd	xii. 19–36.	19–27.
4th	36–47.	xviii. 22–28.
5th Ἀναλήψεως, Ascension Day		
Matins,	Mark xvi. 9–20.	
Liturgy,	Luke xxiv. 36–73.	i. 1–12
6th (παρασκευῇ)	John xiv. 1–10.	xix. 1–8
7th (σαββάτῳ)	10–21.	xx. 7–12

Κυριακῇ ϛ' or 6th Sunday
after Easter τῶν ἁγίων πατέρων ἐν Νικαίᾳ.
xvii. 1–13. 16–38.
2nd day of 7th
week xiv. 27–xv. 7. xxi. 8–14.
3rd xvi. 2–13. 26–32.
4th 15–23. xxiii. 1–11.
5th 23–33. xxv. 13–19.
6th (παρασκευῇ)
xvii. 18–26. xxvii. 1–xxviii. 1.
7th (σαββάτῳ) xxi. 14–25. xxviii. 1–31.

Κυριακῇ τῆς πεντηκοστῆς
Whitsunday
Matins, xx. 19–23.
Liturgy, vii. 37–viii. 12.[1] ii. 1–11.

Ἐκ τοῦ κατὰ Ματθαῖον.

2nd day of 1st week Τῇ ἐπαύριον τῆς πεντηκοστῆς.
Matth. xviii. 10–20. Ephes. v. 8–19.
3rd iv. 25–v. 11.
4th 20–30.
5th 31–41.
6th (παρασκευῇ) vii. 9–18.
7th (σαββάτῳ) v. 42–48. Rom. i. 7–12.

Κυριακῇ α' τῶν ἁγίων πάντων x. 32–33; 37–38; xix. 27–30. Hebr. xi. 33–xii. 2.
2nd day of 2nd week vi. 31–34; vii. 9–14.
3rd vii. 15–21.
4th 21–23.
5th viii. 23–27.
6th (παρασκευῇ) ix. 14–17.
7th (σαββάτῳ) vii. 1–8. Rom. iii. 19–26.

Κυριακῇ β' iv. 18–23. Rom. ii. 10–16.
2nd day of 3rd
week ix. 36–x. 8.
3rd 9–15.
4th 16–22.
5th 23–31.
6th (παρασκευῇ) 32–36; xi. 1.
7th (σαββάτῳ)
vii. 24–viii. 4. Rom. iii. 28–iv. 3.

Κυριακῇ γ' vi. 22–33. Rom. v. 1–10.
2nd day of 4th
week xi. 2–15.
3rd 16–20.
4th 20–26.
5th 27–30.
6th (παρασκευῇ) xii. 1–8.
7th (σαββάτῳ) viii. 14–23. Rom. vi. 11–17.

Κυριακῇ δ' viii. 5–13. Rom. vi. 18–23.
2nd day of 5th
week xii. 9–13.
3rd 14–16; 22–30.
4th 38–45.
5th xii. 46–xiii. 3.
6th (παρασκευῇ) 3–12.
7th (σαββάτῳ) ix. 9–13. Rom. viii. 14–21.

Κυριακῇ ε' viii. 28–ix. 1. Rom. x. 1–10.
2nd day of 6th
week xiii. 10–23.
3rd 24–30.
4th 31–36.
5th 36–43.
6th (παρασκευῇ) 44–54.
7th (σαββάτῳ) ix. 18–26. Rom. ix. 1–5.

Κυριακῇ ϛ ix. 1–8. Rom. xii. 6–14.
2nd day of 7th
week xiii. 54–58.
3rd xiv. 1–13.
4th xiv. 35–xv. 11.
5th 12–21.
6th (παρασκευῇ) 29–31.
7th (σαββάτῳ) x. 37–xi. 1. Rom. xii. 1–3.

Κυριακῇ ζ' xi. 27–35. Rom. xv. 1–7.
2nd day of 8th
week xvi. 1–6.
3rd 6–12.
4th 20–24.
5th 24–28.
6th (παρασκευῇ) xvii. 10–18.
7th (σαββάτῳ) xii. 30–37. Rom. xiii. 1–10.

Κυριακῇ η' xiv. 14–22. 1 Cor. i. 10–18.
2nd day of 9th
week xviii. 1–11.
3rd xviii. 18–20; xix. 1–2; 13–15.
4th xx. 1–16.
5th 17–28.
6th (παρασκευῇ) xxi. 12–14; 17–20.
7th (σαββάτῳ) xv. 32–39. Rom. xiv. 6–9.

[1] The *pericope adulteræ* Jo. vii. 53—viii. 11 is omitted in all the copies we know on the feast of entecost. Whenever read it was on some Saints' Day (*vid. infra, p.* 74, *notes* 2, 3).

Κυριακῇ θ' xiv. 22–34. 1 Cor. iii. 9–17.
2nd day of 10th
week xxi. 18–22.
3rd 23–27.
4th 28–32.
5th 43–46.
6th (παρασκευῇ) xxii. 23–33.
7th (σαββάτῳ)
xvii. 24–xviii. 1. Rom. xv. 30–33.

Κυριακῇ ι' xvii. 14–23. 1 Cor. iv. 9–16.
2nd day of 11th
week xxiii. 13–22.
3rd 23–28.
4th 29–39.
5th xxiv. 13–28.
6th (παρασκευῇ) 27–35; 42–51.
7th (σαββάτῳ) xix. 3–12. 1 Cor. i. 3–9.

Κυριακῇ ια' xviii. 22–35. 1 Cor. ix. 2–12.

Ἐκ τοῦ κατὰ Μάρκον.

2nd day of 12th
week Mark i. 9–15.
3rd 16–22.
4th 23–28.
5th 29–35.
6th (παρασκευῇ) ii. 18–22.
7th (σαββάτῳ)
Matth. xx. 29–34. 1 Cor. i. 26–29.

Κυριακῇ ιβ'
Matth. xix. 16–20. 1 Cor. xv. 1–11.
2nd day of 13th
week Mark iii. 6–12.
3rd 13–21.
4th 20–27.
5th 28–35.
6th (παρασκευῇ) iv. 1–9.
7th (σαββάτῳ)
Matth. xxii. 15–22. 1 Cor. ii. 6–9.

Κυριακῇ ιγ'
Matth. xxi. 33–42. 1 Cor. xvi. 13–24.
2nd day of 14th
week Mark iv. 10–23.
3rd 24–34.
4th 35–41.
5th v. 1–20.
6th (παρασκευῇ) v. 22–24; 35–vi. 1.
7th (σαββάτῳ)
Matth. xxiii. 1–12. 1 Cor. iv. 1–5.

Κυριακῇ ιδ'
Matth. xxii. 2–14. 2 Cor. i. 21–ii. 4.
2nd day of 15th
week Mark v. 24–34.
3rd vi. 1–7.
4th 7–13.
5th 30–45.
6th (παρασκευῇ) 45–53.
7th (σαββάτῳ)
Matth. xxiv. 1–13. 1 Cor. iv. 17–v. 5.

Κυριακῇ ιε'
Matth. xxii. 35–41. 2 Cor. iv. 6–11.
2nd day of 16th
week Mark vi. 54–vii. 3.
3rd 5–16.
4th 14–24.
5th 24–30.
6th (παρασκευῇ) viii. 1–10.
7th (σαββάτῳ)
Matth. xxiv. 34–37; 42–44.
1 Cor. x. 23–28.

[Κυριακῇ ις' (16th) Matth. xxv. 14–30.
σαββάτῳ ιζ' (17th) Matth. xxv. 1–13.
Κυριακῇ ιζ' (17th) Matth. xv. 21–28.]

Ἀρχὴ τῆς ἰνδικτοῦ τοῦ νέου ἔτους, ἤγουν τοῦ εὐαγγελιστοῦ λουκᾶ [Arund. 547, Parham, 18].

Ἐκ τοῦ κατὰ Λουκᾶν [Christ's Coll.].

2nd day of 1st
week Luke iii. 19–22.
3rd 23–iv. 1.
4th 1–15.
5th 16–22.
6th (παρασκευῇ) 22–30.
7th (σαββάτῳ) 31–36.

Κυριακῇ α' v. 1–11.
2nd day of 2nd
week iv. 38–44.
3rd v. 12–16.
4th 33–39.
5th vi. 12–16.
6th (παρασκευῇ) 17–23.
7th (σαββάτῳ) v. 17–26.

Κυριακῇ β' vi. 31–36.
2nd day of 3rd
week 24–30.
3rd 37–45.
4th vi. 46–vii. 1.
5th vii. 17–30.
6th (παρασκευῇ) 31–35
7th (σαββάτῳ) v. 27–32

Κυριακῇ γʹ vii. 11–16.
2nd day of 4th week 36–50.
3rd viii. 1–3.
4th 22–25.
5th ix. 7–11.
6th (παρασκευῇ) 12–18.
7th (σαββάτῳ) vi. 1–10.

Κυριακῇ δʹ viii. 5–15.
2nd day of 5th week ix. 18–22.
3rd 23–27.
4th 43–50.
5th 49–56.
6th (παρασκευῇ) x. 1–15.
7th (σαββάτῳ) vii. 1–10.

Κυριακῇ εʹ xvi. 19–31.
2nd day of 6th week x. 22–24.
3rd xi. 1–9.
4th 9–13.
5th 14–23.
6th (παρασκευῇ) 23–26.
7th (σαββάτῳ) viii. 16–21.

Κυριακῇ ϛʹ viii. 27–35; 38–39.
2nd day of 7th week xi. 29–33.
3rd 34–41.
4th 42–46.
5th 47–xii. 1.
6th (παρασκευῇ) xii. 2–12.
7th (σαββάτῳ) ix. 1–6.

Κυριακῇ ζʹ viii. 41–56.
2nd day of 8th week xii. 13–15; 22–31.
3rd xii. 42–48.
4th 48–59.
5th xiii. 1–9.
6th (παρασκευῇ) 31–35.
7th (σαββάτῳ) ix. 37–48.

Κυριακῇ ηʹ x. 25–37.
2nd day of 9th week xiv. 12–15.
3rd 25–35.
4th xv. 1–10.
5th xvi. 1–9.
6th (παρασκευῇ) xvi. 15–18; xvii. 1–4.
7th (σαββάτῳ) ix. 57–62.

Κυριακῇ θʹ xii. 16–21.
2nd day of 10th week xvii. 20–25.
3rd xvii. 26–37; xviii. 18.
4th xviii. 15–17; 26–30.
5th 31–34.
6th (παρασκευῇ) xix. 12–28.
7th (σαββάτῳ) x. 19–21.

Κυριακῇ ιʹ xiii. 10–17.
2nd day of 11th week xix. 37–44.
3rd 45–48.
4th xx. 1–8.
5th 9–18.
6th (παρασκευῇ) 19–26.
7th (σαββάτῳ) xii. 32–40.

Κυριακῇ ιαʹ xiv. 16–24.
2nd day of 12th week xx. 27–44.
3rd xxi. 12–19.
4th xxi. 5–8; 10–11; 20–24.
5th xxi. 28–33.
6th (παρασκευῇ) xxi. 37–xxii. 8.
7th (σαββάτῳ) xiii. 19–29.

Κυριακῇ ιβʹ xvii. 12–19.
2nd day of 13th week Mark viii. 11–21.
3rd 22–26.
4th 30–34.
5th ix. 10–16.
6th (παρασκευῇ) 33–41.
7th (σαββάτῳ) Luke xiv. 1–11.

Κυριακῇ ιγʹ xviii. 18–27.
2nd day of 14th week Mark ix. 42–x. 1.
3rd x. 2–11.
4th 11–16.
5th 17–27.
6th (παρασκευῇ) 24–32.
7th (σαββάτῳ) Luke xvi. 10–15.

Κυριακῇ ιδʹ xviii. 35–43.
[2nd day of 15th week Mark x. 46–52.
3rd xi. 11–23.
4th 22–26.
5th 27–33.
6th (παρασκευῇ) xii. 1–12.
7th (σαββάτῳ) Luke xvii. 3–10.

Κυριακῇ ιεʹ xix. 1–10.
2nd day of 16th week Mark xii. 13–17.
3rd 18–27.
4th 28–34.
5th 38–44.
6th (παρασκευῇ) xiii. 1–9.
7th (σαββάτῳ) Luke xviii. 1–8.

Κυριακῇ ιϛʹ (*of the Publican*) 9–14.]
2nd day of 17th week Mark xiii. 9–13.
3rd 14–23.
4th 24–31.
5th xiii. 31–xiv. 2.
6th (παρασκευῇ) xiv. 3–9.
7th (σαββάτῳ) Luke xx. 46–xxi. 4.

Κυριακῇ ιζ' (*of the Canaanitess*) Matth. xv. 21–28.

σαββάτῳ πρὸ τῆς ἀποκρέω, Luke xv. 1–10.

Κυριακῇ πρὸ τῆς ἀποκρέω (*of the Prodigal*) Luke xv. 11–32. 1 Thess. v. 14–23.

2nd day of the week of the carnival Mark xi. 1–11.
3rd xiv. 10–42.
4th 43–xv. 1.
5th xv. 1–15.
6th (παρασκευῇ) xv. 20; 22; 25; 33–41.
7th (σαββάτῳ) Luke xxi. 8–9; 25–27; 33–36; 1 Cor. vi. 12–20.

Κυριακῇ τῆς ἀποκρέω Matth. xxv. 31–46. 1 Cor. viii. 8–ix. 2.

2nd day of the week *of the cheese-eater* Luke xix. 29–40; xxii. 7–8; 39.
3rd xxii. 39–xxiii. 1.
4th *deest.*
5th xxiii. 1–43; 44–56.
6th (παρασκευῇ) *deest.*
7th (σαββάτῳ) Matth. vi. 1–13. Rom. xiv. 19–23; xvi. 25–27.

Κυριακῇ τῆς τυροφάγου Matth. vi. 14–21. Rom. xiii. 11–xiv. 4.

Παννυχὶς τῆς ἁγίας νηστείας.

Vigil of Lent (Parh. Christ's.) Matth. vii. 7–11.

Τῶν νηστειῶν (Lent).

σαββάτῳ α'	Mark. ii. 23–iii. 5.	Hebr. i. 1–12.
Κυριακῇ α'	John i. 44–55.	xi. 24–40.
σαββάτῳ β'	Mark i. 35–44.	iii. 12–14.
Κυριακῇ β'	ii. 1–12.	i. 10–ii. 3.
σαββάτῳ γ'	14–17.	x. 32–37.
Κυριακῇ γ'	viii. 34–ix. 1.	iv. 14–v. 6.
σαββάτῳ δ'	vii. 31–37.	vi. 9–12.
Κυριακῇ δ'	ix. 17–31.	13–20.
σαββάτῳ ε'	viii. 27–31.	ix. 24–28.
Κυριακῇ ε'	x. 32–45.	11–14.
σαββάτῳ ς' (*of Lazarus,*)	John xi. 1–45.	xii. 28–xiii. 8.

Κυριακῇ ς' τῶν Βαΐων, Matth. xxi. 1–11; 15–17; [εἰς τὴν λιτήν, Mark x. 46–xi. 11, Burney, 22]. Liturgy, John xii. 1–18. Phil. iv. 4–9.

Τῇ ἁγίᾳ μεγάλῃ (Holy Week).

2nd day { Matins, Matth. xxi. 18–43. Liturgy, xxiv. 3–35.
3rd { Matins, xxii. 15–xxiv. 2. Liturgy, xxiv. 36–xxvi. 2.
4th { Matins, John xii. 17–47. Liturgy, Matth. xxvi. 6–16.
5th { Matins, Luke xxii. 1–36. Liturgy, Matth. xxvi. 1–20.

Εὐαγγέλιον τοῦ νιπτῆρος, John xiii. 3–10. μετὰ τὸ νίψασθαι 12–17; Matth. xxvi. 21–39; Luke xxii. 43, 44; Matth. xxvi. 40–xxvii. 2. 1 Cor. xi. 23–32.

Εὐαγγέλια τῶν ἁγίων πάθων ῑῡ χ̄ῡ (Twelve Gospels of the Passions).

(1) Jo. xiii. 31–xviii. 1. (2) Jo. xviii. 1–28. (3) Matth. xxvi. 57–75. (4) Jo. xviii. 28–xix. 16. (5) Matth. xxvii. 3–32. (6) Mark xv. 16–32. (7) Matth. xxvii. 33–54. (8) Luke xxiii. 32–49. (9) Jo. xix. 25–37. (10) Mark xv. 43–47. (11) Jo. xix. 38–42. (12) Matth. xxvii. 62–66.

Εὐαγγέλια τῶν ὡρῶν τῆς ἁγίας παραμονῆς. (Night-watches of Vigil of Good Friday).

Hour (1) Matth. xxvii. 1–56. (3) Mark xv. 1–41. (6) Luke xxii. 66–xxiii. 49. (9) John xix. 16–37.

Τῇ ἁγίᾳ παραμονῇ (Good Friday) εἰς τὴν λειτουργίαν.

Matth. xxvii. 1–38; Luke xxiii. 39–43; Matth. xxvii. 39–54; John xix. 31–37; Matth. xxvii. 55–61. 1 Cor. i. 18–ii. 2.

Τῷ ἁγίῳ καὶ μεγάλῳ σαββάτῳ (Easter Even).

Matins, Matth. xxvii. 62–66.
1 Cor. v. 6–8.
Evensong, Matth. xxviii. 1–20.
Rom. vi. 3–11.

Εὐαγγέλια ἀναστασιμὰ ἑωθινά (*vid. Suicer Thes. Eccl.* I. 1229), eleven Gospels, used in turn, one every Sunday at Matins.

(1) Matth. xxviii. 16–20. (2) Mark xvi. 1–8. (3) *ib.* 9–20. (4) Luke xxiv. 1–12. (5) *ib.* 12–35. (6) *ib.* 36–52. (7) John xx. 1–10. (8) *ib.* 11–18. (9) *ib.* 19–31. (10) Jo. xxi. 1–14. (11) *ib.* 15–25.

We have now traced the daily service of the Greek Church, as derived from the Gospels, throughout the whole year, from Easter Day to Easter Even, only that in Lent the lessons from the 2nd to the 6th days inclusive are taken from the book of Genesis (*above, p.* 64). The reader will observe that from Easter to Pentecost St John and the Acts are read for seven weeks, or eight Sundays. The first Sunday after Pentecost is the Greek All Saints' Day; but from the Monday next after the day of Pentecost (Whit-Monday) St Matthew is used continuously every day for eleven weeks and as many Sundays. For six weeks more, St Matthew is appointed for the Saturday and Sunday lessons, St Mark for the other days of the week. But inasmuch as St Luke was to be taken up with the new year, the year of the indiction [Arund. 547], which in *this* case must be September 24[1], if all the lessons in Matthew and Mark were not read out by this time (which, unless Easter was very early, would not be the case), they were at once broken off, and (after proper lessons were employed for the Sunday before and the Saturday and Sunday which followed the feast of the elevation of the Cross, Sept. 14) the lessons from St Luke (seventeen weeks and sixteen Sundays in all) were taken up and read on as far as was necessary: only that the 17th Sunday of St Matthew (called from the subject of its Gospel *the Canaanitess*) was always resumed for the Sunday before the Carnival (*πρὸ τῆς ἀποκρέω*), which is also named from its Gospel that of *the Prodigal*, and answers to the Latin *Septuagesima*. Then follow the Sunday of the Carnival (*ἀποκρέω*) or *Sexagesima*, that of *the Cheese-eater* (*τυροφάγου*) or *Quinquagesima*, and the six Sundays in Lent. The whole number of Sunday Gospels in the year (even reckoning the two interpolated about Sept. 14) is thus only fifty-two: but in the Menology or Catalogue of immoveable feasts will be found proper lessons for three Saturdays and Sundays about Christmas and Epiphany, which could either be substituted for, or added to the ordinary Gospels for the year, according as the distance from Easter of one year to Easter in the next exceeded or fell short of fifty-two weeks. The system of lessons from the Acts and Epistles is much simpler than that of the Gospels: it exhibits fifty-two Sundays in the year, without any of the complicated arrangements of the other scheme. Since the Epistles from the Saturday of the 16th week after Pentecost to the Sunday of the Prodigal cannot be set (like the rest) by the side of their corresponding Gospels, they are given separately in the following table:

Κυριακῇ ιϛ'	2 Cor vi. 1–10.	*σαββάτῳ κδ*	2 Cor. xi. 1–6.
σαββάτῳ ιζ'	1 Cor. xiv. 20–25.	*Κυριακῇ κδ'*	Eph. ii. 14–22.
Κυριακῇ ιζ'	2 Cor. vi. 16—viii. 1.	*σαββάτῳ κε'*	Gal. i. 3–10.
σαββάτῳ ιη'	1 Cor. xv. 39–45.	*Κυριακῇ κε'*	Eph. iv. 1–7.
Κυριακῇ ιη'	2 Cor. ix. 6–11.	*σαββάτῳ κϛ'*	Gal. iii. 8–12.
σαββάτῳ ιθ'	1 Cor. xv. 58—xvi. 3.	*Κυριακῇ κϛ'*	Eph. v. 8–19.
Κυριακῇ ιθ'	2 Cor. xi. 31—xii. 9.	*σαββάτῳ κζ'*	Gal. v. 22—vi. 2.
σαββάτῳ κ'	2 Cor. i. 8–11.	*Κυριακῇ κζ'*	Eph. vi. 10–17.
Κυριακῇ κ'	Gal. i. 11–19.	*σαββάτῳ κη'*	Col. i. 9–18.
σαββάτῳ κα'	2 Cor. iii. 12–18.	*Κυριακῇ κη'*	2 Cor. ii. 14—iii. 3.
Κυριακῇ κα'	Gal. ii. 16–20.	*σαββάτῳ κθ'*	Eph. ii. 11–13.
σαββάτῳ κβ'	2 Cor. v. 1–10.	*Κυριακῇ κθ'*	Col. iii. 4–11.
Κυριακῇ κβ'	Gal. vi. 11–18.	*σαββάτῳ λ'*	Eph. v. 1–8.
σαββάτῳ κγ'	2 Cor. viii. 1–5.	*Κυριακῇ λ'*	Col. iii. 12–16.
Κυριακῇ κγ'	Eph. ii. 4–10.	*σαββάτῳ λα'*	Col. i. 2–6.

[1] The more usual indiction, which dates from Sept. 1, is manifestly excluded by the following rubric (Burney, 22, p. 191, and in other copies): *Δέον γινώσκειν ὅτι ἄρχεται ὁ Λουκᾶς ἀναγινώσκεσθαι ἀπὸ τῆς Κυριακῆς μετὰ τὴν ὕψωσιν· τότε γὰρ καὶ ἡ ἰσυμερία* [i.e. *ἰσημερία*] *γίνεται, ὃ καλεῖται νέον ἔτος. Ἢ ὅτι ἀπὸ τὰς* [*τῆς*] *κγ' τοῦ σεπτεμβρίου ὁ Λουκᾶς ἀναγινώσκεται.*

Κυριακῇ λα′	2 Tim. i. 3–9.	σαββάτῳ λδ′	1 Tim. iii. 13—iv. 5.
σαββάτῳ λβ′	Col. ii. 8–12.	Κυριακῇ λδ′	2 Tim. iii. 10–15.
Κυριακῇ λβ′	1 Tim. vi. 11–16.	σαββάτῳ λε′	1 Tim. iii. 1–11.
σαββάτῳ λγ′	1 Tim. ii. 1–7.	Κυριακῇ λε′	2 Tim. ii. 1–10.
Κυριακῇ λγ′	as Κυρ. λα′.	σαββάτῳ λϛ′	2 Tim. ii. 11–19.

ON THE MENOLOGY, OR CALENDAR OF IMMOVEABLE FESTIVALS AND SAINTS' DAYS.

We cannot in this place enter very fully into this portion of the contents of Lectionaries, inasmuch as, for reasons we have assigned above (p. 65), the investigation would be both tedious and difficult. All the great feast-days, however, as well as the commemorations of the Apostles and of a few other Saints, occur alike in all the books, and ought not to be omitted here. We commence with the month of September (the opening of the year at Constantinople), as do all the Lectionaries and Synaxaria we have seen[1].

Sept. 1. Simeon Stylites, Luke iv. 16–22; Col. iii. 12–16.

8. Birthday of the Virgin, Θεοτόκος, Luke x. 38–42; xi. 27, 28; Phil. ii. 5–11.

13. Κυριακῇ πρὸ τῆς ὑψώσεως, Jo. iii. 13–17; Gal. vi. 11–18.

14. Elevation of the Cross, Jo. xix. 6–35; 1 Cor. i. 18–24.

σαββάτῳ μετὰ τὴν ὕψωσιν Jo. viii. 21–30; 1 Cor. i. 26–29.
Κυριακῇ μετὰ τὴν ὕψωσιν Mark viii. 34–ix. 1; Gal. ii. 16–20.

18. Theodora[2], John viii. 3–11 (Parham).

24. Thecla, Matth. xxv. 1–13; 2 Tim. i. 3–9.

Oct. 3. Dionysius the Areopagite, Matth. xiii. 45–54; Act. xvii. 16–34.

6. Thomas the Apostle, Jo. xx. 19–31; 1 Cor. iv. 9–16.

8. Pelagia, John. viii. 3–11.[3]

9. James son of Alphaeus, Matth. x. 1–7; 14; 15.

18. Luke the Evangelist, Luke x. 16–21; Col. iv. 5–19.

23. James, ὁ ἀδελφόθεος, Mark vi. 1–7.

Nov. 8. Michael and Archangels, Luke x. 16–21; Hebr. ii. 2–10.

13. Chrysostom, Jo. x. 9–16; Hebr. vii. 26–viii. 2.

14. Philip the Apostle, Jo. i. 44–55; Act. viii. 26–39.

16. Matthew the Apostle, Matth. ix. 9–13; 1 Cor. iv. 9–16.

25. Clement of Rome, Jo. xv. 17–xvi. 1; Phil. iii. 20–iv. 3.

30. Andrew the Apostle, John i. 35–52; 1 Cor. iv. 9–16.

Dec. 20. Ignatius, ὁ θεόφορος, Mark ix. 33–41; Hebr. iv. 14–v. 6.

Saturday before Christmas, Matth. xiii. 31–58; Gal. iii. 8–12.

Sunday before Christmas, Matth. i. 1–25; Hebr. xi. 9–16.

24. Christmas Eve, Luke ii. 1–20; Hebr. i. 1–12.

25. Christmas Day, Matth. ii. 1–12; Gal. iv. 4–7.

26. Stephen, Matth. ii. 13–23; Hebr. ii. 11–18.

Saturday after Christmas, Matth. xii. 15–21; 1 Tim. vi. 11–16.

Sunday after Christmas, Mark i. 1–8; Gal. i. 11–19.

[1] In the *Menology*, even Arund. 547 has μηνὶ σεπτεμβρίῳ ā· ἀρχὴ τῆς ἰνδίκτου. So Burn. 22 nearly.

[2] *Theodosia* in Codex Cyprius, with the cognate lesson, Luke vii. 36—50.

[3] So Cod. Cyprius, but the Christ's Coll. Evst. removes Pelagia to Aug. 31, and reads Jo. viii. 1—11.

Saturday πρὸ τῶν φώτων, Matth. iii. 1–6; 1 Tim. iii. 13–iv. 5.

Sunday πρὸ τῶν φώτων, Mark i. 1–8; 1 Tim. iii. 13–iv. 5.

Jan. 1. Circumcision, Luke ii. 20; 21; 40–52; 1 Cor. xiii. 12–xiv. 5.

5. Vigil of θεοφανία, Luke iii. 1–18; 1 Cor. ix. 19–x. 4.

6. Θεοφανία (Epiphany) { Matins, Mark i. 9–11. Liturgy, Matt. iii. 13–17. } Titus ii. 11–14.

7. John, ὁ πρόδρομος, John i. 29–34.

Saturday μετὰ τὰ φῶτα, Matth. iv. 1–11; Eph. vi. 10–17.

Sunday μετὰ τὰ φῶτα, Matth. iv. 12–17; Eph. iv. 7–13.

22. Timothy, Matth. x. 32; 33; 37; 38; xix. 27–30; 2 Tim. i. 3–9.

Feb. 2. Presentation of Christ, Luke ii. 22–40; Hebr. vii. 7–17.

3. Simeon ὁ Θεοδόχος, and Anna, Luke ii. 25–38; Hebr. ix. 11–14.

23. Polycarp, John xii. 24–36.

24. Finding of the Head of John the Baptist { Matins, Luke vii. 18–29. Liturgy, Matth. xi. 5–14; 2 Cor. iv. 6–11.

March 25. Annunciation, Luke i. 24–38; Hebr. ii. 11–18.

April 25. Mark the Evangelist, Mark vi. 7–13.

30. James son of Zebedee, Matth. x. 1–7; 14; 15.

May 2. Athanasius, Matth. v. 14–19; Hebr. iv. 14–v. 6.

8. John, ὁ Θεόλογος, Jo. xix. 25–27; xxi. 24, 25; 1 Jo. i. 1–7.

26. Jude the Apostle, Jo. xiv. 21–24.

June 11. Bartholomew and Barnabas the Apostles, Mark vi. 7–13; Acts xi. 19–30.

19. Jude, brother of the Lord, Mark vi. 7–13 or εὐαγγέλιον ἀποστολικόν (Matth. x. 1–8 ?).

24. Birth of John the Baptist, Luke i. 1–25; 57–80; Rom. xiii. 11–xiv. 4.

29. Peter and Paul the Apostles, Matth. xvi. 13–19; 2 Cor. x. 21–xii. 9.

30. The Twelve Apostles, Matth. x. 1–8.

July 22. Mary Magdalene, ἡ μυροφόρος, Mark xvi. 9–20; 2 Tim. ii. 1–10.

Aug. 6. Transfiguration { Matins, Luke ix. 29–36 or Mark ix. 2–9. Liturgy, Matth. xvii. 1–9; 1 Pet. i. 10–19.

20 or 25. Thaddaeus the Apostle, Matth. x. 16–22; 1 Cor. iv. 9–16.

29. Beheading of John the Baptist, Mark vi. 14–30; Acts xiii. 25–32.

Section II.

Description of the Uncial Manuscripts of the Greek Testament.

We proceed to describe in detail the uncial manuscripts of the Greek Testament, arranged separately as copies of the Gospels, of the Acts and Catholic Epistles, of the Pauline Epistles and of the Apocalypse. Including the yet unpublished Codex Sinaiticus (*above*, p. 27) we have already stated the number extant in each portion of the sacred volume (*above*, p. 66). They are usually indicated by the *capital* letters of the English and Greek alphabets, and stand on the list not in the order of their relative value or antiquity (as could have been wished), but mainly as they were applied from time to time to the purposes of Textual criticisms.

Manuscripts of the Gospels.

א (*Aleph*). Codex Sinaiticus, now at St Petersburg, the justly celebrated copy which has recently attracted such general attention in the learned world. From Tischendorf's *Notitia Ed. Cod. Sinaitici* (pp. 5, 6) we gain some insight into the history of its discovery. When travelling in 1844 under the patronage of his own sovereign, the King Frederick Augustus of Saxony, he picked out of a basket full of papers destined to light the oven of the Convent of St Catharine on Mount Sinai, the 43 leaves of the Septuagint which he published in 1846 as the Codex Frederico-Augustanus. These, of course, he easily got for the asking, but finding that further portions of the same codex (e. g. the whole of Isaiah and 1, 4 Maccabees) were extant, he rescued them from their probable fate, by enlightening the brotherhood as to their value. He was permitted to copy one leaf of what yet remained, and departed in the full hope that he should be allowed to purchase the whole; but he had taught the monks a sharp lesson, and neither then, nor on his subsequent visit in 1853, could he gain any tidings of the leaves he had left behind; he even seems to have concluded that they had been carried into Europe by some richer or more fortunate collector. At the beginning of 1859, after the care of the seventh edition of his N. T. was happily over, he went for a third time into the East, under the well-deserved patronage of the Emperor of Russia, the great protector of the Oriental Church; and the treasure which had been twice withdrawn from him as a private traveller, was now (on the occasion of some chance conversation) freely put into the hands of one sent from the champion and benefactor of the oppressed Church. Tischendorf touchingly describes his surprise, his joy, his midnight studies over the priceless volume ("*quippe dormire nefas videbatur*") on that memorable 4th of February, 1859. The rest was easy; he was allowed to copy his prize at Cairo, and ultimately to bring it to Europe, as a tribute of duty and gratitude to the Emperor Alexander II. To that monarch's wise munificence the forthcoming editions (both the larger and the more popular one) will be mainly due.

The Codex Sinaiticus, as we learn from Tischendorf's *Notitia*, consists of 345½ leaves of the same beautiful vellum as the Cod. Frid-Augustanus (*see* p. 20), of which 199 contain portions of the Septuagint version, 147½ the whole New Testament, Barnabas' Epistle, and portions of Hermas' *Shepherd*. Each page comprises four columns (*see* p. 25), with 48 lines in each column, of those continuous, noble, simple uncials (*compare* Plate IV. 11 a *with* 11 b) we have described so minutely in the preceding section (pp. 29—35). The poetical books of the Old Testament, however, being written in στίχοι, admit of only two columns on a page (*above*, p. 45). Since the *Notitia* contains an exact reprint in common Greek type of 18 pages of the codex (nine being taken from the N. T.) as it came from the first hand, we can now form a clear and distinct notion of what we may expect in 1862, only that our knowledge of the actual readings of the manuscript is, of course, still very incomplete. The order of the sacred books is remarkable, though not unprecedented (p. 62). St Paul's Epistles precede the Acts, and among them, that to the Hebrews follows 2 Thess., standing on the same page with it. Breathings and accents there are none: the apostrophus (*see* p. 43), and the single point for punctuation, are entirely absent for pages together, yet occasionally are rather thickly studded, not only in places where a later hand has been unusually busy (e. g. Isaiah i. 1—iii. 2, two pages), but in some others (e.g. in 2 Cor. xii. 20 there are eight stops). Even the words very usually abridged (except $\overline{\theta\sigma}$, $\overline{\kappa\sigma}$, $\overline{\iota\sigma}$, $\overline{\chi\sigma}$, $\overline{\pi\nu\alpha}$ which are constant) are here written in full, as *πατηρ*, *δαυειδ*: the practice varies for *υιος*, *ουρανος*, *ανθρωπος*: we find *ϊσραηλ'*, $\overline{\iota\sigma\lambda}$ or $\overline{\iota\eta\lambda}$: *ϊερουσαλημ'*, $\overline{\iota\eta\mu}$, $\overline{\iota\lambda\mu}$, $\overline{\iota\eta\lambda\mu}$', or $\overline{\upsilon\lambda\mu}$. Tischendorf considers the two points over *iota* and *upsilon* (which are sometimes wanting) as seldom from the first hand: the mark > (*see* p. 44) we note oftener in the Old Testament than in the New. Words are divided at the end of a line as capriciously as can be imagined: thus K in OΥK is repeatedly separated without need. Small letters, of the most perfect shape (*see* p. 44), freely occur in all places, especially at the end of lines, where the — *superscript* almost always represents N (e.g. 17 times in Mark i.1—35). The only other *compendia scribendi* seem to be K_{ι} for *και*, and HN written as in Plate I. No. 3. Numerals are represented by letters, with a straight line placed over them (e. g. $\bar{\mu}$ Mark. i.13). Although there are no capitals, the initial letter of a line which begins a sentence generally stands out from the rank of the rest, which is a step nearer them than we find in Cod. B (*see* p. 44). The titles and subscriptions of the several books are as short as possible (*see* p. 54). Of the *τίτλοι* or *κεφάλαια* majora Tischendorf does not speak; the margin contains the Ammonian sections and Eusebian canons, but he is positive that neither they nor the note *στιχων* $\overline{\rho\pi}$ (*see* p. 45, *note* 2) appended to 2 Thessalonians, are by the original scribe. Correctors of all ages have disfigured the manuscript, some (as he judges) as early as the sixth or seventh century; but for all these points we are necessarily referred to the Prolegomena and detailed Annotations in the fourth volume of his forthcoming edition.

From the transcript of the nine pages of the New Testament (Matth. xxvii. 64—xxviii. 20; Mark i. 1—35; Jo. xxi. 1—25; 2 Cor. xi. 32—xiii. 5; xiii. 5—Gal. i. 17; 2 Thess. ii. 17—Hebr. i. 7; Acts xxviii. 17—31; James i. 1—ii. 6; Apoc. ix. 5—x. 8; xxii. 19—21); from the lithographed *facsimile* of three-fourths of the page containing Luke xxiv. 24—53; and less safely from a loose *sylva lectionum* set down almost at random in the *Notitia*, pp. 14—21, we may form some estimate of the character of Cod. ℵ. From the number of *ὁμοιοτέλευτα*

(p. 9) and other errors, one cannot affirm that it is very carefully written. Its itacisms (*see* p. 10) are of the oldest type, and those not constant; chiefly ι for ει, η υ and οι interchanged. The grammatical forms commonly termed Alexandrian occur, but rather as the exception than the rule. With regard to the more important question as to the class of readings it supports, it cannot be said to give in its exclusive adherence to any of the witnesses hitherto examined. It so lends its grave authority, now to one and now to another, as to convince us more than ever of the futility of seeking to derive the genuine text of the New Testament from any one copy, however ancient and, on the whole, trustworthy. On this whole subject see Chapter VII.

A. CODEX ALEXANDRINUS in the British Museum, where the open volume of the New Testament is publicly shown in the Manuscript room. It was placed in that Library on its formation in 1753, having previously belonged to the king's private collection, from the year 1628, when Cyril Lucar, Patriarch of Constantinople (whose crude attempts to reform the Eastern Church on the model of Geneva provoked the untoward Synod of Bethlehem in 1672), sent this most precious document by our Embassador in Turkey, Sir Thomas Roe, as a truly royal gift to Charles I. An Arabic inscription, several centuries old, at the back of the Table of Contents on the first leaf of the manuscript, states that it was written by the hand of Thecla the Martyr, and given to the Patriarchal Chamber in the year of the Martyrs, 814 [A.D. 1098]. Another, and apparently an earlier inscription, in Moorish-Arabic, declares that the book was dedicated to the Patriarchal Chamber at *Alexandria*. That it was brought from Alexandria by Cyril (who had previously been Patriarch of that see) need not be disputed, though Wetstein, on the doubtful authority of Matthew Muttis of Cyprus, Cyril's deacon, concludes that he procured it from Mount Athos. In the volume itself the Patriarch has written and subscribed the following words: "Liber iste scripturae sacrae N. et V. Test., prout ex traditione habemus, est scriptus manu Theclae, nobilis foeminae Ægyptiae, ante mille et trecentos annos circiter, paulo post Concilium Nicaenum. Nomen Theclae in fine libri erat exaratum, sed extincto Christianismo in Ægypto a Mahometanis, et libri una Christianorum in similem sunt redacti conditionem.

Extinctum ergo et Theclae nomen et laceratum, sed memoria et traditio recens observat." Cyril seems to lean wholly on the Arabic inscription on the first leaf of the volume: independent testimony he would appear to have received none.

This celebrated manuscript, the earliest of first-rate importance applied by scholars to the criticism of the text, and yielding in value to but one or two at the utmost, is now bound in four volumes, whereof three contain the Septuagint version of the Old Testament almost complete, the fourth volume the New Testament with several lamentable defects. St Matthew's Gospel is wanting up to ch. xxv. 6 *ἐξέρχεσθε*, from John vi. 50 *ἵνα* to viii. 52 *λέγει*[1] two leaves are lost, and three leaves from 2 Cor. iv. 13 *ἐπίστευσα* to xii. 6 *ἐξ ἐμοῦ*. All the other books of the New Testament are here entire, the Catholic Epistles following the Acts, that to the Hebrews standing before the Pastoral Epistles (see above, p. 62). After the Apocalypse we find the *only* extant copy of the first or genuine Epistle of Clement of Rome, and a small fragment of a second of suspected authenticity, both in the same hand as the latter part of the New Testament. It would appear also that these two Epistles were designed to form a part of the volume of Scripture, for in the table of contents exhibited on the first leaf of the manuscript under the head Η ΚΑΙΝΗ ΔΙΑΘΗΚΗ, they are represented as immediately following the Apocalypse: *then* is given the number of books, ΟΜΟΥ ΒΙΒΛΙΑ, the numerals being now illegible; and after this, as if distinct from Scripture, the [18] Psalms of Solomon. Such uncanonical works (*ἰδιωτικοὶ ψαλμοὶ...ἀκανόνιστα βιβλία*) were forbidden to be read in churches by the 59th canon of the Council of Laodicea (A.D. 366?); whose 60th canon enumerates the books of the N.T., in the precise order seen in Cod. A, only that the Apocalypse and Clement's Epistles do not stand on the list.

This manuscript is in quarto, about thirteen inches high and ten broad, each page being divided into two columns of fifty lines each, having about twenty letters or upwards in

[1] Yet we may be sure that these two leaves did not contain the *Pericope Adulterae*, Jo. vii. 53—viii. 11. Taking the Elzevir N. T. of 1624, which is printed without breaks for the verses, we count 286 lines of the Elzevir for the two leaves of Cod. A preceding its defect, 288 lines for the two pages which follow it; but 317 lines for the two missing leaves. Deduct the 30 lines containing Jo. vii. 53—viii. 11, and the result for the lost leaves is 287.

a line. These letters are continuously written in uncial characters, without any space between the words, the uncials being of an elegant yet simple form, in a firm and uniform hand, though in some places larger than in others. Specimens of both styles may be seen in our *facsimiles* (Nos. 12, 13)[1], the first, Gen. i. 1, 2, being written in vermillion, the second, Acts xx. 28, in the once black, but now yellowish brown ink of the body of the Codex. The punctuation merely consists of a point placed at the end of a sentence, usually on a level with the top of the preceding letter, but not always; and a vacant space follows the point at the end of a paragraph, the space being proportioned to the break in the sense. Capital letters of various sizes abound at the beginning of books and sections, not painted as in later copies, but written by the original scribe in common ink. As these capitals stand entirely outside the column in the margin (excepting in such rare cases as Gen. i. 1), if the section begins in the middle of a line, the capital is necessarily postponed till the beginning of the next line, whose first letter is always the capital, even though it be in the middle of a word. Vermillion is freely used in the initial lines of books, and has stood the test of time much better than the black ink: the first four lines of each column on the first page of Genesis are in this colour, accompanied with the only breathings and accents in the manuscript (see above, p. 39). The first line of St Mark, the first three of St Luke, the first verse of St John, the opening of the Acts down to δι, and so on for other books, are in vermillion. At the end of each book are neat and unique ornaments in the ink of the first hand: see especially those at the end of St Mark and the Acts. As we have before stated (pp. 49, 51) this codex is the earliest which has the κεφάλαια proper, the Ammonian sections, and the Eusebian canons complete. Lists of the κεφάλαια precede each Gospel, except the first, where they are lost. Their titles stand or have stood at the top of the pages, but the binder has often ruthlessly cut them short, and committed other yet more serious mutilation at the edges. The places at which they begin are

[1] Other facsimiles are given in Woide's edition of the New Testament from this MS. (1786), and in Baber's of the Old Test. (1816). Two specimens of the style of the first Epistle of Clement are exhibited in Canon Jacobson's Patres Apostolici, Vol. I. p. 110 (1838).

indicated throughout, and their numbers are moreover placed in the margin of Luke and John. The Eusebian sections and canons are conspicuous in the margin, and at the beginning of each of these sections a capital letter occurs. The rest of the New Testament has no division into κεφάλαια, as was usual in later times, but paragraphs and capitals as the sense requires.

The palæographic reasons for referring this manuscript to the beginning or middle of the fifth century (the date now very generally acquiesced in) depend in part on the general style of the writing, which is at once firm, elegant and simple; partly on the formation of certain letters, in which respect it holds a middle place between copies of the fourth and sixth centuries. The reader will recall what we have already said (pp. 29—35) as to the shape of *alpha*, *delta*, *epsilon*, *pi*, *sigma*, *phi* and *omega* in the Codex Alexandrinus. Woide, who edited the New Testament, believes that two hands were employed in that volume, changing in the page containing 1 Cor. v—vii., the vellum of the latter portion being thinner and the ink more thick, which has accordingly peeled off or eaten through the vellum in many places. This, however, is a point on which those who know manuscripts best will most hesitate to speak decidedly[1].

The external arguments for fixing the date are less weighty, but all point to the same conclusion. On the evidence for its being written by St Thecla, indeed, no one has cared to lay much stress, though some have thought that the scribe might belong to some monastery dedicated to that holy martyr. Tregelles, however, explains the origin of the Arabic inscription, on which Cyril's statement appears to rest, by remarking that the New Testament in our manuscript at present commences with Matth. xxv. 6, this lesson (Matth. xxv. 1—13) *being that appointed by the Greek Church for the festival of St Thecla* (see above, Menology, p. 74, Sept. 24). The Egyptian, therefore, who wrote this Arabic note, observing the name of Thecla in the now mutilated upper margin of the Codex, where such rubrical notes are commonly placed by later hands, hastily concluded that she wrote the book, and thus has perplexed our

[1] Notice especially what Tregelles says of the Codex Augiensis (Tregelles' Horne Introd. p. 198), where the difference of hand in the leaves removed from their proper place is much more striking than any change in Cod. Alex. Yet even in that case it is likely that one scribe only was engaged.

Biblical critics. It is hardly too much to say that Tregelles' shrewd conjecture seems to be certain, almost to demonstration.

Other more trustworthy reasons for assigning Cod. A to the fifth century may be summed up very briefly. The presence of the canons of Eusebius [A. D. 268—340?], and of the epistle to Marcellinus by the great Athanasius, Patriarch of Alexandria [300?—373], before the Psalms, place a limit in one direction, while the absence of the Euthalian divisions of the Acts and Epistles (see above, p. 53), which came into vogue very soon after 458, and the shortness of the ὑπογραφαὶ (above, p. 54) appear tolerably decisive against a later date than A. D. 450. The insertion of the Epistles of Clement, like those of Barnabas and Hermas in the Cod. Sinaiticus, recalls us to a period when the canon of Scripture was in some particulars a little unsettled, or about the age of the Council of Laodicea 366. Other arguments have been urged both for an earlier and a later date, but they scarcely deserve discussion. Wetstein's objection to the title Θεοτόκος as applied to the Blessed Virgin in the title to her song, added to the Psalms, is quite groundless: that appellation was given to her by both the Gregories in the middle of the fourth century (*vid. Suicer. Thesaur. Eccles.* I. p. 1387), as habitually as it was a century after: nor should we insist much on the contrary on Woide's or Schulz's persuasion that the τρισάγιον (ἅγιος ὁ θεός, ἅγιος ἰσχυρός, ἅγιος ἀθάνατος) would have been found in the ὕμνος ἑωθινὸς after the Psalms, had the manuscript been written as late as the fifth century.

Partial and inaccurate collations of this manuscript were made by Patrick Young, by Alexander Huish, Prebendary of Wells, for Walton's Polyglott, and by some others.

In 1786, Charles Godfrey Woide, preacher at the Dutch Chapel Royal and Assistant Librarian in the British Museum, a distinguished Coptic scholar [d. 1790], published, by the aid of 456 subscribers, a noble folio edition of the New Testament from this manuscript, with valuable Prolegomena, a copy of the text which so far as it has been tested has been found reasonably accurate, notes on the changes made in the codex by later hands, and a minute collation of its readings with the common text as presented in Kuster's edition of Mill's N. T. (1711). In this last point Woide has not been taken as a model by subsequent editors of manuscripts, much to the inconvenience of the student. In 1816—28 the Old Testament portion of the Codex Alexandrinus was published in four folio volumes at the national expense, by the Rev. Henry Hervey Baber, also of the British Museum, the Prolegomena to whose magnificent work are very inferior to Woide's, but contain some additional information. Both these works, and many others like them which we shall have to describe, are printed in an uncial type, bearing some general resemblance to that of their respective originals, but which must not be supposed to convey any adequate notion of their actual appearance. These *quasi-facsimiles* (for they are nothing more), while they add to the cost of the book, seem to answer no useful purpose whatever; and, if taken by an incautious reader for more than they profess to be, will seriously mislead him.

The Codex Alexandrinus has been judged to be carelessly written; many errors of transcription no doubt exist, but not more than in other copies of the highest value (e. g. Cod. ℵ). None other than the ordinary abridgments are found in it (see p. 43): numerals are not expressed by letters except in Apoc. vii. 4; xxi. 17: ι and υ have usually the dots over them at the beginning of a syllable. Of itacisms (see p. 10) it may be doubted whether it contains more than others of the same date: the interchange of ι and ει, η and ι, ε and αι, are the most frequent; but such things are too common to prove anything touching the country of the manuscript. Its external history renders it very likely that it was written at Alexandria, that great manufactory of correct and elegant copies, while Egypt was yet a Christian land: but such forms as λήμψομαι, ἐλάβαμεν, ἔνατος, ἐκαθερίσθη, and others named by Woide, are peculiar to no single nation, but are found repeatedly in Greek-Latin codices, which unquestionably originated in Western Europe. This manuscript is of the very greatest importance to the critic, inasmuch as it exhibits a text more nearly approaching that found in later copies than is read in others of its high antiquity. This topic, however, will be discussed at length in another place (Chap. VII.), and we shall elsewhere (Chap. IX.) consider the testimony Codex A bears in the celebrated passage 1 Tim. iii. 16.

B. CODEX VATICANUS 1209 is one of the oldest vellum manuscripts in existence, and is the glory of the great Vatican

Library at Rome. To these legitimate sources of deep interest must be added the almost romantic curiosity which has been excited by the jealous watchfulness of its official guardians, with whom an honest zeal for its safe preservation seems to have now degenerated into a species of capricious wilfulness, and who have shewn a strange incapacity for making themselves the proper use of a treasure they scarcely permit others more than to gaze upon. This book seems to have been brought into the Vatican Library shortly after its establishment by Pope Nicholas V. who died in 1455, but nothing is known of its previous history. Since the missing portions at the end of the New Testament are said to have been supplied in the fifteenth century from a manuscript belonging to Cardinal Bessarion, we may be allowed to conjecture, if we please, that this learned Greek brought the Codex into the west of Europe. Although this book has not even yet been thoroughly collated, or rendered as available as it might be to the critical student, its general character and appearance are sufficiently well known[1]. It is a quarto volume, of 146 leaves, bound in red morocco, ten and a half inches high, ten broad, four and a half thick. It once contained the whole Bible in Greek, the Old Testament of the Septuagint version (a tolerably fair representation of which was exhibited in the Roman edition as early as 1586), excepting the first forty-six chapters of Genesis (the manuscript begins at *πολιν*, Gen. xlvi. 48) and Psalms cv.—cxxxvii.; the New Testament complete down to Hebr. ix. 14 *καθα*: the rest of the Epistle to the Hebrews, the four Pastoral Epistles[2] (the Catholic Epistles had followed the Acts) and the Apocalypse being written in the later hand alluded to above. The peculiar arrangement of three columns on a page, or six on the opened leaf of the volume is described by eye-witnesses as very striking (see above, p. 25): in the poetical books of the Old Testament

[1] I derive some of the following particulars from two letters in the *Guardian* of August 15 and 22, 1860, signed J. W. B. This writer is the latest I know of who has been allowed to examine the manuscript, to which with great difficulty he obtained access for an hour and a half. An excellent use he has made of his rare though brief opportunity.

[2] It is really a little unworthy of Dr Tregelles to speak of Dr Bloomfield's citations from Cod. B in the Pastoral Epistles as "quotations invented by pure imagination" (Horne Introd. II. p. 159). Intentional fraud is out of the question, and which of us has not fallen into errors just as gross?

(since they are written στιχηρῶς) only two columns fill a page. For this reason it would have been desirable that our *facsimile* (No. 20, derived from Silvestre, Paléogr. Un. No. 60) should have been taken elsewhere than from the Psalms: but since the copper-plates in Mai's larger edition of the Codex Vaticanus, and the uncouth tracing by Zacagni in 1704, still repeated both by Horne and Tregelles, have been strongly censured by recent observers, we were bound to resort to the only one remaining that was not obviously unworthy of its subject. All who have inspected the Codex are loud in the praises of the fine thin vellum, the clear and elegant hand of the first penman, the simplicity of the whole style of the work: capital letters, so frequent in the Codex Alexandrinus, were totally wanting in this document for several centuries. In several of these particulars our manuscript resembles the Herculanean rolls, and thus asserts a just claim to high antiquity, which the absence of the usual divisions into κεφάλαια, of the Ammonian sections and canons of Eusebius, and the substitution in their room of another scheme of chapters of its own (which we have fully described above, p. 47) beyond question tend very powerfully to confirm. Each column contains about forty-two lines, each line from sixteen to eighteen letters, of a size somewhat less than in the Codex Alexandrinus, with no intervals between the words, a space of the breadth of half a letter being left at the end of a sentence, and a little more at the conclusion of a paragraph. It has been doubted whether any of the stops are *primâ manu*, and (contrary to the judgment of Birch and others) the breathings and accents are now generally allowed to have been added by the second hand. This hand, apparently of about the eighth century, retraced, with as much care as such an operation would permit, the faint lines of the original writing (the ink whereof was perhaps never quite black), the remains of which can even now be seen by a keen-sighted reader by the side of the more modern strokes; and anxious at the same time to represent a critical revision of the text, the writer left untouched such words or letters as he wished to reject. In these places, *where no breathings or accents and scarcely any stops*[1] *have ever been detected*, we have an

[1] Hug says *none*, but Tischendorf (Cod. Frid-Aug. Proleg. p. 9) himself detected two in a part that the second scribe had left untouched; though a break often occurs, with no stop by either hand.

opportunity of seeing the manuscript in its primitive condition, before it had been tampered with by the later scribe. There are occasional breaks in the continuity of the writing, every descent in the genealogies of our Lord (Matth. i., Luke iii.), each of the beatitudes (Matth. v.), and of the parables in Matth. xiii., forming a separate paragraph; but such a case will oftentimes not occur for several consecutive pages. The writer's plan was to proceed steadily with a book until it was finished: then to break off from the column he was writing, and to begin the next book on the very next column. Thus only *one* column perfectly blank is found in the whole volume, that which follows ἐφοβοῦντο γάρ in Mark xvi. 8: and since Cod. B is the only one yet known, except Cod. ℵ, that actually omits the last twelve verses of that Gospel, by leaving such a space the scribe has intimated that he was fully aware of their existence, or even found them in the copy from which he wrote (see below, Chap. IX.). The capital letters at the beginning of each book are likewise due to the corrector, who sometimes erased, sometimes merely touched slightly, the original initial letter, which (as in the Herculanean rolls) is no larger than any other. These later capitals in blue or red, $\frac{3}{4}$ of an inch high, and the broad green bar, surmounted with three red crosses, which habitually stands at the head of a book (see our *facsimile*, No. 20, of Psalm i. 1), are in paint, and by the same second hand. Fewer abridgments than usual occur in this venerable copy; e.g. ΔΑΥΕΙΔ is always used, not $\overline{\Delta\mathrm{A}\Delta}$: the formation of *delta, pi, chi;* the loop-like curve on the left side of *alpha*, the absence of points at the extremities of *sigma* or *epsilon*, the length and size of *rho*, *upsilon*, *phi* all point to the FOURTH century as the date of this manuscript. The smaller letters so often found at the end of lines preserve the same firm and simple character as the rest; of the apostrophus, so frequent in Cod. A and some others, we are told nothing here.

Tischendorf says truly enough that something like a history might be written of the futile attempts to collate Cod. B, and a very unprofitable history it would be. The manuscript is first distinctly heard of (for it does not appear to have been used for the Complutensian Polyglott) by Sepulveda, to whose correspondence with Erasmus attention has been seasonably recalled by Tregelles. Writing in 1534, he says, "Est enim Græcum exemplar antiquissimum in Bibliothecâ Vaticanâ, in quo diligentissimè et accuratissimè literis majusculis conscriptum utrumque Testamentum continetur longè diversum a vulgatis exemplaribus:" and after noticing as a weighty proof of its excellence its agreement with the Latin version (multum convenit cum vetere nostrâ translatione) against the common Greek text (vulgatam Græcorum editionem), he furnishes Erasmus with 365 readings as a convincing argument in support of his statements. It would probably be from this list that in his Annotations to the Acts, published in 1535, Erasmus cites the reading *καῦδα*, ch. xxvii. 16, from a Greek codex in the Pontifical Library, since for this reading Cod. B is the only known *Greek* witness. It seems, however, that he had obtained some account of this manuscript from Paul Bombasius as early as 1521 (see Wetstein's Proleg. N. T. I. p. 23). Lucas Brugensis, who published his Notationes in S. Biblia in 1580, and his Commentary on the Four Gospels (dedicated to Cardinal Bellarmine) in 1606, made known certain extracts from Cod. B taken by Werner of Nimuegen; that most imperfect collection was the only source from which Mill and even Wetstein had any knowledge of the contents of this first-rate document. More indeed might have been gleaned from the Barberini readings gathered in or about 1624 (of which we shall speak in the next section), but their real value and character were not known in the lifetime of Wetstein. In 1698 Laurence Alexander Zacagni, Librarian of the Vatican, in his Preface to the Collectanea Monumentorum Veterum Eccles., describes Cod. B, and especially its peculiar division into sections, in a passage cited by Mill (Proleg. § 1480). In 1669 indeed the first real collation of the manuscript had been attempted by Bartolocci, then librarian of the Vatican; from some accident, however, it was never published, though a transcript under the feigned name of Giulio di Sta Anastasia yet remains in the Imperial Library of Paris (MSS. Gr. Supp. 53), where it was first discovered and used by Scholz, and subsequently by Tischendorf and Muralt, the latter of whom (apparently on but slender grounds) regards it as the best hitherto made; others have declared it to be very imperfect, and quite inferior to those of Bentley and Birch. The collation which bears Bentley's name was procured about 1720 by his money and the labour of the Abbate Mico, for the purpose of his projected Greek Testament. When he had found out its defects, by means of an examination of the original by his nephew Thomas Bentley in 1726, our great critic engaged the Abbate Rulotta for 40 scudi to revise Mico's sheets, and especially to note the changes made by the second hand. Rulotta's papers have recently come to light among the Bentley manuscripts in the Library of Trinity College, Cambridge (B. XVII. 20), and have lately proved of signal value; Mico's were published in 1799 at Oxford, by Henry Ford, Prælector of Arabic there, together with some Thebaic fragments of the New Testament, in a volume which (since it was chiefly drawn from Woide's posthumous papers) he was pleased to call an Appendix to the Codex Alexandrinus. A fourth collation of the Vatican MS. was made by Andrew Birch of Copenhagen, and is included in the notes to the first volume of his Greek Testament 1788, or published separately in 1798 and 1801. Birch's collation does not extend to the Gospels of St Luke and St John, and on the whole is less full and exact than Mico's: possibly, though he travelled under the auspices of the King of Denmark, the system of jealous exclusion of strangers from their choicest books had already commenced at Rome. Certain it is that since Birch's day no one not in the confidence of the Papal Court has had fair access to this document. In 1810, however, when, with the other best treasures of the Vatican, Codex B was at Paris, the celebrated critic J. L. Hug sent forth his treatise "de Antiquitate Vaticani Codicis Commentatio," and though even he did not perceive the need of a new and full collation of it, he has the merit of first placing it in the paramount rank it still holds as one of the oldest and most valuable of extant monuments of sacred antiquity. His conclusion respecting its date, not later than the middle of the fourth century, has been acquiesced in with little opposition, though Tischendorf declares rather pithily that he holds this belief "non propter Hugium sed cum Hugio" (Cod. Ephraem. Proleg. p. 19). Some of his reasons, no doubt, are weak enough[1]; but the strength of his

[1] Thus the correspondence of Codex B with what St Basil (c. Eunom. II. 19) states he found in the middle of the fourth century, *ἐν τοῖς παλαιοῖς τῶν ἀντιγράφων*, in Eph. i. 1, viz. *τοῖς οὖσιν* without *ἐν* 'Εφέσῳ, though now read only in this and the Sinai manuscript *primâ manu*, and in one cursive copy *secundâ manu*, seems in itself of but little weight. Another point that has been raised is the position of the Epistle to the Hebrews (see above, p. 62). But this argument can apply only to the elder document from which the Vatican MS. was taken, and wherein

position depends on an *accumulation* of minute particulars, against which there seems nothing to set up which would suggest a lower period. On its return to Rome, this volume was no longer available for the free use and reference of critics. In 1843 Tischendorf, after long and anxious expectation during a visit to Rome that lasted some months, obtained a sight of it for two days of three hours each[1]. In 1844 Edward de Muralt was admitted to the higher privilege of three days or nine hours enjoyment of this treasure, and on the strength of the favour published an edition of the New Testament, *Ad fidem codicis principis Vaticani*, in 1846. Tregelles, who went to Rome in 1845 for the special purpose of consulting it, was treated even worse. He had forearmed himself (as he fondly imagined) with recommendatory letters from Cardinal Wiseman[2], and was often allowed to *see* the manuscript, but hindered from transcribing any of its readings[3]. We are ashamed to record such childish jealousy, yet thankful to believe that treatment thus illiberal could befal a learned stranger in but one city of Christendom.

What the Papal authorities would not entrust to others, they have at least the merit of attempting themselves. As early as 1836 Bishop Wiseman announced in his Lectures on the Connection between Science and Revelation, Vol. II. pp. 187—191, that Cardinal Mai, whose services to classical and ecclesiastical literature were renowned throughout Europe, was engaged on an edition of the Codex Vaticanus, under the immediate sanction of Pope Leo XII. As years passed by and no such work appeared, adverse reports and evil surmises began to take the place of hope, although the Cardinal often spoke of his work as already finished, only that he desired to write full Prolegomena before it

this book unquestionably followed that to the Galatians. In Cod. B it *always* stood in its present place, after 2 Thess., as in the Codices cited p. 62, note 2, to which list add Codd. 189, 196.

[1] Besides the 25 readings Tischendorf observed himself, Cardinal Mai supplied him with 34 more for his N. T. of 1849. His 7th edition of 1859 was enriched by 230 other readings furnished by private friends. Proleg. N. T. pp. cxliii, cxlvi.

[2] *Πέμπε δέ μιν Λυκίηνδε, πόρεν δ' ὅγε σήματα λυγρά,*
Γράψας ἐν πίνακι πτυκτῷ θυμοφθορὰ πολλά.

[3] "They would not let me open it," he adds, "without searching my pocket, and depriving me of pen, ink, and paper.... If I looked at a passage too long the two *prelati* would snatch the book out of my hand." I do not know where Dr Dobbin (Dublin University Magazine, Nov. 1859, p. 614) met with this piquant extract, whose authenticity, however, need not be questioned.

should appear. In September 1855 he died, honoured and ripe in years; and at length, when no more seemed to be looked for in that quarter, five quarto volumes issued from the Roman press in 1858, the New Testament comprising the fifth volume, with a slight and meagre preface by the Cardinal, and a letter to the reader by "Carolus Vercellone, Sodalis Barnabites," which told in a few frank manly words how little accuracy we had to expect in a work, by the publication of which he still persuaded himself he was decorating Mai's memory "novâ usque gloriâ atque splendidiore coronâ" (Tom. I. p. iii). The cause of that long delay now required no explanation. In fact so long as Mai lived the edition never would have appeared; for though he had not patience or special skill enough to accomplish his task well, he was too good a scholar not to know that he had done it very ill. The text is broken up into paragraphs, the numbers of the modern chapters and verses being placed in the margin; the peculiar divisions of the Codex Vaticanus sometimes omitted, sometimes tampered with. The Greek type employed is not an imitation of the uncial in the manuscript (of which circumstance we do not complain), but has modern stops, breathings, accents, ι subscript, &c., as if the venerable document were written yesterday. As regards the orthography it is partially, and only partially modernised; clauses or whole passages omitted in the manuscript are supplied from other sources, although the fact is duly notified[1]; sometimes the readings of the first hand are put in the margin, while those of the second stand in the text, sometimes the contrary: in a word the plan of the work exhibits all the faults such a performance well can have. Nor is the execution at all less objectionable. Although the five volumes were ten years in printing (1828—38), Mai devoted to their superintendence but his scanty spare hours, and even then worked so carelessly that after cancelling a hundred pages for their incurable want of exactness, he was reduced to the shift of making *manual* corrections with moveable types, and projected huge tables of errata, which Vercellone has in some measure tried to supply. When once it is stated that the type was set from some printed Greek Testament, the readings of the Codex itself being inserted as corrections, and the whole revised by means of an assistant

[1] The great gap in the Pauline Epistles (*see* p. 85) is filled up from Vatic. 1761 (Act. 158, Paul. 192) of the eleventh century.

who read the proof-sheets to the Cardinal while he inspected the manuscript; no one will look for accuracy from a method which could not possibly lead to it. Accordingly when Mai's text came to be compared with the collations of Bartolocci, of Mico, of Rulotta and of Birch, or with the scattered readings which had been extracted by others, it was soon discovered that while this edition has added very considerably to our knowledge of the Codex Vaticanus, and often enabled us to form a decision on its readings when the others were at variance; it was in its turn convicted by them of so many errors, oversights, and inconsistencies, that its single evidence can never be used with confidence, especially when it agrees with the commonly received Greek text. Immediately after the appearance of Mai's expensive quartos, an octavo reprint of the New Testament was struck off at Leipsic for certain London booksellers, which proved but a hasty, slovenly and unscholarlike performance, and was put aside in 1859 by a cheap Roman edition in octavo, prepared like the quarto by Mai, prefaced by another graceful and sensible epistle of Vercellone. This last edition was undertaken by the Cardinal, after sad experience had taught him the defects of his larger work, and he took good care to avoid some of the worst of them: the readings of the second hand are usually, though not always, banished to the margin, their number on the whole is increased, gross errors are corrected, omissions supplied, and the Vatican chapters are given faithfully and in full. But Mai's whole procedure in this matter is so truly unfortunate, that in a person whose fame was less solidly grounded, we should impute it to mere helpless incapacity. Not only did he split up the paragraphs of his quarto into the modern chapters and verses (in itself a most undesirable change, see above, p. 59), but by omitting some things and altering others, he introduced almost as many errors as he removed. The last person who is known to have examined the Codex (see above, p. 85, *note* 1), on consulting it for sixteen passages out of hundreds wherein the two are utterly at variance, discovered that the quarto was right in seven of them, the octavo in nine: as if Mai were determined that neither of his editions should supersede the use of the other. Critics of every shade of opinion are unanimous on one point, that a new edition of the Codex Vaticanus is as imperatively needed as ever; one which shall preserve with accuracy all that the first hand has written (transcriptural errors included), shall note in every instance the corrections made by the second hand, and wherever any one of the previous collators is in error, shall expressly state the true reading.

Those who agree the most unreservedly respecting the age of the Codex Vaticanus, vary widely in their estimate of its critical value. By some it has been held in such undue esteem that its readings, if probable in themselves, and supported (or even though not supported) by two or three other copies and versions, have been accepted in preference to the united testimony of all authorities besides: while others have spoken of its text as one of the most vicious extant. Without anticipating what must be discussed hereafter (Chap. VII.) we may say at once, that neither of these views can commend itself to impartial judges: that while we accord to Cod. B as much weight as to any single document in existence, we ought never to forget that it is but one out of many, several of them being nearly (and one quite) as old, and in other respects as worthy of confidence as itself. One marked feature, characteristic of this copy, is the great number of its *omissions*, which has induced Dr Dobbin to speak of it as presenting "an abbreviated text of the New Testament:" and certainly the facts he states on this point are startling enough[1]. He calculates that Codex B leaves out words or whole clauses no less than 330 times in Matthew, 365 in Mark, 439 in Luke, 357 in John, 384 in the Acts, 681 in the surviving Epistles; or 2556 times in all. That no small proportion of these are mere oversights of the scribe seems evident from a circumstance that has only just come to light, namely, that this same scribe has repeatedly written words and clauses *twice over*, a class of mistakes which Mai and the collators have seldom thought fit to notice, inasmuch as the false addition has not been retraced by the second hand, but which by no means enhances our estimate of the care employed in copying this venerable record of primitive Christianity[2]. Hug and others have referred the origin of Codex B to Egypt, but (unlike in this respect to Codex A) its history does not confirm their conjecture, and the argument

[1] Dublin University Magazine, Nov. 1859, p. 620.

[2] J. W. B. (of whom above, p. 85, note 1) cites four specimens of such repetitions: Matth. xxi. 4, 5 words written twice over; *ib.* xxvi. 56, 6 words; Luke i. 37, 3 words or one line; John xvii. 18, 19, 6 words.

derived from orthography or grammatical forms, we have before intimated to be but slight and ambiguous.

C. CODEX EPHRAEMI, No. 9 in the Imperial Library of Paris, is a most valuable palimpsest containing portions of the Septuagint version of the Old Testament on 64 leaves, and fragments of every part of the New on 145 leaves, amounting on the whole to less than two-thirds of the volume[1]. This manuscript seems to have been brought from the East by Andrew John Lascar [d. 1535], a learned Greek patronised by Lorenzo de' Medici; it once belonged to Cardinal Nicolas Ridolphi of that family, was brought into France by Queen Catherine de Medici of evil memory, and so passed into the Royal Library at Paris[2]. The ancient writing is barely legible, having been almost removed about the twelfth century to receive some Greek works of St Ephraem, the great Syrian Father [299—378]; a chemical preparation applied at the instance of Fleck in 1834, though it revived much that was before illegible, has defaced the vellum with stains of various colours, from green and blue to black and brown. The older writing was first noticed by Peter Allix nearly two centuries ago; various readings extracted from it were communicated by Boivin to Kuster, who published them (under the notation of Paris 9) in his edition of Mill's N. T.,

[1] As this manuscript is of first-rate importance it is necessary to subjoin a full list of the passages it contains, that it may not be cited *e silentio* for what it does not exhibit: Matth. i. 2—v. 15; vii. 5—xvii. 26; xviii. 28—xxii. 20; xxiii. 17—xxiv. 10; xxiv. 45—xxv. 30; xxvi. 22—xxvii. 11; xxvii. 47—xxviii. 14; Mark i. 17—vi. 31; viii. 5—xii. 29; xiii. 19—xvi. 20; Luke i. 2—ii. 5; ii. 42—iii. 21; iv. 25—vi. 4; vi. 37—vii. 16; viii. 28—xii. 3; xix. 42—xx. 27; xxi. 21—xxii. 19; xxiii. 25—xxiv. 7; xxiv. 46—53; John i. 1—41; iii. 33—v. 16; vi. 38—vii. 3; viii. 34—ix. 11; xi. 8—46; xiii. 8—xiv. 7; xvi. 21—xviii. 36; xx. 26—xxi. 25; Acts i. 2—iv. 3; v. 35—x. 42; xiii. 1—xvi. 36; xx. 10—xxi. 30; xxii. 21—xxiii. 18; xxiv. 15—xxvi. 19; xxvii. 16—xxviii. 8; Jac. i. 1—iv. 2; 1 Pet. i. 2—iv. 6; 2 Pet. i. 1—1 Jo. iv. 2; 3 Jo. 3—15; Jud. 3—25; Rom. i. 1—ii. 5; iii. 21—ix. 6; x. 15—xi. 31; xiii. 10—1 Cor. vii. 18; ix. 6—xiii. 8; xv. 40—2 Cor. x. 8; Gal. i. 20—vi. 18; Ephes. ii. 18—iv. 17; Phil. i. 22—iii. 5; Col. i. 1—1 Thess. ii. 9; Hebr. ii. 4—vii. 26; ix. 15—x. 24; xii. 15—xiii. 25; 1 Tim. iii. 9—v. 20; vi. 21—Philem. 25; Apoc. i. 1—iii. 19; v. 14—vii. 14; vii. 17—viii. 5; ix. 16—x. 10; xi. 3—xvi. 13; xviii. 2—xix. 5. Of all the books only 2 John and 2 Thess. are entirely lost; about 37 chapters of the Gospels, 10 of the Acts, 42 of the Epistles, 8 of the Apocalypse have perished.

[2] The following Medicean manuscripts seem to have come into the Imperial Library by the same means: Evan. 16. 19. 317. Act. 12. 126. Paul. 164.

1711. A complete collation of the New Testament was first made by Wetstein in 1716, then very young, for Bentley's projected edition, for which labour (as he records the fact himself) he paid Wetstein £50. This collation Wetstein of course used for his own Greek Testament of 1751—2, and though several persons subsequently examined the manuscript, and so became aware that more might be gathered from it, it was not until 1843 that Tischendorf brought out at Leipsic his full and noble edition of the New Testament portion; the Old Testament he published in 1845. Although Tischendorf complains of the typographical errors made in his absence in the former of these two volumes, and has corrected them in the other, they probably comprise by far the most masterly production of this nature up to that date published; it is said too that none but those who have seen Codex C can appreciate the difficulty of decyphering some parts of it[1]. The Prolegomena are especially valuable; the uncial type does not aim at being an imitation, but the *facsimile* (from which a few lines have been copied in Plate 9, No. 24, from 1 Tim. iii. 16) faithfully represents the original, even to the present colour of the ink. In shape Codex C is about the size of Cod. A, but not quite so tall; its vellum is hardly so fine as that of Cod. A and a few others, yet sufficiently good. In this copy there is but one column in a page, which contains from 40 to 46 lines (usually 41), the characters being a little smaller than either A or B, and somewhat more elaborate. Thus the points at the ends of *sigma*, *epsilon*, and especially of the horizontal line of *tau*, are more decided than in Codex A; *delta*, though not so fully formed as in later books, is less simple than in A, the strokes being of less equal thickness, and the base more ornamented. On the other hand, *alpha* and *pi* are nearer the model of Codex B. *Iota* and *upsilon*, which in Cod. A and many other copies, have two dots over them when they commence a syllable, and are sometimes found with one dot, have here a small straight line in its place. There are no breathings or accents by the first hand: the apostrophus is found but rarely, chiefly with Proper names, as $\overline{\delta\alpha\delta}$'. The uncial writing is continuous, the punctuation of Cod. C, like that of A and B, consisting only of a single point, mostly

[1] Canon Wordsworth (N. T. Part IV. p. 159) reminds us of Wetstein's statement (*Bentley's Correspondence*, p. 501) that it had cost him two hours to read one page; so that his £50 were not so easily earned, after all.

but not always put level with the top of the preceding letter; wherever such a point was employed, a space of one letter broad was usually left vacant: these points are most common in the later books of the N. T. The *κεφάλαια* are not placed in the upper margin of the page as in Cod. A, but a list of their *τίτλοι* preceded each Gospel: the so-called Ammonian sections stand in the margin, but not at present the Eusebian canons; though since lines of the text written in vermillion have been thoroughly washed out, the canons (for which that colour was commonly employed) may easily have shared the same fate. There is no trace of chapters in the Acts, Epistles or Apocalypse, and both the titles and subscriptions to the various books are very simple. Capital letters are used quite as freely as in Cod. A, both at the commencement of the Ammonian sections, and in many other places. All these circumstances taken together indicate for Cod. C as early a date as the fifth century, though I see no sufficient cause for deeming it at all older than Cod. A. Alexandria has been assigned as its native country, for the very insufficient reasons stated when we were describing A and B. It is very carefully transcribed, and of its great critical value there is no doubt; its text seems to stand nearly midway between A and B. Three correctors at least have been at work on Cod. C, greatly to the perplexity of the critical collator: they are respectively indicated by Tischendorf as C*, C**, C***. The earliest may have been of the sixth century: the second perhaps of the ninth, who revised such portions only as were adapted to ecclesiastical use; he inserted many accents, the *rough* breathing, and some notes. By him or by the third hand (whose changes are but few) small crosses were interpolated as stops, agreeably to the fashion of their times.

D of the Gospels and Acts, Codex Bezae Graeco-Latinus belongs to the University Library at Cambridge, where the open volume is conspicuously exhibited to visitors in the New Building. It was presented to the University in 1581 by Theodore Beza, for whom and his master Calvin, the heads of that learned body then cherished a veneration which already boded ill for the peace of the English Church[1]. Between the

[1] Very remarkable is the language of the University in returning thanks for the gift: "Nam hoc scito, post unicæ scripturæ sacratissimam cognitionem, nullos

Gospels (whose order was spoken of above, p. 62) and the Acts, the Catholic Epistles once stood, of which only a few verses remain in the Latin version (3 John *v.* 11—15) followed by the words "epistulae Johanis III. explicit, incipit actus apostolorum," as if St Jude's Epistle were displaced or wanting. There are not a few hiatus both in the Greek and Latin texts[1]. The contents of this remarkable document were partially made known by numerous extracts from it, under the designation of *β*, in the margin of Robert Stephens' Greek Testament of 1550, whose history of it is that it was collated for him in Italy by his friends (τὸ δὲ β′ ἐστὶ τὸ ἐν Ἰταλίᾳ ὑπὸ τῶν ἡμετέρων ἀντιβληθὲν φίλων) (Epistle to the Reader)[2]. It is not very easy to reconcile this statement with Beza's account to the University of Cambridge in 1581, wherein he

unquam ex omni memoriâ temporum scriptores extitisse, quos memorabili viro Johanni Calvino tibique præferamus." Kipling's Præf. to Codex Bezæ, p. xxiii.

[1] Matth. i. 1—20; vi. 20—ix. 2; xxvii. 2—12; John i. 16—iii. 26; Acts viii. 29—x. 14; xxi. 2—10; 15—18 (though Wetstein cites several readings from these verses, which must have been extant in his time); xxii. 10—20; 29—xxviii. 31 in the *Greek;* Matth. i. 1—11; vi. 8—viii. 27; xxvi. 65—xxvii. 1; John i. 1—iii. 16; Acts viii. 20—x. 4; xx. 31—xxi. 2; xxii. 2—10; xxii. 20—xxviii. 31 in the *Latin.* The original writing has perished in the following, which are supplied by later hands: Matth. iii. 7—16; Mark xvi. 15—20; John xviii. 14—xx. 13 in the *Greek,* by a scribe not earlier than the tenth century, and Matth. ii. 21—iii. 7; Mark xvi. 6—20; John xviii. 2—xx. 1 in the *Latin,* written in or about the ninth century. A fragment, containing portions of Matth. xxvi. 65—67 (Latin) and xxvii. 2 (Greek), still remains, which however Kipling does not mention.

[2] It is surprising that any one should have questioned the identity of Cod. D with Stephens' *β*. No other manuscript has been discovered which agrees with *β* in the many singular readings and arbitrary additions in support of which it is cited by Stephens. That he omitted so many more than he inserted is no argument against their identity, since we *know* that he did the same in the case of his *α* (the Complutensian Polyglott) and *η* (Codex L, Paris 62). The great inaccuracy of Stephens' *margin* (the text is much better revised) is so visible from these and other well-ascertained instances that no one ought to wonder if *β* is alleged occasionally (not often) for readings which D does not contain. I do not find *β* cited by Stephens after Acts xx. 24, except indeed in Rom. iii. 10, in manifest error, just as in the Apocalypse xix. 14 *ε* (No. 6 of the Gospels), which does not contain this book, is cited instead of *ιε*; or as *ια* is quoted in xiii. 4, *but not elsewhere in the Apocalypse,* undoubtedly in the place of *ιϛ*; or as *ιϛ*, which had broken off at xvii. 8, reappears instead of *ιε* in xx. 3. In the various places named in the last note, wherein the Greek of Cod. D is lost, *β* is cited only at Matth. xxvii. 3, beyond question instead of *η*; and for *part* of the reading in Acts ix. 31, *δ* (to which the whole rightly belongs) being alleged for the other part. In John xix. 6, indeed, where the original Greek is missing, *β* is cited, but it is for a reading actually extant in the modern hand which has there supplied Codex D's defects. The inference to be drawn from this last fact is tolerably evident.

alleges that he obtained the volume in 1562 from the monastery of St Irenæus at Lyons ("oriente ibi civili bello"), where it had long lain buried ("postquam ibi in pulvere diu jacuisset"). This great city, it must be remembered, was sacked in that very year by the infamous Des Adrets, whom it suited to espouse for a while the cause of the Huguenots; and we can hardly doubt that some one who had shared in the plunder of the abbey conveyed this portion of it to Beza, whose influence at that juncture was paramount among the French Reformed[1]. Patrick Young, the librarian of Charles I, who first collated Cod. A and published from it the Epistles of Clement in 1633, had also the honour of being the first to completely examine Cod. D. An unusually full collation was made for Walton's Polyglott by pious Archbishop Ussher, who devoted to these studies the doleful leisure of his latter years. But a manuscript replete as this is with variations from the sacred text beyond all other example could be adequately represented only by being published in full; a design entrusted by the University of Cambridge to Dr Thomas Kipling, afterwards Dean of Peterborough, whose "Codex Theodori Bezae Cantabrigiensis" 1793, 2 vol. fol. (in type imitating the original handwriting much more closely than in Codices AC and the rest), is believed to be a faithful transcript of the text, though the Prolegomena too plainly testify to the editor's pitiable ignorance of sacred criticism, while his frequent habit of placing the readings of the second hand in the text, and those

[1] I cannot understand why Wetstein (N. T. Proleg. Vol. I. 30) should have supposed that Beza *prevaricated* as to the means whereby he procured his manuscript. He was not the man to be at all ashamed of spoiling the Philistines, and the bare mention of Lyons in connexion with the year 1562 would have been abundantly intelligible scarce twenty years afterwards. It is however remarkable that in the last edition of his Annotations (1598) he nowhere calls it Codex Lugdunensis, but *Claromontanus* (notes on Luke xix. 26; Acts xx. 3); for though it might be natural that Beza, at eighty years of age and after the lapse of so long a time, should confound the Lyons copy with his own Codex Claromontanus of St Paul's Epistles (D); yet the only way in which we can account for the Codex Bezæ being collated in *Italy* for Stephens, is by adopting Wetstein's suggestion that it was the actual copy ("antiquissimum codicem Græcum") taken to the Council of Trent in 1546 by William a Prato, Bishop of *Clermont* in Auvergne, to confirm the Latin reading in John xxi. 22, "*sic* eum volo," which D alone is known to do. Some learned man (*ὑπὸ τῶν ἡμετέρων φίλων* does not well suit his son Henry) might have sent to Robert Stephens from Trent the readings of a manuscript to which attention had been thus specially directed.

of the first hand in the notes (a defect we have also noted in Mai's Cod. B) renders his volumes inconvenient for use. Let Kipling be praised for the care and exact diligence his work evinces, but Herbert Marsh [1757—1839] was of all Cambridge men of that period the only one known to be competent for such a task.

The Codex Bezae is a quarto volume 10 inches high by 8 broad; of 414 leaves (whereof 11 are more or less mutilated, and 9 by later hands), with one column on a page, the Greek text and its Latin version being parallel, the Greek on the left, or *verso* of each leaf, and the Latin on the right, opposite to it, on the *recto* of the next. Notwithstanding the Alexandrine forms that abound in it more than in any other copy, and which have been held to prove the Egyptian origin of Codd. ABC, the fact of its having a Latin version sufficiently attests its Western origin. The vellum is not quite equal in fineness to that of a few others. There are thirty-three lines in every page, and these of unequal length, as this manuscript is arranged in *στίχοι*, being the earliest in date that is so. The Latin is placed in the same line and as nearly as possible in the same order as the corresponding Greek. It has not the larger *κεφάλαια* or Eusebian canons, but the Ammonian sections, often incorrectly placed, and obviously in a later hand. The original absence of these divisions is no proof that the book was not at first intended for ecclesiastical use (as some have stated), inasmuch as the sections and canons were constructed for a very different purpose (see above, p. 50), but is another argument for its being copied in the West, perhaps not far from the place where it rested so long. The characters are of the same size as in C, smaller than in AB, but betray a later age than any of these, although the Latin as well as the Greek is written continuously, excepting that in the titles and subscriptions of the several books (as in Codd. DH of St Paul) the words are separated. With regard to the use of capitals, Cod. D agrees with Cod. ℵ (*see* p. 78). As a specimen of the style of this manuscript we subjoin about half a page both of the Greek and Latin (pp. 148, 9, Matth. xxiv. 51—xxv. 6), which the shape of the present volume has compelled us to print lengthwise. The type cast for Kipling's edition, which is here employed, is so wonderfully exact, that it possesses nearly all the advantages of an

ΚΑΙΟΒΡΥΓΜΟCΤΩΝΟΔΟΝΤΩΝ
CΞΗ : ΤΟΤΕΟΜΟΙΩΘΗCΕΤΑΙ·ΗΒΑCΙΛΕΙΑΤΩΝΟΥΡΑΝΩΝ
ΔΕΚΑΠΑΡΘΕΝΟΙC·ΑΙΤΙΝΕCΛΑΒΟΥCΑΙ
ΤΑCΛΑΜΠΑΔΑCΕΑΥΤΩΝ
ΕΞΗΛΘΟΝΕΙCΑΠΑΝΤΗCΙΝΤΟΥΝΥΜΦΙΟΥ
ΚΑΙΤΗCΝΥΜΦΗC
ΠΕΝΤΕΔΕΕΞΑΥΤΩΝΗCΑΝΜΩΡΑΙ
ΚΑΙΠΕΝΤΕΦΡΟΝΙΜΟΙ
ΑΙΟΥΝΜΩΡΑΙΛΑΒΟΥCΑΙ·ΤΑCΛΑΜΠΑΔΑCΑΥΤΩΝ
ΟΥΚΕΛΑΒΟΝΜΕΘΕΑΥΤΩΝΕΛΑΙΟΝ
ΕΝΤΟΙCΑΓΓΕΙΟΙCΑΥΤΩΝ·ΑΙΔΕΦΡΟΝΙΜΟΙ
ΕΛΑΒΟΝΕΛΕΟΝΕΝΤΟΙCΑΓΓΕΙΟΙC
ΜΕΤΑΤΩΝΛΑΜΠΑΔΩΝΑΥΤΩΝ
ΧΡΟΝΙΖΟΝΤΟCΔΕΤΟΥΝΥΜΦΙΟΥ
ΕΝΥCΤΑΞΑΝΠΑCΑΙΚΑΙΕΚΑΘΕΥΔΟΝ
ΜΕCΗCΔΕΝΥΚΤΟC·ΚΡΑΥΓΗΓΕΓΟΝΕΝ

ETSTRIDORDENTIUM
TUNCSIMILABITURREGNUMCAELORUM
DECEMUIRGINIBUS·QUAEACCEPERUNT
LAMPADASSUAS
ETEXIERUNTINOBUIAMSPONSI
ETSPONSAE
QUINQUEAUTEMEXHIS ERANTSTULTAE
ETQUINQUESAPIENTES
STULTAEERGOACCIPIENTES·LAMPADASSUAS
NONACCEPERUNTSECUMOLEUM
INUASISSUIS·SAPIENTESAUTEM
ACCEPERUNTOLEUMINUASISSUIS
CUMLAMPADIBUSSUIS
TARDANTEAUTEMSPONSO
DORMITAUERUNTOMNES·ETDORMIEBANT
MEDIAUTEMNOCTE·CLAMORFACTUSEST

actual *facsimile*. The horizontal strokes to the left, at the bottom of *rho* and *kappa*, are not exaggerated in length, though they are not so fine as in the original: the curves in *phi* almost become angles (see p. 35): the hook to the left of *pi* is sometimes omitted; in other respects the imitation is complete, both in the Greek and Roman letters. In addition to the single point, about three-fourths of the height of a letter up, which often sub-divides the στίχοι in both languages (e.g. ll. 3, 9, 11, 16), the coarser hand which inserted the Ammonian sections (e.g. CΞH or 168 in l. 2) placed double dots (:) after the numerals, and often inserted similar points in the text, before or over the first letter of a section. Each member of the genealogy in Luke iii. forms a separate στίχος, as in Cod B (p. 87): quotations are indicated by throwing the commencement of the lines which contain them, both Greek and Latin, about an inch back (e.g. Matth. xxvi. 31; Mark i. 2; Act. ii. 34; iv. 25). The first three lines of each book, in both languages, were written in bright red ink, which was also employed in the alternate lines of the subscriptions, and in other slight ornaments. The traces of the scribe's needle and lines (*see p.* 24) are very visible, the margin ample, and the volume on the whole in good keeping, though its first extant page (Latin) is much decayed, and it is stained in parts by some chemical mixture that has been applied to it. The portions supplied by a later hand are in the uncial Greek and cursive Latin characters usual at the dates assigned to them. The marginal notes of the Saturday and Sunday lessons (αvvαγvοσμα is the form often used) are in thick letters (of a later date than the Ammonian sections), which *might* have been written by a Copt.

The leaves of the Codex Bezae are arranged in quires of four sheets (or eight leaves) each, the numeral signatures of which are set *primâ manu* low in the margin at the foot of the last page of each (*see p.* 24). It originally consisted of upwards of 64 quires, of which the 1st, 44th, and 64th, have each lost some leaves, the 34th is entire though containing but six leaves, while those signed Γ (3), IΔ (14), KB (22), ME (45)—NB (52), NZ (57), and all after ΞΔ (64), are wholly wanting. It is not easy to surmise what may have been written on the 67 leaves that intervened between MΔ 5 and NΓ 1; the gap ends with

3 John 11 (Greek), but the space is apparently too great for the Catholic Epistles alone, even though we suppose that Jude was inserted (as appears in some catalogues) otherwise than in the last place.

The internal character of the Codex Bezae is a most difficult and indeed an almost inexhaustible theme. No known manuscript contains so many bold and extensive interpolations (six hundred, it is said, in the Acts alone), countenanced, where they are not absolutely unsupported, chiefly by the Old Latin and some of the Syriac versions: its own parallel Latin translation is too servilely accommodated to the Greek text to be regarded as an independent authority, save where its corresponding Greek is lost. So far as the topic can be discussed in an elementary work, it will be touched upon in Chapter VII. For the present we shall simply say with Davidson that "its singularly corrupt text, in connexion with its great antiquity, is a curious problem, which cannot easily be solved" (Biblical Crit. Vol. II. p. 288); though we are not disposed to imitate the blind policy of Beza, who, alarmed by its wide diversities from other copies, however ancient, suggested that "vitandae quorundam offensioni, asservandum potius quam publicandum" (Letter to the University of Cambridge).

Of the manuscripts hitherto described Codd. ℵABC for their critical value, Cod. D for its numberless and strange deviations from other authorities, and all five for their high antiquity, demanded a full description. Of those which follow many contain but a few fragments of the Gospels, and others are so recent in date that they hardly exceed in importance some of the best cursive copies (e.g. FGHSU). None of these need detain us long.

E. Codex Basiliensis (B VI. 21, now K IV. 35) contains the four Gospels, excepting Luke iii. 4—15; xxiv. 47—53, and was written about the middle of the eighth century. Three leaves on which are Luke i. 69—ii. 4; xii. 58—xiii. 12; xv. 5—20 are in a smaller and late hand, above the obliterated fragments of a homily as old as the main body of the manuscript. This copy is one of the best of the second-rate uncials, and might well have been published at length. It was given to a religious house in Basle by Cardinal John de Ragusio, who was sent on a mission to the Greeks by the Council of Basle (1431), and probably brought it from Constantinople. Erasmus overlooked it for later books when preparing his Greek Testament at Basle; indeed it was not brought into the Public Library there before 1559. A collation was sent to Mill by John Battier, Greek Professor at Basle: Mill named it B. 1, and truly declared it to be "probatæ fidei et bonæ notæ." Bengel (who obtained a few extracts from it) calls it Basil. *a*, but its first real collator was Wetstein, whose native town it adorns. Since his time, Tischendorf in 1843, Professor Müller of Basle and Tregelles in 1846, have independently collated it throughout. Judging from the specimen sent to him, Mill (N.T. Proleg. § 1118) thought the hand much like that of Cod. A; the uncial letters (though not so regular or neat) are firm, round and simple: there is but one column of about 24 lines on the page; it has breathings and accents pretty uniformly, and not ill placed; otherwise, from the shape of many of the letters (e.g. *theta*, *facsimile* No. 26, l. 4), it might be judged of earlier date: observe, however, the oblong form of *omicron* where the space is crowded in the first line of the *facsimile*, whereas the older scribes would have retained the circular shape and made the letter very small (*see* p. 36, and *facsim.* No. 11a, l. 4). The single stop in Cod. E, as was stated above (p. 42), changes its place according to the variation of its power, as in other copies of about the same age. The capitals at the beginning of sections stand out in the margin as in Codd. AC. There are no tables of Eusebian canons prefixed to the Gospels, but lists of the larger *κεφάλαια*. These, together with the numbers of the Ammonian sections in the margin and the Eusebian canons beneath them, as well as harmonising references to the other Gospels at the foot of the page (*see above*, p. 51, *note* 2), names of feast days with their Proper lessons, and other liturgical notices, have been inserted (as some think) by a later hand. The value of this codex, as supplying materials for criticism, is considerable. It approaches more nearly than some others of its date to the text now commonly received, and is an excellent witness for it.

F. Codex Boreeli, now in the Public Library at Utrecht, once belonged to John Boreel [d. 1629], Dutch ambassador at the court of King James I. Wetstein obtained some readings from it in 1730, as far as Luke xi, but stated that he knew not where it then was. In 1830 Professor Heringa of Utrecht discovered it in private hands at Arnheim, and procured it for his University Library, where in 1850 Tregelles found it, though with some difficulty, the leaves being torn and all loose in a box, and made a *facsimile;* Tischendorf had looked through it in 1841. In 1843, after Heringa's death, H. E. Vinke published that scholar's *Disputatio de Codice Boreeliano*, which includes a full and exact collation of the text. It contains the Four Gospels with many defects, some of which have been caused since the collation was made which Wetstein published: hence the codex must still sometimes be cited on his authority as F^{w}. In fact there are but 204 leaves and a few fragments remaining, written with two columns of about 19 lines each on the page, in a tall, oblong, upright form: it is referred by Tischendorf to the ninth, by Tregelles to the tenth century. In St Luke there are no less than 24 gaps; in Wetstein's collation it began Matth. vii. 6, but now ix. 1: other hiatus are Matth. xii. 1—44; xiii. 55—xiv. 9; xv. 20—31; xx. 18—xxi. 5; Mark i. 43—ii. 8; ii. 23—iii. 5; xi. 6—26; xiv. 54—xv. 5; xv. 39—xvi. 19; John iii. 5—14; iv. 23—38; v. 18—38; vi. 39—63; vii. 28—viii. 10; x. 32—xi. 3; xi. 40—xii. 3; xii. 14—25: it ends xiii. 34. Few manuscripts have fallen into such unworthy hands. The Eusebian canons are wanting, the Ammonian sections standing without them in the margin. Thus in Mark x. 13 (*see facsimile*, No. 27) the section $\overline{\rho\varsigma}$ (106) has not under it the proper canon β (2). The letters *delta*, *epsilon*, *theta*, *omicron*, and especially the cross-like *psi* are of the most recent uncial form, *phi* is large and bevelled at both ends; the breathings and accents are fully and not incorrectly given.

F^{a}. CODEX COISLIN. 1 is that great copy of the Septuagint Octateuch, the glory of the Coislin Library, first made known by Montfaucon (Biblioth. Coislin. 1715), and illustrated by a *facsimile* in Silvestre's Paléogr. Univ. No. 65. It contains 227 leaves in two columns, 13 inches by 9: the fine massive uncials of the sixth or seventh century are much like Cod. A's in general appearance. In the margin *primâ manu* Wetstein found Acts ix. 24, 25, and so inserted this as Cod. F in his list of MSS. of the Acts. In 1842 Tischendorf observed 19 other passages of the New Testament, which he published in his *Monumenta sacra inedita* (p. 400, &c.) with a *facsimile*. The texts are Matth. v.

48; xii. 48; xxvii. 25; Luke i. 42; ii. 24; xxiii. 21; John v. 35; vi. 53, 55; Acts iv. 33, 34; x. 13, 15; xxii. 22. 1 Cor. vii. 39; xi. 29; 2 Cor. iii. 13; ix. 7; xi. 33; Gal. iv. 21, 22; Col. ii. 16, 17; Hebr. x. 26.

G. Cod. Harleian. 5684 or Wolfii A, H. Cod. Wolfii B. } These two copies were brought from the East by Andrew Erasmus Seidel, purchased by La Croze, and by him presented to J. C. Wolff, who published loose extracts from them both in his *Anecdota Græca* (Vol. III. 1723), and actually mutilated them in 1721 in order to send pieces to Bentley, among whose papers in Trinity College Library (B. XVII. 20) Tregelles found the fragments in 1845 (*Account of the Printed Text*, p. 160). Subsequently Cod. G came with the rest of the Harleian collection into the British Museum; Cod. H, which had long been missing, was brought to light in the Public Library of Hamburgh, through Petersen the Librarian, in 1838. Codd. GH have now been thoroughly collated both by Tischendorf and Tregelles. Cod. G appears to be of the tenth, Cod. H of the ninth century, and is stated to be of higher critical value. Besides the mutilated fragments at Trinity College (Matth. v. 29—31; 39—43 of Cod. G; Luke i. 3—6; 13—15 of Cod. H), many parts of both have perished: viz. in Cod. G 372 verses; Matth. i. 1—vi. 6; vii. 25—viii. 9; viii. 23—ix. 2; xxviii. 18—Mark i. 13; xiv. 19—25; Luke i. 1—13; v. 4—vii. 3; viii. 46—ix. 5; xii. 27—51; xxiv. 41—53; John xviii. 5—19; xix. 4—27 (of which one later hand supplies Matth. xxviii. 18—Mark i. 8; John xviii. 5—19; another Luke xii. 27—51): in Cod. H 679 verses; Matth. i. 1—xv. 30; xxv. 33—xxvi. 3; Mark i. 32—ii. 4; xv. 44—xvi. 14; Luke v. 18—32; vi. 8—22; x. 2—19; John ix. 30—x. 25; xviii. 2—18; xx. 12—25. Cod. G has some Church notes in the margin; Cod. H the Ammonian sections without the Eusebian canons: G however has both sections and canons. Both are written in a somewhat rude style, with breathings and accents rather irregularly placed, as was the fashion of their times; G in two columns of 22 lines each on a page, H with one column of 23 lines. In each the latest form of the uncial letters is very manifest (e.g. *delta*, *theta*), but G is the neater of the two. In G the single point, in H a kind of Maltese cross, are the prevailing marks of punctuation. Our *facsimiles* (Nos. 28 of G, 30 of H) are due to Tregelles; that of G he took from the fragment at Trinity College. Inasmuch as beside Matth. v. 31 ἀρ (ἀρχή) is conspicuous in the margin, and τε της λε (τέλος τῆς λέξεως) stands in the text itself, good scholars may be excused for having mistaken it for a scrap of some Evangelistarium.

I. Cod. Tischendorf. II at St Petersburg, consists of palimpsest fragments found by Tischendorf in 1853 "in the dust of an Eastern library," and published in his new series of *Monumenta sacra*, Vol. I. 1855. On 28 vellum leaves (8 of them on 4 double leaves) Georgian writing is above the partially obliterated Greek, which is for the most part very hard to read. They compose fragments of no less than seven different manuscripts; the first two, of the fifth century, are as old as Codd. AC (the first having scarcely any capital letters and those very slightly larger than the rest); the third fragment seems of the sixth century, nearly of the date of Cod. N (p. 110), about as old as Cod. P (*see* p. 113); the fourth scarcely less ancient: all four, like other palimpsests, have the Ammonian sections without the Eusebian canons (*see* p. 51). Of the Gospels we have 190 verses: viz. (*Frag.* 1) John xi. 50—xii. 9; xv. 12—xvi. 2; xix. 11—24; (*Frag.* 2) Matth. xiv. 13—16; 19—23; xxiv. 37—xxv. 1; xxv. 32—45; xxvi. 31—45; Mark ix. 14—22; xiv. 58—70; (*Frag.* 3) Matth. xvii. 22—xviii. 3; xviii. 11—19; xix. 5—14; Luke xviii. 14—25; John iv. 52—v. 8; xx. 17—26; (*Frag.* 4) Luke vii. 39—49; xxiv. 10—19. The fifth fragment, containing portions of the Acts and St Paul's Epistles (1 Cor. xv. 53—xvi. 9; Tit. i. 1—13; Acts xxviii. 8—17) is as old as the third, if not as the first. The sixth and seventh fragments are of the seventh century: viz. (*Frag.* 5, *of two leaves*) Acts ii. 6—17; xxvi. 7—18; (*Frag.* 7, *of one leaf*) Acts xiii. 39—46. In all seven are 255 verses. All except *Frag.* 6 are in two columns of from 29 to 18 lines each, and unaccentuated; *Frag.* 6 has but one column on a page, with some accents. The first five fragments, so far as they extend, must be placed in the first rank as critical authorities. Tischendorf gives us six *facsimiles* of them in the *Monumenta sacra*, a seventh in *Anecdota sacra et profana*, 1855.

K. Cod. Cyprius or No. 63 of the Imperial Library at Paris, shares only with Codd. MSU the advantage of being a *com-*

plete uncial copy of the Four Gospels. It was brought into the Colbert Library from Cyprus in 1673; Mill inserted its readings from Simon; it was re-examined by Scholz, whose inaccuracies (especially those in his collation of Cod. K in his "*Curæ Criticæ in Historiam textûs Evangeliorum*," *Heidelberg*. 1820) have been strongly denounced by later editors, and I fear with too good reason. The independent collations of Tischendorf and Tregelles have now done all that can be needed for this copy. It is an oblong 4to, in compressed uncials, of about the middle of the ninth century, having one column of about 21 lines on each page, but the hand-writing is irregular and varies much in size. A single point being often found where the sense does not require it, this codex has been thought to have been copied from an older one arranged in *στίχοι*; the ends of each *στίχος* may have been indicated in this manner by the scribe. The subscriptions, *τίτλοι*, Ammonian sections, and indices of the *κεφάλαια* of the last three Gospels are believed to be the work of a later hand: the Eusebian canons are absent. The breathings and accents are *primâ manu*, but often omitted or incorrectly placed. Itacisms and permutations of consonants are very frequent, and the text is of an unusual and interesting character. Scholz regards the directions for the Church lessons, even the *ἀρχαὶ* and *τέλη* in the margin at the beginning and end of lessons, as by the original scribe. He transcribes at length the *ἐκλογάδιον τῶν δ' εὐαγγελιστῶν* and the fragments of a menology prefixed to Cod. K (N. T. Vol. I. pp. 455—493; *see above*, pp. 64, 68—75), of which tables it affords the earliest specimen. The second hand writes at the end *προσδέξη ταύτην* [*τὴν δέλτον*] *ἡ ἁγία θεοτόκος καὶ ὁ ἅγιος Εὐτύχιος*. The style of this copy will be seen from our *facsimile* (No. 29) from Luke xx. 9: the number of the larger chapter (O or 70) stands in the margin, referring to the *τίτλος*, ΠΑΡΑΒΟΛΗ ΑΜΠЄΛѠΝΟϹ at the top of the page. The two stops in l. 2 illustrate the unusual punctuation of this copy.

L. Cod. Regius, No. 62 in the Imperial Library at Paris, is by far the most remarkable document of its age and class. It contains the Four Gospels, except the following passages, Matth. iv. 22—v. 14; xxviii. 17—20; Mark x. 16—30; xv. 2—20; John xxi. 15—25. It was written about the eighth century and consists of 257 leaves 4to, of thick vellum, nearly

6½ inches square, with two columns of 25 lines each on a page, regularly marked, as we so often see, by the *stylus* and ruler. This is doubtless Stephens' η, though he cites it erroneously in Acts xxiv. 7 *bis;* xxv. 14; xxvii. 1; xxviii. 11: it was even then in the Royal Library, although "Roberto Stephano" is marked in the volume. Wetstein collated Cod. L but loosely; Griesbach, who set a very high value on it, studied it with peculiar care; Tischendorf published it in full in his *Monumenta sacra inedita*, 1846. It is but carelessly written, and abounds with errors of the ignorant scribe, who was more probably an Egyptian than a native Greek. The breathings and accents are often deficient, often added wrongly, and placed throughout without rule or propriety. The apostrophus also is common, and frequently out of place; the points are quite irregular, as we have elsewhere stated (p. 42). Capitals occur plentifully, often painted and in questionable taste (see *facsim.* No. 21), and there is a tendency throughout to inelegant ornament. This codex is in bad condition through damp, the ink brown or pale, the uncial letters of a debased oblong shape: *phi* is enormously large and sometimes quite angular (p. 35), other letters are such as might be looked for from its date; neither neat nor remarkably clear. The lessons for Sundays, festivals, &c., ἀρχαὶ and τέλη are marked everywhere in the margin, especially in St Matthew; there are also many corrections and important critical notes (e.g. Mark xvi. 8) in the text or margin, apparently *primâ manu*. Before each Gospel are indices of the κεφάλαια, now imperfect: we find also the τίτλοι at the head and occasionally at the foot of the several pages; the numbers of the κεφάλαια (pointed out by the sign of the cross), Ammonian sections and Eusebian canons in the inner margin[1], often ill put, as if only half understood. The critical weight of this copy may best be discussed hereafter (Chap. VII); it will here suffice barely to mention its resemblance to Cod. B, to the citations of Origen [185—254], and to the margin of the Philoxenian Syriac version [A.D. 616]. Cod. L abounds in what are termed Alexandrian forms, beyond any other copy of its date.

M. COD. CAMPIANUS, No. 48 in the Imperial Library at

[1] In our *facsimile* (No. 21) of John xii. 13, 14, IΔ (14) is the number of the κεφάλαιον περὶ τοῦ ὄνου, ρα (101) of the Ammonian section, Z (7) of the Eusebian Canon.

Paris, contains the Four Gospels complete in a small 4to form, written in very elegant and minute uncials of the end of the ninth century, with two columns of 24 lines each on a page. The Abbé Francis des Camps gave it to Louis XIV, Jan. 1, 1707. This document is Kuster's 2 (1711); it was collated by Wetstein, Scholz and Tregelles; transcribed in 1841 by Tischendorf. Its synaxaria (*see* p. 65) have been published by Scholz in the same place as those of Cod. K, and obviously with great carelessness. Scholia abound in the margin (Tischendorf thinks *primâ manu*) in a very small hand, like in style to the Oxford Plato (Clarke 39, *above*, p. 36): we find too Hippolytus' chronology of the Gospels, Eusebius' canons, and some Arabic scrawled on the last leaf, of which the name of Jerusalem alone has been read. It has breathings, accents pretty fairly given, and a musical notation in red, so frequent in Church manuscripts of the age. Its readings are very good; itacisms and ν ἐφελκυστικὸν are frequent. Tischendorf compares the form of its uncials to those of Cod. V (*below*, p. 117); which, judging from the *facsimile* given by Matthaei, we should deem somewhat less beautiful. From our *facsimile* (No. 31) it will be seen that the round letters are much narrowed, the later form of *delta* quite decided, while *pi* and *beta* might look earlier. Our specimen (Matth. iii. 11) represents the canon A, under the section IA.

N. Codex Purpureus. Only twelve leaves of this beautiful copy remain, and some former possessor must have divided them in order to obtain a better price from three purchasers than from one; four leaves being now in the British Museum (Cotton, C. xv.), six in the Vatican (No. 3785), two at Vienna (Lambec. 2), at the end of a fragment of Genesis in a different hand. The London fragments (Matth. xxvi. 57—65; xxvii. 26—34; John xiv. 2—10; xv. 15—22) were collated by Wetstein on his first visit to England in 1715, and marked in his Greek Testament by the letter J: Scrivener transcribed them in 1845, and announced that they contained 57 various readings, of which Wetstein had given but 5. The Vienna fragment (Luke xxiv. 13—21; 39—49) had long been known by the descriptions of Lambeccius: Wetstein had called it N; Treschow in 1773 and Alter in 1787 had given imperfect collations of it. Scholz first noticed the Vatican leaves (Matth. xix. 6—13; xx. 6—22; xx. 29—xxi. 19), denoted them by Γ, and used some readings extracted by Gaetano Marini. It was reserved for Tischendorf (*Monumenta sacra inedita*, 1846) to publish them all in full, and to determine by actual inspection that they were portions of the same manuscript, of the date of about the end of the sixth century. This book is written on the thinnest vellum (*see* p. 21), dyed purple, and the silver letters (which have turned quite black) were impressed in some way on it, but are too varied in shape, and at the end of the lines in size, to admit the supposition of moveable type being used; as some have thought to be the case in the Codex Argenteus of the Gothic Gospels. The abridgements $\overline{\Theta C}$, $\overline{XC}$ &c. are in gold; and some changes have been made by an ancient second hand. The Ammonian sections and Eusebian canons are faithfully given (*see* p. 53), and the Vatican portion has the 41st, 46th and 47th τίτλοι of St Matthew at the head of the pages (*see* p. 49). Each page has two columns of 16 lines, and the letters (about 10 or 12 in a line) are firm, uniform, bold, and unornamented, though not quite so much so as in a few older documents; their lower extremities are *bevelled* (No. 14). Their size is at least four times that of the letters in Cod. A, the punctuation quite as simple, being a single point (and that usually neglected) level with the top of the letter (see our *facsimile*, No 14, l. 3), and there is no space left between words even after stops. A few letters stand out as capitals at the beginning of lines; of the breathings and accents, if such they be, we have spoken above (p. 41). Letters diminished at the end of a line do not lose their ancient shape, as in many later books: *compendia scribendi* are rare, yet ⊢ stands for N at the end of a line no less than 29 times in the London leaves alone, but ⅄ for αι only once. I at the beginning of a syllable has two dots over it, Υ but one. We have discussed above (pp. 30—35) the shape of the alphabet in N (for by that single letter Tischendorf denotes it), and compared it with others of nearly the same date; *alpha*, *omega*, *lambda* look more ancient than *delta* or *xi*. It exhibits strong Alexandrine forms, e.g. παραλήμψομε, ειχοσαν (the latter condemned *secundâ manu*), and not a few such itacisms as the changes of ι and ει, αι and ε.

N[b]. Musei Brittannici (Addit. 17136) is a 16° volume containing the hymns of Severus in Syriac, and is one of the books recently brought thither from the Nitrian desert. It is a palimpsest, with a second Syriac work written below the first, and under both *four* leaves (117, 118, 127, 128) contain fragments of 16 verses of St John (xiii. 16; 17; 19; 20; 23; 24; 26; 27; xvi. 7; 8; 12; 13; 15; 16; 18; 19). These Tischendorf (and Tregelles about the same time) decyphered with great difficulty, and published in the second volume of his new collection of *Monumenta sacra inedita.* He finds the Ammonian sections, the earliest form of uncial characters, no capital letters, and only the simplest kind of punctuation: and hesitates whether he shall assign the fragment to the 4th or 5th century.

O. No less than seven small fragments have borne this mark. O of Wetstein was given by Anselmo Banduri to Montfaucon, and contains only Luke xviii. 11—14: *this* Tischendorf discards as taken from an Evangelistarium (of the tenth century, as he judges from the writing) chiefly because it wants the Ammonian number at v. 14. In its room he puts for Cod. O Moscow Synod. 120 (Matthaei, 15), a few leaves of about the ninth century (containing the 16 verses, John i. 1—4; xx. 10—13; 15—17; 20—24, with some scholia), used for binding a copy of Chrysostom's Homilies, brought from Mount Athos, and published in Matthaei's Greek Testament with a *facsimile.* Tregelles also will append it to his edition of Cod. Ξ (*see* p. 126). In this fragment we find the cross-like *psi* (p. 35), the interrogative; (Jo. xx. 13), and the comma (*ib. v.* 12). The next five comprise N. T. hymns.

O^{a}. *Magnificat* and *Benedictus* in Greek uncials of the 8th or 9th century, in a Latin book at Wolfenbüttel, is published by Tischendorf, *Anecdota sacr. et prof.* 1855; as is also O^{b}, which contains these two and *Nunc Dimittis*, of the ninth century, and is at Oxford, Bodleian. Misc. Gr. 5 (Auct. D. 4. 1) foll. 313—4[1]. O^{c}. *Magnificat* in the Verona Psalter of the 6th century (the Greek being written in Latin letters), published by Blanchini, (*Vindiciæ Canon. Script.* 1740). O^{d}, O^{e}, both contain the three hymns, O^{d} in the great purple and silver Turin Psalter of the 7th century; O^{e} of the 9th century at St Gall (Cod. 17), partly written in Greek, partly in Latin.

[1] These songs, with 13 others from the Old Testament and Apocrypha, though *partially* written in uncial letters, are included in a volume of Psalms and Hymns, whose prevailing character is early cursive.

P. CODEX GUELPHERBYTANUS A.} These are two palimpsests, discovered by F. A.
Q. .... B.}
Knittel, Archdeacon of Wolfenbüttel, in the Ducal Library of that city, which (together with some fragments of Ulphilas' Gothic version) lie under the more modern writings of Isidore of Seville. He published the whole in 1762, so far at least as he could read them, though Tregelles believed more might be decyphered, and Tischendorf, with his unconquerable energy, has just re-edited the Greek portion in Vol. III. of his *Monumenta sacra inedita* (1860). The volume (called the *Codex Carolinus*) seems to have been once at Bobbio, and has been traced from Weissenburg to Mayence and Prague, till it was bought by a Duke of Brunswick in 1689. Codex P contains, on 43 leaves, 31 fragments of 486 verses, taken from all the four Evangelists[1]; Codex Q, on 13 leaves, 12 fragments of 235 verses from Luke and John[2]; but all can be traced only with great difficulty. A few portions, once written in vermillion, have quite departed, but Tischendorf has made material additions to Knittel's labours, both in extent and accuracy. He assigns P to the sixth, Q to the fifth century. Both are written in two columns, the uncials being bold, round or square, those of Q not a little the smaller. The capitals in P are large and frequent, and both have the Ammonian sections without the canons of Eusebius (but see above, p. 51). The table of τίτλοι found in the volume is written in oblong uncials of a lower date. Itacisms, what are termed Alexandrine forms, and the usual contractions (ΙC, XC, KC, ΘC, YC, ΠΗΡ, ΠΝΑ, ΙΛΗΜ, ΑΝΟC, ΔΑΔ, Mȣ) occur in both copies. From Tischendorf's beautiful *facsimiles* of Codd. PQ we observe that while *delta* is far more elaborate in P than Q, the precise contrary is the case with *pi*. *Epsilon* and *sigma* in P have strong points at all the

[1] Codex P contains Matth. i. 11—21; iii. 13—iv. 19; x. 7—19; x. 42—xi. 11; xiii. 40—50; xiv. 15—xv. 3; xv. 29—39; Mark i. 1—10; iii. 5—17; xiv. 13—24; 48—61; xv. 12—37; Luke i. 1—13; ii. 9—20; vi. 21—42; vii. 32—viii. 2; viii. 31—50; ix. 26—36; x. 36—xi. 4; xii. 34—45; xiv. 14—25; xv. 13—xvi. 22; xviii. 13—39; xx. 21—xxi. 3; xxii. 3—16; xxiii. 20—32; 45—56; xxiv. 14—37; John i. 29—41; ii. 13—25; xxi. 1—11.

[2] Codex Q contains Luke iv. 34—v. 4; vi. 10—26; xii. 6—43; xv. 14—31; xvii. 34—xviii. 15; xviii. 34—xix. 11; xix. 47—xx. 17; xx. 34—xxi. 8; xxii. 27—46; xxiii. 30—49; John xii. 3—20; xiv. 3—22.

extremities; *nu* in each is of the ancient form exhibited in Codd. ℵ NR (*see* p. 33); while in P *alpha* resembles in shape that of our alphabet in Plate II. No. 5, *eta* that in Plate III. No. 7.

R. This letter also, like some that precede, has been used to represent different books by various editors, a practice the inconvenience of which is very manifest. (1) R of Griesbach and Scholz is a fragment of two 4to leaves containing John i. 38—50, at Tübingen (published by Reuss, 1778), which from its thick vellum, want of the Ammonian sections and Eusebian canons, and the general resemblance of its uncials to those of late service books, Tischendorf pronounces to be an Evangelistarium, and puts in its room (2) in his N. T. of 1849, 12 or 14 leaves of a palimpsest in the Royal Library of Naples (*Borbon.* II. C. 15) of the eighth century, under a *Typicum* (see *Suicer*, *Thes. Eccles. Tom.* II. 1335) or Ritual of the Greek Church of the fourteenth century. These are fragments from the first three Evangelists, in oblong uncials, leaning to the right. Tischendorf, by chemical applications, was able in 1843 to read one page, in two columns of 25 lines each (Mark xiv. 32—39), and saw the Ammonian sections in the margin; the Eusebian canons he thinks have been washed out: but in 1859 he calls this fragment W^b, reserving the letter R for (3) Codex Nitriensis, Brit. Museum, Additional 17211, the very important palimpsest containing on 45 leaves about 505 verses of St Luke in 25 fragments[1], under the black, broad Syriac writing of Severus of Antioch against Grammaticus, of the ninth or tenth century. There are two columns of about 25 lines each on a page; for their boldness and simplicity the letters may be referred to the end of the sixth century; we have given a *facsimile* of the manuscript (which cannot be read in parts but with the utmost difficulty[2]), and an alphabet collected from it (Nos. 5, 17). In size and shape the letters are much like those of Codd. INP, only that they are somewhat irregular and straggling: the punctuation

[1] Codex R contains Luke i. 1—13; i. 69—ii. 4; 16—27; iv. 38—v. 5; v. 25—vi. 8; 18—31; vi. 49—vii. 22; viii. 5—15; viii. 25—ix. 1; ix. 12—43; x. 3—16; xi. 4—27; xii. 4—15; 40—52; xiii. 26—xiv. 1; xiv. 12—xv. 1; xv. 13—xvi. 16; xvii. 21—xviii. 10; xviii. 22—xx. 20; xx. 33—47; xxi. 12—xxii. 6; xxii. 8—14; 42—56; xxii. 71—xxiii. 11; xxiii. 38—50.

[2] In our *facsimile* we have not attempted to represent the extreme faintness of the lines, which in parts are only just visible.

is effected by a single point almost level with the top of the letter, as in Cod. N. The Ammonian sections are there without the Eusebian canons, and the first two leaves are devoted to the *τίτλοι* of St Luke. This most important palimpsest is one of the 550 manuscripts brought to England about 1847, from the Syrian convent of S. Mary Deipara, in the Nitrian Desert, 70 miles N. W. of Cairo. When examined at the British Museum by Canon Cureton, then one of the Librarians, he discovered in the same volume, and published in 1851 (with six pages in *facsimile*), a palimpsest of 4000 lines of Homer's Iliad, not in the same hand as St Luke, but quite as ancient. The fragments of St Luke were independently transcribed, with most laudable patience, both by Tregelles in 1854, and by Tischendorf in 1855. The latter has published an edition of them in his *Monumenta sacra inedit.* Vol. II. with a *facsimile.* Tregelles (Horne's Introd. Vol. IV. p. 184) calls attention to a palimpsest fragment of St John's Gospel, of extreme antiquity, on beautiful vellum, with letters much like those of Cod. B, which has been used *more than once* for Syriac writing. This is also one of the Nitrian books (Brit. Mus. Addit. 17136). It contains but 15 verses (John xiii. 16; 17; 19; 20; 23; 24; 26; 27; xvi. 7; 8; 9; 12; 13; 18; 19). The writing is in two columns, with the Ammonian sections, but not the Eusebian canons. One rough breathing is legible here.

S. CODEX VATICANUS 354, contains the four Gospels entire, and is the earliest dated manuscript of the Greek Testament. This is a folio of 234 leaves, written in large oblong or compressed uncials: the Epistle to Carpianus and Eusebian canons are prefixed, and it contains many later corrections, and marginal notes (e.g. Matth. xxvii. 16, 17: *vid. Tischendorf.* N.T.). Luke xxii. 43, 44; John. v. 4; vii. 53—viii. 11 are obelized. At the end we read *ἐγράφει ἡ τιμία δέλτος αὕτη διὰ χειρὸς ἐμοῦ Μιχαὴλ μοναχοῦ ἁμαρτωλοῦ μηνὶ μαρτίω α· ἡμέρα ε΄, ὥρα ϛ΄, ἔτους ϛυνζ. ινδ. ζ* i.e, A.D. 949. "Codicem bis diligenter contulimus," says Birch: but collators in his day (1781—3) seldom noticed orthographical forms or stated where the readings *agree* with the received text: so that a more thorough examination is still required. Tregelles and Tischendorf, when at Rome, only inspected it: the latter states that Birch's *facsimile* (consisting of the obelized Jo. v. 4) is coarsely executed, while Blanchini's is too elegant; he has made another himself.

T. CODEX BORGIANUS 1, now in the Propaganda at Rome (see below Cod. 180 of the Gospels), contains 13 or more 4to leaves of Luke and John, with a Thebaic or Sahidic version at their side, but on the opposite and left page. Each page consists of two columns; a single point indicates a break in the sense, but there are no other divisions. The fragment contains Luke xxii. 20—xxiii. 20; John vi. 28—67; vii. 6—viii. 32 (177 verses, since vii. 53—viii. 11 are wanting). The portion containing St John, both in Greek and Egyptian, was carefully edited at Rome in 1789 by A. A. Giorgi, an Augustinian Eremite: his *facsimile*, however (vii. 35) seems somewhat rough, though Tischendorf (who has inspected the codex) says that its uncials look as if written by a Copt, from their resemblance to Coptic letters: the shapes of *alpha* and *iota* are specially noticeable. Birch had previously collated the Greek text. Notwithstanding the constant presence of the rough and smooth breathing in this copy, Giorgi refers it to the fourth century, Tischendorf to the fifth. The Greek fragment of St Luke was first collated by Mr Bradley H. Alford, and inserted by his brother Dean Alford in the fourth edition of his Greek Testament, Vol. I. (1859). Dr Tregelles had drawn Mr Alford's attention to it, from a hint thrown out by Zoega, in p. 184 of his "Catalogus codd. Copt. MSS. qui in Museo Borgiano Velitris adservantur." Romae 1810.

T^s is used by Tischendorf to indicate a few leaves in Greek and Thebaic, which once belonged to Woide, and were published with his other Thebaic fragments in Ford's Appendix to the Codex Alexandrinus, Oxon. 1799. They contain Luke xii. 15—xiii. 32; John viii. 33—42 (85 verses). From the second fragment it plainly appears (what the similarity of the *facsimiles* had suggested to Tregelles) that T and T^s are parts of the same manuscript, for the page of T^s which contains John viii. 33 in Greek exhibits on its reverse the Thebaic version of John viii. 23—32, of which T affords us only the Greek text. This fact was first noted by Tischendorf (N. T. 1859), who adds that the Coptic scribe blundered much over the Greek: e.g. *βαβουσα* Luke xiii. 21; so *δεκαι* for *δεκα και*, v. 16.

U. Codex Nanianus 1, so called from a former possessor, is now in the Library of St Mark, Venice (I. viii). It contains the four Gospels entire, carefully and luxuriously written in two columns of 21 lines each on the 4to page, scarcely before the tenth century, although the "letters are in general an imitation of those used before the introduction of compressed uncials; but they do not belong to the age when full and round writing was customary or natural, so that the stiffness and want of ease is manifest" (Tregelles' Horne, p. 202). Thus while the small *o* in l. 1 of our *facsimile* (No. 22) is in the oldest style, the oblong *omicrons* creep in at the end of lines 2 and 4. Munter sent some extracts from this copy to Birch, who used them for his edition, and states that the book contains the Eusebian canons. Accordingly in Mark v. 18, B (in error for H) stands under the proper Ammonian section $\overline{\mu\eta}$ (48). Tischendorf in 1843 and Tregelles in 1846 collated Cod. U, thoroughly and independently, and compared their work at Leipsic for the purpose of mutual correction.

V. Codex Mosquensis, of the Holy Synod, is known almost[1] exclusively from Matthaei's Greek Testament: he states, no doubt most truly, that he collated it "bis diligentissimè," and gives a *facsimile* of it, assigning it to the eighth century. Judging from Matthaei's plate, it is hard to say why others have dated it in the ninth. It contained in 1779, when first collated, the Four Gospels in 8vo with the Ammonian sections and Eusebian canons, in uncial letters down to John vii. 39, *ουπω γαρ ην*, and from that point in cursive letters of the 13th century; Matth. v. 44—vi. 12; ix. 18—x. 1 being lost: when recollated but four years later Matth. xxii. 44—xxiii. 35; John xxi. 10—25 had disappeared. Matthaei tells us that the manuscript is written stichometrically, by a diligent scribe: its resemblance to Cod. M has been already mentioned (p. 110). The cursive portion is Matthaei's v, Scholz's Evan. 250.

W[a]. Cod. Reg. Paris 314 consists of but two leaves at the end of another book, containing Luke ix. 34—47; x. 12

[1] I say *almost*, for Bengel's description makes it plain that this is the Moscow manuscript from which F. C. Gross sent him the extracts, that Wetstein copied and numbered Evan. 87. Bengel, however, states that the cursive portion from John vii. onwards bears the date of 6508 or A.D. 1000. Scholz was the first to notice this identity.

—22 (23 verses). Its date is about the eighth century; the uncial letters are firmly written, *delta* and *theta* being of the ordinary oblong shape of that period. Accents and breathings are usually put; all the stops are expressed by a single point, whose position makes no difference in its power (*see* p. 42). This copy was adapted to Church use, but is not an Evangelistarium, inasmuch as it exhibits the Ammonian sections and Eusebian canons[1], and τίτλοι twice at the head of the page. This fragment was brought to light by Scholz, and published by Tischendorf, *Monument. sacra ined.* 1846. He considers the fragment at Naples he had formerly numbered R (2) as another portion of the same copy, and therefore indicates it in his 7th edition of the N. T. (1859) as W^b (*see* p. 114).

W^c is assigned by Tischendorf to three leaves containing Mark ii. 8—16; Luke i. 20—32; 64—79 (35 verses), which have been washed to make a palimpsest, and the writing erased in parts by a knife. There are also some traces of a Latin version, but all these were used up to bind other books in the library of St Gall. They are of the eighth century, and have appeared in Vol. III. of *Monumenta sacra inedita*, with a *facsimile*, whose style closely resembles that of Cod. Δ, and its kindred FG of St Paul's Epistles.

X. Codex Monacensis in the University Library at Munich is a valuable folio manuscript of the end of the ninth or early in the tenth century, containing the Four Gospels (in the order described above p. 62), with serious defects[2], and a commentary (chiefly from Chrysostom) surrounding and interspersed with the text of all but St Mark, in early cursive letters, not unlike (in Tischendorf's judgment) the celebrated Oxford Plato dated 895 (*see* p. 36). The very elegant uncials of Cod. X "are small and upright; though some of them are compressed, they seem

[1] Notwithstanding the Eusebian canons have been washed out of W^b, a strong confirmation of what was conjectured above, p. 51.

[2] Codex X contains Matth. vi. 3—10; vii. 1—ix. 20; ix. 34—xi. 24; xii. 9—xvi. 28; xvii. 14—xviii. 25; xix. 22—xxi. 13; xxi. 28—xxii. 22; xxiii. 27—xxiv. 2; xxiv. 23—35; xxv. 1—30; xxvi. 69—xxvii. 12; Mark vi. 47—Luke i. 37; ii. 19—iii. 38; iv. 21—x. 37; xi. 1—xviii. 43; xx. 46—John ii. 22; vii. 1—xiii. 5; xiii. 20—xv. 25: xvi. 23—xxi. 25. The hiatus in John ii. 22—vii. 1 is supplied on paper in a hand of the twelfth century; Mark xiv. 61—64; xiv. 72—xv. 4; xv. 33—xvi. 6 are illegible in parts, and xvi. 6—8 have perished. Matth. v. 45 survives in the commentary.

as if they were *partial* imitations of those used in very early copies" (Tregelles' Horne p. 195, *facsimile* No. 33). Each page has two columns of about 45 lines each. There are no divisions by τίτλοι or sections, nor notes to serve for ecclesiastical use. This copy has been often removed; the ink has much faded, and its general condition is bad. From a memorandum in the beginning we find that it came from Rome to Ingoldstadt, and that it was at Innsbruck in 1757; from Ingoldstadt it was taken to Landshut, thence to Munich. When it was at Ingoldstadt Griesbach obtained some extracts from it through Dobrowsky for his edition of the Greek Testament; Scholz first collated it, in his usual unhappy way; Tischendorf in 1844, Tregelles in 1846, examined it thoroughly, and compared and verified the results of their independent collations.

Y. CODEX BARBERINI 225 at Rome (in the Library founded by Cardinal Barberini in the 17th century) contains on six large leaves the 137 verses John xvi. 3—xix. 41, of about the eighth century. Tischendorf obtained access to it in 1843 for a few hours, after some difficulty with the Prince Barberini, and published it in his first instalment of *Monumenta sacra inedita*, 1846. Scholz had first noticed, and loosely collated it. A later hand has coarsely retraced the letters, but the ancient writing is plain and good. Accents and breathings are most often neglected or placed wrongly: κ θ τ are frequent at the end of lines. For punctuation one, two, three or even four points are employed, the power of the single point varying as in Codd. E (see pp. 42, 104) Θ or B of the Apocalypse. The Ammonian sections are without the Eusebian canons: and such forms as λήμψεται xvi. 14, λήμψεσθε *v.* 24 occur. These few uncial leaves are prefixed to a cursive copy of the Gospels with Theophylact's commentary (Evan. 392).

Z. CODEX DUBLINENSIS RESCRIPTUS, one of the chief palimpsests extant, contains 290 verses of St Matthew's Gospel in 22 fragments[1]. It was discovered in 1787 by Dr John Barrett, Senior Fellow of Trinity College, Dublin, under some cursive

[1] Codex Z contains Matth. i. 17—ii. 6; ii. 13—20; iv. 4—13; v. 45—vi. 15; vii. 16—viii. 6; x. 40—xi. 18; xii. 43—xiii. 11; xiii. 57—xiv. 18; xv. 13—23; xvii. 9—17; xvii. 26—xviii. 6; xix. 4—12; 21—28; xx. 7—xxi. 8; xxi. 23—45; xxii. 16—25; xxii. 37—xxiii. 3; xxiii. 13—23; xxiv. 15—25; xxv. 1—11; xxvi. 21—29; 62—71.

writing of the 10th century or later, consisting of Chrysostom de Sacerdotio, extracts from Epiphanius, &c. In the same volume are portions of Isaiah and of Gregory Nazianzum, in erased uncial letters, but not so ancient as the fragment of St Matthew. All the 32 leaves of this Gospel that remain were engraved in copper-plate *facsimile* at the expense of Trinity College, and published by Barrett in 1801, furnished with Prolegomena, and the contents of each *facsimile* plate in modern Greek characters, on the opposite page. The *facsimiles* are not very accurate, and the form of the letters is stated to be less free and symmetrical than in the original: yet from these plates (for the want of a better guide) our alphabet (No. 6) and specimen (No. 18) have been taken. The Greek type on the opposite page has not been very well revised, and a comparison with the copper-plate will occasionally convict it of errors, which have been animadverted upon more severely than was quite necessary. The Prolegomena are encumbered with a discussion of our Lord's genealogies quite foreign to the subject, and the tone of scholarship is not very high; but Barrett's judgment on the manuscript is correct in the main, and his conclusion that it is as old as the sixth century, has been generally received. Tregelles in 1853 was permitted to apply a chemical mixture to the vellum, which was already miserably discoloured, apparently from the purple dye: he was thus enabled to add a little to what Barrett had read long since, but he found that in most places which that editor had left blank, the vellum had been cut away or lost: it would no doubt have been better for Barrett to have stated, in each particular case, *why* he had been unable to give the text of the passage. Codex Z, like many others, and for the same orthographical reasons, has been referred to Alexandria as its native country. It is written in 4to, with a single column on a page of from 21 to 23 lines. The Ammonian sections are given, but not the Eusebian canons: the τίτλοι are written at the top of the pages, their numbers being set in the margin. The writing is continuous, the *single* point either rarely found or quite washed out: the abbreviations are very few, and there are no breathings or accents. A space, proportionate to the occasion, is usually left when there is a break in the sense, and capitals extend into the margin when a new section begins. The letters are in a plain, steady, beautiful hand, some 18 or 20 in a line. The shape of *alpha* (which varies a good deal) and especially of *mu* are very peculiar: *phi* is inordinately large: *delta* has an upper curve which is not usual: the same curves appear in *zeta*, *lambda* and *chi*. The characters are less in size than in N, about equal to those in R, much less than in AB.

Γ. CODEX TISCHENDORFIAN. IV. was brought by Tischendorf from an "eastern monastery" (he usually describes the locality of his manuscripts in general terms), and was bought for the Bodleian Library (Auct. T. Infra II. 2) in 1855. It consists of 158 leaves in large quarto, with one column (of 24 not very straight or regular lines) on a page, in uncials of the ninth century, leaning *slightly* back, but otherwise much resembling Cod. K in style (*facsim.* Plate XI. No. 8 a). St Luke's Gospel is complete; the last ten leaves are hurt by damp, though still legible. In St Mark only 105 verses are wanting (iii. 35—vi. 20); about 531 verses of the other Gospels survive[1]. Tischendorf, and Tregelles by his leave, have independently collated this copy, of which Tischendorf gives a *facsimile* in his *Anecdota sacra et profana*, 1855. Some of its peculiar readings are very notable, and few uncials of its date deserve that more careful study, which it has hardly yet received. In 1859 Tischendorf, on his return from his third Eastern journey, took to St Petersburg 99 additional leaves of this self-same manuscript, doubtless procured from the same place as he had obtained the Bodleian portion six years before (*Notitia Cod. Sinait.* p. 53). This copy of the Gospels, though unfortunately in two distant libraries, is now nearly perfect[2], and at the end of St John's Gospel, in the newly-discovered portion, we find an inscription which seems to fix the date: *ετελειωθη ή δέλτος αὕτη μηνι νοεμβριω κζ, ινδ. η̄, ἡμερα ε̄, ωρα β.* Tischendorf, by the aid of Ant. Pilgrami's *Calendarium chronicum medii potissimum ævi monumentis accommodatum*, Vienn. 1781, pp. VII, 11, 105, states that the only year between A.D. 800 and 950, on which the Indiction was 8, and Nov. 27 fell on a Thursday, was 844. In

[1] These are Matth. vi. 16—29; vii. 26—viii. 27; xii. 18—xiv. 15; xx. 25—xxi. 19; xxii. 25—xxiii. 13; John vi. 14—viii. 3; xv. 24—xix. 6.

[2] In the St Petersburg portion are *all* the rest of John, and Matth. i. 1—v. 31; ix. 6—xii. 18; xiv. 15—xx. 25; xxiii. 13—xxviii. 20; or all St Matthew except 115 verses.

the Oxford sheets we find tables of *κεφάλαια* before the Gospels of Matthew and Luke, the *τίτλοι* at the heading of the pages, their numbers *rubro* neatly set in the margin; capitals in red at the commencement of these chapters; the Ammonian sections and Eusebian canons in their usual places, and some liturgical directions. Over the original breathings and accents some late scrawler has in many places put others, in a very careless fashion.

Δ. Codex Sangallensis was first inspected by Gerbert (1773), named by Scholz (N. T. 1830), and made fully known to us by the admirable edition in *lithographed facsimile of every page*, by H. Ch. M. Rettig, published at Zurich, 1836, with copious and satisfactory Prolegomena. It is preserved and was probably transcribed a thousand years since in the great monastery of St Gall in the N.E. of Switzerland. It is rudely written on 197 leaves of coarse vellum 4to, 10 inches by 8¾ in size, with from 20 to 26 (usually 21) lines on each page, in a very peculiar hand, with an *interlinear* Latin version, and contains the four Gospels complete except John xix. 17—35. Before St Matthew's Gospel are placed Prologues, Latin verses, the Eusebian canons in Roman letters, tables of the *κεφάλαια* both in Greek and Latin, &c. Rettig thinks he has traced several different scribes and inks employed on it, which might happen easily enough in the Scriptorium of a monastery; but, if so, their style of writing is very nearly the same, and they doubtless copied from the same archetype, about the same time. He has produced more convincing arguments to shew that Cod. Δ is part of the same book as the Codex Boernerianus, G of St Paul's Epistles. Not only do they exactly resemble each other in their whole arrangement and appearance, but marginal notes by the first hand are found in each, of precisely the same character. Thus the predestinarian doctrines of the heretic Godeschalk [d. 866] are pointed out for refutation at the hard texts, Luke xiii. 24; John xii. 40 in Δ, and six times in G[1]. St Mark's Gospel is stated to

[1] viz. Rom. iii. 5; 1 Cor. ii. 8; 1 Tim. ii. 4; iv. 10; vi. 4; 2 Tim. ii. 15. Equally strong are the notices of Aganon, who is cited 8 times in Δ, 16 (I think) in G. This personage was Bishop of Chartres, and a severe disciplinarian, who died A.D. 941; a fact which does not hinder our assigning Cod. Δ to the ninth century, as Rettig states that all notices of him are by a later hand. There is the less need of multiplying proofs of this kind, as Tregelles has observed a circum-

represent a text different from that of the other Evangelists, and the Latin version (which is clearly *primâ manu*) seems a mixture of the Vulgate with the older Italic, so altered and accommodated to the Greek as to be of little critical value. The penmen seem to have known but little Greek, and to have copied from a manuscript written continuously, for the divisions between the words are sometimes absurdly wrong; there are scarcely any breathings or accents, except about the opening of St Mark, and once an aspirate to ἑπτα; what we find are often falsely placed; and a dot is set in most places regularly at the end of every *Greek* word. The letters have but little tendency to the oblong shape, but *delta* and *theta* are decidedly of the latest uncial type. Here, as in Cod. G, the mark >>> is much used to fill up vacant spaces. The text from which Δ was copied seems to have been arranged in στίχοι, for almost every line has at least one *Greek* capital letter, grotesquely ornamented in colours. We transcribe three lines, taken almost at random, from pp. 80—1 (Matth. xx. 13—15), in order to explain our meaning:

dixit uni eor̄ amice non ījusto tibi n̄ne
ειπεν · μοναδι · αυτων · Εταιρε · ουκ · αδικω · σε · Ουχι

ex denario convenisti mecū tolle tuū et vade
δηναριου συνεφωνησασ · μοι · Αρον · το · σου και υπαγε

volo autē huic novissimo dare sicut et tibi antā non li
Θελω δε τουτω τω εσχατω δουναι ωσ και · σοι · Η · ουκ εξ

It will be observed that while in Cod. Δ a line begins at any place, even in the middle of a word; if the capital letters be assumed to commence the lines, the text divides itself into regular στίχοι. See above pp. 44—46. There are also the τίτλοι, the Ammonian sections and the canons. The letters N and Π, Z and Ξ, T and Θ, P and the Latin R are perpetually confounded. As in the kindred Codd. Augiensis and Boerner. the Latin ſ is much like r. Tregelles has noted ι ascript in Cod. Δ, but this is rare. There is no question that this document was written

stance which proves to a certainty the identity of Codd. Δ and G. When he was at Dresden he found in Cod. G twelve leaves of later writing in precisely the same hand as several that are lithographed by Rettig, because they were attached to Cod. Δ. "Thus," he says, "these MSS. once formed ONE BOOK; and when separated, some of the superfluous leaves with additional writing attached to the former part, and some to the latter" (Tregelles' Horne, p. 197).

by Latin (most probably by *Irish*) monks, in the west of Europe, during the ninth century. See below, Paul. Cod. G.

Θ. Codex Tischendorf. I. was brought from the East by Tischendorf in 1845, published by him in his *Monumenta sacra inedit.* 1846, and deposited in the University Library at Leipsic. It consists of but four leaves (all imperfect) 4to, of very thin vellum, almost too brittle to be touched, so that each leaf is kept separately in glass. It contains about 40 verses; viz. Matth. xiii. 46—55 (in mere shreds); xiv. 8—29; xv. 4—14, with the greater *κεφάλαια* in red; the Ammonian sections and Eusebian canons in the inner margin. A few breathings are *primâ manu*, and many accents by two later correctors. The stops (which are rather numerous) resemble Cod. Y, only that four points are not found in Θ. Tischendorf places it towards the end of the 7th century, assigning Mount Sinai or Lower Egypt for its country. The uncials (especially ЄΘOC) are somewhat oblong, leaning to the right, but the writing is elegant and uniform; *delta* keeps its ancient shape, and the diameter of *theta* does not extend beyond the curve (*see* p. 32).

Λ (1). This letter was applied by Tischendorf in his N.T. of 1849 to two torn fragments of vellum, which he found used in the binding of an Arabic manuscript in the monastery of St Catherine on Mount Sinai. They contain 14 verses; viz. Matth. xx. 8—15; Luke i. 14—20; but since, on removing the vellum from the Arabic book, he found it exhibit a portion of St Matthew on one side of the leaf, of St Luke on the other, he rightly concluded that the fragment belonged to an Evangelistarium, dating from about the ninth century. This fragment he published in the Annales Vindobonenses, 1846, but substituted in its room in his N.T. of 1859 (2).

Codex Tischendorf. III, whose history, so far as we know it, exactly resembles that of Cod. Γ, and like it is now in the Bodleian (Auct. T. Infra i. 1). It contains 157 leaves, but written in two columns of 23 lines each, in small, oblong, clumsy, sloping uncials of the eighth or ninth century (*facsim.* Plate x. No. 8 b). It has the Gospels of St Luke and St John complete, with the subscription to St Mark, each Gospel being preceded by tables of *κεφάλαια*, with the *τίτλοι* at the heads of the pages, the numbers of the *κεφάλαια*, of the Ammonian sections, and of Eusebian canons (these last *rubro*) being set in the margin. There are also scholia interspersed, of some critical value; a portion being in uncial characters. This copy also was described (with a *facsimile*) by Tischendorf, *Anecdota sacra et profana*, 1855, and collated by himself and Tregelles. Its text is said to vary greatly from that common in the later uncials, and to be very like Scholz's 262 (Paris, 53).

Here again the history of this manuscript curiously coincides with that of Cod. Γ. In his *Notitia Cod. Sinaitici*, p. 58, Tischendorf describes an early cursive copy of St Matthew and St Mark (*the subscription to the latter being wanting*), which he took to St Petersburg in 1859, so exactly corresponding in general appearance with Cod. Λ (although that be written in uncial characters), as well as in the style and character of the marginal scholia, often in small uncials, that he pronounces them part of the same codex. Very possibly he *might* have added that he procured the two from the same source: at any rate the subscription to St Matthew at St Petersburg precisely resembles the other three subscriptions at Oxford, and those in Paris 53 (Scholz's 262)[1], with which Tischendorf had previously compared Cod. Λ (N. T. Proleg. p. CLXXVII, 7th edition). These cursive leaves are preceded by Eusebius' Epistle to Carpianus, his table of canons, and a table of the *κεφάλαια* of St Matthew. The *τίτλοι* in uncials head the pages, and their numbers stand in the margin.

From the marginal scholia Tischendorf cites the following notices of the Jewish Gospel, or that according to the Hebrews, which certainly have their value as helping to inform us respecting its nature: Matth. iv. 5, *το ιουδαικον ουκ εχει εις την αγιαν πολιν αλλ εν ιλημ.* xvi. 17, *Βαριωνα· το ιουδαικον υιε ιωαννου.* xviii. 22, *το ιουδαικον εξης εχει μετα το ἑβδομηκοντακις ἑπτα· και γαρ εν τοις προφηταις μετα το χρισθηναι αυτους εν πνι ἁγιω εὑρισκετω* (*sic*) *εν αυτοις λογος ἁμαρτιας*: —an addition which Jerome (*contra Pelag.* III.) expressly cites from the Gospel of the Nazarenes. xxvi. 74, *το ιουδαικον· και ηρνησατο και ωμοσεν και κατηρασατο.* It is plain that this whole matter requires careful discussion, but at present it would seem that the first half of Cod. Λ was written in cursive, the

[1] The subscription to St Matthew stands in *both*: *ευαγγελιον κατα ματθαιον. εγραφη και αντεβληθη εκ των* [*sic*] *ιεροσολυμοις παλαιων αντιγραφων· των εν τω ἁγιω ορει αποκειμενων· εν στιχοις βφιδ· κεφφ. τνε.*

second in uncial letters; if not by the same person, yet on the same plan and at the same place.

Ξ. Codex Zacynthius is a palimpsest in the Library of the British and Foreign Bible Society in London, which, under an Evangelistarium written on coarse vellum in or about the 13th century, contains large portions of St Luke, down to ch. xi. 33, in full well-formed uncials, but surrounded by and often interwoven with large extracts from the Fathers, in a hand so cramped and, as regards the round letters (ЄΘOC) so oblong, that it cannot be earlier than the eighth century. As the arrangement of the matter makes it certain that the commentary is contemporaneous, it must be regarded as the earliest known copy furnished with a catena (*above*, p. 56). This volume, which once belonged to "Il Principe Comuto, Zante," and is marked as *Μνημόσυνον σεβάσματος τοῦ Ἱππέος Ἀντωνίου Κόμητος* 1820, was presented to the Bible Society in 1821 by General Macaulay, who brought it from Zante. Mr Knolleke, one of the Secretaries, seems first to have noticed the older writing, and on the discovery being communicated to Tregelles in 1858, with characteristic eagerness he examined, decyphered and has announced the Scripture text for publication: he doubts whether the small Patristic writing can be read without chemical restoration. Besides the usual *τίτλοι* above the text and other notations of sections, and numbers which refer to the Catena running up from 1 to 100, this copy is remarkable for possessing also the division into chapters, hitherto deemed unique in Cod. B (p. 48). To this notation is commonly prefixed *psi*, formed like a cross, in the fashion of the eighth century (*above*, p. 35). The ancient volume must have been a large folio (14 inches by 11), of which 86 leaves and three half-leaves survive: of course very hard to read. Of the ecclesiastical writers cited by name Chrysostom, Origen and Cyril are the best known. The readings of this codex (which are very valuable) were communicated to Dean Alford for his 4th edition of the N. T., by Dr Tregelles, from whose "Description" our account is abridged. The latter is on the eve of publishing an edition of Cod. Ξ, with a *facsimile*, and the Moscow fragment O (*see* p. 112) appended to it.

The present seems the most fit place for naming six small fragments of the Gospels, &c. in uncial letters, and another manuscript almost complete, brought from the East in 1859 by Tischendorf, and now at St Petersburg. He has not yet distinguished them by any special notation, but they are briefly described in his *Notitia Cod. Sinaitici, Appendix, pp.* 50—2.

(1). Two large leaves, containing 1 Cor. i. 20—ii. 12, elegantly written, without breathings or accents. This and the next three fragments date from about the 6th century.

(2). Six 8vo leaves, containing 20 columns (the outer margins being often much cut) of Coptic-shaped uncials, with vacant spaces instead of stops. There are two columns on a page. They comprise Jo. i. 25—42; ii. 9—iv. 50.

(3). Six leaves of large 8vo, very hard to decypher, having been torn piecemeal from the binding of another book. They contain parts of Matth. xxii. xxiii.; Mark iv. v.

(4). One folio leaf, in style of writing much resembling Cod. N. Containing Matth. xxi. 19—24.

(5). One 8vo leaf of the 7th century, of thick uncials without accents, torn from the wooden cover of a Syriac book. Containing Acts ii. 45—iii. 8.

(6). Half a leaf, written in two columns of the 7th or 8th century, with accents by a later hand. It contains Luke xi. 37—41; 42—45.

(7). May perhaps hereafter be named Σ of the Gospels. It consists of 350 vellum leaves in small 4to, and contains all the Gospels except Matth. iii. 12—iv. 18; xix. 12—xx. 3; John viii. 6—39; 77 verses. A century since it belonged to Parodus, a noble Greek of Smyrna, and the present possessor was persuaded by Tischendorf to present it to the Emperor of Russia. He states that it is of the age of the later uncials (meaning, we presume, the 8th or 9th century), but of higher critical importance than most of them, and much like Cod. K in its rarer readings. Though it is yet uncollated, Tischendorf gives extracts from it of no very striking character. There are many marginal corrections, and John v. 4; viii. 3—6 are *obelized.* In the table of *κεφάλαια* before St Mark, there is a gap after $\overline{λϛ}'$: Mark xvi. 18—20; John xxi. 22—25 are in a later hand. At the end of St Mark, the last Ammonian section inserted is $\overline{σλδ}$ by the side of *ἀναστὰς δὲ v.* 9, with $\bar{η}$ under it for the Eusebian canon (see Chapter IX).

Manuscripts of the Acts and Catholic Epistles.

ℵ. COD. SINAITICUS (described pp. 76—9). A. COD. ALEXANDRINUS (pp. 79—84). B. COD. VATICANUS (pp. 84—93). C. COD. EPHRAEMI (pp. 94—6). D. CODEX BEZAE (pp. 96—103).

E. CODEX LAUDIANUS 35 is one of the most precious treasures preserved in the Bodleian at Oxford. It is a Latin-Greek copy, with two columns on a page, the Latin version holding the post of honour on the *left*, and is written in very short στίχοι, consisting of from one to three words each (p. 45), the Latin words always standing opposite to the corresponding Greek. This peculiar arrangement points decisively to the West of Europe as its country, notwithstanding the abundance of Alexandrian forms has led some to refer it to Egypt. The very large, bold, thick, rude uncials, without break in the words or accents, lead us up to the end of the sixth century as its date. The Latin is not of Jerome's or the Vulgate version, but is made to correspond closely with the Greek, even in its interpolations and rarest various readings. The contrary supposition that the Greek portion of this codex *Latinised*, or had been altered to coincide with the Latin, is inconsistent with the facts of the case. This manuscript contains only the Acts of the Apostles (from xxvi. 29, παυλος to xxviii. 26, πορευθητι being lost), and exhibits a remarkable modification of the text. That the book was once in Sardinia, appears from an edict of Flavius Pancratius, συν θεω απο επαρχων δουξ σαρδινιας, appended (as also is the Apostles' Creed in Latin, and some other foreign matter) in a later hand: Imperial governors ruled in that island with the title of *dux* from the reign of Justinian A.D. 534 to A.D. 749. It was probably among the *Greek* volumes brought into England by the fellow-countryman of St Paul, Theodore of Tarsus, "the grand old man" as he has been recently called by one of kindred spirit to his own (*Dean Hook*, *Lives of the Archbishops of Canterbury*, Vol. I. p. 150), who came to England as Primate at the age of sixty-six A.D. 668, and died in 690. At all events, Mill (*Proleg. N. T.* §. 1022—6) has rendered it all but certain, that the Venerable Bede (d. 735) had this very codex before him, when he wrote his *Expositio Retractata* of the Acts, and Woide (*Notitia Cod. Alex.* p. 156, &c.) has since alleged 32 additional instances of agreement between them. This manuscript, with many others, was presented to the University of Oxford in the year 1636, by its munificent Chancellor, Archbishop Laud. Thomas Hearne, the celebrated antiquary, published a full edition of it in 1715, which is now very scarce, and is known to be far from accurate. Tischendorf purposes to re-edit it at some future period, but it may be hoped, for our national honour, that some English scholar will anticipate him. Cod. E is stated to have capital letters at the commencement of each of the Euthalian sections, but as the capitals occur at other places where the sense is broken, this circumstance does not prove that those sections were known to the scribe. It is in size 9 inches by 7½, and consists of 226 leaves of 23, 24, 25 or 26 lines; the vellum is rather poor in quality, and the ink in many places very faint. There seem to be no stops or breathings, except an aspirate over initial *upsilon* (ὑ) almost invariably. The shape of *xi* is more complicated than usual (see our *facsimile*, No. 25); the other letters (e. g. *delta* or *psi*) such as were common in the sixth or early in the seventh century.

F[a]. COD. COISLIN. 1, see above, p. 105.

G = L of Tischendorf (N. T. 1859). COD. BIBLIOTH. ANGELICAE A. 2. 15, belonging to the Augustinian monks at Rome, formerly Cardinal Passione's, contains the Acts, from viii. 10, μις του θεου to the end, the Catholic Epistles complete, and the Pauline down to Hebr. xiii. 10, οὐκ ἔχουσιν, of a date not earlier than the ninth century. It was collated in part by Blanchini and Birch, in full by Scholz (1820) and F. F. Fleck (1833). Tischendorf in 1843, Tregelles in 1845 collated it independently, and subsequently compared their papers, as they have done in several other instances.

H. COD. MUTINENSIS 196, of the Acts, in the Grand Ducal Library at Modena, is an uncial copy of about the ninth century, defective in Act. i. 1—v. 28; ix. 39—x. 19; xiii. 36—xiv. 3 (all supplied by a recent hand of the fifteenth century), and in xxvii. 4—xxviii. 31 (supplied in uncials of about the eleventh century). The Epistles are in cursive letters of the twelfth century, indicated in the Catholic Epistles by h, in the Pauline by 179. Scholz first collated it loosely, as usual; then Tischendorf in 1843, Tregelles in 1846, afterwards comparing their collations for mutual correction.

I. COD. PETROPOLIT. or Tischendorf. II, see above, p. 107.

K. COD. MOSQUENSIS, S. Synodi No. 98, is Matthaei's g, and came from the monastery of St Dionysius on Mount Athos. It contains the Catholic Epistles entire, but not the Acts; and the Pauline Epistles are defective only in Rom. x. 18—1 Cor. vi. 13; 1 Cor. viii. 7—11. Matthaei alone has collated this document, and judging from his *facsimile* (Cath. Epp. 1782) it seems to belong to the ninth century. This copy is Scholz's Act. 102, Paul. 117.

Manuscripts of the Pauline Epistles.

ℵ. CODEX SINAITICUS (described pp. 76—9). A. COD. ALEXANDRINUS (pp. 79—84). B. COD. VATICANUS (pp. 84—93). C. COD. EPHRAEM. (pp. 94—6).

D. COD. CLAROMONTANUS, No. 107 of the Imperial Library at Paris, is a Greek-Latin copy of St Paul's Epistles, one of the most ancient and important in existence. Like the Cod. Ephraemi in the same Library it has been fortunate in such an editor as Tischendorf, who published it in 1852 with complete Prolegomena, and a *facsimile* traced by Tregelles. Ours (No. 19) is taken from the *Paléographie Universelle*, No. 67, which seemed more delicately executed. This noble volume is in small quarto, written on 533 leaves of the thinnest and finest vellum. The Greek and Latin are both written continuously (except the Latin titles and subscriptions), but in a stichometrical form (*see* p. 46): the Greek, as in Cod. Bezae, stands on the left or first page of the opened book, not on the right, as in the Cod. Laudianus. Each page has but one column of about 21 lines, so that in this copy, as in the Codex Bezae, the Greek and Latin are in parallel lines, but on separate pages. The ink has much faded, or gone off upon the opposite page: otherwise the book is in good condition. It contains all St Paul's Epistles (the Hebrews after Philemon), except Rom. i. 1—7; 27—30, both Greek and Latin: Rom. i. 24—27 in the Latin is supplied in a later but very old hand, as also is 1 Cor. xiv. 13—22 in the Greek: the Latin of 1 Cor. xiv. 8—18; Hebr. xiii. 21—23 is lost. The Epistle to the Hebrews has been erroneously imputed by some to a later scribe, although it is not included in the list of the sacred books, and of the number of their $\sigma\tau\acute{\iota}\chi o\iota$ or *versus*, which stands immediately *before* the Hebrews in this codex[1]: but the same list overlooks the Epistle to the Philippians, which has never been doubted to be St Paul's: in this manuscript, however, the Epistle to the Colossians precedes that to the Philippians. Our earliest notice of it is derived from the Preface to Beza's 3rd edition of the N. T. (20 Feb. 1582): he there describes it as of equal antiquity with his copy of the Gospels (D), and states that it had been found "in Claromontano apud Bellovacos cœnobio," at Clermont near Beauvais. Although Beza sometimes through inadvertence calls his codex of the Gospels Claromontanus, there seems no reason for disputing with Wetstein the correctness of his account (*see* p. 97), though it throws no light on the manuscript's early history. From Beza it passed into the possession of Claude du Puy, Councillor of Paris, probably on Beza's death [1605]: thence to his sons Jacques and Pierre du Puy; before the death of Jacques (who was the King's Librarian) in 1656, it had been bought by Louis XIV. for the Royal Library at Paris. In 1707, John Aymont, an apostate priest, stole 35 leaves; one, which he disposed of in Holland, was restored in 1720 by its possessor Stosch; the rest were sold to that great collector, Harley, Earl of Oxford, but sent back in 1729 by his son, who had learnt their shameful story. Beza made some, but not a considerable use of this document; in Walton's Polyglott were inserted 2245 readings sent by the du Puys to Ussher (*Mill. N. T. Proleg.* § 1284); Wetstein collated it twice in early life (1715—6); Tregelles examined it in 1849, and compared his results with the then unpublished transcript of Tischendorf; which proved on its appearance (1852) the most difficult as well as one of the most important, of his critical works; so hard it had been found at times to determine satisfactorily the original readings of a manuscript, which had been corrected by *nine* different hands, ancient and modern. The date of the codex is doubtless the sixth century, in the middle or towards the end of it. The Latin letters b and d are the latest in form (*facsim.* No. 19),

[1] The names and order of the books of the *New* Testament in this most curious and venerable list stand thus: Matthew, John, Mark, Luke, Romans, 1, 2 Corinth. Galat. E*f*es. 1, 2 Tim. Tit. Colos. *Filimon*, 1, 2 Pet. James, 1, 2, 3 John, Jude, Barnabas' Ep. John's Revelation, Act. Apost., Pastor [Hermas], Actus Paul., Revelatio Petri.

and are much like those in the Cod. Bezae (*see above, p.* 101), which in many points Cod. Claromontanus strongly resembles. We have noticed many of its peculiarities in the preceding section (pp. 30—35), and need not here repeat them. *Delta* and *pi* look even more ancient than in Cod. A: the uncials are simple, square, regular, and beautiful, of about the size of those in Codd. CD, and less than in Cod. B. The stichometry forbids our assigning it to a period earlier than the end of the fifth century (p. 45), while other circumstances connected with the Latin version tend to put it a little lower still. The apostrophus is frequent (p. 43), but there are few stops (p. 46) or abridgements; no breathings or accents are *primâ manu.* Initial letters, placed at the beginning of books or sections, are plain, and not much larger than the rest. The comparative correctness of the Greek text, and its Alexandrine forms, have caused certain critics to refer us as usual to Egypt for its country: the Latin text is more faulty, and shews ignorance of the language: yet what use a Latin version could be except in Africa or Western Europe it were hard to imagine. This Latin is more independent of the Greek, and less altered from it than in Codd. Bezae or Laudian., where it has little critical value: that of Cod. Claromont. better represents the African type of the *Old* Latin. Of the corrections, a few were made by the original scribe when revising; a hand of the 7th century went through the whole (D**); two others follow; then in sharp black uncials of the ninth or tenth century another made more than two thousand changes in the text, and added stops and all the breathings and accents (D***); another D^{**}_{**} (among other changes) added to the Latin subscriptions; D^b supplied Rom. i. 27—30 very early; D^c, a later hand, 1 Cor. xiv. 13—22. Tischendorf distinguishes several others besides these.

E. Cod. Sangermanensis is another Greek-Latin manuscript, and takes its name from the Abbey of St Germain des Prez near Paris. Towards the end of the last century the Abbey (which at the Revolution had been turned into a saltpetre manufactory) was burnt down, and many of its books *lost.* In 1805 Matthaei found this copy, as might have been anticipated, at St Petersburg, where it is now deposited. The volume is a large 4to, the Latin and Greek in parallel columns on the same page, the Greek standing to the left; its uncials are coarse, large and thick, not unlike those in Cod. E of the Acts, but of later shape, with breathings and accents *primâ manu*, of about the tenth century[1]. Mill obtained some extracts from it, and noted its obvious connection with Cod. Claromontanus: Wetstein thoroughly collated it; and not only he but Sabatier and Griesbach perceived that it was, at least in the Greek, nothing better than a mere transcript of Cod. Claromontanus, made by some ignorant person later than the corrector indicated by D$^{**}_{**}$ (p. 132). Muralt's endeavours to shake this conclusion have not satisfied better judges; indeed the facts are too numerous and too plain to be resisted. Thus, while in Rom. iv. 25, Cod. D reads *δικαιωσιν* (accentuated *δικαίωσιν* by D***), in which D$^{**}_{**}$ changes *ν* into *νην*, the writer of Cod. E adopts *δικαίωσινην* with its monstrous accent: in 1 Cor. xv. 5 Cod. D reads *μετα ταυτα τοις ενδεκα*, D*** *εἶτα τοῖς δώδεκα* (observe again the accents), out of which Cod. E makes up *μετα ταυεῖτα τοῖς δώενδεκα.* The Latin version is also borrowed from Cod. D, but is more mixed, and may be of some critical use: the Greek is manifestly worthless, and should long since have been removed from the list of authorities. This copy is defective, Rom. viii. 21—33; xi. 15—25; 1 Tim. i. 1—vi. 15; Hebr. xii. 8—xiii. 25.

F^{a} Cod. Coislin. 1 (*see* p. 105).

F. Cod. Augiensis in the Library of Trinity College, Cambridge (B. 17. 1), is another Greek-Latin manuscript on 136 leaves of good vellum 4to (the *signatures* proving that seven more are lost), 9 inches by 7¼, with the two languages in parallel columns of 28 lines on each page, the Greek being always inside, the Latin next the edge of the book. It is called from the monastery of Augia Dives or Major (Reichenau, or *rich meadow*), on a fertile island in the lower part of Lake Constance, to which it long appertained, and where it may even have been written, a thousand years since. By notices at the beginning and end we can trace it through the hands of G. M. Wepfer of Schaffhausen and of L. Ch. Mieg, who covered many of its pages with Latin notes wretchedly scrawled, but allowed Wetstein to examine it. In 1718 Bentley was induced by Wetstein to buy it at Heidelberg for 250 Dutch

[1] *Facsimiles* of this manuscript are given by Semler in his edition of Wetstein's *Prolegomena* (1764, Nos. 8, 9). Blanchini's estimate of its age (*Evangeliarum Quadruplex, Tom.* II. fol. 591. 2), the 7th century, is certainly too high.

florins, and both he and Wetstein collated the Greek portion, the latter carelessly, but Bentley somewhat more fully in the margin of a Greek Testament (Oxon. 1675), yet preserved in Trinity College (B. 17. 8). Tischendorf in 1842, Tregelles in 1845, re-examined the book (which had been placed where it now is on the death of Bentley's nephew in 1787), and drew attention to the Latin version: in 1859 Scrivener published an edition of the Codex in common type, with Prolegomena and a photograph of one page (1 Tim. iii. 14—iv. 5). The Epistles of St Paul are defective in Rom. i. 1—iii. 19; and the Greek only in 1 Cor. iii. 8—16; vi. 7—14; Col. ii. 1—8; Philem. 21—25; in which four places the Latin stands in its own column with no Greek over-against it. In the Epistle to the Hebrews, the Greek being quite lost, the Latin occupies both columns: this Epistle alone has an Argument, almost verbatim the same as we read in the great Cod. Amiatinus of the Vulgate. At the end of the Epistle, and on the same page (*fol.* 139, *verso*) commences a kind of Postscript (having little connection with the sacred text), the larger portion of which is met with under the title of "Dicta Abbatis Pinophi," in the works of Rabanus Maurus, Archbishop of Mayence, who died in A.D. 856; from which circumstance the Cod. Augiensis has been referred to the ninth century. Palæographical arguments also would lead us to the same conclusion. The Latin version (a modification of the Vulgate in its purest form, though somewhat tampered with in parts to make it suit the Greek text) is written in the cursive minuscule character common in the age of Charlemagne. The Greek must have been taken from an archetype with the words continuously written; for not only are they miserably divided by the unlearned German[1] scribe, but his design (not always acted upon) was to put a single middle point at the end of each word. The Latin is exquisitely written, the Greek uncials are neat, but evidently the work of an unpractised hand, which soon changes from weariness. The shapes of *eta*, *theta*, *pi*, and other testing letters are such as we might have expected from the date; some others have an older look. Contrary to the more ancient custom, capitals, small but numerous, occur in the *middle* of the lines in both languages. Of the ordinary breath-

[1] He betrays his nationality by placing "waltet" *primâ manu* over ἐξουσιάζει, 1 Cor. vii. 4.

ings[1] and accents there are no traces. Here and there we meet with a straight line, inclined between the horizontal and the acute accent, placed over an initial vowel, usually when it should be aspirated, but not always (e.g. *ἴδιον* 1 Cor. vi. 18). Over *ι* and *υ* double or single points, or a comma, are frequently placed, especially if they begin a syllable, and occasionally a large comma or kind of circumflex over *ι*, *ει* and some other vowels or diphthongs. The arrangement of the Greek forbids punctuation there; in the Latin we find the single middle point as a colon, or after an abridgement, the semi-colon (;) sometimes, the note of interrogation (?) when needed. Besides the universal forms of abridgement (*see* p. 43), ϗ and ȣ are frequent in the Greek, but no others: in the Latin the abbreviations are numerous, and some of them unusual: Scrivener (*Cod. Augiensis Proleg. pp.* xxxi—ii) has drawn up a full list of them. This copy abounds as much as any with real variations from the common text, and with numberless errors of the pen, itacisms of vowels, and permutations of consonants. It exhibits many corrections, a few *primâ manu*, some unfortunately very recent, but by far the greater number in a hand little later than the original writer's, which has also inserted over the Greek in 106 places, Latin renderings differing from those in the parallel column, but which in 86 of these 106 instances agree with the Latin of the sister manuscript

G. COD. BOERNERIANUS, so called from a former possessor, but now in the Royal Library at Dresden. In the 16th century it belonged to Paul Junius of Leyden: it was bought dear at the book-sale of Peter Francius, Professor at Amsterdam, in 1705, by C. F. Boerner, a Professor at Leipsic, who lent it to Kuster to enrich his edition of Mill (1711), and subsequently to Bentley. The latter so earnestly wished to purchase it as a companion to Cod. F, that though he received it in 1719, it could not be recovered from him for five years, during which he was constantly offering high sums for it[2]:

[1] In 1 Tim. iv. 2 the Latin h is inserted *secundâ manu* before *υποκρισι*.

[2] Boerner's son tells the tale 30 years afterwards with amusing querulousness in his Catalogus Bibl. Boern. Lips. 1754, p. 6, cited by Matthaei Cod. Boern. p. xviii. But there must have been some misunderstanding on both sides, for it appears from a manuscript note in his copy of the Oxford N. T. of 1675 (Trin. Coll. B. 17. 8), that Bentley considered Cod. G his own property; since after

a copy, but not in Bentley's hand, had been already made (Trin. Coll. B. 17. 2). Cod. G was published in full by Matthaei in 1791, in common type, with two *facsimile* pages; his edition is believed to be very accurate; Anger, Tischendorf, Tregelles, Böttiger and others who have examined it have only expressly indicated two errors[1]. Rettig has abundantly proved that, as it is exactly of the same size, so it once formed part of the same volume with Cod. Δ (*see* p. 122 and note): they must date towards the end of the ninth century, and may very possibly have been written in the monastery of St Gall (where Δ still remains) by some of the Irish monks who flocked to those parts. That Cod. G has been in such hands appears from some very curious Irish lines at the foot of one of Matthaei's plates (fol. 23), which after having long perplexed learned men, have recently been translated by Dr Reeves, the eminent Celtic scholar[2]. All that we have said respecting the form of Cod. Δ applies to this portion of it: the Latin version (a specimen of the Old Latin, but as in Codd. Bezae and Laudianus much changed to suit the Greek) is cursive and interlinear; the Greek uncials coarse and peculiar; the punctuation

describing Cod. F before the Epistle to the Romans as his own, and as commencing at Rom. iii. 19, he adds "Variæ lectiones ex altero *nostro* MSto, ejusdem veteris exemplaris apographo."

[1] viz. μετρους for μερους, Eph. iv. 16; εσκοτισμενος for -μενοι, iv. 18.

[2] Dr Reeves's translation of these verses appears in the Irish Archæological Journal for September 1848, but Dr Todd, the learned Senior Fellow and Librarian of Trinity College, Dublin, has favoured us with the following revision of Dr Reeves's translation of these two stanzas: the second and fourth lines of each stanza rhyme.

Téicht do róim [téicht do róim]	To go to Rome, to go to Rome,
Mór saido beci torbai	Much of trouble, little of profit,
Inrí chondaigi hifoss	The King thou seekest here,
Manimbera latt ni fogbai	If thou bring Him not with thee thou findest not.
Mór báis mór baile	Great folly, great madness,
Mór coll ceilla mór mire	Great ruin of sense, great insanity,
Olais airchenn teicht dóecaib	Since thou hast set out for the sake of going to death,
Beith fó étoil maic Maire.	That thou shouldst be in disobedience to the Son of Mary.

In l. 3 *n* (written in error) is afterwards erased before *hifoss*. The second stanza intimates that as the pilgrimage to Rome is at the risk of life, it is folly not to be at peace with Christ before we set out.

chiefly a stop at the end of words, which have no breathings or accents. Its affinity to the Cod. Augiensis has no parallel in this branch of literature. Scrivener has noted all the differences between them at the foot of each page in his edition of Cod. F: they amount to but 1982 places, whereof 577 are mere blunders of the scribe, 968 changes of vowels or itacisms, 166 interchanges of consonants, 71 grammatical or orthographical forms, the remaining 200 are real various readings, 32 of them relating to the article. While in Cod. F (whose first seven leaves are lost) the text commences at Rom. iii. 19, *μω· λεγει*, this portion is found in Cod. G, except Rom. i. 1—5; ii. 16—25. All the other lacunae of Cod. F occur also in Cod. G, which ends at Philem. 20 *ἐν χρω*: there is no Latin version to supply these gaps in Cod. G, but a blank space is always left sufficient to contain what is missing. At the end of
ad laudicenses incipit epistola
Philemon G writes Π*ροσ λαουδακησασ αρχεται επιστολη*, but neither that writing (which would indeed have been a great curiosity), nor the Epistle to the Hebrews, follows. It is quite plain that one of these manuscripts was not copied immediately from the other, for while they often accord even in the strangest errors of the pen that men unskilled in Greek could fall into, their division of the Greek words, though equally false and absurd, is often quite different: it results therefore that they are independent transcripts of the same venerable archetype (probably some centuries older than themselves) which was written without any division between the words. From the form of the letters and other circumstances Cod. F may be deemed somewhat but not much the older; its corrector *secundâ manu* evidently had both the Greek and the Latin (p. 135) of Cod. G before him, and Rabanus, in whose works the *Dicta Pinophi* are preserved (p. 134), was the great antagonist of Godeschalk, on whom the annotator of Codd. ΔG bears so hard. Cod. G is in 4to, of 99 leaves, with 21 lines in each. The line indicating breathing (if such be its use) and the mark > to fill up spaces (p. 44), are more frequent in it than in F.

H. Cod. Coislin. 202 is a very precious fragment of 14 leaves, 12 of which are in the Imperial Library at Paris, two having found their way to St Petersburg after the hasty removal of the manuscripts from the Abbey of St Germain de Prez, when

Cod. E disappeared (above p. 132). The leaves at Paris contain 1 Cor. x. 22—29; xi. 9—16; 1 Tim. iii. 7—13; Tit. i. 1—3; i. 15—ii. 5; iii. 13—15; Hebr. ii. 11—16; iii. 13—18; iv. 12—15; those at St Petersburg Gal. i. 4—10; ii. 9—14; in all 56 verses. They are in 4to, with large square uncials of about 16 lines on a page, and date from the 6th century. Breathings and accents are added by a later hand, which retouched this copy (*see Sylvestre, Paléogr. Univ.* Nos. 63, 64, *and above*, p. 23). These leaves, which comprise one of our best authorities for stichometrical writing (p. 46), were used in 1218 to bind another book on Mount Athos, and thence came into the library of Coislin, Bishop of Metz. Montfaucon has published Cod. H in his Bibliotheca Coisliniana, but Tischendorf, who has transcribed it, promises a fuller and more accurate edition. The subscriptions, which appear due to Euthalius of Sulci[1], written in vermilion, are not retouched, and consequently have neither spirits nor accents. Besides arguments to the Epistles we copy the following final subscription from Tischendorf (N. T. 1859, p. clxxxix): *ἔγραψα καὶ ἐξεθέμην κατὰ δύναμιν στειχηρὸν· τόδε τὸ τεῦχος παύλου τοῦ ἀποστόλου πρὸς ἐγγραμμὸν καὶ εὐκατάληπττον ἀνάγνωσιν. τῶν καθ' ἡμᾶς ἀδελφῶν· παρῶν ἀπάντων τόλμης συγγνώμην αἰτῶ. εὐχῇ τῇ ὑπὲρ ἐμῶν· τὴν συμπεριφορὰν κομιζόμενος· ἀντεβλήθη δὲ ἡ βίβλος· πρὸς τὸ ἐν καισαρίᾳ ἀντίγραφον τῆς βιβλιοθήκης τοῦ ἁγίου παμφίλου χειρὶ γεγραμμένον αὐτοῦ* (*see above p.* 47).

I. Cod. Tischendorf. II, at St Petersburg (*see p.* 107).

K. Cod. Mosquensis (*see p.* 130). L. Cod. Angelicus at Rome (*see p.* 129).

M. Codex Ruber is peculiar for the beautifully bright red colour of the ink[2], the elegance of the small uncial characters, and the excellency and critical value of the text. Two folio

[1] In reference to what was said above, p. 53, note 1, it is only fair to state that Euthalius is called Ἐπίσκοπος Σούλκης (or Ἐούλκης once in one manuscript) in the titles to his works as edited by L. A. Zacagni (*Collectanea Monument. Veter. Eccles. Græc. ac Latin.* Romae 1698, p. 402). That Euthalius should write in Greek is easily accounted for by his previous connection with Egypt, and it is plain that there was but one town of Sulci, Sardinia being sometimes reckoned a portion of the Roman diocese, sometimes of the Province of Mauritania Secunda (*Bingham's Antiquities*, Vol. III. pp. 152, 201, *edition of* 1838). Zacagni's improbable guess of Ψέλχη near Syene must certainly be rejected, as no place of that name appears in any list of Episcopal sees.

[2] Scholz also describes 196, 362, 366 of the Gospels as written in red ink.

leaves containing Hebr. i. 1—iv. 3; xii. 20—xiii. 25, once belonged to Uffenbach, then to J. C. Wolff, who bequeathed them to the Public Library (Johanneum) of Hamburgh (*see Cod.* H. *of the Gospels, p.* 106). To the same manuscript belong fragments of two leaves used in binding Cod. Harleian. 5613 in the British Museum, and seen at once by Griesbach, who first collated them (*Symbol. Crit.* Tom. II. p. 162 &c.), to be portions of the Hamburgh fragment. Each page in both contains two columns, of 45 lines each in the Hamburgh, of 38 in the London leaves. The latter comprise 1 Cor. xv. 52—2 Cor. i. 15; 2 Cor. x. 13—xii. 5; reckoning both fragments 196 verses in all. Henke in 1800 edited the Hamburgh portion, Tregelles collated it twice, and Tischendorf in 1855 published the text of both in full in his *Anecdota Sacra et Profana.* The letters are a little unusual in form, perhaps about the tenth century in date; but though sometimes joined in the same word, can hardly be called *semicursive.* Our *facsimile* (Plate XI, No. 38) is from the London fragment: the graceful, though peculiar shapes, both of *alpha* and *mu* (*see p.* 33) closely resemble those in some writing of about the same age, added to the venerable Leyden Octateuch, on a page just published in *facsimile* by Tischendorf (*Monum. sacr. ined.* Vol. III). Accents and breathings are given pretty correctly and constantly: *iota* ascript occurs three times (2 Cor. i. 1; 4; Hebr. xiii. 21)[1]; only 10 *itacisms* occur and ν ἐφελκυστικὸν (as it is called) is rare. The usual stop is the single point in its three positions, with a change in power, as in Cod. E of the Gospels. The interrogative (;) occurs once (Hebr. iii. 17), and > is often repeated to fill up space (*see p.* 44), or, in a smaller shape, to mark quotations. After the name of each of the Epistles (2 Cor. and Hebr.) in their titles we read εκτεθειϲα ώς εν πινακι, which Tischendorf thus explains; that whereas it was customary to prefix an argument to each epistle, these words, originally employed to introduce the argument, were retained even when the argument was omitted. Henke's account

[1] Griesbach (*Symbol. Critic.* Vol. II. p. 166) says that in the Harleian fragment "Iota bis tantum aut ter subscribitur, semel postscribitur, plerumque omittitur," overlooking the second postscript. Scrivener repeats this statement about ι subscript (*Cod. Augiens. Introd.* p. lxxii), believing he had verified it: but Tischendorf cannot see the subscripts, nor can Scrivener on again consulting Harl. 5613 for the purpose. Tregelles too says, "I have not seen a *sub*scribed iota in any uncial document" (*Printed Text,* p. 158, *note*).

of the expression looks a little less forced, that this manuscript was set forth ὡς εν πινακι, that is, in vermillion, after the pattern of Imperial letters patent.

N[c]. FRAGMENTA MOSQUENSIA used as early as A.D. 975 in binding a volume of Gregory Nazianzen now at Moscow (S. Synodi 61). Matthaei describes them on Hebr. x. 1: they only contain the 12 verses Hebr. x. 1—3; 3—7; 32—34; 35—38. These very ancient leaves may possibly be as old as the sixth century, for their letters resemble in shape those in Cod. H which the later hand has so coarsely renewed; but are more probably a little later.

Manuscripts of the Apocalypse.

ℵ. CODEX SINAITICUS (described above, pp. 76—79). A. CODEX ALEXANDRINUS (described above, pp. 79—84).

B. CODEX VATICANUS 2066 (formerly 105 in the Library of the Basilian monks in the city) was judiciously substituted by Wetstein for the *modern* portion of the great Vatican MS., which is yet uncollated. It is an uncial copy of about the beginning of the eighth century, and the volume also contains in the same hand homilies of Basil the Great and Gregory of Nyssa, &c. It was first known from a notice and *facsimile* in Blanchini's Evangeliarium Quadruplex (1748), Vol. II. p. 525: Wetstein was promised a collation of it by Cardinal Quirini, who seems to have met with unexpected hindrances, as the papers only arrived after the text of the New Testament was printed, and proved very loose and defective. When Tischendorf was at Rome in 1843, though forbidden to collate it afresh (in consequence, as we now know, of its having been already printed in Mai's unpublished volumes of the Codex Vaticanus), he was permitted to make a *facsimile* of a few verses, and while thus employed he so far contrived to elude the watchful custodian, as to compare the whole manuscript with a modern Greek Testament. The result was given in his *Monumenta sacra inedita* (1846) pp. 407—432, with a good *facsimile;* but (as was natural under the unpromising circumstances) Tregelles in 1845 was able to observe several points which he had overlooked, and more have come to light since Mai's edition has appeared:

on the other hand, the errors of Mai detected by Tischendorf (*N. T. 7th edit. Proleg. p.* cxcii) are yet more numerous, so that a renewed examination of this valuable document is even now desirable.

This Codex is now known to contain the whole of the Apocalypse, a fact which the poor collation that Wetstein managed to procure had rendered doubtful. It is rather an octavo than a folio or quarto; the uncials being of a peculiar kind, simple and unornamented, leaning a little to the right: they hold a sort of middle place between square and oblong characters. The shape of *beta* is peculiar, the two loops to the right nowhere touching each other, and *psi* has degenerated into the form of a cross (*see* Plate III, No. 7): *delta, theta, xi* are also of the latest uncial fashion. The breathings and accents are *primâ manu,* and pretty correct; the rule of the grammarians respecting the change of power of the single point in punctuation according to its change of position (above, p. 42) is now regularly observed. The scarcity of old copies of the Apocalypse renders this uncial of considerable importance, and it much confirms the readings of the older codices AC.

C. CODEX EPHRAEMI (described above pp. 94—96).

SECTION III.

On the Cursive Manuscripts of the Greek Testament.

THE later manuscripts of the Greek Testament, written in cursive characters from the tenth down to the fifteenth century or later, are too numerous to be minutely described in an elementary work like the present. We shall therefore speak of them with all possible brevity, dwelling only on a few which present points of especial interest, and employing certain abridgements, a list of which we subjoin for the reader's convenience.

Abbreviations used in the following Catalogue.

Am. denotes that a manuscript has the Ammonian sections in the margin. *Eus.* that under them stand the Eusebian canons. *Eus. t.* that a table of these canons is prefixed to the Gospels, and if the Epistle to Carpian precede, *Carp.* stands before *Eus. t.* *κεφ.* indicates that the numbers of the *κεφάλαια* majora stand in the margin. *τίτλ.* that the *τίτλοι* are given at the head or foot of the page. *κεφ. t.* that tables of the *κεφάλαια* are prefixed to each book. *lect.* that the book is adapted for Church-reading by notices of the proper lessons, feasts &c. in the margin, or above, or below, or interspersed with the text. *men.* that a menology, or calendar of Saints' Days, is found at the beginning or end of the book. *syn.* that a calendar of the daily lessons throughout the year is given. *mut.* that the copy described is mutilated. *pict.* that it is illuminated with pictures &c. *prol.* that it contains prologues or *ὑποθέσεις* before the several books. The books are all written on parchment or vellum, unless *chart.* (paper) be expressly named.

N. B. The numerals within brackets which immediately follow the name of each manuscript represent the date, whether fixed by a subscription in the book itself, or approximated to by other means: e.g. [XIII] indicates a book of the 13th century. The names within parentheses indicate the collators of each manuscript, and if it has been satisfactorily examined, an asterisk is prefixed to the number by which it is known (see p. 67). If the copy contain other portions of the New Testament, its notation in those portions is always given.

Manuscripts of the Gospels.

*1. (Act. 1, Paul. 1). Codex Basilensis K III. 3 [X] 8°, *prol.*, *syn.*, *pict.* Among the illuminations are what appear to be pictures of the Emperor Leo the Wise [886—911] and his son Constantine Porphyrogenitus. Its later history is the same as that of Cod. E of the Gospels (*see* pp. 103—4): it was known to Erasmus, who but little used or valued it: it was borrowed by Reuchlin, a few extracts given by Bengel (Bas. γ), collated by Wetstein, and recently by C. L. Roth and Tregelles, who have compared their results. Our facsimile (No. 23) gives an excellent notion of the elegant and minute style of writing, which is fully furnished with breathings, accents and ι ascript: there are 38 lines in each page. In the Gospels the text is very remarkable, adhering pretty closely to the uncials Codd. BL and others of that class.

2. Cod. Basil. B VI. 25 [XV.] is the inferior manuscript chiefly used by Erasmus for his first edition of the N. T., with press corrections in his hand. The monks at Basle had bought it for two Rhenish florins; and dear enough, in Michælis' judgment. (Bengel, Bas. *β*, Wetstein).

3. (Act. 3, Paul. 3). Cod. Corsendonck. [XII] 4°, once belonging to a convent at Corsendonck near Turnhout, now in the Imperial Library at Vienna (Forlos. 15, Kollar. 5): *syn., Eus. t., prol., pict.* It was lent to Erasmus for his second edition in 1519, as he testifies on the first leaf (Alter).

4. Cod. Regius 84 [XII] 4°, in the Imperial Library at Paris (designated RI by Tischendorf), was rightly recognised by Lelong as Robert Stephens' γ′ (see Chap. v.) Mill notices its affinity to the Latin versions and the Complutensian edition (*Prol. N. T.* § 1161); *mut.* in Matth. ii. 9—20; John i. 49—iii. 11; 49 verses: it contains *syn.* and extracts from some Fathers (Scholz).

5. (Act. 5, Paul. 5). Regius 106 [XII] is Stephens' δ′: 4°, *prol.* (Wetstein, Scholz).

6. (Act. 6, Paul. 6). Regius 112 [XI] is Stephens' ϵ′; in text it much resembles Codd. 4; 5. 12°, *syn.* with St Chrysostom's Liturgy, *prol., κεφ. t* (Wetstein, Griesbach, Scholz).

7. Regius 71 [XI] is Stephens' ϛ′. 4°, *prol., syn., Eus. t., pict.* (Wetst., Scholz).

8. Regius 49 [XI] fol., seems to be Stephens' ζ′: *Eus. t., syn.* (Wetst., Scholz).

9. Regius 83 [dated A.D. 1168, when "Manuel Porphyrogenitus was ruler of Constantinople, Amauri of Jerusalem, William II. of Sicily"] 4°, is *probably* Stephens' ιβ′, *Eus. t., syn.* It once belonged to Peter Stella (Kuster's Paris 3, Scholz).

10. Regius 91 [XIII or later] 4°, given in 1439 to a library of Canons Regular at Verona by Dorotheus Archbishop of Mitylene, when he came to the Council of Florence. If this be Kuster's Paris 1 he says that it came "ex Bibliothecâ Telleriano-Rhemensi;" Scholz, that it was "antea Joannis Huraultii Boistallerii;" some confusion seems to be attached to this copy. *Syn. Eus., t.* (Wetstein, Griesbach, Scholz).

11. Regius 121—2 [XII or earlier] in two small 8° volumes, neatly written. *Eus. t.* It also once belonged to Teller (Kuster's Paris 4, Scholz).

12. In Wetstein's notation stands for a medley of readings from the manuscripts noted below as 119, 120, and another unknown: *but Scholz's Cod.* 12. is Regius 230 [XI] 4°, *syn., Eus. t., prol., pict.* and a commentary. The next manuscript is the most important since Cod. 1.

13. Regius 50 [XII] 4°, is Kuster's Paris 6, who says that it supplied him with more various readings than all the rest of his Paris manuscripts put together. This, like Codd. 10, 11 once belonged to Teller. It is not correctly written, and still needs careful collation. *Syn., mut.* in Matth. i. 1—ii. 21; xxvi. 33—53; xxvii. 26—xxviii. 10; Mark i. 2—45; Jo. xxi. 2—25; 181 verses (Kuster, Wetstein, Griesbach, Begtrup in 1797).

14. Regius 70 [A.D. 964, the earliest dated cursive: see p. 36, note 2] 8°, once Cardinal Mazarin's; was Kuster's Paris 7. A *facsimile* of this beautiful copy, with round conjoined minuscule letters, regular breathings and accents is given in the Paléographie Universelle, No. 78. *Κεφ. t., pict.* Paschal. Canon, *Carp., Eus. t.* (Kuster, Scholz).

15. Regius 64 [X] 4°, is Kuster's Paris 8. *Eus. t., syn., pict.* very neat (Kuster, Scholz).

16. Regius 54 [XIV] fol., once belonged to the Medici; it has a Latin version in parts; *mut.* Mark xvi. 6—20. *Eus. t., syn., pict.* (Wetstein, Scholz).

17. Regius 55 [XVI] fol., has the Latin Vulgate version: it was neatly written in France by George Hermonymus the Spartan, who settled at Paris in 1472, and became the Greek teacher of Budæus and Reuchlin: it once belonged to Cardinal Bourbon. *Syn., pict.* (Wetstein, Griesbach, Scholz).

18. (Act. 113, Paul. 132, Apoc. 51). Regius 47, bought 1687, but written at Constantinople A.D. 1364 by Nicephorus Cannavus. It is one of the few copies of the whole New Testament (see p. 61), and once belonged to the monastery *τοῦ ζωοδότου χριστοῦ* at Myzithra (Misitra?). *Prol., syn.* psalms, hymns (Scholz).

19. Regius 189 [XII] or Wetstein's 1869, once belonged to the Medici, with a catena to John, and scholia to the other Gospels (Scholz).

20. Regius 188 [XII], brought from the East in 1669. It is carelessly written, and contains catenæ, commentaries and other treatises enumerated by Scholz, who collated most of it. At the end of Mark, Luke and John "dicitur etiam hoc evangelium ex accuratis codicibus esse exscriptum, nec non collatum" (Scholz). A second hand has been busy here.

21. Regius 68 [X] 4°, *pict.*, with *syn.* on paper in a later hand (Scholz).

22. Regius 72, once Colbert. 2467 [XI] 4°, very imperfectly known, but contains remarkable readings. *Mut.* Matth. i. 1—ii. 2 (v. 25 Griesb.); John xiv. 22—xvi. 27; 90 verses. *Lect.* added in 16th century (Wetstein, Scholz).

23. Regius 77, Colbert. 3947 [xi] 4°, with the Latin Vulgate version down to Luke iv. 18. *Mut.* Matth. i. 1—17; Luke xxiv. 46—Jo. ii. 20; xxi. 24, 25; 96 verses (Scholz).

24. Regius 178, Colbert. 4112 [xi] fol., with a commentary, and also *syn.* but in a later hand. *Mut.* Matth. xxvii. 20—Mark iv. 22; 186 verses (Griesb., Scholz).

25. Regius 191, Colbert. 2259 [x] fol., with scholia. Very imperfect, wanting about 715 verses, viz. Matth. xxiii. 1—xxv. 42; Mark i. 1—vii. 36; Luke viii. 31—41; ix. 44—54; x. 39—xi. 4; John xiii. 19?—xxi. 25 (Griesbach, Scholz).

26. Regius 78, Colbert. 4078 [xi] 4°, neatly and correctly written by Paul a priest. Comment., *Eus. t.* (Wetstein, Scholz).

27. Regius 115, Colbert. 6043 [xi] 8°, is Mill's Colb. 1. That critic procured Larroque's collation of Codd. 27—33 (a very imperfect one) for his edition of the New Testament. From Jo. xviii. 3 the text is supplied, cotton *chart.* [xiv]. *Syn.*, *pict.* Extensively altered by a later hand (Wetstein, Scholz).

28. Regius 379, Colbert. 4705 [xi?] 4°, is Mill's Colb. 2, most carelessly written by an ignorant scribe; it often resembles Cod. D, but has many unique readings and interpolations. *Syn.*, *mut.* in 334 verses, viz. Matth. vii. 17—ix. 12; xiv. 33—xvi. 10; xxvi. 70—xxvii. 48; Luke xx. 19—xxii. 46; John xii. 40—xiii. 1; xv. 24—xvi. 12; xviii. 16—28; xx. 20—xxi. 5; 18—25 (Scholz).

29. Regius 89, Colbert. 6066 [xii] 4°, is Mill's Colb. 3, correctly written by a Latin scribe, with very many peculiar corrections by a later hand. Lost leaves in the three later Gospels are supplied [xv]. Scholia, *Eus. t.*, *mut.* Matth. i.—xv. Mill compares its text with that of Cod. 71 *infra* (Scholz).

30. Regius 100, Colbert. 4444 [xvi] 4°, *chart.*, is Mill's Colb. 4, containing *all* the Gospels, by the writer of Cod. 17, whose text it much resembles (Scholz).

31. Regius 94, Colbert. 6083 [xiii] 4°, is also Mill's Colb. 4, but contains all the Gospels with prayers and *pict.* This copy has many erasures (Scholz).

32. Regius 116, Colbert. 6551 [xii] 8°, *lect.*, is Mill's Colb. 5. It begins Matth. x. 22. *Mut.* Matth. xxiv. 15—30; Luke xxii. 35—Jo. iv. 20 (Scholz). Mill misrepresented the contents of Codd. 30—32, through supposing that they contained no more than the small portions which were collated for his use.

*33. (Act. 13, Paul. 17). Regius 14, Colbert. 2844 [xi] fol., is Mill's Colb. 8, containing some of the Prophets and all the New Testament except the Apocalypse. In text it resembles Codd. BDL more than any other cursive manuscript, and whatever may be thought of the character of its readings, they deserve the utmost attention. After Larroque, Wetstein, Griesbach, Begtrup and Scholz, it was most laboriously collated by Tregelles in 1850. From his beautiful tracing our *facsimile* (No. 34) of this manuscript is derived. There are 42 long lines in each page, in a fine round hand, the accents being sometimes neglected, and *eta* unusually like our English letter h. The ends of the leaves are much damaged, and greatly misplaced by the binder; so that the Gospels now stand last, though on comparing the style of handwriting (which undergoes a *gradual* change throughout the volume) at their beginning and end with that in the Prophets which stand first, and the Epistles that should follow them, it is plain that they originally occupied their usual place. The ink too, by reason of the damp, has often left its proper page blank, so that the writing can only be read *set off* on the opposite page, especially in the Acts. Hence it is no wonder that Tregelles should say that of all the manuscripts he has collated "none has ever been so wearisome to the eyes, and exhaustive of every faculty of attention." (*Account of the Printed Account*, p. 162).

The next eight copies, like Cod. H. of St Paul, belonged to that noble collection made by the Chancellor Seguier, and on his death in 1672 bequeathed to Coislin, Bishop of Metz. Montfaucon has described them in his "Bibliotheca Coisliniana," fol. 1715, and all were slightly collated by Wetstein and Scholz.

34. Cod. Coislin. 195 [XI] 4°, elegantly written on Mount Athos, has a catena, *prol.*, *pict.*

35. (Act. 14, Paul. 18, Apoc. 17). Coislin. 199 [XI] fol., contains the whole New Testament, with many corrections.

36. Coislin. 20 [XI], *Eus. t.*, *prol.*, with a commentary, from the *laura* [i. e. convent, *Suicer*, *Thes. Ecc.* Tom. II. 205] of St Athanasius in Mount Athos.

37. Coislin. 21 [XII] 4°, with short scholia, *Eus. t.*, *syn.*, *prol.*, *pict.*

38. (Act. 19, Apoc. 23). Coislin. 200 [XIII] 4°, copied by the Emperor Michael Palaeologus [1259—1282], and by him sent to St Louis [d. 1270], containing all the N. T. except St Paul's Epistles, has been judged by Wetstein to be Stephens' θ′[1]. *Pict.*, *mut.* 143 verses; Matth. xiv. 15—xv. 30; xx. 14—xxi. 27; Mark xii. 3—xiii. 4. A facsimile of this beautiful book is given in the *Paléographie Univer.* No. 84, where it is erroneously called an Evangelistarium.

39. Coislin. 23 [XI], written by the Patriarch Sergius II., and in 1218 at the convent of St Athanasius on Mount Athos. With a Commentary.

40. Coislin. 22 [XI] 4°, once belonged to the monastery of St Nicholas σταυρονικήτας, with a Commentary and *Eus. t.* Ends at John xx. 25.

41. Coislin. 24 [XI] 4°, contains Matthew and Mark with a Commentary.

42. Cod. Medicaeus exhibits many readings of the same class as Codd. 1. 13. 33, but its authority has the less weight, since it has

[1] Stephens includes his θ′ among the copies that αὐτοὶ πανταχόθεν συνηθροίσαμεν, which might suit the case of Coislin. 200, as St Louis would have brought or sent it to France. But how can we account for Stephens citing θ′ repeatedly in St Paul which Coisl. 200 does not contain, and never in the Apocalypse, which it does?

disappeared under circumstances somewhat suspicious. Bernard communicated to Mill these readings, which he had found in the hand of Peter Pithoeus, a former owner, in the margin of Stephens' N. T. of 1550: they professed to be extracted from an "exemplar Regium Medicaeum" (which may be supposed to mean that portion of the King's Library which Catherine de Medici brought to France: above, p. 94), and were inserted under the title of *Med.* in Mill's great work, though he remarked their resemblance to the text of Cod. K (Proleg. N. T. § 1462). The braggart Amelotte [1606—78] professes to have used the manuscript, about the end of the seventeenth century, and states that it was in a college at Troyes; but Scholz could find it neither in that city nor elsewhere.

43. (Act. 54, Paul. 130). Cod. Graec. 4, in the Arsenal of Paris [XI] 4°, in two volumes; the first containing the Gospels with *Eus. t.*, the second the Acts and Epistles. Perhaps written at Ephesus; given by P. de Berzi in 1661 to the Oratory of San Maglorian (Amelotte, Simon, Scholz).

44. Brit. Museum, Addit. 4949 [XI] fol., brought from Mount Athos by the celebrated Caesar de Missy [1703—75], George III's French chaplain, who spent his life in collecting materials for an edition of the N. T. His collation, most imperfectly given by Wetstein, is still preserved with the manuscript. *Syn.*, *men.*, *pict.*, *Am.*, *Eus.*, but no *κεφ.* (Bloomfield, 1860).

45. Cod. Bodleian. Barocc. 31 [XIII] 4°, is Mill's Bodl. 1, a very neat copy, with *Eus. t.*, *κεφ. t.*, *Am.*, *pict.*, subscriptions, and *στίχοι* numbered in Luke (Mill, Griesbach).

46. Bodleian. Barocc. 29 [XI] 4°, Mill's Bodl. 2, with *τὸ νομικὸν* and *τὸ κυριακὸν πάσχα*, *syn.*, *men.*, *Carp.*, *Eus. t.*, *κεφ. t.*, *τίτλοι*, *pict.*, subscriptions, *στίχοι* (Mill, Griesbach).

47. Bodleian. Misc. 9 (Auct. D. 5. 2), [XV] 12°, in a vile hand, *κεφ. t.*, and much foreign matter, is Mill's Bodl. 6 and Bodl. 1 of Walton's Polyglott (Polyglott, Mill).

48. Bodleian. Misc. 1 (Auct. D. 2. 17), [XII] 4°, is Mill's Bodl. 7, having scholia in a later hand, *pict.*, *Eus. t.*, subscriptions with *ῥήματα* and *στίχοι* appended (Mill).

49. Bodleian. Roe 1 [XI] 4°, is also Mill's Roe 1, brought by Sir T. Roe (see p. 79) from Turkey about 1628; it has *Eus. t.*, *κεφ. t.*, *Am.*, *Eus.*, *lect.* (Mill).

50. Bodleian. Laud. 33 [XI] 4°, is Mill's Laud. 1 (see p. 128), surrounded by a catena, and attended with other matter. It begins Matth. ix. 35, and ends at Jo. v. 18; besides which it is mutilated in Matth. xii. 3—24; xxv. 20—31; and Mark xiv. 40—xvi. 20 is by a later hand. It contains many unusual readings (Mill, Griesbach).

51. (Act. 32, Paul. 38). Bodleian. Laud. 31 [XIII] fol., Mill's Laud. 2, whose resemblance to the Complutensian text is pointed out by him (Prol. N. T. § 1437), though, judging from his own collation of Cod. 51, his statement "per omnia penè respondet" is rather too strong. See below, Chap. V. *Syn.*, *κεφ.*, *τίτλοι*, *Am.* (not *Eus.*), *lect.*, *men.*, *prol.*, and other foreign matter. The *present* order

of the contents (see p. 62) is Act., Paul., Cath., Evangelia (Mill, Griesbach), but it ought to be collated afresh.

52. Bodleian. Laud. 3 [dated A.D. 1286] an elegant small 4°, written by νικητας ὁ μαυρωνης, is Mill's Laud. 5, with κεφ. *t.*, *Am.*, *Eus.*, *lect.*, *pict.*, *men.*, subscriptions (Mill, Griesbach).

53. Bodleian. Selden. 53 [XIV] 4°, is Mill's Selden 1, who pronounces it much like Stephens' γ′ (Cod. 4), having κεφ. *t.*, κεφ. (not *Eus.*), and subscriptions (Mill).

54. Bodleian. Selden. 54 [dated A.D. 1338] 4°, Mill's Seld. 2, has the text broken up into paragraphs, beginning with red capitals, *syn.*, *lect.*, κεφ. *t.*, *Am.*, but not *Eus.* (Mill).

55. Bodleian. Selden. 5 [XIII] 4°, Mill's Seld. 3, containing also Judges vi. 1—24 (Grabe, Prol. V. T. III. 6), has *syn.*, *men.*, κεφ. *t.*, κεφ., *pict.*, subscriptions with στίχοι (Mill).

56. Lincoln Coll. Oxon. 18 [XV or later] 4°, *chart.*, was presented about 1502 by Edmund Audley, Bishop of Salisbury: κεφ. *t.*, *prol.*, τίτλοι, and paragraphs *numbered* (viz. Matth. 127, Mark 74, Luke 130, John 67). Walton gives some various readings, but confounds it with Act. 33, Paul. 39, speaking of them as if one "vetustissimum exemplar." It has been recently inspected by Dobbin; (Mill).

57. (Act. 35, Paul. 41). Magdalen Coll. Oxon., Greek 9 [XII] 4°, in a small and beautiful hand. *Mut.* Mark i. 1—11; Rom.; 1, 2 Cor.; Psalms and Hymns follow the Epistles. It has κεφ. *t.*, τίτλοι, *lect.* Collated twice by Dr Hammond, the great commentator, whose papers seem to have been used for Walton's Polyglott (Magd. 1): also examined by Dobbin; (Mill).

58. Nov. Coll. Oxon. 68 [XV or later] 4°, is Walton's and Mill's N. 1. This, like Codd. 56—7, has been accurately examined by Dr Dobbin, for the purpose of his *Collation of the Codex Montfortianus* (London, 1854), with whose readings Codd. 56, 58 have been compared in 1922 places. He has undoubtedly proved the close connection subsisting between the three manuscripts (which had been observed by Mill, *Prol. N. T.* § 1388), though *pace viri tanti dixerim*, he may not have quite demonstrated that they must be direct transcripts from each other. *Syn.*, κεφ. *t.*, *prol.*, τίτλοι, with scholia. The writing is very careless, and those are in error who follow Walton in stating that it contains the Acts and Epistles (Walton's Polyglott, Mill, Dobbin).

*59. Gonville and Caius College, Cambridge, 403 [XII] 4°, an important copy, "textu notabili," as Tischendorf states (much like D. 61. 71), but carelessly written, and exhibiting no less than 81 omissions by ὁμοιοτέλευτον (*see p.* 9). It was very poorly examined for Walton's Polyglott, better though defectively by Mill, seen by Wetstein in 1716, minutely collated by Scrivener in 1860. It once belonged to the House of Friars Minor at Oxford, and was given to Gonville College by Th. Hatcher, M.A. in 1567. It has (whatever Walton asserts) τίτλοι, κεφ., *Am.*, but not *Eus.*, and exhibits many and rare *compendia scribendi*.

60. (Apoc. 10). Cambridge Public Library 553 or Dd. 9. 69 [A.D. 1297] 4°, but the Apocalypse later, and has a few scholia from Arethas about it. This copy is Mill's Moore 1[1], and is still badly known. *Carp.*, *Eus. t.*, *Am.* without *Eus. c.*, and is elegantly written (Mill). The Gospels appear to have been written in the East, the Apocalypse in the West of Europe.

*61. (Act. 34, Paul. 40, Apoc. 92). Codex Montfortianus at Trinity College, Dublin, G. 97 [XV or XVI] 8°, so celebrated in the controversy respecting 1 John v. 7. Its last collator, Dr Orlando Dobbin (*see on Cod.* 58), has discussed in his Introduction every point of interest connected with it. It contains the whole New Testament, apparently the work of three or four successive scribes, on 455 paper leaves, only one of them—that on which 1 Jo. v. 7 stands—being glazed[2], as if to protect it from harm. This manuscript was first heard of between the publication of Erasmus' second (1519) and third (1522) editions of his N. T., and after he had publicly declared, in answer to objectors, that if any *Greek* manuscript could be found containing the passage, he would insert it in his revision of the text; a promise which he fulfilled in 1522. Erasmus describes his authority as "Codex Britannicus," "apud Anglos repertus," and there is the fullest reason to believe that the Cod. Montfortianus is the copy referred to (*see below*, Chap. IX). Its earliest known owner was Froy, a Franciscan friar, then Thomas Clement [fl. 1569], then William Chark [fl. 1582], then Thomas Montfort, D.D. of Cambridge, from whom it derives its name, then Archbishop Ussher, who caused the collation to be made which appears in Walton's Polyglott (Matth. i. 1—Act. xxii. 29; Rom. i.), and presented the manuscript to Trinity College. Dr Barrett appended to his edition of Cod. Z (*see p.* 119) a full collation of the parts left untouched by his predecessors; but since the work of Ussher's friends was known to be very defective, Dobbin has re-collated the whole of that portion which Barrett left unexamined, comparing the readings throughout with Codd. 56, 58 of the Gospels, and Cod. 33 of the Acts. This copy has *τίτλοι*, *Am.*, and the number of *στίχοι* noted at the end of each book, besides which the division by the Latin chapters is employed, a sure proof—if any were needed—of the modern date of the manuscript. There are many corrections by a more recent hand, erasures by the pen, &c. It has been supposed that the Gospels were first written; then the Acts and Epistles (transcribed, in Dobbin's judgment, from Cod. 33); the Apocalypse last; having been added, as Dr Dobbin thinks, from Cod. 69 (*see p.* 151), when they were both in Chark's possession. The text, however, of the Apoca-

[1] On the death of Dr John Moore, Bishop of Ely, in 1714, George I. was induced to buy his books and manuscripts for the Public Library at Cambridge, in acknowledgment of the attachment of the University to the House of Hanover. Every one remembers the epigram which this royal gift provoked.

[2] "We often hear (said a witty and most Reverend Irish Prelate) that the text of the Three Heavenly Witnesses is a *gloss;* and any one that will go into the College Library may see as much for himself."

lypse is not quite the same in the two codices, nor would it be easy, without seeing them together, to verify Dobbin's conjecture, that the titles to the sacred books, in pale red ink, were added by the same person in both manuscripts.

62. Cambridge P. L. 2061 or Kk. 5. 35 [xv] 8°, *chart.*, *men.*, *lect.*, with the *Latin* chapters[1]. This is Walton's *Goog.*; it was brought from the East, and once belonged to Dr Henry Googe, Fellow of Trinity College. The collations of Cod. D. 59. 61. 62 made for the London Polyglott was given to Emmanuel College in 1667, where they yet remain.

63. Cod. Ussher 1, Trin. Coll. Dublin, A. I. 8 [x] fol., with a Commentary. A few extracts were contributed by Henry Dodwell to Bishop Fell's N. T. of 1675; Richard Bulkeley loosely collated it for Mill, Dr Dobbin in 1855 examined St Matthew, and the Rev. John Twycross, of the Charter House, re-collated the whole manuscript in 1858.

64. Ussher 2 belonged, like the preceding, to the illustrious Primate of Ireland, but has been missing from Trin. Coll. Library in Dublin ever since 1742. It was collated, like Cod. 63, by Dodwell for Fell, by Bulkeley for Mill, and with their reports we must now be content. It once belonged to Dr Thomas Goad, and was very neatly, though incorrectly, written in 8°. As the Emmanuel College copy of the Epistles (Act. 53, Paul. 30) never contained the Gospels, for which it is perpetually cited in Walton's Polyglott as *Em.*, the strong resemblance undoubtedly subsisting between *Usser.* 2 and *Em.* led even Mill to suspect that they were in fact the same copy. Since both codices (if they be two) are lost, we have examined both Walton's and Mill's collations with a view to this question. The result is that they are in numberless instances cited together in support of readings in company with other manuscripts; often with a very few or even alone (e. g. Mark ii. 2; iv. 1; ix. 10; 25; Luke iv. 32; viii. 27; Jo. iv. 24; v. 7; xvi. 19; xxi. 1). That *Usser.* 2 and *Em.* are sometimes alleged separately is easily accounted for by the inveterate want of accuracy exhibited by all early collators. Since Mill had access to the papers from which the Polyglott collations were drawn (*Proleg. N. T.* § 1505), we need not wonder if he largely *adds* to Walton's quotations from *Em.* (e. g. Mark viii. 35; xvi. 10; and *many* other places). A real difficulty would arise if *Em.* and *Usser.* 2 were cited as opposing witnesses; and inasmuch as the only two such cases we have been able to discover (Jo. viii. 2; xix. 31) may fairly be imputed to the error of one of the collators, it can hardly be doubted that the two codices are identical. Marsh's objections to this conclusion (*Notes to Michaelis*, Vol. II. pp. 800—802 and *Addenda*) seem by no means decisive.

65. Cod. Harleian. 5776, in the British Museum [XIII] 4°, is Mill's *Cov.* 1, brought from the East in 1677 with four other manuscripts of

[1] Such is Walton's meaning when, to Mill's sore perplexity (*N. T. Proleg.* § 1377), he writes "habet distinctionem ordinariorum κεφαλαίων, sed non quæ Eusebianis canonibus sunt accommodata."

the Greek Testament by Dr John Covell [1637—1722], once English Chaplain at Constantinople, afterwards Master of Christ's College, Cambridge. *Carp.*, *Eus. t.*, κεφ. *t.*, τίτλ., *Am.*, *Eus.*, στίχοι, subscriptions (Mill). This book was presented to Covell in 1674 by Daniel, Bishop of Proconesus. The last verse is supplied by a late hand, the concluding leaf being lost.

66. Cod. Galei Londinensis [no date assigned] 8°, once belonged to Th. Gale, High Master of St Paul's School, but is now lost. *Syn.*, *Carp.* (followed by five vacant leaves for *Eus. t.*), *lect.*, scholia. Known only to (Mill).

67. Bodleian. Miscell. 76 [XI] 4°, is Mill's Hunt. 2, brought from the East by Dr Robert Huntington. *Mut.* Jo. vi. 64—xxi. 25. Κεφ. *t.*, *Eus. c.*, *pict.*, *lect.* (Mill).

68. Lincoln. Coll. Oxon. 17 [XII] 8°, is Mill's Wheel. 1, brought from the East, with two other copies, by George Wheeler, Canon of Durham. *Carp.*, *Eus. t.*, *syn.*, κεφ. *t.*, κεφ. in margin, *Am.*, but not *Eus.* (Mill). The next copy is, after Codd. 1. 33, the most important of all the cursives.

*69. (Act. 31, Paul. 37, Apoc. 14). Codex Leicestrensis [XIV] fol., like Cod. 206, on parchment and paper (*see p.* 21), is now in the library of the Town Council of Leicester. It contains the whole New Testament, except Matth. i. 1—xviii. 15; Act. x. 45—xiv. 17; Jud. 7—25; Apoc. xviii. 7—xxii. 21, but with fragments down to xix. 10. It is written with a reed (*see p.* 24) on 212 complete leaves of 38 lines in a page, in the coarse and strange hand our *facsimile* exhibits (No. 35), *epsilon* being recumbent and almost like *alpha*, and the whole style of writing resembling a careless scrawl. The words Єιμι Ιλєρμου Χαρκου at the top of the first page, in the same beautiful hand that wrote many (*too* many) marginal notes, prove that this codex once belonged to the William Chark, mentioned under Cod. 61 (*p.* 149). In 1640 (Wetstein states 1669) Thomas Hayne, M.A. of Trussington, in that county, gave the book to the Leicester Library. Mill collated it there, as did John Jackson for Wetstein, and some others. Tregelles re-collated it in 1852 for his edition of the Greek Testament, and Scrivener very minutely in 1855; the latter published his results, with a full description of the book itself, in the Appendix to his "Codex Augiensis." No manuscript of its age has a text so remarkable as this: though none of the ordinary divisions into sections, and scarcely any liturgical marks occur throughout, there is evidently a close connection between Cod. 69 and the Church service-books, as well in the interpolations of proper names, particles of time, or whole passages (e. g. Luke xxii. 43, 44 placed after Matth. xxvi. 39) which are common to both, as especially in the titles of the Gospels: ἐκ τοῦ κατὰ μάρκον εὐαγγέλιον (*sic*), &c., being in the very language of the Lectionaries[1]. Tables of κεφάλαια stand before the three later Gospels, with very unusual variations; for which, as well as for the foreign matter inserted and

[1] See the style of the Evangelistaria, as cited above, pp. 68—70; Matthaei's uncials BH and Birch's 178 of the Gospels, described below.

other peculiarities of Cod. 69, see Scrivener's Cod. Augiensis (Introd. pp. XL—XLVII).

70. Cambridge P. L. 2144 or Ll. 2. 13 [XV] *chart.* (*not* in Trinity College), was written, like Codd. 17. 30, by G. Hermonymus for William Bodet, at Paris; it once belonged to Bunckle of London, then to Bp. Moore. Like Cod. 62 it has the Latin chapters (Mill).

71. Lambeth 528 [dated 1160] 265 leaves 4°, is Mill's *Eph.* and Scrivener's g. This elegant copy, which once belonged to an Archbishop of Ephesus, was brought to England in 1675 by Philip Traheron, English Chaplain at Smyrna. Traheron made a careful collation of his manuscript, of which both the rough copy (B. M., Burney 24) and a fair one (Lambeth 528 b) survive. This last Scrivener in 1845 compared with the original, and revised, especially in regard to later corrections, of which there are many. Mill used Traheron's collation very carelessly. *Carp., Eus. t., κεφ. t., τίτλοι, Am., Eus. c., lect.* This copy presents a text full of interest, and much superior to that of the mass of manuscripts.

72. Cod. Harleian. 5647 B. M. [XI] large 4°, an elegant copy with a catena on Matthew, *κεφ. t., τίτλ., κεφ., Am., Eus., pict.*, various readings in the ample margin. Lent by T. Johnson to (Wetstein).

73. Christ-Church Oxford, Wake 26 [XI] 4°, *Eus. t., κεφ. t., Am., Eus., pict.* It is marked "Ex dono Mauri Cordati Principis Hungaro-Walachiae," A° 1724. This and Cod. 74 were once Archbishop Wake's, and were collated for Wetstein by (Jo. Walker, *Wake MS.* 35)[1].

74. *ib.* Wake 20 [XIII] 4°, written by Theodore (*see p.* 37, *note* 2). *Mut.* Matth. i. 1—14; v. 29—vi. 1; 32 verses. It came in 1727 from the Monastery of Παντοκράτωρ, on Mount Athos. *Syn., Carp., Eus. t., τίτλ., κεφ., Am., Eus., lect.*

75. Cod. Genevensis 19 [XI] 4°, *prol., Eus. t., pict.* In text it much resembles Cod. 6. Seen in 1714 by Wetstein, collated by (Scholz, Cellérier, a Professor at Geneva).

76. (Act. 43, Paul. 49). Cod. Caesar-Vindobonensis, Nessel. 300, Lambec. 28 [XI] 4°, *prol., syn., pict.* This copy (the only one known to read αὐτῆς with the Complutensian and other editions in Luke ii. 22) is erroneously called uncial by Mill (Gerhard à Mastricht 1690; Ashe 1691; F. K. Alter 1786).

77. Caesar-Vindobon. Nessel. 114, Lambec. 29 [XI] 4°, very neat; with a Commentary, *prol., Eus. t., pict.*, and (by a later hand) *syn.*

[1] Of the 183 manuscript volumes bequeathed by William Wake, Archbishop of Canterbury [1657—1737] to Christ-Church (of which he had been a Canon), no less than 28 contain portions of the Greek Testament, not more than seven of which have ever appeared in any printed Catalogue. They are all described in the present and the next section from a comparison of Dean Gaisford's MS. Catalogue (1837) with the books themselves, to which Canon Jacobson's kindness gave me access.

It once belonged to Matthias Corvinus, the great King of Hungary (1458—90). Collated in "Tentamen descriptionis codicum," &c. 1773 by (Treschow, and by Alter).

78. Cod. Nicolae Jancovich de Vadass, now in Hungary [XII] 4°, *Eus. t., κεφ. t., τίτλοι, κεφ., lect., syn., pict.* It was once in the library of King Matthias Corvinus: on the sack of Buda by the Turks in 1527, his noble collection of 50,000 volumes was scattered, and about 1686 this book fell into the hands of S. B., then of J. G. Carpzov of Leipsic, at whose sale it was purchased and brought back to its former country. A previous possessor, in the 17th century, was Γεώργιος δεσμοφύλαξ Ναυπλίου. (Collated by C. F. Boerner for Kuster, and "in usum" of Scholz).

79. Cod. Geor. Douzæ (from Constantinople), consulted on John viii. by Gomar at Leyden (perhaps 74 in that Library). *Mut.* with a Latin version.

80. Cod. T. G. Grævii, then Jo. Van der Hagen's [XI], is probably still somewhere in Holland: it is said by Wetstein, who saw it in 1739, to have been collated by Bynæus in 1691. *Prol.*, τίτλοι, κεφ., subscriptions: the Latin chapters were added [XV].

81. Greek manuscripts cited in a Correctorium Bibliorum Latinorum of the XIIIth century[1].

82. Seven unknown Greek manuscripts of St John, three of St Matthew and (apparently) of the other Gospels, cited in Laurentius Valla's "Annotationes in N. T., ex diversorum utriusque linguae, Graecae et Latinae, codicum collatione," written about 1440, edited by Erasmus, Paris 1505. His copies seem modern, and have probably been used by later critics. The whole subject, however, is very carefully examined in the Rev. A. T. Russell's *Memoirs of the life and works of Bp. Andrewes*, pp. 282—310.

83. Cod. Monacensis 518 [XI] 4°, beautifully written, *syn.*, at Munich, whither it was brought from Augsburg (Bengel's August. 1, Scholz).

84. Monacensis 568 [XII] 8°, contains Matthew and Mark. *Mut.* Matth. i. 1—18; xiii. 10—27; 42—xiv. 3; xviii. 25—xix. 9; xxi. 33—xxii. 4; Mark vii. 13—xvi. 20 (Bengel's August. 2, Scholz).

85. Monacensis 569 [XIII] 4°, contains only Matth. viii. 15—ix. 17; xvi. 12—xvii. 20; xxiv. 26—45; xxvi. 25—54; Mark vi. 13—ix. 45; Luke iii. 12—vi. 44; John ix. 11—xii. 5; xix. 6—24; xx. 23—xxi. 9 (Bengel's August. 3, Scholz).

86. Cod. Posoniensis Lycaei Aug. [?]. *Prol., Eus. t.* Once at Buda, but bought in 1183 at Constantinople for the Emperor Alexius II. Comnenus (Bengel, Endlicher).

1 These formal revisions of the Latin Bible were mainly two, one made by the University of Paris with the sanction of the Archbishop of Sens about 1230, and a rival one undertaken by the Mendicant Orders, through Cardinal Hugo de S. Caro (*see above*, p. 59), and adopted at their general Chapter held at Paris in 1256. A Manuscript of the latter was used by Lucas Brugensis and Simon (Wetstein, N. T. Prol. Vol. I. p. 85).

87. Cod. Trevirensis [XII] fol., contains St John's Gospel with a catena, published at length by Cordier at Antwerp. It once belonged to the eminent scholar and mathematician, Cardinal Nicholas of Cuza, on the Moselle, near Trèves [1401—64: *see* Cod. 129]; previously to the monastery of Petra or the Fore-runner at Constantinople[1] (Scholz). Westein's 87 is our 250.

88. Codex of the Gospels, 4°, on vellum, cited as ancient and correct by Joachim Camerarius (who collated it) in his Annotations to the New Testament. It resembles in text Codd. 63. 72. 80.

89. Cod. Gottingensis [dated 1006] fol., with corrections. Collated by A. G. Gehl in 1739, and by Matthaei (No. 20).

90. (Act. 47, Paul. 14). Cod. Jo. Fabri, a Dominican of Deventer [XVI, but copied from a manuscript written by Theodore (*p.* 37, *note* 2) and dated 1293] 4°, *chart.* 2 vol. The Gospels stand John, Luke, Matthew, Mark, the Pauline Epistles precede the Acts; and Jude is written twice, from different copies. This codex (which has belonged to Abr. Hinckelmann of Hamburg, and to Wolff) was collated by Wetstein. Faber [1472—living in 1515] had also compared it with another "very ancient" vellum manuscript of the Gospels presented by Sixtus IV. (1471—84) to Jo. Wessel of Groningen, but which was then at Zvolle. As might be expected, this copy much resembles Cod. 74.

91. Cod. Perronianus [X], of which extracts were sent by Montfaucon to Mill, had been Cardinal Perron's, and before him had belonged to "S. Taurini monasterium Ebroicense" (Evreux).

92. Cod. Faeschii 1 (Act. 49) }
94. Cod. Faeschii 2 } The former contains Mark with Victor's Commentary on vellum, the latter Mark and Luke with a Commentary, on paper. Both belonged to Andrew Faesch, of Basle, and were collated by Wetstein. Their date is not stated.

93. Cod. Grævii of the Gospels, cited by Voss on the Genealogy, Luke iii.

95. Lincoln Coll. Oxon. 16 [XII] fol., is Mill's Wheeler 2. It contains Luke from xi. 2 and John all but 2 or 3 leaves. With Scholia, *syn.* (Mill, Professor Nicoll).

96. Cod. Bodleian. Misc. 8 (Auct. D. 5. 1) [XV] 12°, is Walton's and Mill's *Trit.*, with many rare readings, containing St John with a Commentary, beautifully written by Jo. Trithemius, Abbot of Spanheim [d. 1516]. Received from Abraham Sculter [?] by Geo. Hackwell, 1607 (Walton's Polyglott, Mill, Griesbach).

97. Cod. Hirsaugiensis [1500, by Nicholas, a monk of Hirsau], 12°, on vellum, containing St John, seems but a copy of 96. It once

[1] On fol. 4 we read *ἡ βίβλος αὕτη* (*ἥδε* 178) *τῆς μονῆς τοῦ Προδρόμου* | *τῆς κειμένης ἔγγιστα τῆς Ἀε[αι]τίου* | *ἀρχαϊκὴ δὲ τῇ μονῇ κλῆσις Πέτρα.* Compare Cod. 178 and Montfauc. Palaeogr. Graeca, pp. 39, 110, 305.

belonged to Uffenbach, and is now at Giessen (Bengel[1], Wetstein, Maius, Schulze).

98. Cod. Bodleian. [xii] 4°, *pict.*, E. D. Clarke 5, by whom it was brought from the East. Κεφ. *t.*, τίτλ., *Am.* (not *Eus.*), κεφ., *lect.* It was collated in a few places for Scholz, who substituted it here for Cod. R. (*see p.* 114) of Griesbach.

99. Cod. Lipsiensis, Bibliothec. Paul. [xvi] 4°, Matthaei's 18, contains Matth. iv. 8—v. 27; vi. 2—xv. 30; Luke i. 1—13; *syn.* (Matthaei). Wetstein's 99 is our 155.

100. Cod. Paul. L. B. de Eubeswald [x] 4°, vellum, *mut.* Jo. xxi. 25; *pict.*, κεφ. *t.*, *Eus. t.*, and in a later hand many corrections with scholia and *syn.*, *chart.* J. C. Wagenseil used it in Hungary for Jo. viii. 6. Our description presumes it to be the manuscript now in the University of Pesth, but in the 15th century belonging to Bp. Jo. Pannonius.

101. Cod. Uffenbach. 3 [xvi] 12°, *chart.*, St John στιχήρης (*see p.* 46). So near the Basle (that is, we suppose, Erasmus') edition, that Bengel never cites it. With two others (Paul. M and 52) it was lent by Z. C. Uffenbach, Consul of Frankfort-on-the-Mayn, to Wetstein in 1717, and afterwards to Bengel.

102. Cod. Bibliothecae Medicaeae, a valuable but unknown manuscript with many rare readings, extracted by Wetstein at Amsterdam for Matth. xxiv—Mark viii. 1, from the margin of a copy of Plantin's N. T. 1591, in the library of J. le Long. The Rev. B. F. Westcott is convinced that the manuscript from which these readings were derived is none other than Cod. B. itself.

103. Regius 196 [xi] fol., once Cardinal Mazarin's, seems the same manuscript as that from which Emericus Bigot gave extracts to Curcellaeus' N. T. 1658 (Scholz).

104. Cod. Hieronymi Vignerii [x], from which also Bigot extracted readings, which Wetstein obtained through J. Drieberg in 1744, and published.

105. (Act. 48, Paul. 24). Cod. Ebnerianus, Bodl. Miscell. 136, a beautiful copy [xii] 4°, on 426 leaves of vellum, with 27 lines in each, formerly belonged to Jerome Ebner von Eschenbach of Nuremberg. *Pict.*, *Carp.*, *Eus. t.*, κεφ. *t.*, τίτλ., κεφ., *Am.* (not *Eus.*), the Nicene Creed, all in gold: *syn.*; with *lect.* throughout and *syn.*, *men.* prefixed by Joasaph, a calligraphist, A.D. 1391, who also added John viii. 3—11 at the end of that Gospel. *Facsimile* in Horne's Introduction, and in Tregelles' Horne p. 220 (Schoenleben 1738, Rev. H. O. Coxe).

106. Cod. Winchelsea [x], with many important readings, often resembling the Philoxenian Syriac: believed to be still in the Earl of Winchelsea's Library (Jackson collated it for Wetstein in 1748).

107. Cod. Bodleian. [xiv. and later] 4°, is E. D. Clarke 6, con-

[1] Though 97 once belonged to Uffenbach, 101 better suits Bengel's description of Uffen. 3: they are written on different materials, and the description of their respective texts will not let us suspect them to be the same.

taining the Gospels in different hands: *κεφ. t.*, *pict.* (Like 98, 111, 112, *partially* collated for Scholz). Griesbach's 107 is also 201.

108. Caesar-Vindobonensis, Kollar. 4, Forlos. 5 [XI] fol., 2 vol. With a commentary, *Eus. t.*, *pict.* It seems to have been written at Constantinople, and formerly belonged to Parrhasius, then to the convent of St John de Carbonaria at Naples (Treschow, Alter, Birch, Scholz).

109. Brit. Mus. Addit. 5117 [A. D. 1326] 4°, *syn.*, *Eus. t.*, *men.*, *lect.*, *τίτλοι*, *Am.* (not *Eus.*, *κεφ.*), Mead. 1, then Askew (5115 is Act. 22, 5116 is Paul. 75, in the same hand; different from that employed in the Gospels).

110. Cod. Ravianus, Bibl. Reg. Berolinensis [XVI] 4°, 2 vols., on parchment, once belonging to Jo. Rave of Upsal, has been examined by Wetstein, Griesbach, and G. G. Pappelbaum in 1796. It contains the whole New Testament, and has attracted attention because it has the disputed words in 1 Jo. v. 7. It is now however admitted by all to be a mere transcript of the N. T. in the Complutensian Polyglott with variations from Erasmus or Stephens, and as such should be expunged from our list.

111. Cod. Bodleian. [XII] 4°, Clarke 7, *mut.* Jo. xx. 25—xxi. 25: *κεφ. t.*, *Am.* (not *Eus.*), and

112. Bodleian. [XI] 12°, Clarke 10, *Carp.*, *Eus. t.*, *κεφ. t.*, *τίτλ.*, *Am.* and *Eus.* often in the same line (a very rare arrangement; *see* Wake 21 *below*), *lect.*, *syn.*, *men.*, a very beautiful copy. These two, very partially collated for Scholz, were substituted by him and Tischendorf for collations whose history is not a little curious.

111. (Wetstein). THE VELESIAN READINGS. The Jesuit de la Cerda inserted in his "Adversaria Sacra," cap. XCI (Lyons 1626) a collection of various readings, written in vermilion in the margin of a *Greek* Testament (which from its misprint in 1 Pet. iii. 11, we know to be R. Stephens' of 1550) by Pedro Faxardo, Marquis of Velez, a Spaniard, who had taken them from sixteen manuscripts, eight of which were in the king's library, in the Escurial. It is never stated what codices or how many support each variation. De la Cerda had received the readings from Mariana, the great Jesuit historian of Spain, then lately dead, and appears to have inadvertently added to Mariana's account of their origin, that the sixteen manuscripts were in Greek. These Velesian readings, though suspected from the first even by Mariana by reason of their strange resemblance to the Latin Vulgate and the manuscripts of the Old Latin, were repeated as critical authorities in Walton's Polyglott, 1657, and (contrary to his own better judgment) were retained by Mill in 1707. Wetstein, however (N. T. Proleg. Vol. I. pp. 59—61), and after him Michaelis and Bp. Marsh, have abundantly proved that the various readings must have been collected by Velez from *Latin* manuscripts, and by him translated into Greek, very foolishly perhaps, but not of necessity with a fraudulent design. Certainly, any little weight the Velesian readings may have, must be referred to the Latin, not to the Greek text. Among the various proofs of their Latin origin urged by Wetstein

and others, the following establish the fact beyond the possibility of doubt:

	Greek Text.	Vulgate Text.	Vulgate various reading.	Velesian reading.
Mark viii. 38.	ἐπαισχύνθῃ	confusus fuerit	confessus fuerit	ὁμολογήσῃ
Hebr. xii. 18.	κεκαυμένῳ	accensibilem	accessibilem	προσιτῷ
— xiii. 2.	ἔλαθον	latuerunt	placuerunt	ἤρεσαν
James v. 6.	κατεδικάσατε	addixistis	adduxistis	ἠγάγετε
Apoc. xix. 6.	ὄχλου	turbae	tubae	σάλπιγγος
— xxi. 12.	ἀγγέλους	angelos	angulos	γωνίας

112. (Wetstein). THE BARBERINI READINGS must also be banished from our list of critical authorities, though for a different reason. The collection of various readings from 22 manuscripts (ten of the Gospels, eight of the Acts and Epistles, and four of the Apocalypse), seen by Isaac Vossius in 1642 in the Barberini Library at Rome, was first published in 1673, by Peter Possinus (Poussines), a Jesuit, at the end of a Catena of St Mark. He alleged that the collations were made by John M. Caryophilus [d. 1635], a Cretan, while preparing an edition of the Greek Testament, under the patronage of Paul V. [d. 1621] and Urban VIII. [d. 1644]. As the Barberini readings often favour the Latin version, they fell into the same suspicion as the Velesian: Wetstein, especially (Proleg. Vol. I. pp. 61, 62), after pressing against them some objections more ingenious than solid, declares "lis haec non aliter quam ipsis libris Romae inventis et productis, *quod nunquam credo fiet*, solvi potest." The very papers Wetstein called for were discovered by Birch (Barberini Lib. 209) more than thirty years later, and besides them Caryophilus' petition for the loan of six manuscripts from the Vatican (Codd. BS. 127. 129. 141. 144), which he doubtless obtained and used. The good faith of the collator being thus happily vindicated, we have only to identify his thirteen remaining codices, most of them *probably* being in that very Library, and may then dismiss the Barberini readings as having done their work, and been fairly superseded.

113. Cod. Harleian. 1810 Brit. Mus. [XI] 4°, *prol.*, *Carp.*, *Eus. t.*, *pict.*, *lect.*, *κεφ. t.*, *τίτλ.*, *κεφ.*, *Am.*, *Eus.*, and (in a later hand) *syn.* (Griesbach, Bloomfield): its readings are of more than usual interest, as are those of

114. Harleian. 5540 [XIII] 12°, (*facsimile* in a Greek Testament, published in 1837 by Taylor, London), very elegant, with more recent marginal notes and Matth. xxviii. 19—Mark i. 12 in a later hand. *Mut.* Matth. xvii. 4—18; xxvi. 59—73 (Griesbach, Bloomfield). *Carp.*, *κεφ. t.*, *τίτλ.*, *κεφ.*, *Am.* (not *Eus.*).

115. Harleian. 5559 [XII] 4°, once Bernard Mould's (Smyrna, 1724), with an unusual text. *Mut.* Matth. i. 1—viii. 10; Mark v. 23—36; Luke i. 78—ii. 9; vi. 4—15; John xi. 2—xxi. 25 (Griesbach, Bloomfield). A few more words of John xi. survive: *τίτλ.*, *κεφ.*, *Am.*, and sometimes *Eus.*[1]

[1] In Cod. 115 *Eus.* is usually, in Codd. 116 and 117 but rarely written under *Am.*: these copies therefore were never quite finished.

116. Harleian. 5567 [XII] small 4°, *Eus. t.*, *κεφ. t.*, *τίτλ.*, *Am.*, *lect.*, *syn.*, of some value. It belonged in 1649 to Athanasius a Greek monk, then to B. Mould (Griesbach, Bloomfield).

117. (Apost. 6). Harleian. 5731 [XV] 4°, *chart.*, carelessly written, once belonged to the great Bentley. *Mut.* Matth. i. 1—18: *lect.*, *pict.*, *Carp.*, *Eus. t.*, *κεφ. t.*, *τίτλ.*, *Am.*, *syn.*, fragments of a Lectionary on the last twenty leaves (Griesbach, Bloomfield).

*118. Bodleian. Miscell. 13, Marsh. 24 [XIII] 4°, an important *palimpsest (with the Gospels uppermost)* once the property of Archbishop Marsh of Armagh. *Am.*, *Eus.*, *κεφ. t.*, *lect.* with *syn.*, *men.*, and some of the Psalms on paper. Later hands also supplied Matth. i. 1—vi. 2; Luke xiii. 35—xiv. 20; xviii. 8—xix. 9; John xvi. 25—xxi. 25. Well collated by (Griesbach).

119. Regius 85, Paris [XII] 4°, formerly Teller's of Rheims, is Kuster's Paris 5 (Griesbach).

120. Regius 185 a [XIII] 4°, formerly belonged to St Victor's on the Walls, Paris, and seems to be Stephens' ιδ', whose text (1550) and Colinaeus' (1534) it closely resembles. St Mark is wanting (Griesbach).

121. An important lost codex, once at St Geneviève's, in Paris [dated Sept. 1284, Indiction 12], 4°. *Mut.* Matth. v. 21—viii. 24 (Griesbach).

122. (Act. 177, Paul. 219). Bibl. Lugdunensis-Batavorum [XII] 4°, once Meermann's[1] 116. *Mut.* Act. i. 1—14; xxi. 14—xxii. 28; 1 Jo. iv. 20—Jud. 25; Rom. i. 1—vii. 13; 1 Cor. ii. 7—xiv. 23 (Dermout, Collect. Crit. I. p. 14). Griesbach's 122 is also 97.

123. Caesar-Vindobon. Nessel. 240, Lambec. 30 [XI] 4°, brought from Constantinople by Auger Busbeck; *prol.*, *Eus. t.*, *pict.*, corrections by another hand (Treschow, Alter, Birch).

*124. Caesar-Vindobon. Nessel. 118, Lambec. 31 [XII] 4°, *Eus. t.*, *syn.*, *mut.* Luke xxiii. 31—xxiv. 28, an eclectic copy, with corrections by the first hand (Mark ii. 14; Luke iii. 1, &c). This manuscript (which once belonged to a certain Leo) is considered by Birch the best of the Vienna codices; it resembles the Philoxenian Syriac, old Latin, Codd. DL. I. 13, and especially 69 (Treschow, Alter, Birch).

125. Caesar-Vindobon. Kollar. 6, Forlos. 16 [X] 4°, with many corrections in the margin and between the lines (Treschow, Alter, Birch).

126. Cod. Guelpherbytanus XVI. 16 [XI] carelessly written. *Eus. t.*, *κεφ. t.*, *prol.*, *pict.*, with *lect.*, *syn.* in a later hand, and some quite modern corrections. Matth. xxviii. 18—20 is cruciform, capitals

[1] Meermann's other two manuscripts of the N. T. dispersed at his sale in 1824, are No. 117, 436 of the Gospels (also set down in error as Evangelistarium 153), and No. 118 at Middle-Hill (Act. 178, Paul. 242, Apoc. 87).

often occur in the middle of words, and the text is of an unusual character. Inspected by (Heusinger 1752, Knittel, Tischendorf).

N.B. Codd. 127—181, all at Rome, were inspected, and a few (127. 131. 157) really collated by Birch, when at Rome about 1782. Of 153 Scholz collated the greatest part, and small portions of 138—44; 146—52; 154—57; 159—60; 162; 164—71; 173—75; 177—80.

127. Cod. Vatican. 349 [XI] fol., *Eus. t.*, κεφ. *t.*, a neatly written and important copy, with a few later corrections (e. g. Matth. xxvii. 49).

128. Vat. 356 [XI] fol., *prol.*, κεφ. *t.*, and the numbers of the στίχοι.

129. Vat. 358 [XII] fol., with scholia, and a note on Jo. vii. 53, as we read in Cod. 145 and others. Bought at Constantinople in 1438 by Nicholas de Cuza, Eastern Legate to the Council of Ferrara (*see* Cod. 87).

130. Vat. 359 [XIII] fol., *chart.*, a curious copy, with the Greek and Latin in parallel columns, and the Latin chapters.

131. (Act. 70, Paul. 77, Apoc. 66). Vat. 360 [XI] 4°, contains the whole New Testament, with many remarkable variations, and a text somewhat like that of Aldus' Greek Testament (1518). The manuscript was given to Sixtus V. [1585—90] for the Vatican by "Aldus Manuccius Paulli F. Aldi." The Epistle to the Hebrews stands before 1 Tim. *Carp.*, *Eus. t.*, κεφ. *t.*, of an unusual arrangement (viz. Matth. 74, Mark 46, Luke 57: *see above, p.* 49). This copy contains many itacisms, and corrections *primâ manu.*

132. Vat. 361 [XI] 4°, *Eus. t.*, *pict.*

133. (Act. 71, Paul. 78). Vat. 363 [XI?] 4°, *syn.*, Euthalian prologues.

134. Vat. 364 [XI?] 4°, elegant. *Eus. t.*, *pict.*, titles in gold.

135. Vat. 365 [XI?] 4°, κεφ. *t.*, *pict.* The first 26 of its 174 leaves are later and *chart.*

136. Vat. 665 [XIII] fol., on cotton paper; contains Matthew and Mark with Euthymius' Commentary.

137. Vat. 756 [XI or XII] fol., with a Commentary. At the end we read κσ φραγκισκος ακκιδας ευγενης κολασσευς...ρωμη ηγαγε το παρον βιβλιον ετει απο αδαμ ζϡα [A. D. 1583], μηνι ιουλιῳ, ινδ. ια.

138. Vat. 757 [XII] fol., with Commentary from Origen, &c.

139. Vat. 758 [XII] fol., contains Luke and John with a Commentary.

140. Vat. 1158 [XII] 4°, beautifully written, and given by the Queen of Cyprus to Innocent VII. (1404—6). *Eus. t.*, *pict.* In Luke i. 64 it supports the Complutensian reading, καὶ ἡ γλῶσσα αὐτοῦ διηρθρώθη.

141. (Act. 75, Paul. 86, Apoc. 40). Vat. 1160 [XIII] 4°, 2 vol. contains the whole New Testament, *syn.*, *pict.* The leaves are arranged in quaternions, but separately for each volume.

142. (Act. 76, Paul. 87). Vat. 1210 [XI] 12°, very neat, containing also the Psalms. There are many marginal readings in another ancient hand.

143. Vat. 1229 [XI] fol., with a marginal Commentary. On the first leaf is read της ορθης πιστεως πιστῳ οικονομῳ και φυλακι Παυλῳ τετάρτῳ [1555—59].

144. Vat. 1254 [XI] 8°, *Eus. t.*, κεφ. *t.*

145. Vat. 1548 [XIII] 4°, contains Luke and John. *Mut.* Luke iv. 15—v. 36; Jo. i. 1—26. A later hand has written Luke xvii—xxi, and made many corrections.

146. Palatino-Vatican. 5[1] [XII] fol., contains Matth. and Mark with a Commentary.

147. Palat.-Vat. 89 [XI] 8°, *syn.*

148. Palat.-Vat. 136 [XIII] 4°, with some scholia and unusual readings.

149. (Act. 77, Paul. 88, Apoc. 25). Palat.-Vat. 171 [XIV] fol., *lect.*, contains the whole New Testament.

150. Palat.-Vat. 189 [XI] 16°, *Eus. t.*, *syn.*

151. Palat.-Vat. 220 [XI] 4°, *Eus. t.*, scholia in the margin, and some rare readings (e.g. Jo. xix. 14). The sheets are in 21 quaternions. After Matthew stands εκλογη εν συντομω εκ των συντεθεντων ὑπο Ευσεβιου προς Στεφανον λ.

152. Palat.-Vat. 227 [XIII] 4°, *prol.*, *pict.*

153. Palat.-Vat. 229 [XIII] 4°, on cotton paper. *Prol.*, *syn.*

154. Cod. Alexandrino-Vatican. vel Christinae 28 [*dated* April 14, 1442] 4°, written in Italy on cotton paper, with Theophylact's Commentary. It was given by Christina Queen of Sweden to Alexander VIII. (1689—91).

155. Alex.-Vat. 79 [XI? Birch, XIV Scholz] 12°, with some lessons from St Paul prefixed. Given by Andrew Rivet to Rutgersius, Swedish Embassador to the United Provinces. This copy is Wetstein's 99, the codex Rutgersii cited by Dan. Heinsius in his Exercitat. sacr. in Evangel.

156. Alex.-Vat. 189 [XII] 12°: "ex bibliothecâ Goldasti" is on the first page.

157. Cod. Urbino-Vat. 2 [XII] 8°, deemed by Birch the most important manuscript of the N. T. in the Vatican, except Cod. B. It belonged to the Ducal Library at Urbino, and was brought to Rome by Clement VII. (1523—34). It is very beautifully written on 325 leaves of vellum (Birch, N. T. 1788, gives a *facsimile*), with

[1] A collection presented to Urban VIII. (1623—44) by Maximilian, Elector of Bavaria, from the spoils of the unhappy Elector Palatine, titular King of Bohemia.

Eus. t., *prol.*, certain chronicles, κεφ., τίτλοι and rich ornaments, pictures, &c. in vermilion and gold. On fol. 19 we read underneath two figures Ιωαννης εν χω τω θω πιστος βασιλευς πορφυρογεννητος και αυτοκρατωρ ῥωμαιων, ὁ Κομνηνος, and Αλεξιος εν χω τω θω πιστος βασιλευς πορφυρογεννητος ὁ Κομνηνος. The Emperor John II. the Handsome succeeded his father, the great Alexius, A.D. 1118. For the subscriptions appended to the Gospels in this copy (which also register the number of στίχοι in each of them), see above, p. 47. In text it is akin to Codd. BDL. 69. 106, and especially to 1.

158. Cod. Pii II., Vatic. 53 [XI] 4°, with *Eus. t.*, κεφ. *t.*, and readings in the margin, *primâ manu*. This copy was given to the Library by Pius II. (1458—64).

159. Cod. Barberinianus 8 [XI] 4°, in the Barberini Palace, at Rome, founded above two centuries since by the Cardinal, Francis II, of that name.

160. Barberin. 9 [*dated* 1123] 4°, *syn.*

161. Barberin. 10 [X] 4°, *ending* at Jo. xvi. 4. This copy follows the Latin versions both in its text (Jo. iii. 6) and marginal scholia (Jo. vii. 29). Various readings are often thus noted in its margin.

162. Barberin. 11 [*dated* 13 May, 1153 (ϛχξα), Indict. 1] 4°, written by one Manuel: *Eus. t.*, *pict.*

163. Barberin. 12 [XI] fol., written in Syria. Scholz says it contains only the portions of the Gospels read in Church-lessons, but Birch the four Gospels, with *Eus. t*, κεφ. *t.*, the numbers of ῥήματα and στίχοι to the first three Gospels (*see p.* 57, *note*).

164. Barberin. 13 [*dated* Oct. 1040] 8°, *Eus. t.*, κεφ. *t.*, *syn.*, and numbers of στίχοι. The subscription states that it was written by Leo, a priest and calligrapher, and bought in 1168 by Bartholomew, who compared it with ancient Jerusalem manuscripts on the sacred mount.

165. Barberin. 14 [*dated* 1197] fol., with the Latin Vulgate version, *Eus. t.*, κεφ. *t.*, *syn.* Written for one Archbishop Paul, and given to the Library by Eugenia, daughter of Jo. Pontanus.

166. Barberin. 115 [XIII] 4°, containing only Luke ix. 33—xxiv. 24 and John.

167. Barberin. 208 [XII or XIV] 12°, κεφ. *t.*, *pict.*, subscriptions numbering the στίχοι.

168. Barberin. 211 [XIII] fol., with Theophylact's Commentary.

169. Cod. Vallicellianus B. 133 [XI] 12°, once the property of Achilles Statius, as also was Cod. 171. *Prol.*, *syn.*, *pict.* This codex and the next three are in the Library of St Maria in Vallicella at Rome, and belong to the Fathers of the Oratory of St Philippo Neri.

170. Vallicell. C. 61 [XIII] 4°, *syn.* The end of Luke and most of John is in a later hand.

171. Vallicell. C. 73 [XIV] 8°. Montfaucon ascribes it to [XI].

172. Vallicell. F. 90 [XII] 4°, now only contains the Pentateuch, but from Blanchini, Evan. Quadr. Pt. I. pp. 529—30, we infer that the Gospels were once there.

173. Vatic. 1983, Basil. 22 [XI or XIII] 4°, ending John xiii. 1, seems to have been written in Asia Minor. *Lect.*, *syn.*, *Eus. t.*, the number of ῥήματα and στίχοι being appended to the first three Gospels as in Codd. 163; 164; 167. This codex, and the next four, were brought from the Library of the Basilian monks.

174. Vatic. 2002, Basil. 41 [*dated* 4th hour of Sept. 2, A.D. 1053] 4°, *mut.* Matth. i. 1—ii. 1; Jo. i. 1—27; ending viii. 47. Written by the monk Constantine "tabernis habitante," "cum praeesset praefecturae Georgilas dux Calabriae" (Scholz).

175. (Act. 41, Paul. 194, Apoc. 20) Vat. 2080, Basil. 119 [XII] 4°, contains the whole New Testament (beginning Matth. iv. 17) with scholia to the Acts, between which and the Catholic Epistle stands the Apocalypse (*see p.* 62). There are some marginal corrections *primâ manu* (e.g. Luke xxiv. 13). The Pauline Epistles have Euthalius' subscriptions. Also inspected by Blanchini.

176. Vat. 2113, Basil. 152 [XIII] 4°, *lect.* Begins Matth. x. 13, ends Jo. ii. 1.

177. Vat.?, Basil. 163 [XI] 8°, *mut.* Jo. i. 1—29.

178. Cod. Angelicus A. 1. 5 [XII] fol. *Eus. t.*, *mut.* Jo. xxi. 17—25. Arranged in quaternions, and the titles to the Gospels resemble those in Cod. 69. Codd. 178—9 belong to the Angelica convent of Augustinian Eremites at Rome. Montfaucon (*Palaeogr. Graeca*, pp. 290—1) describes and gives a *facsimile* of Cod. 178. It has on the first leaf the same subscription as we gave under Cod. 87: which Birch and Scholz misunderstand.

179. Angelic. A. 4. 11 [XII] 4°, *Eus. t.*, κεφ. *t.*, *lect.* The last five leaves (214—18) and two others (23, 30) are *chart.*, and in a later hand.

180. (Act. 82, Paul. 92, Apoc. 44) Cod. Bibl. Propagandae 250, Borgiae 2 [XI] 8°, *lect.*; the Gospels were written by one Andreas: the rest of the New Testament and some apocryphal books by one John, November 1284. This manuscript, with Cod. T and Evst. 37, belonged to the Velitran Museum of "Praesul Steph. Borgia, Collegii Urbani de Propaganda Fide a secretis."

181. Cod. Francisci Xavier, Cardinal. de Zelada [XI] fol., with scholia in the margin. This manuscript (from which Birch took extracts) seems now missing.

Codd. 182—198, all in that noble Library at Florence, founded by Cosmo de Medici [d. 1464], increased by his grandson Lorenzo [d. 1492], were very slightly examined by Birch, and subsequently by Scholz.

182. Cod. Laurentianus VI. 11 [XII] 4°.

183. Laurent. VI. 14 [XII] 8°, *pict.*, *Eus. t.*, *men.*, at the end of which is τέλος σὺν Θεῷ ἁγίῳ τοῦ μηνολογίου, ἀμήν· ϛ υιη [i.e. A.D. 910],

which Scholz refers to the date of the *arrangement* of the menology. It might seem more naturally to belong to the manuscript itself.

184. Laurent. VI. 15 [XIII] 4°, *prol.*

185. Laurent. VI. 16 [XII] 4°, *prol.*, *syn.*; written by one Basil.

186. Laurent. VI. 18 [XI] fol., *prol.*, *Eus. t.*, Commentary; written by Leontius, a calligrapher.

187. Laurent. VI. 23 [XII] 4°, *pict.*, with readings in the margin by the first hand.

188. Laurent. VI. 25 [XI] 8°, *syn.*

189. (Act. 141, Paul. 239). Laurent. VI. 27 [XII] 12°, *prol.*, *syn.*, *mut.* at end of John.

190. Laurent. VI. 28 [*dated* July 1285, Ind. 13] 8°.

191. Laurent. VI. 29 [XIII] 8°, *prol.*

192. Laurent. VI. 30 [XIII] 12°, *prol.*

193. Laurent. VI. 32 [XI] 8°, *Eus. t.*, *pict.*, *lect.*

194. Laurent. VI. 33 [XI] fol., *pict.*, and a marginal Catena. Begins Matth. iii. 7.

195. Laurent. VI. 34 [XI] fol., once belonged to the Cistercian convent of S. Salvator de Septimo. *Prol.*, *syn.*, and a Commentary. The date of the year is lost, but the month (May) and indiction (8) remain.

196. Laurent. VIII. 12 [XII] 4°, in red letters (*see* p. 138, *note* 2), *pict.*, with a catena.

197. (Act. 96) Laurent. VIII. 14 [XI] fol., contains the Epistle of James and fragments of Matthew and Mark, with Chrysostom's Commentary.

198. Laurent. 256 [XIII] 4°, on cotton paper, *Eus. t.*, from the library "Ædilium Flor. Ecc."

Codd. 199—203 were inspected, rather than collated, by Birch at Florence; the first two in the Benedictine library of St Maria; the others in that of St Mark, belonging to the Dominican Friars. Scholz could not find any of them, but 201 is Wetstein's 107, Scrivener's m; and 202 is now in the British Museum, Addit. 14774.

199. Cod. S. Mariae, 5 [XII] 4°, *Eus. t.*, with iambic verses and scholia.

200. S. Mariae 6 [X] 4°, *pict.*, *Eus. t.*, *prol.*, *syn.*, with fragments of Gregory against the Arians.

*201. (Act. 91, Paul. 104, Apoc. b^{scr}, or Kelly 94) Cod. Praedicator. S. Marci 701 [*dated* Oct. 7, 1357, Ind. 11], large fol., on 492 leaves. This splendid copy was purchased for the British Museum (where it is numbered Butl. 2, or Addit. 11837) from the heirs of Dr Samuel Butler, Bishop of Lichfield. It contains the whole New Testament; was first cited by Wetstein (107) from notices by Jo. Lamy, in his "de Eruditione Apostolorum," Florence, 1738, glanced at by Birch, and stated by Scholz (N. T. Vol. II. pp. XII, XXVIII) to have been cursorily collated by himself: how that is possible can hardly be understood, as he elsewhere professes his ignorance where the manuscript had gone (N. T. Vol. I. p. LXXII). Scrivener collated the whole volume. There are many changes by a later hand, also *syn.*, *κεφ. t.*, *κεφ.*, *Am.*, *Eus.*, *lect.*, *prol.*, and some foreign matter.

202. Praedicat. S. Marci 705 [XII] 4°, *syn.*

203. Praedicat. S. Marci 707 [XV] 4°, *chart.*, is really in modern Greek. Birch cites it for Jo. vii. 53, but it ought to be expunged from the list.

204. (Act. 92, Paul. 105) Bononiensis Canonic. Regular. 640 [XI] at Bologna (Birch, Scholz).

Codd. 205—217 at Venice, were slightly examined by Birch.

205. (Act. 93, Paul. 106, Apoc. 88) Venet. S. Marci 5 [XV] fol., contains both Testaments, with many peculiar readings. It was written for Cardinal Bessarion (apparently by John Rhosen his librarian), the donor of all these books. C. F. Rink considers it in the *Gospels* a mere copy of Cod. 209 ("Lucubratio Critica in Act. Apost. Epp. C. et P.," Basileae, 1830).

206. (Act. 94, Paul. 107) Venet. 6 [XV] fol., like Cod. 69, is partly on parchment, partly on paper. It contains the whole New Testament, but is not numbered for the Apocalypse.

207. Venet. 8 [X] 4°, *Carp.*, *Eus. t.*, *syn.*, *mut.* at the beginning.

208. Venet. 9 [X] 8°, *Eus. t.*, *κεφ. t.*, of some value, but far less than the important

209. (Act. 95, Paul. 108, Apoc. 46) Venet. 10 [XV] 8°, of the whole New Testament, once Bessarion's, who had it with him at the Council of Florence, 1439, and wrote many notes in it. It would seem that in the Gospels and Apocalypse either Cod. 205 is copied from 209, or *vice versâ*. Rink, who collated them for the Acts and Epistles, states that they differ in those portions. A good collation of one or both is needed; Birch did little, Engelbreth gave him some readings, and Fleck has published *part* of a collation by Heimbach. In the Gospels it is very like Cod. B. The Apocalypse has *prol.* For the unusual order of the books, see above, p. 61.

210. Venet. 27 [X] fol., with a catena.

211. Venet. 539 [XII] 4°, *mut.*, with an Arabic version.

212. Venet. 540 [XII] 8°.

213. Venet. 542 [XI] 8°.

214. Venet. 543 [XIV] 8°, *chart.*, *syn.*

215. Venet. 544 [XI] fol., *Carp.*, *Eus. t.*, with a Commentary.

216. Codex Canonici, brought by him from Corcyra to St Mark's, in a small character [no date assigned].

217. Venet. S. Marci, cl. I. cod. 3, given in 1478 by Peter de Montagnana to the monastery of St John, in Viridario, at Padua [XIII] 4°, in fine condition. *Eus. t.*, *syn.*

Codd. 218—225 are in the Imperial Library at Vienna. Alter and Birch collated them about the same time, the latter but cursorily.

*218. (Act. 65, Paul. 57, Apoc. 33) Caesar-Vindobon. 23, Lambec. 1, Nessel. 23 [XIII] fol., contains both Testaments. *Mut.* Apoc. xiii. 5—xiv. 8; xv. 7—xvii. 2; xviii. 10—xix. 15; ending at xx. 7 λυθήσεται. This important copy, containing many peculiar readings, was described by Treschow, and comprises the text of Alter's inconvenient, though fairly accurate N. T. 1786—7, to be described in Chap. v. Like Cod. 123 it was brought from Constantinople by Busbeck.

219. Lambec. 32, Nessel. 321 [XIII] 8°, *prol.*

220. Lambec. 33, Nessel. 337 [XIV] 12°, in very small letters.

221. Caesar-Vindobon. CXVII. 29, Lambec. 38 [XI] fol., with commentaries (Chrysostom on Matth. John, Victor on Mark, Titus of Bostra on Luke), to which the *portions* of the text here given are accommodated: it begins Matth. i. 11.

222. Lambec. 39, Nessel. 180 [XIV] 4°, on cotton paper, *mut.* Contains *portions* of the Gospels, with a commentary.

223. Lambec. 40, Nessel. 301 [XIV] 4°, contains fragments of Matthew, Luke and John, with a catena. Codd. 221—3 must be cited cautiously: Alter appears to have made no use of them.

224. Caesar-Vindob. Kollar. 8, Forlos. 30 [date not given] 4°, only contains St Matthew. This copy came from Naples.

225. Kollar. 9, Forlos. 31 [*dated* ϛψ or A.D. 1192] 8°, more important. *Syn.*, *men.*

Codd. 226—233 are in the Escurial, described by D. G. Moldenhawer, who collated them about 1783, loosely enough, for Birch's edition, in a temper which by no means disposed him to exaggerate their value (*see below*, Chap. v).

226. (Act. 108, Paul. 228) Codex Escurialensis χ. IV. 17 [XI] 8°, on the finest vellum, richly ornamented, in a small, round, very neat hand. *Eus. t.*, *κεφ. t.*, *lect.*, *pict.*, *τίτλοι*, *κεφ.*, *Eus.* Many corrections were made by a later hand, but the original text is valuable, and the readings sometimes unique. Fairly collated.

227. Escurial. χ. III. 15 [XIII] 4°, *prol.*, *κεφ. t.*, *Am.*, *pict.* A later hand, which dates 1308, has been very busy in making corrections.

228. (Act. 109, Paul. 229) Escurial. χ. IV. 12 [XIV] 8°, *chart.* Once belonged to Nicholas Nathanael of Crete, then to Andreas Darmarius of Epidaurus, a calligrapher. *Eus. t.*, *syn.*[1]

229. Escurial. χ. IV. 21 [*dated* 1140] 8°, written by Basil Argyropolus, a notary. *Mut.* Mark xvi. 15—20; John i. 1—11. *Pict.*, *lect.*; the latter by a hand of about the 14th century, which retraced much of the discoloured ink, and corrected in the margin (since mutilated by the binder) very many *important* readings of the first hand, which often resemble those of ADK I. 72.

230. Escurial. φ. III. 5 [*dated* Oct. 29, 1013, with the wrong Indiction, 11 for 12] 4°, written by Luke a monk and priest, with

[1] Thus, at least, I understand Moldenhawer's description, "Evangeliis et Actis λέξεις subjiciuntur dudum in vulgus notae."

a double *syn.*[1], *Carp.*, *κεφ. t.*, subscriptions with the number of ῥήματα and στίχοι. An interesting copy, deemed by Moldenhawer worthy of closer examination.

231. Escurial. φ. III. 6 [XII] 4°, *lect.*, *Eus. t.* torn, *κεφ. t.*, a picture "quae Marcum mentitur," subscriptions with στίχοι numbered, *syn.*, *men.* There are some marginal glosses by a later hand (which obelizes Jo. vii. 53 *seq.*), and a Latin version over parts of St Matthew.

232. Escurial. φ. III. 7 [XIII] 4°, very elegant but otherwise a poor copy. Double *syn.*, τίτλοι in the margin of Matthew and Luke, but elsewhere kept apart.

233. Escurial. Υ. II. 8 [XI?], like Codd. 69, 206 is partly of parchment, partly paper, in bad condition, and once belonged to Matthew Dandolo, a Venetian noble. It has a catena, and through ligatures, &c. (see p. 38) is hard to read. *Prol.*, *κεφ. t.*, *Eus. t.* (apart), some iambics, and ῥήματα, στίχοι to the first two Gospels.

234. (Act. 57, Paul. 72) Codex Havniensis I. [*dated* 1278] 4°, one of the several copies written by Theodore (*see p.* 37, *note* 2). This copy and Cod. 235 are now in the Royal Library at Copenhagen, but were bought at Venice by F. Rostgaard in 1699. The order of the books in Cod. 234 is described p. 62. *Syn.*, *men.*, *lect.*, with many corrections. (C. G. Hensler, 1784).

235. Havniens. 2 [*dated* 1314] 4°, written by the ἱερομοναχος Philotheus, though very incorrectly; the text agrees much with Codd. DK I. 33 and the Philoxenian Syriac. Κεφ. *t.*, *lect.;* the words are often ill divided and the stops misplaced (Hensler).

236. Readings extracted by Griesbach (*Symbolae Criticae* I. pp. 247—304) from the margin of a copy of Mill's Greek Testament in the Bodleian, either in his own or Thomas Hearne's handwriting. Scrivener (*Cod. Augiensis, Introd.* p. xxxvi) has shewn that they were derived from Evan. 440, which see below.

Codd. 237—259 are nearly all Moscow manuscripts, and were thoroughly collated by C. F. Matthaei, for his N. T. to be described in Chapter V. These Russian codices were for the most part brought from the twenty-two monasteries of Mount Athos by the monk Arsenius, on the suggestion of the Patriarch Nico, in the reign of Michael, son of Alexius (1645—76), and placed in the library of the Holy Synod, at Moscow.

*237. S. Synod 42 [X] fol., Matthaei's d, from Philotheus (monastery) *pict.* with scholia.

*238. Syn. 48 (Mt. e) [XI] fol., with a catena and scholia; only contains Matthew and Mark, but is of good quality.

*239. Syn. 47 (Mt. g) [XI] fol., contains Mark xvi. 2—8; Luke; John to xxi. 23, with scholia.

*240. Syn. 49 (Mt. i) [XII] fol., once belonging to Philotheus, then to Dionysius (monasteries) on Athos, with the Commentary of

[1] By double *syn.* Moldenhawer may be supposed to mean here and in Cod. 232 both *syn.* and *men.*

Euthymius Zigabenus. *Mut.* Mark viii. 12—34; xiv. 17—54; Luke xv. 32—xvi. 8.

*241. (Act. 104, Paul. 120, Apoc. 47) Cod. Dresdensis, once Matthaei's (k) [XI] 4°, *syn.*, the whole N. T., beautifully written, with rare readings.

*242. (Act. 105, Paul. 121, Apoc. 48) Syn. 380 (Mt. l) [XII] 8°, the whole N. T., with Psalms, ᾠδαί, *prol.*, *pict.*, *Eus. t.*

*243. Cod. Typographei S. Syn. 13 (Mt. m) [XIV] fol., on cotton paper, from the Iberian monastery on Athos, contains Matthew and Luke with Theophylact's Commentary.

*244. Typograph. 1 (Mt. n) [XII] fol., *pict.* with Euthymius Zigabenus' Commentary.

*245. Syn. 265 (Mt. o) [*dated* 1199] 4°, from the monastery "Batopedii," written by John, a priest.

*246. Syn. 261 (Mt. p) [XIV] 4°, *chart.*, with marginal various readings. *Mut.* Matth. xii. 41—xiii. 55; John xvii. 24—xviii. 20.

*247. Syn. 373 (Mt. q) [XII] 8°, *syn.*, from Philotheus.

*248. Syn. 264 (Mt. r) [*dated* 1275] 4°, written by Meletius a Beroean for Cyrus Alypius, οἰκόνομος of St George's monastery, in the reign of Michael Palaeologus (1259—82).

*249. Syn. 94 (Mt. s) [XI] fol., from Παντοκράτωρ monastery (as Cod. 74). Contains John with a catena.

*250. Syn. in a box (Mt. v) [XIII] is the cursive portion of Cod. V (*see* p. 117), John vii. 39—xxi. 25. It is also Wetstein's Cod. 87.

*251. Cod. Tabularii Imperial. at Moscow (Mt. x) [XI] 4°, *Eus. t.*, *pict.*

*252. Cod. Dresdensis, once Matthaei's (z) [XI] 4°, with corrections and double readings (as from another copy), but *primâ manu.*

*253. Codex of Nicephorus Archbishop of Cherson, "et Slabinii," (Slaviansk?) formerly belonged to the monastery of St Michael, at Jerusalem (Mt. 10) [XI] fol., with scholia and rare readings.

*254. Codex belonging to Matthaei (11) [XI] fol., from the monastery of St Athanasius. Contains Luke and John with scholia: *pict.*

*255. Syn. 139 (Mt. 12) [XIII] fol., once "Dionysii monachi rhetoris *et amicorum.*" Commentaries of Chrysostom and others, with fragments of the text interspersed.

*256. Typogr. Syn. 3 (Mt. 14) [IX?] fol., scholia on Mark and Luke, with portions of the text.

*257. Syn. 120 (Mt. 15) is Cod. O, described p. 112.

*258. Cod. Dresdensis (Mt. 17) [XIII] 4°, barbarously written: *pict.*

*259. Syn. 45 (Mt. a) [XI] fol., from the Iberian monastery, with a commentary, *syn.*, *Eus. t.* This is one of Matthaei's best manuscripts. His other twenty-two copies contain portions of Chrysostom, for which see Chapter IV.

Codd. 260—469 were added to the list by Scholz (see Chapter v): the very few he professes to have collated thoroughly will be distinguished by *.

260. Codex Regius 51, Paris [XII] fol., once (like Cod. 309) "domini du Fresne," correctly written: *pict.*

261. Reg. 52 [XIV] fol., once at the monastery of the Forerunner at Constantinople (*see p.* 154, *note*). *Lect.*, *mut.* Luke xxiv. 39—53. Matth. i. 1—xi. 1 supplied [XIV] *chart.*

*262. Reg. 53 [X] fol., *syn.*, *Eus. t.*, with rare readings and subscriptions like Cod. Λ (*see above, p.* 124) and Codd. 300, 376, 428.

263. (Act. 117, Paul. 137, Apoc. 54) Reg. 61 [XIII] 4°, *Eus. t.* torn, *Am.*, *pict.* Probably from Asia Minor. It once belonged to Jo. Hurault Boistaller, as did Codd. 301, 306, 314.

264. Reg. 65 [XIII] 4°, with Coptic-like letters, but brought from the East in 1718 by Paul Lucas. The leaves are misplaced in binding, as are those of Cod. 272.

265. Reg. 66 [X] 4°, once belonged to Philibert de la Mare.

266. Reg. 67 [X] 4°, *syn.*

267. Reg. 69 [X] 4°, *lect.*, *mut.* Matth. i. 1—8; Mark i. 1—7; Luke i. 1—8; xxiv. 50—John i. 12.

268. Reg. 73 [XII] 4°, *Eus. t.*, *syn.*, *pict.*

269. Reg. 74 [XI] 4°, *pict.*

270. Reg. 75 [XI] 8°, *syn.*, with a mixed text.

271. Reg. 75[a] [XII] 8°, *Eus. t.*, *pict.*

272. Reg. 76 [XI] 12°, once Melchisedech Thevenot's.

273. Reg. 79, 4°, on vellum [XII], but partly on cotton paper [XIV], contains also some scholia, extracts from Severianus' commentary, annals of the Gospels, *Eus. t.*, a list of the Gospel parables, parts of *syn.*, with a mixed text.

274. Reg. 79[a] [X] 4°, once belonged to Maximus Panagiotes, *protocanon* of the Church at Callipolis (there were many places of this name: but see Cod. 346). *Pict.*, *Eus. t.*, *syn.*, *men.*, *mut.* (but supplied in a later hand, *chart.*) Mark i. 1—17; vi. 21—54; John i. 1—20; iii. 18—iv. 1; vii. 23—42; ix. 10—27; xviii. 12—29.

275. Reg. 80 [XI] 8°, antea Memmianus, *Eus. t.*, *prol.*, portions of *syn.*

276. Reg. 81 [XI] 8°, written by Nicephorus of the monastery Meletius: *Eus. t.*, *pict.*

277. Reg. 81 A [XI] 8°, *Eus. t.*, *pict.*: some portions supplied by a later hand.

278. Reg. 82 [XII] 8°, once Mazarin's, with Armenian inscriptions, *Eus. t.*, *pict.*, *syn.* Matth. xiii. 43—xvii. 5 is in a later hand.

279. Reg. 86 [XII] 12°, this copy and Cod. 294 were brought from Patmos and given to Louis XIV. in 1686 by Joseph Georgeirenus, Archbishop of Samos. *Eus. t.*, *syn.*, *pict.*

280. Reg. 87 [XII] 8°, parts of *syn.*, *prol.*, *mut.* Mark viii. 3—xv. 36.

281. Reg. 88 [XII] 8°, *Eus. t.*, *pict.*, *mut.* Matth. xxviii. 11—20; Luke i. 1—9. Given to the Monastery "Deiparae Hieracis" by the eremite monk Meletius.

282. Reg. 90 [*dated* 1176] 12°.

283. Reg. 92 [XIV] 8°.

284. Reg. 93 [XIII] 8°, *Eus. t.*, *pict.*, *syn.* Once Teller's of Rheims and Peter Stella's.

285. Reg. 95 [XIV] 8°, *pict.*, once Teller's: given by Augustin Justinian to Jo. Tharna of Catana.

286. Reg. 96 [*dated* April 12, 1432, Indiction 10] 8°, by the monk Calistus, with the Paschal canon for the years 1432—1502.

287. Reg. 98 [XV] 8°.

288. Reg. 99 [XVI] 8°, *chart.*, once German Brixius': contains St Luke only.

289. Reg. 100 A [*dated* Feb. 15, 1625] fol., *chart.*, written by Lucas αρχιθυτης.

290. Reg. 108 a [XIII] 4°, on cotton paper; from the Sorbonne: *syn.*

291. Reg. 113 [XII] 8°, *syn.*: belonged to one Nicholas.

292. Reg. 114 [XI] 8°, *syn.*, *pict.*, *mut.* Matth. i. 1—vii. 14; John xix. 14—xxi. 25.

293. Reg. 117 [*dated* Nov. 1373] 16°, *syn.*, *pict.*, written by Manuel for Blasius a monk.

294. Reg. 118 [XIII] 16°, *pict.*, *mut.* Matth. i. 18—xii. 25.

295. Reg. 120 [XIII] 16°, *mut.* Matth. i. 1—11.

296. Reg. 123 [XVI] 16°, written by Angelus Vergecius (*see p.* 38, *note* 2).

297. Reg. 140 a [XII] 12°, *pict.*, *syn.*

298. Reg. 175 a [XII] 8°, from the Jesuits' public library, Lyons: *pict.*, *syn.*

*299. Reg. 177 [XI] fol., an accurately written copy with a mixed text, and scholia which seem to have been written in Syria by a partisan of Theodore of Mopsuestia: *prol.*, *Eus. t.*, *pict.* and other fragments.

*300. Reg. 186 [XI] fol., "olim fonte-blandensis," (Fontainbleau?) contains the first three Gospels, with subscriptions like that of Cod. 262. *Eus. t.*, *syn.*, a catena, "πάρεργα de locis selectis," and in the outer margin Theophylact's Commentary in a later hand.

*301. Reg. 187 [XI] fol., once Boistaller's, a mixed text with a Catena.

302. Reg. 193 [XVI] fol. *chart.*, once Mazarin's: contains fragments of Matthew and Luke with a Commentary.

303. Reg. 194 A [XI] fol., contains vellum fragments of John i—iv; and on cotton paper, dated 1255, Theophylact's Commentary and some iambic verses written by Nicander, a monk.

304. Reg. 194 [XIII] fol., once Teller's: contains Matthew and Mark with a Catena.

305. Reg. 195 [XIII] fol., on cotton paper, once Mazarin's: contains the same as Cod. 304.

306. Reg. 197 [XII] fol., once Boistaller's, contains Matthew and John with Theophylact's Commentary.

307. Reg. 199 [XI] fol., contains Matthew and John with a Commentary.

308. Reg. 200 [XII] fol., once Mazarin's: *mut.*, contains the same as Cod. 307.

309. Reg. 201 [XII] fol., once du Fresne's, has Matthew and John with Chrysostom's Commentary, Luke with that of Titus of Bostra, Mark with Victor's.

310. Reg. 202 [XI] fol., has Matthew with a Catena, once Colbert's (as also were Codd. 267, 273, 279, 281—3, 286—8, 291, 294, 296, 315, 318—9). Given to St Saba's monastery by its Provost Arsenius.

311. Reg. 303 [XII] fol., once Mazarin's: also has Matthew with a Catena.

312. Reg. 206 [*dated* 1308] fol., Mark with Victor's Commentary.

313. Reg. 208 [XIV] fol., *chart.*, *mut.*, once Mazarin's, contains Luke with a Catena.

314. Reg. 209 [XII] fol., once Boistaller's, contains John with a Commentary.

315. Reg. 210 [XIII] fol., has the same contents as Cod. 314. *Mut.* John xiv. 25—xv. 16; xxi. 22—25.

316. Reg. 211 [XII] fol., on cotton paper, brought from Constantinople. Contains John and Luke with a Commentary. *Mut.*

317. Reg. 212 [XII] fol., "olim Medicaeus" (*see* p. 94, *note* 2), contains John x. 9—xxi. 25 with a Catena.

318. Reg. 213 [XIV] fol., has John vii. 1—xxi. 25 with a Commentary.

319. Reg. 231 [XII] 4°, with a Commentary, *mut.*

320. Reg. 232 [XI] 4°, has Luke with a Commentary.

321. Reg. 303 [XIII] 4°.

322. Reg. 315 [XV] 4°.

323. Reg. 118 a [XVI] 4°, contains Matth. vi. vii. and a Greek version of some Arabic fables.

324. (Evst. 97, Apost. 32) Reg. 376 [XIII] 4°, once Mazarin's, together with some lessons from the Acts, Epistles and Gospels, contains also the Gospels complete, *Eus. t.*, *syn.* (on cotton paper), and a chronological list of Emperors from Constantine to Manuel Porphyrogennetus (A.D. 1143).

325. Reg. 377 [XIII] 4°.

326. Reg. 378 [XIV] 4°, contains homilies (ἑρμήνεια) on certain passages or texts (τὸ κείμενον).

327. Reg. 380 [XV] 4°.

328. Reg. 381 [XVI] 4°.

329. Coislin. 19 [XI] 4°, with a Commentary. Described (as also Cod. 331) by Montfaucon.

330. (Act. 132, Paul. 131) Coislin 196 [XI] 8°, from Athos. *Eust. t.*, *prol.*

331. Coislin. 197 [XII] 4°, once Hector D'Ailli's, Bishop of Toul: *syn.*

332. Codex Taurinensis XX. b. IV. 20 [XI] fol., at Turin, *prol.*, *pict.* with a Commentary.

333. Taurin. IV. b. 4 [XIII] fol., on cotton paper, once belonged to Arsenius, Archb. of Monembasia, in the Morea, then to Gabriel, metropolitan of Philadelphia: contains Matthew and John with Nicetas' Catena.

334. Taurin. 43, b. V. 23 [XIV] fol. Matthew and Mark with a Commentary, *prol.*

335. Taurin. 44, b. V. 24 [XVI] fol., *chart.*, *prol.*

336. Taurin. 101, c. IV. 17 [XVI] fol., *chart.*, Luke with a Catena.

337. Taurin. 52, b. V. 32 [XII] fol., parts of Matthew with a Commentary.

338. Taurin. 335, b. I. 3 [XII] 12°, *Eus. t.*, *pict.*

339. (Act. 135, Paul. 170, Apoc. 83) Taurin. 302, c. II. 5 [XIII] 4°, *prol.*, *Eus. t.*, *syn.*, and other matter.

340. Taurin. 344, b. I. 13 [XI]?, with many later corrections.

341. Taurin. 350, b. I. 21 [*dated* 1296] 4°, written by Nicetas Mauron, a reader: *syn.*

342. Taurin. 149, b. II. 3 [XIII] 4°, *Eus. t.*

343. Codex Ambrosianus 13 [XII] 12°, at Milan, written by one Antony; *lect.*, *Eus. t.*, *pict.*

344. Ambros. 16 [XII] 12°, *syn.*, *mut.* John xxi. 12—25. But Luke xiii. 21—xvi. 23; xxi. 12[?]; xxii. 12—23; xxiii. 45—50? are [XIV] *chart.*

345. Ambros. 17 [XI] 12°, *syn.*, *mut.* Matth. i. 1—11.

*346. Ambros. 23 [XII] 4°, carelessly written, with unusual readings. *Mut.* John iii. 6—vii. 52. Bought in 1606 at Gallipoli in Calabria.

347. Ambros. 35 [XII] 8°, *prol.*, *lect.*, correctly written by Constantine Chrysographus.

348. Ambros. B. 56 [*dated* 29 December, 1023] 8°, once "J. V. Pinelli," *syn.*, *Eus. t.*

349. Ambros. 61 [*dated* 1322] 8°, *chart.*, bought at Corfu; *syn.*, *pict.*

350. Ambros. B. 62 [XI] 8°, *pict.*, *syn.* The first four leaves [XVI] *chart.* *Mut.* John xxi. 9—25.

351. Ambros. 70 [XI] 4°, with a Latin version [XV] in many places.

352. Ambros. B. 93 [XII] 4°, brought from Calabria, 1607; *mut.* Matth. i. 1—17; Mark i. 1—15; xvi. 13—20; Luke i. 1—7; xxiv. 43—53; John i. 1—10; xxi. 3—25. Lesson-marks were placed in the margin, and the faded ink retouched [XIV].

353. Ambros. M. 93 [XIII] 4°, with the same Commentary as Cod. 181. *Mut.* John xxi. 24, 25.

354. Venet. 29 [XI] 4°, at Venice, Matthew with Theophylact's Commentary.

355. Venet. 541 [XI] 8°, *Carp., Eus. t.*

356. Venet. 545 [XVI] 4°, *chart.*, contains Titus of Bostra's Catena on Luke, the text of which is occasionally cited.

357. Venet. 28 [XI] fol., Luke and John with a Catena.

358. Mutinensis 9 (II. A. 9) [XIV] 8°, at Modena.

359. Mutin. 242 (III. B. 16) [XIV] 4°.

360. Cod. de Rossi 1, at Parma [XI] 4°, with an unusual text, collated by de Rossi, who once possessed this codex and

361. De Rossi 2 [XIII] 12°.

362. At Florence, Cod. Biblioth. S. Mariae [XIII] fol., Luke with a Catena. Text written in red. This copy, now missing, is cited, like Codd. 201, 370, by Jo. Lamy, *De eruditione Apostolorum*, Florent. 1738, p. 239.

363. (Act. 144, Paul. 180) Laurent. VI. 13 [XIII] 4°, at Florence.

364. Laurent. VI. 24 [XIII] 8°, the style of the characters resembles Sclavonic: some leaves at the beginning and end [XIV].

365. (Act. 145, Paul. 181) Laurent. VI. 36 [XIII] 4°, contains also the Psalms.

366. Laurent. 2607, from S. Maria's [XII] fol., Matthew written in red, with a Catena. *Mut.* at the beginning, with many later marginal notes. This is evidently a portion of the lost Cod. 362.

367. (Act. 146, Paul. 182) Laurent. 2708, also from St Maria's [*dated* 26 Decembr. 1332] 4°, *chart.*, written by one Mark, *syn.* Scholz says "N. T. continet," but the Apocalypse seems wanting.

368. (Act. 150, Paul. 230, Apoc. 84, Apost. 37) Cod. Richardian. 84, also at Florence, "olim Cosmae Oricellarii *et amicorum*" (see Cod. 255) [XV] 8°, *chart.*, contains St John's Gospel, the Apocalypse, the Epistles and lessons from them, with Plato's Epistles, carelessly written.

369. Richard. 90 [XII] 4°, contains Mark vi. 25—ix. 45; x. 17—xvi. 9[?], with a Greek Grammar and Phaedrus' fables.

370. Richard. Plut. K. I. n. 11 [XIV] fol., *chart.*, with Theophylact's Commentary, *mut.* at beginning and end. Described by Lamy (see Cod. 362) p. 232, but now missing.

371. Vatican. 1159 [X] 4°, *Eus. t., pict.*

372. Vat. 1161 [XV] 4°, ends John iii. 1. Beautifully written.

373. Vat. 1423 [XV] fol., *chart.*, "olim Cardinalis Sirleti," with a Catena, *mut.* in fine.

374. Vat. 1445 [XII] fol., with the commentary of Peter of Laodicea. In 1211 one John procured it from Theodosiopolis; there were at least five cities of that name, three of them in Asia Minor.

375. Vat. 1533 [XII] 8°, *Eus. t.*

376. Vat. 1539 [XI] 16°, given by Francis Accidas. With subscriptions resembling those of Codd. Λ, 262, 300.

377. Vat. 1618 [XV] fol., *chart.*, Matthew with a Catena, the other Gospels with questions and answers.

378. Vat. 1658 [XIV] fol., portions from Matthew with Chrysostom's Homilies, and from the prophets.

379. Vat. 1769 [XV] fol., *chart.*, with a Commentary.

380. Vat. 2139 [XV] 4°, *chart.*, *Eus. t.*

381. Palatino-Vat. 20. [XIV] fol., *chart.*, Luke with a Catena.

382. Vat. 2070 [XIII] 4°, "olim Basil.," carelessly written, fragments of John and Luke are placed by the binder before Matthew and Mark. Much is lost.

383, 384, 385, are all Collegii Romani [XVI] 4°, *chart.* with a Commentary.

386. (Act. 151, Paul. 199, Apoc. 70) Vat. Ottobon. 66 [XV] fol., *syn.*, once "Jo. Angeli ducis ab Altamps," as also Codd. 388, 389, 390, Paul. 202.

387. Vat. Ottobon. 204 [XII] 4°.

388. Vat. Ottobon. 212 [XII] 4°, *pict.*, once belonged to Alexius and Theodora.

389. Vat. Ottobon. 297 [XI] 8°.

390. (Act. 164, Paul. 203, Apoc. 71) Vat. Ottobon. 381 [*dated* 1252] 4°, with scholia, *syn.*, *Eus. t.*, was in a Church at Scio A.D. 1359.

391. Vat. Ottobon. 432 [XI, *dated* 13 April, Indiction 8] 4°, *prol.*, with a Commentary. Given to Benedict XIII. (1724—30) by Abachum Andriani, an abbot of Athos. Matth. i. 1—8; Luke i; Jo. vii. 53—viii. 11 were written [XV].

392. Barberin. 225 is the cursive portion of Cod. Y [XII] fol., with Theophylact's Commentary. See above, p. 119.

393. (Act. 167, Paul. 185) Vallicell. E. 22 [XVI] 4°, *chart.*

394. (Act. 170, Paul. 186) Vallicell. F. 17 [*dated* 4 July, 1330, Indict. 13] 4°, *chart.* written by Michael, a priest.

395. Cod. Biblioth. S. Mariae supra Minervam, seu Casanatensis A. R. V. 33 [XII] 4°, at Rome, *pict.*, with marginal corrections, bought about 1765.

396. Cod. Ghigianus, at Rome, R. IV. 6 [XII] 4°, begins Matth. xxiii. 27.

397. Vallicell. C. 4 [XV] fol., *chart.* John with a Catena (described by Blanchini).

398. Taurin. 92. c. IV. 6 [XIII]? select passages with a Catena.

399. Taurin. 109. c. IV. 29 [XV]? *chart.* Commentary, sometimes without the text.

400. (Act. 181, Paul. 220) Cod. Biblio. Berolinensis, "olim Diezii" [xv] 12°, *mut.*, damaged by fire and water, contains Matth. xii. 29—xiii. 2; and the Acts and Epistles, except Act. i. 11—ii. 11; Rom. i. 1—27; 1 Cor. xiv. 12—xv. 46; 2 Cor. i. 1—8; v. 4—19; 1 Tim. iv. 1—Hebr. i. 9. This copy belonged to Henry Benzil, Archbishop of Upsal, then to Laurence Benzelstierna, Bishop of Arosen: it was described by C. Aurivill (1802), collated by G. T. Pappelbaum (1815).

401. Cod. Neapolit. 1. C. 24 [xi] 4°, contains Matthew, Mark vi. 1—xvi. 20, Luke, John i. 1—xii. 1.

402. Neapolit. 1. C. 28 [xv] 8°, *prol.*, *pict.*

403. Neapolit. 1. C. 29 [xii] 8°, on cotton paper, *syn.* Contains Matth. xii. 23—xix. 12; 28—xxviii. 20 (?); Mark, Luke i. 1—v. 21; 36—xxiv. 53 (?); John i. 1—xviii. 36.

404. Cod. "Abbatis Scotti" of Naples [xi] 8°, *prol.*

405. Venetian. Bibl. Cl. i. n. x [xi] 4°, "olim Nanian. 3, antea monasterii SS. Cosmae et Damiani urbis Prusiensis," i.e. Brusa. *Eus. t.*, the leaves utterly disarranged by the binder. (Wiedmann and J. G. J. Braun collated portions of 405—417 for Scholz).

406. Venet. i. 11, Nanian. 4 [xi] 8°, *mut.* Mark iv. 41—v. 14; Luke iii. 16—iv. 4.

407. Venet. i. 12, Nanian. 5 [xi] 8°, contains Luke v. 30—John ix.

408. Venet. S. Marci Bibl. i. 14, Nanian. 7 [xii] 4°, *Eus. t.*, once belonged to St John's monastery, by the Jordan.

409. Venet. i. 15, Nanian. 8 [xii] 4°, *Eus. t.*, *syn.*, with many errors and rare readings.

410. Venet. i. 17, Nanian. 10 [xiii or xiv] 4°, written by one Joasaph a monk, on cotton paper, but *Eus. t.* [xii] on parchment.

411. Venet. Nanian. 11 [xiv] 8°, *Eus. t.*, *syn.*

412. Venet. i. 19, Nanian. 12 [*dated* 1301] 4°, written by Theodore (*see p.* 37, note 2). *Eus. t.*, *syn.*

413. Venet. i. 20, Nanian. 13 [dated 1302, Indiction 15] 4°, once belonged to St Catherine's monastery on Sinai, where Cod. א was found, and is elegantly written by one Theodosius. *Eus. t.*, *pict.*, *syn.*

414. Venet. i. 21, Nanian. 14 [xiv] 4°, *syn.*, written by Philip, a monk.

415. Venet. i. 22, Nanian. 15 [*dated* January 1356] 8°, *syn.*, *pict.*

416. Venet. i. 24, Nanian. 17 [xiv] 4°, begins Matth. xxv. 35, ends John xviii. 7.

417. Venet. i. 25, Nanian. 18 [xiv] 4°, contains the first three Gospels, *mut.* at the beginning and end.

418. Venet. Nanian. 21 [?] 8°, *chart.*, contains Matthew and Mark, *mut.* at the end.

419. A codex formerly at St Michael's, Venice, "prope Murianum" 241, [xi] 4°, ends John xxi. 7 (described by J. B. Mittarelli, Venice 1779). See also Evst. 143.

420. (Schulz's 237) Cod. Messanensis 1 [XIV] 4°, by different hands, with readings from other copies (inspected by Munter, as was Cod. 421).

421. (Act. 176, Paul. 218) Cod. Syracusanus [XII] ?, once Landolini's; *prol.*, *Eus. t.*, is Schulz's 238.

422. Reg. Monacensis 210, at Munich [XI] 4°, *lect.*, *prol.*, *syn.*, written by the monk Joseph, but St John in a later hand (described by Ignatius Hardt).

423. Monacensis 36 [XV] fol., *chart.*, contains Matthew with Nicetas' Catena.

424. Monacensis 83 [XV] fol., *chart.*, contains Luke with the commentary of Titus of Bostra and others.

425. Monacensis 37 [XV] fol., *chart.*, contains John with a very full Catena of Nicetas.

426. Monacensis 473, once Augsburg 9 [XIV] 4°, on cotton paper, contains Luke vi. 17—xi. 26 with Nicetas' Catena, the second of four volumes (δεύτερον τῶν τεσσάρων τεῦχος τῶν εἰς τὸ κατὰ Λουκᾶν ἅγιον εὐαγγέλιον κατὰ συναγωγὴν ἐξηγήσεων).

427. Monacensis 465, Augsburg 10 [XII ?] 4°, written by one Maurus, contains Luke and Mark with Theophylact's Commentary.

428. Monacensis 381, Augsburg 11 [XIII] fol., on cotton paper, so like Cod. 300 as to be a copy from it, or taken from the same manuscripts; with subscriptions like Codd. 262 &c. *pict.*, a Commentary &c.

429. Monacensis 208 [*dated* but a few years later than Cod. 14, June 20, A.D. 978, Indiction 6] 4°, written by John a priest and "ἔκδικος magnae ecclesiae," contains Luke i. 1—ii. 39 with a Catena, questions and answers from Matthew and John, with the text. See above, p. 36, note 2.

430. Monacensis 437 [XI] 4°, contains John with the Catena of Nicetas, metropolitan of Heraclia Serrarum (in Macedonia, now *Xevosna*). Martin Crusius of Tubingen procured it from Leontius, a Cyprian monk, in 1590, and sent it to the library at Augsburg.

431. (Act. 180, Paul. 238.). Cod. Molsheimensis [XII] 12°, *prol.*, *Eus. t.*, with many unusual readings, was brought to Strasburg from the Jesuits' College at Molsheim in Alsace, extracts made by the Jesuit Hermann Goldhagen (N. T. Mogunt. 1753), and collated by Arendt, 1833.

432. Monacensis 99 [XVI] fol., *chart.*, contains Mark with the Commentary of Victor of Antioch.

433. Cod. Bibl. Berolinensis is Schulz's 239 [XII] 4°, brought from the East by W. Ern. de Knobelsdorf, with a mixed text and many errors. It contains Matth. i. 1—21; vi. 12—32; xxii. 25—xxviii. 20; Mark i. 1—v. 29; ix. 21—xiii. 12; Luke viii. 27—John ix. 21; xx. 15—xxi. 25. (G. T. Pappelbaum, 1824).

434. Caesar. Vindobon. 71, Lambec. 42 [XIV] fol., contains Luke with a Catena. Like Codd. 218, &c. bought at Constantinople by Busbeck.

435. Cod. Gronovii 131, at Leyden, is Schulz's 245 [?] 4°, *mut.* Matth. i. 20—ii. 13; xxii. 4—9 (John x. 14—xxi. 25 in a rather *later hand), has a somewhat unusual text* (collated, as also Cod. 122, by J. Dermout, *Collectanea Critica in N. T.* 1825).

436. Cod. Meermann. 117, last traced to some English bookseller, in 1824, described by Montfaucon, Palaeograph. Graec. p. 295, when in the Library of the Jesuits' College of Louis XIV. *lect.* See above, p. 158, note.

437. Cod. Petropolit. [XI], like Cod. E. of the Epistles, one leaf of the Colbert Pentateuch, and some other manuscripts, has found its way from the Coislin library and the Abbey of St Germain des Prez near Paris, to St Petersburg. It was written by Michael Cerularius, Patriarch of Constantinople, and noticed by Matthaei (N. T. III. p. 99, 2nd ed.).

438. Cod. Mus. Brit. 5111—2. (Askew 621) [XI] 4°, two vols. (Bloomfield).

439. Mus. Brit. 5107 (Askew 622) [*dated* April 1159, Ind. 7] fol., written by the monk Nepho, at Athos. *Carp., Eus. t., κεφ. t., pict., τίτλ., κεφ., Am., Eus.* (Bloomfield).

440. (Act. 111, Paul. 221) University Library, Cambridge, 2423 (Mm. 6. 9) is the copy from which Griesbach's readings in Cod. 236 were derived. Described below under Scrivener's v.

441, 442, at Cambridge, must be removed from Scholz's list; they are *printed* editions with manuscript notes. Cod. 441 is Act. 110, Paul. 222; Cod. 442 is Act. 152, Paul. 223.

443. University Libr. Cambridge, 2512 (Nn. 2. 36), once Askew 624,[1] [XI or XII] 4°, *Carp., Eus. t., κεφ. t., τίτλ., Am., Eus., syn., prol.*

444. (Act. 153, Paul. 240) Cod. Harleian. 5796 [XV] 4°, neatly written, *syn.*, sold in 1537 "aspris 500 :[2]" bought at Smyrna in 1722 by Bernard Mould.

445. Harleian. 5736 [*dated* 1506] *chart.*, in the hand "Antonii cujusdam eparchi," once (like Apoc. 31) in the Jesuits' College, Agen, on the Garonne.

446. Harl. 5777 [XV] 4°, *syn. Mut.* Matth. i. 1—17; Mark i. 7—9; Luke i. 1—18; John i. 1—22 by a person who mischievously cut out the ornaments. It is clearly but unskilfully written, and Covell states on the outer leaf that it seems a copy from his manuscript, noted above as Cod. 65. This copy is *Cov. 5* (Bloomfield).

[1] Scholz has a great deal to answer for in the way of negligence, but he does not deserve the imputation brought against him in the Catalogue of the Cambridge Manuscripts (Vol. III. p. 310), of guessing *Askew* to be a College there. Cod. 443 was bought for the University Library in 1775 for £20, at the celebrated book-sale of Anthony Askew [1722—74], the learned physician who projected an edition of Æschylus. See Marsh on Michaelis, Vol. II. pp. 661—2.

[2] The asper or asprum was a mediæval Greek silver coin (derived from *ασπρος, albus*): we may infer its value from a passage cited by Ducange from Vincentius Bellovac. XXX. 75 "quindecim drachmas seu asperos."

447. Harl. 5784 [xv] *Eus. t., men.*, well written, and much like

448. Harl. 5790 [*dated* Rome, 25 April, 1478] fol., *pict.*, elegantly written by John a priest for Francis Cardinal of S. Maria nova.

449. Mus. Brit. 4950—1 [xiii] 12°, 2 vol., clearly and carefully written: once Caesar de Missy's (see Cod. 44). *Prol., κεφ. t., τίτλ., Am., Eus., men., syn.*

450. Codex 1 in the great Greek Monastery at Jerusalem [*dated* 1 July 1043] 8°, *syn., Eus. t.*, neatly written by the reader Euphemius, contains the first three Gospels with an Arabic version. This is Mr Coxe's No. 6, but he calls it 4°, and speaks of it as containing only St Luke's Gospel.

451. Jerusalem 2 [xii] 8°. 452. Jerus. 3 [xiv] 8°.

453. Jerus. 4 [xiv] 8°. 454. Jerus. 5 [xiv] 8°.

455. Jerus. 6 [xiv] 4°, with a Commentary.

456. Jerus. 7 [xiii] 4°, Matthew is neatly written with a Commentary, in golden *uncial* letters (Coxe, No. 43, who dates it [xi]).[1]

457. (Act. 186, Paul. 234) Codex 2 in the Monastery of St Saba (a few miles from Jerusalem, near the Dead Sea) [xiii] 4°, *syn., men.*

458. St Saba 3 [*dated* 1272, Indict. 15] 16°.

459. St Saba 7 [xii] 8°. 460. St Saba 8 [xii] 8°.

461. St Saba 9 [*dated, si qua fides Scholzio*, May 7, A. D. 835, Indict. 13] 8°, neatly written by Nicholas, a monk.

462. (Act. 187, Paul. 235, Apoc. 86) St Saba 10 [xiv] 4°.

463. St Saba 11 [xiv] 4°, *chart.*

464. St Saba 12 [xi] 4°, *chart.* 465. St Saba 19 [xiii] 8°.

466. (Act. 189, Paul. 237, Apoc. 86[2] or 89) St Saba 20 [xiii] 8°.[2]

467. Codex of a monastery at Patmos [xi] 4°.

468. Another at Patmos [xii] 8°, with a Commentary.

469. Another as Patmos [xiv] 4°.[3]

Of this whole list of 210 manuscripts, Scholz collated five entire (262. 299. 300. 301. 346), eleven in the greatest part (260. 270. 271. 277. 284. 285. 298. 324. 353. 382. 428), many in a few places, and not a few seem to have been left untouched.

1 Mr Coxe (*Report to Her Majesty's Government of the Greek Manuscripts yet remaining in the Libraries of the Levant*, 1858) saw fourteen copies of the Gospels in this Monastery: as I can identify but two of them with Scholz's Codd. 450—456, they must be described below, p. 185, only that we may be sure that Scholz's 451—5 are *included* somewhere in Mr Coxe's list.

2 At Mar Saba Mr Coxe found no less than twenty copies of the Gospels, four of them being of the 10th century (*Report* p. 12), with a noble palimpsest of the Orestes and Phoenissae. Here again I must repeat his list (*below* p. 185), as I cannot satisfactorily reconcile his account with Scholz's.

3 At Patmos Coxe saw but five copies of the Gospels: No. 6 [x] 4°, *syn.*, probably Scholz's 467; No. 2 [xii] 4°, with scholia, perhaps Scholz's 468; and No. 21 [xii] fol., which may be Scholz's 469.

The following additions must be made to the above list: we have adopted the notation employed by Tischendorf, N. T. 7th edition.

Edward de Muralt in his N. T. "ad fidem codicis principis Vaticani," 1848, inserts a collation of eleven manuscripts (five of them being Lectionaries), chiefly at St Petersburg.

1^pe. (Petropol. IV. 13) some fragments of Evangelistaria. [IX].

2^pe. (Petrop. VI. 470), the Gospels [IX], a very important copy, especially in St Mark.

3^pe. Lectionary [X], of the Gospels (Petr. VII. 179) and Praxapostolos (Petr. VIII. 80).

4^pe. The Gospels at Moscow, (Mich. Petridae Pogodini 472) [XII or XIII].

5^pe. Psalter (Petr. IX. 1) with the hymns Luke i. 46—55; 68—79; ii. 29—32 [*dated* 994].

6^pe. Evangelistarium (Petr. X. 180) [*dated* Salernum, 1022].

7^pe. (Petr. IX. 3. 471) the Gospels, a valuable copy [*dated* 1062].

8^pe. (Petr. XI. 1. 2. 330) Gospels, Acts and Epistles [XII].

9^pe. (Petr. XI. 3. 181) fragments of an Evangelistarium [XIII].

10^pe. An Evangelistarium of Palaeologus, Panticapaeense [of Kertch?], collated at Odessa.

11^pe. Gospels (Q. v. 1, 15.) [XV].

F. H. Scrivener has published the following in his "Collation of Greek Manuscripts of the Holy Gospels 1853," and "Codex Augiensis" (Appendix) 1859.

a^scr. Archiepiscopal Library, Lambeth 1175 [XI] 4°, *κεφ. t.*, *lect.*, *κεφ.*, *Am.*, *Eus.*, *mut.* Matth. i. 1—13; once at Constantinople, but brought (together with the next five) from the Greek Archipelago by J. D. Carlyle, Professor of Arabic at Cambridge [d. 1804].

b^scr. Lamb. 1176 [XII] small 4°, very elegant: *Carp.*, *Eus. t.*, *pict.*, *lect.*, *κεφ. t.* (these last *chart.*) *τίτλοι*, *Am.*, *Eus.*, *syn.* A copy "eximiae notae," but with many corrections by a later hand, and some foreign matter.

c^scr. Lamb. 1177 [XII] 4°, for valuable readings by far the most important at Lambeth, shamefully ill written, torn and much mutilated[1]: perhaps not all by the same hand. *Κεφ. t.*, (a fragment), *τίτλοι*, *Am.*, *lect.*, portions of *syn.*

d^scr. Lamb. 1178 [XI] large 4°, in a fine hand, splendidly illuminated, and with much curious matter in the subscriptions (see

[1] Matth. iv. 1—vii. 6; xx. 21—xxi. 12; Luke iv. 29—v. 1; 17—33; xvi. 24—xvii. 13; xx. 19—41; John vi. 51—viii. 2; xii. 20—40; xiv. 27—xv. 13; xvii. 9—xviii. 2; xviii. 37—xix. 14.

p. 56). *Mut.* Matth. i. 1—8. *Syn.*, *men.*, *κεφ. t.*, and the other usual divisions. A noble-looking copy.

e^{scr}. Lamb. 1179 [x] 4°, neatly written but in wretched condition beginning Matth. xiii. 53, ending John xiii. 8. Also *mut.* Matth. xvi. 28—xvii. 18; xxiv. 39—xxv. 9; xxvi. 71—xxvii. 14; Mark viii. 32—ix. 9; John xi. 8—30. Carlyle brought it from Trinity Monastery, Chalké. *Κεφ. t.*, *lect.*, *τίτλοι*, *Am.*, *Eus.*

f^{scr}. Lamb. 1192 [XIII] large 4°, from Syria, beautifully written, but tampered with by a later hand. *Mut.* John xvi. 8—22, and a later hand [xv] has supplied Mark iii. 6—21; Luke xii. 48—xiii. 2; John xviii. 27—xxi. 25. *Κεφ. t.*, *τίτλοι*, *Am.*, *Eus.*, *lect.*, *pict.*; at the beginning stand some texts, *περὶ ἀνεξικακίας*. (Re-examined by Bloomfield.)

g^{scr}, is Lamb. 528 and Cod. 71, described above.

h^{scr}. Cod. Arundel 524 in the British Museum, [XI] 4°, was brought to England (with x^{scr} and many others) by the great Earl of Arundel in 1646. *Syn.*, *men.*, *Carp.*, *Eus. t.*, *κεφ. t.*, *τίτλοι*, *Am.*, *Eus.*, *lect.*

i^{scr}. Cod. Trin. Coll. Cantab. B. x. 17 [XIII] 4°, from Athos, bequeathed to Trinity College by Bentley. *Κεφ. t.*, *τίτλοι*, *κεφ.*, *Am.* (not *Eus.*), *lect.*, and (on paper) are *ὑπόθεσις* to St Matthew and *syn.*

j^{scr}. See above Cod. N.

k^{scr}. Cod. Lebanon, Mus. Brit. 11300 [XI] 4°, most elegantly and correctly written, purchased in 1838, and said to come from Caesarea Philippi at the foot of Lebanon. Contains *scholia*, *lect.*, no *syn.*, but all other matter as in Cod. h: the text is broken up into paragraphs. (Re-examined by Bloomfield.)

l^{scr}. (Act. and Paul. g^{scr}) Cod. Wordsworth [XIII] 4°, was bought in 1837 by Dr Christopher Wordsworth, Canon of Westminster, and bears a stamp "Bibliotheca Suchtelen." *Κεφ. t.*, *τίτλοι*, *Am.*, *lect.*, *syn.*, *men.*, *prol.* or *ὑποθέσεις* are prefixed to the Epistles, and scholia of Chrysostom, &c. set in the margin.

m^{scr}. See above Cod. 201. (Re-examined by Bloomfield.)

n^{scr}. (Paul. j^{scr}) Brit. Mus., Burney 18 (purchased in 1818, with many other manuscripts, from the heirs of Dr Charles Burney), contains the Gospels and two leaves of St Paul (Hebr. xii. 17—xiii. 25), written by one Joasaph A. D. 1366, fol., very superb, *lect.*, *κεφ. t.* (but not *τίτλοι*), *Am.*, *Eus.*, some foreign matter, *αποστολοευαγγελια*, and *syn.* or *men.*, both terms being used. Codd. lmn agree pretty closely.

o^{scr}. Brit. Mus. Burney 19 [x] 4°: (*see p.* 37, and Plate III, No. 8c), in the Escurial as late as 1809, singularly void of the usual apparatus.

p^{scr}. Burney 20 [*dated* A. D. 1285, Indict. 13, altered into 985, whose indiction is the same] 4°, written by a monk Theophilus: *pict.*, *Eus. t.*, *κεφ. t.*, *τίτλοι*, *Am.*, *Eus.*, *lect.*, *syn.*, *men.*, the last in a later hand, which has made many corrections: this copy is next in value to Cod. c.

q^{scr}. (Act. and Paul. f^{scr}) Codex Theodori, from the name of the scribe (see p. 37, note 2) [*dated* 1295] 8°, passed from Caesar de Missy into the Duke of Sussex's Library: in 1845 it belonged to the late Wm. Pickering, the much-respected bookseller. *Syn.*, *Carp.*, *Eus. t.*, *κεφ. t.*, *κεφ.*, *Am.*, *lect.*, ὑποθέσεις or *prol.*, and *syn.* before Act. and all Epp., Euthalius περὶ χρόνων, *men.* after Jude; it has many later changes made in the text.

r^{scr}. Burney 21, by the same scribe [*dated* 1292] fol., on cotton paper in a beautiful but formed hand (see p. 37, and Plate VI, No. 15), *syn.*, *prol.* to each Gospel, *κεφ. t.*, *men.* Codd. qr differ in 183 places.

s^{scr}. Burney 23 [XII] 4°, boldly but carelessly written, ends John viii. 14: *mut.* Luke v. 22—ix. 32; xi. 31—xiii. 25; xvii. 24—xviii. 4. *Syn.*, *Carp.*, *κεφ. t.*, *pict.*, *Am.* (not *Eus.*), τίτλοι, with many later changes and weighty readings.

t^{scr}. Lambeth 1350 [XIV] St John on paper, written with a reed (*see p.* 24), appended to a copy of John Damascene "De Fide Orthodoxa": has ὑπόθεσις or *prol.*, *κεφ.*, and a few rubrical directions; carelessly written, and inscribed "T. Wagstaffe ex dono D. Barthol. Cassano e sacerdotibus ecclesiae Graecae, Oct. 20, 1732."

u^{scr}. C. 4 of Archdeacon Todd's Lambeth Catalogue, was a copy of the Gospels, in the Carlyle collection, restored with six others in 1817 to the Patriarch of Jerusalem at Constantinople[1]. The collation of Matthew and Mark by the Rev. G. Bennet is at Lambeth (1255, No. 25).

v^{scr}. Lambeth 1180 [XIV] *chart.*, τίτλοι, *Am.*, *Eus.*, *lect.*, with important variations: restored like Cod. u, but previously collated by Dr Charles Burney in Mark i. 1—iv. 16; John vii. 53—viii. 11 (Lambeth 1223).

v^{scr} (Evan. 440, Act. 111, Paul. 221 of Scholz, Evan. 236; Act. and Paul. 61 of Griesbach; Act. and Paul. o^{scr}) is Mm. 6, 9 of the Cambridge University Library [XII] 4°, in a minute hand, with many unusual readings, especially in the Epistles (*see above* Cod. 236), from Bp. Moore's Library. *Eus. t.*, *syn.* (later), τίτλοι, *Am.* (not *Eus.*), *lect.*, ὑποθέσεις to most of the Epistles: beautifully written with many contractions.

w^{scr}. (Act. and Paul. k^{scr}) Trin. Coll. Cantab. B. x. 16 [*dated* 1316] 4°, *chart.*, was inelegantly written by a monk James on Mount Sinai. *Κεφ. t.*, *Am.*, *Eus.*, *κεφ.*, *lect.*, *prol.* and ὑποθέσεις to the Epistles, *syn.*, *men.*, and much extraneous matter.

---

[1] In Mr Coxe's *Report to Her Majesty's Government*, we find an account (which illness compelled him to give at second hand) of several copies of the Gospels and one palimpsest Evangelistarium, all dated [XII], still remaining in this Prelate's Library. Here doubtless *all* the restored Carlyle books might be found, and their examination would well employ the leisure of some scholar attached to our Embassy at Constantinople.

The following, among many other manuscripts of the Gospels, as yet entirely uncollated, may be added to the catalogue.

tisch[1]. Cod. Tischendorfianus IV in the University Library at Leipsic [x], described in his *Anecdota sacra et profana*, pp. 20—29.

tisch[2]. at St Petersburgh [XII] 4°, *mut.*, *Notitia Cod. Sinait.* p. 60.

tisch[3]. *ibid.* p. 64, [XII] 4°, only 19 leaves, containing Mark viii. 3—ix. 50, also at St Petersburg.

Middle-Hill 13975, once Lord Strangford's, now Sir Th. Phillipps' [XII] fol., a noble copy, the text surrounded with a full commentary in very minute letters.

To G. Haenel (*Catal. Librorum MSS.* Lips. 1830) we owe our knowledge of Codex Atrebatensis of the whole New Testament at Arras [XV] 8°, of another at Poictiers fol., *chart.*; another he states to be at Carpentras, in uncial letters [VI!] 4°, which Tischendorf discovered to be the Evangelistarium he designates as carp[ev]. [IX].

Haenel has also made known to us most of the following: a vellum copy of St John in the Royal Institute at Paris; two copies of the Gospels [XI], in the Hunterian Museum at Glasgow, marked Q. 122, 123, and once Caesar de Missy's: another of St John (with other matter) at the same place S. 8. 141 [XV], all 4°; a copy of the Gospels at Toledo [XIV] 4°; and another in the University Library at Edinburgh [XI] 8°, *κεφ. t.*, *pict.*, in bad condition, brought from the East, and presented in 1650 by Sir John Chiesley.

Scholz also copies from Jo. Lamy's "*Deliciae eruditorum*," Florence 1743, the class-marks of seven manuscripts from some unknown library (vaguely conjectured to be at Trinity Monastery, Chalké, an island ten miles from Constantinople, whence Lambeth 1179 or e[scr] came), whereof one (207) contains the Gospels, Acts and Epistles, another (201) very ancient, Matthew and Mark with a Catena, five (202—206) the Gospels alone. Dr Millingen, however, has recently printed a catalogue of the Library at Chalké, which contains eight copies of the Gospels (1—6; 19; 20), four being bound in silver.

Tischendorf (N. T. 7th edn. Proleg. p. ccxxiv. note 1) names a copy of the Gospels dated 1254, at St Geneviève's in Paris, 4. A. 34. This, however, seems to be Cod. 121, which Scholz reported as missing: though the date is a little different (*see p.* 158).

Of the seven Cambridge manuscripts, enumerated by Scholz (N. T. Vol. I. p. cxix), we find that c)=Evan. 60, e)=Evan 62, f)=Evan. 70: g) seems No. 2154, a *Latin* version of St John with a gloss: d) No. 1673 is Hh. 6. 12, the four Gospels only [XV] 4°, *chart.*, *κεφ. t.*, *prol.* For a)b) Lowes, formerly Askew, memb. 4°, Gospels, Marsh on Michaelis, Vol. II. p. 662, states that they were sold to Mr Lowes, the bookseller, at Askew's sale (*see p.* 176, note 1), and are now lost sight of[1].

[1] We have now traced from Askew's sale Codd. 109, 438, 439, 443 of the Gospels, and the two volumes in the same hand Act. 22, Paul. 75. But besides

The Parham copies of the Gospel are described in a "Catalogue of materials for writing, early writings on tablets and stones, rolled and other Manuscripts and Oriental Manuscript books in the library of Robert Curzon at Parham," fol. 1849, and were slightly inspected by Scrivener in 1855. They are eight. Greek, vellum, No. 6. Gospels, Acts and all the Epistles [XI] 8°, from Caracalla on Athos, with arabesques in red. No. 7. Gospels [IX or X] small 4°, *pict.*, from St Saba. No. 8. Gospels [XI] 4°, with a marginal paraphrase and other matter, from του ξενοφου on Athos. No. 9. Gospels [XI] 4°, with faded red arabesques, from Caracalla. No. 10. Gospels [XI] 8°, *pict.*, from Caracalla. No. 11. Gospels [XII] 8°, from St Saba, as are the next two. No. 12. Gospels [XIII] 8°, with red arabesques. No. 13. Gospels [*dated* 1272] 12°, of which the Catalogue contains a *facsimile.*

In addition to Codd. 73, 74 (*see* p. 152 *and note*) Gaisford in 1837 catalogued, and Scrivener in 1861 inspected the following fourteen copies of the Gospels in the collection of Archbishop Wake, now at Christ Church, Oxford.

No. 12 (Apoc. 26, Apostol. 57) [XI] large folio, was also noted by Scholz, on Gaisford's information, Evangelistarium 187: but this is an error, as the Gospels are contained at full length and in their proper order, with unusually full liturgical matter, *rubro, Eus. t.*, *κεφ. t.*, *τίτλ.*, *Am.*, *Eus.*, *pict.* A *Lectionary* of the Acts and Epistles follows them, and last of all comes the Apocalypse.

No. 21 [XI] fol., brought from Παντοκράτωρ on Athos, 1727. *Prol.*, *Carp.* (later); but *primâ manu*, *Eus. t.*, *κεφ. t.*, *lect.*, *τίτλ.*, *κεφ.*, *Am.*, *Eus.*, the last written in the same line with *Am.*, not beneath them as usual (compare Cod. 112). The scribe's name, Abraham Teudatus, a Patrician (*Montf. Palaeo. Gr.* p. 46), is written cruciform after *Eus. t.*

No. 22 [XIII ?] small fol., in a wretched hand and bad condition, begins Matth. i. 23, ends John xix. 31. *Κεφ. t.*, *Am.* (not *Eus.*); *lect.*, but partly in a later hand.

No. 24 [XI] fol., from Παντοκράτωρ in 1727. *Eus. t.*, *prol.*, *κεφ. t.*, *pict.*, *τίτλ.*, *κεφ.*, *Am.*, *Eus.* in gold. One leaf (John xix. 13—29), and another containing John xxi. 24, 25, are in duplicate at the beginning, *primâ manu.* This copy (as Wake remarks) is in the same style, but less free than

No. 25 [X or XI] 4°, *pict.* (in red ink, nearly faded), *κεφ. t.*, *lect.*, *syn.*, *κεφ.*, and besides them another system of chapters, of which there are 116 in Matthew, 71 in Mark, 114 in Luke, 67 in John. The numbers given in Cod. 56 (see p. 148) are very similar.

the two missing Lowes copies, the priced sale catalogue mentions another manuscript of the Gospels, 2 vol. 12mo, No. 619, bought for £5. 10*s.* by Dr Farmer, who usually purchased for the Cambridge University Library, which does not appear to have been deposited there.

No. 27, *chart.* 8°. Matth. xviii. 9—Mark xiv. 13; Luke vii. 4—John xxi. 13 are [XIII], the rest supplied [XV]. *Lect.*, κεφ. *t.*, τίτλ., κεφ., *Am.*, (not *Eus.*).

No. 28 [XIV] 4°, κεφ. *t.*, τίτλ., κεφ. (not *Am.*, *Eus.*) *syn.*, *lect.*, much of this *in rubro.* Subscribed Θῡ το δωρον και γρηγοριου πονος.

No. 29 [*dated* ϛχ[1]λθ or 1131, Indict. 9] 4°. After some later fragments (Matth. i. 12—v. 3, and other matter) on paper, the older copy begins Matth. v. 29. Κεφ. *t.*, τίτλ., *Am.*, *Eus.*, *lect.*

No. 30 [XII] 4°, ending John xx. 18, neatly written, but in ill condition. Κεφ. *t.*, *Carp.*, *Eus. t.*, τίτλ., *Am.*, *Eus.*, *lect.*, in red, almost obliterated from damp.

No. 31 [XI] 4° small, in a very elegant and minute hand. *Pict.*, κεφ. *t.*, τίτλ. (in gold), κεφ., *Am.* (not *Eus.*), *lect.* full, and in red.

No. 32 [X or XI] 4° small, elegant, and with much gold ornament. *Carp.*, κεφ. *t.*, τίτλ., κεφ., *Am.*, *Eus.*, *pict.*, *prol.*, long subscriptions, *syn.*, *men.*

No. 36 [XII] 4°. Κεφ. *t.* in part, τίτλ., *Am.* (not *Eus.*), *lect.*, *pict.*

No. 39 [XIII] very small 4°, a poor copy, in several hands. Τίτλ., κεφ. only.

No. 40 [XII?] 16°, a beautiful little copy. *Syn.*, κεφ. *t.*, *lect.* in the faintest red, but no other divisions.

No. 34 [XI or XII] large 4°. This remarkable copy (mentioned p. 62, note 1, under Scholz's notation of Wake 2) begins with the ὑποθέσις to 2 Peter, the second leaf contains Acts xvii. 24—xviii. 13 misplaced, then follow the 5 later Catholic Epistles with ὑποθέσεις: then the Apocalypse on the same page as Jude ends, and the ὑποθέσις to the Romans on the same page as the Apocalypse ends, and then the Pauline Epistles. All the Epistles have *prol.*, κεφ. *t.*, and the Euthalian κεφ., with much *lect.* *primâ manu*, and *syn.* later. Last, but seemingly misplaced by the binder, follow the Gospels, ending Luke vi. 42. Here are τίτλ. in the margin by κεφ., *Am.* (not *Eus.*). This copy is Scholz's Act. 190, Paul. 244, Apoc. 27, but unnumbered in the Gospels.

Of these manuscripts Thomas Mangey [1684—1755], the editor of Philo, states on the fly-leaves that he collated Nos. 25, 28, 34 in 1749. Caspar Wetstein collated the Apocalypse in Nos. 12 (to be described in the next Section) and 34 for his relative's great edition; while in the margin of No. 35, a 4° Greek Testament printed at Geneva (1620), is inserted a most laborious collation (preceded by a full description) of eight of the Wake manuscripts with Wetstein's N. T. of 1711, having this title prefixed to them, "Hae Variae lectiones ex MSS. notatae sunt manu et opera Johannis Walkeri, A. 1732:" John Walker (most of whose labours seem never yet to have been used) was doubtless the Vice-Master of Trinity College, Cambridge, where so many of his critical materials

[1] The letter χ is quite illegible, but the Indiction 9 belongs only to A.D. 831, 1131, 1431, and the style of the manuscript leaves no doubt which to choose.

accumulated for the illustrious Bentley are deposited[1]. Of his eight codices, we find on investigation that Walker's C is Wake 26; Walker's 1 is Wake 20 (collations of these two, sent by Walker to Wetstein, comprise Codd. 73, 74, described above); Walker's B is Wake 21; Walker's D is Wake 24, both of the Gospels; Walker's E is Wake 18, his H is Wake 19, both Evangelistaria; Walker's q is Wake 12, of which Caspar Wetstein afterwards examined the Apocalypse (Cod. 26); Walker's W is Wake 38 of the Acts and Epistles, or Scholz's Act. 191, Paul. 245.

To this list we must add the five following copies from the collection of the Abbot M. L. Canonici, purchased at Venice in 1817 for the Bodleian Library, by the late Dr Bandinel.

Canon. Gk. 33 [xv] fol., *chart.*, St Matthew, with the Latin chapters only, once belonged to Anthony Dizomaeus.

Ibid. 34 [*dated* 1515, 1516: *see* p. 37, note 3] 4°, *chart.*, written by Michael Damascenus the Cretan for John Francis Picus of Mirandola, contains the whole N. T., the Apocalypse alone being yet collated (k^{scr}): *mut.* Apoc. ii. 11—23. It has Oecumenius' and Euthalius' *prol.*

Ibid. 36 [xi] 4°, Gospels: *olim Georg. Phlebaris: pict.*, *κεφ. t.*, *syn.*, *men.*

Ibid. 112 [xii] 4°, Gospels well written: *Carp.*, *pict.*, *κεφ. t.*, *lect.*, *syn.*

Ibid. 122 Cod. Illyricus [*dated* 1429] 4°, Gospels in Illyrian with a Greek version later, written in Moldavia by Gabriel, a monk. *Prol.*, *pict.*, *κεφ. t.*, *syn.*, *men.*

The five following also are in the Bodleian and uncollated:

Barocc. 59. 1 [xv] 4°, *chart.*, has six leaves [xi] containing Luke xxiii. 38—xxiv. 53, and *κεφ. t.* of John.

Cromwell 15 [xi] 4°, Gospels well written: this and the next copy were brought from Παντοκράτωρ on Athos, 1727. *Carp.*, *Eus. t.*, *prol.*, *κεφ. t.*, *τίτλ.*, *κεφ.*, *mut.* at end.

Cromwell 16 [xi] 4°, Gospels (followed by the Proper Lessons for the Holy Week), *pict.*, *κεφ. t.*, *Eus. t.*, *Am.*, *Eus.*, *syn.*

Miscell. 17, Auct. D. Infr. 2. 21 [xi] 4°, Gospels, *prol.*, *κεφ. t.*, *Eus.*, *syn.*, in text said to resemble Cod. 71, was presented by S. Smallbrooke in 1800.

[1] This humble friend is said to have rejoiced at the prospect of living in the pages of Pope's *Dunciad*, in company with the great Master of Trinity:

"Before them march'd that awful Aristarch;
Plough'd was his front with many a deep remark:
His hat, which never veiled to human pride,
Walker with reverence took, and laid aside."—*Dunciad*, IV. 203.

And again: "'Walker! our hat'—nor more he deign'd to say,
But stern as Ajax' spectre strode away."—*ibid.* 273.

Miscell. 141, Rawl. Auct. G. 3 [XI] 4°, Gospels and other matter; κεφ. t.

The Rev. H. O. Coxe, now Bodley's Librarian, though quite unable to purchase any of the literary treasures he was commissioned to inspect in 1857[1], has added considerably to our knowledge of manuscripts in the East: those of the Gospels in Greek are the fifty-one following:

(α) In the Library of the Patriarch of Alexandria at Cairo; Shelf 1, No. 2 [XIII] 4°; No. 15 [XI] 4°, *mut.*; No. 16 [XI] 4°, *syn.*, beautifully written; No. 17 [XI] 4°; Shelf 5, No. 68 [X] 4°: and at the Cairo *μετοικία* of St Catherine's on Sinai, No. 7, the Gospels and Psaltery [XVI] fol., *chart.*

(β) At the great Greek Monastery of the Holy Sepulchre at Jerusalem, besides Scholz's Cod. 450 (No. 6) and Cod. 456 (No. 43) are No. 2 [X] 4°, beautifully written; No. 5 [X] 4°; No. 14 [XII] large 4°, with Scholia; No. 17 [XI] 4°, with a few Scholia; No. 31 [XI] 4°, very beautiful; No. 32 [XI] 4°; No. 33 [XII] 4°; No. 40 [XII] 4°, a fine copy of the Gospels, Acts, and all the Epistles; No. 41 [XI] 4°, a beautiful copy; No. 44 [XIV] fol.; No. 45 [XII] 4°, the Gospels and all the Epistles, but only *λέξεις τῶν πράξεων*. No. 46 [XI] small 4°: and at the College of the Holy Cross there, No. 3 [XI] 4°, *syn.*, *κεφ.*

(γ) At St Saba (see p. 177, note 2) No. 27 [XII] fol.; Nos. 52, 53 [XI] 4°, two copies of the Gospels and all the Epistles, No. 52 having *syn.*; No. 54 contains the same [XII] 4°; No. 56 [X] 4° small, Gospels only; as have also Nos. 57—60 [X or XI]; No. 61, five copies of the Gospels [XI] 4°; No. 62, five other copies [XII] 4°. In a kind of lumber-room called the Tower Library, in wretched keeping, are No. 45 [XI] 4°; No. 46 [XII] 4°; No. 47 [XI] small 4°, all of the Gospels.

(δ) Three copies (Nos. 2, 6, 21) at the convent of St John at Patmos[2] seem to be Scholz's Codd. 467—9 (see p. 177, note 3), and must not be reckoned again: there are besides No. 59 [X] 4°; No. 77 [XI] 4°.

[1] Those who venerate the Greek Church for what she has been, or look forward to her future with hope, may well take comfort from the spirit in which Mr Coxe's fair offers of purchase were invariably met. Of the rulers of the Convent of the Holy Sepulchre he writes (*Report to Her Majesty's Government*, p. 10), "They would not entertain the idea for a moment. They had now, they said, become aware of the value of what they possessed, although they admitted that a few years since it was far otherwise, and that a collector would have found little difficulty in obtaining anything he wished for barely more than the asking."

[2] Mr Coxe found the Librarian of the Bodleian peculiarly unpopular at St John's Convent, Patmos; from whose Library E. D. Clarke [1769—1822] had obtained the early dated copy of Plato's Dialogues (now Clarke 39) described above p. 36 and note 3. "The authorities were well acquainted with, and all deplored the loss they had sustained in their Plato, and knew perfectly well where it is now deposited. No money would tempt them to part with their Job." [VII. or VIII.] (*Report to Her Majesty's Government*, p. 27.)

(ε) At Larnaka in Cyprus the Bishop of Citium has one copy [XII] 4°, *syn.*

(ζ) In the Island of Milo, in private hands, one copy neatly written A.D. 1305 by a Cyprian. To all this valuable information Mr Coxe adds, that Le Barbier, an eminent French archaeologist, has lately been making a tour of the Monastic libraries at Athos, with the view of publishing a full account of the manuscript treasures still remaining there.

Dr S. T. Bloomfield has lately published (1860), as a Supplement to the ninth edition of his Greek Testament, "Critical Annotations on the Sacred Text," as an *opus supremum et ultimum*, the last effort of a prolonged, arduous, and honourable literary career. It professes to be grounded on the examination of no less than 70 Manuscripts, 23 at Lambeth, the rest in the British Museum; but in the absence of all formal description of his documents, or definite explanation, we may infer that they were not so much collated throughout, as consulted on the very numerous passages discussed in his work. We have already acknowledged his labours with regard to manuscripts included in the preceding catalogue: but his list embraces also the following codices (making in all 30 of the Gospels), which he has been the first to render available.

Brit. Mus. Addit. 7141 [XIII] 4°, bought 1825, and once Claudius James Rich's. *Carp.*, *Eus. t.*, *κεφ. t.*, *Am.*, *Eus.*, *lect.* in red. No *τίτλ.*, *κεφ.*

B. M. 11836, this and the next two are from Bishop Butler's collection: [XI], small 4°, contains Evan. Act. Cath. Paul. Psalms, &c. *Mut.* Mark i. 1—28; Acts i. 1—23; vii. 8—39; Ps. i. 1—3. *Pict.*, *Eus. t.*, (i.e. a blank space is left for them), *τίτλ.*, *Am.* (not *Eus.*), no *prol.*, *κεφ.* in Epistles.

B. M. 11838 [*dated* 1326, Ind. 9] fol., from Sinai, most beautifully written by Constantine, a monk. *Syn.*, *κεφ. t.*, *pict.*, *lect.*, all in a later hand, *τίτλοι.*

B. M. 11839 [XV] 4°, *chart.*, ill-written, with later marginal notes, and no chapter-divisions. *Lect.;* Matth. iv. 13—xi. 27; Mark i. 1—vi. 1, are later.

B. M. 14774 [XII] *syn.*, is Cod. 202 of Griesbach, from St Mark's, at Florence.

B. M. 15581 [XII] *κεφ. t.*, once Melch. Thevenot's. See above, Cod. 272.

B. M. 16183 [XII] 4°, in a minute hand, bought of Capt. Macdonald in 1846.

B. M. 16184 [XIV] 4°, the whole New Testament.

B. M. 16943 [XI], in a very small hand, *Eus. t.*, *pict.*, from the collection made by the Hon. F. North for the University of Corfu.

B. M. 17469 [XIV] small fol., *syn.*, with an hiatus about 1 Tim. iii. 16. This copy is j^{scr} in the Apocalypse.

B. M. 17741 [XII] 4°, *pict.*, begins Matth. xii. 21, ends John xvii. 13: purchased in 1849.

B. M. 17982 [XIII] 4°, ending John xix. 38 (eight leaves being lost), and believed to contain important readings.

B. M. 18211 [XIII] 4°.

B. M. 19387 [XII], written by one Leo, begins Matth. viii. 12, and was purchased in 1853 from the well-known M. Simonides.

B. M. 19389 [XIII] 12°, St John's Gospel only.

Another copy, B. M. 17470 [*dated* 1034], purchased of H. Rodd in 1848, does not appear to have been collated by Dr Bloomfield.

Harl. 5538, described in the Harleian Catalogue as an Evangelistarium, and numbered by Scholz Evst. 149, I find to be a copy of the Gospels [XIV] 12°, *lect.*, with no κεφ., *Am.*, *Eus.*

There is also a fine fragment of the Gospels [XIV], at Sion College, London.

After deducting 32 duplicates, &c., we have enumerated 601 cursive copies of the Gospels.

Manuscripts of the Acts and Catholic Epistles.

*1. (= Evan. 1).

2. (Paul. 2) Cod. Basil. B. IX. 38? [XII?] 8°, with Theophylact's Commentary, once belonged to the Preaching Friars, then to Amerbach, a printer of Basle. It was the copy on which Erasmus grounded the text of his first edition (1516), and he calls it "exemplar mirè castigatum." It is Mill's B. 2. (Battier, Wetstein).

3. (= Evan. 3).

4. (Paul. 4) Basil. B. 20 [XV] 8°, Mill's B. 3, elegantly written, the Pauline Epistles preceding the Catholic (*see p.* 61). Erasmus made some use of it for revising his text (Battier, Wetstein).

5. (= Evan. 5). 6. (= Evan. 6).

7. (Paul. 9) Paris Reg. 102 [X] 8°, *prol.*, seems to be Stephens' ι', although ι' is cited in error Luke v. 19; John ii. 17: it nearly resembles Cod. 5 and the Latin version.

8. (Paul. 10) Stephens' ια', now missing, cited about 400 times by that editor, in 276 of which it supports the Latin versions (Mill, N.T. Proleg. § 1171). Stephens cites ια' (apparently in error) four times in the Gospels, once in the Apocalypse. (Matth. x. 8; 10; xii. 32; John ii. 17; Apoc. xiii. 4).

9. (Paul. 11) Cod. Vatabli, now in the University Library at Cambridge, 2068 or Kk. 6. 4 [XI]. Bp. Marsh has fully proved that this copy, which once belonged to Stephens' friend Vatablus, Professor of Hebrew at Paris, is his ιγ': this copy also is twice quoted by him in the Gospels (Matth. xxvii. 64; John ii. 17), through mere oversight.

10. (Paul. 12, Apoc. 2) Reg. 237, Stephens' ιε' [X] 4°, neatly written, with *prol.*, scholia and other matter. Lelong identified this, and about five other of Stephens' manuscripts: its value in the Apocalypse is considerable (Wetstein, Scholz).

11. (Paul. 140) Reg. 103 [X] 8°, with scholia, *mut.* Act. ii. 20—31.

12. (Paul. 16, Apoc. 4) Reg. 219 [XI] 4°, neat, with Arethas' Commentary on the Apocalypse, and Oecumenius' on the other books. Like Evan. 16. 19. 317, it once belonged to the Medici: in 1518 it was given by the Greek Janus Lascar "Petro Masieli" of Constance, and was used by Donatus of Verona for an edition of Oecumenius (Wetstein, Scholz).

*13. (= Evan. 33). 14. (= Evan. 35).

15. Coislin. 25 [XI] 4°, described by Montfaucon (as were also Codd. 16—18), compared with Pamphilus' revision (*see p.* 47), *prol.*, and a Commentary digested by Andreas, a priest (Wetstein).

16. (Paul. 19) Coislin. 26 [XI] fol., with a Commentary much like Oecumenius', and a catena of various Fathers: also a life of S. Longinus on two leaves [IX]. It once belonged to the monastery of S. Athanasius on Athos, βίβλιον τῆς τετάρτης θέσεως (Wetstein).

17. (Paul. 21, Apoc. 19) Coisl. 205 [written by Antony, a monk, 1079. Indict. 2] fol., *prol., syn., mut.* 1 Cor. xvi. 17—2 Cor. i. 7; Hebr. xiii. 15—25; with Apoc. i. 1—ii. 5 in a recent hand (Wetstein).

18. (Paul. 22, Apoc. 18) Coislin. 202, 2 [foll. 1—26 XI on vellum, the rest XIII on cotton paper], with scholia to the Acts and Catholic Epistles, Andreas' Commentary to the Apocalypse, *prol.* to St Paul's Epistles (Wetstein).

19. (= Evan. 38).

20. (Paul. 25) Brit. Mus. King's Library, I. B. I, once Westminster 935 [XIV] *chart., prol., mut.*, and in bad condition (Wetstein).

21. (Paul. 26) Cambridge University Libr. Dd. XI. 90 [XIII] 12°, once Jo. Luke's: *mut.* Act. i—xi; xiv. 23—xv. 10; Rom. xv. 14—16; 24—26; xvi. 4—20; 1 Cor. i. 15—iii. 12; 2 Tim. i. 1—ii. 4; Tit. i. 9—ii. 15; ending Philem. 2. *Prol.* to Pauline Epistles only.

22. (Paul. 75 is in the same hand) Brit. Mus. Addit. 5115, once Askew's [XII] 4°, *κεφ. t., prol.*, ending with κεφ. to the Romans: *mut.* Act. i. 1—11: *lect.* is later (Act. i—xx. collated by Paulus for Griesbach, Bloomfield): Scholz's date [IX] is an error.

23. (Paul. 28, Apoc. 6) Bodleian. Barocc. 3 [XI] small 4°, a beautiful little book, written at Ephesus, beginning Act. xi. 13, ending Apoc. xx. 1: *mut.* 1 Pet. iii. 7—23: the opening chapters are supplied in a late hand. With the Euthalian *prol.* and scholia on the Epistles, and a full and unique Commentary on the Apocalypse, edited by J. A. Cramer, 1840 (Mill, Caspar Wetstein, Griesbach).

*24. (Paul. 29) Christ's Coll. Cambridge F. 1. 13 [XII] 4°, *mut.* Act. i. 1—11; xviii. 20—xx. 14; James v. 14—1 Pet. i. 4, and some leaves of this fine copy are torn or decayed: there are also many changes by a later hand (Mill's Cant. 2, Scrivener's 1): unpublished collations were made by Bentley (Trin. Coll. Camb. B. XVII. 10, 11), and Jo. Wigley for Jackson (Jesus Coll. Camb. O. Θ. 1).

25. (Paul. 31, Apoc. 7) Harleian 5537, or Covell. 2 [*dated* Pentecost, 1087, Indict. 10] 4°, an important copy, from the neighbourhood of the Ægean, with the στίχοι numbered, and a lexicon: *mut.*

1 John v. 14—2 John 6 (Mill, Griesbach, Bloomfield, Scrivener in Apoc.).

26. (Paul. 32) Harl. 5557, Covell. 3 [xii] 4°, *mut.* Act. i. 1—11; 1 Cor. xi. 7—xv. 56: *syn.*, *lect.*, *prol.*, *στίχοι*. This copy and the next bear Covell's emblem "*Luceo*," and the date Constantinople, 1675, but he got Cod. 27 from Adrianople. (Mill, Paulus in Act. i—iii. Bloomfield).

27. (Paul. 33) Harl. 5620 [xv] 4°, *chart.*, or Covell. 4, is of some weight: there are no chapter-divisions *p. m.*; the writing is small, and abbreviated (Mill, Griesbach, Bloomfield).

*28. (Paul. 34, Apoc. 8) Harl. 5778, is Covell's 5[1] or Sinai manuscript, [xii] 4°, in wretched condition, and often illegible. *Mut.* Act. i. 1—20; Apoc. vi. 14—viii. 1; xxii. 19—21, perhaps elsewhere (Mill, Bloomfield for Act. Paul., Scrivener for Apoc.).

29. (Paul. 35) Genevensis 20 [xi or xii] 12°, brought from Greece, beautifully but carelessly written, without subscriptions; in text much like Cod. 27 (readings sent to Mill, Scholz).

30. (Paul. 36, Apoc. 9) Bodleian Misc. 74 [xi] 4°, brought from the East by Dr Robert Huntington, beginning Act. xv. 19, *κεφ.*, *prol.* 3 John, Jude, the Apocalypse and St Paul's Epistles, which stand last, are in a somewhat earlier hand than the rest (Mill).

*31. (= Evan. 69).

32. (= Evan. 51) *mut.* 2 Pet. iii. 2—18.

33. (Paul. 39). Lincoln Coll. Oxford 82 [xi or xii] 4°, presented in 1483 by Robert Flemmynge, Dean of Lincoln, a beautiful and interesting codex, with *pict.*, *prol.*, *lect.*, *syn.*, *men.*, and the numbers of the *στίχοι* noted in the subscriptions. *Mut.* 2 Pet. i. 1—15; Rom. i. 1—20 (Walton's Polyglott, Mill, Dobbin *Cod. Montfort.*, who regards it as the manuscript from which this portion of the latter was mainly copied). The Epistle of Jude stands between James and 1 Peter (see p. 103).

*34. (= Evan. 61). 35. (= Evan. 57).

36. New College, Oxford 58 [xiii] 4°, with a Catena of Fathers, enumerated by Mill (N. T. Prol. § 1390), and edited by Cramer, Oxon. 1838: with a valuable text, *prol.*, and *τίτλοι κεφαλαίων* (Walton's Polyglott, Mill).

37. (Paul. 43) New Coll. Oxford 59 [xiii] 4°, erroneously described by Walton, and after him by Wetstein, as part of Evan. 58, a much later manuscript. It is a beautiful copy, *prol.*, with marginal glosses (Walton's Polyglott, Mill, Dobbin).

*38. (Paul. 44) Lugduno-Batav. 77, Mill's Petav. 1 [xiii.] 4°, once Petavius', a Councillor of Paris, given by Queen Christina to Is. Vossius (Mill, Wetstein, Dermout 1825).

39. (Paul. 45, Apoc. 11) Petavii 2, age and present locality not

[1] Covell once marked this codex 5, but afterwards gave it the name of the Sinai MS., reserving 5 for Harl. 5777 or Evan. 446.

stated. *Mut.* Act. i. 1—xviii. 22; James i. 1—v. 17; 3 John 9—Jude 25; 1 Cor. iii. 16—x. 13 (Extracts in Mill; J. Gachon).

40. (Paul. 46, Apoc. 12) Alexandrino-Vat. 179, Petavii 3 [XI] 4°, with a mixed text and the end of Titus (from iii. 3), Philemon and the Apocalypse in a later hand. This copy, given by Christina to Alexander VIII. (1689—91), is of considerable importance, and as containing all Euthalius' labours on the Acts and the Epistles (see p. 53), was largely used by Laur. Zacagni for his edition of his Prologues, &c. (Extracts in Mill, Zacagni, Birch; Griesbach adds, "Gagnaeus eundem sub Dionysiani nomine laudasse creditur.")

41. (= Evan. 175).

*42. (Paul. 48, Apoc. 13. Evst.—Lect. 56). Gymnasium at Frankfort on the Oder, once Seidel's [XI] 4°, carelessly written, with some rare readings: *prol.*, *mut.* Act. ii. 3—34 (xxvii. 19—34 is in a later hand); 2 Pet. i. 1, 2; 1 John v. 11—21; Apoc. xviii. 3—13 (N. Westermann, H. Middeldorp). One leaf of a Lectionary is added, containing Matth. xvii. 16—23; 1 Cor. ix. 2—12. This copy often agrees closely with the Complutensian text and Laud. 31 (Evan. 51) jointly.

43. (= Evan. 76).

44. (Like Evan. 82, Paul. 51, Apoc. 5) certain manuscripts cited by Laurentius Valla.

45. (Paul. 52, Apoc. 16) Uffenbach 1 or 2 [XV] 4°, *chart.*, in two hands, is stated by Tischendorf to be now at Hamburg: with its companion Cod. M of St Paul's Epistles, it was lent to Wetstein in 1717 and to Bengel, by Z. C. Uffenbach. It once belonged to Jo. Ciampini at Rome, is carelessly written, but from a good text; "plura genuina omittens, quam aliena admiscens:" Bengel.

46. (Paul. 55) Monacensis 375 [XI] fol., is Bengel's Augustan. 6, with Oecumenius' Commentary and some rare readings (Bengel, Matthaei, Scholz).

47. (= Evan. 90). 48. (= Evan. 105). 49. (= Evan. 92).

50. (Paul. 8) Stephens' ζ′ is unknown, though it was once in the Royal Library at Paris; that is if Evan. 8, Reg. 49, is Stephens' ζ′ in the Gospels, which may perhaps be doubted. Stephens seldom cites ζ′, or (as Mill puts the case) "textus ipsius fere universus absorptus est in hac Editione" (N. T., Proleg. § 1167)[1].

51. (Paul. 133, Apoc. 52) Paris Reg. 56, once Mazarin's [XII] 4°, *prol.*, *mut.*, Apoc. xxii. 17—21.

52. (Paul. 50) Cod. Rhodiensis, some of whose readings Stunica, the chief of the Complutensian editors (see Chapter v.), cites in controversy with Erasmus: it may have been his own property, and

[1] I find that ζ′ is cited in Stephens' margin 84 times in the Gospels, usually in company with several others, but alone Mark vi. 20; xiv. 15; Luke i. 37. In the Acts it is cited but once (xvii. 5), in the Catholic Epistles 7, in the Pauline 27 times; never in the Apocalypse. Since Cod. 8 contains only the Gospels, Cod. 18 or Reg. 47 of the whole N. T. has been suggested. One hour in the Imperial Library at Paris would suffice to settle the question.

cannot now be identified. Whatever Mill states (on 1 John iii. 16), it is not now at Alcala.

*53. (Paul. 30) Emman. College, Cambr. I. 4. 35 [XII] 16°, only 4½ inches square, the writing being among the minutest and most elegant extant. It is Mill's Cant. 3, Scrivener's n (a *facsimile* is given Plate XI. No. 31 b), and is in bad condition, in parts almost illegible. It begins 2 Pet. ii. 4, and there is an hiatus from 1 John iii. 20 to the middle of Oecumenius' Prologue to the Romans: *mut.* also 1 Cor. xi. 7—xv. 56, and ends Hebr. xi. 27. From 1 Tim. vi. 5 another and far less careful hand begins: but the manuscript exhibits throughout many abbreviations. *Prol.*, κεφ. *t.*, τίτλοι, κεφ., and some marginal notes *primâ manu.* Given to the College "in Testimonium grati animi" by Sam. Wright 1598.

54. (= Evan. 43).

55. Readings of a *second* copy of Jude contained in Cod. 47.

56. (Paul. 59, Apoc. 23). This number was assigned by Wetstein and Griesbach to certain readings of four Medicean manuscripts (only one in the Acts), which like No. 102 of the Gospels, were found by Wetstein in the margin of Rapheleng's Greek Testament (1591). As Birch considers these identical with Codd. 84, 87—9, Scholz substitutes (Paul. 227) Cod. Bodleian., Clarke 4 [XII] 4°, *prol.*, κεφ., *syn.*, *lect.* (extracts &c. by Dean Gaisford).

57. (= Evan. 234).

58. of Wetstein is the same codex as 22; Scholz substitutes (Paul. 224) Bodl., Clarke 9 [XIII] 8°, *lect.*, *mut.* Hebr. xiii. 7—25 (Gaisford).

59. (Paul. 62) Harleian. 5588 [XIII] 4°, cotton paper, *prol.*, full *lect.*, κεφ. On the first leaf we read "liber hospitalis de Cusa trevirencis dioc. R^mi^." See Cod. Evan. 87 (Griesbach, Bloomfield).

60. (Paul. 63, Apoc. 29) Harl. 5613 [*dated* May 1407, Indict. 15] 4° *chart.*, *mut.* Apoc. xxii. 2—18. (Griesbach 55 chapters of Acts and Epp., Griesbach and Scrivener in Apocalypse).

*61. (Paul. 61) comprises extracts made by Griesbach from the margin of a copy of Mill's N. T. in the Bodleian (see Evan. 236), where certain readings are cited under the notation *Hal.* These are now known to be taken from Evan. 440 (p. 176), or Scrivener's v of the Gospels, o of the Acts and Epistles.

62. (Paul. 65) Reg. 60, once Colbert's [XIV] fol., on cotton paper, with scholia, *prol.*, *syn.* (Wetstein, Griesbach, Scholz).

*63. (Paul. 68). Caesar-Vindobon. Nessel. 313, Lambec. 35 [XIV] 8°, with scholia and *prol.* (Treschow, Alter, Birch).

*64. (Paul. 69) C. Vind. Nessel. 303, Lambec. 36 [XII] 8°, carefully written by one John, *prol.*, *syn.*, brought by Auger Busbecke from Constantinople, like Cod. 67 and many others of this collection (Treschow, Alter, Birch).

*65. (= Evan. 218).

*66. (Paul. 67, Apoc. 34) C. Vind. Nessel. 302, Lambec. 34 [XII] 4°, with scholia, *syn.*, and other matter: three several hands have made corrections, which Griesbach regarded as far more valuable than the text (cited by him 66**). *Mut.* Apoc. xv. 6—xvii. 3; xviii. 10—xix. 9; xx. 8—xxii. 21. It once belonged to Arsenius Archbishop of Monembasia (see Evan. 333, Evst. 113), then to Sebastian Tengnagel and Jo. Sambuc (A. C. Hwiid 1785 for the Acts, Treschow, Alter, Birch).

*67. (Paul. 70) C. Vind. Nessel. 221, Lambec. 37 [written by one Leo at Constantinople, December 1331, Indict. 14] 4°, elegant but inaccurate, *prol.*, *syn.* (Treschow, Alter, Birch).

68. (Paul. 73) Upsal., Sparwenfeld 42, is in fact two separate manuscripts, bound together, both of high value. The first part [XII] contains the Acts (commencing viii. 14) Rom. 1 Cor. to xv. 38: the second [XI] begins 1 Cor. xiii. 6, and extends through the Pauline and Catholic Epistles, which follow them (see p. 61). There is a Catena annexed, and the portion in duplicate (1 Cor. xiii. 6—xv. 38) has contradictory readings (P. F. Aurivill [Orville?] 1686).

69. (Paul. 74, Apoc. 30) Guelpherbytanus XVI. 7 at Wolfenbüttel, Aug. 7, 4°, *chart.* also in two hands: the first (Acts and Epistles) [XIII] written by George a monk, the Apocalypse [XIV]. It exhibits a remarkable text, and has many marginal readings and *prol.* (Knittel, Matthaei).

70. (=Evan. 131). 71. (=Evan. 133).

72. (Paul. 79, Apoc. 37) Vatic. 366 [XIII] 4°, *chart.* (This and all from 70 to 97 were slightly collated by Birch, and all except 81, 93—7 by Scholz also).

73. (Paul. 80) Vat. 367 [XI] 4°, an excellent manuscript used by Caryophilus (see p. 157, Evan. 112).

74. Vat. 760 [XII] 4°, only contains the Acts with a Catena.

75. (=Evan. 141). 76. (=Evan 142). 77. (=Evan. 149).

78. (Paul. 89). Alexandrino-Vat. 29 [XII] 4°, a good copy, but *mut.* 2 Cor. xi. 15—xii. 1; Ephes. i. 9—Hebr. xiii. 25.

79. (Paul. 90) Urbino-Vat. 3 [XI] 8°.

80. (Paul. 91, Apoc. 42) Pio-Vat. 50 [XII] 8°.

81. Barberin. 377 [XI] fol., with a Commentary (Birch). Scholz could not find this copy, which has remarkable readings: it contains but one chapter of the Acts and the Catholic Epistles.

82. (=Evan. 180).

83. (Paul. 93) Biblio. Borbon. Reg. at Naples 1 B. 12 [X] 4°, written by Evagrius and compared with Pamphilus' copy at Caesarea (see p. 47 and Cod. 15): the numbers of the στίχοι are sometimes noted in the margin.

84. (Paul. 94) Laurent. IV. 1, at Florence [X] fol., has Chrysostom's Commentary on the Acts, that of Nicetas of Heraclea on all the Epistles.

85. (Paul. 95) Laurent. IV. 5 [XIII] fol., on cotton paper, contains the Acts and *Pauline* Epistles with Theophylact's Commentary.

86. (Paul. 96, Apoc. 75) Laurent. IV. 20 [XI] 8°, with a Commentary.

87. (Paul. 97) Laurent. IV. 29 [X] 4°, with scholia, *prol.*, and a *modern* interlinear Latin version in the Epistles, for beginners.

88. (Paul. 98) Laurent. IV. 31 [XI] 8°, *prol.*, *mut.* in fine Titi.

89. (Paul. 99, Apoc. 45) Laurent. IV. 32, 12°, written by John Tzutzuna, priest and monk, December 1093, Indict. 1, in the reign of Alexius Comnenus, Nicholas being Patriarch of Constantinople. *Prol.*, *syn.*, and a treatise of Dorotheus Bishop of Tyre on the 70 disciples and 12 Apostles (found also in Codd. 10, 179).

90. (=Evan. 197). 91. (=Evan. 201). 92. (=Evan. 204).

*93. (=Evan. 205). *94. (=Evan. 206). *95. (=Evan. 209).

*96. (Paul. 109) Venet. 11 [XI] 4°, an important copy, often resembling Cod. 142, from the monastery of St Michael de Troyna in Sicily. It has both a Latin and Arabic version. *Mut.* Act. i. 1—12; xxv. 21—xxvi. 18; Philemon. Codd. 93—96 of the Acts, 106—112 of St Paul, were collated by G. F. Rink, *Lucubratio Critica in Act. Ap. Epp. Cath. et Paul.* Basilae 1830.

97. (Paul. 241) Biblioth. Guelpherbyt. Gud. gr. 104. 2 [XII] 8°; once belonging to Langer, librarian at Wolfenbüttel, who sent a collation to Griesbach. *Mut.* Act. xvi. 39—xvii. 18, with marginal scholia from Chrysostom and Oecumenius, prayers and dialogues subjoined. Deposited by one Theodoret in the Catechumens' library of the Laura (monastery) of St Athanasius on Athos.

Codd. 98—107 were accurately collated by Matthaei for his N. T.

*98. (Paul. 113) Codex Mosquensis (Mt. a) [XI], once belonged to Jeremias the patriarch of the monastery of Stauronicetas on Athos. Matthaei professes that he chiefly followed this manuscript, which is divided into three parts: viz. a_1 church-lessons from the Acts, so arranged that no verse is lost, with various readings and scholia in the margin: a_2 or simply *a* the text with marginal various readings and scholia: a_3 Church-lessons from the Acts and Epistles.

*99. (Paul. 114) Mosq. Synod. 5 (Mt. c) [*dated* April 1445] fol., *chart.*, from the Iberian monastery on Athos, carelessly written by Theognostus, Metropolitan of Perga and Attalia: *prol.*, *syn.*, and some Patristic writings.

*100. (Paul. 115) Synod. 334 (Mt. d) [XI] 4°, with a Catena and scholia.

*101. (Paul. 116) Synod. 333 (Mt. f) [XIII] 4°, on cotton paper, carefully written, with scholia to the Acts and *prol.*

*102. (Paul. 117) Synod. 98 (Mt. g) [IX?] fol., from the monastery of St Dionysius on Athos, containing the Epistles with a Catena, without the Acts, is highly valued by Matthaei, but does not seem to be an uncial copy. *Mut.* Rom. x. 18—1 Cor. vi. 13; viii. 7—12.

*103. (Paul. 118) Synod. 193 (Mt. h) [XII] fol., from the Iberian monastery on Athos, is a volume of scholia, with the entire text in its margin for Act. i. 1—ix. 12; elsewhere only in fragments after the usual manner of scholia.

*104. (= Evan. 241). *105. (= Evan. 242).

*106. (Paul. 122) Synod. 328 (Mt. m) [xi] 4°, carefully written, from the Batopedion(?) monastery on Athos, has *prol.*, *syn.*, and the Psalms annexed.

*107. (Evst. 57) Cod. Dresdensis 252 (Mt. 19) [xv] 8°, *chart.*, a Euchology, carelessly written by several scribes. It came from Italy, and, like Apoc. 32, once belonged to Loescher, then to the Count de Brühl.

108. (= Evan. 226). 109. (= Evan. 228).

Codd. 110—192 were first added to the list by Scholz, who states that he collated entire 115, 133, 160; in the greater part 120—3, 126, 127, 131, 137, 161—3, 174; the rest slightly or not at all.

110. (= Evan. 441) should be erased from the Catalogue.

*111. (= Ev. 440). This is Scrivener's o Act. and Paul.

112. Cantabrig. 2068 erase: it is the same as Cod. 9.

*113. (= Evan. 18). Codd. 113, 114, 117, being 132, 134, 137, of St Paul, and 51 Apoc. respectively, together with Act. 127 and Paul. 139, 140, 153 have been collated by J. G. Reiche.

*114. (Paul. 134) Reg. 57 [xiii] 4°, a valuable copy, with *prol.*, *syn.*, some portions of the Septuagint version, and prayers for the Greek service.

*115. (Paul. 135) Reg. 58, once Colbert's, as were 118, 121, 122, 124, 128, 129 [xiii] 4°, begins Act. xiv. 27 ends with 2 Tim.; there are no liturgical notes.

116. (Paul. 136, Apoc. 53) Reg. 59, once Teller's [xvi] 4°, *chart.*, *prol.* and scholia to the Catholic Epistles.

*117. (= Evan. 263) of some value.

118. (Paul. 138, Apoc. 55) Reg. 101 [xiii] fol., on cotton paper, with *prol.*, scholia, and other matter. *Mut.* Act. xix. 18—xxii. 17.

119. (Paul. 139, Apoc. 56) Reg. 102 A. [x, but Apoc. xiii] fol., *prol.*, *syn.*, *mut.* 2 Cor. i. 8—ii. 4. The Catholic Epistles follow the Pauline, as would seem to be the case in Cod. 120.

120. (Paul. 141) Reg. 103 A. [xi] fol., *prol.*, much mutilated, beginning Act. xxi. 20 (although v. 38—vi. 7; vii. 6—16; 32—x. 25 are supplied [xiii] on cotton paper), *mut.* Act. xxviii. 23—Rom. ii. 26; Phil. i. 5—1 Thess. iv. 1; v. 26—2 Thess. i. 11; 1 John ii. 11 —iii. 3; 24—v. 14; 2 John; ending 3 John 11.

121. (Paul. 142) Reg. 104 [xiii] fol., on cotton paper, was August. de Thou's before Colbert's: *lect.*, *syn.*

122. (Paul. 143) Reg. 105 [xi] 4°, correctly written, but a mere collection of disarranged fragments, containing Act. xiii. 48—xv. 22; 29—xvi. 36; xvii. 4—xviii. 26; xx. 16—xxviii. 17; 1 Pet. ii. 20—iii. 2; 17—1 John iii. 5; 21—v. 9; 2 John 8—3 John 10; Jude 7 —Rom. iv. 16; 24—vii. 9; 18—1 Cor. i. 28; ii. 13—viii. 1; ix. 6 —xiv. 2; 10—Gal. i. 10; ii. 4—Eph. i. 18; 1 Tim. i. 14—v. 5.

123. (Paul. 144) Reg. 106 A. [xiv] 8°, on cotton paper, with *prol.*, scholia and Church-hymns: *mut.* 1 Pet. i. 9—ii. 7.

124. (Paul. 149, Apoc. 57) Reg. 124 [xvi] 16°, beautifully written by Angelus Vergecius (p. 38, note 2).

125. (Paul. 150) Reg. 125 [xiv] 12°, from Constantinople.

126. (Paul. 153) Reg. 216, from the Medici collection [x] fol., probably written at Constantinople, with *prol.*, and a Catena from Chrysostom, Ammonius, Origen, &c., sometimes in uncial letters, occasionally, especially in Hebr., as late as [xvi].

*127. (Paul. 154) Reg. 217 [xi] fol., one of the important manuscripts collated by Reiche. It has a Catena in the Acts, scholia in the Catholic, Theodoret's Commentary on the Pauline Epistles.

128. (Paul. 155) Reg. 218 [xi] fol., with a Catena.

129. (Paul. 156) Reg. 220 [xiii] fol., a Commentary, the text being sometimes suppressed.

130. Reg. 221 [xii] fol., from the East, with a Catena: *mut.* Act. xx. 38—xxii. 3; 2 Pet. i. 14—iii. 18; 1 John iv. 11—Jude 8.

131. (Paul. 158) Reg. 223, once Boistaller's, contains the Pauline Epistles with *prol.* and a Catena, written A. D. 1045 by Theopemptus, reader and calligrapher, followed by the Acts and Cath. Ep. [xii] fol.

132. (= Evan. 330).

*133. (Paul. 166) Taurinens. 285. i. 40, at Turin [xiii] *chart.*, *pict.*, *prol.*

134. (Paul. 167) Taurin. 315 (now 19) ii. 17 [xi] *prol.*, *mut.* Act. i. ii.

135. (= Evan. 339).

136. (Paul. 169) Taurin. 328 (now 1) ii. 31 [xii], *mut.* in Hebr.

137. (Paul. 176) Ambros. 97, at Milan [xi] 4°, *lect.*, *prol.*, bought at Corfu: so like Cod. D and the margin of the Philoxenian Syriac in the Acts, as to assist us when D is mutilated; especially in additions. *Tischend.*

138. (Paul. 173) Ambros. 102 [xiv] 4°, *chart.*, once J. V. Penelli's; it contains the Epistles only.

139. (Paul. 174) Ambros. 104 [written March 20, 1434, Indict. 12, by one Athanasius] fol., *chart.*, bought at Padua, 1603.

140. (Paul. 215, Apoc. 74) Venet. 546 [partly xi on vellum, partly xiii *chart.*] 4°. The Epistles have a Catena, the Apocalypse a Commentary.

141. (= Evan. 189).

142. (Paul. 178) Mutinensis 243, at Modena [xii] 12°; valuable, but with many errors; but see Cod. 96.

143. Laurent. vi. 5, contains the Catholic Epistles and other matter. Scholz erroneously states that this copy = Evan. 362.

144. (= Evan. 363). 145. (= Evan. 365).

146. (= Evan. 367).

147. (Paul. 183, Apoc. 76) Laurent. IV. 30, at Florence [XII] 8°, *prol.*

148. (Paul. 184) Laurent. 2574 [written 984, Indict. 12, by Theophylact, priest and doctor of law] fol., *prol.*, once belonged to the Benedictine Library of St Mary.

149. Laurent. 176 [XIII] 8°, contains the Catholic Epistles, with a Latin version.

150. (=Evan. 368). 151. (=Evan. 386).

152. (=Evan. 442), erase. 153. (=Evan. 444).

154. (Paul. 187) Vatican. 1270 [XV] 4°, contains the Acts, Catholic Epistles, Rom., 1 Cor., with a Commentary.

155. (Paul. 188) Vat. 1430 [XII] fol., with a Commentary in another hand. It does not contain the Acts, but all the Epistles.

156. (Paul. 190) Vat. 1650 [*dated* Jan. 1073] fol., written for Nicholas Archbishop of Calabria by the cleric Theodore. The Pauline Epistles have a Commentary: it begins Act. v. 4.

157. (Paul. 191) Vat. 1714 [XII] 4°, is a heap of disarranged fragments, containing Act. xviii. 14—xix. 9; xxiv. 11—xxvi. 23; James iii. 1—v. 20; 3 John with κεφ. and ὑπόθεσις to Jude; Rom. vi. 22—viii. 32; xi. 31—xv. 23; 1 Cor. i. 1—iii. 12.

158. (Paul. 192) Vat. 1761 [XI] 4°, *prol.* From this copy Mai supplied the lacunae of Cod. B in the Pauline Epistles (see p. 91, note).

159. Vat. 1968, Basil. 7 [XI] 8°, contains the Acts, James and 1 Peter, with scholia, whose authors' names are given: *mut.* Act. i. 1—v. 29; vi. 14—vii. 11.

*160. (Paul. 193, Apoc. 24) Vat. 2062, Basil. 101 [XI] 4°, with scholia accompanied by the authors' names: it begins Act. xxviii. 19, ends Hebr. ii. 1.

161. (Paul. 198, Apoc. 69) Vat. Ottob. 258 [XIII] 4°, *chart.*, with a Latin version: it begins Act. ii. 27, and the last chapters of the Apocalypse are lost. The latter part was written later [XIV].

162. (Paul. 200) Vat. Ottob. 298 [XV] small 4° or 8°, with the Latin Vulgate version (with which Scholz states that the Greek has been in many places made to harmonise), contains many transpositions of words, and unusual readings introduced by a later hand[1].

[1] Cod. 162 has attracted much attention from the circumstance that it is the only *unsuspected* witness among the Greek manuscripts for the celebrated text 1 John v. 7, whose authenticity will be discussed in Chap. IX. A *facsimile* of the passage in question was traced in 1829 by Cardinal Wiseman for Bishop Burgess, and published by Horne in several editions of his Introduction, as also by Tregelles (Horne, IV. p. 217). If the *facsimile* is at all faithful, this is as rudely and indistinctly written as any manuscript in existence; but the illegible scrawl between the Latin column in the post of honour on the left, and the Greek column on the right, has recently been ascertained by Mr B. H. Alford (who examined the codex at Tregelles' request) to be merely a consequence of the accidental shifting of the tracing paper, too servilely copied by the engraver.

163. (Paul. 201) Vat. Ottob. 325 [XIV] 8°, *chart.*, *mut.* Act. iv. 19—v. 1.

164. (= Evan. 390).

165. Vat. Ottob. 417 [XIV] 8°, *chart.*, contains the Catholic Epistles, works of St Ephraem and others.

166. (Paul. 204, Apoc. 22) Vallicellian. B. 86 [XIII] 12°, written by George, son of Elias, and Joachim a monk.

167. (= Evan. 393).

168. (Paul. 205) Vallicell. F. 13 [XIV] 4°, *chart.*

169. (Paul. 206) Ghigian. R. v. 29, at Rome [*dated* June 12, 1394[1]] fol., written by Joasaph at Constantinople in the monastery τῶν ὁδηγῶν. See Evangelistarium 86.

170. (= Evan. 394).

171, 172 (Paul. 209, 210) are both Collegii Romani [XVI] fol., *chart.*

173. (Paul. 211) Bibl. Borbon. Reg. Naples, with no press mark [XI] 4°, *prol.*, *syn.*, indices of στίχοι and μαρτυρίαι (see p. 54) from Scripture and profane writers. This codex has 1 John v. 7 in the margin, by a recent hand.

174. (Paul. 212) Neapol. 1 C. 26 [XV] 8°, *chart.*

175. (Paul. 216) Messanensis II [XII] 4°, at St Basil's monastery.

176. (= Evan. 421). *177. (= Evan. 122).

178. (Paul. 242, Apoc. 87) Meermann. 118 [XI or XII] 8°, bought at his sale in 1824 by Sir T. Phillipps, Bart. of Middle Hill, Worcestershire. The Pauline Epistles are written smaller than the rest, but in the same clear hand. *Lect.*, κεφ. *t.*, *prol.*, κεφ. (but not in the Apocalypse), flourished rubric capitals. Scrivener fully collated Apoc. (whose text is valuable), the rest slightly. It is sadly mutilated; it begins Act. iv. 24; *mut.* Act. v. 2—16; vi. 2—vii. 2; 16—viii. 10; 38—ix. 13; 26—39; x. 9—22; 43—xiii. 1; xxiii. 32—xxiv. 24; xxviii. 23—James i. 5; iii. 6—iv. 16; 2 Pet. iii. 10—1 John i. 1; iii. 13—iv. 2; Jude 16—25; Rom. xiv. (xvi. 25 there placed)—xv. 14; 1 Cor. iii. 15—xv. 23; 2 Cor. x. 14—xi. 19; xiii. 5—13; Eph. i. 1—ii. 14; v. 29—vi. 24; Col. i. 24—26; ii. 4—7; 2 Thess. i. 1—iii. 5; Hebr. ix. 3—x. 29; Apoc. xiv. 4—14: ending xxi. 12. The ὑποθέσεις and tables of κεφ. before each Epistle have suffered in like manner.

179. (Paul. 128, Apoc. 82) Monacens. 211, once the Bohemian Zomozerab's [XI] 4°, *lect.*, *prol.*, ὑπογραφαί, Dorotheus' treatise (see Cod. 89), fragments of *Eus. t.*, and (in a later hand) marginal scholia to St Paul. The text is very near that commonly received.

*180 (= Evan. 431), important. 181. (= Evan. 400).

182. (Paul. 243) Bibl. of St John's monastery at Patmos [XII] 8°, also another [XIII] 8°.

[1] Scholz says 1344, and Tischendorf corrects few of his gross errors in these Catalogues: but A.M. 6902, which he cites from the manuscript, is A.D. 1394.

183. (Paul. 231) Bibl. of the great Greek monastery at Jerusalem 8 [xiv] 8°. This must be Coxe's No. 7 [x] 4°, beginning Act. xii. 6.

184. (Paul. 232, Apoc. 85) Jerusalem 9 [xiii] 4°, with a Commentary. This is evidently Coxe's No. 15, though he dates it at the end of [x].

185. (Paul. 233) St Saba, Greek monastery, 1 [xi] 12°.

186. (=Evan 457). 187. (=Evan. 462).

188. (Paul. 236) St Saba 15 [xii] 4°. 189. (=Evan. 466).

190. (Paul. 244, Apoc. 27) Christ Church, Oxford, Wake 34 [xi] 4°, is described above, p. 183.

191. (Paul. 245) Christ Church, Wake 38 [xi] 4°, in small and neat characters, from St Saba (brought to England with the other Wake manuscripts in 1731), contains a Catena, and at the end the date 1312 (ἐτελείωθη τὸ παρὸν ἐν ἔτει ϛωκ́) in a later hand. *Syn.*, *prol.*, full *lect.*, *mut.* Act. i. 1—11. (Walker: *see above*, p. 184).

192. (Paul. 246) Christ Church, Wake 37 [xi] 4°, *mut.* Act. xii. 4—xxiii. 32. The last leaf is a palimpsest, and some later leaves are in paper. To this list must be added the following:

*lo[ti] (or p[scr]). B. M. Addit. 20003. Thus Tischendorf indicates the most important cursive copy of the Acts (discovered by him in Egypt in 1853), which he sold to the Trustees of the British Museum 1854. It is dated April 20, 1044, Indict. 12, and was written by one John a monk, in small 4°, with no κεφ. (though the κεφ. *t.* for St James ends the volume), or divisions in the text, but rubrical marks added in a later hand. *Mut.* iv. 8—vii. 17; xvii. 28—xxiii. 9; 297 verses. Independent collations have been made by Tischendorf (*Anecd. sacra et prof.* pp. 7, 8; 130—46), by Tregelles, and by Scrivener (*Cod. Augiens. Introd.* pp. lxviii—lxx). Its value is shewn not so much by the readings in which it stands alone, as by its agreement with the oldest uncial copies, where their testimonies coincide.

The following codices also are described by Scrivener, *Cod. Augiens.* Introd. pp. lv—lxiv, and their collations given in the Appendix.

a[scr] (Paul. a) Lambeth 1182 [xii] 4°, *chart.*, brought (as were also bcde) by Carlyle from a Greek island. A later hand [xiv] supplied Act. i. 1—xii. 3; xiii. 5—15; 2, 3 John, Jude. In this copy and b[scr] the Pauline Epistles precede the Catholic (*see p.* 61). *Lect.*, *pict.*, κεφ., *prol.*, *syn.*, ἀποδημίαι παύλου, ἀντίφωνα for Easter, and other foreign matter. The various readings are interesting, and strongly resemble those of Cod. 69 of the Acts.

b[scr] (Paul. b) Lambeth 1183 [*dated* 1358] 4°, *chart.*, *mut.* 1 Cor. xi. 7—27; 1 Tim. iv. 1—v. 8. *Syn.*, *prol.*, κεφ. *t.*, τίτλοι, κεφ., *lect.*, in a beautiful hand, with many later corrections.

c[scr] (Paul. c) Lambeth 1184 [xv] 4°, *chart.*, *mut.* Act. vii. 52—viii. 25. Having been restored in 1817 (see p. 180, Cod. u), its readings (which, especially in the Catholic Epistles, are very important) are taken from an excellent collation (Lamb. 1255, 10—14) made for Carlyle about 1804 by the Rev. W. Sanderson of Morpeth.

d^scr (Paul. d) Lamb. 1185 [XIV?] 4°, *chart.*, miserably mutilated and ill-written. It must be regarded as a collection of fragments in at least four different hands, pieced together by the most recent scribe. *Mut.* Act. ii. 36—iii. 8; vii. 3—59; xii. 7—25; xiv. 8—27; xviii. 20—xix. 12; xxii. 7—xxiii. 11; 1 Cor. viii. 12—ix. 18; 2 Cor. i. 1—10; Eph. iii. 2—Phil. i. 24; 2 Tim. iv. 12—Tit. i. 6; Hebr. vii. 19—ix. 12. We have 1 Cor. v. 11, 12; 2 Cor. x. 8—15, written by two different persons. *Lect.*, *prol.*, *κεφ. t.*, *syn.*, in wretched disorder.

e^scr seems to have been Lambeth 1181 [XIV] 4° of the Acts, Catholic and Pauline Epistles (as we learn from the Lambeth Catalogue), but having been returned (see p. 180) we have access only to a tolerable collation of Act. i. 1—xxvii. 12, made by the Rev. John Fenton for Carlyle (Lamb. 1255, 27—33). In its text it much resembles Cod. E (see p. 128).

f^scr (= Evan. q^scr). g^scr (= Evan. l^scr).

h^scr (= Evan. 201, Act. 91).

j^scr Brit. Mus. Burney 48 [XIV] fol., *chart.*, *prol.*, *κεφ. t.*, contains the Catholic Epistles (except that of St Jude), with some uncommon variations. This elegant copy begins fol. 221 of Vol. II. of Chrysostom's Homilies on Galat.—Hebrews. k^scr (= Evan. w^scr).

At Middle Hill (see Cod. 178) 7681 is a copy of the Acts and all the Epistles from the Hon. F. North's Collection, dated 1107.

Cod. Boecleri (Paul. 248) [age not stated], on vellum, containing the Acts, Catholic and Pauline Epistles, the last arranged as one book, with a Prologue. It belongs to J. H. Boecler, Professor of History at Strasburg; brought "a Graecis" by Steph. Gerlach, when in the suite of Baron Ungnad, Imperial Embassador to the Porte.

From Haenel's "Catalogus Libr. MSS." (see p. 181) we add the following: Basil. B. VI. 29, fol. contains the Acts, Catholic and twelve Pauline Epistles with short prologues; Basil. B. II. 5, 8°, of the Acts and all the Epistles; six Escurial codices of the Acts: besides the two (p. 181) containing the whole N. T. Add also Lamy's 207 (p. 181), Muralt's 8^po (*see p.* 178) and the Parham copies (*see p.* 182). Including No. 6, which has been described above, these are four; viz. No. 14 [dated A.D. 1009] 4°, from St Saba: a *facsimile* is given in the Catalogue: No. 15 [XI] 4°, from Caracalla, with a marginal paraphrase: No. 16 [?] fol., from Simo Petra on Athos. These three contain the Acts and all the Epistles.

In the Canonici collection at Oxford, besides No. 34 described above (p. 184), is Canon. Gk. 110 [X] 4°, *pict.*, a beautiful copy of the Acts and all the Epistles, with Euthalius' *prol.*, *κεφ.* &c., one leaf from Cyril's Homilies, and two other later (Rev. H. O. Coxe). Add also Bodleian. Miscell. 118, Auct. F. 6. 24 [XIII] 4°, *mut.*, also containing the Acts and all the Epistles: *lect.*, *syn.*, *men.*, and St Paul furnished with Euthalius' matter.

The following fourteen copies were seen by Mr Coxe in the East (*above, p.* 185).

(α) In the Patriarch's Library at Cairo, Shelf 1, No. 8, all the Epistles [XIV] 4°, *chart.* Shelf 4, No. 59, Acts and all the Epistles [XI] 4°. Shelf 5, No. 88, the same, with the Psalter [XI] fol.

(β) At the Greek Monastery at Jerusalem besides Nos. 7, 15, which can be no other than Scholz's 183—4, we must add Nos. 40, 45 from p. 185.

(γ) At St Saba Scholz found five copies, 185—9, and Coxe no larger number; although it is not easy to reconcile their statements. Coxe's No. 20, of the Acts, all the Epistles and Apocalypse [XI] small 4°, a palimpsest on uncials [VII], will ill suit Scholz's 187 or 189. Coxe's No. 35, Acts and all the Epistles [XI] 4°, may be either Scholz's 185 or 188. Coxe's other three contain the Gospels and all the Epistles, No. 52 [XI] small 4°, *syn.*; No. 53 [XI] 4°; No. 54 [XII] 4°. See Scholz's 186.

(δ) At Patmos both Scholz and Coxe observed two copies (Cod. 182), of the Acts and all the Epistles, Coxe's No. 27 [XII] fol., with marginal glosses, and No. 31 [IX] fol.

It will be remarked that Coxe's dates are almost always earlier than Scholz's.

Dr Bloomfield collated ten copies of the Acts in the British Museum. Six have been named in the foregoing list (Codd. 22; 25—8; 59). The others are Addl. 11836, 16184, 17469 described under the head of the Gospels (p. 186), and Addl. 11837 or Act. 91.

Deducting twelve duplicates &c., our list contains 229 cursive manuscripts of the Acts and Catholic Epistles.

Manuscripts of St Paul's Epistles.

*1. (= Evan. 1). 2. (= Act. 2). 3. (= Evan. 3).

4. (= Act. 4). 5. (= Evan. 5). 6. (= Evan. 6).

7. Basil. B. VI. 17[?] 4°, with notes and glosses, ends Hebr. xii. 18.

8. (= Act. 50). 9. (= Act. 7). 10. (= Act. 8).

11. (= Act. 9). 12. (= Act. 10).

13. Certain readings cited by J. le Fevre d'Etaples, in his Commentary on St Paul's Epistles, Paris, 1512.

14. (= Evan. 90). 15. A manuscript cited by Erasmus, belonging to Amandus of Louvain.

16. (= Act. 12). *17. (= Evan. 33).

18. (= Evan. 35). 19. (= Act. 16).

20. Coislin. 27, described (as is Cod. 23) by Montfaucon [X] fol., in bad condition, with *prol.* and a catena, from Athos (Wetstein).

21. (=Act. 17). 22. (=Act. 18).

23. Coislin. 28 from Athos [XI] fol., *prol.* and a Commentary (Wetstein, Scholz).

24. (=Evan. 105). 25. (=Act. 20). 26. (=Act. 21).

27. Cambridge Univ. Libr. 1152, Ff. I. 30 [XI and XIV?], with a Commentary, chiefly Photius': Rom. and 1, 2 Cor. are wanting (Wetstein, 1716).

28. (=Act. 23). *29. (=Act. 24). *30. (=Act. 53).
31. (=Act. 25). 32. (=Act. 26). 33. (=Act. 27).
*34. (=Act. 28). 35. (=Act. 29). 36. (=Act. 30).
*37. (=Evan. 69). 38. (=Evan. 51). 39. (=Act. 33).
*40. (=Evan. 61). 41. (=Evan. 57).

42. Magdalen Coll. Oxford, Greek 7 [XI] fol., contains Rom. 1, 2 Cor. surrounded by Oecumenius' Commentary, *prol.* &c. (Walton's Polyglott, Mill).

43. (=Act. 37). *44. (=Act. 38).
45. (=Act. 39). 46. (=Act. 40).

47. Bodleian. Roe 16, Mill's Roe 2 [XI or XII] fol., with a Patristic Catena, in a small and beautiful hand, and a text much resembling that of Cod. A: its history is the same as that of Evan. 49. The Epistle to the Hebrews precedes 1 Tim.: see p. 62, note. (Mill).

*48. (=Act. 42). 49. (=Evan. 76). 50. (=Act. 52).
51. (=Evan. 82, Act. 44, Apoc. 5). 52. (=Act. 45).

53 of Wetstein is now Paul. Cod. M, the portion containing the Hebrews, or Bengel's Uffenbach 2 or 1 (see p. 139).

54. Monacensis 412 [XII] fol., is Bengel's August. 5, containing Rom. vii. 7—xvi. 24, with a Catena from twenty Greek authors (see Cod. 127), stated by Bengel to resemble that in the Bodleian described by Mill (N. T. Proleg. § 1448).

55. (=Act. 46).

56. Tigurinus, in the Public Library at Zurich, written in 1516, in the hand of the well-known Ulrich Zwingle. This is quite worthless if Wetstein is correct in calling it a transcript of Erasmus' first edition, then just published.

*57. (=Evan. 218). 58. Vat. 165, "olim Cryptoferratensis," of the Monastery of Crypta Ferrata, near Tusculum [XII] (Zacagni).

59 of Wetstein and Griesbach comprises readings of two Medicean manuscripts of the Ephes. and Philipp., derived from the same source as Evan. 102, Act. 56, Apoc. 23: Scholz silently substitutes Coislin. 204 [XI] fol., with a Catena.

60. Codices cited in the Correctorium Bibliorum Latinorum (*see p.* 153, *note*).

*61. (=Act. 61). 62. (=Act. 59). 63. (=Act. 60).

64 of Griesbach is the portion of Cod. M now in the British Museum (see p. 139).

65. (= Act. 62).

66. Various readings extracted by Griesbach from the margin of Harl. 5552, 4°, which itself he thinks but a transcript of Erasmus' first edition (*Symb. Crit.* p. 166).

*67. (= Act. 66). 67** resembles Cod. B. *68. (= Act. 63).

*69. (= Act. 64). *70. (= Act. 67).

71. Caesar-Vindobon. Forlos. 19, Kollar. 10 [XII] 4°, *mut.* Rom. i. 1—9; Titus; Philem., with Hebrews before 1 Tim. (see p. 62, note 2). There is a Commentary and Catechetical lectures of St Cyril of Jerusalem (Alter, Birch).

72. (= Evan. 234). 73. (= Act. 68).

74. (= Act. 69). 75. (Addl. 5116, = Act. 22).

*76. Biblioth. Paulinae Lipsiensis (Mt. s.) [XIII] fol., contains Rom., 1 Cor., Gal. and part of Eph., with Theophylact's Commentary (Matthaei).

Codd. 77—112 were cursorily collated by Birch, and nearly all by Scholz.

77. (= Evan. 131). 78. (= Evan. 133).

79. (= Act. 72). 80. (= Act. 73)[1].

81. Vat. 761 [XII] fol., with Oecumenius' Commentary. The Ep. to the Hebrews is wanting.

82. Vat. 762 [XII] fol., contains Rom., 1, 2 Cor., with a Catena.

83. Vat. 765 [XI] fol., with a Commentary.

84. Vat. 766 [XII] fol., with a Commentary.

85. (Apoc. 39) Vat. 1136 [XIII] fol., contains *first* the Apocalypse (beginning iii. 8) with a Latin version, then St Paul's Epistles, ending 1 Tim. vi. 5, with many unusual readings.

86. (= Evan. 141). 87. (= Evan. 142).

88. (= Evan. 149). 89. (= Act. 78).

90. (= Act. 79). 91. (= Act. 80).

92. (= Evan. 180)[2]. 93. (= Act. 83).

94. (= Act. 84). 95. (= Act. 85).

96. (= Act. 86). 97. (= Act. 87).

98. (= Act. 88). 99. (= Act. 89).

100. Laurent. x. 4 [XII] fol., with a Commentary, and additional scholia [XIV], from the Cistercian Monastery of S. Salvator de Septimo, in the diocese of Florence.

101. Laurent. x. 6 [XI] fol., with *prol.* and a Catena supplying the authors' names.

[1] Birch shews the connexion of Caryophilus with this important copy (which much resembles the Leicester manuscript, Evan. Cod. 69) from James v. 5, and especially from 3 John 5 μισθὸν for πιστὸν, a *lectio singularis*. See p. 157. In this codex, as in those cited p. 62, note 2, Hebr. stands before 1 Tim.

[2] The proper date of the later hand in this copy seems to be A.D. 1274. It is written ψτψπβ, according to Engelberth, which must stand for A.M. 6782.

102. Laurent. x. 7 [XI] fol., *syn.*, a life of Paul, and Catena with such names as Theodoret, Chrysostom, Oecumenius, Severianus, &c.

103. Laurent. x. 19 [XIII] fol., with *syn.* and a Catena. At the end is a date "A. D. 1318, Ind. 1, Timotheus."

*104. (= Evan. 201). 105. (= Evan. 204).

*106. (= Evan. 205). *107. (= Evan. 206).

*108. (= Evan. 209). *109. (= Act. 96).

*110. Venet. 33 [XI] fol., with a Catena, much being taken from Oecumenius (Rink, as also 111, 112: *see* Act. 96).

*111. Venet. 34 [XI] fol., with *prol.* and a Commentary.

*112. Venet. 35 [XI] fol., with a Commentary, a fragment beginning 2 Cor. i. 20, ending Hebr. x. 25; *mut.* 1 Thess. iv. 13—2 Thess. ii. 14.

Codd. 113—124 were collated by Matthaei.

*113. (= Act. 98). *114. (= Act. 99).

*115. (= Act. 100). *116. (= Act. 101).

*117. (= Act. 102). *118. (= Act. 103).

119. Mosq. Synod. 292 (Mt. i) [XII] 4°, from the monastery of Pantocrator on Athos, contains 1, 2 Corinth. with Theophylact's Commentary.

*120. (= Evan. 241). *121. (= Evan. 242).

*122. (= Act. 106).

*123. Synod. 99 (Mt. n) [XI] fol., with scholia, from St Athanasius' monastery on Athos.

*124. Synod. 250 (Mt. q) [XIV] 8°, on cotton paper, from the monastery of Batopedion(?) on Athos, contains Rom. i.—xiii. with Theophylact's Commentary and other writings.

Codd. 125—246 were first catalogued by Scholz, who professes to have collated entire 177—179, in the greater part 157, the rest slightly or not at all.

125. Monacensis 504 at Munich, Reisser 5, once August. 8 [dated 1 Feb. 1387, Indict. 10] 8°, on cotton paper, with Theophylact's Commentary in black ink, and the text (akin to it) in red. Bought by Nicetas "primicerius sceuophylactus" for eight golden ducats of Rhodes[1]. *Mut.* Philemon.

126. Monacens. 455, Reisser 19, Hoeschel 35, once August. 13, is either a copy of Cod. 125, or derived from the same manuscript [dated Feb. 17, Indict. 12, probably 1389] fol., *chart.*, also *mut.* Philem.; with Theophylact's Commentaries, and some homilies of Chrysostom.

127. Monacens. 110 [XVI] fol., *chart.*, once at the Jesuits' College, Munich, contains Rom. vii. 7—ix. 21, with a Catena. It was

[1] The gold ducat coined for the Military order of St John at Rhodes (*see* Ducange) was worth 9s. 6d. English money.

found by Scholz to be, what indeed it professes, a mere copy of part of Cod. 54.

128. (= Act. 179).

129. Monacens. 35 [XVI] fol., *chart.*, with a Catena.

130. (= Evan. 43). 131. (= Evan. 330).

*132. (= Evan. 18: *see* Act. 113). 133. (= Act. 51).

*134. (= Act. 114). 135. (= Act. 115).

136. (= Act. 116). *137. (= Evan. 263).

138. (= Act. 118). *139. (= Act. 119) Reiche, as also

*140. (= Act. 11). 141. (= Act. 120).

142. (= Act. 121). 143. (= Act. 122).

144. (= Act. 123).

145. Reg. 108, once Colbert's, as were 146—8 [XVI] 8°, contains from Philipp. to Timothy, with *prol.*

146. Reg. 109 [XVI] 8°, contains Rom. with *prol.*, and the ὑπόθεσις to 1 Corinth.

147. Reg. 110 [*dated* 1511] 8°, contains 1, 2 Corinth.

148. Reg. 111 [XVI], contains Titus, Philem., Hebrews. Codd. 145—8 are surely the divided portions of the same manuscript.

149. (= Act. 124). 150. (= Act. 125).

151. Reg. 126 [XVI] 12°, written (like 149) by Angelus Vergecius (see p. 38, note 2).

152. (Apoc. 60) Reg. 136[a] [?] 8°, contains the Hebrews, Apoc., and a life of St Alexius.

*153. (= Act. 126) Reiche. 154. (= Act. 127).

155. (= Act. 128). 156. (= Act. 129).

157. Reg. 222, once Colbert's [XI] fol., brought from Constantinople 1676, with *prol.* and a Commentary. *Mut.* Rom. i. 1—11; 21—29; iii. 26—iv. 8; ix. 11—22; 1 Cor. xv. 22—43; Col. i. 1—6.

158. (= Act. 131).

159. (Apoc. 64) Reg. 224 [XI] fol., very elegant. The Pauline Epistles have *prol.* and a Catena, the Apocalypse Arethas' Commentary.

160. Reg. 225 [XVI] fol., *chart.*, a fragment of St Paul with Theophylact's Commentary.

161. Reg. 226 [XVI] fol., *chart.*, contains the Romans with a Commentary.

162. Reg. 227, once Bigot's [XVI] fol., *chart.*, only contains a Catena on 1 Cor. xvi.

163. Reg. 238 [XIII] 8°, from Adrianople, contains Hebr. i—viii. with a Catena.

164. Reg. 849, once a Medicean manuscript [XVI] fol., contains Theodoret's Commentary with the text in the margin.

165. Taurinens. 284, I. 39, at Turin [XVI] *chart.*, contains from 1 Thess. to Hebrews.

166. (= Act. 133). 167. (= Act. 134).

168. Taurin. 325, II. 38 [XII] fol., with *prol.* and a Commentary: it begins Rom. iii. 19.

169. (= Act. 136). 170. (= Evan. 339).

171. Ambros. 6, at Milan [XIII] fol., with a Commentary: it ends Hebr. iv. 7, and Rom. i. 1—2 Cor. v. 19 are later, on cotton paper.

172. Ambros. 15 [XII] fol., with an abridgment of Chrysostom's Commentary: bought at Reggio in Calabria, 1606.

173. (= Act. 138). 174. (= Act. 139).

175. Ambros. 125 [XV] fol., *chart.*, with a continuous Commentary: it was brought from Thessaly.

176. (= Act. 137).

*177. Mutinens. 14 (Ms. II. A. 14), at Modena [XV] 16°.

*178. (= Act. 142).

*179 is Cod. H of Act.: see p. 129. The Pauline Epistles with a Commentary are [XII].

180. (= Evan. 363). 181. (= Evan. 365).

182. (= Evan. 367). 183. (= Act. 147).

184. (= Act. 148). 185. (= Evan. 393).

186. (= Evan. 394). 187. (= Act. 154).

188. (= Act. 155).

189. Vat. 1649 [XIII] fol., with Theodoret's Commentary: Hebr. precedes 1 Tim. (p. 62, note 2).

190. (= Act. 156). 191. (= Act. 157).

192. (= Act. 158). 193. (= Act. 160).

194. (= Evan. 175).

195. Vat. Ottob. 31 [X] fol., *mut.* Rom. and most of 1 Cor.; with a continuous Commentary, and such names as Oecumenius, Theodoret, Methodius, occasionally mentioned.

196. Vat. Ottob. 61 [XV] 8°, *chart.*, with a Commentary: here as in Cod. 189 the Epistle to the Hebrews precedes 1 Tim. So perhaps Cod. 217.

197. (Apoc. 78) Vat. Ottob. 176 [XV] 8°, *chart.*

198. (= Act. 161). 199. (= Evan. 386).

200. (= Act. 162). 201. (= Act. 163).

202. Vat. Ottob. 356 [XV] 4°, *chart.* "olim Aug. ducis ab Altamps," contains Rom. with a Catena.

203. (= Evan. 390). 204. (= Act. 166).

205. (= Act. 168). 206. (= Act. 169).

207. Ghigian. R. v. 32, at Rome [XV] 4°, *chart.*, with a Commentary.

208. Ghigian. VIII. 55 [XI] fol., with Theodoret's Commentary.

209. (= Act. 171). 210. (= Act. 172).

211. (=Act. 173). 212. (=Act. 174).

213. Barberin. 29 [*dated* 1338] *prol.*, scholia.

214. Caesar-Vindobon. theol. 167, Lambec. 46 [XV] 4°, on cotton paper, contains Rom. with a Catena, 1 Corinth. with Chrysostom's and Theodoret's Commentaries, which influence the readings of text.

215. (=Act. 140). 216. (=Act. 175).

217. Bibl. Reg. Panormi (Palermo) [XII] 4°, begins 2 Cor. iv. 18; *mut.* 2 Tim. i. 8—ii. 14; ends Hebr. ii. 9.

218. (=Evan. 421). *219. (=Evan. 122).

220. (=Evan. 400). *221. (=Evan. 440) is o^scr.

222, 223 (=Evan. 441, 442) must be erased.

224. (=Act. 58).

225. (=Act. 112), erase: it is the same as Cod. 11.

226, erase: it is the same as Cod. 27.

227. (=Act. 56 of Scholz). 228. (=Evan. 226).

229. (=Evan. 228). 230. (=Evan. 368).

231. (=Act. 183). 232. (=Act. 184).

233. (=Act. 185). 234. (=Evan. 457).

235. (=Evan. 462). 236. (=Act. 188).

237. (=Evan. 466). 238. (=Evan. 431).

239. (=Evan. 189). 240. (=Evan. 444).

241. (=Act. 97). 242. (=Act. 178).

243. (=Act. 182), two codices. 244. (=Act. 190).

245. (=Act. 191). 246. (=Act. 192).

Tischendorf adds to Scholz's list

247. Library of St Geneviève at Paris, 4, A. 35 [XIV] *all* the Pauline Epistles.

248. Cod. Boecleri, described under Act. p. 199.

To this list we must add the following collated in Scrivener's *Cod. Augiensis, Appendix:* a^scr (=Act. a). b^scr (=Act. b). c^scr (=Act. c). d^scr (=Act. d). e^scr (Apoc. 93) Lambeth 1186 [XI] 4° (see the *facsimile* in the Catalogue of Manuscripts at Lambeth, 1812), begins Rom. xvi. 15, ends Apoc. xix. 4; *mut.* 1 Cor. iv. 19—vi. 1; x. 1—21; Hebr. iii. 14—ix. 19; Apoc. xiv. 16—xv. 7. *Lect.* The Epistles have *prol.*, *τίτλοι*, *κεφ.*, and a few marginal notes. f^scr (=Evan. q^scr). g^scr (=Evan. l^scr). h^scr (=Evan. 201). j^scr (=Evan. n^scr). k^scr (=Evan. w^scr).

Haenel adds the two Basle codices described under the Acts, and four at the Escurial: besides the two (p. 181) containing the whole N. T. There remain Lamy 207 (p. 181); the four Parham copies enumerated above, p. 199; three copies at Oxford (*see p.* 199); five seen by Mr Coxe (p. 200) more than by Scholz; to which we must add Coxe's Patmos No. 24 [XII] 4°, Rom. 1, 2 Cor. with scholia; and Muralt's 8^pe as in the Acts (*see p.* 199).

Dr Bloomfield collated nine codices of the Epistles at the British Museum; viz. the four Covell copies (Paul. 31—34); Addl. 11837 or Paul. 104; Addl. 11836 described p. 186, and Addl. 5540, 5742, 19389.

He does not seem to have touched Addl. 17469 of the whole N. T., save in the Gospels and Acts. There is also at the B. Museum, apparently quite uncollated: Addl. 7142 [XIII] 4°, the Pauline Epistles with marginal scholia, with a life of St Paul prefixed, *prol.*, κεφ. *t.*, τίτλοι, *mut.*, *lect.*, the last mostly *s. m.*

Deducting 14 duplicates &c., we find 283 cursive manuscripts of St Paul's Epistles.

Manuscripts of the Apocalypse.

1. Codex Reuchlini, the only one used by Erasmus (who calls it exemplar vetustissimum), and now lost, contained the Commentary of Andreas of Caesarea, *mut.* xxii. 16—21.

2. (= Act. 10, Stephens' ιε').

3. Codex Stephani ιϛ', unknown; cited only 77 times throughout the Apocalypse in Stephens' edition of 1550, and that very irregularly; only once (xx. 3) after xvii. 8. It was not one of the copies in the King's library, and the four citations noticed by Mill (N. T. Proleg. § 1176) from Luke xxii. 30; 67; 2 Cor. xii. 11; 1 Tim. iii. 3 are probably mere errors of Stephens' press.

4. (= Act. 12).

5. Codices Laurentii Vallae (*see* Evan. 82); the readings of which Erasmus used. 6. (= Act. 23).

*7. (= Act. 25, l^{scr}). *8. (= Act. 28, d^{scr}).

9. (= Act. 30). 10. (= Evan. 60). 11. (= Act. 39).

12. (= Act. 40). *13. (= Act. 42).

*14. (= Evan. 69, f^{scr}).

15. Fragments of ch. iii. iv. annexed to Cod. E Evan. (*see p.* 103), in a later hand. 16. (= Act. 45). 17. (= Evan. 35).

18. (= Act. 18). 19. (= Act. 17).

20. (= Evan. 175), a few extracts made by Blanchini: so Cod. 24.

21, 22 of Wetstein were two unknown French codices, cited by Bentley in his specimen of Apoc. xxii., and his 23 (= Act. 56). Scholz, discarding these three as doubtful, substitutes Cod. 21 Cod. Vallicell. D. 20 [XIV] fol., *chart.*, with Andreas' Comment.: Cod. 22. (= Act. 166): Cod. 23. (= Evan. 38), which he says he collated cursorily. But whatever readings he cites under these three numbers, are simply copied from Wetstein! (Kelly's *Revelation*, Introd. p. xi, note).

24. (= Act. 160). 25. (= Evan. 149).

26. (Apostol. 57). Wake 12 [XI] large folio, brought from Constantinople in 1731, and now in the Library of Christ Church, Oxford, contains the Gospels (*see p.* 182), with lessons from the Acts and Epistles. Codd. 6, 26, 27, 28 were rather loosely collated for Wetstein by his kinsman Caspar Wetstein, chaplain to Frederick, Prince of Wales.

27. (= Act. 190). This copy is fully described above, p. 183.

*28. Cod. Barocc. 48 in the Bodleian, contains mixed matter by several hands (*see p.* 61), and is n^{scr} of the Apocalypse [XV] 4°, *chart.*, *mut.* xvii. 5—xxii. 21: *τίτλοι, κεφ.* (v. 1—5 is repeated in the volume in a different hand). This is an important copy.

*29. (= Act. 60, e^{scr}). 30. (= Act. 69).

*31. Cod. Harleian. 5678 is c^{scr}, but i—viii. had been loosely collated for Griesbach by Paulus [XV] 4°, *chart.* Like Cod. 445 Evan., it once belonged to the Jesuits' College at Agen, and is important for its readings. As in Codd. 28, 32, 35, 38, 43, 49, 50, 58, 60, 65, 68, 81, there is much miscellaneous matter in this volume.

32. Codex Dresdensis, antea Loescheri, deinde Brühlii [x Griesb. xv Scholz] 8°, collated by Dassdorf and Matthaei, seems important. Is this the same codex as Act. 107, Evst. 57? The close resemblance in the text of Codd. 29—32 is somewhat overstated by Griesbach.

*33. (= Evan. 218). *34. (= Act. 66).

35. Caesar-Vindobon. Lambec. 248 [XIV] 4°, with Andreas' Comment.: brought from Constantinople by Busbeck (Alter).

36. Caesar-Vindobon. Forlos. 29, Kollar. 26 [XIV] 8°, ends xix. 20, with Andreas: the text is in *στίχοι* (Alter).

37. (= Act. 72).

*38. Vatic. 579 [XIII] 8°, cotton paper, in the midst of foreign matter. The text (together with some marginal readings *primâ manu*) closely resembles that of Codd. AC, and was collated by Birch, inspected by Scholz and Tregelles, and lately recollated by B. H. Alford (*see on* Cod. T, p. 116).

39. (= Paul. 85). 40. (= Evan. 141).

41. Alexandrino-Vat. 69 [XIV] *chart.*, with extracts from Oecumenius and Andreas' Com. (Birch, Scholz: so Cod. 43).

42. (= Act. 80).

43. Barberini 23 [XIV] 4°, contains xiv. 17—xviii. 20, with a Commentary, together with portions of the Septuagint.

44. (= Evan. 180). 45. (= Act. 89). 46. (= Evan. 209).

*47. (= Evan. 241). *48. (= Evan. 242).

*49. Moscow, Synod. 67 (Mt. o) [XV] fol., *chart.*, with Andreas' Comment., and Gregory Nazianzen's Homilies.

*50. Synod. 206 (Mt. p) [XII] fol., like Evan. 69, 206, 233, is partly of parchment, partly paper, from the Iberian monastery on Athos; it also contains lives of the Saints.

*50². Also from the Iberian monastery [x] is Matthaei's r.

Codd. 51—88 were added to the list by Scholz, of which he professes to have collated Cod. 51 entirely, as Reiche has done after him; Codd. 68, 69, 82 nearly entire; twenty-one others cursorily, the rest (apparently) not at all. Cod. 87 is Scrivener's m, collated in the Apocalypse only.

*51. (= Evan. 18). 52. (= Act. 51). 53. (= Act. 116).

54. (= Evan. 263). 55. (= Act. 118). 56. (= Act. 119).

57. (= Act. 124).

58. Paris, Reg. 19, once Colbert's [XVI] fol., *chart.*, with "Hiob et Justini cohort. ad Graec." Scholz.

59. Reg. 99[a] [XVI] *chart.*, with a Commentary. Once Giles de Noailles'. 60. (= Paul. 152).

61. Reg. 491, once Colbert's [XIII] 4°, on cotton paper, *mut.*, with pieces from Basil, &c.

62. Reg. 239—40 [XVI] 4°, *chart.*, with Andreas' Commentary.

63. Reg. 241, once De Thou's, then Colbert's [XVI] 4°, *chart.*, with Andreas' Comment. 64. (= Paul. 159).

65. University Library at Moscow, 25 (once Coislin's 229) [?], contains xvi. 20—xxii. 21. 66. (= Evan. 131).

67. Vat. 1743 [*dated* 5 Decembr. 1302], with Andreas' Commentary.

68. Vat. 1904 [XI] 4°, contains vii. 17—viii. 12; xx. 1—xxii. 21, with Arethas' Commentary, and much foreign matter. This fragment (as also Cod. 72 according to Scholz, who however never cites it) agrees much with Cod. A. 69. (= Act. 161).

70. (= Evan. 386). 71. (= Evan. 390).

72. Cod. Ghigianus R. iv. 8 [XVI] 8°, *chart.*, with Andreas' Commentary. The same description suits 73, in the Corsini Library 838.

74. (= Act. 140). 75. (= Act. 86). 76. (= Act. 147).

77. Cod. Laurent. vii. 9 at Florence [XV] 4°, *chart.*, with Arethas' Commentary. 78. (= Paul. 197).

79. Cod. Monacensis 248, at Munich; once Sirlet's, the Apostolic chief notary (see Evst. 132) [XVI] 4°, *chart.*, with Andreas' Comment., whose text it follows. That excellent and modest scholar Fred. Sylburg collated it for his edition of Andreas, 1596, one of the last labours of his diligent life.

80. Monacens. 544 (Bengel's Augustan. 7) [XII Sylburg, XIV Scholz, who adds that it once belonged to the Emperor Manuel, who died A.D. 1180[1]] 4°, on cotton paper, with Andreas' Commentary.

81. Monacensis 23 [XVI] fol., *chart.*, with works of Gregory Nyssen, and Andreas' Commentary, used by Theod. Peltanus for his edition of Andreas, Ingoldstadt 1547. Peltanus' marginal notes from this copy were seen by Scholz. 82. (= Act. 179).

83. (= Evan. 339): much like Codd. AC.

[1] Unless indeed he means Manuel II., the son of Palaeologus, who visited England in 1400, the guest and suppliant of Henry IV.

84. (= Evan. 368). 85. (= Act. 184).

86. (= Evan. 462), thrice cited ineunte libro (Tischend.).

86^2. (= Evan. 466). *87. (= Act. 178).

88. (= Evan. 205). 89. Tischend. = 86^2 Scholz.

90. Tischend. = 50^2 Scholz (Mt. r).

91. Mico's collation of the modern Supplement [xv] to the great Cod. B, published in Ford's Appendix to the Codex Alexandrinus 1799.

92. (= Evan. 61) published by Dr Barrett 1801 in his Appendix to Cod. Z, but suspected to be a later addition.

Wm. Kelly, "*The Revelation of John edited in Greek, with a new English Version*" 1860, thus numbers Scrivener's recent collations of six copies not included in the foregoing catalogue:

93. (= Paul. e^{scr}) a^{scr}. 94. (= Evan. 201) b^{scr}.

95. Cod. Parham 17, g^{scr} [xii or xiii] 4°, brought by the Hon. R. Curzon in 1837 from Caracalla on Athos: it contains an epitome of the Commentary of Arethas, in a cramped hand much less distinct than the text, which ends at xx. 11. There are no divisions into chapters.

96. Parham 2, h^{scr} [xiv] 4°, κεφ., on glazed paper, very neat, also from Caracalla, complete and in excellent preservation, with very short scholia here and there.

97, 98 both contain the whole New Testament, without Commentaries, but have hitherto been collated only for this book.

97. Brit. Mus. Addit. 17469, j^{scr} [xiv] fol. (*see* p. 186) is full of interesting variations.

98. Canonici 34 in the Bodleian, k^{scr} [*dated* in the Apocalypse July 18, 1516] 4°, *chart.: see above*, p. 184. The Pauline Epistles (dated Oct. 11, 1515) precede the Acts (*see* p. 61). This copy much resembles Cod. 30, and is of considerable value.

Haenel adds one copy from the Escurial, and the two at Arras and Poictiers (p. 181). Evan. 206, Act. 94, Paul. 107, seems also to contain the Apocalypse, but to be a copy of Cod. 46 (see p. 164).

Mr Coxe saw but two codices of the Apocalypse in the East (Jerusalem No. 15; S. Saba No. 20), though Scholz speaks of one more at St Saba, and no doubt correctly. Dr Bloomfield states that he collated four in the British Museum, but does not name them: they are probably included in our catalogue.

We have enumerated 102 cursive manuscripts of the Apocalypse.

SECTION IV.

On the Lectionaries, or Manuscript Service-books of the Greek Church.

HOWEVER grievously the great mass of cursive manuscripts of the New Testament has been neglected by Biblical critics, the Lectionaries of the Greek Church, partly for causes previously stated (p. 63), have received even less attention at their hands. Yet no sound reason can be alleged for regarding the testimony of these Service-books as of slighter value than that of other witnesses of the same date and character. The necessary changes interpolated in the text at the commencement and sometimes at the end of lessons are so simple and obvious that the least experienced student can make allowance for them: and if the same passage is often given in a different form when repeated in the same Lectionary, although the fact ought to be recorded and borne in mind, this occasional inconsistency must no more militate against the reception of the general evidence of the copy that exhibits it, than it excludes from our roll of critical authorities the works of Origen and other Fathers, in which the selfsame variation is even more the rule than the exception. Dividing, therefore, the Lectionaries that have been hitherto catalogued (which form indeed but a small portion of those known to exist in Eastern monasteries and Western libraries) into Evangelistaria containing the Gospels, and Praxapostoli or Apostoli comprising extracts from the Acts and Epistles, (see p. 63); we purpose to mark with an asterisk the few that have been really collated, including them in the same list with the majority which have been examined superficially, or not at all. Uncial copies (some as late as the eleventh century: see p. 26) will be distinguished by †. The uncial codices of the Gospels amount to 58, those of the Acts and Epistles only to six or perhaps seven, for Cod. 40 is doubtful.

Evangelistaria or Evangeliaria, containing the Gospels.

†1. Regius 278 Paris, once Colbert's [VIII ?] fol., *mut.* (Wetstein, Scholz).

†2. Reg. 280, once Colbert's [IX] fol., *mut.* (Wetstein, Scholz).

†3. Wheeler 3, Lincoln College, Oxford No. 15 [X] 4°, (Mill).

4. Cantab. Dd. 8. 49, or Moore 2 [XI] 4°, *syn., men., cursive* (Mill).

†5. Bodleian. Barocc. 202, or Mill's Bodl. 3 [X ?, but *undated*] *mut.*, initio et fine (Mill, Wetstein).

*†6. (Apostol. 1). Lugduno-Batav. 243, once Scaliger's [XI], *chart.*, with an Arabic version, contains the Praxapostolos, Psalms, and but a few Lessons from the Gospels (Wetstein, Dermout).

7. Reg. 301, once Colbert's, as were 8—12; 14—17 [written by George, a priest, in 1205] fol. (Codd. 7—12; 14—17 were slightly collated by Wetstein, Scholz).

8. Reg. 312 or 302 *teste Tischendorf.* [XIV] fol., written by Cosmas, a monk.

9. Reg. 307 [XIII] fol. 10. Reg. 287 [XI] fol., *mut.*

11. Reg. 309 [XIII] fol., *mut.* 12. Reg. 310 [XIII] fol., *mut.*

†13. Coislin. 31 [X] fol., most beautifully written, the first seven pages in gold, the next fifteen in vermilion, the rest in black ink, *pict.*, described by Montfaucon (Scholz). Wetstein's 13 (Colbert. 1241 or Reg. 1982) contains no Evangelistarium.

14. Reg. 315 [XV] fol., *chart.*

15. Reg. 302 [XIII] fol., *mut.*

16. Reg. 297 [XII] fol., much *mut.*

17. Reg. 279 [XII] fol., *mut.*, (Tischendorf seems to have confounded 13 and 17 in his *N. T. Proleg.* p. ccxvi. 7th edition).

18. Bodl. Laud. Gk. 32, or Laud. D. 121, Mill's Bodl. 4 [XI] fol., much *mut.*, beginning John iv. 53. Codd. 18—22 were partially examined by Griesbach after Mill.

19. (Apost. Paul. 3, Griesbach). Bodl. 3048, or Misc. 10, Auct. D. Infr. 2. 12; Mill's Bodl. 5 [XIII] fol., *mut.*, with musical notes, *rubro:* given in 1661 by Parthenius, Patriarch of Constantinople, to Heneage Finch, Earl of Winchelsea, our Embassador there. This and Cod. 18 are said by Mill to be much like Stephens' ϛ′, Evan. 7.

20. Bodl. Laud. 34, Mill's Laud 4 [written by Onesimus, April 1047, Indiction 15] 4°, *mut.*[1]

[1] Laud. Gk. 36, which in the Bodleian Catalogue is described as an Evangelistarium, is a collection of Church Lessons from the Septuagint read in Lent and the Holy Week, such as we described above, pp. 64, 73. It has red musical notes, and seems *once* to have borne the date A. D. 1028.

21. Bodl. 3386, or Selden 49, Mill's Selden 4 [XIV] 4°, coarsely written; a mere fragment, as is also

22. Bodl. 3384, or Seld. 47, Seld. 5 of Mill [XIV] 4°, *mut.*, with Patristic homilies [XI].

†23. Mead's, then Askew's, then D'Eon's, by whom it was sent to France. Wetstein merely saw it.

†24. Monacensis 383 (August. 4 of Bengel) [X] fol., *mut.* (Bengel, Scholz). Is this the Cod. Radzivil, with slightly sloping uncials, [VIII], of which Silvestre gives a *facsimile* (*Paléogr. Univ.* No. 68)?

25. Mus. Brit. Harleian. 5650 [XII] 4°, a palimpsest, whose later writing is by Nicephorus the reader. The older writing, now illegible, was partly uncial, *mut.*

25[b] represents a few Lessons in the same codex by a later, yet contemporary hand (Bloomfield). Codd. 25—30 were very partially collated by Griesbach.

26. (Apost. 28). Bodleian. 3390, Seld. 1, or Mill's Seld. 2 [XIII] 4°, *mut.* a palimpsest, but the earlier uncial writing is illegible, and the codex in a wretched state, in several hands.

†27. Bodl. 3391, Seld. 2, or Mill's Seld. 3, a palimpsest [IX uncial, XIV later writing] 4°, *mut.*, in large ill-formed characters. Codd. 26, 27 were collated by Mangey, 1749 (*see* p. 183), but his papers appear to be lost.

28. Bodl. Misc. 11, Auct. D Infra 2. 14, Marsh 22 [XIII] 4°, *mut.*, in two careless hands.

29. Bodl. Misc. 12, Auct. D Infra 2. 15, Marsh 23 [XIII] 4°, *mut.* Elegantly written but much worn.

30. (Apost. Paul. 5, Griesbach). Bodl. 296, now Cromwell 11 [the whole written 1225 by Michael, a χωρικὸς καλλιγράφος] 4°, containing Prayers and some Lessons from the Gospels (including εὐαγγέλια ἀναστασιμά: *see* p. 72) and Epistles (Griesbach).

31. Cod. Norimberg. [XII] 4°, (Doederlein). Its readings are stated by Michaelis to resemble those of Codd. DL. 1. 69.

*32. Cod. Gothanus, in the Library of the Duke of Saxe Gotha [XII] fol., carelessly written. Edited by Matthaei, 1791.

†33. Cod. Cardinalis Alex. Albani [IX] 4°, a menology edited by Steph. Ant. Morcelli, Rome 1788.

†34. Monacens. 229, from Mannheim [X] 4°, elegantly written, in three volumes, the contents being in unusual order, and the menology suiting the custom of a monastery on Athos (Rink, Scholz).

Codd. 35—39 were inspected or collated by Birch, 40—43 by Moldenhawer.

35.[1] Vatic. 351 [X or XI] fol., contains only the lessons for holidays.

*†36. Vat. 1067 [XI] fol., a valuable copy, completely collated.

[1] I follow Birch's description. Scholz (whom Horne and Tischendorf merely copy) has given to this Cod. Vat. 351 the date and description which belong to Cod. Vat. 354, or S of the Gospels.

37. (Apost. 7). Propaganda 287, Borgia 3 [xi] 4°, contains only 13 lessons from the Gospels.

38. Laurent. Florent. 1, and

39. Florent. 2, formerly in the Palace, and neatly written, are only once cited by Birch.

†40. Escurial I. [x] 4°, kept with the reliques there as an autograph of St Chrysostom. It was given by Queen Maria of Hungary (who obtained it from Jo. Diassorin) to Philip II. Moldenhawer, who relates its history in a scoffing spirit, was only allowed to see it for a few hours, and collated 15 lessons. The text is of the common type, but in the oblong shape of the letters, false spirits and accents, the red musical notes &c., it resembles Evst. Cod. 1, though its date is somewhat lower.

†41. Escur. χ. III. 12 [x] 4°, very elegant: the menology (as also that of Cod. 43) suited to the use of a Byzantine church.

†42. Escur. χ. III. 13 [ix or x] 4°, *mut.* at the beginning. Two hands appear, the earlier leaning a little to the right.

43. Escur. χ. III. 16 [xi or xii] 4°, *mut.* at the beginning, in large cursive letters, with full *men.*

44. (Apost. 8). Havniens. 3 [xv] *mut.*, and much in a still later hand. Its history resembles that of Evan. 234—5 (Hensler).

†45. Caesar-Vindobon., Lambec. 15, Nessel 5 [x] fol., six leaves from the binding of a law-book: the letters resemble the Tubingen fragment, Griesbach's R (*see* p. 114) or Wetstein's 98 (Alter).

†46. Vindobon. Forlos. 23, Kollar. 7 [ix], on purple vellum, with gold and silver letters. There is a Latin version (Blanchini, Treschow, Alter). Silvestre has a *facsimile, Pal. Univ.* No. 69.

†*47. Moscow, S. Synod. 43 (Matthaei B) [viii] fol., "a barbaro scriptus est, sed ex praestantissimo exemplari," Matthaei, whose codices extend down to 57.

*48. Synod. 44 (Mt. c) [written by Peter, a monk, A.D. 1056] fol., from the Iberian monastery on Athos. In 1312 it belonged to Nicephorus, Metropolitan of Crete.

*49. Typograph. Synod. 11 (Mt. f) [x and later] fol., *pict.* Superior in text to Cod. 48, but much in a later hand.

†*50. Typograph. Synod. 12 (Mt. H) [viii ?] fol. A very valuable copy, whose date Matthaei placed unreasonably high.

*51. Typograph. Syn. 9 (Mt. t) [xvi] 4°, *chart.*

*52. (Apost. 16) Synod. 266 (Mt. ξ) [xiv] 4°, contains an Euchology and ἀποστολοευαγγέλια (*see p.* 63), as also do 53, 54, 55.

*53. (Apost. 17). Synod. 267 (Mt. χ) [xiv or xv] 4°, *chart.*, from the monastery of Simenus on Athos.

*54. (Apost. 18). Synod. 268 (Mt. ψ) [written A.D. 1470, by Dometius, a monk] 4°, *chart.*, from Batopedion monastery on Athos.

*55. (Apost. 19). Typogr. Syn. 47 (Mt. ω) [the Apost. copied at Venice 1602] 4°, *chart.*, wretchedly written.

*56. (Apost. 20). Typogr. Syn. 9 (Mt. 16) [xv or xvi] 16°, *chart.*, fragments of little value. *57. (=Act. 107).

Codd. 58—181 were added to the list by Scholz, who professes to have collated entire Cod. 60; in the greater part 81. 86.

58. Paris Reg. 50 a [xv] 4°, *chart.*, brought from some church in Greece.

59. Reg. 100 A [xvii] fol.

*60. (Apost. 12). Reg. 375, once Colbert's, formerly de Thou's [written A.D. 1022 by Helias, a priest and monk, "in castro de Colonia," for the use of the French monastery of St Denys] 8°; it contains many valuable readings (akin to those of Codd. ADE), but numerous errors.

†61. Reg. 182 [x] 4°, a fragment. 62. Reg. 194 A [xiii] fol.

†63. Reg. 277 [ix] fol., *mut.* at the beginning and end.

†64. Reg. 281 [ix] fol., from Constantinople; many leaves are torn.

†65. Reg. 282 [ix] fol., a palimpsest, with a Church-service in later writing [xiii].

†66. Reg. 283 [ix] fol., also a palimpsest, with the older writing of course misplaced; the later (*fine mut.*) a Church-service [xiii].

†67. Reg. 284 [xi] fol., "optimae notae," with musical marks, &c.

68. Reg. 285, once Colbert's [xi] fol., *mut.*, initio et fine.

69. Reg. 286 [xi] fol., fine *mut.*

70. Reg. 288 [xi] fol., brought from the East in 1669. A few leaves at the beginning and end later, *chart.*

71. Reg. 289, once Colbert's [written July 1066 by John, a priest, for George, a monk] fol., *mut.*, partly on vellum, partly on cotton paper.

72. Reg. 290 [written by Nicholas, 1257] fol. To this codex is appended

†72 b, three uncial leaves [ix] containing John v. 1—11; vi. 61—69; vii. 1—15.

73. Reg. 291 [xii] fol., *mut.*

74. Reg. 292, once Mazarin's [xii] fol.

75. Reg. 293, from the East [xii] fol.

76. Reg. 295, once Colbert's [xii] fol., *mut.*

77. Reg. 296 [xii] fol., from Constantinople.

78. Reg. 298, once Colbert's [xii] fol., *mut.* Some hiatus are supplied later on cotton paper.

79. Reg. 299 [xii] fol., *mut.* initio et fine.

80. Reg. 300 [xii] fol.

81. Reg 305 [XIII] fol., perhaps written in Egypt. Some passages supplied [XV] on cotton paper.

82. (Apost. 31). Reg. 276 [XV] fol., *chart.*, with lessons from the Prophets.

83. (Apost. 21). Reg. 294 [XI] fol.

84. (Apost. 9) Reg. 32 a, and

85. (Apost. 10) Reg. 33 a, both [XII] fol. have lessons from the Old and New Testament.

86. Reg. 311 [written July 1336, Indict. 4, by Charito] fol., given by the monk Ignatius to the monastery τῶν ὁδηγῶν or Θεοτόκου at Constantinople (*see* Act. 169): afterwards it was Boistaller's, and is described by Montfaucon. John vii. 53—viii. 11 is at the end, obelized, and not appointed for any day, as the names of Pelagia or Theodora (*see p.* 74) are not in the menology.

87. Reg. 313, once Colbert's (as were 88—91; 99—101) [XIV] fol.

88. Reg. 314 [XIV] fol. Many verses are omitted, and the arrangement of the lessons is a little unusual.

89. Reg. 316 [XIV] fol., on cotton paper, *mut.* fine.

90. Reg. 317 [written by Stephen, a reader, A.D. 1533. Ind. 6] fol., *chart.*

91. Reg. 318 [XI] fol., a subscription, &c. written in Cyprus by the monk Leontius 1553 (Montfauc. *Palaeo. Graec.* p. 89).

92. (Apost. 35). Reg. 324 [XIII] 4°, on cotton paper, with fragments of the Liturgy of St. Basil.

93. (Apost. 36). Reg. 326 [XIV] 4°, *chart.*, with the Liturgies of SS. Chrysostom and Basil.

94. (Apost. 29). Reg. 330 [XIII] 4°, *mut.*, with an Euchology and part of a Church-service in a later hand [XV].

95. Reg. 374 [XIV] 4°, from Constantinople.

96. Reg. 115ᵃ [XII] 4°, *chart.*, *mut.* initio et fine.

97. (= Evan. 324, Apost. 32) Reg. 376, only the εὐαγγέλια τῶν πάθων (*see p.* 72).

98. Reg. 377, once Mazarin's [XIII] 4°, portions are palimpsest, and the older writing *seems* to belong to an Evangelistarium.

99. Reg. 380 [XV] 4°, *chart.*

100. Reg. 381 [written in A. D. 1550 at Iconium by Michael Maurice] 4°, *chart.*

101. Reg. 303 [XIII] fol.

102. Ambrosian. 62, at Milan [written Sept. 1381 by Stephen, a priest], fol., *chart.* (but two leaves of parchment at the beginning, two at the end), bought at Taranto 1606, *syn.*?

103. Ambros. 67 [XIII] 4°, *pict.*; bought 1606, "Corneliani in Salentinis." See Apost. 46.

104. (Apost. 47). Ambros. 72 [XII] 8°, *mut.* initio et fine: brought from Calabria, 1607.

105. Ambros. 81 [XIII] 8°, carefully written, but the first 19 leaves [XVI] *chart.*

106. Ambros. 91 [XIII] 4°.

107. Venet. 548 [XI] fol.

108. Venet. 549 [XI] fol.

109. Venet. 550 [XI] 4°.

110. Venet. 551 [XI] fol.

†111. Mutinensis 27, at Modena [X] 4°.

112. (Apost. 48). Laurent. 2742, at Florence [XIII] 8°, neat.

113. Laurent. VI. 2 [foll. 1—213, XII; the rest written by one George XIV] fol. Prefixed are verses of Arsenius, Archbishop of Monembasia (see Evan. 333), addressed to Clement VII. (1523—34).

114. Laurent. VI. 7 [XII] fol.

†115. Laurent. VI. 21 [XI] 4°, elegantly written.

†116. Laurent. VI. 31 [X] fol., elegant, musical notes *rubro: facsimile* in Silvestre, *Pal. Univ.* No. 73.

117. Laurent. 244 [XII] fol., most beautifully written in golden cursive letters, *pict.*, once kept among the choicest *κειμήλια* of the Grand Ducal Palace.

†118. Laurent., kept in a chest for special preservation [XI or XII] fol., most elegant. Codd. 117—8 were described by Canon Angelo Bandini, 1787.

119. Vatic. 1155 [XIII] fol.

120. Vat. 1256 [XIII] fol.

121. Vat. 1157 [XIII] fol., very splendid.

122. Vat. 1168 [*dated* August 1175, Indict. 12 (but the proper Indiction is 8)] 4°, written by the monk Germanus for the monk Theodoret.

†123. Vat. 1522 [X] 4°, *pict.*, very correctly written, without points.

124. Vat. 1988, Basil 27 [XIII] 4°, *mut.* initio et fine.

125. Vat. 2017, Basil. 56 [XII] 4°, with a subscription dated 1346.

126. Vat. 2041, Basil. 80 [XII] fol., written by one George.

†127. Vat. 2063, Basil. 102 [IX] 4°, *mut.* initio. The first two leaves of the festival-lessons [XIV].

128. Vat. 2133 [XIV] 4°.

129. Alexandrino-Vat. (Queen Christina's) 12 [XIII] 4°. Foll. 1—40 appear to have been written in France, and have an unusual text: foll. 41—220 [XIII] are by another hand, the other 71 leaves to the end [XV].

†130. Vat. Ottobon. 2 [IX] fol., very beautiful.

131. Vat. Ottob. 175 [XIV] 4°, a fragment.

132. Vat. Ottob. 326 [XV] 4°, in silver letters. Procured at Rome, Sept. 11, 1590, "a Francisco et Accida" of Messina, and given to Cardinal Sirlet.

133. (Apost. 39). Ottob. 416 [XIV] 8°, *chart.*

134. Barberin. 15 [XIII] fol., the first eight and last three leaves being paper.

†135. Barber. 16, a palimpsest [VI. Scholz] 4°, is Tischendorf's barb[ev.], and by him referred to the middle of the 7th century, which is a little earlier date than has hitherto been assigned to Lectionaries (*see above, p.* 63). He has given specimens of its readings in *Monum. sacr. ined.* pp. 207 &c.

136. Barber. 16 [XII], the later writing of the palimpsest Cod. 135.

137. Vallicellian. D. 63, once Peter Polidore's [XII] 4°, *mut.* initio.

138. Neapol. 1. B. 14 [XV] fol., *chart.*, given by Christopher Palaeologus, May 7, 1584, to the Church of St Peter and Paul at Naples.

139. Venet. 12 [X] fol. 140. Venet. 626 [XIII] 4°, *chart.*

141. Venet. Nanian. 2 [XI] fol., from St Catherine's, on Sinai (*see p.* 76).

142. Venet. Nanian. 16 [XIV] 8°, *mut.*

143. Once belonged to the monastery of St Michael, 'prope murianum,' 49, Venice, fol. *mut.*, described by J. B. Mittarelli, 1779.

†144. Cod. Biblio. Malatestianae of Cesena XXVII. 4, now at Rome [X or XII] fol., very splendid.

145. Cod. XXIX. 2, of the same library [XII] fol.

146. Cambridge University Libr. Dd. VIII. 23 [XI] 4°, neatly written for a church at Constantinople.

[147. Mus. Brit. Harleian. 2970 [XI] 4°.

148. Harl. 2994 [XI] 4°. 149. Harl. 5538 [XIV].

Codd. 147—9 should be erased; 147, 148 being in *Latin*, and 149 already described (p. 187) as a manuscript of the Gospels in their proper order.

†*150. Harl. 5598 [written by Constantine, a priest, May 27, 995. Indict. 8] fol., is Scrivener's H, and described in *Cod. Augiensis*, Introd. pp. xlvii—l: for an alphabet formed from it see Plate III. No. 7. It was brought from Constantinople by Dr John Covell, in 1677 (*see above, p.* 150), and by him shewn to Mill (*Proleg. N. T.* § 1426); from Covell it seems to have been purchased (together with his five other copies) by Harley, Earl of Oxford. It is a most splendid specimen of the uncial class of Evangelistaria, and its text presents many instructive variations. At the end are several lessons for special occasions which are not often met with. Collated also by (Bloomfield).

151. Harl. 5785 [XII] fol., a splendid copy, in large, bold, cursive letters, with musical notes in red, and ornaments in gold. At the end is a note, written at Rome in 1699, by L. A. Zacagni (*see* p. 88), certifying that the volume was then more than 700 years old. The date assigned above is more likely.

†152. Harl. 5787 [x] fol., the uncials leaning to the right, a fine copy, with small uncial notes, well meriting collation. It begins John xx. 20, and is *mut.* elsewhere.

153. Meermann. 117 [xi] 4°, justly suspected by Tischendorf to be identical with Evan. 436, should be erased from the list: see p. 158, note.

154. Monacensis 326, once at Mannheim [xiii] fol., written very small and neatly, containing the lessons from the season of Lent (*see p.* 72) to the month of December in the menology (*see p.* 74), which seems adapted to the Constantinopolitan use.

†155. Caesar-Vindobon. Nessel. 209, Lambec. 41 [x] 4°, a palimpsest, over which is written a Commentary on St Matthew [xiv].

156. Vallicellian. D. 4. 1 [?] fol., described by Blanchini, *Evang. Quad.* Pt. i. p. 537; now missing.

157. Bodleian., Clarke 8 [xiii] 4°, Saturday and Sunday lessons, *mut.* initio et fine.

158. Library of the great Greek monastery at Jerusalem, No. 10 [xiv] fol.

159. "Biblioth. monasterii virginum τῆς μεγάλης παναγίας a s. Melana erect." [xiii] fol., very neat, ("non sec. viii. ut monachi putant") Scholz.

160. (Apost. 53) S. Saba 4, written there by one Anthony [xiv] 8°.

161. S. Saba 5 [xv] 8°, *chart.* 162. S. Saba 6 [xv] 16°, *chart.*

163. S. Saba 13 [xiii] 4°, *chart.*, adapted (as also those that follow) to the use of Palestine.

164. S. Saba 14 [xiv] 4°. 165. S. Saba 17 [xv] 4°, *chart.*

166. S. Saba 21 [xiii] fol. 167. S. Saba 22 [xiv] fol.

168. S. Saba 23 [xiii] fol. 169. S. Saba 24 [xiii] fol.

170. S. Saba 25 [xiii] fol.

171. (Apost. 52) S. Saba (unnumbered) [written July 1059, in the monastery of Θεοτόκος by Sergius, a monk of Olympus in Bithynia] 8°.

†172. Library of St John's monastery at Patmos ["iv" Scholz, obviously a misprint] fol.

†173. Patmos [ix] 4°. †174. Patm. [x] 4°.

†175. Patm. [x] 4°. 176. Patm. [xii] 4°.

177. Patm. [xiii] 4°.

178. Patm. [xiv] 4°, in the same Library, but not numbered.

†*179. (Apost. 55) Cod. Trevirensis, in the Cathedral Library [x or xi] 4°, called St Simeon's, and brought by him from Syria in the 11th century, consists chiefly of lessons from the Old Testament. It contains many itacisms and some unusual readings. Edited at Trèves 1834 by B. M. Steininger in his *Codex S. Simeonis exhibens lect. eccl. gr.* DCCC *ann. vetustate insigne.*

†180. Caesar-Vindob. CCIX [IX] 4°, palimpsest, with many itacisms (Scholz, Endlicher). Readings are given by Scholz (N. T. Vol. II. pp. lv—lxiii).

181. (= Apoc. 26, Apost. 57). This is inserted in error: see p. 182, Wake No. 12. (In p. 182, l. 20, read 181 for 187).

The next five are due to Tischendorf.

†* ven$^{\text{ev.}}$ Venetian palimpsest fragments (edited *Mon. sacr. ined.* Vol. I. pp. 199, &c.), assigned to the end of the seventh century (see Cod. 135, p. 218), containing Matth. viii. 32—ix. 1; 9—13; John ii. 15—22; iii. 22—26; vi. 16—26; or 27 verses.

†carp$^{\text{ev.}}$ at Carpentras [IX], examined by Tischendorf in 1843, in consequence of Haenel's assigning it to the 6th century. Extracts are given in *Anecd. sacr. et prof.* pp. 151, &c.

†tisch$^{\text{ev.}}$ Tischendorf. V, in the University Library at Leipsic [VIII or IX], a palimpsest, described *Anecd. sacr. et prof.* pp. 29, &c. [Tischendorf's tubing$^{\text{ev.}}$ is described under Cod. R, p. 114, and Bandur$^{\text{ev.}}$ under Cod. O, p. 112].

†Petrop$^{\text{ev.}}$ [IX] 69 leaves 4°, ill written, but with a remarkable text; the date being tolerably fixed by Arabic matter decidedly more modern, written 401 and 425 of the Hegira (i. e. about A.D. 1011 and 1035) respecting the birth and baptism of the two Holy infants. There are but 10 lessons from St Matthew, and 19 from other parts of the New Testament, enumerated *Notit. Cod. Sinait.* p. 54. This copy has the two leaves on cotton paper, with writing by the first hand, mentioned above, p. 21, note.

Petrop$^{\text{ev. 2}}$ a fragment of 93 leaves [XI or XII] 4°. *Notitia Cod. Sinaitici*, p. 63.

The following were collated by Scrivener:

†*P$^{\text{scr.}}$ Parham 18, the property of the Hon. R. Curzon, who brought it from Caracalla in 1837 (see p. 182) [*dated* June 980, Indict. 8] fol., beautifully written at Ciscissa, in Cappadocia Prima; a note dated 1049 is subjoined by a reviser, who perhaps made the numerous changes in the text, and added two lessons in cursive letters. A facsimile of P is given in Plate XII. No. 32. For this codex, P 2 and z see *Cod. Aug.* Introd. pp. l—lv.

†*P 2$^{\text{scr.}}$ Parham 1 [IX], three folio leaves from the monastery of Docheirou on Athos, containing the 33 verses, Matth. i. 1—11; 11—22; vii. 7, 8; Mark ix. 41; xi. 22—26; Luke ix. 1—4.

†*x$^{\text{scr.}}$ Arundel 547, in the British Museum (see p. 179) [IX] 4°, *mut.* fine, followed by one leaf in a somewhat later hand, containing John viii. 12—19; 21—23. Bentley's previous collation is at Trinity College (B. 17. 8).

*y^{scr} Burney 22, in the British Museum [*dated* A.D. 1319; see *facsimile*, Plate XII. No. 36, and p. 38, note 1] fol., remarkable for its wide departures from the received text, and for that reason often cited by Tischendorf and Alford on the Gospels. Part of the first leaf (John i. 11—13) is on paper and later: x, y are described in *Collations of the Holy Gospels*, Introd. pp. lix—lxiii. Like Evst. 23 it once was D'Eon's.

*z^{scr} Christ's College, Cambridge, F. 1. 8 [XI] fol., is much fuller than most Lectionaries, and contains many minute variations and interesting readings[1]: it exhibits a subscription dated 1261, Indict. 4, much later than the codex, and a note stating that Francis Tayler, Preacher at Christ's Church, Canterbury [the Cathedral], gave it to the College in 1654. There are also 4 lessons from the prophets, and 4 from St Paul. A *facsimile* is given *Cod. Augiens.* Introd. p. lii.

The following Evangelistaria are quite uncollated.

Arundel. 536 [XIII] 4°, *mut.* fine, with musical notes, as usual.

One at Middle Hill (see p. 181) [XII or XIII].

†Bodleian. Canonici Gr. 85 [IX] 4°, much *mut.* The uncials lean a little to the left.

†*Ibid.* 92 [X] large folio, very splendid, with gilt initials.

Ibid. 119 [XV] fol., *chart.*, belonging in 1626 to Nicholas, a priest.

Ibid. 126, p. 252, a small fragment of an Evst.

In E. D. Clarke's collection are four besides Evst. Cod. 157 of Scholz.

Bodl. Clarke 45 [XII] large 4°, splendid but spoiled by damp, with musical notes and bold initial letters *rubro.*

Ibid. 46 [XIII] large 4°, inferior and rudely written: *mut.* initio et fine.

Ibid. 47 [XII] 4°, with musical notes *rubro:* much like 45.

Ibid. 48 [XIII] 4°, carelessly and ill written: *mut.* initio.

The following are also in the Bodleian:

Cromwell 27 [XI] fol., from Athos 1727, once Irene's. *Men.*

Miscell. 119, Auct. F. 6. 25 [A. D. 1067] 4°, once belonged to Constantine Ducas βασιλεύς. It is carelessly written, and is preceded by

†One uncial palimpsest leaf, containing parts of Rom. xiv., Hebr. i. This volume was bought of Payne and Foss, London, in 1820.

Miscell. 140, Rawl. Auct. G. 2 [XI] small 4°, a very beautiful copy, one volume only out of a set of four. Both this codex and Cromw. 27, Miscell. 119 have musical notes *rubro.*

†Barocc. 119 contains five uncial palimpsest leaves in two columns (THE ORDINARY ARRANGEMENT OF EVANGELISTARIA) [X] used for the binding.

Eight of the Wake manuscripts at Christ Church, Oxford (*see p.* 182) are Evangelistaria.

[1] Thus z, with only two other Evangelistaria (6. 13) supports Cod. ℵ and Eusebius in the significant omission of υἱοῦ βαραχίου Matth. xxiii. 35.

†No. 13 contains three uncial leaves [IX], the rest cursive [XI] in a very large, bold, peculiar hand. Two palimpsest leaves at the end have the older writing cursive. A table of lessons is in the handwriting of the venerated Dr Burton, late Regius Professor of Divinity.

No. 14 [XII] fol., with one leaf *chart.*, and two leaves at the beginning and end from the Old Testament, 3 (1) Kings xvii. 12 &c.

No. 15 [*dated* 1068] 4°, the first and last leaves being earlier.

No. 16 [XIII] 4°, *mut.* initio et fine. There are musical notes *rubro:* so also in Nos. 19, 23.

No. 17 [XIII or XIV] 4°, *mut.* fine. Fifteen leaves are supplied *chart.*

No. 18 [XII] fol., ill written. The first leaf contains the history of St Varus and six martyrs. This is Walker's E (*see p.* 184): his H is

No. 19 [XI] 4°. Of this codex the 9th leaf is wanting.

No. 23 [XI ?] fol., an elegant copy.

In the Library of Sion College, in the city of London (*see p.* 187) are three Evangelistaria, viz. Ari. I. 1 [XII]; Ari. I. 4 and Ari. I. 2 [XIV].

The following were seen by Mr Coxe in the East (*see p.* 185).

At Cairo: No. 18. Συναγωγὴ λέξεων ἐκ παλαιᾶς καὶ νέας.

At Jerusalem: No. 12 [XI or XII] fol., which must be Scholz's Evst. 158.

At S. Saba Scholz saw twelve Evangelistaria (Codd. 160—171), two of them containing the Apostolos (Codd. 160, 171); and four Lectionaries of the Apostolos only (Codd. 49—51; 54). Coxe observed but one Apostolos, Tower Libr. No. 52 [XI] 4° with musical notes; and nine Evangelistaria. Some seen at S. Saba by Scholz have perhaps been since taken into Europe, the rather as we know that Parham No. 20 (named below) came from that place.

Coxe's list runs: No. 17 [XII] large 4°; No. 23 [XII] fol.; Nos. 24—6 [XI] fol.; No. 40 [XII] fol. with an Arabic version; Nos. 44, 55 [XII] large 4°; Tower Library No. 12 [XI] 4°.

At Patmos Scholz enumerates seven Evangelistaria (Codd. 172—8), no Lectionary of the Apostolos: Coxe mentions only those four of Scholz's that are uncials (Codd. 172—5), viz. No. 4 [XI] 4°; No. 10 [XI] 4°; No. 22 [XI] fol.; No. 81 [VIII] 4°.

At Milo, in private hands (*see p.* 186) was an Evst. [XII] fol., *mut.*

In the Patriarch of Jerusalem's Library at Constantinople (*see p.* 180, note) an Evst. [XII] 4°, over early writing from Ptolemy.

Of E. de Muralt's collated codices, described p. 178, five are Evangelistaria (†No. 1 apparently uncial), of which one contains also a Praxapostolos.

Seidel's codex at Frankfort-on-Oder (Act. 42, Paul. 48, Apoc. 13, Apost. 56), also contains a lesson, Matth. xvii. 16—23.

Apost. 15, and perhaps Apost. 24, also contain lessons from the Gospels.

Lambeth 1187, 1188, 1189, all [XIII], and 1193, *mut.*, which Dr Bloomfield refers to [IX], have been collated by him. He praises Cod. 1188 as the fullest and most accurate either at Lambeth or the British Museum.

In the British Museum Bloomfield professes to have examined 13 Lectionaries, of which those not before named *appear* to be Additional 536; 1575; 1577; 5153; 11840; 11841; 18212; 19460; 19993. Of these 11840 [XI] 4°, *mut.*, with musical notes, beautifully written, with some other matter; and 11841 [XII] fol., are from Bp. Butler's collection. All these he has not so much collated as inspected; reserving their fuller investigation, he is pleased to say, for Scrivener. "*Cupidum, pater optime, vires deficiunt.*"

There are also uncollated Evangelistaria at Besançon; in the Hunterian Museum at Glasgow, Q. 3, 35, 36 [XI]; one of great splendour at Parham (No. 19), partly written in gold, and perhaps by the Emperor Alexius Comnenus (1081—1118); and another at Parham, No. 20 [XII] fol., from S. Saba, which must be on Scholz's list (Codd. 160—171).

Deducting six duplicates &c., there remain 241 Evangelistaria.

Lectionaries containing the Apostolos or Praxapostolos.

†*1. (= Evst.[1] 6). 2. Brit. Mus. Cotton. Vespas. B. XVIII. [XI] *mut.* initio et fine (Casley)[2]. The Museum Catalogue is wrong in stating that it contains lessons from the Gospels.

3. Readings sent to Mill (*Proleg. N. T.* § 1470) by John Batteley, D.D., as taken from a codex, now missing, in Trinity Hall, Cambridge. The extracts were from 1 Peter and John. Griesbach's Paul. 3 is Bodl. 5 (Evst. 19) cited by Mill only at Hebr. x. 22, 23.

4. Laurent., once at St Mark's, Florence [XI] 4°.

*5. Gottingense 2 (in the University Library), once de Missy's [XV] fol., formerly of the monastery Castamonitum (?) on Athos (Matthaei's v). N.B. Paul. 5 of Griesbach (= Evst. 30).

6. (= Evan. 117) fragments examined by Griesbach (Foll. 183—202).

7. (= Evst. 37). 8. (= Evst. 44).

9. (Evst. 84). 10. (Evst. 85).

11. Paris, Reg, 104[a] [XII] 8°, well written in some monastery of Palestine: with marginal notes in Arabic.

*12. (= Evst. 60).

†*13. Moscow, S. Synod. 4 (Mt. b) [X] fol., important: it would seem to be an uncial, once belonging to the Iberian monastery; renovated by Joakim, a monk, A.D. 1525.

[1] Evst. = Evangelistarium.

[2] In 1721. See Monk's *Life of Bentley*, Vol. II. p. 149.

*14. S. Synod. 291 (Mt. e) [XII] 4°, well written, from the monastery τοῦ ἐσφιγμένου on Athos.

*15. Typogr. Syn. 31 (Mt. tz) [*dated* 1116].

*16. (=Evst. 52). *17. (=Evst. 53).

*18. (=Evst. 54). *19. (=Evst. 55).

*20. (=Evst. 56).

Codd. 21—58 comprise Scholz's additions to the list, of which he describes none as collated entire or in the greater part. He seems, however, to have collated Cod. 12.

21. (=Evst. 83).

22. Reg. 304 [XIII] fol., brought from Constantinople: *mut.* fine.

23. Reg. 306 [XII] fol., *mut.* initio et fine.

24. Reg. 308 [XIII] fol., contains a few lessons from the New Testament, more from the Old: *mut.*

25. Reg. 319, once Colbert's [XI] fol., ill-written, with a Latin version over some portions of the text.

26. Reg. 320 [XII] fol. *mut.*

27. Reg. 321, once Colbert's [XIII] fol., *mut.*, and illegible in parts.

28. (=Evst. 26). 29. (=Evst. 94).

30. Reg. 373 [XIII] 4°, *mut.* initio et fine: with some cotton-paper leaves at the end.

31. (=Evst. 82). 32. (=Evan. 324, Evst. 97).

33. Reg. 382, once Colbert's [XIII] 4°.

34. Reg. 383, once Colbert's [XV] 4°, *chart.* In readings it is much with Apost. 12, and the best copies.

35. (=Evst. 92). 36. (=Evst. 93).

37. (=Evan. 368, Act. 150, Paul. 230, Apoc. 84).

38. Vat. 1528 [XV] 4°, *chart.*, written by the monk Eucholius.

39. (=Evst. 133).

40. Barberini 18 [X] 4°, a palimpsest (probably uncial, though not so stated by Scholz), correctly written, but mostly illegible. The later writing [XIV] contains lessons in the Old Testament, with a few from the Catholic Epistles at the end.

41. Barb. ? [XI] 4°, *mut.*

42. Vallicell. C. 46 [XVI] 4°, *chart.*, with other matter.

43. Richard. 2742 at Florence: seems to be the same as Cod. 48 below, and is not (as Scholz states) Evst. 139.

44, 45. Hunterian Mus. Glasgow, having been bought by Hunter at Caesar de Missy's sale (Nos. 1633—4): 45 is dated A.D. 1199.

46. Ambros. 63 [XIV] 4°, bought (like Evst. 103) in 1606, "Corneliani in Iapygia."

47. (= Evst. 104). 48. (= Evst. 112).

49. S. Saba 16 [XIV] 4°, *chart.*

50. S. Saba 18 [XV] 8°. 51. S. Saba 26 [XIV] fol.

52. (= Evst. 171). 53. (= Evst. 160).

54. S. Saba (unnumbered) [XIII] 4°.

†*55. (= Evst. 179).

56. (= Act. 42, Paul. 48, Apoc. 13 and Evst. —) contains only 1 Cor. ix. 2—12. 57. (= Apoc. 26, Wake 12, p. 182).

58. Wake 33, at Christ Church, Oxford [*dated* 1172] fol., 265 leaves, the ink quite gone in parts.

z^scr (see p. 221) contains four lessons from the Epistles; and de Muralt's Evst. 3^pe (p. 178) is also a Praxapostolos.

Additional copies are:

†*tisch^6. f. Bibl. Univers. Lipsiens. 6. F. (Tischend. v) [IX or X], containing Heb. i. 3—12, published *Anecd. sacr. et prof.* p. 73, &c.

†*Petrop., one leaf of a double palimpsest, now at St Petersburg, the oldest writing [IX] containing Act. xiii. 10; 2 Cor. xi. 21—23, cited by Tischendorf (*N. T. Prol.* p. ccxxvi, 7th edition).

†His new uncial Lectionary at St Petersburg (see p. 220) also contains lessons from all parts of the New Testament; Scholz seems to state the same of Evst. 161, "continet lect. et pericop.," and Coxe of Evst. Cairo 18.

At Lambeth, manuscripts 1190 [XIII], 1191 [XIII] 4°, *mut.* initio et fine, 1194, 1195, 1196, all [XIII] 4°, *mut.* are Lectionaries of the Praxapostolos, which Dr S. T. Bloomfield has collated.

We find Latin versions in 8 uncial and 10 cursive codices; an Arabic version in Evan. 211; 450; Evst. 6; Coxe's Evst. at St Saba, No. 40; Latin and Arabic in Act. 96.

The total number of manuscripts we have recorded in the preceding catalogues are 34 uncial and 601 cursive of the Gospels; 10 uncial and 228[1] cursive of the Acts and Catholic Epistles; 14 uncial and 282 cursive of St Paul; 4 uncial and 102 cursive of the Apocalypse; 58 uncial and 183 cursive Evangelistaria; and 7 uncial, 65 cursive Lectionaries of the Praxapostolos. In calculating this total of 127 uncials and 1461 cursives we have deducted 66 duplicates, and must bear in mind that a few of the codices, whose present locality is unknown, may have reappeared under other heads.

Ὁ μὲν θερισμὸς πολύς, οἱ δὲ ἐργάται ὀλίγοι.

[1] In spite of the utmost care to detect duplicates, I overlooked at p. 193 what I had observed at p. 130, that Scholz's Act. 102, Paul 117 is Tischendorf's *uncial* K of all the Epistles. Hence it becomes necessary to make the requisite changes in the totals at pp. 200, 207.

CHAPTER III.

ON THE ANCIENT VERSIONS OF THE NEW TESTAMENT IN VARIOUS LANGUAGES.

---

1. THE facts stated in the preceding chapter have led us to believe that no extant manuscript of the Greek Testament yet discovered is older than the fourth century, and that those written as early as the sixth century are both few in number, and (with one notable exception) contain but portions, for the most part very small portions, of the sacred volume. When to these considerations we add the well-known circumstance that the most ancient codices vary widely and perpetually from the commonly received text and from each other, it becomes desirable for us to obtain, if possible, some evidence as to the character of those copies of the New Testament which were used by the primitive Christians in times anterior to the date of the most venerable now preserved. Such sources of information, though of a more indirect and precarious kind than manuscripts of the original can supply, are open to us in the *versions* of Holy Scripture, made at the remotest period in the history of the Church, for the use of believers whose native tongue was not Greek. Translations, certainly of the New and probably of the Old Testament, were executed not later than the second century in the Syriac and Latin Tongues, and, so far as their present state enables us to judge of the documents from which they were rendered, they represent to us a modification of the inspired text which existed within a century of the death of the Apostles. Even as the case stands, and although the testimony of versions is peculiarly liable to doubt and error, the Peshito Syriac and Old Latin translations of the Greek Testa-

ment stand with a few of the most ancient manuscripts of the original in the very first rank as authorities and aids for the critical revision of the text.

In a class apart from and next below the Peshito Syriac and Old Latin we may group together the Curetonian Syriac, the Egyptian, the Latin Vulgate, the Gothic, the Armenian and Æthiopic versions, which we name in what seems to be their order in respect to value. Of these the Curetonian will be discussed more fitly hereafter (pp. 236—241); the Egyptian may have been formed, partly in the third, principally in the fourth century; the Latin Vulgate and the Gothic belong to the fourth, the Armenian and possibly the Æthiopic to the fifth. The Philoxenian Syriac, although not brought into its present condition before the beginning of the seventh century, would appear, for reasons that will be detailed hereafter, to hold a place in this class not much lower than the Latin Vulgate.

The third rank must be assigned to the several minor Syriac (so far as their character has been ascertained), to the Georgian and Slavonic, some Arabic, and one of the Persic versions: these are either too recent or uncertain in date, or their text too mixed and corrupt, to merit particular attention. The other Persic (and perhaps one Arabic) version being derived from the Peshito Syriac, and the Anglo-Saxon from the Latin Vulgate, can be applied only to the correction of their respective primary translations.

2. The weight and consideration due to versions of Scripture, considered as materials for critical use, depend but little on their merits as competent representations of the original. A very wretched translation, such as the Philoxenian Syriac, may happen to have high critical value; while an excellent one, like our English Bible, shall possess just none at all. And, in general, the testimony of versions as witnesses to the state of the text is rendered much less considerable than that of manuscripts of the same date, by defects which, though they cleave to some of them far more than to others, are too inherent in their very nature to be absolutely eliminated from any. These defects are so obvious as to need no more than a bare statement, and render a various reading, *supported by versions alone*, of very slight consideration.

(1). It may be found as difficult to arrive at the primitive text of a version, as of the Greek original itself: the variations in its different copies are often quite as considerable, and suspicions of subsequent correction, whether from the Greek or from some other version, are as plausible to raise and as hard to refute. This is preeminently the case in regard to the Latin version, especially in its older form; but the Peshito Syriac, the Armenian, the Georgian and almost every other have been brought into discredit, on grounds more or less reasonable, by those whose purpose it has served to disparage their importance.

(2). Although several of the ancient versions, and particularly the Latin, are rendered more closely to the original than would be thought necessary or indeed tolerable in modern times, yet it is often by no means easy to ascertain the precise Greek words which the translator had in his copy. While versions are always of weight in determining the authenticity of sentences or clauses inserted or omitted by Greek manuscripts[1], and in some instances may be employed even for arranging the order of words, yet every language differs so widely in spirit from every other, and the genius of one version is so much at variance with that of others, that too great caution cannot be used in applying this kind of testimony to the criticism of the Greek. The Aramæan idiom, for example, delights in a graceful redundancy of pronouns, which sometimes affects the style of the Greek Testament itself (e.g. Matth. viii. 1; 5): so that the Syriac should have no influence in deciding a point of this kind, as the translator would naturally follow the usage of his own language, rather than regard the precise wording of his original.

(3). Hence it follows that no one can form a trustworthy judgment respecting the evidence afforded by any version, who is not master of the language in which it is written. A past generation of critics contented themselves with using Latin versions of the Egyptian, Æthiopic, &c., to their own and their readers' cost. The insertion or absence of whole

[1] This use of versions was seen by Jerome (*Praefatio ad Damasum*) "Cum multarum gentium linguis scriptura ante translata, doceat falsa esse quae addita sunt." It is even now the principal service they can perform for the critic.

clauses, indeed, are patent facts which cannot be mistaken, but beyond such matters the unskilled enquirer ought not to venture. The immediate result of this restriction may be to confine the student to the full use of the Syriac and Latin versions; a few Biblical scholars, as Professor Ellicott, have made some progress in the ancient Egyptian; the rest of us must remain satisfied with a confession of ignorance, or apply our best diligence to remedy it.

From this rapid glance over the whole subject of versions, we pass on to consider them severally in detail; not aiming at a full literary history of any of them, which would be unsuitable to our limits and present design, but rather seeking to put the learner in possession of materials for forming an independent estimate of their relative value, and of the internal character of the chief among them.

3. *Syriac Versions.* (1). *The Peshito.*

The Aramæan or Syriac (preserved to this day as their sacred tongue by several Eastern Churches), is an important branch of the great Shemitic family of languages, which as early as Jacob's age existed distinct from the Hebrew (Gen. xxxi. 47). In its present state, it was spoken in the north of Syria and in Upper Mesopotamia, the native region of the patriarch Abraham, about Edessa. It is a more copious, flexible and elegant language than Hebrew (which ceased to be vernacular at the Babylonish captivity) had ever the means of becoming, and is so intimately akin to the Chaldee as spoken at Babylon, and subsequently throughout Palestine, that the latter was popularly known by its name (2 Kings xviii. 26; Isai. xxxvi. 11; Dan. ii. 4). As the Gospel took firm root at Antioch within a few years after the Lord's Ascension (Act. xi. 19—27; xiii. 1, &c.), we might deem it probable that its tidings soon spread from the Greek capital into the native interior, even though we utterly rejected the venerable tradition of Thaddaeus' mission to Abgarus, toparch of Edessa, as well as the fable of that monarch's intercourse with Christ while yet on earth (Eusebius, *Eccl. Hist.* I. 13.; II. 1). At all events we are sure that Christianity flourished in these regions at a very early period; it is even possible that the Syriac Scriptures were seen by

Hegisippus in the second century (Euseb. *Eccl. Hist.* IV. 22); they were familiarly used and claimed as his national version by Ephraem of Edessa (*see p.* 94) in the fourth. Thus the universal belief of later ages, and the very nature of the case, seem to render it unquestionable, that the Syrian Church was possessed of a translation, both of the Old and New Testament, which it used habitually, and, for public worship exclusively, from the second century of our æra downwards: as early as A. D. 170 ὁ Σύρος is cited by Melito on Genes. xxii. 13 (Mill, *Proleg.* § 1239). And the sad history of that distracted Church can leave no room to doubt what that version was. In the middle of the fifth century, the third and fourth general Councils at Ephesus and Chalcedon proved the immediate occasions of dividing the Syrian Christians into three, and eventually into yet more, hostile communions. These grievous divisions have now subsisted for fourteen hundred years, and though the bitterness of controversy has abated, the estrangement of the rival Churches is as complete and hopeless as ever[1]. Yet the same translation of Holy Scripture is read alike in the public assemblies of the Nestorians among the fastnesses of Coordistan, of the Monophysites who are scattered over the plains of Syria, of the Christians of St Thomas along the coast of Malabar, and of the Maronites on the mountain-terraces of Lebanon. Even though these last acknowledged the supremacy of Rome in the twelfth century, and certain Nestorians of Chaldæa in the eighteenth, both societies claimed at the time, and enjoy to this day, the free use of their Syriac translation of Holy Scripture. Manuscripts, too, obtained from each of these rival communions, have flowed from time to time into the libraries of the West, yet they all exhibit a text in every important respect the same; all are without the Apocalypse and four of the Catholic Epistles, which latter we know to have been wanting in the Syriac in the sixth century (*Cosmas Indico-*

[1] All modern accounts of the unorthodox sects of the East confirm Walton's beautiful language two hundred years ago: "Etsi verò, olim in hæreses miserè prolapsi, se a reliquis Ecclesiæ Catholicæ membris separarint, unde justo Dei judicio sub Infidelium jugo oppressi serviunt, qui ipsis dominantur, ex continuis tamen calamitatibus edocti et sapientiores redditi (est enim Schola Crucis Schola Lucis) tandem eorum misertus Misericordiarum Pater eos ad rectam sanamque mentem, rejectis antiquis erroribus, reduxit" (Walt. *Prolegomena,* Wrangham, *Tom.* II. *p.* 500).

pleustes apud Montfaucon, Collectio Nova Patrum et Script. Graec. Tom. II. *p.* 292), a defect, we may observe in passing, which alone is no slight proof of the high antiquity of the version that omits them; all correspond with whatever we know from other sources of that translation which, in contrast with one more recent, was termed "old" (ܩܕܡܝܐ) by Thomas of Harkel A.D. 616, and "Peshito" (ܦܫܝܛܬܐ) the "Simple" by the great Monophysite doctor, Gregory Bar-Hebraeus [1226-86]. Literary history can hardly afford a more powerful case than has been established for the identity of the version of the Syriac now called the *Peshito* with that used by the Eastern Church, long before the great schism had its beginning in the native land of the blessed Gospel.

The first printed edition of this most venerable monument of the Christian faith was published in quarto at Vienna in the year 1555 (some copies are re-dated 1562), at the expense of the Emperor Ferdinand I., on the recommendation and with the active aid of his Chancellor, Albert Widmanstadt, an accomplished person, whose travelling name in Italy was John Lucretius. It was undertaken at the instance of Moses of Mardin, legate from the Monophysite Patriarch Ignatius to Pope Julius III. (1550—55), who seems to have brought with him a manuscript of the Jacobite family, although written at Mosul, for publication in the West: Widmanstadt contributed a second manuscript of his own, though it does not appear whether either or both contained the whole New Testament. This beautiful book, the different portions of which have separate dedications, was edited by Widmanstadt, by Moses, and by W. Postell jointly, in an elegant type of the modern Syriac character, the vowel and diacritic points, especially the *linea occultans*, being frequently dropped, with subscriptions and titles indicating the Jacobite Church lessons in the older, or Estrangelo, letter. It omits, as was natural and right, those books which the Peshito does not contain: viz. the second Epistle of Peter, the second and third of John, that of Jude and the Apocalypse, together with the disputed passage John vii. 53—viii. 11, and the doubtful, or more than doubtful clauses in Matt. xxvii. 35; Acts viii. 37; xv. 34; 1 John v. 7. This *editio princeps* of the Peshito New Testament, though now become very scarce (one half of its thousand copies having been sent into Syria), is held in high and deserved repute, as its text is apparently based on manuscript authority alone.

Immanuel Tremellius, a converted Jew and Professor of Divinity at Heidelberg, published the second edition in folio in 1569, containing the New Testament in Hebrew type, with a literal Latin version, accompanied by the Greek text and Beza's translation of it, with a Chaldee and Syriac grammar annexed. Tremellius used several manuscripts, especially one at Heidelberg, and made from them and his own conjecture many changes, which were not always improvements, in the text; besides admitting some grammatical forms which are Chaldee rather than Syriac. His Latin version has been used as their basis by later editors, down to the time of Schaaf. Tremellius' and Beza's Latin versions were reprinted together, without their respective originals, in 1592. Subsequent editions of the Peshito New Testament were those of the folio Antwerp or Royal Spanish Polyglott of Plantin (1569—72), in Hebrew and Syriac type, revised from a copy dated A. D. 1188, which Postell had brought from the East: two other editions of Plantin in Hebrew type without points (1574, 8°, 1575, 24°), the second containing various readings extracted by Francis Rapheleng from a Cologne manuscript for his own reprints of 1575 and subsequently of 1583: the smaller Paris edition, also in unpointed Hebrew letters, 4°, 1584, by Guy Le Fevre, who prepared the Syriac portion of the Antwerp Polyglott: that of Elias Hutter, in two folio volumes (Nuremberg 1599—1600), in Hebrew characters; this editor ventured to supply in Syriac of his own making, the single passages wanting in the *editio princeps*, and the spurious Epistle to the Laodiceans: Martin Trost's edition (Anhalt-Cöthen, 1621, 4°,) in Syriac characters, with vowel-points and a list of various readings, is much superior to Hutter's.

The magnificent Paris Polyglott (fol. 1645) is the first which gives us the Old Testament portion of the Peshito, though in an incomplete state. The Maronite Gabriel Sionita, who superintended this portion of the Polyglott, made several changes in the system of vowel punctuation, possibly from analogy rather than from manuscript authority, but certainly for the better. His judgment however was much at fault when he inserted as integral portions of the Peshito the version of the four missing Catholic Epistles, which had been published in 1630 by our illustrious oriental scholar, Edward Pococke, from some manuscript in the Bodleian: and another of the Apocalypse, edited at Leyden in 1627 by Louis de Dieu, from an unpromising and recent manuscript, lately examined by Tregelles, in the University Library there (Scaliger MS. 18). Of the two, the version of the Catholic Epistles seems decidedly the older, and both bear much resemblance to the later Syriac or Philoxenian translation, but neither have the smallest claim to be regarded as portions of the Peshito, to which, however, they have unhappily been appended ever since.

Bp. Walton's, or the London Polyglott (fol. 1654—7), affords us little more than a reprint of Sionita's Syriac text, with Trost's various readings appended, but interpolates the text yet further by inserting John vii. 53—viii. 11 from a manuscript (now lost) of Archbishop Ussher, by whom it had been sent to De Dieu before 1631. As this passage is not in the true Philoxenian, we are left to conjecture as to its real date and character, only that De Dieu assures us that the Ussher manuscript contained the *whole* New Testament, which no copy of the Peshito or other Syriac version yet known has been found to do.

Giles Gutbier published at Hamburg (8°, 1664) an edition containing all the interpolated matter, and 1 Joh. v. 7 in addition, from Tremellius' own version, which he inserted in *his* margin. Gutbier used two manuscripts, by one of which, belonging to Constantine L'Empereur, he corrected Sionita's system of punctuation. A glossary, notes and various readings are annexed. The Salzburg edition 12°, 1684, seems a mere reprint of Plantin's; nor does that published at Rome in 1703 for the use of the Maronites, though grounded upon manuscript authority, appear to have much critical value.

A collation of the various readings in all the preceding editions, excepting those of 1684 and 1703, is affixed to the Syriac N. T. of J. Leusden and Ch. Schaaf (4°, Leyden, 1709: with a new title-page 1717). It extends over one hundred pages, and, though most of the changes are very insignificant, is tolerably accurate and of considerable value. This edition contains a revised Latin version, and is usually accompanied with an admirable Syriac Lexicon (it might almost be called a Concordance) of the Peshito New Testament. Its worth, however, is considerably lessened by a fancy of Leusden for pointing the vowels according to the rules of Chaldee rather than of Syriac grammar: after his death, indeed, and from Luke xviii. 27 onwards, this grave mistake was corrected by Schaaf. Of modern editions the most convenient, or certainly the most accessible to English students, are the N. T. Professor Lee prepared in 1816 for the British and Foreign Bible Society with the Eastern Church-lessons noted in Syriac, and that of Greenfield, both in Bagster's Polyglott of 1828, and in a small form, which aims at representing Widmanstadt's text distinct from the subsequent additions derived from other sources. Lee's edition was grounded on a collation of three fresh manuscripts, besides the application of other matter previously available to the revision of the text; but the materials on which he founded his conclusions have never been printed, although their learned collector once intended to do so, and many years afterwards consented to lend them to Scrivener for that purpose; a promise which death ultimately hindered him from redeeming. An edition printed in 1829 by the British and Foreign Bible Society for the Nestorian Christians was based on a single manuscript brought from Mosul by Dr Wolff.

From the foregoing statement it will plainly appear that the Peshito Syriac has not yet received that critical care on the part of editors that its antiquity and importance so urgently demand; such a work in fact is one of the few great tasks yet open to the enterprise of scholars. Nor have we any cause to regret the scantiness of the means at our disposal for its accomplishment. In the Vatican, "ditissimo illo omnium disciplinarum promptuario," as Wiseman calls it in his honest pride (*Horae Syriacae*, p. 151), the master-hand of the Dane Adler [1755—1805] has been engaged on several codices of the Peshito[1], one dated as early as A.D. 548; many more must linger unexamined in the recesses of continental libraries, especially at Paris and Florence. Our own Museum, even before it was enriched from the monasteries of Egypt, possessed several copies of venerable age, one of which has been collated

[1] Novi Testamenti Versiones Syriacae, Simplex, Philoxeniana, et Hierosolymitana...a J. G. Ch. Adler. Hafniae, 1789, 4to.

by Tregelles and others (Rich. 7157[1]); and if "the general result is, that though some materials are certainly thus afforded for the critical revision of the text, by far the greater part of the changes relate to grammatical forms, and particulars of that kind" (Tregelles' *Horne*, p. 264), yet here we have access to the kind of text current among the Nestorians in the eighth century, long before their copies could have been corrupted by intercourse with the Latins. At Cambridge too are deposited two manuscripts, both used by Lee, one of them containing the Old Testament also (Univ. Libr. Ff. 2. 15), thought by some to be written about the seventh century, and brought from the Malabar coast in 1806 by Buchanan: in the Bodleian *at least* the two whose readings were published by Jones in 1805. With such full means of information within our reach it will not be to our credit if a good critical edition of the Peshito be much longer unattempted.

It is not easy to determine why the name of *Peshito* "the simple" should have been given to the oldest Syriac version of Scripture to distinguish it from others that were subsequently made. The term would seem to signify "faithful" rather than "literal;" for in comparison with the Philoxenian it is the very reverse of a close rendering of the original. We shall presently submit to the reader a few extracts from it, contrasted with the same passages in other Syriac versions (*below, pp.* 249—251); for the present we can but assent to the ripe judgment of Michaelis, who after thirty years' study of its contents, declared that he could consult no translation with so much confidence in cases of difficulty and doubt. In regard to the criticism of the text, its connexion with Cod. D and the Latin versions has been often dwelt upon. For its style, composed in the purest dialect of a perspicuous and elegant, if not a very copious language, no version can well be more exempt from the besetting faults of translators, constraint and stiffness of expression: yet while

[1] Of this copy the late Professor Rosen, in the Preface to the Catalogue of Syriac MSS. in the British Museum, 1838, thus writes: "Inter quos ante alios omnes memorabile est N. T. exemplar Nestorianum, liber et antiquitate suâ, quum saeculo octavo scriptus est, et summâ scripturae diligentiâ atque elegantiâ, inter omnia quotquot nobis innotuerunt Syriaca N. T. exemplaria, eximiâ laude dignus. Etenim remotioris etiam aetatis codices Syriacos extare comperimus quidem; sed de nullo nos vel audire vel legere meminimus, qui omnes quos Nestoriani agnoscunt N. T. libros amplecteretur."

remarkable for its ease and freedom, it very seldom becomes loose or paraphrastic. Though a word or two may occasionally be inserted to unravel some involved construction (Act. x. 38; Eph. iii. 1; Col. ii. 14; 1 John i. 1), or to elucidate what else might be obscure (Luke ix. 34; xvi. 8; Acts i. 19; ii. 14; 24; v. 4; xii. 15; Rom. xii. 16; xiv. 1, &c.); yet seldom would its liberty in this particular offend any but the most servile adherent to the letter of the Greek. The Peshito has well been called "the Queen of versions" of Holy Writ, for it is at once the oldest and one of the best of all those, whereby God's Providence has blessed and edified the Church.

(2). *The Curetonian Syriac.*

Dean Alford is bold enough to call this fragment "perhaps the earliest and most important of all the versions" (N. T. *Proleg.* p. 114); and though this estimate may be deemed a little unreasonable, we cannot doubt that its discovery is the most valuable of the many services rendered to sacred and profane literature by Canon Cureton, whose energy and practised sagacity, displayed in his researches among Syriac manuscripts, have been aided by that good fortune which does not always fail those who deserve her smile. The volume which contained these portions of the Gospels (and no other copy of the translation has yet been found) had been brought by Archdeacon Tattam in 1842 from the same monastery as the palimpsest Cod. R described in the last chapter (p. 115). The eighty-two leaves and a half on which what remains of the version is written (although two of them did not reach England till 1847) were picked out by Dr Cureton, then one of the officers in the Manuscript department of the British Museum, from a mass of other matter which had been bound up with them by unlearned possessors, and comprise the Additional MS. 14, 451* of the library they adorn. They are in quarto, with two columns on a page, in a bold hand and Estrangelo or old Syriac character, on vellum originally very white, the single points for stops, some titles, &c. being in red ink; and there are no marks of Church-lessons by the first hand, which Cureton (a most competent judge) assigns to the middle of the fifth century. The fragments contain Matth. i. 1—viii. 22; x. 32—

xxiii. 25; Mark xvi. 17—20; John i. 1—42; iii. 6—vii. 37; xiv. 10—12; 16—18; 19—23; 26—29; Luke ii. 48—iii. 16; vii. 33—xv. 21; xvii. 24—xxiv. 44, or 1786 verses, so arranged that St Mark's Gospel is immediately followed by St John's (*see* p. 62). The Syriac text was printed in fine Estrangelo type in 1848, and freely imparted to such scholars as might need its help; it was not till 1858 that the work was published[1], with a very literal translation into rather bald English (*see above*, p. 8), a beautiful and exact *fac-simile* by Mrs Cureton, and a Preface (pp. xcv), full of interesting or startling matter, which has been criticised in no friendly tone. Indeed, the difficult but unavoidable investigation into the relation his new version bears to the Peshito has been further complicated by Dr Cureton's persuasion that he had discovered in these Syriac fragments a text of St Matthew's Gospel that "to a great extent, has retained the identical terms and expressions which the Apostle himself employed; and that we have here, in our Lord's discourses, to a great extent the very same words as the Divine Author of our holy religion himself uttered in proclaiming the glad tidings of salvation in the Hebrew dialect..."(p. xciii): that here in fact we have to *a great extent* the original of that Hebrew Gospel of St Matthew of which the canonical Greek Gospel is but a translation. It is beside our present purpose to examine in detail the arguments of Dr Cureton on this head[2], and it would be the less necessary in any case, since they seem to have convinced no one save

[1] Remains of a very antient recension of the four Gospels in Syriac, hitherto unknown in Europe, discovered, edited, and translated by William Cureton, D.D. ...Canon of Westminster, 4to, London, 1858.

[2] Less able writers than Dr Cureton have made out a strong, though not I think a convincing case, for the Hebrew origin of St Matthew's Gospel, and thu far his argument is plausible enough. To demonstrate that the version he has discovered is based upon that Hebrew original, at least so far as to be a modification of it and not a translation from the Greek, he has but a single plea that will bear examination, viz. that out of the many readings of the Hebrew or Nazarene Gospel with which we are acquainted (the reader will see three, two of them previously unknown, above p. 125), his manuscript agrees with it in the one particular of inserting the *three kings*, ch. i. 8, though even here the number of *fourteen* generations retained in *v.* 17 shews them to be an interpolation. Such cases as *Juda*, ch. ii. 1; *Ramtha*, *v.* 18; ܕ for ὅτι or the relative, ch. xiii. 16, can prove nothing, as they are common to the Curetonian with the Peshito, from which version they may very well be derived.

himself: but the place his version occupies with reference to the Peshito is a question that cannot be quite passed over, even in an elementary treatise like the present.

Any one who shall compare the verses we have cited from them in parallel columns (pp. 249, 251) will readily admit that the two translations have a common origin, whatever that may be; many other passages, though not perhaps of equal length, might be named where the resemblance is closer still; where for twenty words together the Peshito and the Curetonian shall be positively identical, although the Syriac idiom would admit other words and another order just as naturally as that actually employed. Nor will this conclusion be shaken by the not less manifest fact that, throughout many passages the diversity is so great that no one, with those places alone before him, would be led to suspect any connection between the two versions; for resemblances in such a case furnish a positive proof, not to be weakened by the mere negative presumption supplied by divergencies. Add to this the consideration that the Greek manuscripts from which either version was made or corrected (as the case may prove) were materially different in their character; the Peshito for the most part favouring Cod. A, the Curetonian taking part with Cod. D, or the Old Latin, or often standing quite alone, unsupported by any critical authority whatever; and the reader is then in possession of the whole case, from whose perplexities we have to unravel the decision, which of these two recensions best exhibits the text of the Holy Gospels, as received from the second century downwards by the Syrian Church.

(1). Now it is obvious to remark, in the first place, that the Peshito has the advantage of *possession*, and that too of fourteen centuries standing. The mere fact that the Syriac manuscripts of the rival sects, whether modern or as old as the seventh century, agree with each other and with the citations from Ephraem in all important points, seems to bring the Peshito text, in the same state as we have it at present, up to the fourth century of our æra. Of this version, again, there are many codices, of different ages and widely diffused; of the Curetonian but one, of the fifth century, indeed, so far as the verdict of a most accomplished judge can determine so delicate a question; yet surely not to be much preferred, in respect to antiquity, to Adler's copy of the Peshito in the Vatican, *dated*

A.D. 548. From the Peshito, as the authorised version of the Oriental Church, there are many quotations in Syriac books from Ephraem downwards; can Dr Cureton, the profoundest Syriac scholar in England, allege any *second* citation from the Gospels by a native writer which corresponds with the newly discovered version better than with the old, and which may serve to keep in countenance the statement of Dionysius Barsalibi, late in the twelfth century, "there is found occasionally a Syriac copy made out of the Hebrew, which inserts the three kings in the genealogy" (Matth. i. 8)[1]? With every wish to give to this respectable old writer, and to others who bear testimony to the *same* reading, the consideration that is fairly their due, we can hardly fail to see that the weight of evidence enormously preponderates in the opposite scale.

(2). Dr Cureton will probably admit that in external proof his theory is not strong, but will deem the internal character of the version powerfully in favour of his view. And herein, perhaps, he has been a little helped (if he needed or cared for such aid) by those hostile critics who have thought to annihilate the critical influence of his version, when they had shewn it to be, as a translation, loose, careless, paraphrastic, full of interpolations, for which no authority, or only very bad authority, can be found elsewhere. Not that we quite assent to Tregelles' quaint remark, "unfortunately it has been criticised by those who do not understand the subject, and who have actually regarded its merits as defects" (*Introd. Notice to Part II. of N. T.* p. iii); negligent or licentious renderings (and the Curetonian Syriac is pretty full of them) cannot but lessen a version's usefulness as an instrument of criticism, by increasing our difficulty of reproducing the precise words of the original which the translator had before him; but in another point of view these very faults may still form the main strength of Dr Cureton's case. It is, no doubt, a grave suggestion, that the more polished, accurate, faithful and grammatical of the two versions—and the Peshito richly deserves all this praise—is more likely to have been produced by a careful and gradual revision of one much its inferior in these respects, than the worse to have originated in the mere corruption of the better

[1] Cureton, Preface, pp. xi. xciii.

(*Cureton, Pref.* p. lxxxi). *A priori*, we readily confess that probability inclines this way; but it is a probability which needs the confirmation of facts, and by adverse facts may be utterly set aside. If, for instance, he had demonstrated at length, instead of hinting incidentally and almost by chance, that "upon the comparison of several of the oldest copies now in the British Museum of that very text of the Gospels which has been generally received as the Peshito, the more antient the manuscripts be, the more nearly do they correspond with the text of these Syriac fragments" (Pref. lxxiii) in respect to dialectical peculiarity; more especially if he could have extended his statement to matters more important than bare language or grammar, as he very possibly might have done[1]; it could not be said of Dr Cureton, as now it must be said, that on the most serious plea in his whole argument, he has allowed judgment to pass against him by default.

Meanwhile we ought not to dissemble our conviction that many passages in which the Peshito differs from the Curetonian version bear strong traces of being corruptions on the part of the latter of readings already correctly given by the former; and thus form a class of facts very adverse to the higher authority claimed for the newly discovered translation. Such, for example, is Luke xxiv. 32, where all existing manuscripts (except Cod. D, which has a different reading altogether, *κεκαλυμμένη*) have *ἡ καρδία ἡμῶν καιομένη ἦν*, "our heart was burning within us," which the Peshito rightly translates by ܠܒܢ ܝܩܝܕ ܗܘܐ , while the Curetonian, by the slight change of the Estrangelo *dolath* ܕ into *rish* ܪ, for ܝܩܝܕ "burning," presents us with ܝܩܝܪ "heavy;" a variation supported only by those precarious allies the Thebaic and (apparently) the Armenian versions. Had the passage occurred in St Matthew's Gospel, Dr Cureton would of course have

[1] Dr P. N. Land, of the National Reformed Communion in Holland, who reviewed Cureton's work in the *Journal of Sacred Literature, October*, 1858, very pertinently states that in the Edessene codex of A. D. 548 in the Vatican, as collated by Adler in his *Versiones Syriacae*, "thirty-nine variations from Schaaf's Pĕshîttô occur within the first seven chapters; and among these thirty-nine, twenty-one are literally, and of some others traces are found in Dr C.'s text" (p. 153). This information is given *ex abundanti benevolentiâ*, for Land calls the way Cureton's book is got up "unprincipled" (p. 160), which I trust is Anglo-Dutch for nothing worse than *illogical.*

thrown the error upon the Greek translator, as having misread his Aramaic original; as the matter stands, it is difficult to avoid the conclusion that in this and not a few other passages the careless transcriber of the Curetonian mistook or corrupted the Peshito, rather than that the Peshito amended the defects, real or supposed, of the other. But on this head we can dwell no longer.

On the whole, then, fully admitting the critical value of this newly-discovered document, and feeling much perplexed when we try to account for its origin, we yet see no reason whatever to doubt its decided inferiority *in every respect* to the primitive version still read throughout the Churches of the East.

(3). *The Philoxenian Syriac.*

Of the history of the Philoxenian Syriac version, which embraces the whole New Testament except the Apocalypse, we possess rather exact information, though some points of difficulty may still remain unsolved. Moses of Aghel in Mesopotamia, who translated into Syriac certain works of the Alexandrian Cyril about A. D. 550, describes a version of the "New Testament and Psalter made in Syriac by Polycarp, Rural-Bishop[1] (rest his soul!) for Xenaias of Mabug," &c. This Xenaias or Philoxenus, from whom the translation takes its name, was Monophysite Bishop of Mabug (Hierapolis) in Eastern Syria (488—518), and doubtless wished to provide for his countrymen a more literal translation from the Greek than the Peshito aims at being. His scheme may perhaps have been injudicious, but it is a poor token of the presence of that quality which "thinketh no evil," to assert, without the slightest grounds for the suspicion, "More probable it is that his object was of a less commendable character; and that he meant the version in some way to subserve the advancement of his party[2]." Dr Davidson will have learnt by this time, that one may lie under the imputation of heresy, without being of necessity a bigot or a dunce.

[1] On the order, functions and decay of the Χωρεπίσκοποι, see Bingham's *Antiquities*, Book II., Chapter XIV.

[2] Davidson, *Bibl. Crit.* Vol. II. p. 186.

Our next account of the work is even more definite. At the end of the manuscripts of the Gospels from which the printed text is derived, we read a subscription by the first hand, importing that "this book of the four holy Gospels was translated out of the Greek into Syriac with great diligence and labour...first in the city of Mabug, in the year of Alexander of Macedon 819 (A. D. 508), in the days of the pious Mar Philoxenus, confessor, Bishop of that city. Afterwards it was collated with much diligence by me, the poor Thomas, by the help of two [*or* three] approved and accurate Greek Manuscripts in Antonia, of the great city of Alexandria, in the holy monastery of the Antonians. It was again written out and collated in the aforesaid place in the year of the same Alexander 927 (A. D. 616), Indiction IV. How much toil I spent upon it and its companions, the Lord alone knows"...&c. It is plain that by "its companions" the other parts of the N. T. are meant, for though but one manuscript of the Acts and Epistles in this version survive, a similar subscription (specifying but one manuscript) is annexed to the Catholic Epistles; those of St Paul are defective from Hebr. xi. 27, but two manuscripts are cited in the margin.

That the labour of Thomas (surnamed from Harkel, his native place, and like Philoxenus, subsequently Monophysite bishop of Mabug) was confined to the collation of the manuscripts he names, and whose various readings, usually in Greek characters, with occasional exegetical notes, stand in the margin of all copies but one at Florence, is not a probable opinion. It is likely that he added the asterisks and obeli which abound in the version, and G. H. Bernstein (*De Charklensi N. T. transl. Syriac. Commentatio*, Breslau, 1837) believes that he so modified the text itself, that it only remains in the state in which Polycarp left it in one codex now at Rome, which he collated for a few chapters of St John. From this and other copies yet uncollated, as well as from quotations met with in Syriac writers, it may possibly appear that the difference between the state of the version before and after the recension of Thomas of Harkel is more considerable than from his own expressions we might have anticipated.

We are reminded by Tregelles, who is always ready to give every one his due, that our own Pococke in 1630, in the

Preface to his edition of the Catholic Epistles wanting in the Peshito (*see p.* 233), both quotes an extract from Dionysius Barsalibi, Bishop of Amida (Diarbekr), in the twelfth century (*see p.* 239), which mentions this version, and even shews some acquaintance with its peculiar character. Although again brought to notice in the comprehensive Bibliotheca Orientalis (1719—28), of the elder J. S. Assemani [1687—1768], the Philoxenian attracted no attention until 1730, in which year Samuel Palmer sent from Diarbekr to Dr Gloucester Ridley four Syriac manuscripts, two of which proved to belong to this translation, both containing the Gospels, one of them being the only extant copy of the Acts and all the Epistles. Fortunately Ridley [1702—1774] was a man of some learning and acuteness, or these precious codices might have lain disregarded as other copies of the same version had long done in Italy; so that though he did not choose, in spite of his fair preferment in the Church, to incur the risk of publishing them in full, he communicated his discovery to Wetstein, who came to England once more, in 1746, for the purpose of collating them for his edition of the N. T., then soon to appear: he could spare, however, but fourteen days for the task, which was far too short a time, and the more so as the Estrangelo character was new to him. In 1761 Ridley produced his tract, *De Syriacarum N. F. Versionum Indole atque Usu Dissertatio*, and on his death his manuscripts went to New College, of which society he had been a Fellow. The care of publishing them was then undertaken by the Delegates of the Oxford Press, who selected for their editor Joseph White [1746—1814], then Fellow of Wadham College, and Professor of Arabic, afterwards Canon of Christ Church, who, though now, I fear, chiefly remembered for the most foolish action of his life, was an industrious, able and genuine scholar. Under his care the Gospels appeared in 2 vol. 4°, 1788[1], with a Latin version and satisfactory Prolegomena; the Acts and Catholic Epp. in 1799, the Pauline in 1803. Meanwhile Storr

[1] Sacrorum Evangeliorum Versio Syriaca Philoxeniana, ex Codd. MSS. Ridleianis in Bibliotheca Novi Collegii Oxon. repositis; nunc primum edita, cum Interpretatione Latinâ et Annotationibus Josephi White. Oxonii e Typographeo Clarendoniano, 1778. 2 tom. 4°. And so for the two later volumes. Ridley named that one of his manuscripts which contains only the Gospels Codex Barsalibaei, as notes of revision by that writer are found in it (e. g. John vii. 53—viii. 11).

(*Observat. super N. T. vers. Syr.* 1772) and Adler (*N. T. Version. Syr.* 1789) had examined and described seven or eight continental codices of the Gospels in this version, some of which are thought superior to White's.

The characteristic feature of the Philoxenian is its excessive closeness to the original: it is probably the most servile version of Scripture ever made. Specimens of it will appear on pp. 249—251, by the side of those from other translations, which will abundantly justify this statement. The Peshito is beyond doubt taken as its basis, and is violently changed in order to force it into rigorous conformity with the very letter of the Greek. In the twenty verses of Matth. xxviii we note 76 such alterations: three of them seem to concern various readings (*vv.* 2; 18; and 5 *marg.*); six are inversions in the order; about five are substitutions of words for others that may have grown obsolete: the rest are of the most frivolous description, the definite state of nouns being placed for the absolute, or *vice versâ;* the Greek article represented by the Syriac pronoun; the inseparable pronominal affixes (that delicate peculiarity of the Aramæan dialects) retrenched or discarded; the most unmeaning changes made in the tenses of verbs, and the lesser particles. Its very defects, however, as a version give it weight as a textual authority: there can be no hesitation about the readings of the copies from which such a book was made. While those employed for the version itself in the sixth century resembled more nearly our modern printed editions, the three or more codices used by Thomas at Alexandria must have been nearly akin to Cod. D (especially in the Acts), and next to D, support B L 1. 33. 69.

The asterisks (⁜) and obeli (ܢ ÷) of this version will be observed in our specimens (pp. 250—1), and seem to be due to Thomas of Harkel. Like the similar marks in Origen's *Hexapla* (from which they were doubtless borrowed), they have been miserably displaced by copyists; so that their real purpose is a little uncertain. Wetstein, and after him even Storr and Adler, refer them to changes made in the Philoxenian from the Peshito: White more plausibly considers the asterisk to intimate an addition to the text, the obelus to recommend a removal from it.

(4). *The Jerusalem Syriac.*

Of this version but one manuscript has been discovered, and that virtually by Adler, who collated, described and copied a portion of it (Matth. xxvii. 3—32) for that great work in a small compass, his *N. T. Versiones Syriacae:* S. E. Assemani the nephew had merely inserted it in his Vatican Catalogue (1756). It is a partial Lectionary of the Gospels in the Vatican (MS. Syr. 19), on 196 quarto thick vellum leaves, written in two columns in a rude hand (F being expressed by ܦ, P by Ƥ), with rubric notes of Church-lessons in the *Carshunic*, i. e. bad Arabic in Syriac letters. From a subscription we learn that the scribe was Elias, a presbyter of Abydos, who wrote it in the Monastery of the Abbot Moses at Antioch, in the year of Alexander 1341, or A. D. 1030. Adler gives a poor *facsimile* (Matth. xxvii. 12—22): the character is peculiar, and all diacritic points (even that distinguishing *dolath* from *rish*), as as well as many other changes, are thought to be by a later hand. Tregelles confirms Assemani's statement, which Adler had disputed, that the first six leaves, shewing traces of Greek writings buried beneath the Syriac, proceeded from another scribe. The remarkable point, however, about this version (which seems to be made from the Greek, and is quite independent of the Peshito) is the peculiar dialect it exhibits, and which has suggested its name. Its grammatical forms are far less Syriac than Chaldee, which latter it resembles even in that characteristic particular, the prefixing of *yud*, not *nun*, to the third person masculine of the future of verbs[1]; the most ordinary words it employs can be illustrated only from the Chaldee portions of the Old Testament, from the Jerusalem Targum, or the Talmud[2]. Adler's account of the translation

[1] Thus also the termination of the definite state plural of nouns is made in ܝܐ for ܐ: the third person affix to plural nouns in ܘܝ for ܘܗ̱ܝ.

[2] Thus in the compass of the six verses we have cited from Adler (*below, p.* 250) occur not only the Greek words ܩܝܪܘܣܐ (καιρὸς) *v.* 3, and ܢܘܣܐ (ναὸς) *v.* 5, which are common enough in all Syriac books, but such Chaldaisms as ܕܝ for ܕܝܢ, δὲ (*vv.* 4, 6, 7); ܟܡܝܢ, *v.* 3, "when;" ܬܗܐ, *v.* 3, "repented;" ܐܕܡܐ for ܕܡܐ, *vv.* 4, 6, 8, "blood;" ܠܢܢܗ, *v.* 4, "to us;" ܓܪܡܐ, *v.* 5, "himself;"

and its copyist is not very flattering "satis constat dialectum esse incultam et inconcinnam......orthographiam autem vagam, inconstantem, arbitrariam, et ab imperito librario rescribendo et corrigendo denuo impeditam" (*Vers. Syr.* p. 149). As it is mentioned by no Syriac writer, it was probably used but in a few remote churches of Lebanon or Galilee: but though (to employ the words of Porter) "in elegance far surpassed by the Peshito; in closeness of adherence to the original by the Philoxenian" (*Principles of Textual Criticism*, Belfast, 1848, p. 356); it has its value, and that not inconsiderable, as a witness to the state of the text at the time it was turned into Syriac; whether, with Adler, we regard it as derived from a complete version of the Gospels made not later than the sixth century, or with Tischendorf refer it to the fifth, or with Tregelles (who examined the codex at Rome) it be thought a mere translation of some Greek Evangelistarium of a more recent date. Of all the Syriac books, this copy and Barsalibi's recension of the Philoxenian (*see* p. 243 note) alone contain John vii. 53—viii. 11; the Lectionary giving it as the Proper Lesson for Oct. 8, St Pelagia's day (*see above*, p. 74). In general its readings much resemble those of Codd. BD, siding with B 85 times, with D 79; but with D *alone* 11 times, with B alone but 3.

(5). Akin to this Jerusalem version, as Tischendorf suspects, and certainly resembling it in the shape of its letters, is a palimpsest fragment brought by him "from the East" (*see p.* 121), and now at St Petersburg, briefly described in his *Anecdota sacra et profana*, p. 13, and there illustrated by a *facsimile*. He assigns its date to the fifth century, but it yet remains to be collated.

(6). *The Karkaphensian Syriac.*

Assemani (*Biblioth. Orient.* Tom. II. p. 283), on the authority of Gregory Barhebraeus (*above* p. 231), mentions a Syriac version of the N. T., other than the Peshito and Philoxenian,

ܕܡܝܢ, *v.* 6, "price" (Pesh. has ܛܝܡܝܗܘܢ, Philox. ܛܝ̈ܡܬܐ, τιμή); ܠܟܢ, *v.* 8, "therefore;" ܗܐܘ̇, *v.* 8, "this," made up of Syr. ܗܘ̇ and Chald. ܗܐ.

which was named "Karkaphensian" (ܟܪܟܦܝܐ), whether because it was used by Syrians of the *mountains*, or from *Carcuf*, a city of Mesopotamia. Adler (*Vers. Syr.* p. 33) was inclined to believe that Barhebraeus meant rather a revised manuscript than a separate translation, but Cardinal Wiseman, in the course of those youthful studies which gave such seemly, precocious, deceitful promise (*Horae Syriacae*, Rom. 1828), discovered in the Vatican (MS. Syr. 153) a Syriac translation of both Testaments, with the several portions of the New standing in the following order; Acts, James, 1 Peter, 1 John, the fourteen Epistles of St Paul, and then the Gospels (*see p.* 62), these being the only books contained in the Peshito (*see p.* 231). On being compared with that venerable translation, the Vat. 153 was found to resemble it much, (though the Peshito is somewhat less literal), only that in Proper Names and Greek words it follows the more exact Philoxenian. In the margin also are placed by the first hand many readings indicated by the notation ܦܫ, which turns out to mean the Peshito. The codex is on thick yellow vellum, in large folio, with the two columns so usual in Syriac writing; the ink, especially the points in vermilion, has often grown pale, and it has been carefully retouched by a later hand; the original document being all the work of one scribe: some of the marginal notes refer to various readings. There are several long and tedious subscriptions in the volume, whereof one states that the copy was written "in the year of the Greeks 1291 (A. D. 980) in the [Monophysite] monastery of Aaron on [mount] Sigara, in the jurisdiction of Calisura, in the days of the Patriarchs John and Menna, by David a deacon of Urin in the jurisdiction of Gera" [Γέρρα, near Beroea or Aleppo]. It may be remarked that Assemani has inserted a letter in the Bibliotheca Orientalis from John the Monophysite Patriarch [of Antioch] to his brother Patriarch, Menna of Alexandria. This manuscript, of which Wiseman gives a rather rude *facsimile*, is deemed by him of great importance in tracing the history of the Syriac vowel-points. He names other manuscripts (e.g. Barberini 101) which seem to belong to this version, and reserves a full collation for that more convenient season which in his tumultuous life is yet to come. We subjoin Matth. i. 19 in four versions, wherein the close connexion of the Karkaphensian with the Peshito is very manifest. The vowel points of the Karkaphensian are irregularly put, and deserve notice.

PESHITO.	KARKAPHENSIAN.
ܝܘܣܦ ܕܝܢ ܒܥܠܗ ܟܐܢܐ ܗܘܐ. ܘܠܐ ܨܒܐ ܗܘܐ ܕܢܦܪܣܝܗ. ܘܐܬܪܥܝ ܕܒܛܘܫܝܐ ܢܫܪܝܗ.	ܝܘܣܦ ܕܝܢ ܒܥܠܗ ܟܐܢܐ ܗܘܐ. ܘܠܐ ܨܒܐ ܗܘܐ ܕܢܦܪܣܝܗ. ܘܐܬܪܥܝ ܗܘܐ ܕܒܛܘܫܝܐ ܢܫܪܝܗ.

CURETONIAN.	PHILOXENIAN.
ܝܘܣܦ ܕܝܢ ܡܛܠ ܕܓܒܪܐ ܗܘܐ ܟܐܢܐ ܠܐ ܨܒܐ ܗܘܐ ܕܢܦܪܣܝܗ ܠܡܪܝܡ ܘܐܬܪܥܝ ܗܘܐ ܕܒܛܘܫܝܐ ܢܫܒܩܝܗ.	ܝܘܣܦ ܕܝܢ ܗܘ ܓܒܪܐ ܕܝܠܗ ܕܟܐܢܐ ܐܝܬܘܗܝ ܗܘܐ : ܘܠܐ ܨܒܐ ܗܘܐ ܕܢܦܪܣܝܗ : ܐܬܪܥܝ ܕܒܛܘܫܝܐ ܢܫܪܝܗ. *Marg.* παραδειγματίσαι.

We have now traced the history of the several Syriac versions, so far at least as to afford the reader some general idea of their relative importance as materials for the correction of the sacred text. On pp. 249—251 are given parallel versions of Matth. xii. 1—4; Mark xvi. 17—20 from the Peshito, the Curetonian, and the Philoxenian, the only versions yet published in full; for Matth. xxvii. 3—8, in the room of the Curetonian, which is here lost, we have substituted the Jerusalem Syriac; and have retained throughout Thomas' marginal notes to the Philoxenian, its asterisks and obeli. We have been compelled to employ the common Syriac type, though every manuscript of respectable antiquity is written in the Estrangelo character. Even from these slight specimens the servile strictness of the Philoxenian, and some leading characteristics of the other versions, will readily be apprehended by an attentive student (e. g. Cureton. Matth. xii. 1; 4; Mark xvi. 18; 20).

PESHITO.

(1) ܒܗܘ ܙܒܢܐ: ܡܗܠܟ ܗܘܐ
ܝܫܘܥ ܒܫܒܬܐ ܒܝܬ ܙܪ̈ܥܐ.
ܘܬܠܡܝܕܘܗܝ ܟܦܢܘ : ܘܫܪܝܘ
ܡܠܓܝܢ ܫܒܠ̈ܐ ܘܐܟܠܝܢ. (2) ܦܪ̈ܝܫܐ
ܕܝܢ ܟܕ ܚܙܘ ܐܢܘܢ ܐܡܪܝܢ ܠܗ. ܗܐ
ܬܠܡܝ̈ܕܝܟ ܥܒܕܝܢ ܡܕܡ ܕܠܐ ܫܠܝܛ
ܠܡܥܒܕ ܒܫܒܬܐ. (3) ܗܘ ܕܝܢ ܐܡܪ
ܠܗܘܢ. ܠܐ ܩܪܝܬܘܢ ܡܢܐ ܥܒܕ ܕܘܝܕ
ܟܕ ܟܦܢ ܘܐܠܝܢ ܕܥܡܗ: (4) ܐܝܟܢܐ
ܥܠ ܠܒܝܬܐ ܕܐܠܗܐ : ܘܠܚܡܐ
ܕܦܬܘܪܗ ܕܡܪܝܐ ܐܟܠ : ܗܘ ܕܠܐ ܫܠܝܛ
ܗܘܐ ܠܗ ܠܡܐܟܠܗ. ܘܠܐ ܠܐܝܠܝܢ
ܕܥܡܗ. ܐܠܐ ܐܢ ܠܟܗܢ̈ܐ ܒܠܚܘܕܝܗܘܢ.

CURETONIAN.

(1) ܒܗܘ ܙܒܢܐ ܡܗܠܟ ܗܘܐ
ܝܫܘܥ ܒܫܒܬܐ ܒܝܬ ܙܪܥܐ.
ܘܬܠܡܝܕܘܗܝ ܟܦܢܘ. ܘܫܪܝܘ ܡܠܓܝܢ
ܫܒܠܐ ܘܡܦܪܟܝܢ ܒܐܝܕܝܗܘܢ ܘܐܟܠܝܢ.
(2) ܟܕ ܚܙܘ ܐܢܘܢ ܦܪܝܫܐ ܐܡܪܝܢ ܠܗ.
ܗܐ ܬܠܡܝܕܝܟ ܥܒܕܝܢ ܡܕܡ ܕܠܐ
ܫܠܝܛ ܠܡܥܒܕ. (3) ܐܡܪ ܠܗܘܢ ܠܐ
ܩܪܝܬܘܢ ܡܢܐ ܥܒܕ ܕܘܝܕ ܟܕ ܟܦܢ
ܘܐܠܝܢ ܕܥܡܗ. (4) ܐܝܟܢܐ ܥܠ
ܠܒܝܬܗ ܕܐܠܗܐ. ܘܐܟܠ ܡܢ ܠܚܡ
ܐܦܐ. ܕܠܐ ܠܗ ܫܠܝܛ ܗܘܐ ܠܡܐܟܠܘ
ܐܦܠܐ ܠܐܝܠܝܢ ܕܥܡܗ. ܐܠܐ ܐܢ ܠܟܗܢܐ
ܒܠܚܘܕ.

PHILOXENIAN.

(1) ܒܗܘ ܙܒܢܐ : ܡܗܠܟ ܗܘܐ
ܝܫܘܥ ܒܫܒܬܐ ܒܝܬ ܙܪܥܐ.
ܘܬܠܡܝܕܘܗܝ ܕܝܢ ܟܦܢܘ : ܘܫܪܝܘ
ܡܠܓܝܢ ܫܒܠܐ ܘܐܟܠܝܢ. (2) ܦܪܝܫܐ
ܕܝܢ ܟܕ ܚܙܘ ܐܡܪܘ ܠܗ . ܗܐ
ܬܠܡܝܕܝܟ ܥܒܕܝܢ ܗܘ ܡܕܡ ܕܠܐ ܫܠܝܛ
ܠܡܥܒܕ ܒܫܒܬܐ. (3) ܗܘ ܕܝܢ ܐܡܪ
ܠܗܘܢ. ܠܐ ܩܪܝܬܘܢ ܡܢܐ ܥܒܕ ܕܘܝܕ.
ܟܕ ܟܦܢ[1] ܘܐܠܝܢ ܕܥܡܗ : (4) ܐܝܟܢܐ
ܥܠ ܠܒܝܬܗ ܕܐܠܗܐ : ܘܠܚܡܐ
ܕܣܝܡܘܬܐ[2] ܩܕܡ ܐܟܠ : ܗܘ ܕܠܐ
ܫܠܝܛ ܗܘܐ ܠܗ ܠܡܐܟܠܗ ܘܠܐ
ܠܗܢܘܢ ܕܥܡܗ : ܐܠܐ ܐܢ ܠܟܗܢܐ
ܒܠܚܘܕܝܗܘܢ.

[1] Margo, ܗܘ

[2] Marg. προθησεως ܐܘ ܕܝܢ ܕܣܝܡܘܬܐ ܗܘܘ ܩܕܡ ܐܠܗܐ.

PESHITO.

(3) ܗܝܕܝܢ ܝܗܘܕܐ ܡܫܠܡܢܐ. ܟܕ
ܚܙܐ ܕܐܬܚܝܒ ܝܫܘܥ ܐܬܬܘܝ. ܘܐܙܠ
ܐܗܦܟ ܗܠܝܢ ܬܠܬܝܢ ܕܟܣܦܐ ܠܪ̈ܒܝ
ܟܗܢܐ ܘܠܩܫܝܫܐ. (4) ܘܐܡܪ. ܚܛܝܬ
ܕܐܫܠܡܬ ܕܡܐ ܙܟܝܐ. ܗܢܘܢ ܕܝܢ ܐܡܪܘ
ܠܗ. ܠܢ ܡܐ ܠܢ. ܐܢܬ ܝܕܥ ܐܢܬ.
(5) ܘܫܕܐ ܟܣܦܐ ܒܗܝܟܠܐ ܘܫܢܝ.
ܘܐܙܠ ܚܢܩ ܢܦܫܗ. (6) ܪ̈ܒܝ ܟܗܢܐ
ܕܝܢ ܢܣܒܘܗܝ ܠܟܣܦܐ ܘܐܡܪܘ. ܠܐ
ܫܠܝܛ ܠܡܪܡܝܘܗܝ ܒܝܬ ܩܘܪܒܢܐ.
ܡܛܠ ܕܛܝܡܐ ܕܕܡܐ ܗܘ. (7) ܘܡܠܟܐ
ܢܣܒܘ: ܘܙܒܢܘ ܒܗ ܐܓܘܪܣܐ ܕܦܚܪܐ
ܠܒܝܬ ܩܒܘܪܐ ܕܐܟܣܢܝܐ. (8) ܡܛܠ
ܗܢܐ ܐܬܩܪܝ ܐܓܘܪܣܐ ܗܘ: ܩܪܝܬܐ
ܕܕܡܐ ܥܕܡܐ ܠܝܘܡܢܐ.

JERUSALEM SYRIAC.

(3) ܒܢܬܗ ܚܙܘܬܐ ܒܒܝܢ ܡܢ ܣܦܪܐ
ܝܗܘܕܗ ܕܡܫܠܡ ܢܬܗ ܕܐܬܚܝܒ ܠܗܘܐ
ܘܐܬܒ ܬܠܬܝܢ ܕܟܣܦܐ ܠܪܒܢܐ ܕܟܗܢܐ
ܘܩܫܝܫܐ. (4) ܘܐܡܪ ܐܣܬܟܠܬ ܕܡܣܪܬ
ܐܕܡܐ ܙܟܝܐ ✤ ܗܢܘܢ ܕܝܢ ܐܡܪܘ ܡܐ
ܠܟܠܝܬܗ ܐܬ ܬܚܡܐ ✤ (5) ܘܪܡܐ ܟܣܦܐ
ܒܗܝܟܠܐ ܘܐܙܠ ܚܢܩ ܢܦܫܗ ✤ (6) ܪܒܢܐ
ܕܟܗܢܐ ܕܝܢ ܢܣܒܘ ܟܣܦܐ ܘܐܡܪܘ ܠܐ
ܫܠܝܛ ܕܢܪܡܐ ܢܬܗ ܒܩܘܪܒܢܐ ✤
ܡܛܠ ܕܗܘ ܕܡܝ ܕܐܕܡܐ (7) ܢܣܒܘ
ܕܝܢ ܡܠܟܐ (ܡܠܟܘ *s. m.*) ܘܙܒܢܘ
ܒܗܘܢ ܚܩܠܗ ܕܦܚܪܐ ܠܡܩܒܪܐ
ܠܐܟܣܢܝܐ (8) ܡܛܠ ܗܕܐ ܐܬܩܪܝ ܚܩܠܐ
ܗܘܐ ܚܩܠ ܐܕܡܐ ܥܕ ܝܘܡܐ.

[See p. 245, notes 1, 2.]

PHILOXENIAN.

(3) ܗܝܕܝܢ ܟܕ ܚܙܐ ܝܗܘܕܐ ܗܘ
ܕܐܫܠܡܗ ܕܐܬܚܝܒ: ܟܕ ܐܬܬܘܝ:
ܐܗܦܟ ܗܠܝܢ ܬܠܬܝܢ ܟܣܦܐ ܠܪ̈ܒܝ
ܟܗܢܐ ܘܠܩܫܝܫܐ (4) ܟܕ ܐܡܪ:
ܚܛܝܬ ܕܐܫܠܡܬ ܕܡܐ [1]ܙܟܝܐ. ܗܢܘܢ
ܕܝܢ ܐܡܪܘ. ܡܢܐ ܠܘܬܢ. ܐܢܬ [2]ܬܚܙܐ.
(5) ܘܟܕ ܫܕܐ ܐܢܘܢ ܠܟܣܦܐ ܒܗܝܟܠܐ:
ܫܢܐ ܘܐܙܠ [3]ܚܢܩ ܗܘ ܠܗ.
(6) ܪ̈ܒܝ ܟܗܢܐ ܕܝܢ ܟܕ ܢܣܒܘ ܐܢܘܢ
ܠܟܣܦܐ ܐܡܪܘ: ܠܐ ܫܠܝܛ ܠܡܪܡܝܘ
[4]ܠܩܘܪܒܢ: ܡܛܠ ܕܛܝܡܐ ܕܕܡܐ
ܐܝܬܝܗܘܢ. (7) ܟܕ ܕܝܢ ܡܠܟܐ ܢܣܒܘ:
ܙܒܢܘ ܡܢܗܘܢ ܐܓܘܪܣܐ [5]ܕܦܚܪܐ
ܠܩܒܪܐ ܕܐܟܣܢܝܐ. (8) ܡܛܠ
ܗܕܐ ܐܬܩܪܝ ܗܘ ܐܓܘܪܣܐ ܗܘ:
ܐܓܘܪܣܐ ܕܕܡܐ ܥܕܡܐ ܠܝܘܡܢܐ.

Marg. [1] αθωον. [2] οψη. [3] απηγξατο. [4] κορβαναν. [5] κεραμεως.

PESHITO.

(17) ܐܬܘܬܐ ܕܝܢ ܠܐܝܠܝܢ
ܕܡܗܝܡܢܝܢ ܗܠܝܢ ܢܩܦܢ. ܒܫܡܝ
ܫܐܕܐ ܢܦܩܘܢ ܘܒܠܫܢܐ ܚܕܬܬܐ ܢܡܠܠܘܢ.
(18) ܘܚܘܘܬܐ ܢܫܩܠܘܢ. ܘܐܢ ܣܡܐ
ܕܡܘܬܐ ܢܫܬܘܢ ܠܐ ܢܗܪܐ ܐܢܘܢ.
ܘܐܝܕܝܗܘܢ ܢܣܝܡܘܢ ܥܠ ܟܪܝܗܐ
ܘܢܬܚܠܡܘܢ. (19) ܝܫܘܥ ܕܝܢ ܡܪܢ:
ܡܢ ܒܬܪ ܕܡܠܠ ܥܡܗܘܢ ܠܫܡܝܐ
ܣܠܩ. ܘܝܬܒ ܡܢ ܝܡܝܢܐ ܕܐܠܗܐ.
(20) ܗܢܘܢ ܕܝܢ ܢܦܩܘ ܘܐܟܪܙܘ ܒܟܠ
ܕܘܟ. ܘܡܪܢ ܡܥܕܪ ܗܘܐ ܠܗܘܢ:
ܘܡܫܪܪ ܡܠܝܗܘܢ ܒܐܬܘܬܐ ܕܥܒܕܝܢ
ܗܘܘ.

CURETONIAN.

(17) ܕܡܗܝܡܢܝܢ ܒܝ. ܗܠܝܢ
ܒܫܡܝ ܕܝܘܐ ܢܦܩܘܢ. ܒܠܫܢܐ
ܚܕܬܐ ܢܡܠܠܘܢ. (18) ܚܘܘܬܐ ܢܫܩܠܘܢ
ܒܐܝܕܝܗܘܢ ܘܐܢ ܡܕܡ ܣܡܐ ܕܡܘܬܐ
ܢܫܬܘܢ ܠܐ ܢܚܒܠ ܐܢܘܢ . ܥܠ ܟܪܝܗܐ
ܢܣܝܡܘܢ ܐܝܕܝܗܘܢ ܘܢܬܚܠܡܘܢ. (19) ܡܪܢ
ܕܝܢ ܝܫܘܥ ܡܢ ܒܬܪ ܕܦܩܕ
ܠܬܠܡܝܕܘܗܝ ܐܣܬܠܩ ܠܫܡܝܐ.
ܘܝܬܒ ܡܢ ܝܡܝܢܐ ܕܐܠܗܐ. (20) ܗܢܘܢ
ܕܝܢ ܢܦܩܘ ܘܐܟܪܙܘ ܒܟܠܗ ܕܘܟܐ. ܟܕ
ܡܪܢ ܡܥܕܪ ܠܗܘܢ ܒܟܠ. ܘܡܫܪܪܗܘܢ
ܡܠܬܗ ܗܘܐ ܒܐܬܘܬܐ ܕܥܒܕܝܢ ܗܘܘ. . .

PHILOXENIAN.

(17) ܐܬܘܬܐ ܕܝܢ ܠܗܢܘܢ ܕܡܗܝܡܢܝܢ
ܗܠܝܢ ܢܩܦܢ. ܒܫܡܝ ܕܝܠܝ ܕܝܘܐ
ܢܦܩܘܢ. ܒܠܫܢܐ ܚܕܬܐ ܢܡܠܠܘܢ.
(18) ⁜ ܘܒܐܝܕܝܐ ܠܐ ܚܘܘܬܐ ܢܫܩܠܘܢ.
ܘܐܢ ÷ ܣܡܐ ܠܐ ܡܡܝܬܢܐ ܡܕܡ ܢܫܬܘܢ
ܠܐ ܢܚܒܠ ܐܢܘܢ. ܥܠ ܟܪܝܗܐ ܐܝܕܝܐ
ܢܣܝܡܘܢ : ܘܬܗܘܐ ܠܗܘܢ ⁜ (19) ܗܘ
ܡܢ ܗܟܝܠ ܡܪܝܐ ܝܫܘܥ : ܒܬܪ
ܕܡܠܠ ܥܡܗܘܢ ܐܣܬܠܩ ܠܫܡܝܐ ܘܝܬܒ
ܡܢ ܝܡܝܢܐ ܕܐܠܗܐ ⁜ (20) ܗܢܘܢ
ܕܝܢ ܟܕ ܢܦܩܘ ܐܟܪܙܘ ܒܟܠ ܕܘܟܐ :
ܟܕ ܡܪܝܐ ܡܥܕܪ ܗܘܐ ܘܡܠܬܐ ܡܫܪܪ
ܗܘܐ : ܒܝܕ ܐܬܘܬܐ ܕܢܩܦܢ
ܗܘܝ.

4. The Latin Versions. (1). *The Old Latin, previous to Jerome's revision.*

Since we know that a branch of the Christian Church existed at Rome "many years" before St Paul's first visit to that city (Rom. xv. 23), and already flourished there towards the end of the first century, it seems reasonable to conjecture that the earliest Latin version of Holy Scripture was made for the use of believers in the capital, or at all events in other parts of Italy (Heb. xiii. 24). There are, moreover, passages in the works of the two great Western Fathers of the fourth century, Jerome [345?—420] and Augustine [354—430], whose obvious and literal meaning might lead us to conclude that there existed in their time *many* Latin translations, quite independent in their origin, and used almost indifferently by the faithful. Their statements are very well known, but must needs be cited anew, as bearing directly on the point now at issue. When Jerome, in that Preface to the Gospels which he addressed to Pope Damasus (366—84), anticipates but too surely the unpopularity of his revision of them among the people of his own generation, he consoles himself by the reflection that the variations of previous versions prove the unfaithfulness of them all: "verum non esse quod variat, etiam maledicorum testimonio comprobatur." Then follows his celebrated assertion: "Si enim Latinis exemplaribus fides est adhibenda, respondeant quibus: tot enim sunt exemplaria penè quot codices." The testimony of Augustine seems even more explicit, and at first sight conclusive. In his treatise *De Doctrinâ Christianâ* (Lib. II. capp. 11—15), when speaking of "Latinorum interpretum infinita varietas," and "interpretum numerositas," as not without their benefit to an attentive reader, he uses these strong expressions: "Qui enim Scripturas ex Hebraeâ linguâ in Graecam verterunt, numerari possunt, Latini autem interpretes nullo modo. Ut enim cuique primis fidei temporibus in manus venit codex Graecus, et aliquantulum facultatis sibi utriusque linguae habere videbatur, ausus est interpretari" (c. 11); and he soon after specifies a particular version as preferable to the rest: "In ipsis autem interpretationibus Itala[1] caeteris praeferatur. Nam est verborum tenacior cum perspicuitate sententiae" (c. 14—5). And, indeed, the variations subsisting between the several extant manuscripts of the Old Latin are so wide and so perpetual, as in the judgment of no less eminent a critic than Ernesti (*Instit. Interpretis*, Pt. III. Chap. IV. § 11, *Terrot's translation*) "to prove an original diversity of versions." Such is, no doubt, the *primâ facie* view of the whole case.

When, however, the several codices of the version or versions antecedent to Jerome's revision came to be studied by Sabatier and Blanchini, and through their labours to be placed within the reach of all scholars[2], it was soon perceived, that with many points of difference between them, there were evident traces of a common source from which all originally sprung: and on a question of this kind occasional divergency, however extensive, cannot weaken the impression produced by resemblance, if it be too close or too constant to be attributed to chance (*see above, p.* 238). A single example out of thousands, taken almost at random, will best illustrate our meaning (Matth. xx. 1, 2). "Simile est enim...[regn]um caelorum homini patri familias, qui exiit primo mane conducere operarios in vineam suam. Conventione autem facta cum operariis ex denario diurno, misit eos in vineam suam." Thus stand the verses in the Vercelli manuscript, the oldest and probably the best monument of the Latin before Jerome. In the other copies there is pretty much variation; five or six omit *enim*, one reads *autem* in its room: one spells *coelorum*; in one *pater* is inserted before *exiit*; two have *exivit*; one reads *primâ mane*; one (Tischendorf's Codex Palatinus) begins v. 2 more idiomatically, "et convenit illi cum operariis denario diurno et misit..."; one adds *operari* after *misit eos*. The general form of the construc-

[1] For *Itala* Bentley boldly conjectured *et illa*, changing the following *nam* into *quae*; Potter more plausibly suggests *usitata* for *Itala*: but alteration is quite needless.

[2] "Bibliorum Sacrorum Latinae Versiones Antiquae, seu Vetus Italica, et ceterae quaecunque in Codicibus MSS. et Antiquorum Libris reperiri potuerunt... Operâ et studio D. Petri Sabatier. Romae 1743—9, fol. 3 tom.," and the far superior work, "Evangeliarium Quadruplex Latinae Versionis Antiquae, seu Veteris Italicae, editum ex Codicibus Manuscriptis...a Josepho Blanchino. Romae 1749. fol., 2 tom."

tion, however, is the same in all; all (except the Latin of Cod. D, which hardly belongs to this class of documents: *see p.* 103) retain the characteristic "*denario diurno*": so that the result of the whole, and of innumerable like instances, is a conviction that they are all but offshoots from one parent stock, modifications more or less accidental of one single primitive version. Now when, this fact fairly established, we look back again to the language employed by Jerome and Augustine, we can easily see that, with some allowance for his habit of rhetorical exaggeration, the former may mean no more than that the scattered copies (*exemplaria*) of the one Old Latin translation vary widely from each other; and though the assertions of Augustine are too positive to be thus disposed of, yet he is here speaking, not from his personal knowledge so much as from vague conjecture; of what had been done not in his own time, but "in the first ages of our faith;" and the illustrious Bishop of Hippo, with all his earnest godliness, his spiritual discernment and mighty strength of reasoning, must yield place as a Biblical critic and an investigator of Christian history to many (Eusebius or Jerome for example) who were far his inferiors in intellectual power.

On one point, however, Augustine must be received as a competent and most sufficient witness. We cannot hesitate to believe that one of the several translations or recensions current towards the end of the fourth century was distinguished from the rest by the name of *Itala*, and in his judgment deserved praise for its clearness and fidelity. It was long regarded as certain that in Augustine's *Italic* we might find the Old Latin version in its purest form, and that it had obtained that appellation from Italy, the native country of the Latin language and literature, where Walton thinks it likely that it had been used from the very beginning of the Church, "cum Ecclesia Latina sine versione Latinâ esse non potuerit" (Proleg. x. 1). Mill, indeed, who bestowed great pains on the subject, reminds us that the first Christians at Rome were composed to so great an extent of Jewish and other foreigners whose vernacular tongue was Greek, that the need of a Latin translation of Scripture would not at first be felt; yet even he could not place its date later than the Pontificate of Pius I. (142—57), the first Bishop of Rome after Clement that bears a Latin name (Mill. *Proleg.*

§ 377). It was not till attention had been specially directed to the style of the Old Latin version that scholars began to suspect its AFRICAN origin, of which no hint had been given by early ecclesiastical writers, and which possesses in itself no great inherent probability. This opinion, which had obtained favour with Eichhorn and some others before him, may be considered as demonstrated by Cardinal Wiseman, in a brief and fugitive pamphlet entitled "*Two letters on some parts of the controversy concerning* 1 *John* v. 7," *Rome,* 1835, since republished in his *Essays on various subjects,* Vol. I. 1853. So far as his argument rests on the exclusively Greek character of the primitive Roman Church, a fact which Mill seems to have insisted on quite enough, it may not bring conviction to the reflecting reader. Even though the early Bishops of Rome were of foreign origin, though Clement towards the end of the first, Caius the presbyter late in the second century, who are proved by their names to be Latins, yet chose to write in Greek; it does not at all follow that the Church contained not many humbler members, both Romans and Italians, ignorant of any language except Latin, for whose instruction a Latin version would still be urgently required. On the ground of internal evidence, however, Wiseman has made out a case which all who have followed him, Lachmann, Tischendorf, Davidson, Tregelles, accept as irresistible: indeed it is not easy to draw any other conclusion from his elaborate comparison of the words, the phrases, and grammatical constructions of the Latin version of Holy Scripture, with the parallel instances by which they can be illustrated from African writers, and from them only (*Essays*, Vol. I. pp. 46—66). It is impossible to exhibit any adequate abridgement of an investigation which owes all its cogency to the number and variety of minute particulars, each one weak enough by itself, the whole comprising a mass of evidence which cannot be gainsayed. As the earliest citations from the Old Latin are found in the ancient translation of Irenaeus, and the African fathers Tertullian [150?—220?] and Cyprian [d. 258]; so from the study of Tertullian and other Latin authors natives of North Africa, especially of the Roman proconsular province of that name, we may understand the genius and character of the peculiar dialect in which it is composed; such writers are Appuleius in the second century, Arnobius, Lactantius and

Augustine of the fourth. In their works, as in the Old Latin version, are preserved a multitude of words which occur in no Italian author so late as Cicero: constructions (e.g. *dominantur eorum* Luke xxii. 25; *faciam vos fieri* Matth. iv. 19) or forms of verbs (*sive consolamur...sive exhortamur* 2 Cor. i. 6) abound, which at Rome had long been obsolete; while the palpable lack of classic polish is not ill atoned for by a certain terseness and vigour which characterises this whole class of writers, but never degenerates into vulgarity or absolute barbarism.

Besides the vestiges of the Old Latin translation detected by Sabatier and others in the Latin Fathers and Apologists from Tertullian down to Augustine, the following manuscripts of the version are extant, and have been cited by critics since the appearance of Lachmann's edition (1842—50) by the small italic letters of the alphabet.

Manuscripts of the Gospels.

a. CODEX VERCELLENSIS [IV] at Vercelli, said to have been written by Eusebius Bishop of Vercellae and Martyr. *Mut.* in many letters and words throughout, and entirely wanting in Matth. xxv. 1—16; Mark i. 22—34; iv. 17—24; xv. 15—xvi. 7 (xvi. 7—20 in a later hand from Jerome's Vulgate); Luke i. 1—12; xi. 12—25; xii. 38—59. Published by J. A. Irici (*Sacrosanctus Evangeliorum Codex S. Eusebii Magni*), Milan 1748, and by Blanchini on the left-hand page of his *Evangeliarium Quadruplex;* the latter gives a *facsimile,* but Tregelles states that Irici represents the mutilated fragments the more accurately.

b. COD. VERONENSIS [IV or V] at Verona, also in Blanchini's *Evang. Quadruplex,* on the right-hand page. *Mut.* Matth. i. 1—11; xv. 12—23; xxiii. 18—27; Mark xiii. 9—19; 24—xvi. 20; Luke xix. 26—xxi. 29; John vii. 44—viii. 12 *erased.*

c. COD. COLBERT. [XI] at Paris, very important though so late; edited in full by Sabatier (see p. 253 note 2), but beyond the Gospels the version is Jerome's, and in a later hand.

d. CODEX BEZAE, its Latin version: see pp. 96—103, and for its *mut.* p. 97, note 1.

e. COD. PALATINUS [IV or V] at Vienna, on purple vellum, with gold and silver letters, as are Codd. *bfi,* edited by Tischendorf (*Evangelium Palatinum ineditum*), Leipsic, 1847. The order of the books plainly stands Matthew, John, Luke, Mark (the usual order in these Latin codices, see p. 62), but only the following portions are extant:

Matth. xii. 49—xiii. 13; 24—xiv. 11 (*with breaks*); 22—xxiv. 49; xxviii. 2—John xviii. 12; 25—Luke viii. 30; 48—xi. 4; 24—53; Mark i. 20—iv. 8; 19—vi. 9; xii. 37—40; xiii. 2, 3; 24—27; 33—36: i. e. 2627 verses, including all John but 13 verses, all Luke but 38.

f. COD. BRIXIANUS [VI] at Brescia, edited by Blanchini beneath Cod. *b.* *Mut.* Mark xii. 5—xiii. 32; xiv. 70—xvi. 20.

ff[1], *ff*[2]. CODD. CORBEIENSES, very ancient, once at the Abbey of Corbey in Picardy. Of *ff*[1] T. Martianay edited St Matthew and St James (*Vulgata Antiqua Latina et Itala versio ev. Matth. et ep. Jacobi*...Paris 1695), the first of any portion of the Old Latin, and Blanchini repeated it underneath Cod. *a*, giving in its place the text of *ff*[2] in the other Gospels: but Sabatier cites *ff*[1] in Mark i. 1—v. 18 and *ff*[2] in all parts except Matth. i—xi, and a few other places, wherein it is *mut.*

g[1], *g*[2]. CODD. SANGERMANENSES, like Paul. E (p. 132) and others, once at the Abbey of St Germain des Prez, near Paris; very ancient. Blanchini repeated the readings of these from Martianay in the margin of Cod. *ff*[1] of St Matthew, but Sabatier gave the variations of both throughout the Gospels: *g*[2] is not often cited by him, and seems *mut.*

h. COD. CLAROMONTANUS [IV or V] bought for the Vatican by Pius VI. (1774—99), contains only St Matthew in the Old Latin, the other Gospels in Jerome's revision. *Mut.* Matth. i. 1—iii. 15; xiv. 33—xviii. 12. Sabatier gave extracts and Mai published St Matthew in full in his *Script. Vet. nova collectio Vaticana*, Tom. III. p. 257, Rom. 1828.

i. COD. VINDOBONENSIS [V or VI] brought from Naples to Vienna, contains Luke x. 6—xxiii. 10 ("evangel. secundum Lucanum" it is termed); Mark ii. 17—iii. 29; iv. 4—x. 1; 33—xiv. 36; xv. 33—40. This valuable codex has been published by Alter and Paulus in Germany in such a form that Tregelles has been obliged to resort to Blanchini's and Griesbach's extracts, though Tischendorf has used Alter's publication[1].

k. COD. BOBBIENSIS [IV or V] brought from Bobbio to Turin. It is valuable, and contains Mark viii. 19—xvi. 8, followed by Matth. i. 1—iii. 10; iv. 2—xiv. 17; xv. 20—xvi. 1; 5—7. It was most wretchedly edited by F. F. Fleck in 1837, and not very well by Tischendorf in the Wiener Jahrbücher 1847, but he promises a separate and more correct publication.

l. COD. RHEDIGERIANUS [VII] at St Elizabeth's church, Breslau; *mut.*, especially in St John. J. E. Scheibel in 1763 published Matthew and Mark, far from correctly: D. Schulz wrote a Dissertation on it in 1814, and inserted his collation of it in his edition of Griesbach's N. T. Vol. I. 1827.

[1] His citation is from Alter, "N. Repert. d. bibl. u. morgenl. Literatur," III. 115—170, and to Paulus' *Memorabilia*, VII. p. 58—96 (Tischend. N. T. Prol. p. 244, 7th edn.).

m. This letter indicates the readings extracted by Mai (*Spicilegium Romanum*, 1843, Tom. IX. pp. 61—86) from a "Speculum" [VI or VII] which has been ascribed to Augustine, and is unique for containing extracts from the whole N. T. except St Mark, 3 John, Hebrews, and Philemon. It is in the Monastery of Santa Croce, or Bibliotheca Sessoriana (No. 58) at Rome. Wiseman drew attention to it in his celebrated "Two Letters," 1835 (*see* p. 255), because it contains 1 John v. 7 in two different places. Both he and Mai furnish *facsimiles.* This "Speculum" (published in full by Mai, *Patrum Nova Collectio*, Vol. I. pt. 2, 1852) consists of extracts from both Testaments, arranged in chapters under various heads or topics.

For the next four we are indebted to Tischendorf, who inserts them in his 7th edition (N. T. Proleg. p. 245), and purposes to edit them in full.

n. COD. SANGALLENSIS [V or IV] at St Gall (*see* p. 112). It contains Matth. xvii. 1—5; 14—18; xvii. 19—xviii. 20; xix. 21—xx. 7; 7—23 (*defective*); 23—xxi. 3; xxvi. 56—60; 69—74; xxvii. 3; 62—64; 66—xxviii. 2; 8—20; Mark vii. 13—31; viii. 32—ix. 9; xiii. 2—20; xv. 22—xvi. 13; 199 verses.

o, p are other fragments at St Gall: *o* [VII?] contains Mark xvi. 14—20 in a hand of the Merovingian period: *p* [VII or VIII] contains John xi. 14—44; it seems part of a lectionary in a Scottish (i. e. Irish) hand, and from a specimen Tischendorf gives would appear to be very loose and paraphrastic.

q. COD. MONACENSIS [VI] at Munich. *Mut.* Matth. iii. 15—iv. 25; v. 25—vi. 4; 28—vii. 8; John x. 11—xii. 39; Luke xxiii. 22—36; xxiv. 11—39; Mark i. 7—22; xv. 5—36: an important copy.

Add to this list Cod. δ, the interlinear Latin of Cod. Δ (see p. 123), whatever be its value. Also Luke xvii. 3—29; xviii. 39—xix. 47; xx. 46—xxi. 22, &c. [V] just published at Milan in *Monumenta Sacra et Profana, ex Codd. praesertim Bibl. Ambrosian.*

In the Acts we have Codd. *dm* as in the Gospels: *e* the Latin version of Cod. E of the Acts (*see above, p.* 128), and *s* COD. BOBBIENSIS, now at Vienna [V?], containing palimpsest fragments of Acts xxiii, xxvii, xxviii: edited by Tischendorf and Eichenfeld (*Wiener Jahrbücher*, 1847).

In the Catholic Epistles are *ff* (Martianay) of St James and *m* as in the Gospels; *s* as in the Acts, containing James i. 1—5; iii. 13—18; iv. 1; 2; v. 19; 20; 1 Pet. i. 1—12.

In the Pauline Epistles we have *m* as in the Gospels. Codd. *d, e, f, g* are the Latin versions of Codd. DEFG of St Paul, described above, Cod. D, p. 130; Cod. E, p. 132; Cod. F, p. 133; Cod. G, p. 135. Sabatier had given extracts from *de*, though not very carefully: *f* (if we except the interlinear Latin, *see p.* 135) rather belongs to Jerome's recension.

gue. COD. GUELFERBYTANUS [VI], fragments of Rom. xi. 33—xii. 5; 17—xiii. 1; xiv. 9—20; xv. 3—13 (33 verses), found in the great Gothic palimpsest at Wolfenbüttel (*see p.* 113), and published with the other matter by Knittel in 1762, and more fully by Tischendorf, *Anecdota sacra et profana*, p. 153, &c.

r. COD. FRISINGENSIS [VI or V] on the covers of some books at Munich. These precious fragments (1 Cor. i. 1—27; 28—iii. 5; xv. 14—43; xvi. 12—24; 2 Cor. i. 1—10; iii. 17—v. 1; ix. 10—xi. 21; Phil. iv. 11—23; 1 Thess. i. 1—10; 179 verses), were discovered by J. A. Schmeller, were read and will be published by Tischendorf.

In the Apocalypse we have only *m* of the Gospels, and large extracts in the Commentary of Primasius, an African writer of the sixth century, first cited by Sabatier.

These twenty-nine (or, counting the same copy more than once, thirty-six) codices, compared with what extracts we obtain from the Latin Fathers, comprise all we know of the version before Jerome. Codd. *abc* and the fragments of *i* have been deemed to represent the Old Latin in its primitive form, as it originated in Africa, and agree remarkably with Cod. D and the Curetonian Syriac, in regard to interpolations, and improbable or ill-supported readings: so far as they represent a text as old as the second century, they prove that some manuscripts of that early date had already been largely corrupted. Cod. *e*, also, though the specimens we shall give below (pp. 267, 268) shew extensive divergency from the rest, often bears a striking resemblance to Cod. *d* and its parallel Greek. There are, however, copies (Cod. *f* for instance) of which Lachmann speaks, which "ab Afrâ suâ origine mirum quantum discrepent, et cum inimicissimis quasi colludant" (*N. T. Proleg.* Vol. I. p. xiii); and since these best agree with the quotations of Augustine, who commended the *Italic* version (see p. 254), and counselled that "emendatis non emendati cedant" (*De Doct. Chr.* Lib. II. c. 14), and that "Latinis quibuslibet emendandis, Graeci adhibeantur" (ib. c. 15); it has been inferred, not improbably, though on somewhat precarious grounds, that such codices are of the *Italic* recension, formed perhaps in the North of Italy, by correcting the elder *African* from Greek manuscripts of a more approved class. It is obvious, however, that little dependence can be placed on a theory thus slenderly supported[1], nor would the critical value of the *Italic* be diminished

[1] I do not perceive the cogency of what Lachmann says that "Wisemanus egregie demonstravit" (*N. T. Proleg.* Vol. I. p. xiii) on this head from Augustine's argument against Faustus, the *African* Manichaean (*Advers. Faust.* Lib. XI. c. 2). That heretic adopted the principle we are so familiar with now, of accepting just so much of Scripture as suited his purpose, and no more: "*Inde probo hoc illius esse, illud non esse, quia hoc pro me sonat, illud contra me.*" Augustine,

17—2

were we certain that it had sprung from a revision made by the aid of such Greek codices as were the most highly esteemed in the third or fourth century. Of the remaining copies, Codd. *hm?n*, each with many peculiarities of its own, are assigned to the African family, *k* and *q* (which Tischendorf praises highly) to the Italic, though *k* has been amended from "a Greek text more Alexandrian than that which had been the original basis of the Latin version" (Tregelles' *Horne*, p. 239), and is otherwise remarkable, especially for a habit of abridging whole passages. Cod. *l* is said to possess a mixed text, and ff^2, g^1, g^2 to be of but little use, so far as they have been cited. It is evident that much of this division is arbitrary, and that the whole subject needs renewed and close investigation.

(2). *Jerome's revised Latin Version, commonly called the Vulgate.*

The extensive variations then existing between different copies of the Old Latin version, and the obvious corruptions which had crept into some of them, prompted Damasus, Bishop of Rome, in A.D. 382, to commit the important task of a formal revision of the New, and probably of the Old Testament, to Jerome, a presbyter born at Stridon on the confines of Dalmatia and Pannonia, probably a little earlier than A.D. 345. This learned, fervent and holy man had just returned to Rome, where he had been educated, from his hermitage in Bethlehem, and in the early ripeness of his high reputation undertook a work for which he was specially qualified, and whose delicate nature he well understood[1]. Whatever prudence and moderation could do (although these were not the peculiar excellences of his

of course, insists in reply on the evidence of "exemplaria veriora, vel plurium codicum vel antiquorum vel linguae praecedentis" [i. e. the Greek],..."vel ex aliarum regionum codicibus, unde ipsa doctrina commeavit." How all this tends to prove that Faustus used African, Augustine Italic manuscripts, is not easily understood.

[1] "Novum opus me facere cogis ex veteri: ut post exemplaria Scripturarum toto orbe dispersa, quasi quidam arbiter sedeam: et quia inter se variant, quae sint illa quae cum Graeca consentiant veritate, decernam. Pius labor, sed periculosa praesumptio, judicare de caeteris, ipsum ab omnibus judicandum: senis mutare linguam, et canescentem jam mundum ad initia retrahere parvulorum." Praef. ad Damasum.

character) to remove objections or relieve the scruples of the simple, were not neglected by Jerome, who not only made as few changes as possible in the Old Latin when correcting its text by the help of "ancient" Greek manuscripts[1], but left untouched many words and forms of expression, and not a few grammatical irregularities, which in a new translation (as his own subsequent version of the Hebrew Scriptures makes clear) he would most certainly have avoided. The four Gospels, as they stand in the Greek rather than the Latin order (*see p.* 256), revised but not re-translated on this wise principle, appeared in A.D. 384, accompanied with his celebrated Preface to Damasus ("summus sacerdos"), who died that same year. Notwithstanding his other literary engagements, it is probable enough that his recension of the whole New Testament for public use was completed A.D. 385, though the proof alleged by Mill (*N. T. Proleg.* § 862), and others after his example, hardly meets the case. In the next year (A. D. 386), in his Commentary on Galat., Ephes., Titus and Philem., he indulges in more freedom of alteration as a translator than he had previously deemed advisable; while his new version of the Old Testament from the Hebrew (completed about A. D. 405) is not founded at all on the Old Latin, which was made from the Greek Septuagint; the Psalter excepted, which he executed at Rome at the same date, and in the same spirit, as the Gospels. The boldness of his attempt in regard to the Old Testament is that portion of his labours which *alone* Augustine disapproved[2] (August. *ad Hieron.* Ep. x. Tom. II. p. 18, Lugd. 1586, A. D. 403), and indeed it was never received entire by the Western Church, which long preferred his slight revision of the Old Latin, made at some earlier period of his life. Gradually, however, Jerome's recension of the whole Bible gained ground, as well through the growing influence of the Church of Rome,

1 "[Evangelia] Codicum Graecorum emendata collatione, sed veterum, quae ne multum a lectionis Latinae consuetudine discreparent, ita calamo temperavimus, ut his tantum quae sensum videbantur mutare correctis, reliqua manere pateremur ut fuerant." *Ibid.* For a signal instance see below, Chap. IX., note on Matth. xxi. 31.

2 To his well-known censure of Jerome's rendering of the Old Testament from the Hebrew, Augustine adds, "Proinde non parvas Deo gratias agimus de opere tuo, quod Evangelium ex Graeco interpretatus es: quia pene in omnibus nulla offensio est, cum Scripturam Graecam contulerimus."

as from its own intrinsic merits: so that when in course of time it came to take the place of the older version, it also took its name of the *Vulgate*, or common translation. Cassiodorus indeed, in the middle of the sixth century, is said to have compared the new and old Latin (of the New, perhaps of both Testaments) in parallel columns, which thus became partially mixed in not a few codices: but Gregory the Great (590—604), while confessing that his Church used both ("quia sedes Apostolica, cui auctore Deo praesideo, utraque utitur," *Epist. Dedic. ad Leandrum*, c. 5) awarded so decided a preference to Jerome's translation from the Hebrew, that this form of his Old Testament version, not without some mixture with his translation from the Septuagint (Walton, *Prol.* x. pp. 242—244, Wrangham), and his Psalter and New Testament as revised from the Old Latin, came at length to comprise the Vulgate Bible, the only shape in which Holy Scripture was accessible in Western Europe (except to a few scattered scholars) during the long night of the Middle Ages. To guard it from accidental or wilful corruption, Charlemagne (A. D. 797) caused our countryman Alcuin to review and correct certain copies, more than one of which are supposed even yet to survive (e.g. one in the British Museum, another described by Blanchini, in the "Bibliotheca Vallicellensis" at Rome, which belongs to the Fathers of the Oratory of S. Philip Neri). Our Primate and benefactor, the Lombard Lanfranc (1069—89) attempted a similar task (Mill, *N. T. Proleg.* § 1058); the aim too of the several subsequent "Correctoria Bibliorum" (*see above*, p. 153, note) was directed to the same good end. These remedies, as applied to written copies, were of course but partial and temporary; yet they were all that seemed possible before the invention of printing. The firstfruits of the press, as it was very right they should be, were Latin Bibles; the earliest (of which some eighteen copies remain) a splendid and beautiful volume, published in Germany about 1452. Of the many editions which followed, that in the Complutensian Polyglott (1514 &c.: *see* Chapter V.) may be named as very elegant; but in none of these does much attention seem to have been paid to the purity of the text. Hence when the Council of Trent in 1546 had declared that "haec ipsa vetus et vulgata editio, quae longo tot saeculorum usu in ipsa ecclesia probata est," should be chosen "ex omnibus Latinis editionibus quae circumferuntur sacrorum librorum," and "in publicis lectionibus, disputationibus, praedicationibus, et expositionibus pro *authentica* habeatur" (Sess. IV. Can. 2); after assigning the lowest sense possible to that ambiguous term "authentic[1]," it became the manifest duty of the Church of Rome to provide for its members the most correct recension of the Vulgate that skill and diligence could produce: in fact the Council went on to direct that "posthàc Scriptura sacra, potissimùm verò haec ipsa vetus et vulgata editio, quam emendatissimè imprimatur." Yet it was not until the Latin Bible had been left upwards of fifty years longer to the enterprise of private persons (e. g. R. Stephens in 1540, who gave various readings from 13 manuscripts; Jo. Hentenius in the Louvain Bible of 1547; F. Lucas Brugensis in 1573, 1584, &c.), that Sixtus V. (1585—90), apparently after personally bestowing much laudable pains on the work, which had been in preparation during the time of his three immediate predecessors, sent forth what we might term his Authorised Edition in 1590; not only commanding in the Bull prefixed to the volume that it should be taken as the standard of all future reprints, but even that all copies should be corrected by it; and that all things contrary thereto in any manuscript or printed book, which for its elegance might still be preserved, be of no weight or authority. Yet this edition (which in places had itself received manual corrections by pen or by paper pasted over it) was soon found so faulty that it was called in to make room for another but two years afterwards (1592) published by Clement VIII. (1592—1605), from which it differs in many places. The high tone adopted by both these Popes, and especially by Sixtus, who had yet to learn that "there is no papal road to criticism" (Tregelles' *Horne*, Vol. IV. p. 251), afforded a rare opportunity to their enemies for upbraiding them on the palpable failure of at least one of them. Thomas James, in his *Bellum Papale sive Concordia Discors* (London 1600), gives a long and curious list of the differences of the Sixtine and Clementine Bibles, very humorous perhaps as a kind of *argumentum ad homines*, but not a little

[1] I must confess I see nothing unreasonable in the statements of the Roman doctors cited by Walton, Proleg. x. Wrangham, Tom. II. pp. 249—262.

unbecoming when the subject is remembered to be an earnest attempt to improve the accuracy of a great and widely-spread version of Holy Scripture. One thing, however, is certain, that neither the Sixtine nor Clementine editions (the latter of which retains its place of paramount authority in the Roman Church) was prepared on any intelligent principles of criticism, or furnishes us with such a text as the best manuscripts of Jerome's Vulgate supply to our hands.

It was easy to enumerate all known codices of the Latin before Jerome (pp. 256—9): those of his own version in the libraries of Western Europe are absolutely countless: they probably much exceed in number those of the Greek Testament, certainly those of any other work whatever. By the aid of the oldest and best of them Bentley proposed, Lachmann and Tregelles to some extent have accomplished, the arduous task of reducing the Vulgate from its Clementine form to the condition in which Jerome left it. A very few of the best documents they have employed are all that need to be described here.

am. Codex Amiatinus, brought into the Laurentian Library at Florence from the Cistercian Monastery of Monte Amiatino, in Tuscany. It contains both Testaments, nearly perfect, in a fine hand, stichometrically written by the Abbot Servandus, about A.D. 541. A. M. Bandini first particularly noticed it (though from a memorandum appended to it we find it had been looked at—hardly much used—in 1587—90, for the Sixtine edition); the New Testament was wretchedly edited by the unfortunate F. F. Fleck in 1840; collated by Tischendorf 1843, and by Tregelles 1846 (del Furia re-collating the codex in the places at which the two differed); published by Tischendorf 1850, and again 1854. The Old Testament is yet in a great measure unexamined. The Latin text of Tregelles' N. T. (see Chapter v.) is based on this, doubtless the best manuscript of the Vulgate.

fuld. Codex Fuldensis, of about the same age, is in the Abbey of Fulda in Hesse Cassel. It contains the New Testament, all in the same hand, written by order of Victor Bishop of Capua, who himself corrected it, and subscribed to the Acts the date, A.D. 546. The Gospels are arranged in a kind of Harmony which diminishes their critical value. It was described by Schanna 1723 (*Vindemiae Literariae Collectio*, p. 218), collated by Lachmann and his coadjutor Ph. Buttmann in 1839 for the Latin portion of his N. T. (see Chapter v.), and will be edited by Ern. Ranke.

tol. Codex Toletanus, at Toledo [?] of both Testaments, in Gothic letters. Collated in 1588 for Sixtus' Bible by Christ. Palomares, whose papers were published by Blanchini, *Vindiciae Canonicarum Scripturarum*, 1740.

for. CODEX FOROJULIENSIS [VI] at Friuli. Blanchini (*Evangeliarium Quadruplex*, Appendix) published three of the Gospels (*mut.* John xix. 29—40; xx. 19—xxi. 25). St Mark's Gospel is partly at Venice in a wretched plight, partly (xii. 21—xvi. 20) at Prague. This last portion was edited by Dobrowsky, 1778.

per. Fragments of St Luke (i. 26—ii. 46; iii. 4—16; iv. 9—22; 28—v. 36; viii. 11—xii. 7) at Perugia, somewhat carelessly edited by Blanchini, *Evan. Quadr.* Appendix.

harl. COD. HARLEIAN. 1775 [VII] Gospels partially collated by Griesbach, *Symbol. Crit.* I. 305—26.

Tregelles cites for the Gospels (N. T. 1857, 1860) no more than the above-named: the following, taken from Tischendorf's list (*N. T. Prol.* pp. 248—51), are less known, or else of slighter value.

and. Gospels at St Andrew's, Avignon: in Martianay 1695, Calmet 1726. *bodl.* Bodleian 857 [VII] fragments of N. T. inspected by Mill and Tisch. *cav.* From the Trinity Monastery di Cava, near Naples [VIII] N. T.: used by Tisch. for 1 John v. 7, and by the Abb. de Rozan, 1822. *demid.* Of the whole Bible [XII], from old sources, edited by Matthaei (N. T.) in the Act. Epp. Apoc.: it belonged to Paul Demidov. *em.* from St Emmeram's, Ratisbon; now at Munich [dated 870]. Collated by P. C. Sanftl, 1786. Contains the Gospels, as does also *erl.* At Erlangen, used by Sanftl. *flor.* Floriacensis, a Lectionary in Sabatier. *fos.* Fossatensis of the Gospels [VIII?], used at St Germain's by Sabatier. *gat.* Gospels at S. Gatien's, Tours [VIII] in Calmet, Sabatier, Blanchini. *gue lect.* A Wolfenbüttel palimpsest [V], seen by Tisch. *harl.* Harleian. 1772 [XIII], a text much mixed with the Old Latin, contains all the Epistles except 3 John and Jude (but Jude [XI] of a different text) and Apoc. (*mut.* xiv. 16—fin.). Collated by Griesbach, *Sym. Crit.* I. pp. 326—82. *jac.* St James, Gospels [IX] used by Sanftl. *ing.* Gospels brought from Ingoldstadt to Munich [VII], begins Matth. xxii. 39; *mut.* elsewhere. Seemiller 1784, Tisch. 1844. *Lc. brug.* Readings extracted by Lucas Brugensis (see p. 153, note) from *Correctoria Bibliorum Latinorum*, and used by Sabatier. These readings are reprinted at length from the Antwerp Polyglott 1569—72 in Walton's *Polyglott*, Tom. VI. xvii. p. 30. *lips.* 4, 5, 6. Three Leipsic copies of Apoc., collated in Matthaei's N. T. 1785. *lux.* Luxoviensis, a lectionary; Mabillon 1729, Sabatier. *mar.* Caesar Vindob. 287 [*dated* 1079] written by Mariana the Scot (i. e. Irishman). St Paul's Epistles, collated in Alter's N. T. Vol. II. pp. 1040—80. *mm.* "Majoris Monasterii (Marmoutier 87)" [X] Gospels collated by Calmet, Sabatier, Blanchini. *mt.* Gospels at St Martin's, Tours [VIII], Sabatier used it for all but St Matthew. *reg.* Several copies of the Gospels examined by Sabatier at Paris, one fragment in purple and gold from St Germains [VII] by Tischendorf. *san.* Fragments at St Gall of the Gospels and St Paul, the latter palimpsests [VI], a very pure text, brought to light by Tisch. 1857, who states that some leaves of the Gospels are at Zurich. *taur.* Gospels at Turin [VII], Tischendorf, *Anecd. sacr. et prof.* p. 160; used by him in St Mark. *trevir.* Gospels at Trèves, mentioned by Sanftl. *trin.* Trinity Coll. Cambridge, B. 10. 5. [IX] begins 1 Cor. vii. 32, ends about 1 Thess. Readings sent by Rev. F. J. A. Hort to Tregelles. *vat.* "S. Mich. Breviar. Moz., Vat. olim reginae Suec. 11" cited in *Magnificat* and *Benedictus*, Luke i, by Tischendorf after Sabatier. The papers collected by Bentley for his edition of the N. T. (see Chapter v.), now at Trinity College, Cambridge, may also be expected to prove serviceable in restoring the Latin Vulgate[1].

On the whole it will probably be found that both as a translation and as an aid to the criticism of the Greek text of the New Testament, the Vulgate is far superior to the Old Latin, which was either formed from manuscripts early interpolated, or (what is far more likely) was corrupted at a later period. Jerome would probably allow great influence to the revised Greek codices of Origen, of Pierius and Pamphilus, to which he occasionally refers with approbation[2]; and since his copies were of a character that Augustine also viewed with favour[3], we have no right to doubt that, so far as Jerome deemed it prudent or necessary to correct the current Latin text, he followed the Greek manuscripts most highly esteemed, at least in the West, at the end of the fourth century. The connection between the several forms of the Latin, before and after Jerome's recension, may be better seen by the following specimens.

In the diction of these several codices, notwithstanding many individual peculiarities, there is enough to convince us (as we saw above, p. 253) that they all had the same remote origin. On the whole *f* comes nearest to Jerome's version, and *a* nearer than *bce*, which have much in common, though *e* is farthest removed from the Vulgate, being the loosest and least grammatical of them all: *d* seldom agrees with any.

[1] For the honour of Irish scholars the Book of Armagh, at Trinity College, Dublin, ought to be added to our catalogue. It is the only complete Irish copy of the Latin New Testament, the Pauline Epistles following the Gospels, then the Catholic Epistles, the Apocalypse, and lastly the Acts: to the Colossians the Epistle to the Laodiceans is subjoined (see Cod. G, p. 137). It dates about 807. The Evangelists seem to stand in the usual *Greek* order.

[2] The passages are cited at length in that curious medley of exact learning and bad reasoning, Dr Nolan's *Inquiry into the Integrity of the Greek Vulgate*, 1815, pp. 171, 100, 85, &c. The principal are *Com. in Matth.* xxiv. [*v.* 36], Hier. Tom. VI. p. 54, and *Cat. Script. Eccl.*, Pamphilus, Tom. I. p. 128.

[3] To the words quoted, p. 261, note 2, Augustine immediately adds: "Unde, si quispiam veteri falsitati contensiosius faverit, prolatis collatisque codicibus, vel docetur facillimè, vel refellitur."

a. Codex Vercellensis (Marc. ii. 1—5).

(1) Et cum introisset iterum in Capharnaum post dies, cognitum est quod in domo esset; (2) et protinus convenerunt multi, in tantum ut jam non posset capere usque ad januam, et loquebatur illis verbum. (3) Et veniunt ad eum, adferentes paralyticum, qui tollebatur a quatuor. (4) Et cum non possent accedere propter turbam, ascendentes, denudaverunt tectum, ubi erat Jesus; et dimiserunt grabattum ubi paralyticus decumbebat. (5) Cum vidisset autem Jesus fidem illorum, ait paralytico, Fili, remittuntur tibi peccata tua.

b. Codex Veronensis.

(1) Et iterum benit Capharnaum post dies: et auditum est quod in domo esset; (2) et convenerunt multi, ita ut jam nec ad januam caperet, et loquebatur ad eos verbum. (3) Et veniunt ad illum, ferentes paralyticum in grabatto. (4) Et, cum accedere non possent prae multitudine, detexerunt tectum, ubi erat; et summiserunt grabbatum, in quo paralyticus jacebat. (5) Cum vidisset autem Jesus fidem illorum, ait paralytico: Fili, remissa sunt tibi peccata.

c. Codex Colbertinus.

(1) Et cum venisset Capharnaum post dies, auditum est quod in domo esset, (2) et confestim convenerunt ad eum multi, ita ut non caperet eos introitus januae, et loquebatur ad eos verbum. (3) Venerunt autem ad eum portantes in lecto paralyticum, (4) Et cum non possent accedere prae turba, denudaverunt tecta ubi erat Jesus: et summiserunt grabatum in quo paralyticus jacebat. (5) Cum vidisset autem Jesus fidem illorum, ait paralytico, Fili remittuntur tibi peccata tua.

e. Codex Palatinus.

(1) Et venit iterum in capharnaum post dies· et auditum est quoniam domi est (2) et continuo collecti sunt multi ita ut nō caperet domus et loquebatur illis verbum. (3) Et venerunt ad illum portantes in grabatto paralyticum (4) et cum non possent accedere prae Turbam denudaverunt tectum ubi erat ih̄s et summiserunt grabattum in quo paralyticus jacebat· (5) et cum vidisset ih̄s fidem illorum dixit paralytico fili remittūtur tibi peccata.

f. Codex Brixiensis.

(1) Et iterum intravit Capharnaum post dies· et auditum est quod in domo esset. (2) et confestim convenerunt multi. ita ut non caperet usque ad januam. et loquebatur eis verbum. (3) Et venerunt ad eum portantes in grabato paralyticum inter quatuor. (4) Et cum offerre eum non possent prae turba, nudaverunt tectum ubi erat jesus. et patefacientes. submiserunt grabatum. in quo paralyticus jacebat. (5) Cum vidisset autem Jesus fidem illorum. ait paralytico Fili dimissa sunt tibi peccata tua.

am. Codex Amiatinus (*Vulg.*)

(1) Et iterum intravit Capharnaum post dies; et auditum est quod in domo esset, (2) et convenerunt multi, ita ut non caperet neque ad januam, et loquebatur eis verbum. (3) Et venerunt ferentes ad eum paralyticum qui a quattuor portabatur. (4) Et cum non possent offerre eum illi prae turba, nudaverunt tectum ubi erat, et patefacientes summiserunt grabatum in quo paralyticus jacebat. (5) Cum vidisset autem Jesus fidem illorum, ait paralytico Filii [*lege* Fili *cum editis*] dimittuntur tibi peccata.

N. B. The Clementine Vulgate reads *v.* 3, ad eum ferentes. *v.* 5, autem vidisset. *v.* 5, tibi peccata tua.

The criticism of the text would lead us to much the same conclusion. In v. 1 *f am.* read πάλιν εἰσῆλθεν, *b* (apparently) πάλιν ἦλθεν, *c* ἐλθὼν (omitting πάλιν), *e* ἦλθε πάλιν, *a* εἰσελθὼν πάλιν: in v. 3 αἰρόμενον ὑπὸ τεσσάρων is read only in *af am*, and that with some variation: *cef* insert ἐν κραβάτῳ (-ττῳ *b*) before παραλυτικόν, *b* after it; in *a am.* it is quite absent: in v. 5 σοι αἱ ἁμαρτίαι σου is given fully in *acf*, and the Clementine Vulgate, σου is omitted in the other three. Other instances will readily present themselves to a careful reader.

We will now transcribe John vii. 53—viii. 11 from *ce am*, with the variations of *for.* in the last. The passage is wholly omitted in *af*, and has been erased from *b*.

c. CODEX COLBERTINUS.

(53) Et reversi sunt unusquisque in domum suam. (viii. 1) Jesus autem ascendit in montem oliveti. (2) Et mane cum factum esset, iterum venit in templo, et universus populus conveniebat ad eum, et cum consedisset, docebat eos. (3) Scribae autem et Pharisaei adduxerunt ad eum mulierem in adulterio deprehensam, quam cum statuissent in medio (4) dixerunt ad Jesum Magister haec mulier deprehensa est in adulterio. (5) In lege autem praecepit nobis Moyses, ut qui in adulterio deprehenditur, lapidetur. Tu autem quid dicis de eâ? (6) Haec ideo dicebant tentantes eum, ut haberent causam accusandi eum. Jesus autem, inclinato capite, digito scribebat in terrâ (7) Cum autem perseverarent interrogantes eum, erexit se, et dicit eis: Qui sine peccato est vestrum, primus in illam lapidem jaciat. (8) Et iterum se inclinans, scribebat in terra. (9)

e. CODEX PALATINUS.

(53) Et abierunt singuli ad domos suas. (viii. 1) Ihs autem abiit in montem oliveti. (2) deluculo autem reversus est in templo et omnis plebs veniebat ad eum et sedens docebat eos. (3) et adduxerunt autem scribae et farisaei mulierem in adulterio depraehensam· et cum statuissent eam in medio (4) dixerunt Illi magister haec mulier depraehensa est sponte maecata. (5) in lege autē nobis moyses mandavit hujusmodi lapidare tu ergo quid dicis. (6) hoc enim dicebant temptantes eum ut haberent quo modo eum accusarent. Ihs autem inclinato capite digito supra terram scribebat (7) cum ergo perseverarent interrogantes eum adlebavit capud et dixit illis· si quis vestrum sine peccato est ipse prior super illā iniciat lapidem. (8) Et iterum inclinato capite supra terram scribebat. (9) Illi autem cum audissent unus post unum exiebant, incipientes a senioribus et

am. for. CODD. AMIAT. FOROJULIENSIS.

(53) Et reversi sunt unusquisque in domum suam· (viii. 1) Jesus autem perrexit in montem oliveti: (2) et diluculo iterum venit in templum, et omnis populus venit ad eum, et sedens docebat eos. (3) Adducunt autem scribae et Pharisaei mulierem in adulterio deprehensam et statuerunt eam in medio (4) et dixerunt ei Magister, haec mulier modo deprehensa est in adulterio. (5) In lege autem Moses (Moyses *for.*) mandavit nobis hujusmodi lapidare: tu ergo quid dicis? (6) Haec autem dicebant temtantes (temptantes *for.*) eum, ut possent accusare eum. Jesus autem inclinans se deorsum digito scribebat in terra. (7) Cum autem perseverarent interrogantes eum, erexit se et dixit eis, Qui sine peccato est vestrum, primus in illam lapidem mittat. (8) Et iterum se inclinans scribebat in terra. (9) Audientes autem unus post unum exiebant, incipientes

Illi igitur cum audissent, paulatim secedebant singuli, incipientes a senioribus omnes recesserunt: et relictus est solus: et ecce mulier illa in medio erat stans. (10) Cumque se erexisset Jesus, dixit ad mulierem: Ubi sunt? nemo te condemnavit? (11) Quae dixit, Nemo Domine. Dixit autem illi Jesus: Nec ego te condemnabo: Vade, et ex hoc jam noli peccare.

relictus est ihs solus et muLier in medio. (10) Cum adlevasset autem capud ihs dixit ei. mulier ubi sunt nemo te judicavit. (11) Dixit et illa nemo dne. dixit autem ihs ad illam nec ego te judico. i et amplius noli peccare.

(incipiens *Am. p. m.*) a senioribus, et remansit solus et mulier in medio stans. (10) Erigens autem se Jesus dixit ei Mulier, ubi sunt? (+ qui te accusant? *for.*) nemo te condemnavit? (11) Quae dixit Nemo domine. Dixit autem Jesus (– Dixit autem Jesus *for.*) Nec ego te condemnabo: vade et amplius jam noli peccare.

N. B. The Clementine Vulgate reads *v.* 7, ergo (*pro* autem); *v.* 9, exibant; + Jesus (*post* solus); *v.* 10, ubi sunt qui te accusabant; *v.* 11 jam amplius[1].

[1] It will easily appear from the foregoing statements that much requires to be done before the subject of the Latin versions, their origin, genius and mutual relations, can be said to be exhausted. The Rev. Henry Craik of Bristol, in his scholarlike and useful little treatise on *The Hebrew Language*, 1860, classifies the several heads of such an investigation in the following

Prospectus of a Monograph on the Vulgate.

CHAP.

I. Origin and History of the Vulgate.

II. General Characteristics of that Ancient Version.

III. Past and Present condition of its Text, with particular reference to the Codex Amiatinus.

IV. Leading instances in which the Vulgate has preserved readings which the labours of recent critics have proved to be genuine, as being possessed of higher critical authority than the corresponding readings of the received Greek Text, from which, for the most part, our own Translation was derived.

V. Leading Instances of erroneous renderings referrible to the fact of the Translator having mistaken the meaning of the Original.

VI. Leading instances in which the Vulgate misrepresents the meaning of the inspired writer, through having followed an erroneous Hebrew or Greek Text.

VII. Influence of the LXX. upon the Vulgate Version of the Old Testament.

* * * * *

APPENDIX.

A. On the Latinity of the Vulgate, and its more remarkable deviations from the phraseology of the Classic Writers.

B. Review of the effects on the Mediæval Theology resulting out of the use of the Vulgate Version, during the dark ages, and reflex effects of the Mediæval Theology on the mode of interpreting the Vulgate.

C. Terms and phraseology, derived from the Vulgate, still retained in modern English, and influence of that Version on certain modes of expression current among Protestant Theologians.

Craik, *Hebrew Language*, pp. 121—2.

Of the remaining versions the Persic, Arabic, and one or two others, are of almost no service to the critic; and those who do not understand the languages in which the remainder are written, cannot be too careful in applying their alleged evidence to the revision of the text, except in the case of their testifying to the addition or omission of whole sentences, or smaller clauses, and sometimes of single words. A brief description will suffice even for the most important among them, the rather as all our information has been obtained at second hand.

5. The Egyptian Versions.

The term *Coptic* (derived from *Coptos* a town in Upper Egypt) is popularly applied to that modification of the ancient Egyptian language which sprung from its mixture with the Greek, under the influence of its sovereigns of the Macedonian dynasty, and of the foreign colony at Alexandria. The only surviving memorials of the Coptic (now displaced by Arabic as the vernacular tongue) are the sacred books yet used in their public worship by the handful of Egyptian Christians, a poor, despised, and oppressed people, that yet survive the tyranny of the infidels. In the early centuries of our aera two (some have thought three) dialects seem to have been in general use, that of lower Egypt, styled from the great native capital, the *Memphitic;* and that of Upper Egypt, now called the *Thebaic*, from the chief city in that region, but formerly (with less strict propriety) the *Sahidic*, from the Arabic name for that part of the country. So far as we understand the main point of difference between the two dialects, it consists in the Thebaic, as that of the more remote province, being less corrupted from the Greek than the Memphitic. At what period the Holy Scriptures were first translated into either of them, or how far they have come down to us without material alteration, are points on which no definite information has yet been obtained. We have fragments of the Thebaic version in Cod. T of the Greek Gospels (*see p.* 116) that have been assigned to the fourth and are not later than the fifth century. Eusebius (*Hist. Eccles.* Lib. VIII. Cap. 9) was an eyewitness to the terrible sufferings of the Christians in the Thebaid throughout Diocletian's persecution (A.D. 303—313); when "not for a few days, but during a space of years" (ἐπὶ μακρὸν ὅλων ἐτῶν διάστημα) ten, twenty, even a hundred of all ages were martyred at once. If a few of them (as Phileas, Bishop of Thmui, and Philoromus) were wise and noble, the mass were evidently of lowly rank; and it seems unreasonable to doubt that for these faithful souls a native version of Holy Scripture would have been made before the end of the third century[1]. In the lower province, where Greek was more generally known, the Memphitic might date perhaps somewhat later; though even more than a century after Constantine (A.D. 451), Calosirius, the native Bishop of a city then bearing a Greek name (Arsinoe), subscribed the Acts of the Council of Chalcedon through an interpreter; and Pachomius (about A.D. 350) drew up in Coptic the rules for the Egyptian monks. Beyond this point history or plausible conjecture will not carry us.

(1). The Memphitic Version (*Cop.* or *Memph.*).

Although this version (*not* the Thebaic) seems to be that exclusively used in the Public Services of the Copts, it was not known in Europe till Dr Th. Marshall, Rector of Lincoln College (1672—85), contributed to Bp. Fell's Oxford N. T. of 1675 many readings collected from eight Coptic manuscripts in his possession, but now in the Bodleian. Marshall was hindered by death from completing his projected edition of the Gospels. Mill (*N. T. Proleg.* § 1406, 1462), however, not only used his papers, but a collation he procured from Louis Piques of three other copies at Paris (*ibid.* § 1508). In 1716 David Wilkins, a Prussian, published at Oxford his "*N. T. Ægyp-*

[1] That some of the native Christians could speak no language but their own, besides the high probability of the fact itself, appears from a passage in one of Zoega's Coptic manuscripts to which attention was called by Hug (*Introduction*, Vol. II. p. 408, Wait's translation). The Roman Prefect is travelling through Upper Egypt in search of Christians, when one presents himself of his own accord: "deinceps praeses ex tribunali *per interpretem* cum eo collocutus cum ei ut sacrificaret persuadere non potuisset, sententiam his verbis pertulit; Isaac Tiphrenus nomi Panan, quoniam mori vult pro nomine Jesu, jubeo ut caput ejus gladio recidatur" (Zoega, *Cat. Codd. Memph.* n. XIX. pp. 20, 21).

tiacum vulgo Copticum" from the Bodleian manuscripts compared with others at Paris and the Vatican; but Coptic scholars are agreed in pronouncing him most imperfectly acquainted with the language, and his accompanying Latin translation quite untrustworthy. Although portions of the Memphitic Old Testament (especially the Psalter) have been several times printed, we were long dependent on Wilkins for what was known of the New: but in 1846—7, M. G. Schwartze, a very competent critic, put forth the Gospels (*Quatuor Evangelia in Dialecto linguae Copticae Memphitica*) with a text revised by the aid of six *modern* codices (transcribed by Petraeus in 1622 from copies of the tenth century and later) at Berlin, and placed at the foot of each page a collation of his Memphitic readings with the Greek Testaments of Tischendorf (1841) and Lachmann (1842). On Schwartze's death the work was continued by P. Boetticher (*Acta Apostolorum, Epp.* 1851—2), in such a shape as to be useless to those who do not study Coptic, and utterly unsatisfactory to those who do. So much remains to be done for the Memphitic that Mill's readings cannot yet be regarded as obsolete.

(2). The Thebaic Version (*Sah.* or *Theb.*),

though but a collection of fragments, is considered more ancient and has fallen into far more skilful hands: the codices too are much more venerable in respect of age [v, vi]. C. G. Woide, the editor of Cod. A (*see* p. 83), projected an edition of this version, which he did not live to execute, but his papers, published by Ford in the *Appendix to the Codex Alexandrinus* 1799, exhibit the fullest collection of materials from all parts of the N. T. Mingarelli, *Ægyptiorum Codicum reliquiae, Venetiis in Bibliothecâ Nanianâ asservatae* (Bononiae, Fasc. I. II. 1785; Fasc. III. 1790); Georgi in his edition of Cod. T, 1789 (*see* p. 116); F. Münter, *Commentatio de Indole Versionis N. T. Sahidicae* (Hafniae 1789), each contributed further portions, sometimes citing readings from passages as yet unprinted, while G. Zoega, in his work cited above (pp. 116, 271, note), has indicated sources from which more might be drawn:

Schwartze made use of all within his reach for the illustration of the Memphitic Gospels[1].

(3). The Basmuric Fragments

Were published by W. F. Engelbreth, *Fragmenta Basmuro-Coptica V. et N. Test.* (Havniae, 1811), with *facsimiles*, from a very old manuscript in the Borgian Museum at Velitrae. Münter and Giorgi had previously edited portions, as also had Zoega in his Catalogue a year before (*see p.* 116). Besides small fragments of the Old Testament, there are the following parts of the New: John iv. 28—34; 36—40; 43—53; 1 Cor. vi. 19—ix. 16; xiv. 33—xv. 35; Eph. vi. 18—Phil. ii. 2; 1 Thess. i. 1—iii. 6; Hebr. v. 5—x. 22. This version is manifestly based on the Thebaic, from which it differs in but a few dialectic peculiarities, and has therefore no great weight except in places where the Thebaic is lost. It has its name of *Basmuric* from the circumstance that the third dialect of the Egyptian was so termed by the Arabs, the other two being the *Sahidic* or Thebaic and the *Bahiric* or Memphitic.

[1] Exclusively of a few portions of the Old Testament, the following fragments of the Thebaic have been published by one or other of the above-named critics: Matth i. 1—iv. 11; v. 14—20; 25; 26; vi. 5—15; 19—26; vii. 7—29; viii. 1—10; 14; 36; 41; xi. 14; 28; 30; xiii. 9; xvi. 21—28; xvii. 1—xxi. 15; xxii. 6—xxiii. 10; xxiv. 4; 5; 15; 22; 36; 43; xxv. 34—xxvii. 45; Mark ix. 2—8; xi. 1—10; 29—xv. 32; xvi. 20; Luke iv. 1—13; viii. 36—56; ix. 1—41; xi. 5—13; xii. 5—59; xiii. 1—35; xiv. 1—11; xv. 1—10; 11—32; xvi. 16—25; xviii. 9—14; xxii. 9—xxiv. 40; John iv. 5—30; v. 1—3; 5—14; vi. 15—58; 68—viii. 31; 40—59; ix. 1—xiii. 1; xvii. 6—26; xviii. 1; 2; 6—9; 15—40; xix. 1—xx. 30; Acts i. 1—xxiv. 19; 24; 25; xxvii. 27—38; James i. 2; 12; 26; 27; ii. 1—4; 8—23; iii. 3—6; iv. 11—17; v. 7—20; 1 Pet. i. 3; 13—21; ii. 7; 9; 13; 19—25; iii. 8; 15; 22; iv. 1; 7—14; 2 Pet. i. 1—21; ii. 1—3; 12—22; iii. 1—18; 1 John 1—10; ii. 1—v. 21; 2 John—Jude 20; Rom. i. 25; vi. 12—19; vii. 21—25; viii. 1—15; x. 14—21; xi. 1—11; xiii. 7—14; xiv. 1—4; 17—23; 1 Cor. i. 31; ii. 1—11; iii. 10—21; ix. 1—xii. 9; 12; xiii. 13; xiv. 1—4; 8—17; 27; 28; 2 Cor. vi. 1—10; x. 5; xii. 9—21; xiii. 1; Gal. iv. 19; 21—31; v. 1; 22—26; vi. 1—16; Eph. i. 18; iv. 9; 10; 17—32; v. 1—5; Col. iii. 5—17; 1 Thess. iv. 16; 1 Tim. i. 14—20; ii. 1—15; iii. 1—16; v. 21—25; vi. 1—21; 2 Tim. i. 1—16; ii. 19—26; iii. 5; Hebr. ii. 11; 16—18; iii. 1—21; xi. 11—22; xii. 1—9; 18—27; Apoc. i. 8; iii. 7; xx. 4. These very slight reliques of the Apocalypse in the Thebaic are the more interesting, since doubts have been cast on the antiquity of the Memphitic version of it as edited by Wilkins. Mill (*N. T. Proleg.* § 1406) states that none of the Bodleian manuscripts contain that book, though one in the Vatican is said to do so.

Some have referred the use of this version to the East of the Delta (Bashmur), but its affinity with the Thebaic is far closer than with the Memphitic, so that Giorgi, Munter, &c. have fixed on the Oasis of Ammon as its most probable country (vid. *Engelbreth*, *Proleg.* § 3).

There seems no cause for doubting that the Thebaic and Memphitic are independent versions, both made from the Greek, the latter being composed in the more polished and correct style. Yet the superior antiquity of the manuscripts of the Thebaic, and its consequent exemption from the chance of later alterations, bestow on it, so far as it is extant, the higher critical value.

6. The Gothic Version (Goth.).

The history of the Goths, who from the wilds of Scandinavia overran the fairest regions of Europe, has been traced by the master-hand of Gibbon (*Decline and Fall*, Chapters x. xxvi. xxxi., &c.), and need not here be repeated. While the nation was yet seated in Moesia, Ulphilas or Wulfilas [318—388], a Cappadocian, who succeeded their first Bishop Theophilus in A. D. 348, though himself an Arian and a teacher of that subtle heresy to his adopted countrymen, became their benefactor, by translating both the Old[1] and New Testament into the Gothic, a dialect of the great Teutonic stock of languages, having previously invented or adapted an alphabet expressly for their use. There can be no question, from internal evidence, that the Old Testament was rendered from the Septuagint, the New from the Greek original: but the existing manuscripts testify to some corruption from Latin sources, very naturally arising during the occupation of Italy by the Goths in the fifth century. These venerable documents are principally three.

(1) Codex Argenteus, the most precious treasure of the University of Upsal, in the mother-country of the Gothic tribes. It appears to be the same copy as Ant. Morillon saw at Werden in Westphalia towards the end of the sixteenth century, and was taken by the Swedes at the siege of Prague

[1] "But he prudently suppressed the four books of Kings, as they might tend to irritate the fierce and sanguinary spirit of the barbarians." Gibbon, chap. xxxvii.

in 1648. Queen Christina gave it to her librarian, Isaac Vossius, and from him it was very rightly purchased about 1662 by the Swedish nation and deposited at Upsal. This superb codex contains fragments of the Gospels (in the Latin order, Matthew, John, Luke, Mark, see p. 62) on 188 leaves 4to (out of about 320) of purple vellum, the bold, uncial, Gothic letters being in silver, sometimes in gold, of course much faded, and so regular that some have imagined, though erroneously, that they were impressed with a stamp (see p. 111). The date assigned to it is the fifth or early in the sixth century, although the several words are divided, and some various readings stand in the margin *primâ manu*. (2) CODEX CAROLINUS, described above for Codd. PQ (p. 113) and for the Old Latin *gue* (p. 258), contains in Gothic about forty verses of the Epistle to the Romans, first published by Knittel, 1762. (3) Palimpsest fragments of five codices, apparently like Cod. Carolinus, from Bobbio, and of about the same date, discovered by Mai in 1817 in the Ambrosian Library at Milan, and published by him and Count C. O. Castiglione ("*Ulphilae Partium Ineditarum...Specimen*," Milan, 1819). The manuscripts are minutely described and illustrated by a rude *facsimile* in Horne's *Introduction*, and after him in Tregelles' *Horne*, Vol. IV. pp. 304—7. Unlike the Codex Argenteus (at least if we trust Dr E. D. Clarke's *facsimile* of the latter) the words in Mai's palimpsests are continuous: they contain parts of Esther, Nehemiah (apparently no portion of the books of *Kings*), a few passages of the Gospels, and much of St Paul. H. F. Massmann ("*Ulfilas*," Stuttgart, 1855) also added from an exposition a few verses of St John.

These fragments (for such they still must be called)[1], in spite of the influence of the Latin, approach nearer the received text, in respect of their readings, than the Egyptian or one or

[1] Matth. iii. 11; v. 8; 15—vi. 32; vii. 12—x. 1; 23—xi. 25; xxv. 38—xxvi. 3; 65—xxvii. 19; 42—65; Mark. i. 1—xii. 38; xiii. 16—29; xiv. 4—16; 41—xvi. 12; Luke i. 1—x. 30; xiv. 9—xvi. 24; xvii. 3—xx. 46; John i. 29; iii. 3—32; v. 21—23; 35—38; 45—xii. 49; xiii. 11—xix. 13; Rom. vi. 23; vii. 1—viii. 10; 34—xiv. 20; xv. 3—13; xvi. 21—24; 1 Cor. i. 12—25; iv. 2—12; v. 3—vi. 1; vii. 5—28; viii. 9—ix. 9; 19—x. 4; 15—xi. 6; 21—31; xii. 10—22; xiii. 1—12; xiv. 20—Gal. i. 7; 20—iii. 6; 27—Eph. v. 11; 17—29; vi. 8—24; Phil. i. 14—ii. 8; 22—iv. 17; Col. i. 6—29; ii. 11—iv. 19; 1 Thess. ii. 10—2 Thess. ii. 4; 15—1 Tim. vi. 16; 2 Tim. i. 1—iv. 16; Tit. i. 1—ii. 1; Philem. 11—23, but no portion of the Acts, Hebrews, Catholic Epistles, or Apocalypse.

two other versions of about the same age; and from their similiarity in language to the German, have been much studied in that country. The fullest and best edition of the whole collected is by H. C. de Gabelentz and T. Loebe ("*Ulfilas. Vet. et N. Testamenti versionis Gothicae fragmenta quae supersunt*," Leipsic, 1843), and of the Codex Argenteus singly that of And. Uppström (with a good *facsimile*), Upsal, 1854. This scholar published separately in 1857 ten leaves of the manuscript which had been stolen between 1821 and 1834, and were restored through him by the penitent thief on his death-bed. The Gothic Gospels, however, had been cited as early as 1675 in Fell's *N. T.*, and more fully in Mill's, through Francis Junius' edition (with Marshall's critical notes), printed at Dort in 1665, from Derrer's accurate transcript of the Upsal manuscript, made in or about 1655, when it was in Isaac Vossius' possession. Other editions of the Codex Argenteus were published by G. Stiernhielm in 1671: by E. Lye at the Clarendon Press in 1750 from the revision of Eric Benzel, Archbishop of Upsal: and (with the addition of the fragments in the Codex Carolinus) by Jo. Ihre in 1763, and by J. C. Zahn in 1805.

7. The Armenian Version (Arm.).

If the Gothic dates from the fourth century, the Armenian seems to belong to the fifth. Earlier it could not be, as Miesrob, who actually invented an alphabet for his nation, which had previously used the Syriac characters and the Peshito version, was enabled to undertake a vernacular translation direct from the Greek, only by the aid of manuscripts brought from the Council of Ephesus (A. D. 431) by Joseph and Eznak ("Johannes Ekelensis et Josephus Palnensis," as Tischendorf calls them), who, together with the historian of Armenia, Moses Chorenensis, were associated with Miesrob in this godly labour (*Moses Chor.* Lib. III. cap. 61). By the diligence of these men the whole Bible was translated into their native tongue, the Old Testament from the Septuagint, the New (as Louis Piques saw long ago, *Mill, N. T. Proleg.* § 1404) direct from the Greek; although many traces of the influence of the old Syriac yet survive, as might be expected from the early habits of the translators. Two circumstances detract considerably from the critical value of this version, even to the few who can use it with confidence; viz. that like the Memphitic its existing codices are comparatively modern, and differ widely in the text they represent; and that their very close resemblance to the Vulgate Latin has lent countenance to a tradition, in itself sufficiently probable, that on the submission of the Armenian Church to that of Rome, King Haitho (1224—70) revised the Armenian version by the Latin: it seems to be ascertained that he did translate into Armenian and insert into his national Bible the Prefaces in the Vulgate which are ascribed to Jerome.

The first printed edition of the Armenian Bible is that of Bishop Uscan or Oscan of Erivan, who had been sent into the West for that purpose by a synod of Armenian prelates in 1662, under the sanction of their Patriarch (arm. usc.). After vain attempts to obtain aid at Rome, Uscan (whether that be a proper name or a local appellative) published his volume at Amsterdam in 1666, from which were derived several reprints, and the various readings furnished to Mill by Piques, and to Wetstein by La Croze. The *best* edition is that of Zohrab, *N. T.* 1789, *Biblia*, 1805 (arm. zoh.), on the basis of a Cilician codex [XIV], compared with twenty others of the N. T., and eight of the whole Bible, printed at Venice at the expense of the Armenian College of the monks of the island of St Lazarus. This last edition Griesbach was enabled to use for critical purposes by the help of Bredenkamp of Hamburg; Scholz, by means of Cirbied, Armenian Professor at Paris, and the Mechitarist monks at Vienna; Tregelles, through the aid of a close comparison with the Greek text, instituted for him by Dr Charles Rieu of the British Museum. It should be added that Zohrab does not acknowledge any systematic corruption of the Armenian from the Latin Bible, and that only one of his eighteen copies of the Epistle contains 1 John v. 7, which had appeared in Uscan's book. Aucher of St Lazarus informed Tischendorf in 1843 that his Society was preparing another edition of the Bible, from fresh and (we may trust) more ancient authorities.

8. THE ÆTHIOPIC VERSION (Æth.).

The Æthiopic language is akin to the Arabic and others of the Shemitic family; it was formerly spoken in Abyssinia, especially in the province of Axoum (where it was called *Gheez*, or "the free," Walton, *Proleg.* XV. c. 10), though it has now given place to a later dialect, the Amharic. Without resting on the rhetorical statement of Chrysostom, that in his time the Scriptures had been translated into the tongues of the Syrian and Egyptian, *the Indian*, the Persian and Æthiopian, and "ten thousand other nations[1]," such a version must have been much needed shortly after the conversion of the Abyssinians by Frumentius in the fourth century. Dillmann attributes it to that age: Gildemeister, however, and other Orientalists, assign it to the sixth or seventh century, and its surviving codices are even more modern [XV] than those of the Memphitic or Armenian. The Old Testament (which has not yet been published in full) was made from the Septuagint (Walt. *Proleg.* XV. c. 10, III.), the New Testament obviously from the Greek and by a person imperfectly acquainted with that language, though Gildemeister, a Professor at Marburg (who collated portions of the Æthiopic for Tischendorf's *N. T.* of 1859), remarks that it must in that case have been largely interpolated from Syriac or Arabic sources. In fact the version is so tautological, confused, and unequal in style (that of St Paul in particular often degenerating into a paraphrase), that some have thought our present text to be a compound of two several translations, and even Tregelles supposes that "there was originally *one version* of the Gospels, afterwards compared with Greek MSS. of a *different* class; and the MSS. in general bearing proofs of containing a text *modified* by such comparison; while others contain throughout *conflate* readings" (Tregelles' *Horne,* Vol. IV. p. 320). It is obvious how great caution is needed in applying this version to the criticism of the N. T. Yet this was the earliest printed of all the Eastern versions. The Psalms were published at Rome, 1513; the New Testament (except the first thirteen Epistles of St Paul, which followed the year after) at Rome, 1548, by native editors ("Memores estote nostrum...Tesfa-Sionis Malhesini, Tensea Waldi, et Zaslaski," as runs the subscription to St Matthew), who for

[1] Ἀλλὰ καὶ Σύροι καὶ Αἰγύπτιοι καὶ Ἰνδοὶ καὶ Πέρσαι καὶ Αἰθίοπες καὶ μύρια ἕτερα ἔθνη, εἰς τὴν αὐτῶν μεταβαλόντες γλῶτταν τὰ παρὰ τούτου δόγματα εἰσαχθέντα, ἔμαθον βάρβαροι φιλοσοφεῖν. II Hom. in Johan., Opera (Montfaucon) Tom. VIII. p. 10.

want of manuscripts themselves translated Act. ix. 29—x. 32; xxvi. 8—xxviii. 31. In Walton's Polyglott the New Testament was reprinted with many faults, and an unusually bad Latin translation by Dudley Loftus, from which Mill and his successors derived their various readings. C. A. Bode published a new or revised version of the Æthiopic N. T. given in the Polyglott (Brunswick, 1753), and in what he good-naturedly calls his "*Pseudo-critica Millio-Bengeliana*" (Halle, 1767—9), corrects some of the errors of those great scholars. Lastly, in 1826—30 in London, Th. Pell Platt, A.M., edited for the British and Foreign Bible Society, "*Nov. Testament... Æthiopicè, ad codicum manuscriptorum fidem.*" Respecting these codices and their readings, at least in the Gospels, Mr Platt gave Tregelles some loose notes, and the latter engaged L. A. Prevost, of the British Museum, to collate Walton's and Platt's texts with the Greek for the use of his N. T., as Tischendorf is similarly indebted to Gildemeister. Mr Platt's edition, being purely of a practical character, is so unsystematic in its employment of manuscripts as to be nearly useless to Biblical critics.

The remaining versions may sometimes be consulted with advantage for a special object, but for the general purposes of critical science they are of little weight. A very short notice will suffice for all of them.

9. THE GEORGIAN (Georg.) or Iberian (Iber.) version of the whole Bible, assigned to the sixth century, is written in a language very little known, and was published at Moscow in 1743 from manuscripts said to be extensively corrupted from the Slavonic. It is doubtful whether it was made from the Greek or Armenian. Both Scholz and Tischendorf saw ancient and perhaps purer codices at the monastery of the Holy Cross at Jerusalem, which may afford us a hope of restoring this version to something like its primitive state. J. H. Petermann edited Philemon as a specimen (Berlin, 1844), and from F. C. Alter's description of its readings (*Ueber Georgianische Literat.*, 1798) it appears that the present text contains even such plain interpolations as 1 John v. 7.

10. THE SLAVONIC VERSION (Sl.), though made as late as the ninth century, was rendered from the best Greek codices of that age, although it would seem to have been subsequently altered from the Latin; or (as Tischendorf thinks) from other sources. Two Greek brothers, Cyril and Methodius, converted about A.D. 870, those tribes of the great Slavonic race that were settled about the Danube in Moravia and its neighbourhood. They then proceeded to translate the Bible (or certainly the New Testament) into Slavonic, for which barbarous tongue Cyril (like Ulfilas and Miesrob before him) had previously constructed an alphabet. This version was brought into Russia on the conversion of Wladimir, its Grand Duke, in 988, in which country it received many changes (perhaps with a view to modernise the style) from the fourteenth century downwards. The oldest manuscript of the *whole* Bible is dated 1499, and the first printed Bible, 1581. Of the New Testament there are many codices, of widely differing recensions, some few as old as the tenth or eleventh century; e.g. an Evangelistarium, dated 1056, and the Gospels at Rheims [x], on which the Kings of France used to take the coronation oath. These were fully described and in part collated by J. Dobrowsky for Griesbach's *N. T.*, 2nd ed. See also Tischendorf, *N. T.*, 7th ed. Proleg. pp. 253—5.

11. ANGLO-SAXON VERSIONS (Sax.) of the New Testament and parts of the Old (e. g. the Psalms) were numerous and apparently independent, dating from the eighth to the eleventh century, but can only be applied to the criticism of the Latin Vulgate, from which they are all rendered. Manuscripts in this language abound in English libraries (Tischendorf names one in the British Museum with the interlinear Latin, which he attributes to the eighth century), but even of the N. T. the Gospels alone are printed. For them Mill uses Marshall's edition of 1665 in parallel columns with the Gothic (*see* p. 276), and Tischendorf that published by Benj. Thorpe, London, 1842.

12. A FRANKISH VERSION (Fr.) of St Matthew, from a manuscript of the ninth century at St Gall, in the Frankish dialect of the Teutonic, was published by J. A. Schmeller in 1827. Tischendorf (*Proleg. N. T.* p. 225) thinks it worthy of

examination, but does not state whether it was translated from the Greek or Latin: the latter is the more probable.

13. PERSIC VERSIONS (Pers.) of the Gospels only, in print, are two: (1) one in Walton's *Polyglott* ($pers^p$) with a Latin version by Samuel Clarke (which C. A. Bode thought it worth his while to reconstruct, Helmstadt, 1750—51, with a learned Preface), obviously made from the Peshito Syriac (which the Persians had long used) "interprete Symone F. Joseph Taurinensi," and taken from a single manuscript belonging to E. Pococke, *probably* dated A.D. 1341. This version may prove of some use in restoring the text of the Peshito. (2) The second, though apparently modern [XIV?], was made from the Greek ($pers^w$). It was commenced in 1652 by Abraham Wheelocke, Professor of Arabic and Anglo-Saxon and University Librarian at Cambridge, at the expense of Sir Th. Adams, the generous and loyal alderman of London. The basis (as appears from the volume itself) was an Oxford codex (probably Laud. A. 96 of the old notation), which Wheelocke, in his elaborate notes at the end of each chapter, compared with Pococke's and a third manuscript at Cambridge (Gg. v. 26), dated 1014 of the Hegira (A.D. 1607). On Wheelocke's death in 1653 only 108 pages (to Matth. xviii. 6) were printed, but his whole text and Latin version being found ready for the press, the book was published with a second title page, dated London, 1657, and a short Preface by an anonymous editor (said to be one Pierson), who in lieu of Wheelocke's notes, which break off after Matth. xvii, appended a simple collation of the Pococke manuscript from that place. The Persians have older versions, parts of both Testaments, still unpublished.

14. ARABIC VERSIONS (Arab.) are many, though of the slightest possible critical importance: their literary history, therefore, need not be traced with much minuteness of detail. It is known that John, Bishop of Seville, translated the Bible (from the Latin Vulgate, it is thought) into Arabic, A.D. 719 (Walton, *Proleg.* XIV. c. 18), and Tischendorf enumerates several manuscripts brought by himself and others from the East, assigned by competent judges to the eighth and following centuries (*N. T. Proleg.* 1859, pp. 236—9). The printed edi-

tions of the New Testament portion are, (1) The Roman edition of the Gospels, from the Medicean press, 1590—1 (ar^{r}), edited by J. Baptista Raymundi, some copies having a Latin version by Gabriel Sionita, who was engaged on the work described below as (3) fifty years later (Mill, *Proleg.* § 1295). T. W. J. Juynboll (Leyden, 1838) holds that this edition, and the text of a Franeker codex of the Gospels, belong to the version of John of Seville. (2) The whole N. T., from a Scaliger manuscript, and (in the Gospels) from a second dated 988 of the aera of the Martyrs, or A.D. 1272[1], edited at Leyden by Th. Erpenius [1584—1624] in 1616 (ar^{e}). (3) The N. T. of the Paris Polyglott (ar^{p}), 1645. (4) The N. T. in the London Polyglott, 1657. (5) The N. T., Peshito and Arabic, in the Carshunic character (i. e. the Arabic in Syriac letters, *see* p. 245), Rome, 1703, based on a manuscript brought from Cyprus. Editions published by the Propaganda, *Biblia*, Rome, 1672, and altered from the Latin, and by our venerable Society for Promoting Christian Knowledge, *N. T.*, London, 1727, and altered from the original Greek, both designed for circulation in the East, need not be considered.

Since the *Dissertatio inaug. critica de Evan. Arab.* of G. C. Storr appeared (Tübingen, 1775) it seems to have been acknowledged that the several published editions of the Gospels have sprung from one version, and that taken from the Greek, though now sadly mixed and confused: Juynboll, however, has rendered it probable that its original was the Latin, which was subsequently corrected by the Greek. The Acts and Epistles in Erpenius' N. T. were certainly made from the Peshito; his Apocalypse seems to have been derived from the Memphitic: but in both Polyglotts all except the Gospels are undoubtedly from the Greek. A list of Greek manuscripts attended with Arabic versions is given above, p. 225.

[1] This manuscript of the Gospels only, together with seventy others which once belonged to Erpenius, was bought for the University of Cambridge by its Chancellor, George Villiers, Duke of Buckingham, just before his murder in 1628. It is now in the University Library, Gg. v. 33, and in the margin of its subscription we find "·i· anno Christi 1272" in Erpenius' handwriting. Pr. Lee (who did not know its history) inferred its identity with Erpenius' codex from the subscription, and other internal marks (*Prolegomena to Bagster's Polyglott*, p. 31, note). There is a second copy of the Gospels in the same Library, Gg. v. 27, with an inscription by the Patriarch Cyril Lucar (*see* p. 79), dated 1618.

*

CHAPTER IV.

ON THE CITATIONS FROM THE GREEK NEW TESTAMENT, OR ITS VERSIONS, MADE BY EARLY ECCLESIASTICAL WRITERS, ESPECIALLY BY THE CHRISTIAN FATHERS.

---

1. WE might at first sight be inclined to suppose that the numerous quotations from the New Testament contained in the remains of the Fathers of the Church and other Christian writers from the first century of our æra downwards, would be more useful even than the early versions, for enabling us to determine the character of the text of Scripture current in those primitive times, from which no manuscripts of the original have come down to us. Unquestionably the testimony afforded by these venerable writings will be free from some of the objections which so much diminish the value of translations for critical purposes (*see above*, p. 228); but not to insist on the fact that many important passages of the New Testament have not been cited at all in any very ancient work now extant, this species of evidence will be received with increasing distrust, the more familiar we become with its uncertain and precarious nature. Not only is this kind of testimony fragmentary and not (like that of versions) continuous, so that it often fails us where we should most wish for information: but the Fathers were better theologians than critics; they frequently quoted loosely or from memory, often no more of a passage than their immediate purpose required; what they actually wrote has been found peculiarly liable to change on the part of copyists and unskilful editors; they can therefore be implicitly trusted, even as to the manuscripts which lay before them, only in the comparatively few places wherein their own direct appeal to

their codices, or the course of their argument, or the current of their exposition, renders it manifest what readings they approved. In other cases, the same author perpetually cites the self-same text under two or more various forms; in the Gospels it is often impossible to determine to which of the three earlier ones reference is made; and, on the whole, Scriptural quotations from ecclesiastical writers are of so much less consideration than ancient translations, that where they are single and unsupported, they may safely be disregarded altogether. An *express* citation, however, by a really careful Father of the first four or five centuries (as Origen, for example), if supported by manuscript authority, and countenanced by the best versions, claims our respectful attention, and powerfully vindicates the reading which it favours.

2. The practice of illustrating the various readings of Scripture from the reliques of Christian antiquity is so obvious and reasonable, that all who have written critical annotations on the sacred text have resorted to it, from Erasmus downwards: the Greek or Latin commentators are appealed to in four out of the five marginal notes found in the Complutensian N.T. (see below, p. 290). When Bishop Fell, however, came to prepare the first edition of the Greek Testament attended with any considerable apparatus for improving the text (see Chapter v.), he expressly rejected "S. Textus loca ab antiquis Patribus aliter quam pro recepto more laudata," from which the toil of such a task did not so much deter him, "quam cogitatio quod minus utile esset futurum iisdem insistere." (*N. T.* 1675, *Praef.*). "Venerandi enim illi scriptores," he adds, "de verborum apicibus non multum soliciti, ex memoriâ quae ad institutum suum factura videbantur passim allegabant; unde factum ut de priscâ lectione ex illorum scriptis nil ferè certi potuerit hauriri." It is certainly to the credit of Mill's sagacity that he did not follow his patron's example by setting aside Patristic testimony in so curt and compendious a manner, yet I would not speak with him (*N. T. Proleg.* § 1478) of Bp. Fell's "praepropera opinio": he merely stated as *universally* true what for the most part certainly is so. No one can study Mill's *Prolegomena* without being conscious of the fact, that the portion of them relating to the history of the text, as gathered from ecclesiastical writers, and the accumulation of that mass of quotations from

the Fathers which stands below his Scripture text, must have been, what he asserts, the result of some years' labour (*N. T. Proleg.* § 1513): yet these are just the parts of his celebrated work that have given the least satisfaction. The field indeed is too vast to be occupied by one man, or by many men, within the space of a few years. A whole library of authors has to be thoroughly searched; each cited passage must be patiently examined; the fallacious help of *indices* should be renounced; the text of the very writers is to be corrected, so far as may be, by the collation of better manuscripts than the printed editions are usually based upon; and all this with the knowledge that codices of the Fathers are for the most part of much lower date than those of Scripture which we desire to amend by their aid; not many are older than the tenth century, the far greater part are considerably more modern.

3. To Griesbach must be assigned the merit of being the earliest editor of the Greek Testament who saw, or at least who acted upon the principle, that it is far more profitable as well as more scholarlike to do one thing well, than to attempt more than can be performed completely and with accuracy. He was led by certain textual theories he had adopted (which we shall best describe hereafter: see Chapter v.) to a close examination of the works of Origen, the most celebrated Biblical critic of antiquity. The result, published in the second volume of his *Symbolae Criticae*, is a lasting monument both of his industry and acuteness; and, if not quite faultless in point of correctness, deserves to be taken as a model by his successors. What Griesbach has done for Origen, has hitherto not been imitated by others for writers of little less importance, such as Clement of Alexandria, or Eusebius, Athanasius or the Cyrils; and until that be accomplished, we cannot use the citations derived from their works with any high degree of confidence. Tregelles, of whose Greek Testament we shall presently speak (Chapter v.), has evidently bestowed much pains on his Patristic citations; they are at once more definite, more numerous, and yet more select than those of his predecessors; to Eusebius of Caesarea, especially to those portions of his works which have been recently edited or brought to light, he has paid great attention: Chrysostom, however, has been grievously neglected, although the subjects of a large portion of his writings, the

early date of some of his codices[1], the extensive collations of Matthaei, and the excellent modern editions of most of his Homilies, might have sufficed to commend him to our particular regard. The custom, commenced by Lachmann, and adopted by Tregelles (though not as yet uniformly by Tischendorf), of recording the exact edition, volume, and page of the writer quoted, and in important cases of copying his very words, cannot be too much praised: we would suggest, however, the expediency of further indicating by an asterisk or some such mark, those passages about which there can be no ambiguity as to the reading adopted by the author, in order to distinguish them from others which are of infinitely less weight and importance.

4. It may be convenient to subjoin an alphabetical list of the ecclesiastical writers, both Greek and Latin (with the usual abridgements for their names), which are the most often cited in critical editions of the New Testament. The Latin authors are printed in italics, and unless they happen to appeal unequivocally to the evidence of Greek codices, are available only for the correction of their vernacular translation. The dates annexed *chiefly* indicate the death of persons they refer to. Fuller details are given by Tischendorf, *Proleg. N. T.* pp. 257—69, 7th edition.

Ambrose Bp. of Milan, A.D. 397 (Ambr.)
Ambrosiaster (the false Ambrose, perhaps *Hilary* the Deacon)—fl. 384? (Ambrst.)
Ammonius of Alexandria, 220 (Ammon.)
Andreas of Crete, 7th century (probably not the same person as)
Andreas Bishop of Caesarea, 6th century? (And.)
Arethas Bp of Caesarea Capp., 10th century? (Areth.)
Arnobius of Africa, 306 (Arnob.)
Athanasius Bp. of Alexandria, 373 (Ath.)
Athenagoras of Athens, 177 (Athen.)
Augustine Bp. of Hippo, 430 (Aug.)
Barnabas, 1st or 2nd century? (Barn.)
Basil Bp. of Caesarea, 379 (Bas.)
Basil of Seleucia, fl. 440 (Bas. Sel.)
Bede the Venerable, d. 735 (Bede).
Caesarius of Constantinople, 368 (Caes.)
Canons Apostolic, 3rd century (Canon.)
Cassiodorus, 575 (Cassiod.)
Chromatius Bp. of Aquileia, 402 (Chrom.)
Chrysostom Bp. of Constantinople, 407 (Chrys.)
Clement Bp. of Alexandria, fl. 194 (Clem.)
Clement Bp. of Rome, fl. 90 (Clem. Rom.)
Constitutiones Apostolicae, 3rd century (Constit.)

[1] Tischendorf (*N. T. Proleg.* p. 256, 7th edition) speaks of one Wolfenbüttel manuscript containing the homilies on St Matthew of the sixth century, which he is to publish in his *Monum. sacra*, Tom. v.

Cosmas Indicopleustes, 535 (Cosm.)
Cyprian Bp. of Carthage, 258 (Cypr.)
Cyril Bp. of Alexandria, 444 (Cyr.)
Cyril Bp. of Jerusalem, 386 (Cyr. Jer.)
Damascenus John, 730 (Damasc.)
Didymus of Alexandria, 370 (Did.)
Dionysius Bp. of Alexandria, 265 (Dion.)
Dionysius (Pseudo-) Areopagita, 5th century (Dion. Areop.)
Ephraem the Syrian, 378 (Ephr.)
Epiphanius Bp. of Cyprus, 403 (Epiph.)
Eusebius Bp. of Caesarea, 340 (Eus.)
Euthalius Bp. of Sulci? 458 (Euthal.)
Euthymius Zigabenus, 1116 (Euthym.)
Evagrius of Pontus, 380 (Evagr.)
Gregory the Great Bp. of Rome, 605 (Greg.)
Gregory Bp. of Nazianzus, 389 (Naz.)
Gregory Bp. of Nyssa, 371 (Nyss.)
Gregory Thaumaturgus Bp. of Neocaesarea, 243 (Thauma.)
Hieronymus (Jerome), 430 (Hier.) or (Jer.)
Hilary Bp. of Poictiers, fl. 354 (Hil.)
Hippolytus Bp. of Portus, fl. 220 (Hip.)
Ignatius Bp. of Antioch, 107 (Ign.)
Irenaeus Bp. of Lyons, 178; chiefly extant in an old Latin version (Iren.)
Isidore of Pelusium, 412 (Isid.)
Justin Martyr, 164 (Just.)
Juvencus, 330 (Juv.)
Lactantius, 306 (Lact.)
Lucifer Bp. of Cagliari, 367 (Luc.)
Marcion the heretic, 130? (Mcion), cited by Epiphanius (Mcion-e) and *Tertullian* (Mcion-*t*).
Maximus Taurinensis, 466 (Max. Taur.)
Maximus the Confessor, 662 (Max. Conf.)
Methodius, fl. 300 (Meth.)
Oecumenius Bishop of Tricca, 10th century? (Oecu.)
Origen, b. 185, d. 254 (Or.)
Pamphilus the Martyr, 308 (Pamph.)
Peter Bp. of Alexandria, 311 (Petr.)
Photius Bp. of Constantinople, 891 (Phot.)
Polycarp Bp. of Smyrna, 166 (Polyc.)
Primasius Bp. of Adrumetum, fl. 550 (Prim.)
Prudentius 406 (Prud.)
Rufinus of Aquileia, 397 (Ruf.)
Severianus, a Syrian Bp., 409 (Sevrn.)
Socrates } Church } fl. 440 (Soc.)
Sozomen } Historians, } 450 (Soz.)
Suidas the lexicographer, 980? (Suid.)
Tatian of Antioch, 172 (Tat.)
Tertullian of Africa, fl. 200 (Tert.)
Theodore Bp. of Mopsuestia, 428 (Thdor. Mops.)
Theodoret Bp. of Cyrus or Cyrrhus in Comagene, 458 (Thdrt.)
Theophilus Bp. of Antioch, 182 (Thph. Ant.)
Theophylact Arch. of Bulgaria, 1071 (Theophyl.)
Tichonius? the Donatist, fl. 390 (Tich.)
Titus Bp. of Bostra, fl. 370 (Tit. Bost.)
Victor of Antioch, 401 (Vict. Ant.)
Victor Bp. of Tunis, 565 (Vict. Tun.)
Victorinus Bp. of Pettau, 303 (Victorin.)
Vigilius of Thapsus, 484 (Vigil.)

CHAPTER V.

ON THE EARLY PRINTED, AND LATER CRITICAL EDITIONS OF THE GREEK NEW TESTAMENT.

IT would be quite foreign to our present design, to attempt to notice all the editions of the New Testament in Greek which have appeared in the course of the last three centuries and a half, nor would a volume suffice for such a labour. We will limit our attention, therefore, to those early editions which have contributed to form our commonly received text, and to such others of more recent date as not only exhibit a revised text, but contain an accession of fresh critical materials for its more complete emendation.

Since the Latin Bible of 1452 was the first production of the new-born printing-press (*see* p. 262), and the Jews had published the Hebrew Bible in 1488, we must impute it to the general ignorance of Greek among divines in Western Europe, that although the two songs *Magnificat* and *Benedictus* (Luke i.) were annexed to a Greek Psalter which appeared at Venice in 1486, and the first six chapters of St John's Gospel were published at Venice by Aldus Manutius in 1504, and John vi. 1—14 at Tübingen in 1514, the first *printed* edition of the whole N. T. in the original is that contained in

1. THE COMPLUTENSIAN POLYGLOTT[1] (6 Vol. folio), the munificent design of Francis Ximenes de Cisneros [1437—1517] Cardinal Archbishop of Toledo, and Regent of Castile (1506—17). This truly eminent person, six years of whose humble youth were spent in a dungeon through the caprice of

[1] Novum Testamentum Grece et Latine in academia complutensi noviter impressum, Tom. v.

one of his predecessors in the Primacy of Spain, experienced what we have seen so conspicuously illustrated in our own times, that long imprisonment ripens the intellect which it fails to extinguish. Entering the Franciscan order in 1482, he carried the ascetic habit of his profession to the throne of Toledo and the palace of his sovereign. Becoming in 1492 Confessor to Queen Isabella the Catholic, and Primate three years later, he devoted to pure charity or to public purposes the enormous revenues of his see; founding the University at Alcala de Henares in New Castile, where he had gone to school, and defraying the cost of an expedition which as Regent he led to Oran against the Moors. In 1502 he conceived the plan of the first Polyglott Bible, to celebrate the birth of him who afterwards became the Emperor Charles V., and gathered in his University of Alcala (*Complutum*) as many manuscripts as he could procure, with men he deemed equal to the task, of whom James Lopez de Stunica (subsequently known for his controversy with Erasmus) was the principal; others being Æ. Antonio of Lebrixa, Demetrius Ducas of Crete, and Ferdinand of Valladolid ("*Pintianus*"). The whole outlay of Cardinal Ximenes on the Polyglott is stated to have exceeded 50,000 ducats or about £23,000, a vast sum in those days:—but his yearly income as Primate was four times as great. The first volume printed, Tom. v., contained the New Testament in two parallel columns, Greek and Latin, the latter that modification of the Vulgate then current: the colophon on the last page of the Apocalypse states that it was completed January 10, 1514, the printer being Arnald William de Brocario. Tom. vi., comprising a Lexicon, indices, &c. bears date March 17, 1515; Tom. i—iv. of the Old Testament and Apocrypha, 1517, (Tom. iv., July 10), on November 8 of which year the Cardinal died, full of honours and good deeds. This event must have retarded the publication of the whole, since Pope Leo's licence was not granted until March 22, 1520, and Erasmus did not see the book before 1522. As but six hundred copies were printed, this Polyglott must from the first have been scarce and dear, and is not always met with in Public Libraries.

The Apocryphal books, like the N. T., are of course given only in two languages; in the Old Testament the Latin Vulgate holds the chief place in the middle, between the Hebrew and the Septuagint Greek[1]. The Greek type in the other volumes is of the common character, with the usual breathings and accents; in the fifth, or New Testament volume, it is quite different, being modelled after the fashion of manuscripts of about the thirteenth century, very bold and elegant (see Plate IX. No. 37), without breathings, and accentuated according to a system defended and explained in a bilingual preface πρὸς τοὺς ἐντευξομένους, but never heard of before or since: monosyllables have no accent, in other words the *tone* syllable receives the acute, the grave and circumflex being discarded. The Latin is in a noble church-character, references are made from the one text to the other by means of small letters, and where in either column there is a void space, in consequence of words omitted or otherwise, it is filled up by such curves as are seen in the bottom line of our specimen. The foreign matter in this volume consists of the short Preface in Latin and Greek, Eusebius Carpiano (but without the Canons), Jerome's letter to Damasus (*see* pp. 252, 261), with the ordinary Latin Prologues and Arguments before each book. St Paul's Epistles precede the Acts, as in Codd. ℵ. 61. 69. 90, &c. (*see* p. 61), and before them stand the ἀποδημία παύλου, Euthalii περὶ χρόνων (*see* p. 57), the ordinary ὑποθέσεις to all the 21 Epistles (grouped together), with Theodoret's *prologues* subjoined to 13 of the ὑποθέσεις. By the side of the Latin text are numerous parallel passages, and there are also five marginal notes (on Matth. vi. 13; 1 Cor. xiii. 3; xv. 31; 51; 1 John v. 7). The only divisions are the common Latin chapters, subdivided by the letters A, B, C, D, &c. (*see* p. 59). Copies of laudatory verses[2], an interpretation of Proper Names, and a Greek Lexicon of the N. T. close the volume.

[1] Quite enough has been made of that piece of grim Spanish humour, "Mediam autem inter has latinam beati Hieronymi translationem velut inter Synagogam et Orientalem Ecclesiam posuimus: tanquam duos hinc et inde latrones, medium autem Jesum, hoc est Romanam sive latinam Ecclesiam collocantes" (Prol. Tom. I.). The editors plainly meant no disparagement to the original Scriptures, *as such;* but they had persuaded themselves that Hebrew codices had been corrupted by the Jew, the Septuagint by the schismatical Greek, and so clung to the Latin as the only form (even before the Council of Trent) in which the Bible was known or studied in Western Europe.

[2] Of these, two copies are in Greek, three in Latin Elegiacs. I subjoin those of the native Greek editor, Demetrius Ducas, as a rather favourable specimen of verse composition in that age: the fantastic mode of accentuation described above was clearly not *his* work.

It has long been debated among critics, what manuscripts were used by the Complutensian editors, especially in the N. T. Ximenes is reported to have spent 4000 ducats in the purchase of manuscripts; in the Preface to the N. T. we are assured that "non quevis exemplaria impressioni huic archetypa fuisse: sed antiquissima emendatissimaque: ac tante preterea vetustatis: ut fidem eis abrogare nefas videatur: Que sanctissimus in Christo pater et dominus noster Leo decimus pontifex maximus, huic instituto favere cupiens ex apostolica bibliotheca educta misit..." Yet these last expressions can hardly refer to the N.T., inasmuch as Leo X. was not elected Pope till March 11, 1513, and the N. T. was *completed* Jan. 10 of the very next year[1]. Add to this that Vercellone, whose services to sacred literature have been spoken of above (pp. 91—2) has recently brought to light the fact that only two manuscripts are known to have been sent to the Cardinal from the Vatican in the first year of Leo, and neither of them (Vat. 330, 346) contained any part of the N. T.[2] The only one of the Complutensian codices specified by Stunica, the Cod. Rhodiensis (Act. 52, *see* p. 190), has entirely disappeared, and from a Catalogue of the thirty volumes of Biblical manuscripts once in the library at Alcala, but now at Madrid, communicated in 1846 by Don José Gutierrez, the Librarian, we find that they consist exclusively of Latin and

Ειπράξεις ὅσιαι ἀρετῆτε βροτοὺς ἐς ὄλυμπον,
ἐσμακάρων χῶρον καὶ βίον οἶδεν ἄγειν,
ἀρχιερεὺς ξιμένης θεῖος πέλει. ἔργα γὰρ αὐτοῦ
ἥδε βίβλος. θνητοῖς ἄξια δῶρα τάδε.

[1] Tregelles (*Account of the Printed Text*, p. 7, note) states that he was *elected* Febr. 28, crowned March 11: Sir Harris Nicholas (*Chronology of History*, p. 194) that he was elected March 11, without naming the date of his coronation as usual, but mentioning that "Leo X, in his letters, dated the commencement of his pontificate before his coronation."

[2] The following is the document (a curiosity in its way) as cited by Vercellone: "Anno primo Leonis PP. X. Reverendiss. Dom. Franciscus Card. Toletanus de mandato SS. D. N. Papae habuit ex bibliotheca a Dom. Phaedro Bibliothecario duo volumina graeca: unum in quo continentur libri infrascripti; videlicet Proverbia Salomonis, Ecclesiastes, Cant. Cant., Job, Sapientia, Ecclesiasticus, Esdras, Tobias, Judith. Sunt in eo folia quingenta et duodecim ex papyro in nigro. Fuit extractum ex blancho primo bibliothecae graecae communis. Mandatum Pontificis super concessione dictorum librorum registratum fuit in Camera Apostolica per D. Franciscum De Attavantes Notarium, ubi etiam annotata est obligatio. Promisit restituere intra annum sub poena ducentorum ducatorum."—"Restituit die 9 Julii, MDXVIII. Ita est. Fr. Zenobius Bibliothecarius."

Hebrew books, with the exception of two which contain portions of the Septuagint in Greek[1]. Thus we seem cut off from all hope of obtaining direct information as to the age, character and present locality of the materials employed for the Greek text of this edition.

It is obvious, however, that in the course of twelve years (1502—14), Ximenes may have obtained *transcripts* of codices he did not himself possess, and since some of the more remarkable readings of the Complutensian are found in but one or two manuscripts (e. g. Luke i. 64 in Codd. 140, 251; ii. 22 in Cod. 76), such copies should of course be narrowly watched. We have pointed out above (p. 190) the resemblance that Seidel's codex (Act. 42, Paul. 48, Apoc. 13) bears to this edition: see too Cod. 4 of the Gospels. Mill first noticed its affinity to Laud. 2 or Evan. 51, Act. 32, Paul. 38 (*see* p. 147), and though this is somewhat remote in the Gospels, throughout the Acts and Epistles it is close and indubitable[2]. We see, therefore, no cause for believing that either Cod. B, or any manuscript much resembling it in character, or any other document of high antiquity or first-rate importance, was employed by the editors of this Polyglott. The text it exhibits does not widely differ from that of most codices written from the tenth century downwards.

That it was corrupted from the parallel Latin version was contended by Wetstein and others on very insufficient grounds.

[1] The Catalogue is copied at length by Tregelles (*Account of the Printed Text*, pp. 15—18). It is scarcely worth while to repeat the silly story taken up by Moldenhawer, whose admiration of *las cosas de España* was not extravagantly high, that the Alcala manuscripts had been sold to make sky-rockets about 1749; to which Sir John Bowring pleasantly adds in 1819, "To celebrate the arrival of some worthless grandee." Gutierrez's recent list comprehends all the codices named in the University Catalogue made in 1745; and we may hope that the Governor of Hong Kong no longer believes that *all* grandees are worthless.

[2] Thus in St Mark the Complutensian varies from Laud. 2 in 51 places, and nowhere agrees with it except in company with a mass of other copies. In the Acts on the contrary they agree 139 times, and differ but 41, some of their *loci singulares* being quite decisive: e. g. x. 17; 21; xii. 12; xvii. 31; xx. 38; xxiv. 16; 1 Pet. iii. 12; 14; 2 Pet. i. 11. In most of these places Seidel's Codex, in some of them Act. 69, and *in nearly all* Cod. Havn. 1 (Evan. 234, Act. 57, Paul. 72) are with Laud. 2. On testing this last at the Bodleian in some forty places, I found Mill's collation reasonably accurate. As might have been expected, his Oxford manuscripts were examined much the best.

Even the Latinism βεελζεβοὺβ Matth. x. 25, seems a mere inadvertence, and is corrected immediately afterwards (xii. 24, 27), as well as in the four other places wherein it is used. We need not deny that 1 John v. 7 was interpolated, and probably translated from the Vulgate, and a few other cases have a suspicious look (Rom. xvi. 5; 2 Cor. v. 10; vi. 15; and especially Gal. iii. 19); the articles too are employed as if they were unfamiliar to the editor (e. g. Acts xxi. 4; 8): yet we must emphatically deny that on the whole the Latin Vulgate had an appreciable effect upon the Greek. This point had been demonstrated to the satisfaction of Michaelis and of Marsh by Goeze[1], in whose short tract many readings of Cod. Laud. 2 are also examined. In the more exact collation of the N. T. which we have made with the common text (*Elzevir* 1624), and which will be printed in the Appendix to the present Chapter, out of 2777 places *in all*, wherein the Complutensian edition differs from that of Elzevir (viz. 1046 in the Gospels, 576 in the Pauline Epistles, 541 in the Acts and Catholic Epistles, 614 in the Apocalypse), in no less than 849 (distinguished in our collation by †) the Latin is at variance with the Greek; in the majority of the rest the difference cannot be expressed in another language. Since the Complutensian N. T. could only have been published from manuscripts, it deserves more minute examination than it has received from Mill or Wetstein; and it were much to be desired that similar collations could be made of several other early editions, especially the five of Erasmus.

Since this Polyglott has been said to be very inaccurately printed, it is necessary to state that we have noted just 50 pure errors of the press; in one place, moreover (Hebr. vii. 3), the Euthalian κεφάλαιον has crept into the text. All the usual peculiarities observable in later manuscripts are here, e.g. 224 itacisms (chiefly ω for ο, η for ει, ει for ι, υ for η, οι for ει, and *vice versâ*); 32 instances of ν ἐφελκυστικόν, or the superabundant ν, before a consonant; 15 instances of the hiatus for the lack of ν before a vowel; ουτως is sometimes found before a consonant, but ουτω 68 times; ουκ and ουχ are interchanged 12 times. The following forms, found in many manuscripts, and here retained,

[1] Goeze's "Defence of the Complutensian Bible" 1766 was not added to the Library of the British Museum till 1857. He published a "Continuation" in 1769.

may shew that the grammatical forms of the Greek were not yet settled among scholars; παρήγγελεν Mark vi. 8; διάγγελε Luke ix. 60; καταγγέλειν Acts iv. 2; διαγγέλων Acts xxi. 26; καταγγέλων 1 Cor. ii. 1; παραγγέλω 1 Cor. vii. 10; αναγγέλων 2 Cor. vii. 7; παραγγέλομεν 2 Thess. iii. 4; παράγγελε 1 Tim. iv. 11; v. 7; vi. 17. The augment is omitted 9 times (Matth. xi. 17; Acts vii. 42; xxvi. 32; Rom. i. 2; Gal. ii. 13; 1 Tim. vi. 10; 2 Tim. i. 16; Apoc. iv. 8; xii. 17); the reduplication twice (John xi. 52; 1 Cor. xi. 5): μέλλω and μέλει are confounded Mark iv. 38; Acts xviii. 17; Apoc. iii. 2; xii. 4. Other forms (some of them would be called Alexandrine, see Chap. VIII.) are παμπόλου Mark viii. 1; νηρέαν Rom. xvi. 15; εξαιρείτε 1 Cor. v. 13; αποκτένει 2 Cor. iii. 6; *passim;* στιχούμεν Gal. v. 25; είπα Hebr. iii. 10; ευράμενος *ibid.* ix. 12; απεσχέσθαι 1 Pet. ii. 11; καταλειπόντες 2 Pet. ii. 15; περιβαλλείται Apoc. iii. 5; δειγνύντος *ibid.* xxii. 8. We have in 31 places cited changes in the punctuation, but the stops are placed carelessly in the Greek, being (.), (,), rarely (·), never (;). In the Latin the stops are pretty regular, but the abbreviations very numerous, even such purely arbitrary forms as $\overline{\text{xps}}$ for *Christus.* In the Greek σ often stands at the end of a word for ς, ϊ and often ϋ or ῡ are set at the beginning of syllables, and there are no ι *ascript* or *subscript,* and no capital letters except at the beginning of a chapter, when they are often flourished.

All the forms enumerated above we have recorded in our collation, and numbered among the 2777 variations from the Elzevir text: the following are also derived from the general practice of manuscripts, and occurring perpetually, are here named once for all: απάρτι, απάρχης, δαν (for δ' ἂν), ειμή, εξαυτής, επιτοαυτό, εφόσον, εωσότου, καίτοιγε, καθημέραν, κατιδίαν, κατόναρ, μεθήμων, μέντοι, ουμή, τουτέστι; and for the most part διαπαντός, διατί, διατούτο, είτις, ουκέτι; sometimes we meet with such forms as παραφύσιν, and once (Mark xiv. 7) ευποιήσαι, Vulg. *benefacere.*

2. ERASMUS' NEW TESTAMENT was by six years the earlier published, though it was printed two years later than the Complutensian. Its editor, both in character and fortunes, presents a striking contrast with Ximenes; yet what he lacked of the Castilian's firmness he more than atoned for by his true love of learning, and the cheerfulness of spirit that struggled patiently, if not boldly, with adversity. Desiderius Erasmus (ἐράσμιος, i.e. Gerald) was born at Rotterdam in 1465, or, perhaps, a year or two later, the illegitimate son of reputable and (but for that sin) of virtuous parents. Soon left an orphan, he was reluctantly forced to take the minor orders, and entered the priesthood in 1492. Thenceforward his was the hard life of a solitary and wandering man of letters, earning a precarious subsistence from booksellers or pupils, now learning Greek at

Oxford (but *αὐτοδίδακτος*)[1], now teaching it at Cambridge (1510); losing by his reckless wit the friends his vast erudition had won; restless and unfrugal, perhaps, yet always labouring faithfully and with diligence. He was in England when John Froben, a celebrated publisher at Basle, moved by the report of the forthcoming Spanish Bible, and eager to forestall it, made application to Erasmus, through a common friend, to undertake immediately an edition of the N. T.: "*se daturum pollicetur, quantum alius quisquam*," is the argument employed. This proposal was sent on April 17, 1515, before which time Erasmus had no doubt prepared numerous annotations to illustrate a revised Latin version he had long projected. On September 11 it was yet unsettled whether this improved version should stand by the Greek in a parallel column (the plan actually adopted), or be printed separately: yet the colophon at the end of Erasmus' first edition, a large folio of 675 pages, is dated February, 1516; the end of the Annotations, March 1, 1516; Erasmus' dedication to Leo X., Feb. 1, 1516; and Froben's Preface, full of joyful hope and honest pride in the friendship of the first of living authors, Feb. 24, 1516. Well might Erasmus, who had besides other literary engagements to occupy his time, declare subsequently that the volume "praecipitatum fuit verius quam editum;" yet both on the title-page, and in his dedication to the Pope, he allows himself to employ widely different language[2]. When we read the assurance he addressed to Leo, "Novum ut vocant testamentum universum ad Graecae originis fidem recognovimus, idque non temere neque levi opera, sed adhibitis in

[1] Bp. Middleton may have lost sight of this pregnant fact when he wrote of Erasmus, "an acquaintance with Greek criticism was certainly not among his best acquirements, as his Greek Testament plainly proves: indeed he seems not to have had a very happy talent for languages" (*Doctrine of the Greek Article*, p. 395, 3rd edition).

[2] The title page is long and rather boastful. "Novum Instrumentum omne, diligenter ab Erasmo Roterodamo recognitum et emendatum, non solum ad graecam veritatem, verum etiam ad multorum utriusque linguae codicum, eorumque veterum simul et emendatorum fidem, postremo ad probatissimorum autorum citationem, emendationem, et interpretationem, praecipue, Origenis, Chrysostomi, Cyrilli, Vulgarii [i. e. Theophylact, Archbishop of *B*ulgaria], Hieronymi, Cypriani, Ambrosii, Hilarii, Augustini, una cum Annotationibus, quae lectorem doceant, quid qua ratione mutatum sit. Quisquis igitur amas veram theologiam, lege, cognosce, ac deinde judica. Neque statim offendere, si quid mutatum offenderis, sed expende, num in melius mutatum sit. Apud inclytam Germaniae Basilaeam."

consilium compluribus utriusque linguae codicibus, nec iis sane quibuslibet, sed vetustissimis simul et emendatissimis," it is almost painful to be obliged to remember that a portion of ten months at the utmost could have been devoted by Erasmus to the text, the Latin version and the notes; while the only manuscripts he can be imagined to have used are Codd. Evan. 2, Act. Paul. 2, with occasional reference to Evan. Act. Paul. 1 and Act. Paul. 4 (all still at Basle, and described, Chap. II. sect. III.) for the remainder of the New Testament, and to Apoc. 1 (now lost) alone for the Apocalypse. All these, excepting Evan. Act. Paul. 1, were neither ancient nor particularly valuable, and of Cod. 1 he made but small account. As Apoc. 1 was mutilated in the last six verses, Erasmus turned these into the Greek from the Latin; and some portions of his version, which are found (however some editors may speak vaguely, *see p.* 67) *in no one known Greek manuscript whatever*, still cleave to our received text[1].

When Ximenes, in the last year of his life, was shewn Erasmus' edition, which had thus got the start of his own, and his editor, Stunica, sought to depreciate it, the noble old man replied, "would God that all the Lord's people were prophets! produce better, if thou canst; condemn not the industry of another[2]." His generous confidence in his own work was not misplaced. He had many advantages over the poor scholar and the enterprising printer of Basle, and had not let them pass unimproved. The typographical errors of the Complutensian Greek have been stated (p. 293); Erasmus' first edition is in that respect the most faulty book I know. Œcolampadius, or John Hausschein [1482—1531], afterwards of some note as a Lutheran, had undertaken this department for him, and was glad enough to serve under such a chief; but Froben's hot haste gave him little leisure to do his part. We must, however, impute it to design that *ι subscript*, which is elsewhere placed quite correctly, is here set under *η* in the plural of the subjunctive mood active, not in the singular (e. g. James ii. 3, *ἐπιβλέψῃτε, εἴπῃτε bis*, but v. 2, *εἰσέλθη bis*). With regard to the text, the difference between the two editions is very wide in

[1] Such are *ὀρθρινὸς* Apoc. xxii, v. 16; *ἐλθέ bis, ἐλθέτω, λαμβανέτω τὸ* v. 17; *συμμαρτυροῦμαι γὰρ, ἐπιτιθῇ πρὸς ταῦτα,—τῷ (ante βιβλίῳ)* v. 18; *ἀφαιρῇ, βίβλου, ἀφαιρήσει, βίβλου secund., καὶ ult.,—τῷ (ante βιβλίῳ)* v. 19; *ἡμῶν, ὑμῶν* v. 21.

[2] Tregelles, *Account of the Printed Text*, p. 19.

the Apocalypse, the text of the Complutensian being decidedly preferable; elsewhere they resemble each other more closely, and while we fully admit the error of Stunica and his colleagues in translating from the Latin version into Greek 1 John v. 7, it would appear that Erasmus has elsewhere acted in the same manner, not merely in cases which for the moment admitted no choice, but in places where no such necessity existed: thus in Acts ix. 5, 6, the words from *σκληρόν* to *πρὸς αὐτόν* are interpolated from the Vulgate, partly by the help of Acts xxvi. 14 (*see* p. 12).

Erasmus died at Basle in 1536, having lived to publish four editions besides that of 1516. The second has enlarged annotations, and very truly bears on its title the statement, "multo quam antehac diligentius ab Er. Rot. recognitum;" for a large portion of the misprints, and not a few readings of the first edition are herein corrected, chiefly on the authority of a fresh codex, Evan. Act. Paul. 3 (*see* p. 143). The colophon to the Apocalypse is dated 1518, Froben's Epistle to the reader, Feb. 5, 1519. In this edition *ι* subscript is set right; *Carp.*, *Eus. t.*, *κεφ. t.*, *Am.*, *Eus.* (see p. 142), are added in the Gospels; Dorotheus' *Lives of the Evangelists* (*see* Cod. Act. 89, p. 193), and the Euthalian *κεφάλαια* are given in both editions in Rom. 1, 2 Corinth. only, but the Latin chapters are represented throughout. Of these two editions put together 3300 copies were printed. The third edition (1522) is chiefly remarkable for its insertion of 1 John v. 7 in the Greek text, under the circumstances described p. 149, in consequence of his controversy with Stunica, and with a much weaker antagonist, Edward Lee, afterwards Archbishop of York, who objected to his omission of a passage which no Greek codex was then known to contain. This edition also was said to be "tertio jam ac diligentius...recognitum," and contains also "Capita argumentorum contra morosos quosdam ac indoctos," which he subsequently found reason to enlarge. The fourth edition (dated, March 1527) contains the text in three parallel columns, the Greek, the Latin Vulgate, and Erasmus' recension of it. He had seen the Complutensian Polyglott in 1522, shortly after the publication of his third edition, and had now the good sense to avail himself of its aid in the improvement of the text, especially in the Apocalypse, wherein he amended from it at least ninety readings. His last edition of 1535 once more discarded the Latin Vulgate, and differs very little from the fourth as regards the text[1].

A minute collation of all Erasmus' editions is a desideratum we may one day hope to see supplied. All who have followed Mill over any portion of the vast field he endeavoured to occupy, will feel certain that his statements respecting their divergencies are much below the truth: such as they are, we repeat them for want of more accurate information. He estimates that Erasmus' second edition contains 330 changes from the first for the better, 70 for the worse (*Proleg. N. T.* § 1134); that the third differs from the second in 118 places (*ibid.* § 1138); the fourth from the third in 113 places, 90 being those from the Apocalypse just spoken of (*ibid.* § 1141); the fifth differs from the fourth only four times (*ibid.* § 1150).

3. In 1518 appeared the *Graeca Biblia* at Venice, from the celebrated press of Aldus, which professes to be grounded on a collation of most ancient copies. However this may be in the Old Testament, it follows Erasmus so closely in the New as to reproduce his very errors of the press (Mill, *N. T. Proleg.* § 1122), though it is stated to differ from him in about 200 places, for the better or worse. If this edition was really revised by means of manuscripts (*see p.* 159, Cod. 131) rather than by mere conjecture, we know not what they were, or how far intelligently employed. Another edition out of the many which now began to swarm, wherein the testimony of manuscripts is believed to have been followed, is that of Simon Colinaeus, Paris 1534, in which the text is an eclectic mixture of the Complutensian and Erasmian. Mill states (*Proleg.* § 1144) that in about 150 places Colinaeus deserts them both, and that his variations are usually supported by the evidence of known codices (Evan. 119, 120 at Paris have been suggested), though a few still remain which may perhaps be deemed conjectural.

[1] I never saw the Basle manuscripts, and probably Dean Alford has been more fortunate, otherwise I do not think he has evidence for his statement that "Erasmus tampered with the readings of the very few MSS. which he collated" (N. T. Vol. I. Proleg. p. 74, 4th edition). The truth is, that to save time and trouble, he used them as *copy* for the press, as was intimated above, p. 143. For this purpose corrections would of course be necessary (those made by Erasmus were all too few), and he might fairly say, in the words cited by Wetstein (*Proleg.* p. 127), "se codices suos praecastigasse." Any wanton "tampering" with the text I am loth to admit, unless for better reasons than I yet know of.

4. The editions of Robert Stephens, mainly by reason of their exquisite beauty, have exercised a far wider influence than these, and Stephens' third or folio edition of 1550 is by many regarded as the received or standard text. This eminent and resolute man [1503—59] early commenced his useful career as a printer at Paris, and having incurred the enmity of the Doctors of the Sorbonne for his editions of the Latin Vulgate (*see* p. 263), was yet protected and patronised by Francis I. [d. 1547] and his son Henry II. It was from the Royal Press that his three principal editions of the Greek N. T. were issued, the fourth and last being published in 1551 at Geneva, to which town he finally withdrew the next year, and made public profession of the Protestant opinions which had long been gathering strength in his mind. The editions of 1546, 1549 are small 12° in size, most elegantly printed with type cast at the expense of Francis: the opening words of the Preface common to both, "*O mirificam* Regis nostri optimi et praestantissimi principis liberalitatem"...have given them the name by which they are known among connoisseurs. Erasmus and his services to sacred learning Stephens does not so much as name, nor indeed did he as yet adopt him for a model: he speaks of "codices ipsa vetustatis specie pene adorandos" which he had met with in the King's Library, by which, he boldly adds "ita hunc nostrum recensuimus, ut nullam omnino literam secus esse pateremur quam plures, iique meliores libri, tanquam testes, comprobarent." The Complutensian, as he admits, assisted him greatly, and he notes its close connection with the readings of his manuscripts. Mill assures us (*Proleg.* § 1220) that Stephens' first and second editions differ but in 67 places. In the folio or third edition of 1550 the various readings of the codices, obscurely referred to in the Preface to that of 1546, are entered in the margin. This fine volume derives much importance from its being the earliest ever published with critical apparatus. In the Preface, written after the example of the Complutensian editors both in Greek and Latin, his authorities are declared to be sixteen; viz. *α′* the Spanish Polyglott; *β′*, which we have already discussed (*above, p.* 97, *note* 2); *γ′*, *δ′*, *ε′*, *ϛ′*, *ζ′*, *η′*, *ι′*, *ιε′* taken from King Henry II.'s Library; the rest (i. e. *θ′*, *ια′*, *ιβ′*, *ιγ′*, *ιδ′*, *ιϛ′*) are those *ἃ αὐτοὶ πανταχόθεν συνηθροίσαμεν*, or, as the Latin runs, "quae undique corrogare licuit:" these, of course, were not necessarily

his own; one at least (ιγ', Act. 9, Paul. 11, see p. 187) we are sure was not. Although Robert Stephens professed to have collated the whole sixteen for his two previous editions, and that too ὡς οἷόν τε ἦν ἐπιμελέστατα, this part of his work is now known to be due to his son Henry [1528—98], who in 1546 was only eighteen years old. The degree of accuracy attained in this collation may be estimated from the single instance of the Complutensian, a book printed in very clear type, widely circulated, and highly valued by Stephens himself. Deducting mere *errata*, itacisms and such like, it differs from his third edition in more than 2300 places, of which (including cases where π or πάντες stands for *all* his copies) it is cited correctly 554 times (viz. 164 in the Gospels, 94 in St Paul, 76 in the Acts and Catholic Epistles, 220 in the Apocalypse), and falsely no less than 56 times, again including errors from a too general use of πάντες[1]. I would not say with some that these authorities stand in the margin more for parade than use, yet the text is perpetually at variance with the majority of them, and in 119 places with them all[2]. If we trust ourselves once more to the guidance of Mill (*Proleg.* § 1228), the folio of 1550 departs from its smaller predecessors of 1546, 1549, in 284 readings, chiefly to adopt the text of Erasmus' fifth edition, but even now the Complutensian is preferred in the Apocalypse, and with good reason. Of his other fifteen authorities, ια' (=Act. 8) and ιϛ' (=Apoc. 3) have never been identified, but were among the six in private hands: β' certainly is Cod. D or Bezae; the learned have tried, and on the whole successfully, to recognise the remainder, especially those in the Royal (or Imperial) Library at Paris. In that great collection Lelong has satisfied us that γ' is probably Evan. 4; δ' is certainly Evan. 5; ε' Evan. 6; ϛ' Evan. 7; η' Evan. L; ζ' he believed to be Evan. 8, but see above, p. 190, note; ι' appears to be Act. 7. Of

[1] Mill says that Stephens' citations of the Complutensian are 598, Marsh 578, of which 48, or one in twelve, are false; but we have tried to be as exact as possible. Certainly some of Stephens' inaccuracies are rather slight, viz. Act. ix. 6; xv. 29; xxv. 5; xxviii. 3; Eph. iv. 32; Col. iii. 20; Apoc. i. 12; ii. 1; 20; 24; iii. 2; 4; 7; 12; iv. 8; xv. 2. β seems to be put for α Matth. x. 25.

[2] viz. in the Gospels 81, Paul 20, Act. Cath. 17, Apoc. 1 (ch. vii. 5), but for the Apocalypse the margin had only three authorities, α', ιε', ιϛ' (ιϛ' ending xvii. 8), whose united readings Stephens rejects no less than 54 times: see, moreover, above, p. 97, note 2.

those in the possession of individuals in Stephens' time, Bp. Marsh (who in his *Letters to Mr Archdeacon Travis*, 1795, was led to examine this subject very carefully) has proved that ιγ′ is Act. 9 (*see* p. 187); Wetstein thought θ′ was Evan. 38 (*but see* p. 146, note); Scholz seems to approve of Wetstein's conjecture which Griesbach doubted (*N.T.Proleg.* Sect. I. p. xxxviii), that ιβ′ is Evan. 9: Griesbach rightly considers ιδ′ to be Evan. 120; ιε′ was seen by Lelong to be Act. 10: these last four are all *now* in the Imperial Library. It has been the more difficult to settle them, as Robert Stephens did not even print all the materials that Henry had gathered; many of whose various readings were published subsequently by Beza from the collator's own manuscript, which itself must have been very defective. With all its faults, however, this edition of 1550 was a foundation on which others might hereafter build, and was unquestionably of great use in directing the attention of students to the authorities on which alone the true text of Scripture is based. R. Stephens' smaller edition, published at Geneva 1551, is said to contain the Greek text of 1550 almost unchanged, between the Vulgate and Erasmus' Latin versions. In this volume we first find our present division of the N. T. into verses (*see above*, p. 60).

We annex to our description of the earlier editions the following collation of St James' Epistle, as it is represented in Erasmus' first edition, with Stephens' N. T. of 1550, in order to illustrate the gradual process by which the text was moulded into its present shape. It will be remembered that the Complutensian (a collation of which is given in the Appendix to this Chapter), was not *published* till after Erasmus' third edition. The references within brackets [ ] are made to those editions in which the false reading of 1516 was continued: when no brackets follow, the error or variation was corrected in Erasmus' *second* edition[1].

Ἐπιστολὴ τοῦ ἁγίου ἀποστόλου ἰακώβου. [— *ἀποστόλου* Er. 2, 3, 4, 5]. Η *του αγίου ιακώβου επιστολή καθολική* C. *Ἰακώβου ἐπιστολὴ καθολικὴ* S. 1, 2, 3. Jacob. i. 2. *περιπέσητε.* 5. *ειδέτις.* 6. *διαδρινόμενος* *secund.* *κλυδῶνι* [Er. 2, 3, 4, 5]. 7. — *ὁ* [Er. 2, 3, 4, 5]. 11. *οὕτως* [Er. 2, 3, 4, 5]. 12. *ζοῆς.* 13. — *τοῦ* [Er. 2, 3, 4, 5, C., S. 1, 2]. 14 *ἐπιθυμίας,* 19. *ως τε* [Er. 2]. 22. — *μόνον* [*habent* Er. 2, &c. *non autem* Er. 5]. 24. *ὁ ποιὸς.* 26. *ἀλλὰ* [Er. 2, 3, 4, 5, C]. ii. 2. *εἰσέλθη* *bis.* 3. *ἐπιβλέψητε.* *εἴπητε* *bis.* *ὑπὼ.* 6. *ἠτιμάσετε* [*ητοιμάσατε* C]. *οὐχ᾽ οἱ* [*οὐχ᾽ οἱ* Er. 2, 3, 4: *οὐχ οἱ* 5]. 10. *ὅς τις* [Er. 2, 3, 4, 5]. 11. *μοιχεύσης.* *φονεύσης.* 12. *οὕτως* *bis* [Er. 2, 3, 4, 5: *οὕπως* *secund.*

[1] Er. represents Erasmus, C. the Complutensian, S. Stephens.

3]. *κρίνασθαι* [Er. 2]. 16. *δέτις* [Er. 2]. *δῷτε*. 17, 26. *οὕτως* [Er. 2, 3, 4, 5]. 19. *πιστεύουσιν*. 21, 23. *ἅβρααμ* [Er. 2, S.]. 25. *ῥαὰβ*. iii. 1. [*κρῖμα omnes, praeter* C.]. 2. *οὗτος*. 3. – *αὐτῶν* [Er. 2]. 5. *οὕτως* [Er. 2, 3, 4, 5]. 6. + *τὸ* (*ante πῦρ*) [Er. 2, 3, 4, 5]. 7. *τὲ prim*. *δομάζεται*. 8. *θανατοφόρου* [Er. 2, 3, 4, 5]. 10. *οὕτως* [Er. 2, 3, 4, 5, C.]. 12. *σύκα* [Er. 2, 3, 4, 5, C., S. 1]. *οὐδὲ μία* [Er. 2, 3, 4]. *ἁλικὸν* [Er. 2, 3, 4, 5 : *αλικόν* C.]. 17. *πρωτόν μεν*, iv. 2. – *δὲ* [Er. 2, 3, 4, 5 : *και ουκ έχετε* (– *δε*) C.]. 3. *διό τι* [Er. 2, 3]. *δαπανήσητε*. 4. *μοιχοι*. – *οὖν* [Er. 2, 3, 4, 5]. *βουληθῆ*. 6. – *διὸ λέγει ad fin. vers*. [Er. 2, 3, 4, 5]. 8. *ἐγγΐζατε* [Er. 2, 3]. 14. *οὐκ. ἔσται* [Er. 2, C.]. 15. *θελήση*. v. 2. – *καὶ* [Er. 2, 3, 4, 5]. 7. *ἰδοὺ*. – *ἂν* [Er. 2, 3, 4, 5]. 9. *κριθῆτε* [C., S. 1, 2]. + *ὁ* (*ante κριτής*) [Er. 2, 3, 4, 5, C., S. 1, 2]. 12. [*εἰς ὑπόκρισιν omnes*]. *πέσητε*. 16. *ἰάθητε*. 17. Ηλίας [Er. 2, 4, C. : Ἡλίας 3, 5 : Ἠλίας S. 1, 2, 3]. *ἄνθροπος*. 19. *πλανηθῆ*. *ἐπιστρέψη*. – *τις secund*. [Er. 2]. Τῆς *τοῦ ἁγίου ἀποστόλου* [– *ἀποστ*. Er. 2, 3, 4] *ἰακώβου ἐπιστολῆς τέλος*. *Deest subscriptio in* Er. 5, S. 1, 2.

It will be remarked, that while the great mass of the errata in Er. 1, both in spelling and accents, are corrected by Er. 2, most of the peculiarities of reading run through his five editions (see especially i. 7; iii. 8; 12; iv. 6; v. 2), and are amended from the Complutensian by Stephens. Twice Stephens' third edition is at variance with all the preceding (i. 13; v. 9), in each case with relation to the article, his margin being silent. In St James alone too Er. 5 appears to differ from Er. 4 in *at least* four places; no hopeful sign of Mill's accuracy (above, p. 298).

5. Theodore de Bèze [1519—1605], a native of Vezelai in the Nivernois, after a licentious youth, resigned his ecclesiastical preferments at the age of 29 to retire with the wife of his early choice to Geneva, the little city to which the genius of one man has given so prominent a place in the history of the sixteenth century. His noble birth and knowledge of the world, aided by the impression produced at the Conference at Poissy (1561) by his eloquence and learning, easily gained for Beza the chief place among the French Reformed on the death of their teacher Calvin in 1564. Of his services in connexion with the two Codd. D, we have elsewhere spoken (pp. 96—8; 131): he put forth himself, at long intervals, five editions of the N. T. (1565, 1576, 1582, 1589, 1598), with his own elegant Latin version (first published 1556), the Latin Vulgate, and Annotations. A better commentator perhaps than a critic, but most conspicuous as the earnest leader of a religious party, Beza neither sought very anxiously after fresh materials for correcting the text, nor made any great use of what were ready at hand, his own two great codices, the papers of Henry Stephens' (*see* p. 301), and Tremellius' Latin version of the Peshito (*see* p. 232). All his

editions (of which we shall give some specimens) vary somewhat from Stephens' folio and from each other, yet there is no material difference between any of them. He exhibits a tendency, not the less blameworthy because his extreme theological views would tempt him to it, towards choosing that reading out of several which might best suit his own preconceived opinions. Thus in Luke ii. 22 he adopts (and our Authorised English version condescends to follow his judgment) τοῦ καθαρισμοῦ αὐτῆς from the Complutensian, for which he could have known of no manuscript authority whatever: *ejus* of the Vulgate would most naturally be rendered by αὐτοῦ (*see Campbell in loc.*). Wetstein calculates that Beza's text differs from Stephens' in some fifty places (an estimate we shall find below the mark), and that either in his translation or his Annotations he departs from Stephens' Greek text in 150 passages (Wetst. *N. T. Proleg.* Tom. II. p. 7).

6. The brothers Bonaventure and Abraham Elzevir set up a printing press at Leyden which maintained its reputation for elegance and correctness throughout the greater part of the seventeenth century. One of their minute editions, so much prized by bibliomanists, was a Greek Testament, 24°, 1624, alleging on the title-page (there is no Preface whatever) to be *ex Regiis aliisque optimis editionibus cum curâ expressum:* by *Regiis*, we presume, Stephens' editions are meant, and especially that of 1550. The supposed accuracy (for which its good name is not quite deserved) and great neatness of the little book procured for it much popularity. When this edition was exhausted, a second appeared in 1633, having the verses broken up into separate sentences, instead of their numbers being indicated in the margin, as in 1624: in the Preface it seems to allude to Beza's N. T., without directly naming him: "Ex regiis ac *caeteris editionibus*, quae maxime ac prae caeteris nunc omnibus probantur." To this edition is prefixed, as in 1624, a table of quotations (πίναξ μαρτυριῶν) from the Old Testament, to which is now added tables of the κεφάλαια of the Gospels, ἔκθεσις κεφαλαίων of the Acts and all the Epistles. Of the person entrusted with its superintendence we know nothing; nearly all his readings are found either in Stephens' or Beza's N. T. (he seems to lean to the latter in preference); but he speaks of the edition of 1624 as that "omnibus acceptam;" and boldly states,

with a confidence which no doubt helped on its own accomplishment, "textum ergo habes nunc ab omnibus receptum, in quo nihil immutatum aut corruptum damus." His other profession, that of superior correctness, is also a little premature: "ut si quae, vel minutissimae in nostro, aut in iis, quos secuti sumus libris, superessent mendae, cum judicio ac cura tollerentur." Although some of the worst misprints of the edition of 1624 are amended (Matth. vi. 34; Col. ii. 13; 1 Thess. ii. 17; 2 Pet. i. 7), others just as gross are retained (Act. ix. 3; Rom. vii. 2; xiii. 5; 1 Cor. xiii. 3; 2 Cor. iv. 4; v. 19; Hebr. xii. 9; Apoc. xviii. 16): ἐθύθη in 1 Cor. v. 7 should not be reckoned as an erratum, since it was adopted from design by Beza, and after him by both Elzevir editions. Of real various readings between the two Elzevirs, we mark but six instances (in the first five that of 1633 follows the Complutensian); viz. Mark iv. 18; viii. 24; Luke xii. 20; John iii. 6 *bis*; 2 Tim. i. 12; Apoc. xvi. 5, to be noticed below in their proper places.

Since Stephens' edition of 1550, and that of the Elzevirs, have been taken as the standard or *Received* text, the former chiefly in England, the latter on the continent, and inasmuch as nearly all collated manuscripts have been compared with one or the other of these, it becomes absolutely necessary to know the precise points in which they differ from each other, even to the minutest errors of the press. Mill (*N. T. Proleg.* 1307) observed but twelve such variations; Tischendorf gives a catalogue of 150 (*N. T. Proleg.* p. lxxxv, 7th ed.): it is hoped that the following list of 286 places will be found tolerably exact; *mere* errata as regards the breathings or accents it seemed needless to include.

Collation of Stephens' N. T. 1550, with the Complutensian (C), Beza's of 1565 (B), and Elzevir's (E[1] of 1624, E[2] of 1633).

	Stephens, 1550.	Elzevir, 1624.
Matth. i. 1.	Ἀβραάμ *passim.*	Ἀβραάμ *passim.*
vi. 34.	μεριμνήσητε C B E².	μεριμνήσετε *errore.*
viii. 4.	ἀλλ' B.	ἀλλὰ C.
x. 4.	Ἰσκαριώτης C.	ὁ Ἰσκαριώτης B.
xii. 18.	ᾑρέτισα B.	ᾑρέτισα.
xviii. 30.	ἀλλὰ C.	ἀλλ' B.
xix. 1.	τῆς Γαλιλαίας C B.	Γαλιλαίας.

	Stephens, 1550.	Elzevir, 1624.
Matth. xx. 15.	εἰ ὁ ὀφθ. C.	ἢ ὁ ὀφθ. B.
22.	ὁ δὲ *errore.*	δὲ ὁ C B.
xxi. 7.	ἐπεκάθισεν C.	ἐπεκάθισαν B.
xxiii. 13, 14.	οὐαὶ δὲ ὑμῖν Γραμ. καὶ φαρ. ὑποκρ. ὅτι κατεσθίετε...... οὐαὶ ὑμῖν Γ. καὶ φαρ. ὑποκρ. ὅτι κλείετε......C.	οὐαὶ δὲ ὑμῖν Γραμ. καὶ φαρισ. ὑποκρ. ὅτι κλείετε...... οὐαὶ ὑμῖν Γ. καὶ φαρ. ὑποκρ. ὅτι κατ--εσθίετε...... B.
xxiv. 9.	τῶν ἐθνῶν C B.	ἐθνῶν.
15.	ἑστὸς C.	ἑστὼς B.
34.	λέγω C B E^2.	λέγων *errore.*
xxv. 2.	καὶ αἱ πέντε C.	καὶ πέντε B.
Marc. i. 21.	τὴν συναγωγὴν C B.	συναγωγὴν.
27.	αὐτοὺς.	αὐτοὺς B.
ii. 7.	οὕτω C B.	οὕτως.
iv. 18.	—οὗτοί εἰσιν *secund.* C E^2, *non* S B E^1.	
vi. 9.	ἐνδύσησθε C.	ἐνδύσασθαι B.
29.	τῷ μνημείῳ.	μνημείῳ C B.
viii. 3.	ἥκασι C.	ἥκουσι B.
24.	—ὅτι *et* ὁρῶ C E^2, *non* S B E^1.	
27.	οἱ μαθηταὶ C B E^2.	ὁ μαθηταὶ *errore.*
ix. 16.	αὐτοὺς B 1589 (εαυτούς C).	αὐτοὺς B.
38.	τῷ ὀνόματι C.	ἐν τῷ ὀνόματι B.
40.	ὑμῶν *bis* C.	ἡμῶν *bis* B.
45.	γέεναν *errore.*	γέενναν C B.
x. 25.	εἰσελθεῖν C.	διελθεῖν B.
xi. 14.	μηδεὶς C.	οὐδεὶς B.
xii. 20.	ἑπτὰ C.	ἑπτὰ οὖν B.
xiii. 14.	ἑστὸς C.	ἑστὼς B.
28.	ἐκφυῇ.	ἐκφύῃ C B.
xiv. 54.	τὸ φῶς C B.	φῶς.
xv. 32.	Ἰσραὴλ *hic tantum.*	Ἰσραήλ.
xvi. 20.	ἀμὴν C.	*deest* B.
Luc. ii. 22.	αὐτῶν	αὐτῆς C B.
iii. 23.	Ἠλὶ	Ἡλί.
33.	Ἐσρὼμ C.	Ἐσρὼν B.
vii. 12.	αὕτη ἦν χήρα	αὕτη χήρα (αὐτῇ χήρᾳ C B).
ibid.	ἱκανὸς C.	ἱκανὸς ἦν B.
viii. 29.	παρήγγελλε C B.	παρήγγειλε.
x. 6.	υἱὸς C B.	ὁ υἱός.
13.	Χωραζὶν C.	Χοραζὶν B.
19.	ἀδικήσῃ C.	ἀδικήσει B.
22.	καὶ στραφεὶς πρὸς τοὺς μαθητὰς εἶπε C: *deest* B.	
xi. 12.	αἰτήσῃ C B.	αἰτήσει.
33.	κρυπτὸν B.	κρυπτὴν C.
ibid.	ἀλλ' C B.	ἀλλά.
xii. 18.	γενήματα C.	γεννήματα B.

	Stephens, 1550.	Elzevir, 1624.
Luc. xii. 20.	ἄφρον C E^{2}, *non* S B E^{1}.	
xiii. 8.	κοπρίαν B.	κοπρία C.
19.	ὃν C B.	ὅ.
xv. 26.	παίδων αὐτοῦ	παίδων C B.
xvii. 1.	τοῦ μὴ C B 1589.	μὴ B 1565.
26.	τοῦ υἱοῦ C B.	υἱοῦ.
35.	μία C.	ἡ μία B.
36.	*versus deest.*	*habent* C B.
xviii. 3.	χήρα δὲ C.	χήρα δέ τις B.
xix. 4.	συκομωραίαν B. συκομωρέαν C.	συκομορέαν.
xx. 31.	οὐ κατέλιπον C.	καὶ οὐ κατέλιπον B.
47.	μακρᾷ	μακρὰ B.
xxii. 45.	μαθητὰς C.	μαθητὰς αὐτοῦ B.
xxiii. 11.	ἐσθῆτα B.	ἐσθῆτα.
xxiv. 4.	ἐσθήσεσιν B.	ἐσθήσεσιν.
xxiv. 27.	περὶ ἑαυτοῦ C.	περὶ αὐτοῦ B.
Johan. i. 28.	Βηθαβαρᾶ B (βηθανία C).	Βηθαβαρᾷ.
ii. 1, 11.	Κανᾷ.	Κανᾶ B.
iii. 6 *bis.*	γεγεννημένον C B E^{2}.	γεγενημένον E^{1}.
iv. 5.	Συχὰρ C.	Σιχὰρ B.
23.	αὐτόν.	αὐτὸν B.
51.	οἱ δοῦλοι C B E^{2}.	οἱ δοῦλος *errore.*
v. 7.	πρὸς	πρὸ C B.
vi. 28.	ποιοῦμεν B.	ποιῶμεν C.
vii. 27.	ἔρχηται C B.	ἔρχεται, *etiam* E^{2}.
38.	ῥεύσουσιν C B.	ῥεύσουσι.
viii. 25.	ὅτι C.	ὅ,τι B.
59.	οὕτω	οὕτως C B.
ix. 10.	σου οἱ C.	σοι οἱ B.
xii. 17.	ὅτε C B.	ὅτι.
32.	ἑλκύσω B.	ἐλκύσω.
xiii. 30, 31.	νὺξ ὅτε ἐξῆλθε C.	νύξ. Ὅτε οὖν ἐξῆλθε B.
xiv. 11.	ἐν ἐμοί	ἐν ἐμοὶ ἐστὶν C B.
xvi. 33.	ἕξετε *errore* (ἔχετε *in corrig.*).	ἕξετε B. ἔχετε C.
xviii. 1.	κέδρων.	Κέδρων B.
20.	πάντοτε C.	πάντοθεν B.
24.	ἀπέστειλαν C.	ἀπέστειλαν οὖν B.
xix. 7.	Θεοῦ C.	τοῦ Θεοῦ B.
31.	ἐκείνου B.	ἐκείνη C.
xxi. 2.	Ναθανὴλ *errore.*	Ναθαναὴλ C B.
Act. ii. 36.	καὶ Κύριον C.	Κύριον B.
iv. 32.	οὐδὲ C E^{2}.	οὐδ' B.
v. 12.	ἐγένετο.	ἐγίνετο C B.
vi. 3.	καταστήσομεν C B.	καταστήσωμεν.
vii. 26.	τῇ τε C.	τῇ δὲ B.
44.	ἐν *secund. errore transfertur in locum post* διαδεξάμενοι, *v.* 45.	*non ita* C B E.
viii. 19.	ἂν	ἐὰν C B.
ix. 3.	περιήστραψεν C B.	περιέστραψεν *errore.*

	Stephens, 1550.	Elzevir, 1624.
Act. ix. 24.	τὰ πύλας *errore.*	τὰς πύλας C B.
35.	Σαρωνᾶν C.	Σάρωνα B.
xiv. 8.	περιπεπατήκει C B.	περιεπεπατήκει.
xv. 32.	Ἰούδας τε C.	Ἰούδας δὲ B.
xvi. 4.	πρεσβυτέρων C B E².	πρεσβυπέρων *errore.*
11.	Σαμοθρᾴκην	Σαμοθράκην B.
17.	ἡμῖν ὁδὸν C.	ὑμῖν ὁδὸν B.
xvii. 25.	κατὰ πάντα C.	καὶ τὰ πάντα B.
xix. 27.	μέλλειν δὲ C.	μέλλειν τε B.
33.	προβαλόντων B.	προβαλλόντων C.
xxi. 3.	ἀναφάναντες	ἀναφανέντες C B.
8.	ἦλθον	ἤλθομεν C B.
xxiii. 15.	διαγνώσκειν *errore.*	διαγινώσκειν C B.
16.	τὸ ἔνεδρον C.	τὴν ἐνέδραν B.
xxiv. 13.	παραστῆσαί με	παραστῆσαι C B.
14.	τοῖς προφήταις C.	ἐν τοῖς προφήταις B.
18.	τινὲς δὲ	τινὲς C B.
19.	δεῖ C.	ἔδει B.
xxvi. 8.	τί ἄπιστον C.	τί; ἄπιστον B.
20.	ἀπαγγέλλων	ἀπήγγελλον C B.
xxvii. 13.	Ἄσσον	ἄσσον (ᾆσσον B).
xxviii. 13.	ειν *prim. errore.*	εἰς C B.
Rom. i. 27.	ἄρρενες *prim.* C B.	ἄρσενες *prim.*
17 *et* xi. 22.	ἴδε	ἰδὲ (ειδε C).
vi. 10 *bis.*	ὃ B.	ὁ.
vii. 2.	τοῦ νόμου τοῦ ἀνδρὸς C B.	τοῦ ἀνδρός.
6.	ἀποθανόντες C.	ἀποθανόντος B.
viii. 11.	τὸ ἐνοικοῦν αὐτοῦ πνεῦμα	τοῦ ἐνοικοῦντος αὐτοῦ πνεύματος C B.
21.	ἐπ' ἐλπίδι· (C ,).	·ἐπ' ἐλπίδι B.
ix. 19.	τῷ γὰρ βουλήματι C B.	τῷ βουλήματι.
x. 6.	ἐν τῇ καρδίᾳ C B.	ἐν καρδίᾳ.
xi. 2.	Ἠλίᾳ	Ἡλίᾳ.
31.	ὑμετέρῳ C B.	ἡμετέρῳ.
33.	Ὦ	Ὢ.
xii. 5.	καθεῖς (καθεἱς C).	καθ εἷς B.
11.	καιρῷ	Κυρίῳ C B.
xiii. 5.	ὑποτάσσεσθαι B (υποτασεσθε C).	προτάσσεσθαι *errore.*
xvi. 5.	Ἐπαινετὸν C.	Ἐπαίνετον B.
20.	*deest* ἀμήν C.	*habet* B.
1 Cor. i. 29.	καυχήσηται C B.	καυχήσεται.
iii. 15.	οὕτω	οὕτως C B.
v. 7.	ἐτύθη C.	ἐθύθη B.
11.	ἢ πόρνος	ᾖ πόρνος B.
vi. 14.	ἡμᾶς C B.	ὑμᾶς.
vii. 4.	ἐκ *errore pro* οὐκ *primo.*	οὐκ C B.
5.	συνέρχησθε C B 1565.	συνέρχεσθε B 1598.
29.	ὁ καιρὸς C.	ὅτι ὁ καιρὸς B.

	Stephens, 1550.	Elzevir, 1624.
1 Cor. vii. 29.	·τὸ λοιπόν ἐστιν ἵνα C.	τὸ λοιπόν ἐστιν· ἵνα B.
ibid.	οἱ ἔχοντες C B.	ἔχοντες.
ix. 1.	ἡμεῖς *errore.*	ὑμεῖς C B.
27.	δουλαγαγῶ *errore.*	δουλαγωγῶ C B.
xi. 22.	ὑμᾶς ἐν τούτῳ; οὐκ C.	ὑμᾶς; ἐν τούτῳ οὐκ B.
xii. 23.	ἀτιμότερα C B.	ἀτιμώτερα.
xiii. 2.	οὐθὲν C.	οὐδὲν B.
3.	ψωμίσω C.	ψωμίζω B.
xiv. 15.	*fin.* τῷ νοῒ C B.	νοΐ.
27.	ἀναμέρος	ἀνὰ μέρος C B.
xv. 2.	εἰκῆ B.	εἰκῇ.
31.	ἡμετέραν B 1565.	ὑμετέραν C B 1582.
xvi. 10.	ἐγάζεται *errore.*	ἐργάζεται C B.
2 Cor. iii. 3.	ἀλλ' C B.	ἀλλά.
iv. 4.	τῆς δόξης C B.	τὸν δ.
v. 4.	ἐπειδὴ	ἐφ' ᾧ C B.
19.	θέμενος C B.	θήμενος *errore.*
vi. 15.	βελίαρ	Βελίαλ B (βελιάλ C).
vii. 12.	ὑμῶν τὴν ὑπὲρ ἡμῶν	ἡμῶν τὴν ὑπὲρ ὑμῶν C B.
16.	χαίρω C.	χαίρω οὖν B.
viii. 8.	ὑμετέρας C B.	ἡμετέρας, *etiam* E[2].
20.	ἀδρότητι	ἀδρότητι B.
xi. 1.	ἀνείχεσθε (B 1589) μου μικρὸν τῇ ἀφροσύνῃ C.	ἠνείχεσθέ μου μικρὸν τι τῆς ἀφροσύνης B.
10.	σφραγίσεται	φραγήσεται C B.
xiii. 4.	καὶ γὰρ ἡμεῖς C.	καὶ γὰρ καὶ ἡμεῖς B.
Galat. iii. 8.	ἐνευλογηθήσονται C.	εὐλογηθήσονται B.
iv. 7.	ὑμᾶς θέλουσιν C.	ἡμᾶς θέλουσιν B.
v. 2.	Ἴδε C.	Ἰδὲ B.
Ephes. i. 3.	Χριστῷ	ἐν Χριστῷ C B.
iv. 25.	ἀλλήλοιν *errore.*	ἀλλήλων C B.
Phil. i. 23.	πολλῷ C.	πολλῷ γὰρ B.
iv. 2.	Εὐωδίαν	Εὐοδίαν C B.
Col. i. 2.	Κολασσαῖς	Κολοσσαῖς C B.
ii. 13.	συνεζωοποίησε E[2] (-σεν ὑμᾶς C), *at* συνεζωποίησε S B E[1].	
ibid.	χαρισάμενος ἡμῖν C.	χαρισάμενος ὑμῖν B.
1 Thess. ii. 15.	ὑμᾶς	ἡμᾶς C B.
17.	ἀπορφανισθέντες C B E[2].	ἀποφανισθέντες E[1].
1 Tim. i. 4.	οἰκονομίαν C.	οἰκοδομίαν B.
ii. 13.	Εὖα	Εὖα B.
iii. 2.	νηφάλεον	νηφάλιον C B.
11.	νηφαλέους (*non* Tit. ii. 2)	νηφαλίους C B.
2 Tim. i. 5.	Εὐνείκῃ.	Εὐνίκῃ C B.
12.	παρακαταθήκην C E[2], *at* παραθήκην S B E[1].	
iv. 13.	φαιλόνην.	φελόνην C B.

	Stephens, 1550.	Elzevir, 1624.
Tit. ii. 7.	*fin.* ἀφθαρσίαν C.	*deest* B.
10.	ὑμῶν	ἡμῶν C B.
Philem. 7.	χάριν B 1589.	χαρὰν C B 1565.
Hebr. i. 12.	ἐλίξεις	ἑλίξεις B.
iv. 15.	πεπειραμένον C.	πεπειρασμένον B.
vii. 1.	τοῦ ὑψίστου B.	ὑψίστου C.
viii. 9.	μου τῆς χειρὸς C B.	τῆς χειρὸς.
ix. 2.	ἀγία	ἅγια C B.
12.	εὑράμενος C B.	εὑρόμενος.
x. 2.	ἐπεὶ οὐκ ἂν ;	ἐπεὶ ἂν · C B.
10.	οἱ διὰ τῆς προσφορᾶς C.	διὰ τῆς προσφορᾶς B.
xii. 9.	ἐνετρεπόμεθα C B.	ἐντρεπόμεθα *errore.*
22, 23.	μυριάσιν ἀγγέλων πανηγύρει, C.	μυριάσιν ἀγγέλων, Πανηγύρει B.
Jacob. iv. 13.	Σήμερον καὶ C.	Σήμερον ἢ B.
	πορευσώμεθα...ποιήσωμεν...	πορευσόμεθα...ποιήσομεν...
	ἐμπορευσώμεθα...κερδήσωμεν C.	ἐμπορευσόμεθα..κερδήσομεν..B.
15.	ποιήσωμεν C.	ποιήσομεν B.
v. 12.	εἰς ὑπόκρισιν C.	ὑπὸ κρίσιν B.
1 Pet. i. 3.	ἡμᾶς C B.	ὑμᾶς.
ii. 21.	ἡμῶν, ἡμῖν B 1582 (ημών, υμίν C).	ὑμῶν, ὑμῖν B 1565.
iii. 11.	*omittit* ἀγαθόν· ζητησάτω *errore.*	*habent* C B.
21.	ὃ	Ὦ (ω C, Ω B).
iv. 8.	ἀγάπη	ἡ ἀγάπη C B.
13.	καθὸ C.	καθὼς B.
2 Pet. i. 1.	σωτῆρος C.	σωτῆρος ἡμῶν B.
7.	φιλαδελφίαν C B E[2].	φλιαδελφίαν E[1].
ii. 12.	γεγενημένα C.	γεγεννημένα B.
18.	ἀσελγείαις C.	ἐν ἀσελγείαις B.
iii. 7.	αὐτοῦ λόγῳ C.	τῷ αὐτῷ λόγῳ B.
1 Johan. i. 4.	χαρὰ ἡμῶν C.	χαρὰ ὑμῶν B.
ii. 29.	γεγένηται	γεγέννηται C B.
iv. 14.	μαρτοῦμεν S, *non* C B E.	
v. 14.	ὑμῶν S.	ἡμῶν C B.
2 Johan. 3.	μεθ' ἡμῶν C.	μεθ' ὑμῶν B.
5.	γράφω	γράφων C B.
3 Johan. 7.	ὀνόματος	ὀνόματος αὐτοῦ C B.
Jud. 9.	Ἐπιτιμήσαι B.	Ἐπιτιμῆσαί.
19.	ἀποδιορίζοντες C.	ἀποδιορίζοντες ἑαυτοὺς B.
24.	φυλάξαι αὐτοὺς C.	φυλάξαι ὑμᾶς B.
Apoc. i. 20.	ἑπτὰ B.	ἑπτὰ *prim., errore.*
ii. 5.	τάχει	ταχὺ C B.
14.	ἐν τῷ Βαλὰκ	τὸν Βαλὰκ C B.
iii. 1.	πνεύματα	ἑπτὰ πνεύματα C B.
12.	ναῷ C B.	λαῷ *errore, etiam* E[2].
ibid.	ἡ καταβαίνουσα.	ἣ καταβαίνει C B.

	Stephens, 1550.	Elzevir, 1624.
Apoc. iv. 3.	ὅμοιος ὁράσει (2° loco).	ὁμοία ὁράσει C B.
10.	προσκυνοῦσι...βάλλουσι C.	προσκυνήσουσι C B...βαλοῦσι B.
v. 11.	*omittit* καὶ ἦν ὁ ἀριθμὸς αὐτῶν μυριάδες μυριάδων	*habent* C B.
vii. 3.	σφραγίζωμεν	σφραγίσωμεν C B.
7.	Ἰσαχὰρ C B.	Ἰσασχὰρ, *etiam* E².
10.	τῷ καθημένῳ ἐπὶ τοῦ θρόνου τοῦ Θεοῦ ἡμῶν	τῷ Θεῷ ἡμῶν τῷ καθημένῳ ἐπὶ τοῦ θρόνου C B.
17.	ἀναμέσον	ἀνὰ μέσον C B.
viii. 5.	τὸ λιβανωτὸν...αὐτὸ	τὸν λιβανωτὸν...αὐτὸν C B.
11.	τὸ τρίτον	τὸ τρίτον τῶν ὑδάτων C B.
xi. 1.	*omittit* καὶ ὁ ἄγγελος εἱστήκει	*habet* B. καὶ εἱστήκει ο ἄγγελος C.
2.	ἔσωθεν	ἔξωθεν C B.
xiii. 3.	ἐθαυμάσθη ἐν ὅλῃ τῇ γῇ	ἐθαύμασεν ὅλη ἡ γῆ C B.
5.	ποιῆσαι B 1589.	πόλεμον ποιῆσαι C B 1565.
xiv. 8.	Βαβυλὼν C B E².	Βαβουλών.
18.	τῆς γῆς	τῆς ἀμπέλου τῆς γῆς C B.
xvi. 5.	ἐσόμενος (*pro* ὅσιος) E², *non* C S B E¹.	
14.	ἐκπορεύεσθαι	ἃ ἐκπορεύεται C B.
xviii. 16.	κεχρυσωμένη C B.	κεχρυσωμένοι, *etiam* E².
xix. 1.	φωνὴν	ὡς φωνὴν C B.
4.	ἔπεσαν	ἔπεσον C B.
6.	λέγοντας	λεγόντων C B.
14.	ἐν τῷ οὐρανῷ	τὰ ἐν τῷ οὐρανῷ C B.
xx. 4.	τὴν εἰκόνα	τῇ εἰκόνι C B.
ibid.	Χριστοῦ	τοῦ Χριστοῦ C B.
xxi. 16.	σταδίων	σταδίους C B.
20.	ἔνατος C.	ἔννατος B.
xxii. 8.	ἔπεσα	ἔπεσον C B.

Ναζαρὲτ *habent* C St., Ναζαρὲθ B *omnibus locis:* Elz. *autem* Ναζαρὲτ Matth. ii. 23; iv. 13; Ναζαρὲθ Matth. xxi. 11; Marc. i. 9; Luc. i. 26; ii. 4; 39; 51; iv. 16; Johan. i. 46; 47; Act. x. 38.

Ἡσαῦ *legit* St. Rom. ix. 13; Hebr. xii. 16: Ἠσαῦ Hebr. xi. 20: Elz. *contrarium omnino.*

Ἱεριχὼ *semper* St.: *etiam* Elz. Marc. x. 46 *bis;* Hebr. xi. 30: *at* Ἰεριχὼ Elz. Matth. xx. 29; Luc. x. 30; xviii. 35; xix. 1.

Variant St. Elz. *inter* κρῖμα *et* κρίμα: *hoc tuentur* Codd. EKMUΓ *alii*, Marc. xii. 40; *illud vero* Æschyl. *Suppl.* 391: οὐκ εὔκριτον τὸ κρῖμα· μή μ' αἱροῦ κριτήν.

Quod ad ν ἐφελκυστικόν, *ut vocant, pertinet, in sequentibus variant* St. Bez. Elz.

Matth. xii. 50.	*fin.* ἐστὶν C S.	ἐστί B E.
xv. 27.	εἶπε, ναὶ C S B.	εἶπεν, ναὶ E.
xxiv. 5, 6.	πλανήσουσι. μελλήσετε C S.	πλανήσουσιν. Μελλήσετε B E.
[xxvi. 18.	ἐστι, πρός B.	ἐστιν, πρός S E.]
Marc. xi. 18.	ἀπολέσουσιν· ἐφοβοῦντο C S.	ἀπολέσουσι· ἐφοβοῦντο B E.
[Luc. x. 32, 33.	ἀντιπαρῆλθε. Σαμαρείτης C B.	ἀντιπαρῆλθεν. Σαμαρείτης S E.]

Johan. iii. 31, 32.	ἐστί, καὶ C S.	ἐστίν. Καὶ B E.
Act. ii. 7.	εἰσιν οἱ C S B.	εἰσι οἱ E.
xxii. 14.	εἶπεν 'Ο C S.	εἶπε 'Ο B E.
[1 Cor. xv. 28, 29.	πᾶσιν. 'Επεὶ C B.	πᾶσι. Επεὶ S E.]
1 Thess. v. 7, 8.	μεθύουσι. 'Ημεῖς S.	μεθύουσιν. 'Ημεῖς B E.
2 Thess. iii. 3.	ἐστι ὁ S.	ἐστιν ὁ B E.
1 Johan. v. 8.	εἰσι. Εἰ S.	εἰσιν. Εἰ B E.
Apoc. ii. 14.	ἐδίδασκεν τὸν Βαλὰκ B E^1 E^2.	
xiv. 20.	ἐξῆλθεν αἷμα C S B.	ἐξῆλθε αἷμα E.
xxi. 16.	ἐστιν ὅσον S B.	ἐστι ὅσον E.

In the following places Beza's editions differ both from the Stephanic text of 1550 and from that of the Elzevirs. This list is somewhat incomplete.

Matth. i. 11. +ἐγέννησε τὸν 'Ιακείμ· 'Ιακεὶμ δὲ (*post* 'Ιωσίας δὲ) 1565, *non* 1582. Marc. xv. 43. −ἦν 1589. Luc. i. 35. +ἐκ σοῦ (*post* γεννώμενον) 1589. v. 7. +παρά τι (*post* ὥστε) 1582. vi. 37. −μὴ *secund.* 1589. Johan. xix. 12 αὐτὸν 1589 (*sic passim*), *non* 1598. Act. iv. 27. +ἐν τῇ πόλει ταύτῃ (*post* ἀληθείας) 1589, *non* 1565. xvi. 7 *fin.* +'Ιησοῦ 1589. xxii. 25. προέτειναν 1589. xxv. 6. +οὐ (*ante* πλείους) 1589. xxvii. 3 +τοὺς (*ante* φίλους) 1565. Rom. v. 17. ἐνὶ (*pro* τοῦ ἑνὸς *prim.*) 1589. xv. 7. +τοῦ (*ante* Θεοῦ) 1589. iii. 3. ἡμῖν (*pro* ὑμῖν) 1589, 1598. x. 28. −καὶ (*post* μηνύσαντα) 1589, 1598. xv. 23. +τοῦ (*ante* Χριστου) 1565. 2 Cor. i. 6 *post* σωτηρίας *prim. habet* εἴτε παρακαλούμεθα *usque ad* παρακλήσεως, *omisso* τῆς σωτηρίας *secund. ante* τῆς ἐνερ. 1589. iii. 1. ἢ (*pro* εἰ) 1589. 14. ὅτι *pro* ὅ τι 1565, 1589. viii. 24. −καὶ *secund.* 1589. Col. i. 2. +'Ιησοῦ (*post* Χριστῷ) 1589. 7. ἡμῶν (*pro* ὑμῶν) 1565. 24. ὃς (*pro* ὃ) 1589. 1 Thess. ii. 12. μαρτυρόμενοι 1565. 2 Thess. iii. 5. τὴν (*ante* ὑπομονὴν) 1565. 1 Tim. iv. 12. μηθεὶς 1589, *non* 1598. Hebr. ix. 1. −σκηνὴ 1589. Jac. ii. 18. χωρὶς (*pro* ἐκ *prim.*) 1589. v. 9. +ὁ (*ante* κριτὴς) 1565: *sic* Er. C. 1 Pet. i. 4. ὑμᾶς (*pro* ἡμᾶς) 1589. ii. 21. +καὶ (*post* γὰρ) 1589. 1 Johan. ii. 23. *fin.* +ὁ ὁμολογῶν τὸν υἱὸν καὶ τὸν πατέρα ἔχει 1589. iii. 16. +τοῦ Θεοῦ (*post* ἀγάπην) 1589, *sic* C. Jud. *v.* 12. +ὑμῖν (*post* συνευωχούμενοι) 1565.

The following is the result of a collation in the Apocalypse of Beza 1565 with St. and Elz. i. 11. +ἑπτὰ (*ante* ἐκκλησίας). ii. 14. ἐδίδαξε. 20. πλανᾷν τοὺς (*pro* πλανᾶσθαι). iii. 17. +ὁ (*ante* ἐλεεινός). iv. 3. σαρδίῳ. 8. ἓν καθ' ἓν αὐτῶν ἔχον. v. 7. −τὸ. 14. ἔπεσον. vii. 11. πληρωθῶσι. 13. ἔπεσον. 14. +ὁ (*ante* οὐρανὸς). vii. 2. ἀναβαίνοντα. 14. αὐτὰς (*pro* στολὰς αὐτῶν *secund.*). viii. 6. +οἱ (*ante* ἔχοντες). 10. +τῶν (*ante* ὑδάτων). 11. ἐγένετο. +τῶν (*ante* ἀνθρώπων). ix. 5. βασανίσωσι. 11. +ὁ (*ante* 'Απολλύων). 19. ἡ γὰρ ἐξουσία τῶν ἵππων ἐν τῷ στόματι αὐτῶν ἐστι, καὶ ἐν ταῖς οὐραῖς αὐτῶν· αἱ γὰρ... x. 7. ἀλλ'. xi. 2. τεσσαρακονταδύο (*sic* xiii. 5). 16. ἔπεσον. xii. 14. ὅπως τρέφηται. 24. αὐτὴν (*pro* ταύτην). 8. +τοῦ (*ante* ἐσφαγμένου). 13. καὶ πῦρ ἵνα καταβαίνῃ (−ποιῇ). xiv. 1, 3. τεσσαρακοντατέσσαρες. 7. +ὡς (*ante* κιθαρῳδῶν). 7. +τὴν (*ante* θάλασσαν). 10. πίεται οἴνου ἐκ τοῦ θυμοῦ. 12. +τοῦ (*ante* 'Ιησοῦ). xvii. 4. ἦν (*pro* ἡ *secund*). 10. ἔπεσον. xviii. 6. −καὶ *secund.* 10, 15, 17. ἀπομακρόθεν. xxi. 7. −ὁ (*ante* υἱὸς) 1589. xxii. 12. μετ' ἐμέ. 20. Καὶ (*pro* Ναί).

7. R. Stephens was the first to bring together any considerable body of manuscript evidence, however negligently or capriciously he may have applied it to the emendation of the sacred text. A succession of English scholars was now ready to follow him in the same path, the only direct and sure one in criticism; and for about eighty years our countrymen maintained the foremost place in this important branch of Biblical learning. Their van was led by Brian Walton [1600—61], afterwards Bishop of Chester, who published in 1657 the London Polyglott, which he had planned twelve years before, as at once the solace and meet employment of himself and a worthy band of colleagues during that sad season when Christ's Church in England was for a while trodden in the dust, and its ministers languished in silence and deep poverty. The fifth of his huge folios was devoted to the N. T. in six languages, viz. Stephens' Greek text of 1550, the Peshito-Syriac, the Latin Vulgate, the Æthiopic, Arabic, and (in the Gospels only) the Persic. The exclusively critical apparatus, with which alone we are concerned, consists of the readings of Cod. A set at the foot of the Greek text (*see* pp. 66, 83); and in the sixth or supplementary volume of Lucas Brugensis' notes on various readings of the Gospels in Greek and Latin; of those given by the Louvain divines in their edition of the Vulgate (*see* p. 263, and Walton, *Polygl. Tom.* VI. No. XVII.); and especially of a collation of sixteen authorities, whereof all but three had never been used before (Walton, Tom. VI. No. XVI). These various readings had been gathered by the care and diligence of Archbishop Ussher [1580—1656], then living in studious and devout retirement near London. They are (1) *Steph.* the sixteen copies extracted from Stephens' margin (*see* p. 300): (2) *Cant.* or Evan. D (p. 98): (3) *Clar.* or Paul. D (p. 131): (4) *Gon.* or Evan. 59 (p. 148): (5) *Em.* or Evan. 64 (p. 150), and also Act. 53 (p. 191): (6) *Goog.* or Evan. 62 (p. 150): (7) *Mont.* or Evan. 61 (p. 149): (8) *Lin.* or Evan. 56 (p. 148), and also Act. 33 (p. 189): (9) *Magd.* 1 or Evan. 57 (p. 148): (10) *Magd.* 2 or Paul. 42 (p. 201): (11) *Nov.* 1 or Evan. 58 (p. 148): (12) *Nov.* 2 or Act. 36 (p. 189): (13) *Bodl.* 1 or Evan. 47 (p. 147): (14) *Trit.* or *Bodl.* 2, Evan. 96 (p. 154): (15) *March. Veles.*, the Velesian readings, described above, pp. 156—7: (16) *Bib. Wech.*, the Wechelian readings, which deserve no more regard

than the Velesian: they were derived from the margin of a Bible printed at Frankfort, 1597, by the heirs of And. Wechel. It is indifferent whether they be referred to Francis Junius (p. 276), or F. Sylburg (p. 209) as editors, since all the readings in the N.T. are found in Stephens' margin, or in the early editions.

Walton was thus enabled to publish very extensive additions to the existing stock of materials. That he did not try by their means to form thus early a corrected text, is not at all to be regretted; the time for that attempt was not yet arrived. He cannot, however, be absolved from the charge to which R. Stephens had been before amenable (p. 300), of suppressing a large portion of the collations which had been sent him. The Rev. C. B. Scott recently found in the Library of Emmanuel College, Cambridge, the readings of Codd. D. 59, 61, 62, prepared for Walton (Dobbin, *Cod. Montfort.* Introd. p. 21), which Mill had access to, and in his N.T. made good use of, as well as of Ussher's other papers (Mill, *Proleg.* § 1505).

8. Steph. Curcellaeus or Courcelles published his N.T. at Amsterdam in 1658, before he had seen Walton's Polyglott. The peculiar merit of his book arises from his marginal collection of parallel texts, which are more copious than those of his predecessors, yet not too many for convenient use: later editors have been thankful to take them as a basis for their own. There are many various readings (some from two or three fresh manuscripts) at the foot of each page, or thrown into an appendix; mingled with certain rash conjectures which betray a Socinian bias: but since the authorities are not cited for each separate reading, his critical labours were as good as wasted.[1]

A more important step in advance was taken in the Greek Testament in 8vo, issued from the Oxford University Press in 1675. This elegant volume (whose Greek text is Stephens') was superintended by John Fell [1625—86], Dean of Christ-Church, soon afterwards Bishop of Oxford, the biographer of

[1] "Stephani Curcellaei annotationes variantium lectionum, pro variantibus lectionibus non habendae, quia ille non notat codices, unde eas habeat, an ex manuscriptis, an vero ex impressis exemplaribus. Possunt etiam pro uno codice haberi." Canon XIII. pp. 11, 69—70 of the *N. T.* by *G. D. T. M. D.* (see below, p. 319).

saint-like Hammond, himself one of the most learned and munificent, if not quite the most popular Prelate, of that golden age of the English Church, in whose behalf Anthony à Wood designates him "the most zealous man of his time." His brief yet interesting Preface not only discusses the causes of various readings[1], and describes the materials used for his edition, but touches on that weak and ignorant prejudice which had been already raised against the collection of such variations in the text of Scripture; and that too sometimes by persons like John Owen[2] the Puritan, intrusive Dean of Christ-Church under Cromwell, who, but that we are loth to doubt his integrity, would hardly be deemed a victim of the panic he sought to spread. In reply to all objectors the Bishop pleads the comparative insignificance of the change produced by various readings on the general sense of Holy Writ, and especially that God hath dealt so bountifully with his people "ut necessaria quaeque et ad salutis summam facientia in S. literis saepius repeterentur; ita ut si forte quidpiam minus commode alicubi expressum, id damnum aliunde reparari possit" (*Praef.* p. 1). On this assurance we may well rest in peace. This edition is more valuable for the impulse it gave to subsequent investigators than for the richness of its own stores of fresh materials; although it is stated on the title-page to be derived "*ex plus* 100 *MSS. Codicibus.*" Patristic testimony, as we have seen, Bishop Fell rather undervalued (p. 284): the use of versions he clearly perceived, yet of those at that time available, he only attends to the Gothic and Coptic as revised by Marshall (pp. 271, 276): his list of manuscripts, hitherto untouched, is very scanty. To those used by Walton we can add only *R*, the Barberini readings, then just published (p. 157); *B*, twelve Bodleian codices "quorum plerique

[1] Fell imputes the origin of various readings to the causes brought under heads (9), (4), (6), (8), (17), (7) in the first Chapter of the present volume, adding one which does not seem very probable, that accidental slips once made were retained and propagated through a superstitious feeling of misplaced reverence, citing in illustration Apoc. xxii. 18, 19. He alleges also the well-known subscription of Irenaeus, preserved by Eusebius, which will best be considered hereafter (Chap. VII.); and remarks, with whatever truth, that contrary to the practice of the Jews and Muhammedans in regard to their sacred books, it was allowed "e vulgo quibusvis, calamo pariter et manu profanis, sacra ista [N. T.] tractare" (*Praef.* p. 4).

[2] *Considerations on the Biblia Polyglotta*, 1659: to which Walton rejoined, sharply enough, in *The Considerator considered*, also in 1659.

intacti prius," in no-wise described, and cited only by the number of them which may countenance each variation; *U*, the two Ussher manuscripts Evan. 63, 64 (p. 150) as collated by H. Dodwell; three copies from the Library of Petavius (*P*, Act. 38, 39, 40, pp. 189, 190), a fourth from St Germains (*Ge*, Paul. E, p. 133), the readings of these four were furnished by Joh. Gachon. Yet this slight volume (for so we must needs regard it) was the legitimate parent of one of the noblest works in the whole range of Biblical literature,

9. NOVUM TESTAMENTUM GRAECUM of Dr John Mill, Oxford, 1707, in folio. This able and laborious critic, born in 1645, quitted his native village in Westmoreland at sixteen for Queen's College, Oxford, of which society he became a Fellow, and was conspicuous there both as a scholar and a ready extemporary preacher. In 1685 his College appointed him Principal of its affiliated Hall, St Edmund's, so honourably distinguished for the Biblical studies of its members, but Mill had by that time made good progress in his Greek Testament, on which he gladly spent the last thirty years of his life, dying suddenly in 1707, a fortnight after its publication. His attention was first called to the subject by his friend, Dr Edward Bernard, the Savilian Professor at Oxford, whom he vividly represents, as setting before him an outline of the work, and encouraging him to attempt its accomplishment. "Vides, Amice mi, opus...omnium, mihi crede, longè dignissimum, cui in hoc aetatis tuae flore, robur animi tui, vigilias ac studia liberaliter impendas" (*Proleg.* § 1417). Ignorant as yet both of the magnitude and difficulty of his task, Mill boldly undertook it about 1677, and his efforts soon obtained the countenance of Bp Fell, who promised to defray the expense of printing, and, mindful of the frailty of life, urged him to go to press before his papers were quite ready to meet the public eye. When about 24 chapters of St Matthew had been completed, Bp Fell died prematurely in 1686, and the *book* seems to have languished for many following years from lack of means, though the *editor* was busy all the while in gathering and arranging his materials, especially for the Prolegomena, which well deserve to be called "marmore perenniora." As late as 1704 John Sharp [1644—1714], Archbishop of York, whose remonstrances to Queen Anne some years subse-

quently hindered the ribald wit that wrote *A Tale of a Tub* from polluting the episcopal throne of an English see, obtained from her for Mill a stall at Canterbury, and the royal command to prosecute his N. T. forthwith. The preferment came just in time. Three years afterwards the volume was given to the Christian world, and its author's course was already finished: his life's work well ended, he had entered upon his rest. He was spared the pain of reading the unfair attack alike on his book and its subject by our eminent Commentator, Daniel Whitby (*Examen Variantium Lectionum*, 1710), and of witnessing the unscrupulous use of Whitby's arguments made by the sceptic Anthony Collins in his *Discourse of Free Thinking*, 1713.

Dr Mill's services to Biblical criticism surpass in extent and value those rendered by any other, except perhaps one man yet living. A large proportion of his care and pains, as we have seen (p. 284), was bestowed on the Fathers and ancient writers of every description who have used and cited Scripture. The versions are usually considered his weakest point: although he first accorded to the Vulgate and its prototype the Old Latin the importance they deserve, his knowledge of Syriac was rather slight, and for the other Eastern tongues, if he was not more ignorant than his successors, he had not discovered how little Latin translations of the Æthiopic, &c. can be trusted. As a collator of manuscripts the list subjoined will bear full testimony to his industry: without seeking to repeat details we have entered into elsewhere (Chap. II. Sect. III.), it is right to state that he has either himself re-examined, or otherwise represented more fully and exactly, the codices that had been previously used for the London Polyglott and the Oxford N. T. of 1675. Still it would be wrong to dissemble that Mill's style of collation is not such as the strictness of modern scholarship demands. He seldom notices at all such various readings as arise from the transposition of words, insertion or omission of the Greek article, homoeoteleuta (*see* p. 9), itacisms (p. 10), or manifest errors of the pen; while in respect to general accuracy he is as much inferior to those who have trod in his steps, as he rises above Stephens and Ussher, or the persons employed by Walton and Fell. It has been my fortune to collate not a few manuscripts after this great critic, and I have elsewhere been obliged to notice these plain facts, I would fain trust in no disparaging temper. During the many years that Mill's N. T. has been my daily companion, my reverence for that diligent and earnest man has been constantly growing: the principles of internal evidence which guided his choice between conflicting authorities (see below, Chap. VI.) were simple (as indeed they ought to be), but applied with rare judgment, sagacity, and moderation: his zeal was unflagging, his treatment of his sacred subject deeply reverential. Of the criticism of the N. T. in the hands of Dr John Mill it may be said, that he found the edifice of wood, and left it marble.

The following Catalogue of the manuscripts known to Mill exhibits the abridged form in which he cites them (*see* p. 66), together with the more usual notation, whereby they are described in Chapter II. Sect. II.—IV. of this volume; and will tend, it is believed, to facilitate the use of Mill's N. T.

Alex..........Cod. A.
Barb. ......Evan. 112, Wetstein
Baroc. ......Act. 23
B. 1 ....Evan. E
B. 2 ....Act. 2
B. 3 ....Act. 4
Bodl. 1......Evan. 45
Bodl. 2......Evan. 46
Bodl. 3......Evst. 5
Bodl. 4......Evst. 18
Bodl. 5......Evst. 19
Bodl. 6......Evan. 47
Bodl. 7......Evan. 48
Bu. ....Evan. 70
Cant. ......Evan. Act. D
Cant. 2......Act. 24
Cant. 3......Act. 53
Clar. ......Paul. D.
Colb. 1 ......Evan. 27
Colb. 2 ......Evan. 28
Colb. 3 ......Evan. 29
Colb. 4 ......Evan. 30, 31
Colb. 5 ......Evan. 32
Colb. 6 ... } Act. 13
Colb. 7 ... } Paul. 17
Colb. 8 ... } Evan. 33
Colb. 9 = Colb. 1
Colb. 10 = Colb. 2
Colb. 11 = Colb. 1
Cov. 1 ......Evan. 65
Cov. 2 ......Act. 25
Cov. 3 ......Act. 26
Cov. 4 ......Act. 27
Cov. 5 *Sin*...Act. 28
Cypr. ......Evan. K
Em. ....*videas* p. 150
Eph. ....Evan. 71
Gal. ....Evan. 66
Ger. ....Paul. E
Genev. ......Act. 29
Go. ....Evan. 62
Gon. ....Evan. 59
Hunt. 1 ...Act. 30
Hunt. 2 ...Evan. 67
L. ....Evan. 69
Laud. 1 ...Evan. 50
Laud. 2 ...Evan. 51
Laud. 3 ...Act. E
Laud. 4 ...Evst. 20
Laud. 5 ...Evan. 52
Lin. ....Evan. 56
Lin. 2 ......Act. 33
M. 1 ....Evan. 60
M. 2 ....Evst. 4.
Magd. 1 ...Evan. 57
Magd. 2 ...Paul. 42
Med..........Evan. 42
Mont. ......Evan. 61
N. 1.........Evan. 58
N. 1 ....Act. 37
N. 2 ....Act. 36
Per. ....Evan. 91
Pet. 1 ......Act. 38
Pet. 2 ......Act. 39
Pet. 3 ......Act. 40
Roe. 1 ......Evan. 49
Roe. 2 ......Paul. 47
Seld. 1 ......Evan. 53
Seld. 2 ......Evan. 54
Seld. 3 ......Evan. 55
Seld. 4 ......Evst. 21
Seld. 5 ......Evst. 22
Steph. codices XVI. *videas* pp. 299—300.
Trin. ......Apost. 3
Trit..........Evan. 96
Vat. ....Cod. B
Vel. ....Evan. 111, Wetstein
Vien. ......Evan. 76
Usser. 1 ...Evan. 63
Usser. 2 ...Evan. 64
Wheel. 1 ...Evan. 68
Wheel. 2 ...Evan. 95
Wheel. 3 ...Evst. 3
Wech. videas pp. 312—3.

Mill merely drew from other sources *Barb., Steph., Vel., Wech.*; the copies deposited abroad (*B* 1—3; *Clar., Colb.* 1—11; *Cypr., Genev., Med., Per., Pet.* 1—3, *Vat., Vien.*) and *Trin.* or Apost. 3 he only knew from readings sent to him; all the rest, not being included in Walton's list (p. 312), and several of them also, he collated for himself.

The Prolegomena of Mill, divided into three parts:—(1) on the Canon of the New Testament; (2) on the History of the Text, including the quotations of the Fathers (*see p.* 285) and the early editions; and (3) on the plan and contents of his own work —though by this time too far behind the present state of knowledge to bear reprinting—comprise a monument of learning such as the world has seldom seen, and contain much information the student will not even now easily find elsewhere. Although Mill perpetually pronounces his judgment on the character of disputed readings, especially in his Prolegomena, which were printed long after some portions of the body of the work, yet he only aims at reproducing Stephens' text of 1550, though in a few places he departs from it, whether by accident or design[1].

In 1710 Ludolph Küster, a Westphalian, republished Mill's Greek Testament in folio, at Rotterdam (with a new title-page, Leipsic 1723, Amsterdam 1746), arranging in its proper place the matter cast by Mill into his Appendix, as having reached him too late to stand in his critical notes, and adding to those notes the readings of twelve fresh manuscripts, ten collated by himself, which he describes in a Preface well worth reading. Nine of these codices are in the Imperial Library at Paris (viz. *Paris.* 1, which *seems* to be Evan. 10; *Paris.* 2 = Evan. M; *Paris.* 3 = Evan. 9; *Paris.* 4 = Evan. 11; *Paris.* 5 = Evan. 119; *Paris.* 6 = Evan. 13; *Paris.* 7 = Evan. 14; *Paris.* 8 = Evan. 15; *Paris.* 9 = the great Cod. C); *Lips.* = Evan. 78 was collated by Boerner; *Seidel.* = Act. 42 by Westermann; *Boerner.* = Paul. G (*see p.* 135) by Küster himself. He keeps his own notes separate from Mill's by prefixing and affixing the marks ⸗, ⸗, and his collations both of his own codices and early editions will be found more complete than Mill's.

10. In the next year after Küster's Mill (1711) appeared at Amsterdam, from the press of the Wetsteins, a small N. T., 8°, containing all the critical matter of the Oxford edition of

[1] As Mill's text is sometimes reprinted in England as if it were quite identical with the commonly received text, it is right to note the following passages wherein it does not coincide with Stephens' of 1550, besides that it corrects his typographical errors: Matth. xx. 15; 22; xxiv. 15; Mark ix. 16; xi. 22; xv. 29; Luke vii. 12 *bis;* x. 6; xvii. 1; John viii. 4; 25; xiii. 30, 31; xix. 7; Act. ii. 36; xiv. 8; Rom. xvi. 11; 1 Cor. iii. 15; x. 10; xv. 28; 2 Cor. vi. 16; Eph. iv. 25; Tit. ii. 10; 1 Pet. iii. 11; 21; iv. 8; 2 Pet. ii. 12; Apoc. xx. 4.

1675, a collation of one Vienna manuscript (*Caes.* = Evan. 76), 43 canons "secundum quos variantes lectiones N. T. examinandae," and discussions upon them, with other matter, forming a convenient manual, the whole by G. D. T. M. D., which being interpreted means Gerard de Trajecto Mosae Doctor, this Gerard à Mästrich being a Syndic of Bremen. A second and somewhat improved edition was published in 1735, but ere that date the book must have become quite superseded.

We have to return to England once more, where the criticism of the New Testament had engrossed the attention of RICHARD BENTLEY [1662—1742], whose elevation to the enviable post of Master of Trinity College, Cambridge, in 1699, was a just recognition of his supremacy in the English world of letters. As early as 1691 he had felt a keen interest in sacred criticism, and in his "*Epistola ad Johannem Millium*" had urged that editor, in language fraught with eloquence and native vigour, to hasten on the work (whose accomplishment was eventually left to others) of publishing side by side on the opened leaf Codd. A. D (*Bezae*) D (*Clarom.*) E (*Laud.*). For many years Bentley's laurels were won on other fields, and it was not till his friend was dead, and his admirable labours were exposed to the obloquy of opponents (some honest though unwise, others hating Mill because they hated the Scriptures which he sought to illustrate), that our Aristarchus exerted his giant strength to crush the infidel and to put the ignorant to silence. In his "*Remarks upon a late Discourse of Free Thinking in a letter to F*[*rancis*] *H*[*are*] *D.D. by Phileleutherus Lipsiensis*," 1713, Bentley displayed that intimate familiarity with the whole subject of various readings, their causes, extent, and consequences (*see above*, p. 7), which has rendered his occasional treatise more truly valued (as it was far more important) than the world-renowned "*Dissertation upon the Epistles of Phalaris*" itself. As his years were now hastening on, and the evening of life was beginning to draw nigh, it was seemly that the first scholar of his age should seek for his rare abilities an employment more entirely suited to his sacred office than even the most successful cultivation of classical learning; and so, about this time, he came to project what he henceforth regarded as his greatest effort, an edition of the Greek New Testament. In 1716 we find him in conference with J. J. Wetstein (then very young) and seeking his aid in procuring collations. In the same year he addressed his memorable Letter to Wm. Wake [1657—1737], Archbishop of Canterbury (whose own mind was full of the subject), wherein he explains, with characteristic energy and precision, the principles on which he proposed to execute his great scheme. As these principles must be reviewed in Chap. VII, we will but touch upon them now. His theory, then, was built upon the notion that the oldest manuscripts of the Greek original and of Jerome's Latin version resemble each other so marvellously, even in the very order of the words, that by this agreement he could restore the text as it stood in the fourth century, "so that there shall not be twenty words, or even particles, difference." "By taking two thousand errors out of the Pope's [i. e. the Clementine] Vulgate, and as many out of the Protestant Pope Stephens's [1550], I can set out an edition of each in columns, without using any book under nine hundred years old, that shall so exactly agree word for word, and, what at first amazed me, order for order, that no two tallies, nor two indentures, can agree better." In 1720, some progress having been made in the task of collation, chiefly at Paris, by John Walker, Vice-Master of Trinity (*see pp.* 183—4), Bentley published his *Proposals for Printing*[1] a work which "he consecrates, as a *κειμήλιον*, a *κτῆμα ἐσαεὶ*, a *charter*, a *magna charta*, to the whole Christian Church; to last when all the ancient MSS. here quoted may be lost and extinguished." Alas for the emptiness of human anticipations! Of this noble design, projected by one of the most diligent, by one of the most highly gifted men our dear mother Cambridge ever nourished, nothing now remains but a few scattered notices in treatises on Textual Criticism, and large undigested stores of various readings and random observations, accumulated in his College Library; papers which no real student ever glanced through, but with a heart saddened—almost sickened—at the sight of so much labour lost[2]. The

[1] These *Proposals* are very properly reprinted by Tischendorf (*N. T. Proleg.* LXXXVII—XCVI, 7th edition) together with the specimen chapter. The full title was to have been: "Η ΚΑΙΝΗ ΔΙΑΘΗΚΗ Graece. Novum Testamentum Versionis Vulgatae, per s^tum^ Hieronymum ad vetusta exemplaria Graeca castigatae et exactae. Utrumque ex antiquissimis Codd. MSS., cum Graecis tum Latinis, edidit Richardus Bentleius."

[2] The following work is just announced: BENTLEII CRITICA SACRA. Notes on the Greek and Latin Text of the New Testament, extracted from the Bentley MSS. in Trinity College Library. With the Abbé Rulotta's Collation of the

specimen chapter (Apocalypse xxii.) which accompanied his *Proposals* shews clearly how little had yet been done towards arranging the materials that had been collected; codices are cited there, and in many of his loose notes, not separately and by name, as in Mill's volume, but mostly as "*Anglicus unus, tres codd. veterrimi, Gall. quatuor, Germ. unus,*" &c., in the rough fashion of the Oxford N. T. of 1675. Though Bentley lived on till 1742, little appears to have been done for the Greek Testament after 1721 (Walker's Oxford collations of 1732 seem to have been on his own account: *see p.* 183); and we cannot but believe that nothing less than the manifest impossibility of maintaining the principles which his *Letter* of 1716 enunciated, and his *Proposals* of 1720 scarcely modified, in the face of the evidence which his growing mass of collations bore against them, could have had power enough to break off in the midst that labour of love from which he had looked for undying fame[1].

11. The text and version of W. or Daniel Mace (*The New Testament in Greek and English*, 2 vol. 8°, 1729) are alike unworthy of serious notice, and have long since been forgotten. And now original research in the science of Biblical criticism, so far as the New Testament is concerned, seems to have left the shores of England, to return no more for upwards of a century[2]; and we must look to Germany if we wish to trace the further

Vatican MSS [? MS: *see p.* 89], a specimen of Bentley's intended edition, and an account of all his Collations. Edited, with the permission of the Master and Seniors, by the Rev. A. A. Ellis, M.A. late Fellow and Junior Dean of Trinity College, Cambridge. *Nearly ready.*

1 "This thought has now so engaged me, and in a manner inslaved me, that *vae mihi* unless I do it. Nothing but sickness (by the blessing of God) shall hinder me from prosecuting it to the end" (*Bentley to Wake*, 1716: *Correspondence*, p. 508).

2 I cannot help borrowing the language of the lamented Dr Donaldson, used with reference to an entirely different department of study, in the opening of one of his earliest and by far his most enduring work: "It may be stated as a fact worthy of observation in the literary history of modern Europe, that generally, when one of our countrymen has made the first advance in any branch of knowledge, we have acquiesced in what he has done, and have left the further improvement of the subject to our neighbours on the continent. The man of genius always finds an utterance, for he is urged on by an irresistible impulse—a conviction that it is his duty and vocation to speak: but we too often want those who shall follow in his steps, clear up what he has left obscure, and complete his unfinished labours" (*New Cratylus*, p. 1).

progress of investigations which our countrymen had so auspiciously begun. The first considerable effort made on the continent was

The New Testament of John Albert Bengel, 4°, Tubingen, 1734[1]: his *Prodromus N. T. Gr. rectè cautèque adornandi*" had appeared as early as 1725. This devout and truly able man [1687—1752], who held the office (whatever might be its functions) of Abbot of Alpirspach in the *Lutheran* communion of Würtemberg, though more generally known as an interpreter of Scripture from his valuable *Gnomon Novi Testamenti*, yet left the stamp of his mind deeply imprinted on the criticism of the sacred volume. As a collator his merits were not high; nearly all his sixteen codices have required and obtained fresh examination from those who came after him[2]. His text (which he arranged in convenient paragraphs, *see p.* 60) is the earliest important specimen of intentional departure from the received type; hence he imposes on himself the strange restriction of admitting into it no reading (excepting in the Apocalypse) which had not appeared in one or more of the editions that preceded his own. He pronounces his opinion on other *select* variations by placing them in his lower margin with Greek numerals attached to them, according as he judged them decidedly better (*α*), or somewhat more likely (*β*), than those which stand in his text: or equal to them (*γ*); or a little (*δ*), or considerably (*ε*) inferior. This notation has advantages which might well have commended it to the attention of succeeding editors. In his *Apparatus Criticus*, also, at the end of his volume, he first set the example, now generally followed, of recording the testimony in favour of a received reading, as well as that against it.

[1] The full title is "Ἡ καινὴ διαθήκη. Novum Testamentum Graecum ita adornatum ut Textus probatarum editionum medullam, Margo variantium lectionum in suas classes distributarum locorumque parallelorum delectum, Apparatus subjunctus criseos sacrae Millianae praesertim compendium limam supplementum ac fructum exhibeat, inserviente J. A. B."

[2] They consist of seven Augsburg codices (*Aug.* 1 = Evan. 83; *Aug.* 2 = Evan. 84; *Aug.* 3 = Evan. 85; *Aug.* 4 = Evst. 24; *Aug.* 5 = Paul. 54; *Aug.* 6 = Act. 46; *Aug.* 7 = Apoc. 80); *Poson.* = Evan. 86; extracts sent by Isel from three Basle copies (*Bas.* α = Evan. E; *Bas.* β = Evan. 2; *Bas.* γ = Evan. 1); *Hirsaug.* = Evan. 97; *Mosc.* = Evan. V, see p. 117, note: extracts sent by F. C. Gross. To these add Uffenbach's three, *Uffen.* 2 or 1 = Paul. M; *Uffen.* 1 or 2 = Act. 45; *Uffen.* 3 = Evan. 101.

But the peculiar importance of Bengel's N. T. is due to the critical principles developed therein. Not only was his native acuteness of great service to him, when weighing the conflicting probabilities of internal evidence (see Chap. VI.), but in his fertile mind sprang up the germ of that theory of *families* or *recensions*, which was afterwards expanded by J. S. Semler [1725—91], and grew to such formidable dimensions in the skilful hands of Griesbach. An attentive student of the discrepant readings of the N. T., even in the limited extent they had hitherto been collected, could hardly fail to discern that certain manuscripts, versions, and ecclesiastical writers, bear a certain affinity with each other; so that one of them shall seldom be cited in support of a variation (not being a manifest and gross error of the copyist), unless accompanied by several of its kindred. The inference is direct and clear, that documents which thus withdraw themselves from the general mass of authorities, must have sprung from some common source, distinct from those, which in characteristic readings they but seldom resemble. It occurred, therefore, to Bengel as a hopeful mode of making good progress in the criticism of the N. T., to reduce all extant testimony into "companies, families, tribes, and nations," and thus to simplify the process of settling the sacred text by setting class over against class, and trying to estimate the genius of each, and the relative importance they may severally lay claim to. He wishes to divide all extant documents into two nations: the *Asiatic*, chiefly written in Constantinople and its neighbourhood, which he was inclined to disparage; and the *African*, comprising the few of a better type (*Apparatus Criticus*, p. 669, 2nd edition, 1763). Various circumstances hindered Bengel from working out his principle, among which he condescends to set his dread of exposing his task to senseless ridicule[1]; yet no one can doubt that it comprehends the elements

[1] It is worth while to quote at length Bengel's terse and vigorous statement of his principle: "Posset variarum lectionum ortus, per singulos codices, per paria codicum, per syzygias minores majoresque, per familias, tribus, nationesque illorum, investigari et repraesentari: et inde propinquitates discessionesque codicum ad schematismos quosdam reduci, et schematismorum aliquae concordantiae fieri; atque ita res tota per tabulam quandam quasi genealogicam oculis subjici, ad quam tabulam quaelibet varietas insignior cum agmine suorum codicum, ad convincendos etiam tardissimos dubitatores exigeretur. Magnam conjectanea nostra sylvam habent: sed manum de tabulâ, ne risuum periculo exponatur veritas.

of what is both reasonable and true; however difficult it has subsequently proved to adjust the details of any consistent scheme. For the rest, Bengel's critical verdicts, always considered in relation to his age and opportunities, deserve strong commendation. He saw the paramount worth of Cod. A, the only great uncial then much known (*N. T., Apparat. Crit.* pp. 390—401); the high character of the Latin version, and the necessity for revising its text by means of manuscripts (*ibid.* p. 391), he readily conceded, after Bentley's example. His mean estimate of the Greek-Latin codices (Evan. Act. D; Act. E; Paul. DG) may not find equal favour in the eyes of all his admirers: he pronounces them "re verâ bilingues;" which for their perpetual and wilful interpolations "non pro codicibus, sed pro rhapsodiis, haberi debeant" (*ibid.* p. 386).

12. The next step in advance was made by John James Wetstein [1693—1754], a native of Basle, whose edition of the Greek New Testament ("cum lectionibus Variantibus Codicum MSS., Editionum aliarum, Versionum et Patrum, necnon Commentario pleniore ex Scriptoribus veteribus, Hebraeis, Graecis et Latinis, historiam et vim verborum illustrante") appeared in two volumes folio, Amsterdam, 1751—2. The genius, the character, and (it must in justice be added) the worldly fortunes of Wetstein were widely different from those of the good Abbot of Alpirspach. His taste for Biblical studies shewed itself early. When ordained pastor at the age of twenty he delivered a disputation, "De variis N. T. Lectionibus," and zeal for this fascinating pursuit became at length with him a passion: the master-passion which consoled and dignified a roving, troubled, unprosperous life. In 1714 his eager search for manuscripts led him to Paris, in 1715—6 and again in 1720 he visited England, and was employed by Bentley in collecting materials for his projected edition (*see p.* 95), but he seems to have imbibed few of that great man's principles: the interval between them, both in age and station, almost forbad much sympathy. On

Bene est, quod praetergredi montem hunc, et planiore via pervenire datur ad codices discriminandos. Datur autem per hanc regulam aequissimam: Quo saepius non modo singuli codices, sed etiam syzygiae minores eorum vel majores, in aberrationes manifestas tendunt; eo levius ferunt testimonium in discrepantiis difficilioribus, eoque magis lectio ab eis deserta, tanquam genuina retineri debet" (*N. T., Apparat. Crit.* p. 387).

his return home he gradually became suspected of Socinian tendencies, and it must be feared with too much justice; so that in the end he was deposed from the pastorate (1730), driven into exile, and after having been compelled to serve in a position the least favourable to the cultivation of learning, that of a military chaplain, he obtained at length (1733) a Professorship among the Remonstrants at Amsterdam (in succession to the celebrated Leclerc), and there continued till his death in 1754, having made his third visit to England in 1746 (*see p.* 243). His *Prolegomena*, first published in 1730, and afterwards, in an altered form, prefixed to his N. T., present a painful image both of the man and his circumstances. His restless energy, his undaunted industry, his violent temper, his love of paradox, his assertion for himself of perfect freedom of thought, his silly prejudice against Jesuits and bigots, his enmities, his wrongs, his ill-requited labours, at once excite our respect and our pity: while they all help to make his writings a sort of unconscious autobiography, rather interesting than agreeable. *Non sic itur ad astra*, whether morally or intellectually; yet Wetstein's services to sacred literature were of no common order. His philological annotations, wherein the matter and phraseology of the inspired writers are illustrated by copious—too copious—quotations from all kinds of authors, classical, Patristic or Rabbinical, have proved an inexhaustible storehouse from which later writers have drawn liberally and sometimes without due acknowledgement; but many of the passages are of such a tenor as (to use Tregelles' very gentle language respecting them) "only excite surprise at their being found on the same page as the text of the New Testament" (*Account of Printed Text*, p. 76). The critical portion of his work, however, is far more valuable, and in this department Wetstein must be placed in the very first rank, inferior (if to any) but to one or two of the highest names. He first cited the manuscripts under the notation by which they are commonly known (*see* p. 66), his list already embracing A—O, 1—112 of the Gospels; A—G, 1—58 of the Acts; A—H, 1—60 of St Paul; A—C, 1—28 of the Apocalypse; 1—24 Evangelistaria; 1—4 of the Apostolos. Of these Wetstein himself collated about one hundred and two[1], if not as fully or

[1] We here reckon separately, as we believe is both usual and convenient, every distinct portion of the N. T. contained in a manuscript. Thus Codd. C or 69 Evan. will each count for four.

accurately as is now expected, yet with far greater care than had hitherto been usual: about eleven were examined for him by other hands. On the versions and early editions he has likewise bestowed great pains; with the Fathers he has been less successful. His text was that of Elzevir, not very exactly printed (e.g. ὦ Θεόφιλε is entirely omitted, Act. i. 1, where there is no various reading), and immediately below it he placed such readings of his manuscripts as he judged preferable to those received: the readings approved by Wetstein (which do not amount to five hundred, and those chiefly in the Apocalypse) were inserted in the text of a Greek Testament published in London 1763, 2 vol., by W. Bowyer, the learned printer.

Wetstein's Prolegomena have also been reproduced by J. S. Semler (Halle, 1764), with good notes and *facsimiles* of certain manuscripts, and more recently, in a compressed and modernized form, by J. A. Lotze (Rotterdam 1831), a book which neither for design nor execution can be much praised. The truth is that both the style and the subject-matter of much that Wetstein wrote are things of the past. In his earlier edition of his Prolegomena (1730) he had spoken of the oldest Greek uncial copies as they deserve; he was even disposed to take Cod. A as the basis of his text. By the time his N. T. was ready, twenty years later, he had come to include it, with all the older codices of the original, under a general charge of being conformed to the *Latin* version. That such a tendency may be detected in some of the codices accompanied by a Latin translation, is both possible in itself, and not inconsistent with their general spirit; but he has scattered abroad his imputations capriciously and almost at random, so as greatly to diminish the weight of his own decisions. Cod. A, in particular, has been fully cleared of the charge of Latinising by Woide, in his excellent *Prolegomena* (§ 6: *see p.* 83). His thorough contempt for that critic prevented Wetstein from giving adequate attention to Bengel's theory of families; indeed he can hardly be said to have rejected a scheme which he scorned to investigate with patience. On the other hand no portion of his labours is more valuable than the "Animadversiones et Cautiones ad examen variarum lectionum N. T. necessariae," (N. T. Tom. II. p. 851—74), which might be discussed more suitably in the next chapter. In this tract his natural good sense and extensive knowledge of authorities of every class have gone far to correct that impetuous temperament which was ever too ready to substitute plausible conjecture in the room of ascertained facts.

13. During the twenty years immediately ensuing on the publication of Wetstein's volumes, little was attempted in the way of enlarging or improving the domain he had secured for Biblical science. In England the attention of critics was directed, and on the whole successfully, to the criticism of the Hebrew Scriptures; in Germany, the younger (J. D.) Michaelis [1717—91] reigned supreme, and he seems to have deemed it the highest effort of scholarship to sit in judgment on the labours of others. In process of time, however, the researches of John James Griesbach [1745—1812], a native of Hesse Darmstadt, and a pupil of Semler and J. A. Ernesti [1707—81] (whose manual *Institutio Interpretis N. T.* 1761 has not long been superseded), began to attract general notice. Like Wetstein, he made a literary tour in England early in life (1769) and with far more profit; returning to Halle as a Professor, he published before he was thirty (1774—5) his first edition of the N.T., which contained the well-defined embryo of his future and more elaborate speculations. It will be convenient to reserve the examination of his views until we have described the investigations of several collators who unknowingly (and in one instance, no doubt very unwillingly) were busy in gathering stores which he was to turn to his own use.

(1) Christian Frederick Matthaei, a Thuringian [1744—1811], was appointed, on the recommendation of his tutor Ernesti, to the Professorship of Classical Literature at Moscow: so far as philology is concerned, he probably merited Bp. Middleton's praise, as "the most accurate scholar who ever edited the N. T." (*Doctrine of the Greek Article*, p. 244, 3rd edition). At Moscow he found a large number of Greek manuscripts, both Biblical and Patristic, originally brought from Athos (*see* p. 166), quite uncollated, and almost entirely unknown in the west of Europe. With laudable resolution he set himself to examine them, and gradually formed the scheme of publishing an edition of the New Testament by the aid of materials so precious and abundant. All authors that deserve that honourable name may be presumed to learn not a little, even on the subject they know best, while preparing an

important work for the public eye; but Matthaei was as yet ignorant of the first principles of the critical art; and beginning thus late, there was much, of a very elementary character, which he never understood at all. When he commenced writing he had not seen the volumes of Mill or Wetstein; and to this significant fact we must impute that inability which clave to him to the last, of discriminating the relative age and value of his own or others' codices. The palaeographical portion of the science, indeed, he gradually acquired from the study of his documents, and the many *facsimiles* of them he represents in his edition; but what can be thought of his judgment, when he persisted in asserting the intrinsic superiority of Cod. 69 of the Acts [XIII, *see* p. 192] to the great uncials AC? (*N. T.* Tom. XII. p. 222)[1]. Hence it results that Matthaei's text, which of course he moulded on his own views, must be held in slight esteem: his services as a collator comprehend his whole claim (and that no trifling one) to our thankful regard. To him solely we are indebted for Evan. V; 237—259; Act. 98—107; Paul. 113—124; Apoc. 47—50[2]; Evst. 47—57; Apost. 13—20; nearly all at Moscow: the whole seventy, together with the citations of Scripture in about thirty manuscripts of Chrysostom, being so fully and accurately collated, that the reader need not be at a loss whether any particular copy supports or opposes the reading in the common text. Matthaei's further services in connection with Cod. G Paul. (p. 136) and a few others (Act. 69, Paul. 76, Apoc. 32, &c.) have been noticed in their proper places. To his Greek text was annexed the Latin Vulgate (the only version, in its present state, he professes to regard, Tom. XI. p. xii.) from the Cod. Demidovianus (see p. 265). The first volume of this edition appeared in 1782, after it had been already eight years in preparation: this comprised the Catholic Epistles. The rest of the work was published at intervals during the next six years, in eleven more thin parts 8°, the whole series being closed by St Matthew and Mark

1 One other specimen of Matthaei's critical skill will suffice: he is speaking of his Cod. H, which is our Evst. 50 (*see* p. 214). "Hic Codex scriptus est literis quadratis, estque eorum omnium, qui adhuc in Europa innotuerunt et vetustissimus et praestantissimus. Insanus quidem fuerit, qui cum hoc aut Cod. V [p. 117] comparare, aut aequiparare voluerit Codd. Alexandr. Clar. Germ. Boern. Cant. [Evan. AD, Paul. ADEG], qui sine ullo dubio pessimè ex scholiis et Versione Latinâ Vulgatâ interpolati sunt" (*N. T.*, Tom. IX. p. 254).

in 1788. Each volume has a Preface, much descriptive matter, and twenty-nine *facsimiles* of Manuscripts, the whole in complete and almost hopeless disorder, and the general title-page absurdly long. Hence his critical principles (if such they may be termed) must be picked up piecemeal; and it is not very pleasant to observe the sort of influence which hostile controversy exercised over his mind and temper. While yet fresh at his task (1782), anticipating the fair fame his most profitable researches had so well earned, Matthaei is frank, calm and rational: even at a later period J. D. Michaelis is, in his estimation, the keenest of living judges of codices, and he says so the rather "quod ille vir doctissimus multis modis me, *quâ de causâ ipse ignoro*, partim jocosè, partim seriò, vexavit." (Tom. II. 1788, p. xxxi): Bengel, whose sentiments were very dissimilar from those of the Moscow Professor, "pro acumine, diligentiâ et religione suâ," would have arrived at other conclusions, had his Augsburg codices been better (*ibid.* p. xxx). But for Griesbach and his recension-theory no terms of insult are strong enough; "risum vel adeo pueris debet ille Halensis criticus," who never saw, "*ut credibile est*," a manuscript even of the tenth century (*ibid.* p. xxiii), yet presumes to dictate to those who have collated seventy. The unhappy consequence was, that one who had taken up this employment in an earnest and candid spirit, possessed with the simple desire to promote the study of sacred literature, could devise no fitter commencement for his latest Preface than this: "Laborem igitur molestum invidiosum et infamem, inter convicia ranarum et latratus canum, aut ferreâ patientiâ aut invictâ pertinaciâ his quindecim annis vel sustinui, vel utcunque potui, perfeci, vel denique fastidio et taedio, ut fortasse non nulli opinantur, deposui et abjeci" (Tom. I. *Praef.* p. 1): he could find no purer cause for thankfulness, than (what we might have imagined but a very slight mercy) that he had never been commended by those "of whom to be dispraised is no small praise;" or (to use his own more vigorous language) "quod nemo scurra...nemo denique de grege novorum theologorum, hanc qualemcunque operam meam ausus est ore impuro suo, laudeque contumeliosâ comprobare." Matthaei's second edition in three volumes (without the Latin and most of the critical notes) bears date 1803—7.

(2) The next, and a far less considerable contribution to

our knowledge of manuscripts of the N. T., was made by Francis Karl Alter [1749—1804] a Jesuit, born in Silesia, and Professor of Greek at Vienna. His plan was novel, and, to those who are compelled to use his edition (*N. T. Graecum, ad Codicem Vindobonensem Graecè expressum*, 8°, Vienna, 2 tom., 1786—7), inconvenient to the last degree. Adopting for his standard a valuable, but not very ancient or remarkable, manuscript in the Imperial Library (Evan. 218, Act. 65, Paul. 57, Apoc. 33), he prints this copy at full length, retaining even the ν ἐφελκυστικὸν when it is found in his model, but not (as it would seem) all the itacisms or errors of the scribe. With this text he collates in *separate* Appendices twenty-one other manuscripts in the same great Library, comprising twelve copies of the Gospels (Codd. N. (*part*), 3. 76. 77. 108. 123. 124. 125. 219. 220. 224. 225); six of the Acts &c. (3. 43. 63—4; 6—7); seven of St Paul (3. 49. 67 —71); three of the Apocalypse (34. 35. 36), and two Evangelistaria (45. 46). He also gives readings from Wilkin's Coptic version, four Slavonic codices and one Old Latin (*i: see p.* 257). In employing this ill-digested mass, it is necessary to turn to a different place for every manuscript to be consulted, and Alter's silence in any passage must be understood to indicate resemblance to his standard, Evan. 218, and not to the common text. As this silence is very often clearly due to the collator's mere oversight, Griesbach set the example of citing these manuscripts in such cases within marks of parenthesis: thus "218 (108. 220)" indicates that the reading in question is certainly found in Cod. 218, and (so far as we may infer *ex Alteri silentio*) not improbably in the other two. Most of these Vienna codices were about the same time examined rather slightly by Andrew Birch.

(3) This eminent person, who afterwards bore successively the titles of Bishop of Lolland, Falster, and Aarhuus, in the Lutheran communion established in Denmark, was one of a company of learned men sent by the liberal care of Christian VII. to examine Biblical manuscripts in various countries. Adler (Chap. III. *see* pp. 234, 245) pursued his Oriental studies at Rome and elsewhere; D. G. Moldenhawer and O. G. Tychsen were sent into Spain in 1783—4; Birch travelled on the same good errand 1781—3 through Italy and Germany. The combined results of their investigations were arranged and published by Birch, whose folio edition of the Four Gospels,

with Stephens' text of 1550, and the various readings of himself and his associates, full descriptive Prolegomena and *facsimiles* of seven manuscripts (Codd. S. 157 Evan; and five in Syriac), appeared at Copenhagen in 1788. Seven years afterwards (1795) a fire destroyed the Royal Printing-house, the type, paper and unsold stock of the first volume, the collations of the rest of the N. T. having very nearly shared the same fate. These poor fragments were collected by Birch into two small 8vo volumes, those relating to the Acts and Epistles in 1798, to the Apocalypse (with *facsimiles* of Codd. 37, 42) in 1800. In 1801 he revised and re-edited the various readings of the Gospels, in a form to correspond with those of the rest of the N. T. Nothing can be better calculated to win respect and confidence than the whole tone of Birch's several Prolegomena: he displays at once a proper sense of the difficulties of his task, and a consciousness that he had done his utmost to conquer them[1]. It is indeed much to be regretted that, for some cause he does not wish to explain, he accomplished but little for Cod. B (*see p.* 89); many of the manuscripts on his long list were beyond question examined but very superficially; yet he was the first to open to us the literary treasures of the Vatican, of Florence, and of Venice. He more or less inspected the uncials Cod. B, Codd. ST of the Gospels, Cod. G of the Acts, which is Paul. L. His catalogue of cursives comprises Codd. 127—225 of the Gospels; Codd. 63—7, 70—96 of the Acts; Codd. 67—71, 77—112 of St Paul; Codd. 33—4, 37—46 of the Apocalypse; Evangelistaria 35—39; Apostolos 7, 8: in all 191 copies, a few of which were thoroughly collated (e.g. Evan. S. 127. 131. 157. Evst. 36). Of Adler's labours we have spoken elsewhere (pp. 234, 245); they are incorporated in Birch's work, and prefaced with a short notice (Birch, *Proleg.* p. lxxxv.) by their author, a real and modest scholar. Moldenhawer's portion of the common task was discharged in another spirit. Received at the Escurial with courtesy and good-will, his colleague Tychsen and he spent four whole

1 "Conscius sum mihi, me omnem et diligentiam et intentionem adhibuisse, ut haec editio quam emendatissima in manus eruditorum perveniret, utque in hoc opere, in quo ingenio non fuit locus, curae testimonium promererem; nulla tamen mihi est fiducia, me omnia, quae exigi possint, peregisse. Vix enim potest esse ulla tam perpetua legentis intentio, quae non obtutu continuo fatigetur, praesertim in tali genere, quod tam multis, saepe parvis, observationibus constat." (*Lecturis Editor*, p. v. 1788.) Well could I testify to the truth of these last words!

months in turning over a collection of 760 Greek manuscripts, of which only 20 related to the Greek Testament. They lacked neither leisure, nor opportunity, nor competent knowledge; but they were full of dislike for Spain and its religion, of overweening conceit, and of implicit trust in Griesbach and his recensions. The whole paper contributed by Moldenhawer to Birch's *Prolegomena* (pp. lxi—lxxxiv) is very disappointing, while its arrogance is almost intolerable. What he effected for other portions of the N. T. I have not been able to trace (226, 228 Evan., which contain the Acts and Epistles are but nominally on Scholz's list for those books); the fire at Copenhagen may probably have destroyed his notes. Of the Gospels he collated eight codices (226—233), and four Evangelistaria (40—43), most of them being dismissed, after a cursory review, with some expression of hearty contempt. To Codd. 226, 229, 230 alone was he disposed to pay any attention; of the rest, whether "he soon restored them to their primitive obscurity" (p. lxxi), or "bade them sweet and holy rest among the reliques of Saints and Martyrs" (p. lxvii), he may be understood to say, once for all, "Omnino nemo, qui horum librorum rationem ac indolem...perspectam habet, ex iis lectionis varietatem operosè eruere aggredietur, nec, si quam inde conquisiverit, operae pretium fecisse a peritis arbitris existimabitur" (p. lxxiv). It was not thus that Matthaei dealt with the manuscripts at Moscow.

14. Such were the materials ready for Griesbach's use when he projected his second and principal edition of the Greek Testament (Vol. I. 1796, Vol. II. 1806). Not that he was backward in adding to the store of various readings by means of his own diligence. His *Symbolae Criticae*[1] (Vol. I. 1785, Vol. II. 1793) contained, together with the readings extracted from Origen (see above, Chap. IV. p. 285), collations, in whole or part, of many copies of various portions of the N. T. Besides inspecting Codd. AD (Evan.), and carefully examining Cod. C,[2] he consulted no less than 26 codices (including GL) of the Gospels, 10 (including E) of the Acts, &c., 15 (including DEH) of St Paul, one of

[1] *Symbolae Criticae ad supplendas et corrigendas variarum N. T. lectionum Collectiones. Accedit multorum N. T. Codicum Graecorum descriptio et examen.*

[2] Yet Tischendorf (*N. T. Proleg.* p. xcvii, 7th ed.) states that he only added two readings (Mark vi. 2; 4) to those given by Wetstein.

the Apocalypse (Cod. 29), twelve Lectionaries of the Gospels, and two of the Apostolos, far the greater part of them being deposited in England. It was not, however, his purpose to exhibit in his N. T. (designed, as it was, for general use) all the readings he had himself recorded elsewhere, much less the whole mass accumulated by the pains of Mill or Wetstein, Matthaei or Birch. The distinctive end at which he aims is to form such a selection from the matter their works contain, as to enable the theological student to decide for himself on the genuineness or corruption of any given reading, by the aid of principles which he devotes his best efforts to establish. Between the text (in which every departure from the Elzevir edition of 1624 is plainly indicated by its being printed in smaller type) and the critical notes at the foot of each page, intervenes a narrow space or inner margin, to receive those portions of the common text which Griesbach has rejected, and such variations of his authorities as he judges of equal weight with the received readings which he retains, or but little inferior to them. These decisions he intimates by several symbols, not quite so simple as those employed by Bengel (*see p.* 322), but conceived in a similar spirit; and he has carried his system somewhat further in his small or manual edition, published at Leipsic 1805, which may be conceived to represent his last thoughts in regard to the recension of the Greek text of the N. T. But though we may trace some slight discrepancies of opinion between his earliest[1] and his latest works[2], as might well be looked for in a literary career of forty years, yet the theory of his youth was maintained, and defended, and temperately applied by Griesbach even to the last. From Bengel and Semler (*see p.* 323) he had taken up the belief that manuscripts, versions, and ecclesiastical writers divided themselves, with respect to the character of their testimony, into races or families. This principle he strove to reduce to practice by marshalling all his authorities under their respective heads, and then regarding the evidence, not of individuals, but of the classes to which they belong. The advantage of some such arrangement is sufficiently manifest, if only it could be made to rest on grounds in themselves certain, or, at all

1 *Dissertatio critica de Codicibus quatuor Evangeliorum Origenianis*, Halae, 1771: *Curae in historiam textus Graeci epistolarum Paulinarum*, Jenae, 1777.

2 *Commentarius Criticus in textum. Gr. N. T.*, Pt. I. 1798; Pt. II. 1811.

events, probable. We should then possess some better guide in our choice between conflicting readings, than the very rough and unsatisfactory process of counting the *number* of witnesses produced on either side. It is not that such a mode of conducting critical enquiries would not be very convenient, that Griesbach's theory is universally abandoned by modern scholars, but that there is no valid reason for believing it to be true.

At the onset of his labours, indeed, this acute and candid enquirer was disposed to divide all extant materials into five or six different families; he afterwards limited them to *three,* the Alexandrine, the Western, and the Byzantine recensions. The standard of the Alexandrine text he conceived to be Origen; who, although his works were written in Palestine, was assumed to have brought with him into exile copies of Scripture, similar to those used in his native city. To this family would belong a few manuscripts of the earliest date, and confessedly of the highest character, Codd. ABC; Cod. L of the Gospels, the Egyptian and some lesser versions. The Western recension would survive in Cod. D of the Gospels and Acts, in the other ancient copies which contained a Latin translation, in the Old Latin and Vulgate versions, and in the Latin Fathers. The vast majority of manuscripts (comprising perhaps nineteen-twentieths of the whole), together with the larger proportion of versions and Patristic writings, were grouped into the Byzantine class, as having prevailed generally in the Patriarchate of Constantinople. To this last class Griesbach hardly professed to accord as much weight as to either of the others, nor if he had done so, would the result have been materially different. The joint testimony of two classes was, *caeteris paribus,* always to prevail; and since the very few documents which comprise the Alexandrine and Western recensions seldom agree with the Byzantine even when at variance with each other, the numerous codices which make up the third family would thus have about as much share in fixing the text of Scripture, as the poor citizens whose host was included in one of Servius Tullius' lower classes towards counterbalancing the votes of the wealthy few that composed his first or second[1].

[1] The following specimen of a reading, *possessing no internal excellence,* preferred or favoured by Griesbach on the slightest evidence, will serve to illustrate

Inasmuch as the manuscripts on which our received text was based must, beyond question, be referred to his Byzantine family, wide as were the variations of Griesbach's revised text from that of Elzevir, had his theory been pushed to its legitimate consequences, the changes it required would have been greater still. The very plan of his work, however, seemed to reserve a slight preference for the received text *as such*, in cases of doubt and difficulty; and this editor, with a calmness and sagacity which may well be called judicial, was usually disposed to relax his stern mechanical law when persuaded by reasons founded on internal probabilities, which (as we cheerfully admit) few men have been found able to estimate with so much patience and discrimination. The plain fact is, that while disciples like Moldenhawer and persons who knew less than he, were regarding Griesbach's system as self-evidently true, their wiser master must have had many a misgiving as to the safety of that imposing structure his rare ingenuity had built upon the sand. The very essence of his theory consisted in there being not two distinct families, but *three;* the majority deciding in all cases of dispute. Yet he hardly attempted, certainly neither he nor any one after him succeeded in the attempt, to separate the Alexandrine from the Western family, without resorting to arguments which would prove that there are as many classes as there are manuscripts of early date. The supposed accordance of the readings of Origen, so elaborately scrutinised for this purpose by Griesbach (*see* p. 285), with Cod. A, on which our editor lays the greatest stress, has been shewn by Archbishop Laurence (*Remarks on Griesbach's Systematic Classification*, 1814), to be in a high degree imaginary[1]. It must have been

the dangerous tendency of his system, had it been consistently acted upon throughout. In Matth. xxvii. 4 for ἀθῷον he indicates the mere gloss δίκαιον as equal or preferable, on the authority of the *later* margin of Cod. B, of Cod. L, the Thebaic, Armenian, and Latin versions and Fathers, and Origen in four places (ἀθῷον once). He adds the Syriac, but this is an error, as regards the Peshito or Philoxenian; the Jerusalem may countenance him (see p. 250); though in such a case the testimony of versions is precarious on either side. Here, however, Griesbach defends δίκαιον against all likelihood, because BL Origen are Alexandrine, the Latin versions Western.

[1] Laurence, in the Appendix to his *Remarks*, shews that while Cod. A agrees with Origen against the received text in 154 places, and disagrees with the two united in 140, it sides with the received text against Origen in no less than 444 passages.

in anticipation of some such researches, and in a partial knowledge of their sure results, that Griesbach was driven to that violent and most unlikely hypothesis, that Cod. A follows the Byzantine class of authorities in the Gospels, the Western in the Acts and Catholic Epistles, and the Alexandrine in St Paul.

It seems needless to dwell longer on speculations which, however attractive and once widely received, will scarcely again find an advocate. Griesbach's text can no more be regarded as satisfactory, though it is far less objectionable than such a system as his would have made it in unskilful hands. His industry, his moderation, his fairness to opponents, who (like Matthaei) had shewn him little forbearance, we may all imitate to our profit. His logical acuteness and keen intellectual perception fall to the lot of few; and though they may have helped to lead him into error, and have even kept him from retracing his steps, yet on the whole they were worthily exercised in the good cause of promoting a knowledge of God's truth, and of keeping alive, in an evil and unbelieving age, an enlightened interest in Holy Scripture, and the studies which it serves to consecrate[1].

15. Of a widely different order of mind was John Martin Augustine Scholz [d. 1852], Roman Catholic Dean of Theology in the mixed University of Bonn. It would have been well for the progress of sacred learning and for his own reputation had the accuracy and ability of this editor borne some proportion to his zeal and obvious anxiety to be useful. His first essay was his "*Curae Criticae in historiam textûs Evangeliorum*," in two dissertations, Heidelberg, 4°, 1820, containing notices of 48 Paris manuscripts (nine of them hitherto unknown) of which he had fully collated seventeen: the second Dissertation is devoted to Cod. K of the Gospels (*see* p. 108). In 1823 appeared his "*Biblisch-Kritische Reise*," Leipsic, 8°, Biblico-Critical Travels in France, Switzerland, Italy, Palestine and the Archipelago, which Schulz laid under contribution for his improved edition of Griesbach's first volume[1]. Scholz's "N. T. Graece," 4°, was published at Leipsic, Vol. I. 1830 (Gospels), Vol. II. 1836.

[1] David Schulz published at Berlin 1827, 8vo, a third and much improved edition of his N. T., Vol. I. (Gospels), containing also collations of certain additional manuscripts, unknown to Griesbach.

The accession of fresh materials made known in these works is almost marvellous: Scholz was the first to indicate Codd. 260—469 of the Gospels; 110—192 of the Acts, &c.; 125—246 of St Paul; 51—89 of the Apocalypse; 58—181 Evangelistaria; 21—58 Lectionaries of the Apostolos; in all 616 cursive codices. His additions to the list of the uncials comprise only the three fragments of the Gospels W[a] Y and the Vatican leaves of N (*see* p. 110). Of those examined previously by others he paid most attention to Evan. KX (M also for its synaxaria), and G Act. (which is L Paul.); he moreover inspected slightly 82 cursive codices of the Gospels after Wetstein, Birch and the rest; collated entire five (Codd. 4. 19. 25. 28. 33), and twelve in the greater part. In the Acts, &c. he inspected 27 of those known before, partially collated two; in St Paul he collated partially two, slightly 29; in the Apocalypse 16, cursorily enough it would seem (*see* p. 207, Codd. 21—3): of the Lectionaries he touched more or less 13 of the Gospels, 4 of the Apostolos. On turning to the 616 codices Scholz placed on the list for the first time, we find that he collated entire but 13 (viz. five of the Gospels, three of the Acts, &c., three of St Paul, one each of the Apocalypse and Evangelistaria): a few of the rest he examined throughout the greater part; many in only a few chapters; while some were set down from printed Catalogues, whose plenteous errors we have used our best endeavours to correct, so far as the means were within our reach.

Yet after making a large deduction from our first impressions of the *amount* of labour performed by Scholz, enough and more than enough would remain to entitle him to our lasting gratitude, if it were possible to place any tolerable reliance on the correctness of his results. Those who are, however superficially, acquainted with the nature of such pursuits, will readily believe that faultless accuracy in representing myriads of minute details is not to be looked for by the most diligent and careful critic. Oversights will mar the perfection of the most highly finished of human efforts; but if adequate care and pains shall have been bestowed on detecting them, such blemishes as still linger unremoved are no real subject of reproach, and do not greatly mar the value of the work which contains them. But in the case of Scholz's Greek Testament the fair indulgence we must all hope for is abused beyond the bounds of reason or moderation. The student who

22

has had much experience of his volumes, especially if he has ever compared the collations there given with the original manuscripts, will never dream of resorting to them for information he can expect to gain elsewhere, or rest with confidence on a statement of fact merely because Scholz asserts it. J. Scott Porter (*Principles of Textual Criticism*, Belfast, 1848, pp. 263—6) and Tischendorf (*N. T. Proleg.* C—II. 7th edition) have dwelt upon his strange blunders, his blind inconsistencies, and his habitual practice of copying from his predecessors without investigation and without acknowledgment; so that it is needless for us to repeat or enlarge on that ungracious task[1]: but it is our duty to put the student once for all on his guard against what could not fail to mislead him, and to express our sorrow that twelve years and more of hard and persevering toil should, through mere heedlessness, have been nearly thrown away.

As was natural in a pupil of J. L. Hug of Freyburg (*see p.* 89), who had himself tried to build a theory of recensions on very slender grounds, Dr Scholz attempted to settle the text of the N. T., upon principles which must be regarded as a modification of those of Griesbach. In his earliest work, like that great critic, he had been disposed to divide all extant authorities into five separate classes; but he soon reduced them to two; the Alexandrine and the Constantinopolitan. In the Alexandrine family he included the whole of Griesbach's Western recension, from which indeed it is vain to distinguish it by any broad line of demarcation: to the other family he referred the great mass of more recent documents which compose Griesbach's third or Byzantine class; and to this family he was inclined to give the preference over the other, as well from the internal excellency of its readings, as because it represents the uniform text which had become traditional throughout the Greek Church. That such a standard, public, and authorised text existed he seems to have taken for granted without much enquiry. "Codices qui hoc nomen [Constantinopolitanum] habent," he writes, "parum inter

[1] One of Porter's examples is almost amusing. It was Scholz's constant habit to copy Griesbach's lists of critical authorities (errors, misprints and all) without giving the reader any warning that they are not the fruit of his own labours. The note he borrowed from Griesbach on 1 Tim. iii. 16, contains the words "uti docuimus in Symbolis criticis:" this too Scholz appropriates (Tom. II. p. 334, col. 2) so as to claim the *Symbolae Criticae* of the Halle Professor as his own!

se dissentiunt. Conferas, quaeso, longè plerosque quos huic classi adhaerere dixi, atque lectiones diversas viginti trigintave in totidem capitibus vix reperies, unde conjicias eos esse accuratissimè descriptos, eorumque antigrapha parum inter se discrepasse" (N. T. *Proleg.* Vol. I. § 55). It might have occurred to one who had spent so many years in studying Greek manuscripts, that this marvellous concord between the different Byzantine witnesses (which is striking enough, no doubt, as we turn over the pages of his Greek Testament) is after all due to nothing so much as to the haste and carelessness of collators. The more closely the cursive copies of Scripture are examined, the more does the individual character of each of them become developed. With certain points of general resemblance, whereby they are distinguished from the older documents of the Alexandrine class, they abound with mutual variations so numerous and perpetual as to vouch for the independent origin of nearly all of them, and to have "swept away at once and for ever" (Tregelles' *Account of Printed Text*, p. 180) the fancy of a standard Constantinopolitan text, and every inference that had been grounded upon its presumed existence. If (as we firmly believe) the less ancient codices ought to have their proper weight and appreciable influence in fixing the true text of Scripture, our favourable estimate of them must rest on other arguments than Scholz has urged in their behalf.

Since this editor's system of recensions differed thus widely from Griesbach's, in suppressing altogether one of his three classes, and in yielding to the third, which the other slighted, a decided preference over its surviving rival, it might have been imagined that the consequences of such discrepancy in theory would have been strongly marked in their effects on his text. That such is not the case, at least to any considerable extent (especially in his second volume), must be imputed in part to Griesbach's prudent reserve in carrying out his principles to extremity (*see p.* 335), but yet more to Scholz's vacillation and evident weakness of judgment. In fact, on his last visit to England in 1845, he distributed among Biblical students here a "*Commentatio de virtutibus et vitiis utriusque codicum N. T. familiae*," that he had just delivered on the occasion of some Encaenia at Bonn, in which (after various statements that display either ignorance or inattention respecting the ordinary phaenomena of manuscripts which in a veteran collator is really unaccountable[1]), he declares his purpose, chiefly it would seem from considerations of internal evidence, that if ever it should be his lot to prepare another edition of the New Testament, "se plerasque codicum Alexandrinorum lectiones illas quas in margine interiore textui editionis suae Alexandrinas dixit, in textum recepturum" (p. 14). The text which its constructor distrusted, has but small claim on the faith of others.

16. "*Novum Testamentum Graece et Latine, Carolus Lachmannus recensuit, Philippus Buttmannus Ph. F. Graecae lectionis auctoritates apposuit*" is the simple title-page of a work, by one of the first philologists of his time, the first volume of which (containing the Gospels) appeared at Berlin (8°) 1842, the second and concluding one in 1850, whose boldness and originality have procured it, for good or ill, a prominent place in the history of the sacred text. Lachmann had published as early as 1831 a small edition containing only the text of the N. T., with a list of the readings, wherein he differs from that of Elzevir, preceded by a notice of his plan not exceeding a few lines in length, itself so obscurely worded that even to those who happened to understand his meaning it must have read like a riddle whose solution they had been told beforehand; and referring us for fuller information to what he strangely considers "a more convenient place," a German periodical of the preceding year's date[2]. Au-

[1] Some of these statements are discussed in Scrivener's *Collation of the Greek Manuscripts of the Holy Gospels*, Introd. pp. lxix.—lxxi.

[2] The following is the *whole* of this notice, which we reprint after Tregelles' example: "De ratione et consilio hujus editionis loco commodiore expositum est (*Theol. Studien und Kritiken*, 1830, pp. 817—845). Hic satis erit dixisse, editorem nusquam judicium suum, sed consuetudinem antiquissimarum orientis ecclesiarum secutum esse. Hanc quoties minus constantem fuisse animadvertit, quantum fieri potuit quae Italorum et Afrorum consensu comprobarentur praetulit: ubi pervagatam omnium auctorum discrepantiam deprehendit, partim uncis partim in marginibus indicavit. Quo factum est ut vulgatae et his proximis duobus saeculis *receptae lectionis* ratio haberi non posset. Hujus diversitatis hic in fine libri adjecta est, quoniam ea res doctis judicibus necessaria esse videbatur." Here we have one of Lachmann's leading peculiarities—his absolute disregard of the received readings—hinted at in an incidental manner:—the influence he was disposed to accord to the Latin versions when his chief authorities were at variance is pretty clearly indicated; but no one would guess that by "custom of the oldest Churches of the East" he intends the few very ancient codices comprising Gries-

thors who take so little pains to explain their fundamental principles of criticism, especially if (as in this case) these are novel and unexpected, can hardly wonder when their drift and purpose are imperfectly apprehended; so that a little volume, which we now learn had cost Lachmann five years of thought and labour, was confounded, even by the learned, with the common, hasty and superficial reprints. Nor was the difficulty much removed on the publication of the first volume of his larger book. It was then seen, indeed, how clean a sweep he had made of the great mass of Greek manuscripts usually cited in critical editions:—in fact he rejects all in a heap excepting Codd. ABC, the fragments PQTZ (and for some purposes D) of the Gospels; DE of the Acts only; DGH of St Paul:—but even now he treats the scheme of his work as if it were already familiarly known, and spends his time in discursive controversy with his opponents and reviewers, whom he chastises with a heartiness which in this country we imputed to downright malice, till Dr Tregelles was so good as to instruct us that in Lachmann it was but "a tone of pleasantry," the horseplay of coarse German wit (*Account of Printed Text*, p. 112). The supplementary Prolegomena which preface his second volume of 1850 are certainly more explicit: both from what they teach and from the practical examples they contain, they have probably helped others, as well as myself, in gaining a nearer insight into his whole design.

It seems, then, to have been Lachmann's purpose, discarding the slightest regard for the *textus receptus* as such, to endeavour to bring the sacred text back to the condition in which it existed during the fourth century, and this in the first instance by documentary aid alone, careless for the moment whether the sense produced be probable or improbable, good or bad; but solely looking to his authorities, and following them implicitly wheresoever the numerical majority might carry him. For accomplishing this purpose he possessed but one Greek copy written as early as the fourth century, Cod. B; and of that he not only knew less than has since come to light (and even this is insufficient), but he did not avail himself of Bartolocci's papers (*see p.* 88), to which Scholz had already drawn attention. His other

bach's Alexandrine class, and not the great mass of authorities, gathered from the Churches of Syria, Asia Minor, and Constantinople, of which that critic's Byzantine family was made up.

codices were not of the fourth century at all, but varying in date from the fifth (ACT) to the ninth (G); and even of these few (of C more especially) his assistant or colleague Buttmann's representation was loose, careless, and unsatisfactory. Of the Greek Fathers, the scanty Greek remains of Irenaeus and the works of Origen are all that are employed; but considerable weight is given to the readings of the Latin version. The Vulgate is printed at length as revised, after a fashion, by Lachmann himself, from the Codices Fuldensis and Amiatinus (*see p.* 264): the Old Latin manuscripts *abc*, together with the Latin versions accompanying the Greek copies which he receives[1], are regarded as primary authorities; of the Western Fathers he quotes Cyprian, Hilary of Poictiers, Lucifer of Cagliari, and in the Apocalypse Primasius also (*h*). The Syriac and Egyptian translations he considers himself excused from attending to, by reason of his ignorance of their respective languages.

The consequence of this voluntary poverty where our manuscript treasures are so abundant, of this deliberate rejection of the testimony of many hundreds of documents, of various countries, dates and characters, may be told in a few words. Lachmann's text seldom rests on more than four Greek codices, very often on three, not unfrequently on two; in Matth. vi. 20—vii. 5, and in 165 out of the 405 verses of the Apocalypse on but *one*. It would have been a grievous thing indeed if we really had no better means of ascertaining the true readings of the N. T. than are contained in this editor's scanty roll; and he who for the sake of some private theory, shall presume to shut out from his mind the great mass of information God's Providence has preserved for our use, will hardly be thought to have chosen the most hopeful method for bringing himself or others to the knowledge of the truth.

But supposing, for the sake of argument, that Lachmann had availed himself to the utmost of the materials he has selected, and that they were adequate for the purpose of leading him up to the state of the text as it existed in the fourth century, would he have made any real advance in the criticism of the sacred volume? Is it not quite evident, even from the

[1] These are *d* for Cod. Bezae, *e* for Cod. Laud. 35, *f* for Paul. Cod. D, *ff* for Paul. Cod. E (whose Latin translation is cited independently, *see* p. 133), *g* for Paul. Cod. G.

authorities contained in his notes, that copies in that age varied as widely—nay even more widely—than they did in later times? that the main corruptions and interpolations which perplex the student in Cod. D and its Latin allies, crept in at a period anterior to the age of Constantine? From the Preface to his second volume (1850) it plainly appears (what might, perhaps, have been gathered by an esoteric pupil from the Preface to his first, pp. v, xxxiii), that he regarded this fourth-century text, founded as it was on documentary evidence alone, as purely provisional; as mere subject-matter on which individual *conjecture* might advantageously operate (Praef. 1850, p. v). Of the many examples wherewith he illustrates his principle we must be content with producing one, as an ample specimen both of Lachmann's plan and of his judgment in reducing it to practice. In Matth. xxvii. 28 for ἐκδύσαντες, which gives a perfectly good sense, and seems absolutely required by τὰ ἱμάτια αὐτοῦ in *v.* 31, BD*abc* read ἐνδύσαντες, a variation either borrowed from Mark xv. 17, or more probably a mere error of the pen. Had the whole range of manuscripts, versions, and Fathers been searched, no other testimony in favour of ἐνδύσαντες could have been found save Cod. 157, *ff*² of the old Latin, the Latin version of Origen, and one codex of Chrysostom. Against these we might set the vast mass of witnesses, exceeding those on the opposite side by full a hundred to one; yet because Cod. A and the Latin Vulgate alone are on Lachmann's list, he is compelled by his system to place ἐνδύσαντες in the text as the reading of his authorities, reserving to himself the privilege of removing it on the ground of its palpable impropriety: and all this because he wishes to keep the "recensio" of the text distinct from the "emendatio" of the sense (Praef. 1850, p. vi). Surely it were a far more reasonable, as well as a more convenient process, to have reviewed from the first the entire case on both sides, and if the documentary evidence were not unevenly balanced, or internal evidence strongly preponderated in one scale, to place in the text once for all the reading which upon the whole should appear best suited to the passage, and most sufficiently established by authority.

But while we cannot accord to Lachmann the praise of wisdom in his design, or of over-much industry and care in the execution of it (see Tischend. *N. T. Proleg.* pp. cvii—cxii), yet we would not dissemble or extenuate the power his edition has exerted over candid and enquiring minds. Earnest, single-hearted, a true scholar both in spirit and accomplishments, he has had the merit of restoring the Latin versions to their proper rank in the criticism of the N. T., which since the failure of Bentley's schemes they seem to have partially lost. No one will hereafter claim for the received text any further weight than it is entitled to as the representative of the manuscripts on which it was constructed: and the principle of recurring exclusively to a few ancient documents in preference to the many (so engaging from its very simplicity), which may be said to have virtually originated with him, has not been without influence with some who condemn the most strongly his hasty and one-sided, though consistent application of it.

17. We have now but to enumerate the labours of two living critics (for Lachmann was lost to us in 1851), whose signal services to theological learning have been often mentioned in these pages. Of those labours it will suffice to give a brief summary in this place, reserving the respective systems on which they revised the text for fuller discussion in Chapter VII.

"*Novum Testamentum Graece. Ad antiquos testes denuo recensuit, apparatum criticum omni studio perfectum apposuit, commentationem isagogicam praetexuit Ænoth. Frid. Const. Tischendorf, editio septima:*" Lipsiae, 1859, 2 Vols. 8vo. This is beyond question the most full and complete edition of the Greek Testament, containing the results of the latest collations and discoveries, and as copious a body of various readings as is compatible with the design of adapting it for general use: though Tischendorf's notes are not sufficiently minute (as regards the cursive manuscripts) to supersede the need of perpetually consulting the labours of preceding critics. His earliest work in connexion with Biblical studies was a small edition of the N. T. (12mo, 1841) completed at Leipsic in 1840, which, although greatly inferior to his subsequent works, merited the encouragement which it procured for him, and the praises of D. Schulz, which he so gratefully remembers. Soon afterwards he set out on his first literary journey: "quod quidem tam pauper suscepi," he ingenuously declares, "ut pro paenula quam portabam solvere non possem;" and, while busily engaged on Cod. C, prepared three other editions of the N. T., which appeared in 1843 at Paris, all of them being booksellers' speculations on which, perhaps, he now sets no high value; one dedicated to Guizot, the Protestant statesman, a second (having the Greek text placed in a parallel column with the Latin Vulgate, and somewhat altered to suit it) dedicated to Denys Affre, the Archbishop of Paris, who fell so nobly at the barricades in June 1848. His third edition of that year contained the Greek text of the second edition, without the Latin Vulgate. It is needless to enlarge upon the history of his travels, so well described by Tischendorf in the Preface to his seventh edition; it will be enough to state that he thrice visited England (1842, 1849, 1855), and thrice went into the East (*see* pp. 76—7), where his chief discovery—that of the Cod. Sinaiticus—was ultimately made. In 1849 came forth his second Leipsic or fifth edition of the N. T., being a very considerable advance upon that of 1841, though, in its earlier pages more especially, still very defective, and even as a manual scarce worthy of his rapidly growing fame. The sixth edition was one stereotyped for Tauchnitz in 1850, representing the text of 1849 slightly revised: the seventh, and by far the most important, was issued in parts at Leipsic during the four years 1856—9. It is indeed a monument of persevering industry which the world has not often seen surpassed.

Yet it may truly be asserted that the reputation of Tischendorf as a Biblical scholar rests less on his critical editions of the N. T. than on the texts of the chief uncial authorities which in rapid succession he has given to the world. In 1843 was published the New Testament, in 1845 the Old Testament portion of *Codex Ephraemi Syri rescriptus* (Cod. C, *see* p. 95), 2 vol. 4to, in uncial type, with elaborate Prolegomena, notes and *facsimiles*. In 1846 appeared *Monumenta sacra inedita*, 4to, containing transcripts of Codd. $F^{a}LNW^{a}Y\Theta$ of the Gospels, and B of the Apocalypse; the plan and apparatus of this volume and of nearly all that follow are the same as in the Codex Ephraemi. In 1846 he published the *Codex Friderico-Augustanus* (*see* p. 27) in lithographed *facsimile* throughout: in 1847 the "*Evangelium Palatinum ineditum*" of the old Latin (*e*, see p. 256): in 1850 and again in 1854 less splendid but good and useful editions of the *Codex Amiatinus* of the Latin Vulgate (*am.* see p. 264). *Codex Claromontanus* (D of St Paul), 1852 (see p. 131), was of precisely the same character as Cod. Ephraemi, &c., but *Anecdota sacra et profana*, 1855, exhibit a more miscellaneous character, comprising (together with other matter) transcripts of O^{a} of the Gospels, M of St Paul; a collation of lo^{ti} of the Acts (see p. 198), *the only cursive copy he seems to have examined;* notices and *facsimiles* of Codd. ΙΓΛ $tisch.^{1}$ (p. 181) of the Gospels, and the lectionaries $tisch.^{ev}$ (p. 220), $tisch.^{e, f}$ (p. 225). Next was commenced a new series of *Monumenta sacra inedita* (to consist of five volumes), on the same plan as the book of 1846. Much of this is devoted to codices of the Septuagint version, to which Tischendorf has paid great attention; but Vol. I. (1855) contains transcripts of Codd. I, $ven.^{ev}$ (p. 220); Vol. II. (1857) of Codd. $N^{b}R$; Vol. III. (1860) of Codd. PQW^{c}, all of the Gospels. He is now engaged on what he doubtless regards as his master-work, the edition of Cod. א (*see pp.* 28, 77), of which, and of other treasures (*see pp.* 127, 181, 220, 225) which he brought to St Petersburg from his last Eastern journey, we have had a foretaste in the *Notitia Codicis Sinaitici*, 1860. To this long and varied catalogue must yet be added exact collations of Codd. EGHKMUX Gospels, EGH Acts, FHL of St Paul, all made for his editions of the N. T.

The consideration of the text of Tischendorf's editions of 1849 and 1859 will be resumed in Chapter VII. To the *general* accuracy of his collations every one who has followed him over a portion of his vast field can bear and is bound to bear cheerful testimony. For practical purposes his correctness is quite sufficient, even though one or two who have accomplished very much less may have excelled in this respect some at least of his later works. By the unflinching exertions and persevering labour of full twenty years Constantine Tischendorf has well earned—and long may he live to enjoy—the name of THE FIRST BIBLICAL CRITIC IN EUROPE.

18. "*The Greek New Testament, edited from ancient authorities; with the various readings of all the ancient MSS., the ancient versions, and earlier ecclesiastical writers (to Eusebius inclusive); together with the Latin version of Jerome, from the Codex Amiatinus of the sixth century. By Samuel Prideaux Tregelles, LL.D.*" 4to.

The esteemed author of the unfinished work of which the above is the full title, first became generally known as the editor of *The Book of Revelation in Greek, edited from ancient authorities; with a new English Version*, 1844: and, in spite of some obvious blemishes and defects, his attempt was received in the English Church with the gratitude and respect to which his thorough earnestness and independent views justly entitled him. He had arranged in his own mind the plan of a Greek Testament as early as 1838, which he announced on the publication of the Apocalypse, and now set himself vigorously to accomplish. His fruitless endeavour to collate Cod. B has already been mentioned (p. 90), but when on the continent in 1845—6 and again in 1849—50 he thoroughly examined all the manuscripts he could meet with, that fell within the compass of his design. In 1854 he published a volume full of valuable information, and intended as a formal exposition of his critical principles, intituled *An Account of the Printed Text of the Greek New Testament:* in 1856 he re-wrote, rather than re-edited, that portion of the Rev. T. Hartwell Horne's well-known *Introduction to the Critical Study and Knowledge of the Holy Scriptures* which relates to the New Testament, under the title of *An Introduction to the Textual Criticism of the New Testament*, &c.[1] In 1857 appeared the Gospels of SS. Matthew and Mark, as the First Part of his *Greek New Testament* (pp. 1—216); early in 1861 the Second Part, containing SS. Luke and John (pp. 217—488), with but a few pages of "Introductory Notice" in each. Every one who venerates the spectacle of time and substance freely bestowed in the best of causes, without the prospect or indeed the possibility of earthly reward, will grieve to know that the further prosecution of his *opus magnum* is for a while suspended by Dr Tregelles' serious illness.

Except Cod. Ξ (which is yet in the press: see pp. 112, 126) this critic has not edited in full the text of any document, but his renewed collations of manuscripts are very extensive: viz. Codd. EGHKMN^{b}RUXZΓΛ 1. 33. 69 of the Gospels; GH 1. 13. 31. lo^{ti} of the Acts; DFLM 1. 17. 37 of St Paul, 14 of the Apocalypse, *Am.* of the Vulgate. Having followed Tregelles through the whole of Cod. 69 (Act. 31, Paul. 37, Apoc.

[1] A pamphlet of 36 pages appeared late in 1860, called *Additions to the Fourth Volume of the Introduction to the Holy Scriptures*, &c., by S. P. T.

14) I am able to speak positively of his scrupulous accuracy, and in regard to other manuscripts now in England it will be found that where Tischendorf and Tregelles differ, the latter is seldom in the wrong. To the versions and Fathers (especially to Origen and Eusebius) he has devoted great attention. His volume is a beautiful specimen of typography, and its arrangement is very convenient, particularly his happy expedient for shewing at every open leaf the precise authorities that are extant at that place.

The peculiarity of his system is intimated, rather than stated, in the title-page of his Greek N. T. It consists in resorting to "ancient authorities" alone in the construction of his revised text; and in refusing not only to the received text, but to the great mass of manuscripts also, all voice in determining the true readings. This scheme, although from the history he gives of his work (*Account of Printed Text*, pp. 153 &c.), it was apparently devised independently of Lachmann, is in fact essentially his plan, after those parts of it are withdrawn which are manifestly indefensible. Tregelles' "ancient authorities" are thus reduced to those manuscripts which, not being Lectionaries, happen to be written in uncial characters, with the remarkable exception of Codd. 1. 33. 69 of the Gospels, lo[ti] of the Acts, which he admits because they "preserve an ancient text." We shall hereafter enquire (Chap. VII.) whether the text of the N. T. can safely be grounded on a basis so narrow as that of Tregelles.

In the course of the last ten or fifteen years the criticism of the N. T. has been rapidly regaining its old place among the favourite pursuits of the English clergy. Its progress is the more hopeful because it has engaged the minds chiefly of men yet in the prime of life, from whose zeal and matured energy we may confidently look, in God's good season, for further instruction in this grave and divine study.

APPENDIX TO CHAPTER V.

COLLATION OF THE COMPLUTENSIAN POLYGLOTT N. T. 1514, WITH THAT OF ELZEVIR, 1624.

N.B. † *prefixed to a Greek reading shews that it is at variance with the parallel Latin Vulgate* (*see* *p.* 293).

MATTH. tit.† + ἅγιον (*ante* ευαγ.). I. 1. δαυίδ (*sic* vv. 6 *bis*, 17 *bis*, 20). 6. σολομώνα. 15. †ματθάμ *bis*. II. 2. τον αστέρα αυτού. 5. ούτως. 11. †είδον. III. 5. –ἡ *prim*. 8. καρπόν άξιον. 11. †–καὶ πυρί. 13. εις (*pro* ἐπὶ). IV. 7. πάλιν. γέγραπται. 10. + οπίσω μου (*post* ύπαγε). 12. παρεδώθη. 18. †–ὁ ἰησοῦς. V. 6. πινώντες. 12. ούτως (*sic* vv. 16, 19). 17. νομήσητε. 19. διδάξει *prim*. 22. γέεναν (*non* vv. 29, 30). 23. και εκεί. 27. – τοῖς ἀρχαίοις. 28. αυτήν (*pro* αὐτῆς). 44. τοις μισοίσιν. 45. + τοις (*ante* ουρανοίς). 47. †φίλους (*pro* ἀδελφοὺς). ούτως. VI. 13. *fin*. πονηρού + αμήν[1]. 15. † + ο ουράνιος (*ante* αφήσει). 18. *fin*. – ἐν τῷ φανερῷ. 24. †μαμωνά. 29. + ο (*ante* σολομών). 34. μεριμνήσητε. VII. 6. δότε. 10. *init*. + η (*aut si*). 12. ούτως (*non* v. 17). ούτως (*pro* οὗτος: *hec*). 14. Τί (*pro* ὅτι: *Quam*). VIII. 5. αυτώ (*pro* τῷ ἰησοῦ). 8. λόγω. 11. ανακληθήσονται. 12. –ὁ *prim*. 14. εισελθών. 15. *fin*. αυτώ. 17. ανέλαβε (*accepit*). [28. γεργεσηνών *gerasenorum*]. IX. 5. †σου. 13. αλλά. 17. αμφότεροι. 18. + εις (*ante* ελθών). 27. δαυιδ. 33. –ὅτι. 35. – ἐν τῷ λαῷ. 36. εσκυλμένοι (*vexati:* pro ἐκλελ). X. 2. εισί (*pro* ἐστι). 4. – ὁ *secund*. 8. – νεκροὺς ἐγείρετε

[1] In exemplaribus grecorum post hec verba orationis dominice vz. Et libera nos a malo: statim sequitur ὅτι σου εστιν η βασιλεια και η δύναμις και η δόξα εις τους αιώνας. Id est. Quoniam tuum est regnum et potentia et gloria in secula. Sed advertendum quod in missa grecorum postquam chorus dicit illa verba orationis dominice, s (scilicet), Et libera nos a malo: sacerdos respondet ista verba supra dicta, s. quoniam tuum est regnum, &c. et dicunt greci quod solus sacerdos potest pronunciare illa verba et non alius. et sic magis credibile videtur quod ista verba non sint de integritate orationis dominice: sed quod vicio aliquorum scriptorum fuerunt hic inserta nam videntes quod publice dicerentur in missa crediderunt esse de textu, et lz (licet) beatus chrisostomus in suis commentariis super Mattheum home. 20. exponat ista verba tam quam si essent de textu: verisimiliter tamen presumitur jam suis temporibus originalia in isto passu fuisse corrupta ex quo nullus latinorum ēt [etiam?] ex antiquissimis interpretibus sive tractatoribus legatur de his verbis aliquam fecisse mentionem.

(habet Lat. ante *leprosos*). 10. †ράβδους. 12. *fin.* + λέγοντες. ειρήνη τω οίκω τούτω. 13. εισελθετω (*veniet*). 19. λαλήσετε (*pro* -σητε). 25. βεελζεβούβ (-*bub*). [*Steph.* β, errore pro α]. απεκάλεσαν (*vocaverunt*). οικειακούς. 28. φοβείσθε (*pro* -θῆτε). αποκτενόντων. 31. †πολλώ. 36. οικειακοί. XI. 8. βασιλείων (*regum*). 10. εστίν. 16. παιδίοις. αγορά. 17. ορχήσασθε. 21. χωραζίν (*sic*). βηθσαϊδά. XII. 3. δαυίδ. 6. †μείζον. 8. †– καὶ. 13. †+ τω εξηραμμένην έχοντι την χείρα. (*ante* έκτεινον). απεκατεστάθη. 14. απωλέσωσιν. 21. †–ἐν. 23. ο χριστός ο υιός δαυίδ. 24, 27 [βεελζεβούλ, at -*bub*]. 32. εάν (*pro* ἂν *prim*). τω νυν (*pro* τούτῳ τῷ: *hoc*). 35. –τῆς καρδίας. – τὰ *prim.* + τὰ (*ante* πονηρά). 36. αποδώσουσιν υπέρ (*pro* περὶ: *de*). [37. *errat Mill.*]. 38. †θέλωμεν. 42. σολομώνος *bis*. 43. ουκ. 44. υποστρέψω (*revertar*). 50. ποιήσει. εστίν. XIII. 3. σπείραι. [4. *errat Mill.*]. 13. συνιούσιν. 14. –ἐπ' (*in*). 15. ιάσομαι. 24. σπείραντι (*qui seminavit*). 27. –τὰ. 28. συλλέξομεν (*colligimus*). 30. –τῷ. 32. + πάντων (*post* μείζον). †κατελθείν. [33. ενέκρυψεν]. 40. καίεται (*comburuntur*). – τούτου. 54. εκπλήσσεσθαι. XIV. 11. †η κεφαλή αυτού ηνέχθη. 12. εξελθόντες (*venientes*). 13. κατιδίαν (*sic* v. 23). 14. επ αυτοίς (*eis*). 19. ανακληθήναι. – καὶ *secund.* 31. καὶ ευθέως (– δὲ). 36. + †καν (*ante* μόνον: *vel*). XV. 4. –σου. 12. + οι (*ante* ακούσαντες: *errat Mill.*). 14. εμπεσουνται (*cadent*). 22. †+ τις (*post* γυνή). δαυίδ. 23. + αυτώ (*post* προσελθόντες: *ei* (sic)). 27. είπε. 31. εδόξαζον (*magnificabant*). + του (*ante* ισραήλ). 32. [ημέρας]. 34. †+ αυτώ (*post* είπον). 39. ανέβη (*ascendit*). XVI. 1. υποδείξαι (*ostenderet*). 24. ακολουθήτω. 25. †απολέσει (*pro* -ῃ). 28. γεύσονται. XVII. 1. κατιδίαν (*sic* v. 19). 14. αυτόν (*pro* αὐτῷ *secund.*). 27. αναβαίνοντα (*qui ascenderit*). XVIII. 4. ταπεινώσει. 6. [ἐπὶ]. 10. διαπαντός. 12. ενενήκοντα εννέα, (*sic*). 13. ενενήκοντα εννέα. 15. αμάρτη. 19. †+ αμήν (*post* πάλιν). 25. †αυτώ (*pro* αὐτοῦ *prim.*). 28. ει τι (pro ὅ,τι: *quod*). 29. †– πάντα. 30. αλλά. 35. ούτως. XIX. 1. + της (*ante* γαλιλαίας). 5. †+ αυτού (*post* πατέρα). 8. ούτως. 9. – εἰ (*nisi*). γαμήσει. 12. εγενήθησαν. ούτως. 13. προσηνέχθησαν. 19. + σου (*post* μητέρα). 26. *fin.* † – ἐστι. 28. [desunt puncta]. δώδεκα θρόνων. 29. οικίαν. 30. + οι (*ante* έσχατοι *secund.*). XX. 2. †και συμφωνήσας (– δὲ). 3. – τὴν. 5. ενάτην. 15. ει (*pro* ἢ *secund.*: *An*). 17. κατιδίαν. 21. †ευωνίμων (*non* v. 23) †+ σου. 22. †η (*pro* καὶ: *deest clausula in Lat.*). 26. †έσται (*pro* ἔστω: *sit*). 27. έσται (*pro* ἔστω: *erit*). 30, 31. δαυίδ. 34. σπλαχνισθείς. XXI. 1. †βηθσφαγή. 2. κατέναντι. †δεδεμένον. 3. †αποστέλλει. 7. †επεκάθισεν. 9. δαυίδ (*sic* v. 15). 11. †ναζαρέτ. 14. †χωλοί και τυφλοί. 22. εάν (*pro* ἂν). 25. διά τι. 28. + τις (*ante* είχε). είπεν. 29. απήλθεν. 39. †εξέβαλον αυτόν. 41. εκδώσεται. XXII. 1, *capiti* XXI *adjungit.* πάλιν, 7. †και ακούσας ο βασιλεύς + εκείνος. 9. εάν (*pro* ἂν). 13. χείρας και πόδας. 19. προνήνεγκαν. 34. επιτοαυτό. 37. έφη (*pro* εἶπεν: *ait*). 39. †αύτη. 42, 43, 45. δαυίδ. 46. ηδύνατο. επερωτάν. XXIII. 3. εάν (*pro* ἂν). 13, 14. ότι κατεσθίετε κ.τ.λ. *ante* ότι κλείετε κ.τ.λ. 21. †κατοικήσαντι. 25. *fin.* αδικίας (*immundicia*). 30. †ότι ει ήμεθα (sic: *at* ήμεν *sequens*). 36. †+ ότι (*ante* ήξει). †πάντα ταύτα. 37. αποκτένουσα. 39. απάρτι. XXIV. 2. ταύτα πάντα. – μὴ *secund.* 3. κατιδίαν. υμίν. 5. πλανήσουσι. 9. + των (*ante* εθνών). 15. εστός. 17. †τα (*pro* τι). 18. το ιμάτιον.

20. —ἐν. 21. απαρχής. 31. + και (*ante* φωνής). 33. ούτως. ταύτα πάντα. 34. λέγω. 36. —τῆς *secund.* XXV. 1. [†*fin.*+*et sponse* Lat.]. 2. + αι (*ante* πέντε *secund.*). 3. αυτών (*pro* ἑαυτῶν *prim.*). 9. αρκέσει. [13. †εν η κ.τ.λ.]. 19. λόγον μετ αυτών. 24. είπεν. 29. δοκεί έχειν (*pro* ἔχει). 30. εκβάλετε. 32. συναχθήσονται. 37. πινώντα. 40. αποκριθείς. εφοσον (*sic* v. 45). 44. — αὐτῷ. XXVI. 4. δόλω κρατήσωσι. 9. + τοις (*ante* πτωχοίς). 15. και εγώ. 18. εστί. 29. απάρτι. 35. απαρνήσωμαι. †+δε (*post* ομοίως). 39. ουκ. 40. ούτως,. 48. †παραδούς. εστίν. 52. *fin.* †αποθανούνται. 54. ούτως. 55. καθ· ημέραν. 59. †θανατώσωσιν αυτόν. 63. —τοῦ *secund.* 64. απάρτι. 70. απάντων (*omnibus*). 71. †αυτοίς (*pro* τοῖς). 74. καταθεματίζειν (*detestari*). 75. —τοῦ *secund.* αλέκτωρα. XXVII. 1. όπως αυτόν θανατώσωσιν. 13. καταμαρτυρούσιν. 15. τω όχλω ένα. 17. (*non* vv. 16, 20, 21, 26). Βαραβάν. 22. †+ουν (*post* λέγει). 33. ο (*pro* ὅς). 35. βάλοντες. †—ἵνα πληρωθῇ κ.τ.λ. 41. †+και φαρισαίων (*post* πρεσβυτέρων). 42. πιστεύσομεν. †+επ. 44. *fin.* αυτόν. 45. ενάτης. 46. ενάτην. †λιμά. τουτέστι. ίνα τι. 64. [†νυκτός]. XXVIII. 9. —ὁ. 19. †—οὖν. Subscr. τέλος του κατά ματθαίον αγίου ευαγγελίου.

Marc. †+άγιον (*ante* ευαγγ.). I. [2. †τοις προφήταις *esaia propheta*]. 6. +ο (*ante* ιωάννης). 9. +ο (*ante* ιησούς). †ναζαρέτ. 16. †+του σίμωνος (*ante* βάλλοντας). 21. +την (*ante* συναγωγήν). εδίδασκεν. 27. εαυτούς (*se*). 30. +του (*ante* σίμωνος). 33. συνηγμένη (*congregata*). 35. †+ο ιησούς (*post* απήλθεν). πνοσεύχετο. 37. †σε ζητούσι. 38. εκεί (*pro* κἀκεῖ). 43. ευθέως,. 44. —μηδὲν. αλλά. 45. έξωθεν (*foris*). II. 1. †εισήλθε πάλιν. 4. [κράββατον]. 7. ούτω. 8. †+αυτοί (*post* ούτως). 9. σου (*pro* σοι: *tibi peccata tua*). τον κράββατον σου. 12. ευθέως ηγέρθη. 15. θελώναι. 18. διά τι. νηστεύουσιν *bis.* 25. δαυίδ. έσχεν. 26. [*habet* του]. III. 3. το (*pro* τῷ *secund.*). 7. ηκολούθησεν. —τῆς *secund.* 9. προσκαρτερεί. 12. φανερόν αυτόν. 18. †βαρτολομαίον. 27. ουδείς δύναται (—οὐ). *fin.* διαρπάση. 32. †+και αι αδελφαί σου (*ante* ἔξω). 35. †μου αδελφός. IV. 4. †—τοῦ οὐρανοῦ. 9. —αὐτοῖς. 17. ευθύς. 18. †—οὗτοί εἰσιν *secund.* (*sic Elzev.* 1633). 30. παραβαλούμεν. 31. κόκκον. 33. εδύναντο. 34. κατιδίαν. 37. λέλαψ. επέβαλεν (*mittebat*). 38. μέλλει. 40. ούτως. V. [1. †γαδ. *geras.*]. 3. μνήμασι. 5. εν τοις μνήμασι και εν τοις όρεσι. 6. έδραμεν. 11. προς τω όρει (*circa montem*). 16. †διηγήσαντο δε (—καὶ). 19. πεποίηκε (*fecerit*). 29. *fin.* †+αυτής. 40. πάντας (*omnibus*). VI. 2. †—ὅτι. 8. παρήγγελεν. 9. ενδύσησθε (*induerentur*). 11. εάν (*pro* ἂν). 13. †εξέβαλον. 15. —ἤ. 16. —ὁ. 17. —τῇ. 23. —μὲ. 25. εξαυτής. 31. κατιδίαν (*sic* v. 32). ευκαίρουν. 33. —οἱ ὄχλοι. ήλθον (*pro* συνῆλθον: *pervenerunt*). 37. †δηναρίων διακοσίων. 44. —ὡσεὶ. 53. γεννησαρέτ (*genesareth*). VII. 6. ισαΐας. 13. παραδώσει. 18. ούτως. 22. ασέλγειαι. 25. —αὐτῆς. 26. σύρα φοινίκισσα (*syrophenissa*). εκβάλη. 32. μογγιλάλον. 33. επιλαβόμενος (*apprehendens*). κατιδίαν. VIII. 1. παμπόλου. 2. [ημέρας]. 3. νήστις. ήκασι. 13. —τὸ *prim.* *Jungit* vv. 18, 19. 19. κλασμάτων πλήρεις. 22. βηθσαϊδά. 24. —ὅτι *et* ὁρῶ (*sic Elz.* 1633). 25. ανέβλεψε (*videret*). 34. ακολουθείν (*pro* ἐλθεῖν). 35. την εαυτού ψυχήν. 38. —ἂν. IX. 2. —τὸν *tert.* κατιδίαν. 6. λαλήσει. έμφοβοι (*exterriti*). 8. ειμή (*pro* ἀλλὰ). 16. εαυτούς. 19. είπεν (*pro* λέγει: *dixit*). εωσπότε *bis.* 22. +το (*ante* πυρ). το ύδωρ. 27. της χειρός αυτού (—αὐτὸν *prim.*). 28.

κατιδίαν. 37. †παιδίων τοιούτων. ουχ. 38. †–ἐν. 40. υμών *bis*. 41. –τῷ. 42. εάν (*pro* αν). +τούτων (*post* μικρών) *sic*. X. 1. Και εκείθεν. 2. –οἱ. επηρώτων. 6. *fin.* †+και είπεν. 17. τις (*pro* εἶς). 21. –τοῖς. 24. –τοῖς *secund.* 25. †+γαρ (*ante* ἐστί). †εισελθείν (*pro* διελθεῖν). 27. –τῷ *prim.* 28. †ήρξατο δε (–καὶ). 29. †και αποκριθείς (–δὲ). +ένεκεν (*ante* του εναγ.). 31. –οἱ. 32. αυτών.(*pro* αὐτοὺς). 43. ούτως. υμών διάκονος. 44. εάν (*pro* ἂν). 47. δαυίδ (*sic* v. 48). 51. ραβουνί (*sic*). 52. †ηκολούθησε. XI. 1. †βηθσφαγή. 3. †αποστέλλει. 5. εστώτων. 10. δαυίδ. 11. –καὶ *secund.* 14. μηδείς. φάγη. 17. έθνεσι. 18. απολέσωσιν. 22. +ο (*ante* ιησούς). 23. πιστεύσει. 24. αιτήσθε. 29. και εγώ. 32. αλλ (–ἐὰν: *si*) *sic*. XII. 5. δαίροντες. αποκτένοντες. 7. προς αυτούς (*adinvicem*). 13. –τῶν *secund.* 20. †–οὖν. 23. †–οὖν. 25. εκγαμίσκονται. 27. ο θεός θεός νεκρών αλλά ζώντων (*deus* semel tantum Lat.). 28. †–αὐτοῖς. [28, 29. πασών]. 32. †–Θεός. 33. –τῶν *secund.* 35, 36, 37. δαυίδ. 36. –τῷ *prim.* et *secund.* λέγει (*pro* εἶπεν *secund.*: *dixit*). 37. –ὁ (*multa*). 39. πρωτοκλησίας. 41. †έβαλον. 43. είπεν (*pro* λέγει: *ait*). †βαλλόντων (*qui miserunt*). XIII. 1. +εκ (*post* εις). 2. αποκριθείς ο ιησούς. 3. κατιδίαν. 4. ταύτα πάντα. 9. *Jungit* συν. *et* δαρ. 14. εστός. 15. –τὴν. 28. όταν δη ο κλάδος αυτής (–ἤδη: *cum jam ramus ejus*). 32. –τῆς *secund.* +τω (*ante* ουρανῷ). XIV. 6. *fin.* εν εμοι (*in me*). 7. ευποιήσαι. 8. έσχεν. 9. εάν (*pro* ἂν). 12. †ετοιμάσομεν. 15. ανώγαιον. 22. +και (*ante* ευλογήσας). 28. υμών (*sic* X. 32: *non* XVI. 7). 29. +εν σοι (*ante* αλλ). 30. +συ (*ante* σήμερον). πρινή. 31. απαρνήσωμαι. 32. προσεύξομαι. 33. –τὸν *secund.* 34. *fin.* †+μετ εμού. 45. χαίρε (*pro* ραββί *prim.*). 49. καθημέραν. 51. †ηκολούθησεν. 54. +το (*ante* φῶς). 60. –τὸ. 62. †εκ δεξιών καθήμενον. 64. †ένοχον είναι. 66. †παιδίσκων (*non* -ών). 68. ούτε (*pro* οὐδὲ). 72. το ρήμα ο. αλέκτωρα. XV. 3. †*fin.*+αυτός δε ουδέν απεκρίνατο. 18. †+και λέγειν (*ante* χαίρε). ο βασιλεύς. 22. †γολγοθάν. 24. †διαμερίζονται. 31. –δὲ. 33. ενάτης. 34. ενάτη. †λιμά. 40. –καὶ *secund.* 43. +.και (*ante* τολμήσας: *et audacter*). 44. τέθνηκεν. †*fin.* πάλαι απέθανε: *jam mortuus esset* (vid. Mill.). 46. αγωρασας. ενείλισε. XVI. 1. –ἡ τοῦ. ηγώρασαν. αλείψωσι τον ιησούν. 8. –ταχὺ. 9. +ο ιησούς (*ante* πρωΐ). †+και (*post* ης). 18. βλάψη. 20. *fin.* †+αμήν. Τέλος του κατά μάρκον αγίου ευαγγελίου.

Luc. Προοίμιον του αγίου λουκά εις το αυτού ευαγγέλιον. I. 2. παρέδωσαν. *Post* v. 4 *legitur* Το κατά λουκάν άγιον ευαγγέλιον Cap. I. [5. †*passim.* –ετ.]. 25. ούτως. 26. †ναζαρέτ. 27. δαυίδ (*sic* vv. 32, 69). 35. +εκ σου (*ante* άγιον). 36. γήρει. 44. †εσκίρτησε το βρέφος εν αγαλλιάσει. 64. †+διηρθρώθη (*ante* και ελαλει). II. 4. †ναζαρέτ (*sic* vv. 39, 51). δαυίδ *bis* (*sic* v. 11). 5. εγγύω (*pregnante*). 8. +τας (*ante* φυλακάς). 12. –τῇ. 15. άνθωρποι. †+εις (*post* έως). 20. υπέστρεψαν. 21. †αυτόν (*pro* τὸ παιδίον). [22. αυτής: *ejus*]. 25. †ην άγιον. 36. φροφήτις. 37. †αυτή. ογδοηκοντατεσσάρων. 39. εαυτών. 40. *fin.* αυτόν. III. 1. πέντε και δεκάτω. †λησανίου. αβιλινής. 2. †επι αρχιερέως. 19. του αδελφού αυτού φιλίππου. 22. ευδόκησα. 23. †–ὁ ἰησοῦς. [*desunt puncta*]. 27. †ιωανάν, *sic* (*johanna*). 33. [αμιναδάβ]. εσρώμ. 34. †θάρρα. 35. †σερούχ. IV. 1. πλήρης πνεύματος αγίου. 4. –ὁ. 7. εμού. †πάσα. 8. –γὰρ. 9. –ὁ. 11. †–ὅτι. 14. κατ (*pro* καθ'). 16. †ναζαρέτ. 18. είνεκεν. εναγγελίσασθαι. 25. –δὲ. 27. †+εξ (*ante* αυτών). 29. –τῆς *secund.* 35. –τὸ *secund.* 38. πενθερά δε (–ἡ). [40. †δύνοντος: *cum occidisset*]. V. [1. †γεννησαρέτ]. 6. †πλῆθος ιχθύων. 7. συλαβέσθαι. 8. γόνασιν ιησού. 19. –διὰ (*qua parte*). 29. –ὁ. 30. +των (*ante* τελωνών). 36. †–ἐπίβλημα *secund.*). VI. 3. δαυίδ. 6. –καὶ *prim.* 7. –αὐτὸν. †+αυτόν (*post* θεραπεύσει). 9. υμάς· Τι (*vòs si licet*). *fin.* †αποκτείναι. 10. είπεν αυτώ (–τῷ ἀνθρώπῳ). ούτως. 22. ένεκεν. 23. χάρητε. 26. –ὑμῖν. είπωσιν υμάς. †–πάντες. 27. αλλά. 28. †–καὶ. 34. –οἱ. 35. οι υιοί υψίστου. VII. 2. έμελλε. [4. παρέξει: *prestes*]. 6. †μου υπό την στέγην. 7. αλλ. 9. ουτε. 12. †και αυτή. –ἦν (*post* ικανός). 16. †πάντας (*omnes*). 19. έπεμψεν. 24. †τοις όχλοις (–πρὸς). 31. †–εἶπε δὲ ὁ Κύριος. 34. φίλος τελωνών. 44. της (*pro* τοῖς). [48. †σου: *tibi*]. VIII. 5. εαυτού. 15. *fin.* †+ταύτα λέγων εφώνει, ο έχων ώτα ακούειν ακουέτω. 18. εαν (*pro* ἂν) *bis.* 19. εδύναντο. [20. †λεγόντων]. 24. επιστάτα *semel tantum.* 29. παρήγγελλε. 34. γενόμενον. [†απελθόντες]. 38. τα δαιμόνια εξεληλύθει. 43. †ιατροίς (–εἰς). 49. †+δε (*post* έτι). 51. †και ιωάννην και ιάκωβον. IX. 5. εάν (*pro* ἂν). 7. από των (*pro* εκ: *a*). 9. –ὁ. 10. κατιδίαν. 13. †ιχθύες δύο. †αγοράσομεν. 15. ούτως. 20. –ὁ. 23. †–καθ' ἡμέραν. 24. εάν (*pro* ἂν *prim.*). 27. εστώτων. 28. –τὸν. [†ιω: και ιακ.]. 33. μίαν μωσεί. 36. εωράκασι. 38. επίβλεψαι. 40. εκβάλωσιν. 41. †τον υιόν σου ώδε. 47. παιδίον. 49. –τὰ. 54. εποίησεν. 60. διάγγελε. 62. †ο ιησούς προς αυτόν. άρωτρον. X. 2. εκβάλη. 4. βαλλάντιον. 6. –μὲν. –ὁ. 11. –τὸν *secund.* 13. χωραζίν. 19. †αδικήση. 20. –μᾶλλον. 22. *init.* †+και στραφείς προς τους μαθητάς είπε. μοι παρεδόθη. 23. κατιδίαν. 32. αντιπαρήλθε. 34. –αὐτὸν *secund.* 35. ότι. 36. †πλησίον δοκεί σοι. 39. †των λόγων. 41. †ο ιησούς είπεν αυτή (*dixit illi dominus*). XI. [2. †*non cum* Lat.]. 6. †–μου. 8. †όσον. 11. δώσει (*pro* ἐπιδώσει *prim.*). η (*pro* εἰ: *aut*). 12. αιτήση. 13. †δώματα αγαθά. [15. *sic* vv. 18, 19. †–ούλ]. 17. τα διανοήματα αυτών. μερισθείσα (*divisum*). 18. εμερίσθη (*divisus est*). 24. ευρίσκων. 25. ελθών. 27. †και εγένετο. 29. εστίν. 31. σολομώνος *bis.* 33. [κρυπτήν]. αλλ. 34. –καὶ *prim.* 44. –οἱ *secund.* 53. †συνέχειν (*insistere*). 54. †–καὶ. XII. 1. †πρώτον. προσεχ. (*deest* πρώ. Lat.). 3. ταμιείοις (*non* v. 24). 4. αποκτενόντων. 7. †πολλώ (*cf.* Mtt. x. 31). *fin.* +υμείς. 8. †εν εαυτώ. 11. †απολογήσεσθε. 18. γενήματα. 20. άφρον. 33. βαλλάντια. 38. ούτως. 39. –ἂν *secund.* 47. †αυτού (*pro* ἑαυτοῦ: *sui*). 53. επί (*pro* ἐφ'). 54. ούτως. 56. του ουρανού και της γης. 58. *Jungit* εν τη οδώ *cum praeced.* βάλη σε. 59. τον (*pro* τὸ). XIII. 6. ζητών καρπόν. 7. ουκ. [8. κόπρια]. 11. ασθενίας (*non* v. 12). 15. υποκριταί. 19. ον (*pro* ὃ). 20. *init.* †–καὶ. 21. έκρυψεν. 28. †όψεσθε. 29. –ἀπὸ *secund.* 34. αποκτέννουσα. †+επισυνάγει (*post* όρνις). 35. λέγω δε (–ἀμὴν). XIV. 4. απέλυσεν. 10. ανάπεσε. 15. †άριστον. 18. απομιάς. 21. τυφλούς και χωλούς. 26. †αυτού (*pro* ἑαυτοῦ *prim.*). είναι μαθητής. 27. †είναι μου. 28. +ο (*ante* θέλων). 32. †πόρρω αυτού. XV. 4. ενενήκοντα εννέα (*sic* v. 7). 7. ούτως (*sic* v. 10). 20. †αυτου (*pro* ἑαυτοῦ). [26. –αὐτοῦ]. XVI. 4. †μεταστώ. 9. †εκλείπητε (*defeceritis*). 15. †*fin.* ην: *errat Millius.* 19. καθημέραν. 26. ένθεν (*pro* εντεῦθεν: *hinc*). XVII. 1. +του (*ante* μη). 4. †–ἐπί σε. 7. ανάπεσε. 9. †–αὐτῷ. 10. ούτως. †οφειλομεν.

17. εννέ. 21. †–ἢ. 22. †+καὶ (*ante* πρὸς). 23. †–ἢ (*et*). 24. υπουρανόν *bis*. –καὶ. 26. –τοῦ *prim*. +του (*ante* υιού). 34. –ὁ *prim*. 35. –ἡ *prim*. [36. *habet*]. 37. +και (*ante* οι αετοί). XVIII. 3. †–τις. 5. υποπιάζη. 7. †ποιήση. 8. *init*. +ναι (*autem*). 9. –καὶ *prim*. 14. η γαρ εκείνος (*ab illo*). 28. –ὁ. 33. †τη τρίτη ημέρα. 38. δαυίδ (*sic* v. 39). XIX. 4. †προσδραμών. συκομωρέαν. –δι' (*inde*). έμελλε. 7. πάντες. 10. ζητείσαι. 15. †?–καὶ *secund*. 23. †τοις τραπεζίταις (*pro* ἐπὶ τ. τρ). †ελθών εγώ. 29. †βηθσφαγή. 47. καθημέραν. 48. †ποιήσουσιν. XX. 5. †–οὖν. 9. †–τις. 19. †–τὸν λαόν. 28. μωυσής. 31. †επτά ου καπέλιπον (–καὶ). 35. εκγαμίζονται (*non* v. 34: *errat Millius*). 37. μωυσής. .κύριον (*sic* Lat.). 41, 42, 44. δαυίδ. XXI. 2. †τινά και. 3. αύτη η πτωχή. 6. επί λίθον. 16. †και συγγενών και φίλων και αδελφών. 26. †+εν (*ante* τη οικουμένη). 34. βαρηθώσιν. 36. †–ταῦτα. XXII. 3. –ὁ. 9. †ετοιμάσομεν. 12. ανώγαιον. 18. γενήματος. 26. ουκ. 30. †καθίσεσθε. 34. †φωνήση. 35. βαλλαντίου. 36. βαλλαντίον. †πωλήσει. †αγοράσει. 44. υδρώς. 45. †–αὐτοῦ. 47. αυτούς (*pro* αὐτῶν). *fin*. †+τούτο γαρ σημείον δεδώκει αυτοίς. ον αν φιλήσω, αυτός εστίν. 52. προς (*pro* ἐπ'). 53. καθημέραν. 54. –αὐτὸν *secund*. (–καὶ εἰσήγαγον αὐτὸν Lat.). 60. –ὁ (*ante* αλέκτωρ). 66. †απήγαγον (*duxerunt*). *fin*. αυτών. XXIII. 8. †έτι (*pro* τι). 12. –ὁ *secund*. 18. παμπληθή. 25. †–αὐτοῖς. 26. –τοῦ *prim*. 38. +η (*ante* επιγραφή). 44. ενάτης. 51. –καὶ (*post* ος). 54. †–καὶ *secund*. 55. –καὶ *prim*. XXIV. 1. βαθέως. 4. †άνδρες δύο. [12. *desunt puncta*]. 18. †–ἐν *prim*. 24. ούτως. 27. *fin*. εαυτού. 36. +και (*ante* αυτός:—καὶ αὐτὸς Lat.). 42. μελισσείου. [43. †*non cum* Lat.). 46. ούτως *bis*. Τέλος του κατά λουκάν αγίου ευαγγελίου.

Το κατά ιωάννην άγιον ευαγγέλιον. JOHANN. I. 18. μονογεννής. 28. βηθανία (*pro* Βηθαβαρᾷ). 40. †–δὲ. 42. †μεσίαν.—ὁ. 44. ο ιησούς *transfert in locum ante* ακολούθει. 46. –τοῦ. †ναζαρέτ: *sic* v. 47. 49. –ὁ. 52. απάρτι. II. 5. ότι. λέγει. 15. †σχοινίου. 17. †καταφάγεται. 19. –ὁ. 22. +των (*ante* νεκρών). [†αυτοίς]. 23. +τοις (*ante* ιεροσολύμοις). III. 5. –ὁ. 6. γεγεννημένον *bis*. 10. –ὁ. 23. †σαλήμ. [25. ιουδαίων]. 31. *fin*. εστί. 36. +την (*post* όψεται). [†μενεί]. IV. 1. ιησούς (*pro* Κύριος). 3. †απήλθεν (–πάλιν). 5. –τῆς. συχάρ. ου (*pro* ὃ). 13. –ὁ *prim*. 14. διψήσει. 15. έρχομαι (*veniam*). 20. εν τω όρει τούτω. 25. †μεσίας. 31. †+αυτού (*post* μαθηταί): *sic* v. 33†. 35. ουκ. †–ἔτι. τετράμηνος. 41. +εις αυτόν (*post* επίστευσαν). 46. †πάλιν ο ιησούς (*iterum* tantum). 47. †αυτόν (*pro* αὐτοῦ). 50. +ο (*ante* ιησούς *secund*.). V. 1. +η (*ante* εορτή). 2. †έστη. 4. εταράσσετο το (*movebatur*). 5. τριακονταοκτώ. 7. βάλη. 21. ούτως. 35. προς ώραν αγαλλιαθήναι. 46. μωσεί. VI. 6. ήμελλε. 8. –ὁ. 15. †πάλιν ανεχώρησεν. 24. –καὶ *prim*. [28. †ποιώμεν]. 29. –ὁ. 37. †εκβάλλω. 39. αλλ. 45. –τοῦ. †ακούων. 52. οι ιουδαίοι προς αλλήλους. 58. †+μου (*post* τρωγων). 65. έλεγεν. 70. †–ὁ ἰησοῦς. 71. έμελλεν. VII. 12. †–δὲ. 16 †+ουν (*post* απεκρίθη). 21. –ὁ. 26. –ἀληθῶς *secund*. 27. έρχηται. 29. –δὲ (†*deest glossa Latina*). 31. –τούτων. 32. †υπηρέτας οι φαρισαίοι και οι αρχιερείς. 33. †–αὐτοῖς. 38. ρεύσουσιν. 39. –ὁ. 41. †–δὲ. 42. δαυίδ *bis*. VIII. 3. (*Nullum suspicionis vestigium*). επί μοιχεία κατειλημμένην. 4. †ταύτην εύρομεν επαυτοφόρω μοιχευομένην. 5. †+ημών (*ante* μωσής). †–ήμῖν. 6. †κατηγορίαν κατ. *fin.* †+μη προσποιούμενος. 9. [†*habet* και υπό κ.τ.λ.]. καθείς. *fin.* †ούσα. 10. †–ή γυνή. 11. +από του νυν (*ante* μηκέτι). 12. αυτοίς ο ιησούς. †περιπατήση.. 14. η που (*pro* και που *secund.*). 25. ότι. 39. †εποιείτε (–ἂν: *facite*). 44. +του (*ante* πατρός). 52. †γεύσηται. [59. ούτως: *non cum* Lat.]. IX. 3. –ό. 10. †σου (*pro* σοι). 15. επέθηκε μοι επί τους οφθαλμούς. 17. λέγουσι ουν. 20. †+δε (*post* απεκρίθησαν) 21. περί εαυτού. 26. ανέωξε. 28. †–οὖν. 29. μωσεί. εστι. 36. †+και (*ante* τις). 40. υμείς *errore*. X. 8. –πρὸ ἐμοῦ. 12. ουχ *prim.* 22. –τοῖς. 23. σολομώνος (–τοῦ). XI. 7. +αυτού (*post* μαθηταίς). 9. –ό. †ώραι εισί. 15. αλλά. 19. +την (*ante* μάρθαν). 20. –ό. 21. –ή. 24. +η (*ante* μάρθα). 32. †αυτού εις τους πόδας. 45. †όσα (*pro* ἃ). 48. ούτως. 52. διασκορπισμένα. συναγάγει. 54. εφραίμ. 56. μετά. XII. 2. ανακειμένων συν. 5. διά τι. 6. έμελλεν. 13. –ό *secund.* 14. εκάθησεν. επ αυτώ. 16. το πρώτον. 17. ότε (*pro* ὅτι). 30. –ό. 31. –τούτου *prim.* 34. –ὅτι *secund.* 50. ούτως. XIII. 8. ουχ. 15. δέδωκα. 19. απάρτι. 30, 31. †ην δε νυξ ότε εξήλθε (–οὖν). 36. +εγώ (*ante* υπάγω). με (*pro* μοι *prim.*). 37. –ό. 38. †φωνήση. XIV. 7. απάρτι. [11. *cum Elz.*]. 13. ότι. 22. †+και (*ante* τι). 23. –ό. 30. †–τούτου. 31. ούτως. XV. 4. ούτος (*pro* οὕτως). 6. +το (*ante* πυρ). 16. ότι. XVI. 3. †–ὑμῖν. 7. +εγώ (*ante* μη). 15. †λαμβάνει (*non* v. 14). 16. –ἐγὼ. 33. †έχετε (*pro* ἕξετε). XVII. 2. δώσει. [7. έγνωκαν]. 11. †ω (*pro* οὓς). 20. †πιστευόντων. 24. δέδωκας (*pro* ἔδωκας). XVIII. 8. –ό. 11. †–σου. 20. †πάντοτε (*pro* πάντοθεν: *omnes*). 24. †–οὖν (*et*). 25. †+ουν (*post* ηρνήσατο). 28. πρωΐ. 32. έμελλεν. 36. –ό. 38. εξήλθεν. 40. †–πάλιν. XIX. 6. +αυτόν (*post* σταύρωσον *secund.*). 7. –τοῦ. 11. –ό. 12. εαυτόν. 13. [†τούτον τον λόγον]. γαβαθά. 16. †*fin.* ήγαγον. 20. †ο τόπος της πόλεως. 26. ίδε (*non* v. 27). 27. †+εκείνος (*post* μαθητής). 30. έλαβεν. [31. εκείνη]. 34. ευθέως. 35. εστίν η μαρτυρία αυτού. 36. +απ (*ante* αυτού). 38. †–δὲ.–ό *prim.* 39. το πρώτον. ως. 40. †+εν (*ante* οθονίοις). XX. 14. –ό. 15. έθηκας αυτόν. 16. †ραβουνί. 28. –ό *prim.* 29. †–θωμᾶ. 31. –ό *prim.* XXI. 3. †ενέβησαν. 5. μήτι. 11. πεντήκοντα τριών. 21. –ό. Τέλος του κατά ιωάννην αγίου ευαγγελίου. *Sequuntur* αποδημία τοῦ ἁγίου παύλου τοῦ ἀποστόλου: Ευθαλίου διακόνου περὶ τῶν χρόνων: ὑποθέσεις *Epistolarum omnium: Prefatio sancti hieronymi presbyteri in omnes Epistolas beati Pauli Apostoli: Prologus specialis in ep. ad Rom.*

Η του αγίου παύλου προς ρωμαίους επιστολή. ROMAN. I. 2. προεπαγγείλατο. 3. δαυίδ. 10. είπως. 13. τινά καρπόν. –καὶ *secund.* 15. ούτως. 26. παραφύσιν. 27. †–τε. άρρενες (*prim.*). 32. συνευδοκούσιν. II. 5. †+και (*ante* δικαιοκρισίας). 7. επιζητούσι (*quaerentibus*). 17. *init.* ει δε. καυχάση (*non* v. 23). 29. –τοῦ. III. 10. †–ὅτι. 26. †ιησούν (*iesu xpi*). IV. 4. –τὸ. 6. δαυίδ. 7. αφείθησαν. 8. †–οὐ (*non*). 12. τῆς πίστεως της εν τη ακροβυστία. V. [1. †έχομεν]. 3. –ή. 13. +τω (*ante* κόσμω). 14. μωυσέος. 15. ούτως (*non* vv. 18, 19, 21, VI. 4, 11). VI. 6. †υμων. 17. †υπακούσετε (*errat Millius*). 19. ούτως. VII. 1. εφόσον. 2. +του νόμου (*ante* του ανδρός). 4. †+ανδρί (*ante* ετέρω). 6. †αποθανόντες (*mortis*). 7. †+ότι (*post* ερούμεν). 9. †έζησεν. 23. +εν (*ante* τω νόμω *secund.*). VIII. [11. †διά του: *propter*]. 21. *Jungit* επ ελπίδι *cum praecedent.* 23. †συστενάζομεν. 26. προσευξόμεθα. †υπέρ υμών. (*errat Mill.*). 28. +το (*ante* αγαθόν). IX. 11. πρόθεσις του θεού. 12. ερρέθη. 15. μωυσεί. 19. +γαρ (*ante* βουλήματι). 26. ερρέθη. 29. †*init.* – καὶ. 33. †+ εγώ (*ante* τίθημι). X. 1. τον (*pro* τοῦ). 5. μωυσής. 6. + τη (*ante* καρδία). 6, 7, 8. τουτέστι. 11. †+ ότι (*ante* πας). 19. μωυσής. †παραζηλώ. XI. 7. τούτο. 9. δαυίδ. 10. σύγκαψον. 11. σοτηρία. 13. εφόσον. 14. είπω. 19. –οἱ. 21. μήπως. φείσεται. 30. ποτέ και υμείς. απειθία *hic.* 31. υμετέρω. XII. 5. καθείς. [11. κυρίω]. XIII. 1. υπό (*pro* ἀπὸ: *a*). 5. ανάγκη υποτάσεσθε. (*errat Mill.*). 9. †–οὐ ψευδομαρτυρήσεις. 10. του (*pro* τῷ). ου κατεργάζεται. 11. †–γὰρ. 14. ποιήσθε. XIV. 3. †αυτών. 6. +και (*ante* ο εσθίων). 9. †έζησεν. 11. †+ επουρανιών και επιγείων και καταχθονίων (*post* γόνυ). 14. †χριστώ (*pro* Κυρίῳ). αυτου (*pro* ἑαυτοῦ). 15. απέθανεν. 22. σεαυτόν. 23. *fin.* εστί. XV. 2. –γὰρ. υμών. 4. †+διά (*ante* της παρακλ.). 7. υμάς. 8. χριστόν ιησούν. 9. +κύριε (*post* έθνεσι). 12. ελπιούσι. 14. †άλλους. 17. +τον (*ante* θεόν). 18. †+ και (*ante* λόγω: *in*). 23. επιποθείαν. 24. ισπανίαν. 26. μακεδωνία. 28. ισπανίαν. XVI. [3. †πρίσκιλλαν]. 5. επαινετόν. μοι (*mihi*). 9. στάχην. 11. ηρωδίωνα. 15. φιλολόγον. †νηρέαν. 20. – ἀμήν. 27. – ῷ. – ἡ. [αμήν]. *Subscript:* τέλος της προς ρωμαίους επιστολής: *Sequuntur Prologus et Argument. in* 1 *Cor.*

Η του αγίου παύλου προς κορινθίους πρώτη επιστολή. 1 COR. I. 9. †του κυρίου ημών ιησού χριστού. 18. – ὁ *prim.* 29. καυχήσηται. †του θεού (*pro* αὐτοῦ). II. 1. καταγγέλων. 5. †ημών. 12. οίδωμεν. III. 1. υμίν λαλήσαι. 2. εδύνασθε. 4. λέγει. 11. – ὁ. [15. ούτως]. IV. 11. γυμνιτεύομεν. V. 5. *fin.* + χριστού. 7. ετύθη. 11. [η: *est*]. †η λοίδορος η πλεονέκτης η ειδωλολάτρης. 13. εξαιρείτε (*auferte*). VI. 5. ένι (*pro* ἔστιν). 7. †–ἐν. 10. – οὐ *secund.* 14. ημάς. 16. *init* †–ἢ. VII. 4. ομοίος (*non* v. 3). 5. ειμήτι. συνέρχησθε. 10. παραγγέλω. 19. εστί *bis.* 24. –τῷ. 29. –ὅτι. .*ante* το. +οι (*ante* έχοντες). 33. †–δὲ. 34. .μεμέρισται. (*et divisus est*). +και (*ante* η γυνή). 35. ευπάρεδρον. 38. ποιή *prim.* 39. †–αὐτῆς *secund.* VIII. 8. †περισσεύωμεν (*abundabimus*). IX. 8. λέγω (*pro* λαλῶ). 9. νόμω μωσέως. 10. –ὁ *prim.* 11. θερίσωμεν. 14. ούτως. 23. συκοινωνός. 26. δαίρων. 27. υποπιάζω. X. 2. μωυσήν. 7. ώσπερ. +του (*ante* φαγείν). 8. είκοσι τρείς. 14. διό. †αδελφοί μου αγαπητοί. ειδωλολατρίας. 19. *Jungit,* φημί ότι. 30. – δὲ. XI. 2. παραδώσεις. 4. †εαυτού κεφαλήν. 5. ξυρημένη. 9. εκκτίσθη. 10. διατούτο. 14. εστίν. 18. – τῇ. 19. †εν υμίν αιρεσείς είναι. 22. τούτω,. 27. + του (*ante* αίματος)). 32. + του (*ante* κυρίου). XII. 2. +ότε (*post* ότι). 21. + ο (*ante* οφθαλμός). 23. ατιμότερα. 26. †συμπάσχη. †συγχαίρη. XIII. 2. ουθέν. 3. ψωμίσω[1]. 9. †δε (*pro* γὰρ). XIV. 5. διερμηνεύει. 15. + τω (*ante* νοῒ *secund.*). 26. γινέσθω. 29. †– δὲ. 31. + έκαστοι (*post* ένα). 33. αλλά. 34. αυτοίς. 35. εθέλουσιν. † εστίν εν εκκλησία γυναιξί. 37. – τοῦ. 39. †+ μου (*post* αδελφοί).

[1] *Ad* καυθήσωμαι *margo habet:* In aliis exemplaribus grecis habetur καυχήσωμαι. Id est glorier, ut ait beatus Hieronymus super epistola ad galatas capit. 5. vide ibi.

XV. 2. ,ει κατέχετε,. 7. έπειτα (*pro* εἶτα). 15. †+ημείς (*ante* ψευδομάρτυρες). 23. +του (*ante* χριστού). 27. δηλονότι. 28. πάσιν. 30. †+κατά (*ante* πάσαν). 31. [υμετέραν][1]. 33. χριστά. 34. †υμών. 39. –σὰρξ *tertium*. 49. φορέσωμεν[2]. XVI. 2. ότι. εάν (*pro* ἂν). γίνονται. 5. μακεδωνίαν *bis*. 11. εξουθενήσει. 16. τιούτοις. Τέλος της προς κορινθίους πρώτης επιστολής.

Prol. Argum. ad 2 Cor. Η του αγίου παύλου προς κορινθίους δευτέρα επιστολή. 2 CORINTH. I. 5. +του (*ante* χριστού *secund.*). †περισσεύη. 6. †και η ελπίς ημών βεβαία υπέρ υμών *transfertur in locum post* πάσχομεν, είτε παρακαλούμεθα κ.τ.λ. *post posito: aliter* Lat. 8. υμάς (*pro* ἡμᾶς). 9. αλλ. 11. †*fin.* υμών. 13. αλλή. 14. *fin.* ημών ιησού χριστού. 15. ελθείν προς υμάς. +το (*ante* πρότερον). 16. †ελθείν (*pro* διελθεῖν). 20. +του (*ante* θεού). 21. †υμάς συν ημίν. 23. ουκ έτι. II. 1. †εν λύπη προς υμάς ελθείν (*in tristitia venire ad vos*). 3. λύπην επί λύπη σχώ. 5. αλλά. 17. †λοιποί (*pro* πολλοί). III. 3. αλλ. σαρκικαίς. 6. αποκτένει. 7. μωϋσέος. 9. †περισσεύσει. 10. †ου (*pro* οὐδὲ: *nec*). 13. μωϋσής. 14. ότι. 15. μωϋσής. IV. 4. †*fin.* +του αοράτου. 14. εξεγερεί. 16. εικαί. έσω (*pro* ἔσωθεν). V. 3. είγε. [4. εφ ω]. 10. κομίση τε. ιδία (*pro* διὰ: *propria*). 12. αλλ. καυχήσεως. 16. †αλλά και νυν ουκέτι. 17. τα πάντα καινά (*malè Mill.*). 19. θέμενος. 21. γενώμεθα. VI. [15. βελιάλ: –*al*: *malè Mill.*). VII. 6. †–ὁ Θεὸς. 7. αναγγέλων. 8. εικαί *ter*. 10. †–ἡ δὲ τοῦ κόσμου *ad fin. vers.* 11. +εν (*ante* υμίν). 12. εικαί. ένεκεν *ter*. [*caetera cum Elz.*]. 16. –οὖν. VIII. 8. υμετέρας. 15. †ω (*pro* ὁ) *bis*. 18. –ὁ. 24. –καὶ *secund.* IX. 4. έλθωσιν. 5. ως (*pro* ὥσπερ). 10. [*puncta cum Elz.*]. γενήματα. 12. λειτουργείας. X. 9. +δε (*post* ίνα). 10. †παρρησία (*pro* παρουσία). 12. συνιούσι. 16. υπερεπέκεινα. XI. 1. ανείχεσθε. †–τι. τη αφροσύνη. 2. †ζήλω θεού. 4. ανείχεσθε. 9. πρωσανεπλήρωσαν. 16. καγώ μικρόν τι. 20. δαίρει. 28. καθημέραν. 31. †–ἡμῶν. XII. [1. †*cum Elz.*]. 12. κατείργασται. 13. εστί. 14. +τούτο (*post* τρίτον). † κατενάρκησα. αλλά. 20. †έρις. 21. ταπεινώσει. XIII. 1. *init.* +ιδού. 3. δύναται. 4. –καὶ *tert.* 5. ειμήτι. +άρα (*ante* αδόκιμοι). 9. κατάρτησιν. 11. +της (*ante* ειρήνης). 12. φιλήματι αγίω. Τέλος της προς κορινθίους δευτέρας επιστολής.

Sequitur Argum. (*non Prol.*) *ad Galatas.* (*Sic etiam ad Eph., Phil. Coloss.* 1, 2 *Thess.* 1, 2 *Tim. Tit. Philem. Hebr.*). Η του αγίου παύλου προς γαλάτας επιστολή. GALAT. I. 4. περί (*pro* ὑπὲρ). 9. υμίν (*pro* ὑμᾶς). 12. παρ. 14. +μου (*post* συνηλικιώτας). 16. έθνεσι. II. 2. κατιδίαν. 6. †τε (*pro* ποτε). +ο (*ante* θεός). συλλαμβάνει (*accipit*). 10. +δε (*post* μόνον). 12. συνίσθιεν. 13. συνυποκρίθησαν. †–καὶ *tert.* 14. ου (*pro* οὐκ *secund.*). III. 1. εβάσκηνεν (–τῇ). 4. –καὶ. 8. ενευλογηθήσονται. 10. εισίν *bis*. 11. +τω (*ante* νόμω). 13. γινόμενος. 15. †–ἀδελφοὶ. 16. ερρέθησαν. †–καὶ *secund.* †–σου. 19. *Punct.*

[1] *Margo habet:* Per vestram gloriam: est modus jurandi in greco.

[2] *v.* 51. *Margo habet:* Alia litta greca habet πάντες μενουν κοιμηθησόμεθα αλλου· πάντες αλλαγησομεθα. Id est omnes quidem igitur dormiemus: sed non omnes immutabimur. Vide de hoc beatum Hieronymum in epistola ad Minerium et alexandrum de resurrectione carnis. [*Compl. cum Elz.*: Omnes quidem resurgemus: sed non omnes immutabimur. *Lat.*]

post ουν. αχρισού. διαταγείσα (*ordinata*). 21. – ἂν. 22. – τὰ. πιστεύουσιν. 23. †– δὲ. †υπό νόμου (*sub lege*). 26. †– γὰρ. 28. ουδ *secund.* 29. †– ὑμεῖς. + του (*ante* χριστού). – καὶ. IV. 3. ούτως. 4. ήλθεν. † γεννώμενον (*pro* γενομ. *prim.*). *fin.* νόμου. 6. ότε (*pro* ὅτι: *quum*). 7. αλλά. 17. υμας (*pro* ἡμᾶς). *fin.* ζηλούσθε. 23. † και (*pro* ἀλλ'). 26. εστίν *bis.* 29. ούτως. 30. έκβαλλε. κληρονομήσει. V. 1. + ὁ (*ante* χριστός). ηλευθέρωσεν. Στήκετε (*sic*). 2. ίδε. οφελήσει. 3. †*fin.* ποιήσας (*legis faciende*). 7. ενέκοψε. 9. ζημοί (*at* ζυμή). 12. αποκόψωνται. 15. † μήπω υπ. 17. αντίκεινται. 18. † από νόμου. 19. πορνία. 20. ειδωλολατρία. φαρμακία. 21. άπερ λέγω (*pro* ἃ προλέγω). 23. εστίν. 24. παθήμασιν. (Cap. VI. *incipit cum* V. 25). 25. στιχούμεν (*errat Mill.*) 26. γενώμεθα. † προσκαλούμενοι. VI. 1. † προσληφθή. 2. – τοῦ. 13. περιτετμημένοι. Τέλος της προς γαλάτας επιστολής.

Η του αγίου παύλου προς εφεσιόυς επιστολή. EPHES. I. 10. – τε. 12. – τῆς. 18. καρδίας (*pro* διανοίας). 20. + των (*ante* νεκρών). 23. + τα (*ante* πάντα). II. 21. – ἡ. III. 1. †– τῶν ἐθνῶν. 2. + καὶ (*post* είγε: *si tamen*). 5. – ἐν. *fin.* †+ αγίω. 6. συγκληρόνομα. 8. †– τῶν ἁγίων. 9. οικονομία (*pro* κοινωνία). IV. 4. ημών (*pro* ὑμῶν). 6. ημίν (*pro* ὑμῖν). 13. † καταντήσομεν. 16. † ποιήται. 27. μήδε. 28. + ιδίαις (*ante* χερσίν: *suis*). 32. † χριστός (*pro* θεὸς ἐν χριστῷ). *fin.* ημίν (*pro* ὑμῖν). V. 21. χριστού (*pro* θεοῦ). 23. – ὁ *prim.* 29. αλλά. VI. 2. † εστί πρώτη εντολή. 5. – τῆς. 7. + ως (*post* δουλευόντες). 9. + και (*post* υμών). 19. δοθή. [21. *habet* πάντα: *errat Millius*]. Τέλος της προς εφεσιόυς επιστολής.

Η του αγίου παύλου προς φιλιππησίους επιστολή. PHILIPP. I. 6. χριστού ιησού. 7. + εν (*ante* τη απολογία). 14. + του θεού (*ante* λόγον). 23. † δε (*pro* γὰρ *prim.*). – γὰρ *secund.* 30. είδετε. II. 1. † ει τις σπλάγχνα. 4. † το ετέρων. 12. †+ μου (*post* υπηκούσατε). – ὡς. †+ και (*ante* νυν). 14. † οργής (*pro* γογγυσμῶν). 18. δε. 21. – τοῦ. 23. εξ αυτής. 27. αλλά. III. 3. † θεού. 12. †*fin.* κυρίου ιησού χριστού. 19. – ὁ. IV. 1. ούτως. [2. ευοδίαν]. 3. *init.* ναι (*etiam*). 10. † φρονείτε (*pro* ἐφρ.). 12. και (*pro* δὲ). 15. †– δὲ. 23. †– ἡμῶν. Τέλος της προς φιλιππησίους επιστολής.

Η του αγίου παύλου προς κολασσαείς επιστολή. (Lat. † *Colossenses*). COLOSS. I. [2. κολοσσαίς]. 6. + και αυξανόμενον (*ante* καθώς). 7. – καὶ. 12. + θεώ και (*ante* πατρί). 14. – διὰ τοῦ αἵματος αὐτοῦ. 18. εστί *prim.* – ἡ. 20. – τὰ *prim.* 27. – τοῦ. 28. – πάντα ἄνθρωπον *secund.* †– τέλειον. II. 4. πειθανολογία. 12. – τῶν. 13. † συνεζωόποιησεν υμᾶς. † ημίν (*pro* ὑμῖν). 14. ήρεν. 17. – τοῦ. 21. † μη (*pro* μηδὲ) *bis.* III. 12. οικτιρμού. 13. έχει. † ημίν (*pro* ὑμῖν). 16. χάριτι,. 17. ότι (*sic* v. 23). 18. – ἰδίοις. 20. εν (*pro* τῷ: *errant Steph. Mill.*). 24. †– ὅτι. απολήψεσθαι. IV. 1. παρέχετε. 3. †+ και (*ante* ημίν). Τέλος της προς κολασσαείς επιστολής.

Η του αγίου παύλου προς θεσσαλονικείς πρώτη επιστολή. 1 THESS. I. 3. αδιαλείπτως,. 5. †– ἐν *tert.* 8. + εν τη (*ante* αχαΐα). † έχειν ημάς. 9. έσχομεν. II. 2. – καὶ. 4. ούτως. 6. από (*pro* ἀπ'). 8. † ημών (*pro* ἡμῖν). 12. μαρτυρόμενοι. 14. τα αυτά. [15. ημάς]. 17. απορφ. 20. – ἡ *secund.* III. 3. το (*pro* τῷ). 6. αγαθήν,. 7. † ημῶν (*pro* ὑμῶν). 10. εκ περισσού. IV. 6. προείπομεν. ημίν. [8. ημάς: *errant Steph. Mill.*]. 12. περιπατείτε. 13. θέλομεν. V. 8. †+ υιοί (*post* όντες). 13. εκ περισσού. 21. †δοκιμάζοντες. 24. †*fin.* + την ελπίδα υμών βεβαίαν. Τέλος της προς θεσσαλονικείς πρώτης επιστολής.

Η του αγίου παύλου προς θεσσαλονικείς δευτέρα επιστολή. 2 THESS. I. 7. † + χριστού (*ante* απ). 9. − τοῦ. 10. πιστεύσασιν. II. 4. αποδεικνύοντα. 16. υμάς (*pro* ἡμᾶς). †διδούς. III. 4. παραγγέλομεν. 5. + την (*ante* υπομονήν). 6. παρέλαβον. 16. διαπαντός. 17. ούτως. Τέλος της προς θεσσαλονικείς δευτέρας επιστολής.

[*Argument:* 1 *Tim.*:....scribens ei a laodicia per tychicum diaconem]. Η του αγιου παύλου προς τιμόθεον πρώτη επιστολή. 1 TIM. I. 1. †θεού πατρός και σωτήρος ημών ιησού χριστού (−Κυρίου). 4. †οικονομίαν. 9. οιδώς. πατρολώαις. μητρολώαις. 12. †ενδυναμούντι. † − ιησού. 13. αλλά. 16. πρώτον (*primo*). 17. μόνω, σοφώ. † − καὶ. II. 5. † ιησούς χριστός. 9. † + αργυρίω (*post* πλέγμασιν). III. 2. [νηφάλιον]. 11. [-λίους]. IV. 1. πλάνης. *Jungit* εν υποκρίσει, *cum* δαιμονίων. 6. χριστού ιησού. εκτρεφόμενος (*enutritus*). 11. παράγγελε. 12. γενού. V. 7. παράγγελε. 10. †η (*pro* εἰ *secund.*). 14. † + χήρας (*ante* γαμεῖν). VI. 5. διαπαρατριβαί. 7. δηλονότι. 8. αρκεσθησώμεθα. 9. ανονήτους. 10. αποπλανήθησαν. 12. − καὶ *prim.* 15. †δείξη. 16. † − καὶ. 17. παράγγελε. πάντα πλουσίως. Τέλος της προς Τιμόθεον πρώτης επιστολής.

Η του αγίου παύλου προς Τιμόθεον δευτέρα επιστολή. 2 TIM. I. 1. † − ἰησοῦ χριστοῦ. †*Jungit vv.* 3, 4. 4. πλησθώ. 5. λωΐδη. [ευνίκη]. 12. παρακαταθήκην. 14. παραθήκην (*depositum vv.* 12, 14). 16. επαισχύνθη. II. 8. δαυίδ. 19. κυρίου (*pro* χριστοῦ). 24, 25. *Jungit* ανεξίκακον *cum* εν πραότητι. III. 2. − οἱ. φυλάργυροι. 6. αιχμαλωτίζοντες. − τὰ. 8. ούτω. 9. †πλείστον. 11. εγένοντο. 17. εξηρτυμένος. IV. 1. † + ημων (*post* κυρίου). 10. †κρίσκης. 11. άγαγε. 13. [φελ.]. 18. επουρανίον. 19. πρίσκιλλαν. Τέλος της προς τιμόθεον δευτέρας επιστολής.

Η του αγίου παύλου προς τίτον επιστολή. TITUS I. 6. ασωτείας. 11. †οίκους όλους. 15. μεμιαμένοις (*errat Mill.*). II. 5. βλασφημείται. 7. *fin.* † + αφθαρσίαν. 8. ημών. [10. ημών]. III. 8. − τῷ. Τέλος της προς Τίτον επιστολής.

Η του αγίου παύλου προς φιλήμονα επιστολή. PHILEM. 6. + έργου (*ante* αγαθού). †εν ημίν. 7. [χαράν]. 23. † − ἰησοῦ. Τέλος της προς φιλήμονα επιστολής.

Η του αγίου παύλου προς εβραίους επιστολή. HEBR. I. 1. εσχάτου. 3. † + του θρόνου (*post* δεξιά). II. 1. μήποτε (*sic* IV. 1; IX. 17). III. 1. †ιησούν χριστόν. 2. μωϋσής. 3. μωϋσήν. καθόσον. 5. μωυσής. 10. είπα. 13. †εξ υμών τις. 16. μωυσέος. 17. έπεσον. 19. †βλέπωμεν. IV. 2. †εκείνοι. συγκεκραμένους. 4. ούτως. 7. δαυίδ. 8. †αυτός. 15. πεπειραμένον. V. 4. † − ὁ *prim.* − ὁ *secund.* VI. 9. κρείσσονα. 14. ημήν. VII. 1. [− τοῦ *secund.*]. ω (*pro* ὁ *secund.*). 3. *fin.* † + εν ω ότι και του αβραάμ προετιμήθη (*e capite Euthaliano*). 5. εξεληλυθότες (*quamquam et ipsi exierint*). 14. μωϋσής. 20. καθόσον. 25. υπερεντυγχάνειν αυτών. VIII. 5. μωϋσής. †ποιήσεις. 6. τετύχηκε. † − καὶ. 9. + μου (*post* επιλαβομένου). 11. †πολίτην (*pro* πλησίον). IX. 2. [άγια]. 8. πεφανώσθαι. 9. τούτον (*pro* τὸν *secund.*). 12. ευράμενος. 14. ημών (*pro* ὑμῶν). 16. διατιθεμένου. 19. μωύσέος. − τῷ. [22. *errat Mill.*]. 23. επουρανία. *fin.* ταύταις. 27. καθόσον. 28. ούτω και. X. 2. [επεί αν]. 9. †το θέλημα σου, ο θεός μου. 10. †+οι (*ante* διά). –τοῦ *secund.* 11. †αρχιερεύς. 18. αυτών (*pro* τούτων). 28. μωϋσέος. 33. αναστρεφωμένων. 34. –ἐν *prim.* (*vos habere*). 39. †–ψυχῆς. XI. 3. †εκφαινομένων. 4. [λαλεῖται, *loquitur*]. 5. μετατέθηκεν. 8. †εξελθών. ἔμελλε. 9. †+αβραάμ (*post* παρώκησεν). 11. +στεῖρα οὖσα (*post* σάρρα: *sterilis*). 12. ως η (*pro* ὡσεὶ) ἄμος. 13. –καὶ πεισθέντες. 23. μωϋσῆς (*sic v.* 24). 26. αιγύπτου (–ἐν: *egyptiorum*). 32. δαυίδ. XII. 1. †απερίστατον (*at in glossario* ευπερίστατον *tantum*). 2. κεκάθικεν (*sedet*). 3. †ουν (*pro* γὰρ). 8. ουκ. 9. ενετρεπόμεθα. 13. τραχιάς. [19. *habet* μη: *errant Steph. Mill.*]. 20. –ἢ βολίδι κατατοξευθήσεται. 21. μωϋσῆς. 22, 23. *Jungit* αγγέλων πανηγύρει. 24. κρείττον. 25. –τῆς. †ουρανού. 28. †λατρεύομεν. XIII. 14. †μένουσαν (*pro* μέλλουσαν). 20. *fin.* +χριστόν. 21. †–τῶν αἰώνων. Τέλος της προς εβραίους επιστολῆς.

Sequitur "prefatio beati Hieronymi presbyteri in librum actuum apostolorum:" *item* "alius prologus." Αι πράξεις των αποστόλων του αγίου λουκά του ευαγγελιστού. ACT. I. 15. επιτοαυτό (*sic* II. 1; 44; III. 1; IV. 26). 15. είκοσι. 16. δαυίδ. 18. –τοῦ. 24. ον εξελέξω εκ τούτων των δύο ένα. 26. συγκατεψυφίσθη. II. 7. †–πάντες *prim.* εισίν. 8. εγενήθημεν. 10. λιβύας. 17. †ενυπνίοις. 25. δαυίδ. διαπαντός. 29. δαυίδ (*sic v.* 34). 31. ουκ εγκατελείφθη. 35. εκδεξιών. 36. +και (*ante* κύριον). 37. †ποιήσωμεν. 44. πιστεύσαντες. 47. καθημέραν (*non* v. 46; III. 2). III. 3. †–λαβεῖν. 11. σολομώνος. 18. ούτως. 20. †προκεχειρισμένον. 21. +των (*ante* αγίων). 23. εάν (*pro* ἂν). 24. κατήγγειλαν. 25. +εν (*ante* τω). IV. 2. καταγγέλειν. †των (*pro* τὴν ἐκ). 7. –τῷ. 12. †+εν (*ante* ουδενί). †ουδέν (*pro* οὔτε). έτερον εστίν. 17. †ανθρώπω. 19. ιωαννής (*sic*). 21. †κολάσονται. 25. δαυίδ. 25. ινατί. 29. τανύν. 30. –σε. 32. ουδέ. 33. +χριστού (*post* ιησού). 37. †αυτού (*pro* αὐτῷ). V. 3. διά τι. 5. +ο (*ante* ανανίας). 12. [εγίνετο]. σολομώνος. [15. †*Non cum Lat.*]. 17. σαδδουκαίον. 21. λε (*pro* δὲ *prim.*). 23. επί (*pro* ἐν: *cum*). –ἔξω. 24. †αρχιερεύς (*pro* Ἱερεὺς). οι αρχιερεύς (*pro* -εῖς). 29. –ὁ. 30. διεχειρήσασθε. 32. πρεύμα. 36. †+μέγαν (*post* εαυτόν). προσεκλήθη (*consensit*). 38. τανύν. 40. δήραντες. 41. κατηξιώθησαν υπέρ του ονόματος του (*sic*) ιησού (–αὐτοῦ). 42. †επαύσαντο. VI. 3. †καταστήσομεν. 11. μωϋσήν. 13. –τούτου. *Cap.* VII. *incipit* v. 2, ἄνδρες. VII. 2. πρινή. 4. και εκείθεν. μετώκησεν. 5. δούναι αυτώ. 11. ουκ. 13. –τῷ *secund.* 14. †εβδομηκονταπέντε ψυχαίς. 16. ω (*pro* ὃ). 18. ήδη. 22. μωϋσής (*non vv.* 20, 29). αιγπτίων. †–ἐν *secund. fin.* +αυτού. 26. τε (*pro* δὲ). 31. μωϋσής. †εθαύμαζε. 32. μωϋσής. 36. †αιγύπτω. 37. †ημών (*pro* ὑμῶν *prim.*). †–αὐτοῦ ἀκούσεσθε. 40. μωϋσής. 42. προσενέγκατε. 43. ρεφάν. 44. μωϋσή. 45. δαυίδ. 46. ενώπιων. [48. ουχ]. 58. +του (*ante* καλουμένου). VIII. 1. δε (*pro* τε). 7. φωνή μεγάλη. 12. –τοῦ *tert.* 13. †δυνάμεις καὶ σημεία μεγάλα γινόμενα. [19. εάν]. 25. †διαμαρτυρόμενοι. 28. †–καὶ *secund.* 30. †προδραμών. 31. μη της. 32. ανοίγη. 37. †*deest versus.* IX. 3. περιήστραψεν. 5, 6. †–σκληρόν *usque ad* αὐτόν. +αλλά (*ante* ανάστηθι). 13. –ὁ. 19. ενίσχυσε. 22. †παύλος. συνέχεε. 25. δαβόντες. 26. εν (*pro* εἰς). 28. †–καὶ ἐκπορευόμενος. εἰσ (*pro* ἐν *prim.*). 32. λύδαν. 35. λύδαν. την σαρωνάν. 38. λύδης. X. 3. ως (*pro* ὡσεὶ). 5. +τινά (*post* σίμωνα). 6. †–οὗτος *ad fin. vers.* 8.

— τὴν. 15. εκδευτέρου (*sic* XI. 9). 17. †+και μαθόντες (*post* διερωτήσαντες). 18. —ὁ. 19. †διενθυμουμένου. 21. †—πρὸς αὐτὸν, *at habet in sequentibus* είπε προς αυτούς. 22. †όχλου (*pro* ὅλου). 23. —τῆς. 25. †ελθείν. 26. ήγειρεν αυτόν. 33. εξ αυτής (*sic* XI. 11). 38. †ναζαρέτ. 39. †+και (*post* ον). 48. +ιησού (*post* κυρίου). XI. 21. †+του ιάσθαι αυτούς (*ante* πολύς). 22. εις αντιόχειαν (—ἕως) *sic*. 26. πρώτων. 29. ευπορείτο. ιουδα α (*sic*). XII. 5. †περί (*pro* ὑπὲρ: *pro*). 6. έμελλε προαγαγείν αυτόν. 8. ούτως. 9. †γενόμενον. 11. —τῆς. 12. †+αδελφοί (*post* συνηθροισμένοι). 15. οι δε έλεγον. 19. †τε (*pro* δὲ). 22. †φωνή θεού. 23. —τὴν. σκωληκώβρωτος. 25. †+εις αντιόχειαν (*post* ιερουσαλήμ). XIII. 2. †—τε. 8. ούτως. 11. —τοῦ. 13. ιερουσαλήμ. 17. †—ἐν τῇ παροικίᾳ. [18. -τοφ-]. [19. -δότ-]. 22. δαυίδ *bis*. 24. +του (*ante* ισραήλ). 27. —ἐν. 29. πάντα. 34. †+αυτόν (*post* υποστρέφειν). δαυίδ (*sic v.* 36). 40. επέλθοι. 41. †+και επιβλέψατε (*post* θαυμάσατε). †—ἔργον *secund.* ο (*pro* ᾧ). 42. +αυτών (*post* δὲ). †τα αυτά ρήματα. 44. †τε (*pro* δὲ). 48. έχαιρε. XIV. 3. —καὶ (*ante* διδόντι). [7. †*non cum* Lat.]. 8. περιπεπατήκει. 10. †+σοι λέγω εν τω ονόματι του κυρίου ιησού χριστου (*post* φωνή). 17. καίτοιγε. 19. †*init.* διατριβόντων δε αυτών και διδασκόντων επήλθον (—δὲ). έσυραν. 20. †αυτών (*pro* αὐτὸν). XV. 1. μωυσέος. 2. †ζητήσεως (*pro* συζητ.). 5. μωσέως. 11. +του (*ante* κυρίου). 12. †το πλήθος άπαν. 16. δαυίδ. 17. †πάντα ταύτα,. 18. †α εστί γνωστά απ αιώνος αυτώ. διό κ.τ.λ. 21. μωϋσής. 22. —τῷ. †βαρσαββάν (*non* I. 23). 24. †—ἐξ ἡμῶν. 25. εκλεξαμένοις. παύλου. 29. †+και όσα μη θέλετε εαυτοίς γίνεσθαι, ετέροις μη ποιείτε (*post* πορνείας). †πράξατε. 32. †τε (*pro* δὲ). 34. αυτόθι. 40. εξήλθεν. XVI. 1. †—ἐκεῖ. 4. †επορεύοντο. [πρεσβυτέρων]. 5. καθημέραν. 9. μακεδωνίαν (*sic v.* 10). 12. μακεδωνίας (*non* XVIII. 5). κολώνεια. †αυτή (*pro* ταύτῃ). 15. †είναι τω κυρίω. 17. †έκραξε. †ημίν (*pro* ὑμίν). 19. —τὸν *secund.* 22. τα ιμάτια αυτών. 24. εσοτέραν. 29. εισεπίδησε. 33. †—πάντες. 36. απήγγειλεν. 37. δήραντες. 40. προσ (*pro* εἰς: *ad*). XVII. 5. *init.* †προσλαβόμενοι δε οι ιουδαίοι οι απειθούντες των αγοραίων τινας άνδρας κ.τ.λ. (—ζηλώσαντες δὲ). 7. †—εἶναι. 10. —τε. †απήεσαν των ιουδαίων. 11. †+των άλλων (*post* ευγενέστεροι). καθημέραν. 13. —τῇ. 18. †+και (*post* τινές δε). †—αὐτοῖς. 25. †κατά (*pro* καὶ τὰ). 26. προστεταγμένους. 28. †ημάς (*pro* ὑμᾶς). 31. †παρασχείν. XVIII. 14. †αδίκημα τι ην. 17. έμελλεν. 18. κεχρέαις. 21. αλλά. 23. †τους μαθητάς πάντας. 24. †όνομα. 26. την οδόν του θεού. XIX. 13. επεχείρισαν. 16. †κατακυριεύσαν. 27. †ιερόν αρτέμιδος. ουθέν. δε (*pro* τε: *et*). 29. —τοῦ. [33. -λλ-]. 34. επιγνόντες. 36. πράσσειν. 37. θεόν. 38. έχουσι προς τίνα λόγον. 40. †δούναι. XX. 4. +πύρρου (*post* σώπατρος). γάϊος,. 5. †προσελθόντες (*non v.* 13). 6. άχρι. 7. —τοῦ. 8. ου ήμεν. 10. θορυβήσθε. 13. ούτως. 14. μιτυλίνην. 15. τρογγυλίω. 21. —τὴν *secund.* 23. +μοι (*ante* λέγον). 26. †+και (*post* διό). 28. +κυρίου και (*ante* θεού). 32. τα νυν. 34. †—δὲ. 35. τον λόγον. μάλλον διδόναι. 38. †—προέπεμπον *ad fin. vers.* XXI. 1. κώ. 2. διαπερόν. [3. -έντες]. 4. —τοὺς. 8. —οἱ περὶ τὸν Παῦλον. [ήλθομεν]. —τοῦ *secund.* 11. τους πόδας και τας χείρας. ούτως. 13. τε (*pro* δὲ). †ετοίμως έχω εις ιερουσαλήμ. 15. επισκευασάμενοι (*preparati*). 16. †αγαγόντες. 20. θεόν (*pro* κύριον). 21. μη δε. 26. διαγγέλων. 29. εωρακότεσ. 32. εξ αυτής. 33. †εγγίσας δε (– τότε). 37. †– τι. 40. αναβάθμων. XXII. 1. νυνί. 3. πρατρώου. 5. †– καὶ *prim.* μοι μαρτυρεί. 6. εγγύζοντι. 9. την φωνήν δε. 12. ευλαβής (*timoratus*). + εν δαμασκώ (*ante* ιουδαίων). 14. είπεν. 19. δαίρων. 20. † πρωτομάρτυρος. †– καὶ *quart.* 22. † καθήκεν. 23. κραζόντων. 25. προέτειναν. 27. †– εἰ. 29. – δὲ. XXIII. 1. – ὁ. 7. † των σαδδουκαίων και φαρισαίων. 9. †+ και (*ante* πνεύμα). 10. καταβήναι και. 11. † δει σε. 14. – τοῖς *secund.* 15. καταγάγη αυτόν. 16. το ένεδρον. 17. νεανίσκον. 19. κατιδίαν. 22. επέλυσε (*dimisit*). 24. φίληκα [† *caetera non cum* Lat.]. 26. φίληκι. 30. εξ αυτής. 35. – τοῦ. XXIV. 3. φίληξ. 6. κρίναι. 7. βία πολλή (– μετὰ). † αφείλετο και προς σε απέστειλε (*pro* ἀπήγαγε). 8. †+ και (*post* κελεύσας). †– ἐπί σε. 9. συνεπέθεντο. 10. † τε (*pro* δὲ). 11. †– ἢ. [13, †18. *cum Elz.*]. 14. – ἐν. 16. † έχων. †– διαπαντός. 19. † δεί. 20. †– εἰ. 22. φίληξ. † ανεβάλλετο. 24. φίληξ. τη ιδία γυναικί (– αὐτοῦ). + ιησούν (*post* χριστόν). 25. φίληξ. λαβών. 26. – δὲ. 27. φίληξ *bis.* δε (*pro* τε). XXV. 2. ανεφάνισαν (*adierunt*: ενεφ. *v.* 15). † ο τε (*pro* ὁ). 5. + άτοπον (*post* τούτω). 6. † οκτώ (*pro* δέκα). 7. αιτιώματα. 8. †– τι. 14. † διέτριβεν. φίληκος. 16. πρινή. 17. – αὐτῶν. 19. δυσειδαιμονίας (*non* XVII. 22). 20. – εἰς. 21. εωσού. XXVI. 2. επί σου μέλλων απολογείσθαι. 3. † ηθών. 7. βασιλεύς. – τῶν. 8. τι άπ. *jungit.* 16. οίδες. 17. † εγώ (*pro* νῦν). 19. βασιλεύς (*non v.* 27). 20. [απήγγελλον]. † μετάνοιαν (*pro* μετανοεῖν). 22. μαρτυρόμενος. 25. αλλά. 26. .ουδέ (*pro* οὐδέν· οὐ). εν γωνία πεπραγμένον τούτο εστί. 32. ηδύνατο. επικέκλητο. XXVII. 2. αδραμυτηνώ. 3. †– τε. φιλανθρόπως. + τους (*ante* φίλους). 5. † κατήχθημεν (*pro* κατήλθομεν). 10. φορτίου. 11. εκατοντάρχης. 15. επιδιδόντες. 17. σύρτην. 23. ταύτη τη νυκτί. 28. οργυάς *bis.* 29. εκπέσωμεν. 36. †– πάντες. 37. εβδομήκοντα εξ. 39. † δυνατόν. 40. αρτέμωνα. 42. διαφύγη. 43. βουλεύματος (*prohibuit fieri*). XXVIII. 3. [εκ] . διεξελθούσα (*processisset*). 11. †? ήχθημεν. αλεξανδρηνώ. 20. † ιδείν υμάς. 26. είπον. 27. εκάμυσαν. 29. ζήτησιν. Τέλος των πράξεων των αγίων αποστόλων.

Sequuntur Prol. argum. "*in septem epistolas canonicas:*" "*Argument. in epistolam canonicam beati Jacobi apostoli.*" Η του αγίου ιακώβου επιστολή καθολική (*Lat.* "canonica"). Jacob. I. 5. ουκ (*pro* μὴ). 12. † υπομενεί. 13. – τοῦ. 21. πραότητι (*non* III. 13). 26. † εν υμίν είναι. αλλά. 27. – τῷ. πατέρι. II. 5. †– τούτου. 6. † ητοιμάσατε. 8. βασιλεικόν. εαυτόν. [11. *errat Mill.*] 13. – καὶ. έλεον *secund.* 20. εστί. III. 3. ίδε (*non v.* 4). 10. †+ αγαπητοί (*post* μου). ούτως. 12. αλικόν. 13. *init.* †+ ει. 17. †– καὶ *prim.* IV. 2. πολεμείτε και ουκ έχετε (– δὲ). 6. † κύριος *sic* (*pro* ὁ θεὸς). 12. [† *cum Elz.*] *at* + δε (*post* συ). 13. † πορευσώμεθα, ποιήσωμεν, εμπορευσώμεθα, κερδήσωμεν. 14. έσται. + και (*post* δε). 15. † ποιήσωμεν. V. 3. † *Jungit* ὡς πυρ εθησαυρίσατε. 4. υφ (*pro* ἀφ'). 7. αυτόν (*pro* αὐτῷ). 9. κριθήτε. + ο (*ante* κριτής). 10. αδελφοί μου της κακοπαθείας. 11. πολυευσπλαγχνος. † εστί (– ὁ κύριος). 12. † εισ υπόκρισιν. 14. προσκαλεσάτω. 18. υιετόν. Τέλος της του αγίου ιακώβου καθολικής επιστολής.

Argum. 1 Pet.: *sic deinceps* 2 Pet. 1. 2, 3. Jo. Jud. Η του αγίου πέτρου καθολική πρώτη επιστολή. 1 Pet. I. 3. ημάς (*pro* ὑμᾶς). 4. υμάς (*pro* ἡμᾶς). 9. πίστεος. 11. προμαρτυρούμενον. 12. υμίν (*pro* ἡμῖν). 23. θεού ζώντος. II. 2. άρτι γέννητα. 5. † θυσίας πνευματικάς. 6. διότι (– καὶ). 11. απέσχεσθαι. 12. έχοντες καλήν εν τοις έθνεσιν. 16. + του (*ante* θεού). 21. † + και (*post* γαρ). ημών (*pro* ὑμῶν), *at* υμίν *seq.* 25. *fin.* ημών. III. 1. † κερδηθήσονται. 6. † εγεννήθητε. 7. † ζώσης. εγκόπτεσθαι. 12. – οἱ. *fin.* † + του εξολοθρεύσαι αυτούς εκ γης. 14. εικαί. πάσχετε. 16. καταλαλούσιν. 17. θέλοι. 18. – τῷ *secund.* 20. ότε απεξεδέχετο. 21. † ω αντίτυπον νυν και ημάς. 22. † αποταγέντων. IV. 3. † υμίν (*pro* ἡμῖν). ειδωλολατρίαις. 4. ασωτείας. 11. † ως (*pro* ἧς). 12. πειρασμών. 13. καθό. 14. † αναπέπαυται. 19. αυτών. V. 1. † ως (*pro* ὁ *prim.*). 3. μήδε. [5. *errat Mill.*]. 8. † – ὅτι. 9. † – ἐπιτελεῖσθαι. 10. † υμάς (*pro* ἡμᾶς). [*verba seq.* †]. 13. † ασπάσεται. Τέλος της του αγίου πέτρου πρώτης επιστολής.

Η του αγίου πέτρου καθολική δευτέρα επιστολή. 2 Pet. I. 1. σίμων. σοτήρος. – ἡμῶν *secund.* 2. + χριστού (*ante* ιησού) *sic.* 4. † τα τίμια ημίν και μέγιστα. 5. δι (*pro* δὲ *prim.*). 7. φιλαδ. 11. αιωνίαν. † – καὶ σωτῆρος. 12. † αεί υμάς. 13. εφόσον. 16. † γεννηθέντες. 19. διαυγάσει. 21. αλλά. – οἱ. II. 2. ασελγείαις (*pro* ἀπωλείαις). 3. † νυστάξει. 4. τηρουμένους. 5. αλλά. 9. † πειρασμών. κρίσεος. 10. κυριότητας. 12. γεγενημένα. 14. πλεονεξίας. 15. καταλειπόντες (*derelinquentes*) *sic.* – τὴν. 18. – ἐν *secund.* (*Jungit* σαρκ. ασελ.). ολίγον (*pro* ὄντως). 20. † οι (*pro* εἰ) *sic.* III. 1. † διαγείρω. 2. υμών (*pro* ἡμῶν). 3. επιθυμίας αυτών. 4. ούτωσ. 7. † αυτού (*pro* αὐτῷ). 8. † *fin.* μία ημέρα. 12. τακήσεται. 13. † αυτού επάγγελμα. 18. – καὶ *quart.* Τέλος της του αγίου πέτρου καθολικής δευτέρας επιστολής.

1. 2. 3 Johan. Η του αγίου ιωάννου (*sic in* 1 Joh.) καθολική {πρώτη / δευτέρα / τρίτη} επιστολή. 1 Johan. I. 1. † υμών (*pro* ἡμῶν *secund.*). 2. † επαγγέλλομεν (*non v.* 3). 4. † ημών (*pro* ὑμῶν). 5. † έστιν αύτη. 6. † ψευδώμεθα. II. 11. † ετύφλωσεν αυτού τους οφθαλμούς. 14. – ἔγραψα *usque ad* ἀπ' ἀρχῆς (*sic* Lat.). [23. † *cum Elz.*]. 27. † διδάσκη (*pro* -ει). 29. † ίδητε. [-νν-]. III. 2. όμιοι. 6. ουκ *prim.* 10. εστί εκ. 16. + του θεού (*post* αγάπην). 17. δαν. † – ἀπ' αὐτοῦ. † μενεί. 18. + τη (*ante* γλώσση). 23. † *fin.* – ἡμῖν. 24. † + μένει (*post* αυτώ *secund.*). έδωκεν ημίν. IV. 2. γινώσκεται (*sic* Lat.). 3. – τὸν. † – τὸ. 9. απέστειλεν (*non v.* 14). 16. † *fin.* + μένει. 21. † – ὁ. V. 4. † υμών (*pro* ἡμῶν). 6. [ισ ο χσ]. – τῷ *tert.*[1] 7. † + και (*post* πατήρ). *fin.*

[1] *Ad v.* 7 *notatur*: Sanctus thomas in expositione secunde decretalis de suma trinitate et fide catholica tractans istum passum contra abbatem Joachim ut Tres sunt qui testimonium dant in celo. pater: verbum: et spiritus sanctus: dicit ad litteram verba sequentia. Et ad insinuandam unitatem trium personarum subditur et hii tres unum sunt. Quod quidem dicitur propter essentie unitatem. Sed hoc Joachim perverse trahere volens ad unitatem charitatis et consensus inducebat consequentem auctoritatem. Nam subditur ibidem: et tres sunt qui testimonium dant in terra. s. spiritus: aqua: et sanguis. Et in quibusdam libris additur: et hii tres unum sunt. Sed hoc in veris exemplaribus non habetur: sed dicitur esse appositum ab hereticis arrianis ad pervertendum intellectum sanum auctoritatis premisse de unitate essentie trium personarum. Hec beatus thomas ubi supra.

και οἱ τρεις εις το εν εισι (*et hi tres unum sunt*). 8. επί της γης (*in terra*). – καὶ οἱ τρεῖς *ad fin. vers. Sic etiam* Lat. 10. εν αυτώ (*in se*). 13. † αιώνιον έχετε. [14. ημών]. 15. εάν (*pro* ἂν). 20. + θεόν (*post* αληθινόν: *sic* Lat.). – ἡ. 1. 2. 3. JOHAN. Τέλος της του αγίου ιωάννου καθολικής { πρώτης / δευτέρας / τρίτης } επιστολής.

2. JOHAN. [2. † μεθ ημών]. 3. [υμών]. ἀπό (*pro* παρὰ *prim.* : *a*). [5. γράφων]. 8. † + καλά (*post* ειργασάμεθα). [† *non cum* Lat.]. 12. εβουλήθην.

3. JOHAN. [7. *cum Elz.*]. 8. γενώμεθα (*simus*). 10. † υπομνήσων. 11. – δὲ. 15. † *fin.* + αμήν.

Η του αγίου ιούδα καθολική επιστολή. JUD. 1. † χριστού ιησού. 3. – τῇ. 4. † θεόν και δεσπότην τον κύρ. 7. †, δίκην. 9. μωϋσέος. σε (*pro* σοι). 12. † + υμίν (*ante* αφόβως). παραφερόμεναι (*conferuntur*). φθινοπώρινα. 13. – τὸν. 14. αγίαις μυριάσιν. 15. ελέγξαι. 18. επιθυμίας εαυτών. 19. † – ἑαυτούς. 20. ημών (*pro* ὑμῶν). 24. † αυτούς (*pro* ὑμᾶς). κατ ενώπιον. [† 23, 24 *caetera cum Elz.*]. 25. † – θεῷ. Τέλος της του αγίου ιούδα καθολικής επιστολής.

Prologi duo, et Arg. in Apocal. Αποκάλυψις του αγίου αποστόλου και ευαγγελιστού ιωάννου του θεολόγου. APOC. I. 2. – τε. † *fin.* + και άτινα εισί και α χρη γενέσθαι μετά ταύτα. 3. προφητίας. 4. – τοῦ. 6. βασιλείαν (*pro* βασιλεῖς καὶ). 8. άλφα. † – ἀρχὴ καὶ τέλος. λέγει κύριος ο θεός. 9. – καὶ *prim.* κοινωνός. – ἐν τῇ *secund.* εν χριστώ ιησού (*pro* ιῦ χῦ). 10. † φωνήν οπίσω μου. 11. – ἐγώ εἰμι *usque ad* ἔσχατος καί. + επτά (*ante* εκκλησίαις). † – ταῖς ἐν Ἀσίᾳ. 12. † + εκεί (*ante* επέστρεψα). ελάλει. 13. μαζοίς. 16. χειρί αυτού. 17. † ότι (*pro* ὅτε). – μοι. 18. του θανάτου και του άδου. 19. + ουν (*post* γράψον). γενέσθαι. II. 1. † της εκκλησίας εφέσω. 2. – σου *secund.* επείρασας. τους λέγοντας εαυτούς αποστόλους είναι. 3. – καὶ *tert.* – κεκοπίακας. *fin.* και ουκ εκοπίασας (*pro* καὶ οὐ κέκμηκας). 4. αλλά. [5. † ταχύ]. 7. – αὐτῷ. *fin.* + μου. 8. της εν σμύρνη εκκλησίας. 9. αλλά πλούσιος (– δὲ). 10. † + δη (*post* ιδού). ο διάβολος εξ υμών. 11. τω (*pro* τὸ). 13. † – καὶ *quart.* ο σατανάς κατοικεί. 14. † εδίδαξε. [τον β.]. 15. ομοίως (*pro* ὃ μισῶ) *cum sequent.* 17. κενόν. οίδεν (*pro* ἔγνω). 19. † και την πίστιν και την διακονίαν. – καὶ *sext.* 20. † – ὀλίγα. αφείς (*pro* ἐᾷς: *permittis*). † + σου την (*post* γυναίκα). ιεζάβελ. η λέγει. † και διδάσκει και πλανά τους. φαγείν ειδωλόθυτα. 21. *Post* μετανοήση: και ου θέλει μετανοήσαι εκ της πορνείας αυτής. 22. † – ἐγὼ. *fin.* αυτής. 24. † τοις (*pro* καὶ *prim.*). † – καὶ *secund.* βαθέα. 27. συντριβήσεται. III. 1. [επτά πν.] – τὸ. 2. † έμελες αποβαλείν. *fin.* + μου. 3. [*errat Steph.*]. 4. *init.* + αλλ. † ολίγα έχεις. – καὶ *prim.* 5. περιβαλλείται. ομολογήσω. 7. κλειν. δαυίδ. † ο ανοίγων και ουδείς κλείσει αυτήν ο μη ο ανοίγων, και ουδείς ανοίξει. 8. ην (*pro* καὶ *prim.*). 9. † ήξουσι. † – ἐγὼ. 11. † – Ἰδού. 12. ναώ. επ αυτού. 14. της εν λαοδικεία εκκλησίας. 15. ης (*pro* εἴης). 16. † ου ζεστός ούτε ψυχρός. 17. † – ὅτι *secund.* + ο (*ante* ελεεινός). 18. † χρυσίον παρ εμού. – καὶ *secund.* † κολούριον. + επι (*ante* τους οφθ.). 20. † + και (*ante* εισελεύσομαι). IV. 1. ανεωγμένη. 3. † – καὶ ὁ καθήμενος ἦν. σαρδίω. [ομοία]. 4. εικοσιτέσσαρες (– καὶ). εικοσιτέσσαρας (– καὶ). – ἔσχον. 5. φωναί και βρονταί.

† + αυτού (*ante* αι). εισίν επτά (– τὰ). 6. ως θάλασσα υελίνη. 8. εν καθέν αυτών (*singula eorum*). έχον. γέμουσιν. † άγιος *novies.* 9. δώσει. 10. εικοσιτέσσαρες (– καὶ). † βάλλουσι. 11. † ο κύριος και ο θεός ημών ο άγιος (*pro* κύριε). V. 1. έξωθεν (*pro* ὄπισθεν: *foris*). 2. † – ἐστιν. 3. εδύνατο. 4. πολύ. 5. – ὢν. δαυίδ. † – λῦσαι. 6. εσφαγισμένον. † α (*pro* οἵ). πνεύματα του θεού αποστελλόμενα (– τὰ). 7. – τὸ βιβλίον, *at* + βιβλίον *in fin. vers.* 8. – οἱ. 10. † αυτούς (*pro* ἡμᾶς). † βασιλεύουσιν. 11. † + ως (*ante* φωνήν). κύκλω. [† *caetera cum Elz.*]. 12. εσφαγισμένον. 13. επί (*pro* ἐν *secund.*) της γης. πάντας (*pro* πάντα) *cum sequent.* † *fin.* + αμήν. 14. † λέγοντα το (*pro* ἔλεγον). † – εἰκοσιτέσσαρες. έπεσον. † – ζῶντι κ.τ.λ. VI. 1. † ότι (*pro* ὅτε). + επτά (*ante* σφραγίδων). φωνή. † – καὶ βλέπε. 2. επ αυτόν. 3. † ότι (*pro* ὅτε: *non* vv. 7, 9). † – καὶ βλέπε. 4. επ αυτόν. εκ (*pro* ἀπὸ: *de*). † – καὶ *tert.* 5. την σφραγίδα την τρίτην. † – καὶ βλέπε. επ αυτόν εχον. 7. † την τετάρτην σφραγίδα. λέγοντος. † – καὶ βλέπε. 8. – ὁ *secund.* αυτώ (*pro* αὐτοῖς). επί το τέταρτον της γης αποκτείναι. 9. † των ανθρώπων των εσφαγισμένων. † + του αρνίου (*post* μαρτυρίαν). 10. † έκραξαν. – ὁ *tert.* εκ (*pro* ἀπὸ: *de*). 11. † – καὶ ἐδόθησαν *usque ad* λευκαί. † εδόθη (*pro* ἐρρέθη). † – μικρόν. πληρωθώσι. 12. † + και (*ante* ότε). † – ἰδοὺ. † μέλας εγένετο. [† *in sequent. errat Steph.*]. 13. έπεσον. 14. + ο (*ante* ουρανός). ελισσόμενον. 15. οι χιλίαρχοι και οι πλούσιοι. ισχυροί (*pro* δυνατοὶ). VII. 1. † τούτο (*pro* ταῦτα). 2. αναβαίνοντα. 3. † αδικήσατε. μετόπων. 4. † των αριθμών. εκατόν και τεσσαράκοντα τέσσαρες. 5. δώδεκα *passim.* ρουβείν. † *deest* ἐσφραγισμένοι *decies in vv.* 5—8: *legitur primo et ultimo loco.* 6. † μανασή. 7. ισαχάρ. 9. – αὐτὸν. εδύνατο. 10. † κράζουσι. 11. ειστήκεισαν. τα πρόσωπα. 12. – ἡ *septim.* 14. είπον (*pro* εἴρηκα). + μου (*post* κύριε). αυτάς (*pro* στολὰς αὐτῶν *secund.*). 15. επί τω θρόνω. 16. πινάσουσιν. ουδ ουμή πέση. 17. ζωής. εκ (*pro* ἀπὸ: *ab*). VIII. 3. του θυσιαστηρίου *prim.* [5. *cum Elz.*]. 6. + οι (*ante* έχοντες). 7. † – ἄγγελος. + εν (*ante* αίματι). + και το τρίτον της γης κατεκάη (*post* γῆν). † – καὶ τὸ τρίτον τῶν δένδρων κατεκάη. 8. † – πυρὶ. 9. – τῶν *secund.* διεφθάρησαν. 10. + των (*ante* υδάτων). 11. + ο (*ante* άψινθος). εγένετο. + των (*ante* ανθρώπων). 13. αετού (*pro* ἀγγέλου). πετομένου. † + τρις (*post* μεγάλη: ve *bis* Lat.). IX. 2. † καιομένης (*pro* μεγάλης). 4. αυτοίς (*pro* -αῖς). 5. βασανίσωσι. πλήξη (*pro* παίσῃ). 6. † ζητούσιν. ουμή (*pro* ουχ). [ευρήσουσιν]. † απ αυτών ο θάνατος. 7. † ητοιμασμένα. † χρυσοί (*pro* ὅμοιοι χρυσῷ). 10. † και (*pro* ἦν). † εξουσίαν έχουσι του (*pro* καὶ ἡ ἐξουσία αὐτῶν). 11. † έχουσαι βασιλέα επ αυτών (– καὶ). – τὸν. † αββαδών. εν δε (– καὶ). + ο (*ante* απολλύων). *fin.* †. 12. έρχεται. 14. † ο έχων (*pro* ὃς εἶχε). 15. † – καὶ ἡμέραν. 16. των στρατευμάτων του ίππου. † – δύο. † – καὶ *secund.* 17. ωράσει. ιακινθίνους. 18. από (*pro* ὑπὸ: *et ab*). + πληγών (*ante* τούτων). – ἐκ † *secund. et tert.* 19. η γαρ εξουσία των ίππων (– αὐτῶν *prim.*). εστί. + και εν ταις ουραίς αυτών (*post* εστί). όμοιοι. 20. † ου (*pro* οὔτε). + τα (*ante* είδωλα). 21. φαρμακιών. X. 1. † – ἄλλον. + η (*ante* ίρις). + αυτού (*post* κεφαλής). 2. βιβλιδάριον. της θαλάσσης. της γης. 4. † – τὰς φωνὰς ἑαυτῶν. † – μοι. † και μετά ταύτα γράφεις. 5. † + την δεξίαν (*post* αυτού). 6. † ουκ έτι έσται. 7. αλλ. – καὶ. † ο (*pro* ὡς). ευηγγελίσατο τους δούλους αυτού τους προφήτας (*per*). 8. βιβλιδάριον. ανεωγμένον. + του (*ante* αγγέλου). 9. βιβλιδάριον (*sic*

v. 10). 11. + επί (*ante* έθνεσι). XI. 1. † ειστήκει ο άγγελος. 2. έξωθεν (*foris*), *at* έξωθεν (*pro sequens* έξω: *foras*). † μετρήσεις. τεσσαρακονταδύο. 4. + αι (*ante* δύο *secund.*). κυρίου (*pro* θεοῦ). 5. είτις *bis.* θέλει. θέλει αυτούς *secund.* ούτως. 6. υετός βρέχη. † τας ημέρας. της προφητείας αυτών. † + εν (*ante* πάση πληγή). 7. μετ αυτών πόλεμον. 8. + της (*ante* πόλεως). σώδομα. αυτών (*pro* ἡμῶν). 9. † βλέπουσιν. † – καὶ (*ante* ήμισυ). (*non v.* 11). ουχ. † μνήμα. 10. † χαίρουσιν. 11. – τὰς. επέπεσεν. 12. † ήκουσα. φωνής μεγάλης. λεγούσης. 13. † ημέρα (*pro* ὥρᾳ). 14. † η ουαί η τρίτη ιδού. 15. εγένετο η βασιλεία. 16. – καὶ *secund.* έπεσον. [17. *errat Steph.*]. 19. † του κυρίου (*pro* αὐτοῦ *prim.*). † – καὶ σεισμὸς. XII. 2. έκραζεν. 3. επτά διαδήματα. 4. μελούσης τίκτειν. 5. ποιμανείν. ηρπάγη. + προσ (*ante* τον θρόνον). 6. † + εκεί (*post* έχει). εκτρέφωσιν. 7. † του πολεμήσαι (*pro* ἐπολέμησαν). μετά (*pro* κατὰ: *cum*). 8. † ίσχυσεν. ουδέ (*pro* οὔτε). † αυτώ (*pro* αὐτῶν). 9. – ὁ (*ante* σατανάς). 10. εν τω ουρανώ λέγουσαν. 12. – τοῖς κατοικοῦσι. τη γη και τη θαλάσση. 13. – τὴν *prim.* 14. † όπως τρέφηται (*pro* ὅπου τρέφεται). 15. εκ του στόματος αυτού οπίσω της γυναικός. αυτήν (*pro* ταύτην). 17. οργίσθη. † – χριστοῦ. XIII. 1. † κέρατα δέκα και κεφαλάς επτά. ονόματα. [2. άρκτου]. 3. † – εἶδον. + εκ (*post* μίαν). ωσεί (*pro* ὡς). 4. τω δράκοντι τω δεδωκότι την. τω θηρίω (*pro* τὸ θηρίον). και τις δυνατός. 5. † βλασφημίαν. τεσσάρακοντα δύο. 7. † ποιήσαι πόλεμον. 8. † το όνομα. τω βιβλίω. + του (*ante* εσφαγμένου). 10. † *init.* είτις έχει αιχμαλωσίαν υπάγει (– αἰχμαλωσίαν συνάγει εἰς). 12. εποίει (*pro* ποιεῖ *secund.*). † εν αυτή κατοικούντας. 13. † και πυρ, ίνα εκ του ουρανού καταβαίνη (– ποιῇ). επί (*pro* εἰς: *in terram*). 14. † + τους εμούς (*post* πλανά). οικόνα. (*non v.* 15). † είχε. 15. † πνεύμα δούναι. και ίνα (*pro* ἵνα καὶ). – ἡ. † ποιεί τους μη προσκυνούντας τη εικόνι (– ὅσοι ἂν). 16. δώσιν. † χαράγματα. μετόπων. 18. – τὸν *prim.* † εστίν εξακόσιοι εξήκοντα εξ. XIV. 1. τεσσαράκοντα τέσσαρες. + αυτού και το όνομα (*post* όνομα). 2. η φωνή ην (*pro* φωνὴν *quart.*). + ως (*ante* κιθαρωδών). 3. † – ὡς. εδύνατο. τεσσαράκοντα τέσσαρες. 4. † + γαρ (*post* όπου). † + υπό ιησού (*ante* ηγοράσθησαν). 5. † ψεύδος (*pro* δόλος). † εισί (– ἐνώπιον τοῦ θρόνου τοῦ θεοῦ). 6. πετόμενον. ευαγγελίσασθαι. καθημένους (*pro* κατοικοῦντας). + επί (*ante* παν). 7. λέγων. + την (*ante* θάλασσαν). 8. † + δεύτερος (*post* άγγελος). βαβυλών. – ἡ πόλις. † – ὅτι. + τα (*ante* έθνη). 9. † άλλος άγγελος τρίτος. είτις προσκυνεί το θηρίον. 11. † εις αιώνας αιώνων αναβαίνει. είτις. 12. + του (*ante* ιησού). 13. *Jungit* απάρτι λέγει. † λέγει ναι. 15. φωνή μεγάλη. ήλθεν (– σοι). 19. *fin.* τον μέγαν. 20. έξωθεν (*pro* ἔξω: *extra*). εξήλθεν. XV. 2. νελίνην *bis.* † πυρί μεμιγμένην. – ἐκ τοῦ χαράγματος αὐτοῦ. 3. μωϋσέος του δ. εθνών (*pro* ἁγίων). 4. άγιος ει (*pro* ὅσιος: *pius es*). 5. † – ἰδοὺ. 6. + οι (*ante* έχοντες). † ουρανού (*pro* ναοῦ). † + οι ήσαν (*ante* ενδεδ.). † + και (*ante* καθαρόν). περιεσζωσμένοι. 8. † – ἑπτὰ *secund.* XVI. 1. – καὶ *secund.* 2. † τους προσκυνούντας τη εικόνι αυτού. 4. εξέχεε. † – εἰς *secund.* 5. † – κύριε. – καὶ *tert.* 6. † – γὰρ. 7. – ἄλλου. 9. † + οι άνθρωποι (*post* εβλασφήμησαν). + την (*ante* εξουσίαν). 12. – τὸν *tert.* 13. ως βάτραχοι (*pro* ὅμοια βατράχοις). 14. – τῆς γῆς καὶ. + τον (*ante* πόλεμον). παντοκράτωρος. 16. – τὸν *prim.* αρμαγεδών. 18. † αστραπαί και βρονται και φωναί. αφού. XVII. 1. – μοι. 2. οι κατοικούντες την γην εκ του *οίνου της πορνείας αυτής.* 4. *ην* (*pro* *ἡ* *secund.*). † *πορφύραν.* † *κόκκινον.* † — *καὶ* *tert.* † *και τα ακάθαρτα της.* 5. † *πόρνων.* 8. *init.* + *το. ότι.* †. *και πάρεσται.* (*sic*). 9. *επτά όρη εισίν.* 10. *έπεσον.* — *καὶ* *secund.* 13. *αυτών.* † *διδόασιν.* 16. † *και* (*pro* *ἐπὶ*). † + *ποιήσουσιν αυτήν* (*post* *γυμνήν*). 17. † *γνώμην μίαν. τελεσθήσονται οι λόγοι.* XVIII. 1. + *άλλον* (*ante* *άγγελον*). 2. † *εν ισχυρά φωνή* (— *ἰσχύϊ* *et* *μεγάλῃ*). 3. † *του θυμού του οίνου.* † *πεπότικε.* 4. *και εκ των πληγών αυτής ίνα μη λάβητε.* 5. *εκολλήθησαν* (*pervenerunt*). † + *αυτής* (*post* *εμνημόνευσεν*). 7. † — *καὶ πένθος* *prim.* + *ότι* (*ante* *κάθημαι*). 8. *κρίνας.* 9. *init.* *και κλαύσουσι και κόψονται επ αυτήν.* 10. — *ἐν.* 12. *πορφυρού.* 13. *ραίδων.* 14. *απώλοντο* (*pro* *ἀπῆλθεν* *secund.*). † *ουμή ευρήσεις.* 16. *κεχρυσωμένη.* 17. + *ο* (*ante* *επί*). *πλέων* (*pro* *ὁ ὅμιλος*). 18. *βλέποντες* (*pro* *ὁρῶντες*). 19. † + *και* (*ante* *λέγοντες*). + *τα* (*ante* *πλοία*). 20. *επ αυτή.* † + *και οι* (*ante* *απόστολοι*). 24. *αίματα.* XIX. 1. *λεγόντων. και η δύναμις και η δόξα* (— *καὶ ἡ τιμὴ*). *του θεού* (— *Κυρίῳ*). 2. *διέφθειρε.* — *τῆς.* 3. † *είρηκεν.* 4. *εικοσιτέσσαρες* (— *καὶ*). 5. — *καὶ* *tert.* 6. + *ημών* (*post* *θεός*). 8. *λαμπρόν και καθαρόν.* † *των αγίων εστί.* 10. — *τοῦ* *prim.* 12. † — *ὡς.* † + *ονόματα γεγραμμένα και* (*post* *έχων*). 14. *επί ίπ.* † — *καὶ* *secund.* 15. + *δίστομος* (*ante* *οξεία*). *πατάξῃ.* — *καὶ* *ult.* 16. — *τὸ* *secund.* 17. *πετομένοις. συνάχθητε* († — *καὶ*). *fin.* † *το μέγα του θεού.* 18. + *τε* (*post* *ελευθέρων*). *μικρών τε* (— *καὶ* *septim.*). 20. *μετ αυτού* (*pro* *μετὰ τούτου*). — *τῷ* (*ante* *θείω*). 21. *εξελθούσῃ* (*pro* *ἐκπορευομένῃ*). XX. 1. *κλείν.* 2. † *ο σατανάς ο πλανών την οικουμένην όλην και έδ.* 3. *έκλεισε* (— *αὐτὸν* *secund.*). *πλανά έτι τα έθνη.* 4. — *τὰ* (*ante* *χίλια*). 5. † *και οι λοιποί* (— *δὲ*). *έζησαν. άχρι* (*pro* *ἕως*). 6. *ο δεύτερος θάνατος.* 8. + *τον* (*ante* *πόλεμον*). 9. *εκύκλευσαν.* † *εκ του ουρανού από του θεού.* 10. + *και* (*post* *όπου*). 11. *μέγαν λευκόν. επ αυτόν.* † *ο ουρανός και η γη.* 12. *τους μεγάλους και τους μικρούς. θρόνου* (*pro* *θεοῦ*). *ανεώχθησαν. άλλο βιβλίον. ανεώχθη.* 13. † *εαυτών* (*pro* *ἐν αὐτοῖς*). 14. *ο θάνατος ο δεύτερος.* *fin.* † + *η λίμνη του πυρός.* XXI. 2. † — *ἐγὼ Ἰωάννης.* † *εἶδον* *ponitur ante* *καταβαίνουσαν.* 3. *λαός.* † — *θεὸς αὐτῶν.* 4. † — *ὁ θεὸς.* 5. *ποιώ πάντα.* 6. † *γέγονα το α και το ω.* — *ἡ.* — *τὸ* *tert.* 7. *ταύτα* (*pro* *πάντα*). — *ὁ* *secund.* 8. *init.* *τοις δε δειλοίς.* † + *αμαρτωλοίς και* (*ante* *εβδελ.*). *φαρμακοίς. εστίν ο θάνατος ο δεύτερος.* 9. *ήλθεν* (— *πρός με*). + *εκ* (*post* *εις*). — *τὰς* (*ante* *γεμούσας*). † *την γυναίκα την νύμφην του αρνίου.* 10. — *τὴν* (*ante* *αγίαν*). 11. † — *καὶ.* † *κρυσταλίζοντι.* 12. — *τε.* 13. *init.* *από. ανατολών.* + *και* (*ante* *από* *secund.*, *tert.*, *quart.*). 14. *και επ αυτών δώδεκα ονόματα των δώδ.* 15. + *μέτρον* (*ante* *κάλαμον*). † — *καὶ τὸ τεῖχος αὐτῆς.* 16. † — *τοσοῦτόν ἐστιν.* — *καὶ* (*post* *όσον*). † + *δώδεκα* (*etiam post* *χιλιάδων*). 18. *όμοιον νέλω.* 20. *σαρδώνυξ. ένατος.* † *υακίνθινος.* 21. *ύελος διαυγής.* 24. *και περιπατήσουσι τα έθνη διά του φωτός αυτής* (— *τῶν σωζομένων*). 27. *κοινόν.* XXII. 1. † *ποταμόν καθαρόν.* 2. — *ἕνα. αποδιδούς.* 3. *κατάθεμα.* † *εκεί* (*pro* *ἔτι*). 5. *φωτιεί.* 6. *λέγει* (*pro* *εἶπέ*). *πνευμάτων των* (*pro* *αγίων*). 8. *καγώ. ο ακούων και βλέπων ταύτα. δειγνύντος.* 9. † — *γάρ.* † — *καὶ* (*ante* *των τηρ.*). 10. *εστί.* 11. *ρυπαρός ρυπαρευθήτω.* † *δικαιοσύνην ποιησάτω* (*pro* *δικαιωθήτω*). 12. *init.* — *καὶ. έσται αυτού.* 13. † — *ειμι. άλφα.* 15. — *δὲ.* — *ὁ.* 16. *δαυίδ.* *fin.* *ο πρωϊνός* (*pro* *καὶ ὀρθρινός*). 17. *έρχου* (*pro* *ἐλθέ*) *bis.* *ερχέσθω* (*pro* *ἐλθέτω*). † — *καὶ* *ult.* *λαβέτω* (— *τὸ* *sequens*). 18. † *μαρτυρώ.* † *εγώ* (*pro* *γὰρ*). *επιθή. επ αυτά* (*pro* πρὸς ταῦτα). † επιθήσαι. † επ αυτόν ο θεός. †+ επτά (*ante* πληγάς). + τω (*ante* βιβλίω). 19. αφέλη. του βιβλίου. αφέλοι. † του ξύλου (*pro* βίβλου *secund.*). †– καὶ *ult.* + τω (*ante* βιβλίω). 21. †– ἡμῶν. † των αγίων (*pro* ὑμῶν). Τέλος της αποκαλύψεως[1].

[1] The fullest collation of any portion of the Complutensian N.T. which has hitherto appeared is that of the Apocalypse contained in Tregelles' *Book of Revelation* mentioned above, p. 347. On comparing pp. 364—8 of the present volume with Tregelles' notes, I find that we differ in 66 places. Out of these Tregelles is quite wrong in xi. 17; 19; xviii. 3: he cites inaccurately in xii. 17; xv. 3; xviii. 5; 17; xxi. 8: in 19 instances he overlooks various readings of the Complutensian: the remaining cases refer to itacisms and peculiarities of spelling, which it was not his purpose to record.

Deo Gratias.

CHAPTER VI.

ON THE LAWS OF INTERNAL EVIDENCE, AND THE LIMITS OF THEIR LEGITIMATE USE.

WE have now described, in some detail, the several species of external testimony available for the textual criticism of the New Testament, whether comprising manuscripts of the original Greek (Chap. II.), or ancient translations from it (Chap. III.), or citations from Scripture made by ecclesiastical writers (Chap. IV.). We have, moreover, indicated the chief editions wherein all these materials are recorded for our use, and the principles that have guided their several editors in applying them to the revision of the text (Chap. V.). One source of information, formerly deemed quite legitimate, has been designedly passed by. It is now agreed among competent judges that *Conjectural Emendation* must never be resorted to, even in passages of acknowledged difficulty, in the absence of proof that the reading thus substituted for the common one is actually supported by some trustworthy document. Those that have been hazarded aforetime by eminent scholars, when but few codices were known or actually collated, have seldom, very seldom, been confirmed by subsequent researches: and the time has now fully come that, in the possession of abundant stores of variations collected from memorials of almost every age and country, we are fully authorised in believing that the reading which no manuscript, or old version, or primitive Father has borne witness to, however plausible and (for some purposes) convenient, cannot safely be accepted as genuine or even as probable[1].

[1] Bentley, the last great critic who paid much regard to conjectural emendations, promised in his Prospectus of 1720 (*see* p. 320) that "If the author has anything to suggest towards a change of the text, not supported by any copies

In no wise less dangerous than bare conjecture, destitute of external evidence, is the device of Lachmann (*see* p. 343) for unsettling by means of emendation (*emendando*), without reference to the balance of conflicting testimony, the very text he had previously fixed by revision (*recensendo*) through the means of critical authorities: in fact the earlier process is but so much trouble misemployed, if its results are liable to be put aside by abstract judgment or individual prejudices. Not that the most sober and cautious critic would disparage the fair use of internal evidence, or withhold their proper influence from those reasonable considerations which in practice cannot, and in speculation ought not to be shut out from every subject on which the mind seeks to form an intelligent opinion. Whether we will or not, we unconsciously and almost instinctively adopt that one of two opposite statements, *in themselves pretty equally attested to*, which we judge the better suited to recognised phænomena, and to the common course of things. I know of no person who has affected to construct a text of the N. T. on diplomatic grounds exclusively, without paying some regard to the character of the sense produced; nor, were the experiment tried, would any one find it easy to dispense with discretion and the dictates of good sense: nature would prove too strong for the dogmas of a wayward theory. "It is difficult not to indulge in *subjectiveness*[1], at least in some measure," writes Dr Tregelles (*Account of Printed Text*, p. 109): and (thus qualified) we may add that it is one of those difficulties a sane man would not wish to overcome.

The foregoing remarks may tend to explain the broad distinction between mere conjectural emendation, which must be utterly discarded, and that just use of internal testimony which he is the best critic who most judiciously employs. They so far resemble each other, as they are both the product of the

now extant, he will offer it separate in his *Prolegomena.*" It is really worth while to turn over Wm Bowyer's *Critical Conjectures and Observations on the N. T.*, or the Summary of them contained in Knappe's N. T. of 1797, if only to see the utter fruitlessness of the attempt to illustrate Scripture by ingenious guess-work. The best (*e. g.* πορκείας for πορνείας Act. xv. 20, 29), no less than the most tasteless and stupid (*e.g.* νηνεμίαν for νηστείαν Act. xxvii. 9) in the whole collection, are hopelessly condemned by the deep silence of a host of authorities which have since come to light.

[1] I am afraid I also must crave leave to use this rather affected but convenient term.

reasoning faculty exercising itself on the sacred words of Scripture: they differ in this essential feature, that the one proceeds in ignorance or disregard of evidence from without, while the office of the other has no place unless where external evidence be evenly, or any rate not very unevenly, balanced. What degree of preponderance in favour of one out of several readings (all of them affording some tolerable sense) shall entitle it to reception as a matter of right; to what extent canons of subjective criticism may be allowed to eke out the scantiness of documentary authority; are points that cannot well be defined with strict accuracy. Men's decisions respecting them will always vary according to their temperament and intellectual habits; the judgment of the same person (the rather if he be by constitution a little unstable) will fluctuate from time to time as to the same evidence brought to bear on the self-same passage. Though the *canons* or rules of internal testimony be themselves grounded either on principles of common sense, or on certain peculiarities which all may mark in the documents from which our direct proofs are derived (*see below*, p. 376); yet has it been found by experience (what indeed we might have looked for beforehand), that in spite, perhaps in consequence, of their extreme simplicity, the application of these canons has proved a searching test of the tact, the sagacity, and judicial acumen of all that handle them. For the other functions of an editor accuracy and learning, diligence and zeal are sufficient: but the delicate adjustment of conflicting probabilities calls for no mean exercise of a critical genius. This innate faculty we lack in Wetstein, and notably in Scholz; it was highly developed in Mill and Bengel, and still more in Griesbach. His well-known power in this respect is the main cause of our deep regret for the failure of Bentley's projected work, with all its faults whether of plan or execution.

Nearly all the following rules of internal evidence, being founded in the nature of things, are alike applicable to all subjects of literary investigation, though their general principles may need some modification in the particular instance of the Greek Testament.

I. Proclivi Scriptioni praestat ardua: the more difficult the reading the more likely it is to be genuine. It would seem more probable that the copyist tried to explain an obscure passage, or relieve a hard construction, than to make that perplexed which before was easy: thus in John vii. 39, Lachmann's addition of δεδομένον to οὔπω γὰρ ἦν πνεῦμα ἅγιον is very improbable, though countenanced by Cod. B and (of course) by the versions. This is Bengel's prime canon, and although Wetstein is pleased to deride it (*N. T.* Vol. I. *Proleg.* p. 157), he was himself ultimately obliged to lay down something nearly to the same effect[1]. Yet this excellent rule may easily be applied on a wrong occasion, and is only true *caeteris paribus*, where manuscripts or versions lend strong support to the harder form. "To force readings into the text merely because they are difficult, is to adulterate the divine text with human alloy; it is to obtrude upon the reader of Scripture the solecisms of faltering copyists, in the place of the word of God (Wordsworth, *N. T.* Vol. I. *Preface*, p. xii.). See Chap. IX. note on Matth. xxi. 28—31.

II. That reading out of several is preferable, from which all the rest may have been derived, although it could not be derived from any of them. Tischendorf (*N. T. Proleg.* p. xlii. 7th edition) might well say that this would be "omnium regularum principium," if its application were less precarious. Of his own two examples the former is too weakly vouched for to be listened to, save by way of illustration. In Matthew xxiv. 38 he and Alford would simply read ἐν ταῖς ἡμέραις τοῦ κατακλυσμοῦ on the very feeble evidence of Cod. L, one uncial Evst. (13), *a . e . ff*[1], the Thebaic version and Origen (in two places); because the copyists, knowing that the eating and drinking and marrying took place not in the days of the flood, but before them (καὶ οὐκ ἔγνωσαν ἕως ἦλθεν ὁ κατακλυσμὸς *v.* 39), would strive to evade the difficulty, such as it was, by adopting one of the several forms found in our copies: ἡμέραις πρὸ τοῦ κατακλ., or ἡμέραις ταῖς πρὸ τοῦ κατακλ., or ἡμέραις ἐκείναις πρὸ τοῦ

[1] "VII. Inter duas variantes lectiones, si quae est εὐφωνότερος aut planior aut Graecantior, alteri non protinus praeferenda est, sed contra saepius. VIII. Lectio exhibens locutionem minus usitatam, sed alioqui subjectae materiae convenientem, praeferenda est alteri, quae, cum aeque conveniens sit, tamen phrasim habet minus insolentem, usuque magis tritam." Wetstein's whole tract, *Animadversiones et Cautiones ad examen variarum lectionum N. T. necessariae* (N. T. Vol. II. pp. 851—874) deserves attentive study. See also the 43 *Canones Critici* and their *Confirmatio* in the N. T. of G. D. T. M. D. (*above*, p. 319).

κατακλ., or ἡμέραις ἐκείναις ταῖς πρὸ τοῦ κατακλ., or even ἡμέραις τοῦ νῶε. In his second example Tischendorf is more fortunate, unless indeed we choose to refer it rather to Bengel's canon. James iii. 12 certainly ought to run μὴ δύναται, ἀδελφοί μου, συκῆ ἐλαίας ποιῆσαι, ἢ ἄμπελος σῦκα; οὔτε (*vel* οὐδὲ) ἁλυκὸν γλυκὺ ποιῆσαι ὕδωρ, as in Codd. ABC, *not less* than six good cursives, the Vulgate and other versions. To soften the ruggedness of this construction, a few copies prefixed οὕτως to οὔτε or οὐδὲ, while others inserted the whole clause οὕτως οὐδεμία πηγὴ ἁλυκὸν καὶ before γλυκὺ ποιῆσαι ὕδωρ. Another fair instance may be seen in Chap. IX., note on Col. II. 2.

III. "Brevior lectio, nisi testium vetustorum et gravium auctoritate penitus destituatur, praeferenda est verbosiori. Librarii enim multò proniores ad addendum fuerunt, quam ad omittendum" (Griesbach, *N. T. Proleg.* p. lxiv. Vol. I.). This canon bears an influential part in the system of Griesbach and his successors, and by the aid of Cod. B (*see* p. 93) and a few others, has brought great changes into the text. Mr Green too (*Course of Developed Criticism on Text of N. T.*) sometimes carries it to excess in his desire to remove what he considers *accretions*. It is so far true that scribes were prone to receive marginal notes into the text which they were originally designed only to explain or enforce (e. g. 1 John v. 7)[1]; or sought to amplify a brief account from a fuller narrative of the same event found elsewhere, whether in the same book (e. g. Act. ix. 5 compared with xxvi. 14), or in the parallel passage of one of the other synoptical Gospels. In quotations, also, from the Old Testament the shorter form is always the more probably correct. Circumstances too will be supplied which were deemed essential for the preservation of historical truth (e. g. Act. viii. 37), or names of persons and places may be inserted from the Lectionaries (*see* pp. 11, 211): to this head also we must refer the graver and more deliberate interpolations so frequently met with in Cod. D and a few other documents. Yet it is just as true that words and clauses are sometimes wilfully

[1] "Though the theory of explanatory interpolations of marginal glosses into the text of the N. T. has been sometimes carried too far (*e. g.* by *Wassenberg* in *Valcken.* Schol. in N. T. Tom. I.), yet probably this has been the most fertile source of error in some MSS. of the Sacred Volume." (Wordsworth, *N. T.*, on 2 Cor. iii. 3.) Yes, in *some* MSS.

omitted for the sake of removing apparent difficulties (e. g. *υἱοῦ βαραχίου*, Matth. xxiii. 35 in Cod. ℵ and a few others), and that the negligent loss of whole passages through *ὁμοιοτέλευτον* (*see* p. 9) is common to manuscripts of every age and character. On the whole, therefore, the indiscriminate rejection of portions of the text regarded as supplementary, on the evidence of but a few authorities, must be viewed with considerable distrust and suspicion.

IV. That reading of a passage is preferable which best suits the peculiar style, manner, and habits of thought of the author; it being the tendency of copyists to overlook the idiosyncrasies of the writer. Thus in editing Herodotus an Ionic form is more eligible than an Attic one equally well attested, while in the Greek Testament an Alexandrine termination should be chosen under similar circumstances. Yet even this canon has a double edge: habit or the love of critical correction will sometimes lead the scribe to change the text to his author's more usual style, as well as to depart from it through inadvertence.

V. Attention must be paid to the genius and usage of each several authority, in assigning the weight due to it in a particular instance. Thus the testimony of Cod. B is of the less influence in omissions, that of Cod. D (Bezae) in additions, inasmuch as the tendency of the former is to abridge, that of the latter to amplify the sacred text. The value of versions and ecclesiastical writers also much depends on the degree of care and critical skill which they display.

Every one of the foregoing rules might be applied *mutatis mutandis* to the emendation of the text of any author whose works have suffered alteration since they left his hands: the next (so far as it is true) is peculiar to the case of Holy Scripture.

VI. "Inter plures unius loci lectiones ea pro suspectâ merito habetur, quae orthodoxorum dogmatibus manifestè prae caeteris favet" (Griesbach, *N. T. Proleg.* p. lxvi. Vol. I.). I cite this canon from Griesbach for the sake of annexing Archbishop Magee's very pertinent corollary: "from which, at least, it is reasonable to infer, that whatever readings, in favour of the Orthodox opinion, may have had *his* sanction, have not been preferred by him from any bias in behalf of Orthodoxy" (*Discourses on Atonement and Sacrifice*, Vol. III. p. 212). Alford says that the rule, "sound in the main," does not hold good, when, "*whichever reading is adopted, the orthodox meaning is legitimate*, but *the adoption of the stronger orthodox reading is absolutely incompatible with the heretical meaning*,—then it is probable that *such stronger orthodox reading was the original*" (*N. T. Proleg.* Vol. I. p. 83, note 6): instancing Act. xx. 28, where the weaker reading τὴν ἐκκλησίαν τοῦ κυρίου would quite satisfy the orthodox, while the alternative reading τοῦ θεοῦ "would have been certain to be altered by the heretics." But in truth there seems no good ground for believing that the rule is "sound in the main," though two or three such instances as 1 Tim. iii. 16 and the insertion of θεὸν in Jude *v.* 4 may seem to countenance it (*see above*, p. 16). We dissent altogether from Griesbach's statement "Scimus enim, lectiones quascunque, etiam manifestò falsas, dummodo orthodoxorum placitis patrocinarentur, inde a tertii seculi initiis mordicus defensas seduloque propagatas, caeteras autem ejusdem loci lectiones, quae dogmati ecclesiastico nil praesidii afferrent, haereticorum perfidiae attributas temere fuisse" (Griesb. *ubi supra*), if he means that the orthodox *forged* those great texts, which, *believing them to be authentic*, it was surely innocent and even incumbent on them to employ[1]. The Church of Christ "inde a tertii seculi initiis" has had her faults, many and grievous, but she never did nor shall fail in her duty as a faithful "witness and keeper of Holy Writ." But while vindicating the copyists of Scripture from all wilful tampering with the text, we need not deny that they, like others of their craft, preferred that one out of several extant readings that seemed to give the fullest and most emphatic sense: hence Davidson would fain account for the addition ἐκ τῆς σαρκὸς αὐτοῦ καὶ ἐκ τῶν ὀστέων αὐτοῦ (which, however, is apparently genuine) in Eph. v. 30. Since the mediæval scribes belonged almost universally to the monastic orders, we

[1] Griesbach's "etiam manifestò falsas" can allude only to 1 John v. 7: yet it is a strong point against the authenticity of that passage that it is *not* cited by Greek writers, who did not find it in their copies, but only by the Latins who did. I am sorry that Dean Alford thought this sentence worth reprinting.

will not dispute the truth of Griesbach's rule, "Lectio prae aliis sensum pietati (praesertim monasticae) alendae aptum fundens, suspecta est," though its scope is doubtless very limited[1]. Their habit of composing and transcribing Homilies has also been supposed to have led them to give a hortatory form to positive commands or dogmatic statements (see p. 15), but there is much weight in Wordsworth's remark, that "such suppositions as these have a tendency to destroy the credit of the ancient MSS.; and if such surmises were true, those MSS. would hardly be worth the pains of collating them" (*note on* 1 Cor. xv. 49).

VII. "Apparent probabilities of erroneous transcription, permutation of letters, itacism and so forth," have been designated by Professor Ellicott "*paradiplomatic* evidence" (*Preface to the Galatians*, p. xvii. 1st ed.), as distinguished from the "*diplomatic*" testimony of codices, versions, &c. This species of evidence, which can hardly be deemed internal, must have considerable influence in numerous cases, and will be used the most skilfully by such as have considerable practical acquaintance with the rough materials of criticism. We have anticipated what can be laid before inexperienced readers on this topic in our first Chapter, when discussing the sources of various readings[2]: in fact, so far as canons of internal or of paradiplomatic evidence are at all trustworthy, they instruct us in the reverse

[1] Alford's only *definite* example is found but in a single cursive (4) in Rom. xiv. 17, *οὐ γάρ ἐστιν ἡ βασιλεία τοῦ Θεοῦ βρῶσις καὶ πόσις, ἀλλὰ δικαιοσύνη καὶ ἄσκησις καὶ εἰρ.* Tregelles (*Account of Printed Text*, p. 222) adds 1 Cor. vii. 5; Act. x. 30; Rom. xii. 13(!).

[2] See (6) p. 9; (7) p. 10; (17) p. 14; (18) p. 15. The uncial characters most liable to be confounded by scribes (*see p.* 9) are ΑΔΛ, ЄC, ΟΘ, ΝΠ, and less probably ΓΙΤ. I was lately shewn an article in a foreign Classical periodical, written by Professor Kuenen, the co-editor of the Leyden reprint of the N. T. portion of Cod. B; which (unless regarded as a mere *jeu d'esprit*) would serve to prove that the race of conjectural emendators is not so completely extinct as I had supposed (*see p.* 369). By a dexterous interchange of letters of nearly the same form (Δ for Α, Є for C, Ι for Τ, C for Є, Κ for ΙC, Τ for Ι) this Dutch Bentley—and he well deserves the name—suggests for ΑCΤЄΙΟC *τῷ θεῷ* Act. vii. 20 [compare Hebr. xi. 23] the common-place ΔЄΚΤΟC *τῷ θεῷ*, from Act. x. 35. Each one of the *six* necessary changes Kuenen profusely illustrates by examples, and even the reverse substitution of *δεκτὸς* for *ἀστεῖος* from Alciphron: but in the absence of all manuscript authority for the very smallest of these several permutations in Act. vii. 20, he excites in us no other feeling than a sort of grudging admiration of his misplaced ingenuity.

process to that aimed at in Chap. I.; the latter shewing by what means the pure text of the inspired writings was brought into its present state of *partial* corruption, the former promising us some guidance while we seek to retrace its once downward course back to the fountain-head of primeval truth[1]. To what has been previously stated in regard to paradiplomatic testimony it may possibly be worth while to add Griesbach's caution "lectiones RHYTHMI fallaciâ facillimè explicandae, nullius sunt pretii" (*N. T. Proleg.* p. lxvi.), a fact whereof 2 Cor. iii. 3 affords a memorable example. Here the perfectly absurd reading ἐν πλαξὶ καρδίαις σαρκίναις, by dint of the rhyming termination, is received by Lachmann in the place of καρδίας, on the authority of Codd. ℵABCDEGL, perhaps a majority of cursive copies (seven out of Scrivener's twelve), and that abject slave of manuscripts, the Philoxenian Syriac. Codd. FK have καρδίας[2].

It has been said that "when the cause of a various reading is known, the variation usually disappears[3]." This language may seem extravagant, yet it hardly exaggerates what may be effected by internal evidence, when it is clear, simple, and unambiguous. It is, therefore, much to be lamented that this is seldom the case in practice. Readings that we should uphold in virtue of one canon, are very frequently (perhaps in a majority of really doubtful passages) brought into suspicion by means of another; yet they shall each of them be perfectly sound and reasonable in their proper sphere. An instance in point is Matth. v. 22, where the external evidence is divided. Codd. ℵB (in Δ *secundâ manu*) 48. 198, Origen *twice*, the Aethiopic and Vulgate omit εἰκῇ after πᾶς ὁ ὀργιζόμενος τῷ ἀδελφῷ αὐτοῦ, Jerome fairly stating that it is "in quibusdam codicibus," not "in veris," which may be supposed to be Origen's (*above*, p. 266), and therefore removing it from his revised Latin version. It is found however in *all* other extant copies (including DEKLMSUVΔ. 1. 33, all the Syriac and Old Latin copies, the Memphitic, Armenian and Gothic versions), in

[1] Thus Canon I. of this Chapter includes (12) p. 12; (19) p. 15: Canon III. includes (2), (3) p. 8; (4) p. 9; (8), (9), (10) pp. 11, 12: while (13) p. 13 comes under Canon IV; (20) p. 15 under Canon VI.

[2] Mai's smaller edition of Cod. B also has καρδίας, but this I presume is only one of those injudicious corrections of the original which go so far towards making his labours useless. In his first or larger edition he gives καρδίαις.

[3] *Canon Criticus* XXIV, N. T. by G. D. T. M. D. p. 12, 1735: see above, p. 319.

Eusebius, the Latin Fathers from Irenaeus, and even in the old Latin version of Origen himself; the later authorities for once uniting with Cod. D and its associates against the two oldest manuscripts extant. Under such circumstances the suggestions of internal evidence would be precious indeed, were not that just as equivocal as diplomatic proof. "Griesbach and Meyer," says Dean Alford, "hold it to have been expunged from motives of moral rigorism:—De Wette to have been inserted to soften the apparent rigour of the precept." Our sixth Canon is here opposed to our first. The important yet precarious and strictly auxiliary nature of rules of internal evidence will not now escape the attentive student; he may find them exemplified very slightly and imperfectly in the ninth Chapter of this volume, but more fully by all recent critical editors of the Greek Testament; except Tregelles, who usually passes them by in silence, though to some extent they influence his decisions; and Lachmann, in the formation of whose provisional text (*see pp.* 343, 370) they have had no share. We will close this investigation by citing a few of those crisp little periods (conceived in the same spirit as our own remarks) wherewith Davidson is wont to inform and sometimes perhaps to amuse his admirers:

"Readings must be judged on internal grounds. One can hardly avoid doing so. It is natural and almost unavoidable. It must be admitted indeed that the choice of readings on internal evidence is liable to abuse. Arbitrary caprice may characterise it. It may degenerate into simple *subjectivity*. But though the temptation to misapply it be great, it must not be laid aside.... While allowing superior weight to the external sources of evidence, we feel the pressing necessity of the subjective. Here, as in other instances, the objective and subjective should accompany and modify one another. They cannot be rightly separated." (*Biblical Criticism*, Vol. II. p. 374, 1852.)

CHAPTER VII.

ON THE HISTORY OF THE TEXT AND OF THE PRINCIPAL SCHEMES THAT HAVE BEEN PROPOSED FOR RESTORING IT TO ITS PRIMITIVE STATE, INCLUDING RECENT VIEWS OF COMPARATIVE CRITICISM.

AN adequate discussion of the subject of the present Chapter would need a treatise by itself, and has been the single theme of several elaborate works. We shall here limit ourselves to the examination of those more prominent topics, a clear understanding of which is essential for the establishment of trustworthy principles in the application of *external* evidence to the correction of the text of the New Testament. The use of *internal* evidence has been sufficiently considered in the preceding Chapter.

1. It was stated at the commencement of this volume that the autographs of the sacred writers "perished utterly in the very infancy of Christian history" (p. 2): nor can any other conclusion be safely drawn from the general silence of the earliest Fathers, and from their constant habit of appealing to "ancient and approved copies[1]," when a reference to the originals, if extant, would have put an end to all controversy on the subject of various readings. Dismissing one passage in the genuine Epistles of Ignatius (d. 107), which has no real connexion with the matter[2], the only allusion to the autographs of Scripture

[1] e.g. Irenaeus, *Contra Haereses*, v. 30. 1, for which see below, p. 383: the early date renders this testimony most weighty.

[2] In deference to Lardner and others, who have supposed that Ignatius refers to the sacred autographs, we subjoin the sentence in dispute. Ἐπεὶ ἤκουσά τινων λεγόντων, ὅτι ἐὰν μὴ ἐν τοῖς ἀρχαίοις εὔρω, ἐν τῷ εὐαγγελίῳ οὐ πιστεύω· καὶ λέγοντός

met with in the primitive ages is the well-known declaration of Tertullian (fl. 200). "Percurre Ecclesias Apostolicas, apud quas ipsae adhuc Cathedrae Apostolorum suis locis praesident, apud quas ipsae Authenticae Literae eorum recitantur, sonantes vocem, et repraesentantes faciem uniuscujusque. Proximè est tibi Achaia, habes Corinthum. Si non longè es a Macedoniâ, habes Philippos, habes Thessalonicenses. Si potes in Asiam tendere, habes Ephesum. Si autem Italiae adjaces, habes Romam..." (*De Praescriptione Haereticorum*, c. 36). Attempts have been made, indeed, and that by very eminent writers, to reduce the term "*Authenticae Literae*" to mean nothing more than "genuine, unadulterated Epistles," or even the authentic Greek as opposed to the Latin translation. It seems enough to reply with Ernesti, that any such non-natural sense is absolutely excluded by the word "*ipsae*," which would be utterly absurd, if "genuine" only were intended (*Institutes*, Pt. III. Ch. II. 3)[1]: yet the African Tertullian was too little likely to be well informed on this subject, to entitle his rhetorical statement to any real attention[2]. We need not try to explain away

μου αὐτοῖς, ὅτι γέγραπται, ἀπεκρίθησάν μοι, ὅτι πρόκειται. Ἐμοὶ δὲ ἀρχεῖά ἐστιν Ἰησοῦς Χριστὸς κ. τ. λ. (*Ad Philadelph.* c. 8). On account of ἀρχεῖα in the succeeding clause, ἀρχείοις has been suggested as a substitute for the manuscript reading ἀρχαίοις, and so the interpolators of the genuine Epistle have written: but without denying that a play on the words was designed between ἀρχαίοις and ἀρχεῖα, both copies of the old Latin version maintain the distinction made in the Medicaean Greek ("si non in veteribus invenio" and "Mihi autem principium est Jesus Christus"), and any difficulty as to the sense lies not in ἀρχαίοις but in πρόκειται. Chevallier's translation of the passage is perfectly intelligible, "Because I have heard some say, Unless I find it in the ancient writings, I will not believe in the Gospel. And when I said to them, It is written [in the Gospel], they answered me 'It is found written before [in the Law].'" Gainsayers set the first covenant in opposition to the second and better one.

[1] Compare too Jerome's expression "ipsa authentica" (*Comment. in Epist. ad Titum*), when speaking of the autographs of Origen's Hexapla: below p. 388.

[2] The view I take is Coleridge's too (*Table Talk*, p. 89, 2nd ed.). "I beg Tertullian's pardon; but among his many *bravuras*, he says something about St Paul's autograph. Origen expressly declares the reverse;" referring, I suppose, to the passage cited below, p. 384. Bp. Kaye, the very excellencies of whose character almost unfitted him for entering into the spirit of Tertullian, observes: "Since the whole passage is evidently nothing more than a declamatory mode of stating the weight which he attached to the authority of the Apostolic Churches; to infer from it that the very chairs in which the Apostles sat, or that the very Epistles which they wrote, then actually existed at Corinth, Ephesus, Rome, &c., would be only to betray a total ignorance of Tertullian's style" (Kaye's *Ecclesias-*

his obvious meaning, but may fairly demur to the evidence of this honest, but impetuous and wrong-headed man. We have no faith in the continued existence of autographs, which are vouched for on no better authority than the real or apparent exigency of *his* argument[1].

2. Besides the undesigned and, to a great extent, unavoidable differences subsisting between manuscripts of the New Testament within a century of its being written, the wilful corruptions introduced by heretics soon became a cause of loud complaint in the primitive ages of the Church. Dionysius, Bishop of Corinth, addressing the Church of Rome and Soter its Bishop (168—176), complains that even his own letters had been tampered with: *καὶ ταύτας οἱ τοῦ διαβόλου ἀπόστολοι ζιζανίων γεγέμικαν, ἃ μὲν ἐξαιροῦντες, ἃ δὲ προστιθέντες· οἷς τὸ οὐαὶ κεῖται*: adding, however, the far graver offence, *οὐ θαυμαστὸν ἄρα εἰ καὶ τῶν κυριακῶν ῥαδιουργῆσαί τινες ἐπιβέβληνται γραφῶν* (Euseb. *Ecc. Hist.* IV. 23), where *αἱ κυριακαὶ γραφαὶ* can be no other than the Holy Scriptures. Nor was the evil new in the age of Dionysius. Not to mention the Gnostics Basilides (A.D. 130?) and Valentinus (150?) who published additions to the sacred text which were avowedly of their own composition, Marcion of Pontus, the arch-heretic of that period, coming

tical History...illustrated from the writings of Tertullian, p. 313, 2nd ed.). Just so: the autographs were no more in those cities than the chairs were: but it suited the purpose of the moment to suppose that they were extant; and, *knowing nothing to the contrary*, he boldly sends the reader in search of them.

[1] I do not observe, as some have thought, that Eusebius (*Hist. Eccl.* V. 10) intimates that the copy of St Matthew's Gospel in Hebrew letters, left by St Bartholomew in India, was the Evangelist's autograph; and the notion that St Mark wrote with his own hand the Latin fragments now at Venice (*for.*, see p. 265) is unworthy of serious notice. The statement twice made in the *Chronicon Paschale* of Alexandria, compiled in the sixth century, *but full of ancient fragments*, that ὡσεὶ τριτὴ was the true reading of John xix. 14 "καθὼς τὰ ἀκριβῆ βιβλία περιέχει, αὐτό τε τὸ ἰδιόχειρον τοῦ εὐαγγελιστοῦ ὅπερ μέχρι τοῦ νῦν πεφύλακται χάριτι Θεοῦ ἐν τῇ ἐφεσίων ἁγιωτάτῃ ἐκκλησίᾳ καὶ ὑπὸ τῶν πιστῶν ἐκεῖσε προσκυνεῖται" (Dindorf, *Chron. Pasch.* pp. 11 and 411) is simply incredible. Isaac Casaubon, however, a most unimpeachable witness, says that this passage, and another which he cites, were found by himself in a fine fragment of the Paschal treatise of *Peter Bp. of Alexandria and martyr* [d. 311], which he got from Andrew Darmarius, a Greek merchant. Casaubon adds to the assertion of Peter "Hec ille. Ego non ignoro quid adversus hanc sententiam possit disputari: de quo judicium esto eruditorum" (*Exercit. in Annal. Eccles.* pp. 464, 670, London 1614).

to Rome on the death of its Bishop Hyginus (142)[1], brought with him that mutilated and falsified copy of the New Testament, against which the Fathers of the second century exerted all their powers, and whose general contents are known to us chiefly through the writings of Tertullian and subsequently of Epiphanius. It can hardly be said that Marcion deserves very particular mention in relating the history of the sacred text. Some of the variations from the common readings which his opponents detected were doubtless taken from manuscripts in circulation at the time, and, being adopted through no private preferences of his own, are justly available for critical purposes. Thus in 1 Thess. ii. 15 Tertullian, who saw only *τοὺς προφήτας* in his own copies, objects to Marcion's reading *τοὺς ἰδίους προφήτας* ("licet *suos* adjectio sit haeretici"), although *ἰδίους* stands in the received text, in Codd. KL (DE in later hands) and all cursives except seven, the Gothic, both Syriac versions, Chrysostom and Theodoret. Here the heretic's testimony is useful in shewing the high antiquity of *ἰδίους*, even though ABDEFG, seven cursives, the Vulgate, Armenian, Æthiopic, and all three Egyptian versions, join with Origen, Lachmann and Tischendorf in rejecting it, some of them perhaps in compliance with Tertullian's decision. In similar instances the evidence of Marcion, as to a matter of fact to which he could attach no kind of importance, is well worth recording: but where on the contrary the dogmas of his own miserable system are touched, or no codices or other witnesses countenance his changes (as is perpetually the case in his edition of St Luke, the only Gospel—and that maimed and interpolated from the others—he seems to have acknowledged at all) his blasphemous extravagance may very well be forgotten. In such cases he does not so much as profess to follow anything more respectable than the capricious devices of his misguided fancy.

3. Nothing throws so strong a light on the real state of the text in the latter half of the second century as the single notice of Irenaeus (d. 178) on Apoc. xiii. 18 (*see above*, p. 379, note 1). This eminent person, the glory of the Western Church in his own age, whose five books against Heresies (though chiefly extant but in a bald old Latin version) are among the most precious

[1] "Necdum quoque Marcion Ponticus de Ponto emersisset, cujus magister Cerdon sub Hygino tunc episcopo, qui in Urbe nonus fuit, Romam venit: quem Marcion secutus..." Cyprian. *Epist.* 74. Cf. Euseb. *Eccl. Hist.* IV. 10, 11.

reliques of Christian antiquity, had been privileged in his youth to enjoy the friendly intercourse of his master Polycarp, who himself had conversed familiarly with St John and others that had seen the Lord (Euseb. *Ecc. Hist.* v. 20). Yet even Irenaeus, though removed but by one stage from the very Apostles, possessed (if we except a bare tradition) no other means of settling discordant readings than are now open to ourselves; to search out the best copies and exercise the judgment on their contents. His *locus classicus* must needs be cited in full, the Latin throughout, the Greek in such portions as survive. The question is whether St John wrote χξϛʹ (666), or χιϛʹ (616).

"His autem sic se habentibus, et in omnibus antiquis et probatissimis et veteribus scripturis numero hoc posito, et testimonium perhibentibus his qui facie ad faciem Johannem viderunt (*τούτων δὲ οὕτως ἐχόντων, καὶ ἐν πᾶσι δὲ τοῖς σπουδαίοις καὶ ἀρχαίοις ἀντιγράφοις τοῦ ἀριθμοῦ τούτου κειμένου, καὶ μαρτυρούντων αὐτῶν ἐκείνων τῶν κατ' ὄψιν τὸν Ἰωάννην ἑωρακότων, καὶ τοῦ λόγου διδάσκοντος ἡμᾶς ὅτι ὁ ἀριθμὸς τοῦ ὀνόματος τοῦ θηρίου κατὰ τὴν τῶν Ἑλλήνων ψῆφον διὰ τῶν ἐν αὐτῷ γραμμάτων ἐμφαίνεται*), et ratione docente nos quoniam numerus nominis bestiae, secundum Graecorum computationem, per literas quae in eo sunt sexcentos habebit et sexaginta et sex (*ἐσφάλησάν τινες ἐπακολουθήσαντες ἰδιωτισμῷ καὶ τὸν μέσον ἠθέτησαν, ἀριθμὸν τοῦ ὀνόματος ν' ψήφισμα ἀφελόντες καὶ ἀντὶ τῶν ἓξ δεκάδων μίαν δεκάδα βουλόμενοι εἶναι*): ignoro quomodo erraverunt quidam sequentes idiotismum et medium frustrantes numerum nominis, quinquaginta numeros deducentes, pro sex decadis unam decadem volentes esse. Hoc autem arbitror scriptorum peccatum fuisse, ut solet fieri, quoniam et per literas numeri ponuntur, facilè literam Graecam quae sexaginta enuntiat numerum, in iota Graecorum literam expansam. Sed his quidem qui simpliciter et sine malitia hoc fecerunt, arbitramur veniam dari a Deo." (*Contr. Haeres.* v. 30. 1: Harvey, Vol. II. pp. 406—7.)

Here we obtain at once the authority of Irenaeus for receiving the Apocalypse as the work of St John; we discern the living interest its contents had for the Christians of the second century, up to the *traditional* preservation of its minutest readings; we recognise the fact that numbers even then were represented by letters; and the far more important one that the original autograph of the Apocalypse was already so completely lost, that a thought of it never entered the mind of the writer, though the book had not been composed one hundred years, perhaps not more than seventy[1].

[1] Irenaeus' anxiety that his own works should be kept free from corruption, and the value then attached to the labours of the corrector, are plainly seen in a

4. Clement of Alexandria is the next writer who claims our attention (fl. 194). Though his works abound with citations from Scripture, on the whole not too carefully made ("in adducendis N. T. locis creber est et *castus*," is rather too high praise, Mill, *Proleg.* § 627), the most has not yet been made of the information he supplies (*see* p. 285). He also complains of those who tamper with (or metaphrase) the Gospels for their own sinister ends, and affords us one specimen of their evil diligence[1]. His pupil Origen's [185—254] is the highest name among the critics and expositors of the early Church; he is perpetually engaged in the discussion of various readings of the New Testament, and employs language in describing the then existing state of the text, which would be deemed strong if applied even to its present condition, after the changes which sixteen more centuries must needs have produced. His statements are familiar enough to Biblical enquirers, but, though often repeated, cannot be rightly omitted here. Seldom have such warmth of fancy and so bold a grasp of mind been united with the life-long patient industry which procured for this famous man the honourable appellation of *Adamantius*. Respecting the sacred autographs, their fate or their continued existence, he seems to have had no information, and to have entertained no curiosity: they had simply passed by and were out of reach. Had it not been for the diversities of copies in all the Gospels on other points (he writes)—*καὶ εἰ μὲν μὴ καὶ περὶ ἄλλων πολλῶν διαφωνία ἦν πρὸς ἄλληλα τῶν ἀντιγράφων*—he should not have ventured

remarkable subscription preserved by Eusebius (*Eccl. Hist.* v. 20), which illustrates what was said above, pp. 46—7. *Ὁρκίζω σε τὸν μεταγραψόμενον τὸ βίβλιον τοῦτο, κατὰ τοῦ κυρίου ἡμῶν ἰησοῦ χριστοῦ, καὶ κατὰ τῆς ἐνδόξου παρουσίας αὐτοῦ, ἧς ἔρχεται κρῖναι ζῶντας καὶ νεκρούς, ἵνα ἀντιβάλλῃς ὃ μετεγράψω, καὶ κατορθώσῃς αὐτὸ πρὸς τὸ ἀντίγραφον τοῦτο, ὅθεν μετεγράψω ἐπιμελῶς, καὶ τὸν ὅρκον τοῦτον ὁμοίως μεταγράψῃς, καὶ θήσεις ἐν τῷ ἀντιγράφῳ.* Here the copyist (*ὁ μεταγράφων*) is assumed to be the same person as the reviser or corrector.

[1] *Μακάριοι, φησίν, οἱ δεδιωγμένοι ἕνεκεν δικαιοσύνης, ὅτι αὐτοὶ υἱοὶ Θεοῦ κληθήσονται· ἤ, ὥς τινες τῶν μετατιθέντων τὰ Εὐαγγέλια, Μακάριοι, φησίν, οἱ δεδιωγμένοι ὑπὸ τῆς δικαιοσύνης, ὅτι αὐτοὶ ἔσονται τέλειοι· καί, μακάριοι οἱ δεδιωγμένοι ἕνεκα ἐμοῦ, ὅτι ἕξουσι τόπον ὅπου οὐ διωχθήσονται* (*Stromata*, IV. 6). Tregelles (*Horne*, p. 39, note 2) pertinently remarks that Clement, in the very act of censuring others, subjoins the close of Matth. v. 9 to *v.* 10, and elsewhere himself ventures on liberties no less extravagant, as when he thus quotes Matth. xix. 24 (or Luke xviii. 25): *πειστέον οὖν πολλῷ μᾶλλον τῇ γραφῇ λεγούσῃ, Θᾶττον κάμηλον διὰ τρυπήματος βελόνης διελεύσεσθαι, ἢ πλούσιον φιλοσοφεῖν* (*Stromata*, II. 5).

to object to the authenticity of a certain passage (Matth. xix. 19) on internal grounds: *νυνὶ δὲ δηλονότι πολλὴ γέγονεν ἡ τῶν ἀντιγράφων διαφορά, εἴτε ἀπὸ ῥαθυμίας τινων γραφέων, εἴτε ἀπὸ τόλμης τινων μοχθηρᾶς τῆς διορθώσεως τῶν γραφομένων, εἴτε καὶ ἀπὸ τῶν τὰ ἑαυτοῖς δοκοῦντα ἐν τῇ διορθώσει προστιθέντων ἢ ἀφαιρούντων* (Comment. on Matth. Tom. III. p. 671, *De la Rue*). "But now," saith he, "great in truth has become the diversity of copies, be it from the negligence of certain scribes, or from the evil daring of some who correct what is written, or from those who in correcting add or take away what they think fit[1]:" just like Irenaeus had previously described revisers of the text as "qui peritiores apostolis volunt esse" (*Contra Haeres.* IV. 6. 1).

5. Nor can it easily be denied that the various readings of the New Testament current from the middle of the second to the middle of the third century, were neither fewer nor less considerable than such language would lead us to anticipate. Though no surviving manuscript of the Old Latin version dates before the fourth century, and most of them belong to a still later age, yet the general correspondence of their text with that used by the first Latin Fathers is a sufficient voucher for its high antiquity (*see* pp. 252—5). The connexion subsisting between this Latin version and the Curetonian Syriac and Codex Bezae proves that the text of these documents is considerably older than the vellum on which they are written; the Peshito Syriac also, most probably the very earliest of all translations (*see* pp. 229—231), though approaching far nearer to the Received text than they, sufficiently resembles these authorities in many peculiar readings to exhibit the general tone and character of *one* class of manuscripts extant

[1] In this place (contrary to what might have been inferred from the language of Irenaeus, cited above, p. 383 note) the copyist (*γραφεὺς*) is clearly distinct from the corrector (*διορθωτής*), who either alters the words that stand in the text, or adds to and subtracts from them. In the masterly Preface to Kuenen and Cobet's *N. T. ad fidem Cod. Vaticani*, Leyden, 1860, pp. xxvii—xxxiv, will be found most of the passages we have used that bear on the subject, with the following from Classical writers, "Nota est Strabonis querela XIII. p. 609 de bibliopolis, qui libros edebant *γραφεῦσι φαύλοις χρώμενοι, καὶ οὐκ ἀντιβάλλοντες*.... Sic in Demosthenis Codice Monacensi ad finem Orationis XI annotatum est *Διωρθώθη πρὸς δύο Ἀττικιανά*, id est, *correctus est* (hic liber) *ex duobus codicibus ab Attico* (nobili calligrapho) *descriptis*." Just as at the end of each of Terence's plays the manuscripts read "Calliopius recensui."

in the second century, two hundred years anterior to Codd. ℵB. Now it may be said without extravagance that no set of Scriptural records affords a text less probable in itself, less sustained by any rational principles of external evidence, than that of Cod. D, of the Latin codices and (so far as it accords with them) of Cureton's Syriac. Interpolations, as insipid in themselves as unsupported by other evidence, abound in them all: additions so little in accordance with the genuine spirit of Holy Writ that some critics (though I, for one, profess no skill in such alchemy) have declared them to be as easily separable from the text which they encumber, as the foot-notes appended to a modern book are from the main body of the work (*Account of the Printed Text*, p. 138 note). It is no less true to fact than paradoxical in sound, that the worst corruptions to which the New Testament has ever been subjected, originated within a hundred years after it was composed; that Irenaeus and the African Fathers and the whole Western, with a portion of the Syrian Church, used far inferior manuscripts to those employed by Stunica, or Erasmus, or Stephens thirteen centuries later, when moulding the Textus Receptus. What passage in the Holy Gospels would be more jealously guarded than the record of the heavenly voice at the Lord's Baptism? Yet Augustine (*De Consensu Evangelist.* II. 14) marked a variation which he thought might be found "in aliquibus fide dignis exemplaribus," though not "in antiquioribus codicibus Graecis," where in the place of ἐν σοὶ ηὐδόκησα (Luke iii. 22) the words ἐγὼ σήμερον γεγέννηκά σε are substituted from Psalm ii. 7 (so also Faustus apud Augustin.; *Enchiridion ad Laurentium* c. 49). The only Greek copy which maintains this important reading is D: it is met with moreover in *abc* (in *d* of course) *ff*[2] *primâ manu*, and *l*, whose united evidence leaves not a doubt of its existence in the primitive Old Latin; whence it is cited by Hilary three times, by Lactantius and Juvencus. Among the Greeks it is known but to Methodius, and to those very early writers, Justin Martyr and Clement of Alexandria, who seem to have derived the corruption (for such it must doubtless be regarded) from the Ebionite Gospel (Epiphan. *Haer.* XXI. 13)[1].

[1] Considering that Cod. D and the Latin manuscripts contain the variation in Luke iii. 22, but not in Matth. iii. 17, we ought not to doubt that Justin Martyr (p. 331. B, Ed. Paris, 1636) and Clement (p. 113, Ed. Potter) refer to the former. Hence Bp. Kaye (*Account of the Writings of Clement*, p. 410) should not have

So again of the doubtful passages we shall examine in Chapter IX, Irenaeus cites Act. viii. 37 without the least misgiving, though the spuriousness of the verse can hardly be doubted; and expressly testifies to a reading in Matth. i. 18 which will now perhaps be upheld by no one. It is hard to believe that 1 John v. 7 was not cited by Cyprian, and even the interpolation in Matth. xx. 28 was widely known and received. Many other examples might be produced from the most venerable Christian writers, in which they countenance variations (and those not arbitrary, but resting on some sort of authority) which no modern critic has ever attempted to vindicate.

6. When we come down to the fourth century, our information grows at once more definite and trustworthy. Copies of Scripture had been extensively destroyed during the long and terrible period of affliction that preceded the conversion of Constantine. In the very edict which marked the beginning of Diocletian's persecution, it is ordered that the holy writings should be burnt (τὰς γραφὰς ἀφανεῖς πυρὶ γενέσθαι, Eusebius, *Eccl. Hist.* VIII. 2); and the cruel decree was so rigidly enforced that a special name of reproach (*traditores*), together with the heaviest censures of the Church, was laid upon those Christians who betrayed the sacred trust (Bingham, *Antiquities*, Book XVI, Ch. VI. 25). At such a period critical revision or even the ordinary care of devout transcribers must have disappeared before the pressure of the times; fresh copies of the New Testament would have to be made in haste to supply the room of those seized by the enemies of our Faith; and when made they were to circulate by stealth among persons whose lives were in jeopardy every hour. Hence arose the need, when the tempest was overpast, of transcribing many new manuscripts of the New Testament, the rather as the Church was now receiving vast accessions of converts within her pale. Eusebius of Caesarea, the Ecclesiastical Historian, seems to have taken the lead in this happy labour; his extensive learning, which by the aid of certain other less commendable qualities had placed him high in Constantine's favour, rendered it natural that the Emperor should employ his services for furnishing with fifty copies of Scripture the Churches of his new capital, Constan-

produced this passage among others to shew (what in itself is quite true) that "Clement frequently quotes from memory."

tinople (*see above*, p. 25, note 1). Eusebius' deep interest in Biblical studies is exhibited in several of his surviving works, as well as in his Canons for harmonising the Gospels (*see* p. 50): and he would naturally betake himself for the text of his fifty codices to the Library founded at his Episcopal city of Caesarea by the martyr Pamphilus, the dear friend from whom he derived his own familiar appellation *Eusebius Pamphili.* Into this Library Pamphilus had gathered manuscripts of Origen as well as of other theologians, of which Eusebius made an index (τοὺς πίνακας παρεθέμην: *Eccles. Hist.* VI. 32); from this collection Cod. H of St Paul and others are stated to have been derived, nay even Cod. ℵ in its Old Testament portion (*see* p. 47 and note), which is expressly declared to have been corrected to the Hexapla of Origen. Indeed we know from Jerome (*Comment. in Epist. ad Tit.*) that the very autograph ("ipsa authentica") of Origen's Hexapla was used by himself at Caesarea, and Montfaucon (*Praeliminaria in Hexapl.* Chap. I. 5) cites from one manuscript the following subscription to Ezekiel, Ὁ Εὐσέβιος ἐγὼ σχόλια παρέθηκα. Πάμφιλος καὶ Εὐσέβιος ἐδιωρθώσαντο.

7. We are thus warranted, as well from direct evidence as from the analogy of the Old Testament, to believe that Eusebius mainly resorted for his Constantinopolitan Church-books to the codices of Pamphilus, which might once have belonged to Origen. What critical corrections (if any) he ventured to make in the text on his own judgment is not so clear. Not that there is the least cause to believe, with Dr Nolan (*Inquiry into the Integrity of the Greek Vulgate*, p. 27) that Eusebius had either the power or the will to suppress or tamper with the great doctrinal texts 1 John v. 7; 1 Tim. iii. 16; Acts xx. 28; yet we cannot deny that his prepossessions may have tempted him to arbitrary alterations in other passages, which had no direct bearing on the controversies of his age. Codd. ℵB are quite old enough to have been copied under his inspection, and it is certainly very remarkable that these two early manuscripts omit one whole paragraph (Mark xvi. 9—16) with his sanction, if not after his example (*see below*, Chap. IX). Thus also in Matth. xxiii. 35 Cod. ℵ, with no other countenance than we have before mentioned (p. 221, note), discards υἱοῦ βαραχίου, for which change Eusebius (*silentio*) is literally the only authority among the Fa-

thers, Irenaeus and even Origen retaining the words, in spite of their obvious difficulty. When we shall come to know more of this venerable codex, its agreement with the readings of Eusebius may become more decided than we are yet aware of. All we can see of it at present shows considerable resemblance to its contemporary B, with as considerable departures from it, while "the state of the text, as proceeding from the first scribe, may be regarded as *very rough*" (Tregelles, *N. T.* Part II. p. 2). The relation in which Cod. א stands to the other four chief manuscripts of the Gospels, may be partially estimated from the transcript of four pages already published by Tischendorf (*see* p. 78). Of the 312 variations from the common text therein noted, א stands alone in 45, in 8 agrees with ABCD united (much of C, however, is lost in these passages), with ABC together 31 times, with ABD 14, with AB 13, with D alone 10, with B alone but once (Mark i. 27), with C alone once: with several authorities against AB 39 times, with A against B 52, with B against A 98. Hence the discovery of this precious document has so far done little to uphold Cod. B (which seems the more correctly written, and probably the more valuable of the two) in its more characteristic and singular readings, but has made the mutual divergencies of the very oldest critical authorities more patent and perplexing than ever.

8. Codd. אB were apparently anterior to the age of Jerome, the latest ecclesiastical writer whose testimony need be dwelt upon, since from his time downwards the stream of extant and direct manuscript evidence, beginning with Codd. AC, flows on without interruption. Jerome's attention was directed to the criticism of the Greek Testament by his early Biblical studies, and the knowledge he thus obtained had full scope for its exercise when he was engaged on revising the Old Latin version (*see* p. 261). In his so often cited *Praefatio ad Damasum*, prefixed to his recension of the Gospels, he complains of certain "codices, quos a Luciano et Hesychio nuncupatos, paucorum hominum asserit perversa contentio," and those not of the Old Testament alone, but also of the New. This obscure and passing notice of corrupt and (apparently) interpolated copies has been made the foundation of more than one theory as fanciful as ingenious. Jerome further informs us that he had adopted in his translation

the Canons which Eusebius "Alexandrinum secutus Ammonium" (*see pp.* 50—3) had invented, or first brought into vogue; stating, and in his usual fashion somewhat exaggerating[1], an evil these Canons helped to remedy, the mixing up of the matter peculiar to one Evangelist in the narrative of another (*see p.* 11). Hence we might naturally expect that the Greek manuscripts he would view with special favour, were the same as Eusebius had approved before him. In the scattered notices throughout his works, Jerome sometimes speaks but vaguely of "quaedam exemplaria tam Graeca quam Latina" (Luke xxii. 43—4, almost in the words of Hilary, his senior); or appeals to readings "in quibusdam exemplaribus et maximè in Graecis codicibus" (Mark xvi. 14): occasionally we hear of "multi et Graeci et Latini codices" (John vii. 53), or "vera exemplaria" (Matth. v. 22; xxi. 31), or "antiqua exemplaria" (Luke ix. 23), without specifying in which language: Mark xvi. 9—20 "in raris fertur Evangeliis," since "omnes Graeciae libri paene" do not contain it[2]. In two places, however, he gives a more definite account of the copies he most regarded. In Galat. iii. 1 τῇ ἀληθείᾳ μὴ πείθεσθαι is omitted by Jerome, because it is not contained "in exemplaribus Adamantii," although (as he elsewhere informs us) "et Graeca exemplaria hoc errore confusa sint." The other passage has been alluded to already (p. 266): in some Latin copies of Matth. xxiv. 36 *neque filius* is added, "quum in Graecis, et maxime Adamantii et Pierii exemplaribus, hoc non habeatur adscriptum." Pierius the presbyter of Alexandria, elsewhere called by Jerome "the younger Origen" (*Cat. Scriptt. Eccl.* I. p. 128), has been deprived by fortune of the honour due to his merit and learning. A contemporary, perhaps the teacher of Pamphilus (Euseb. *Eccl. Hist.* VII. 32) at Caesarea, his copies of Scripture would naturally be preserved with those of Origen in the great Library of that city. Here they were doubtless seen by Jerome when, to his deep joy, he found Origen's writings copied in Pamphilus' hand

[1] Magnus siquidem hic in nostris codicibus error inolevit, dum quod in eadem re alius Evangelista plus dixit, in alio, quia minus putaverint, addiderunt. Vel dum eundem sensum alius aliter expressit, ille qui unum e quatuor primum legerat, ad ejus exemplum ceteros quoque existimaverit emendandos. *Unde accidit ut apud nos mixta sint omnia* (*Praef. ad Damasum*).

[2] The precise references may be seen in Tischendorf's, and for the most part more exactly in Tregelles' *N. T.* That on Matth. xxiv. 36 is Tom VII. p. 199, or VI. p. 54; on Galat. iii. 1 is Tom. VII. pp. 418, 487.

(*Cat. Scriptt. Eccl., ubi supra*), which volumes Acacius and Euzoius, elder contemporaries of Jerome himself, had taken pious care to repair and renew (*ibid.* I. p. 131; *ad Marcel. Ep.* CXLI). It is not therefore wonderful if, employing as they did and setting a high value on precisely the same manuscripts of the N. T., the readings approved by Origen, Eusebius and Jerome should closely agree.

9. Epiphanius [d. 403], who wrote at about the same period as Jerome, distinguishes in his note on Luke xxii. 44 (Tom. II. p. 36) between the uncorrected copies (ἀδιορθώτοις), and those used by the Orthodox[1]. Of the function of the "corrector" (διορθωτής) of an ancient manuscript we have spoken several times before (pp. 46, 383 note, 385 note): but a system was devised by Professor J. L. Hug of Freyburg in 1808 (*Einleitung*), and maintained, though with some modifications, by J. F. Eichhorn, which assigned to these occasional, and (as they would seem to be) unsystematic labours of the reviser, a foremost place in the criticism of the N. T. Hug conceived that the process of corruption had been going on so rapidly and uniformly from the Apostolic age downwards, that by the middle of the third century the state of the text in the general mass of codices had degenerated into the form exhibited in Codd. D. 1. 13. 69. 124 of the Gospels, the Old Latin and Thebaic (he would now have added the Curetonian Syriac) versions, and to some extent in the Peshito and in the citations of Clement of Alexandria and of Origen in his early works. To this uncorrected text he gave the name of κοινὴ ἔκδοσις, and that it existed, substantially in the interpolated shape now seen in Cod. D, the Old Latin and Cureton's Syriac, as early as the second century, need not be doubted. What we may fairly dispute is that it ever had extensive circulation or fair repute in the Churches whose vernacular

[1] This same writer testifies to a practice already partially employed, of using breathings, accents, and stops in copies of Holy Scripture. 'Ἐπειδὴ δέ τινες κατὰ προσῳδίαν ἔστιξαν τὰς γραφὰς καὶ περὶ τῶν προσῳδῶν τάδε· ὀξεῖα ΄, δασεῖα ‘, βαρεῖα ‵, ψιλὴ ’, περισπωμένη ˆ, ἀπόστροφος ’, μακρὰ —, ὑφὲν ‿, βραχεῖα ᵕ, ὑποδιαστολή , . Ὡσαύτως καὶ περὶ τῶν λοιπῶν σημείων κ.τ.λ. (Epiphan. *De Mensur.* c. 2, Tom. III. p. 237 Migne). This passage may tend to confirm the statements made above, pp. 39—41, respecting the presence of such marks in very ancient codices, though on the whole I would not quite vouch for Sir F. Madden's opinion as regards Cod. A.

language was Greek. This "common edition" Hug supposes to have received three separate emendations in the middle of the third century; one by Origen in Palestine, which he thinks Jerome adopted and approved; two others by Hesychius and Lucian (a presbyter of Antioch and Martyr), in Egypt and Syria respectively, both which Jerome condemned (*see* p. 389), and Pope Gelasius (492—6) declared to be apocryphal[1]. To Origen's recension he referred such copies as A. K. M. 42. 106. 114. 116. 253 of the Gospels, the Philoxenian Syriac, the quotations of Chrysostom and Theodoret: to Hesychius the Alexandrine codices BCL; to Lucian the Byzantine documents EFGHSV and the mass of later books. The practical effect of this elaborate theory would be to accord to Cod. A a higher place among our authorities than some recent editors have granted it; its correspondence with Origen in many characteristic readings would thus be admitted and accounted for. But in truth Hug's whole scheme is utterly baseless, as regards historical fact, and most insufficiently sustained by internal proof. Jerome's slight and *solitary* mention of the copies of Lucian and Hesychius abundantly evinces their narrow circulation and the low esteem in which they were held; and even Eichhorn perceived that there was no evidence whatever to shew that Origen had attempted a formal revision of the text. The passages cited above, both from Eusebius and Jerome (*see pp.* 388, 390)—and no others are known to bear on the subject—will carry us no farther than this:—that these Fathers had access to codices of the N. T. once possessed by Adamantius, and here and there, perhaps, retouched by his hand. The manuscripts copied by Pamphilus (p. 390) were those of Origen's own works; and while we have full and detailed accounts of what he accomplished for the Greek versions of the Old Testament, no hint has been thrown out by any ancient writer that he carried his pious labour into the criticism of the New. On the contrary, he seems to disclaim the task in a

[1] "Evangelia, quae falsavit Lucianus apocrypha." "Evangelia quae falsavit Esitius [*alii* Hesychius *vel* Isicius] apocrypha," occur separately in the course of a long list of spurious books (such as the Gospels of Thaddaeus, Matthias, Peter, James, that "nomine Thomae quo utuntur Manichaei," &c.) in Appendix III. to Gelasius' works in Migne's *Patrologia*, Tom. LIX. p. 162 [A. D. 494]. But the authenticity of these decrees is far from certain, and as we hear of these falsified Gospels nowhere else, Gelasius' knowledge of them might have been derived from what he had read in Jerome's *Praef. ad Damasum*.

sentence now extant only in the old Latin version of his works, where to a notice of his attempt to remove diversity of reading from codices of the Septuagint by the help of "the other editions" (κριτηρίῳ χρησάμενοι ταῖς λοιπαῖς ἐκδόσεσιν, i.e. the versions of Aquila and the rest), he is represented to add "In exemplaribus autem Novi Testamenti, hoc ipsum me posse facere sine periculo non putavi" (Origen, Tom. III. p. 671).

10. Hug's system of recensions was devised as a corrective to those of Bengel (*see* p. 323) and Griesbach (p. 334), which have been adequately discussed in Chapter v. The veteran Griesbach spent his last effort as a writer in bringing to notice the weak points of Hug's case, and in claiming him, where he rightly could, as a welcome ally[1]. But neither did Hug's scheme, nor that propounded by Scholz some years later (*see* p. 338), obtain the general credit and acceptance which had once been conceded to Griesbach's. It was by this time plainly seen that not only were such theories unsupported by historical testimony (to which indeed the Professor of Halle had been too wise to lay claim), but that they failed to account for more than a part, and that usually a small part, of the phenomena disclosed by minute study of our critical materials. All that can be inferred from searching into the history of the sacred text amounts to no more than this: that extensive variations, arising no doubt from the wide circulation of the New Testament in different regions and among nations of diverse languages, subsisted from the earliest period to which our records extend. Beyond this point our investigations cannot be carried, without indulging in

[1] Griesbach rejoices to have Hug's assent "in eo, in quo disputationis de veteribus N. T. recensionibus cardo vertitur; nempe extitisse, inde a secundo et tertio seculo, plures sacri textûs recensiones, quarum una, si Evangelia spectes, supersit in Codice D, altera in Codd. BCL, alia in Codd. EFGHS et quae sunt reliqua" (*Meletemata*, p. lxviii, prefixed to *Commentarius Criticus*, Pars II. 1811). I suppose that Tregelles must have overlooked this decisive passage (probably the last its author wrote for the public eye) when he states that Griesbach now "virtually gave up his system" as regards the possibility of "drawing an actual line of distinction between his Alexandrian and Western recensions" (*Account of Printed Text*, p. 91). He certainly shows, throughout his *Commentarius Criticus*, that Origen does not lend him the support he had once anticipated; but he still held that the theory of a triple recension was the very *hinge* on which the whole question turned, and clung to that theory as tenaciously as ever.

pleasant speculations which may amuse the fancy, but cannot inform the sober judgment.

Yet is it true that we are thus cast upon the wide ocean without a compass or a guide? Can no clue be found that may conduct us through the tangled maze? Is there no other method of settling the text of the New Testament than by collecting and marshalling and scrutinizing the testimony of thousands of separate documents, now agreeing, now at issue with each other:—manuscripts, versions, ecclesiastical writers, whose mutual connexion and interdependence, so far as they exist (and to some extent they do and *must* exist), defy all our skill and industry to detect and estimate them aright? This would surely be a discouraging view of critical science as applied to the sacred volume, and it is by no means warranted by proved and admitted facts. Elaborate systems have failed, as might have been looked for from the first: it was premature to frame them in the present stage of enquiry, while the knowledge we possess of the actual contents of our extant authorities is imperfect, vague and fragmentary; while our conclusions are liable to be disturbed from time to time by the rapid accession of fresh materials, of whose character we are still quite ignorant. But if we be incompetent to devise theories on a grand or imposing scale, a more modest and a safer course is open. Men of the present generation may be disqualified for taking a general survey of the whole domain of this branch of divine learning, who may yet be employed, serviceably and with honour, in cultivating each one for himself some limited and humble field of special research, to which his taste, his abilities or opportunities have attached him: those persons may usefully improve a farm, that cannot hope to conquer a kingdom. Of the long array of uncollated manuscripts which swell our catalogues (*see* p. 225), let the student choose from the mass a few within his reach which he may deem worthy of complete examination; or exhaust the information some ecclesiastical writer of the first six centuries can afford; or contribute what he can to an exact acquaintance with some good ancient version, ascertaining the genius of its language and (where this is attainable) the literary history of its text[1]. If, in the course of such quiet

[1] Professor Ellicott has done good service to the Church in directing fresh attention to the ancient translations, and animating the languid and superficial

labours, he shall mark (as a patient observer will find cause to mark) resemblances and affinities more than accidental, between documents of widely different ages and countries; he will not only be contributing to the common stock what cannot fail to be available hereafter as raw material, but will be helping to solve that great problem which has hitherto in part eluded the most earnest enquiries, the investigation of the true laws and principles of COMPARATIVE CRITICISM.

The last-mentioned term has been happily applied by Tregelles to that delicate and important process, whereby we seek to determine the *comparative* value, and trace the mutual relation, of authorities of every kind upon which the original text of the N. T. is based. Thus explained (and in this enlarged sense scholars have willingly accepted it[1]), its researches may be pursued with diligence and interest, without reference to the maintenance or refutation of any particular system or scheme of recensions. The mode of procedure is experimental and tentative, rather than dogmatical; the facts it gradually develops will eventually (as we trust) put us on the right road, although for the present we meet with much that is uncertain, perplexing, ambiguous. It has already enabled critics in some degree to

theologians of the day by his own researches (*see* p. 229) as well in our kindred tongue the Gothic, as in those "somewhat intractable languages" the Coptic and Ethiopic. The versions are full as valuable in aid of the criticism of the N. T. as of its interpretation, to which he chiefly applies them.

[1] "I do not accept Mr Scrivener as an accurate expositor of my views, and as having introduced the *term* 'Comparative Criticism,' I may reasonably ask that it may, if used at all, be employed according to my own definition" (Tregelles, *Additions to the Fourth volume of Horne's Introduction*, p. 756). I should be really grieved to misrepresent my respected fellow-labourer, and subjoin his definition, as set down in the two several passages to which he refers. I had thought it somewhat less simple, though much to the same purport, as that given above in the text. "By *Comparative* Criticism I mean such an investigation as shows what the character of a document is,—not simply from its age, whether known or supposed,—but from its actual readings being shown to be in accordance or not with certain other documents" (*Account of Printed Text*, p. 132). "We thus reach the mode of demonstrating the value of documents by *Comparative Criticism;* that is, by showing, in cases of explicit ancient testimony, what MSS. and versions do, as a fact, accord with readings so established; and thus we are able, as to the text in general, to rely with especial confidence on the witnesses whose character has thus been proved" (*Horne*, p. 148). As to his reiterated assertion that by "comparative criticism" he intends "not the single evidence of *one* MS., *one* version, or *one* Father" (*Additions*, p. 756), I ask with unaffected innocence, who ever supposed or assumed that he *did* mean any thing of the sort?

classify the documents with which they have to deal; it may possibly lead them, at some future period, to the establishment of principles more general, and therefore more simple, than we can now conceive likely or even possible to be attained to.

11. In the course of investigations thus difficult and precarious, designed to throw light on a matter of such vast consequence as the genuine condition of the text of Scripture, one thing would appear almost too clear for argument, too self-evident to be disputed,—that it is both our wisdom and our duty *to weigh the momentous subject at issue in all its parts*, shutting out from the mind no source of information which can reasonably be supposed capable of influencing our decision. Nor can such a course become less right or expedient because it must perforce involve us in laborious, extensive and prolonged examination of a vast store of varied and voluminous testimony: it is essential that divines strive to come to definite conclusions respecting disputed points of sacred criticism; it is not necessary that these conclusions be drawn within a certain limited period, either this year, or even in the lifetime of our generation. Hence such a plan as that advocated by Lachmann (*see* pp. 341—2), for abridging the trouble of investigation by the arbitrary rejection of the great mass of existing evidence, must needs be condemned for its rashness by those who think their utmost pains well bestowed in such a cause; nor can we consistently praise the determination of others, who, shunning the more obvious errors into which Lachmann fell, yet follow his example in constructing the text of the N. T. on a foundation somewhat less narrow, but scarcely more firm than his. As the true science of Biblical criticism is in real danger of suffering harm from the efforts of men of this school, it cannot be out of place if we examine the pleas which have been urged in vindication of their scheme, and assign (as briefly as we may) our reasons for believing that its apologists are but labouring in vain.

12. The most conspicuous and uncompromising advocate of the system referred to, is Dr S. P. Tregelles, whose edition of the Greek Testament, now brought down to the end of the Gospels, has been described in Chap. v. (pp. 346—8). This industrious and earnest man has effectually persuaded himself

that more than nine-tenths of our extant manuscripts and other authorities should be utterly rejected and lost sight of, when we come to amend the text, and try to restore it to its primitive purity. The true readings of the Greek N. T., according to his notion, *must be sought exclusively in the most ancient documents, especially in the earliest uncial codices.* From this proposition it follows, as a corollary at once direct and unavoidable, that "the mass of recent documents [i. e. those written in cursive characters from the tenth century downwards] possess no determining voice, in a question as to what we should receive as genuine readings" (*Account of Printed Text*, p. 138). "We are able," he boldly adds, "to take the *few* documents whose evidence is *proved* to be trustworthy, and safely discard from present consideration the eighty-nine ninetieths, or whatever else their numerical proportion may be" (*ibid.*). Nor has he shrunk from acting on this principle firmly and consistently, in the prosecution of that work on which his reputation must mainly rest, his edition of the Greek Testament. In constructing his text, and in arranging the authorities for it in his notes, he treats the Lectionaries and the great mass of cursive manuscripts *as if they had no existence.* The readings of three select copies in the Gospels, to which will be added a fourth in the Acts (*see* p. 348), are carefully recorded, and are allowed at least their due weight in the decision of critical questions; but these copies have attained such distinction on internal grounds alone; because the text they preserve approaches that which in the editor's judgment an ancient text ought to be. Of the uncial documents which he retains, several are as recent as the tenth or eleventh century (Evan. FGSUX), and it is very hard to perceive why *they* deserve more attention, on the score of age, than the numerous cursives extant, which bear the same date[1]. Tregelles' preference of these uncials cannot be owing to the *character* in which they are written; for this plea (in itself too puerile for grave discussion) would have compelled him to employ about 65 of the Lectionaries he discards (*see* p. 211); yet I have tried in vain to frame reasons for his procedure in this respect less open to the charge of arbitrary caprice.

[1] *Dated* cursive codices of the eleventh century (as may be seen from Chap. II., Sect. III.) are quite common. A list of those dated in the tenth is given p. 36, note 2.

13. *Brevis vita, ars longa.* For this lawful cause, if for no other, the most ardent student of Biblical criticism would fain embrace some such system as Dr Tregelles advocates, if only he could do so in tolerable safety. The process of investigation might thus be diminished twenty-fold, and the whole subject brought within a compass not too vast for one man's diligence or the space of an ordinary life-time. The simplicity and comparative facility of this process of resorting to the few for instruction hitherto supposed to be diffused among the many, has created in its favour a strong and not unnatural prejudice, which has yielded, so far as it has yet yielded at all, to nothing but the stubborn opposition of indisputable facts. It will also readily be admitted, that certain principles, not indeed peculiar to this theory, but brought by it into greater prominence, are themselves most reasonable and true. No one need question, for example, that "if the reading of the ancient authorities in general is unanimous, there can be but little doubt that it should be followed, whatever may be the later testimonies; for it is most improbable that the independent testimony of early MSS., versions and Fathers should accord with regard to something entirely groundless" (Tregelles, *N. T.*, *Introductory Notice*, p. 2). No living man, possessed of a tincture of scholarship, would dream of setting up testimony exclusively modern against the "unanimous" voice of antiquity. The point on which we insist, and find it so difficult to impress on Dr Tregelles and his allies, is briefly this:—that the evidence of his "ancient authorities" is anything but unanimous; that they are perpetually at variance with each other, even if you limit the term "ancient" within the narrowest bounds. Shall it include, among the manuscripts of the Gospels, none but the five oldest copies Codd. א ABCD? The reader has but to open the first recent critical work he shall meet with, to see them scarcely ever in unison; perpetually divided two against three, or perhaps four against one. All the readings these venerable monuments contained must of course be *ancient*, or they would not be found there; but they cannot all be true. So again, if our search be extended to the versions and primitive Fathers, the same phenomenon unfolds itself, to our grievous perplexity and disappointment. How much is contained in Cureton's Syriac or the Old Latin for which no Greek original can now be alleged? Do

not the earliest ecclesiastical writers describe readings as existing and current in their copies, of which few traces can be met with at present[1]? Dean Alford, who throws himself heartily into the debate in defence of Tregelles' views, proposes to us the question, "What right have we to set virtually aside...*the agreement in the main of our oldest uncials*, at the distance of one or two centuries,—of which, owing probably to the results of persecution, we have no MS. remains,—*with the citations of the primitive fathers, and with the earliest versions?*" (*N. T. Proleg.* Vol. I. p. 91, 4th edn.). We answer without hesitation, *no right whatever:* where the oldest of these authorities really agree, we accept their united testimony as practically conclusive; it is not at all our design, as the Dean seems to apprehend, to "seek our readings from the later uncials, supported as they usually are by the mass of cursive MSS.;" but to employ their confessedly secondary evidence in those numberless instances, when their elder brethren are hopelessly at variance. This course, indeed, has just been adopted by Alford himself not only in the case of the Apocalypse, where the great scarcity of uncials might almost force the cursives upon his attention, but of the Catholic Epistles, and (if I mistake not his purpose in a forthcoming edition) of the Pauline Epistles also. In this part of his work, the cursive collations, first of Scrivener, then of his predecessors, are cited in Alford's margin wherever the uncials differ from each other; yet it is not easy to reconcile this practice (which surely deserves to be imitated) with his summary rejection, even in his last edition of the Gospels, of *all* cursive testimony except Codd. 1. 33. 69. Evst. y^{scr}. We do not claim for the recent documents the high consideration and deference fitly reserved for a few of the oldest; just as little do we think it right to pass them by in silence, and allow to them no more weight or importance than if they had never been written. If Dean Alford's latest practice is more to be regarded than his theory of two years old, *confitentem habes reum* that the course he pursued in the Gospels is less likely to lead to trustworthy results than the other.

[1] e.g. Matth. i. 18; Act. viii. 37 for Irenaeus: Act. xiii. 33 for Origen. It is rare indeed that the express testimony of a Father is so fully confirmed by the oldest copies as in John i. 28, where Βηθανίᾳ, said by Origen to be σχεδὸν ἐν πᾶσι τοῖς ἀντιγράφοις, actually appears in ℵ* ABC*.

14. On one point, I think, we are still at issue, the *degree* in which the most ancient documents are at variance with each other. Resuming from Alford the context which we cited above (p. 399), we next read "I say, the agreement *in the main:*—for Mr Scrivener's instances of discrepancy are in vain used by him to produce an impression, which we know would be contrary to the fact in the majority of instances" (Alford, *ubi supra*). But is it really so? I am fully aware that in a field so wide as the criticism of the N.T., those who dexterously select their examples may prove just what they will. More anxious, therefore, to convince opponents than to fight with shadows or beat the air, I determined that the instances I discussed should be chosen by Dr Tregelles, rather than by me. He had alleged seventy-two passages from various parts of the N. T., as a kind of sample of some two or three thousand he reckons to exist there, wherein "the more valuable ancient versions (or some of them) agree in a particular reading or in which such a reading has *distinct* patristic testimony, and the mass of MSS. stand in opposition to such a lection, [while] there are certain copies which *habitually* uphold the older reading" (*Account of Printed Text*, p. 148). Taking as an adequate specimen of the whole (and that, with no consciousness of unhandsome dealing) those seven of Tregelles' texts which are contained in the Gospel of St Mark (*Codex Augiensis, Introd.* pp. ix. *seq.*), I endeavoured to prove that in each one of these cases the *ancient* evidence was not unevenly balanced, whatever might be pronounced the true reading in each separate passage; that the mass of the later evidence was almost always as well supported by *old* manuscripts, versions and Fathers, as was the reading it opposed. If, as Dean Alford states, these "instances of discrepancy produce an impression contrary to the fact in the majority of instances," the fault of unskilful selection rests not with me: if on the other hand they shall prove fair specimens of the whole list, we submit that their impartial consideration will uphold a principle which it was certainly not Tregelles' purpose to help to maintain. When, however, an objection has been taken to the sufficiency of one set of illustrations of a principle, the shortest and only satisfactory method is at once to lay them aside, and substitute for them others which may be less exposed to doubt. Dean Alford holds it just and necessary that the Curetonian Syriac "on the testimony of which

Tregelles very much relies," should form an element in this inquiry, our new series of examples shall consist of *the first twelve* passages in the Gospels, extant as well in that version as in Codd. ABCD, the readings of which in Cod. ℵ have hitherto been made known by Tischendorf in his *Notitia Cod. Sinaitici* (see above, pp. 28, 77). Undue selection, it is presumed, will thus be deemed impossible; and in setting forth the exact state of the evidence on both sides in the most concise form that may be attainable, we trust to enable the reader to judge for himself whether in these instances, taken up at random, the mass of ancient documents as a rule conspire to lead us one way, the more recent another[1].

(1) Luke viii. 30. λεγιων ℵ*B^{2}D*L, Pesh. Cure. Philox. Syriac (ܠܓܝܘܢ) Memph., and of course the Latin versions: λεγειων B* *teste Mai*: λεγαιων ℵ^{2}D^2: λεγεων ACEFGHKMRSUVXΓΔΛΞ, all known cursives, the margin of the Philoxenian and the Received text.

(2) *Ibid. v.* 37. Γεργεσηνων ℵ*ℵ^{3}C^{2}LPX. 1. 13. 22. 33. 118. 131. 157. 209. 251 (Scholia in 237. 239. 259), Memph. Arm. Aeth. Arab.: Γερασηνων BC*D, Theb., all Latin versions (even those in Δ. 130): Γεσινῶν 69: Γαδαρηνων with the common text ℵ^{2}AEGHK MRSUVΓΔΛ and all other cursives (γαδαρινων b^{scr}), Pesh. *Cure.* Philox. Syriac, Goth.

(3) *Ibid. v.* 38. εδεετο of the Received text ℵ*C*EGHKMRSU VΓΔΛ, all cursives except one: εδειτο ℵ^{2}BC^{2}LX, 33. Cyr.: εδεειτο AP: ηρωτα D. Versions here and in (5) are useless to us.

(4) Luke ix. 13. αρτουσ πεντε ℵ: αρτοι πεντε B: επτα αρτοι C: πεντε αρτοι Received text, ADΞ. &c., in fact all manuscripts and versions, including Cureton's.

(5) *Ibid. v.* 19. ειπαν ℵBD, Lachmann, Tischendorf, Tregelles, Alford: ειπον Received text with ACEGHKLMRSUVXΓΔΛΞ, all cursives.

(6) *Ibid. v.* 23. καθημεραν of the Received text is found in ℵ*ℵ^{3}ABKLMRΞ 1. 13. 33. 69. 124. 131. 251. 253, Scrivener's avw, Evst. 48. z^{scr}, and no doubt in many others, where, because there is no variation from the common text, its presence was not expressly noted. It is rendered in all three Syriac versions (though the margin of Philox. marks its absence from some copies), Theb. Memph. Goth. Arm. (Aeth. after the next και) *f. g'.* Vulg. Jerome has it once expressly, as the reading of old copies (*see p.* 390), and on Matth. x. 38 names it as the reading of *another* Gospel, which is

[1] A*, B*, &c. mean readings of A, B, &c. by the first hand; A^2, B^2, &c. by a second; A^3, B^3, &c. by a yet later hand.

not likely to be Mark viii. 34. Καθ' ἡμέραν is omitted in CDEF^{w}GH SUVXΓΔΛ, 17 out of 22 cursives collated by Scrivener, and some 120 others: in *a. b. c. e. ff*^{2}. *l. q.* of the Old Latin, Sax. (after some codices of Vulg.), *Origen*, Chr.(?), and others.

(7) *Ibid. v.* 26: λογους of the Received text appears in ℵABCΞ, all known codices and versions except D, Old Latin *a. e. l.*, Cureton's Syriac (ܘܒܡܠܝ ?? ܕܝܠܝ ܐܢܘܢ), and Origen I. 298. Origen *silently* reads λόγους[1] I. 296, though the context does not require it.

(8) *Ibid. v.* 34. επεσκιαζεν ℵBL Evst. 47. x^{scr}, perhaps 1^{pe}. 10^{pe}. (*uncial* Lectionaries) and *a*: επεσκιασεν of the Received text ACDE FGHKMPRSUVXΓΔΛ, all cursives, all versions (except *a*), even Cureton's Syriac. In Matth. xvii. 5, D* alone reads the imperfect.

(9) Luke x. 1. The first και of the common text (after κυριος) is rejected by BLΞ. 3. Pesh. Syriac (which has "from his disciples" in its room), Memph. Aeth.: it is found in ℵACD, the whole mass of codices, Cureton's, the Philox., and the Latin versions, Eusebius and Tertullian.

(10) *Ibid.* The next variation is more interesting. To ἑτερους ἑβδομηκοντα of the Received text, δυο is added by BDMR[2]. 1 (Tregelles). 42. (γρ^{αι} καὶ, ἑβδομήκοντα δύο of Stephens' margin of 1550 must refer to his *β* or Cod. D), Cureton's Syriac, Arm., Old Latin, *a. c. e. l.*, the Latin of Cod. 130 (see above, Luke viii. 37), and Vulg. But δυο is omitted in ℵACEGHKLSUVXΓΔΛΞ ("et ACLΛΞ in indice capitum" Tregelles), all cursives, Pesh. and Philox. Syriac, Memph., Goth., Aeth., Old Latin *b. f.*, Irenaeus and Tertullian very expressly, Eusebius *ter.* The "Recognitions" falsely ascribed to Clement of Rome, Epiphanius, Hilary, Augustine and some others receive δυο.

(11) *Ibid.* ανα δυο δυο is read by BK. 13. 50. 51. 53. 54. 57. 63. 64. 69. 91. 114. 116. 122^{2}. 145. 239. 248. 253. 254. 256. 300. 346, Scrivener's adpvw, the Philoxenian margin (but obelized, *see* p. 244). Pesh. and Cure. have "two two" without a preposition: but this is the proper mode of rendering ἀνὰ δύο in their language (cf. Mark vi. 39; 40, Greek and Pesh.). Yet ανα δυο of the Received text is found in ℵACDEGHLMSUVXΓΔΛΞ, the majority of cursives, in Eusebius twice. "Binos" of *a. b. c. e. f.* Vulg. may seem ambiguous, but leans to the common reading.

(12) *Ibid. v.* 25. και of the Received text is omitted before λέγων in ℵBLΞ*e*, Cureton's Syriac, Memph. All other authorities have it (including ACD and every known cursive manuscript), the two other Syriac versions &c.

1 "In Orig. quidem I. 298 dubitari potest an recte τοὺς ἐμοὺς legatur, quum praecedat οὔτε ἐπαισχυντέον αὐτὸν ἢ τοὺς λόγους αὐτοῦ. Sed continuo pergitur: καὶ ὁ ιϛ̄...καὶ οἱ μιμηταὶ δὲ αὐτοῦ. Atque quo ante loco (I. 296) τοὺς ἐμοὺς λόγους invenitur, contextu certè non requiritur, λόγους." Tischend. *in loc.* ed. 1859.

2 The text of R is lost from ix. 43 to x. 3, but in the prefixed table of τίτλοι we read, κεφ. λδ'. περὶ τῶν ἀναδειχθέντων οβ'.

15. These specimens will surely suffice for the purpose in hand, and they are the first twelve we meet with wherein the readings of ℵ ABCD and the Curetonian Syriac are as yet available. I believe that Dean Alford will see that we have changed the *venue* without much disturbing the verdict. Indeed, since our previous instances were *selected* by Tregelles, while the present are taken just as they stand in the open volume, it is not surprising if these examples from St Luke prove more favourable to the views we are urging than the others we examined in St Mark. The extent of this "wonderful" harmony of the most venerable uncial documents with the earliest versions, ecclesiastical writers and each other, may now be estimated by the facts before us. The two oldest manuscripts are ℵ B: in these 12 places they differ seven times and agree 5 times. Next in age and value to these two are AC; it may be questioned indeed whether they be much inferior, as critical authorities, and they are certainly not a century younger than the best manuscript extant. Now A supports the Received text in 11 of these readings, C in 9, even ℵ 6 times, B but twice. The Curetonian Syriac, too, on which so much (and I will not say an undue) stress is lain, divides its countenance pretty impartially: it is found in company with D (whose affinity to it is well known, *see* p. 103) six times, with A 5, with ℵ 4, with B 3, and C 2. The peculiarities which distinguish D from other documents of its date and importance do not much appear in these examples: it coincides with ℵ 4 times, with A 5, with B 3, with C 6: twice it affords a *lectio singularis* among Greek manuscripts, once with the aid of the Curetonian. Nor are the few later uncials, which usually do service to Cod. B, so constant in their allegiance as some might have anticipated. Cod. L, which in the seven passages chosen by Tregelles from St Mark (*Cod. Augiens. Introd.* pp. IX, X, XIII), never failed its ally save when there is an hiatus, now deserts it six times out of the twelve: Cod. Δ, which in St Mark sided with B five times out of seven, now never favours it, except when all others do. The readings of Codd. R Ξ, &c., if scrutinized with the same minuteness, will exhibit much the same result. Cod. Ξ, especially, which has been justly commended by Tregelles for "the goodness of its text," though defective in three of these twelve places, accords with the Received text against Cod. B in 5 out of the remaining

nine, with B against it twice, and twice with the two united. In certain cases a good number of cursive manuscripts support the form upheld by B, and (as in Luke x. 1, *ava δυο δυο*) much help to recommend it, by shewing that the variation it presents was widely diffused; sometimes the reading of Cod. B, being further sustained by others of the first rank and by some valuable cursives (Luke ix. 23), has been received into the *textus receptus*, and no doubt rightly received, in spite of the opposition of the mass of later codices both uncial and cursive.

As regards the testimony of the Fathers the passages we have lighted upon are not peculiarly instructive, and yet we have enough to enable us to see how precarious and unsteady is the help they can afford in the settlement of the sacred text. They supply information valuable indeed for the purpose of illustrating each separate variation, but far too slight and uncertain to be the groundwork of a theory or system of recensions. Occasionally (as in the case of Origen in Luke ix. 26) it is hard to say on which side their testimony should be ranged; at other times (as with Jerome in Luke ix. 23) they simply attest the antiquity of both forms in a doubtful passage; while the most prominent instance in which they can be applied in the examples we are considering is Luke x. 1 (10), wherein the two chief witnesses of the second century[1] adhere not to the reading of the minority of copies whereof Cod. B is the Coryphaeus, but to that of the numerical majority, headed as it is by Codd. ℵ ACD.

16. We are now in a condition to re-assert not less confidently than ever, that the few most ancient records, whether manuscripts, versions or Fathers, do *not* so closely agree among themselves, as to supersede all further investigation, and to render it needless so much as to examine the contents of later

[1] Post enim duodecim apostolos septuaginta alios Dominus noster ante se misisse invenitur; *septuaginta autem nec octonario numero, neque denario* (Irenaeus 146, Massuet). Tertullian, just a little later, compares the Apostles with the twelve wells at Elim (Exod. xv. 27), the seventy with the threescore and ten palm trees there (*adv. Marc.* IV. 24). Yet in the Recognitions of Clement, usually assigned to the second or third century, the number adopted is seventy-two, "vel hoc modo recognitâ imagine Moysis" and of his elders, traditionally set down as 72.

and more numerous authorities. As in the affairs of common life, a previous resolution to exclude from the mind all but one portion (and that in the matter before us a *small* portion) of the facts of the case, can never lead to historical or scientific truth, so he who ventures to discard nine-tenths or more of the extant testimony which bears upon the text of Scripture, must end in producing a work that will not satisfy the reasonable expectations of the thorough student, and may not long satisfy himself[1]. Not that we maintain, or that any sober critic ever did maintain, that numerical majority should decide a question of criticism, or that the ancient few should be overborne by the mere mass of the more recent many: still less would we assign to a codex of the fourteenth century the same weight as rightfully pertains to one of the fourth; such a course would be as unreasonable as anything we have found cause to complain of in the argument of our opponents. But not less startling is the proposition that numbers shall possess no determining voice whatever in deciding a question of various readings, and that a handful of documents such as Codd. BL, the Old Latin version, the Curetonian Syriac and the writings of Origen, if they would but present us with a testimony tolerably consistent and uniform (which in point of fact they refuse to do) should have power to silence all the evidence which can be mustered against them, however venerable in age, or recommended by a long train of authorities of various countries, extended over the course of full a thousand years. If to deny these principles, and to withhold our confidence from the conclusions they would lead to, be indeed "to take as truth the plaint of the old tragedian, ἄνω ποταμῶν ἱερῶν χωροῦσι παγαί" (*Alford*, N. T. *Proleg.* p. 92), and to force the stream back again to its source; we must bear contentedly for the time the imputation of folly, and as the science of Biblical criti-

[1] Very pertinent to this matter is a striking extract from Reiche, given in Bloomfield's *Critical Annotations on the Sacred Text*, p. 5, note: "In multis sanè N. T. locis lectionis variae, iisque gravissimi argumenti, de verâ scripturâ judicium firmum et absolutum, quo acquiescere possis, ferri nequit, nisi omnium subsidiorum nostrorum alicujus auctoritatis suffragia, et interna veri falsique indicia, diligenter explorata, justâ lance expendantur...Quod in causâ est, ut re non satis omni ex parte circumspectâ, non solum critici tantopere inter se dissentiant, sed etiam singuli sententiam suam toties retractant atque commutent." Partial views are in candid minds the fruitful parents of a vacillating judgment.

cism becomes more widely and accurately known, we promise ourselves many companions in our reproach.

17. It only remains to speak of the second of the "two wonderful facts" which have persuaded Dean Alford to construct anew his text of the N. T., without regard to the readings of cursive or later uncial codices; namely, "*The very general concurrence of the character of text of our earliest MSS., versions, and Fathers, with that text which the soundest critical principles lead us to adopt*" (*ibid. p.* 91). What those critical principles are may partly appear from the terms in which he speaks of the Received text, as having attained its present form by the process "of crumbling down salient points, softening irregularities, conforming differences, and [I am sorry he should think it right to add, *see p.* 375] favouring prevalent doctrines" (*ibid.* p. 92). In other words, Alford regards the text of Cod. B and its compeers as more probable on internal grounds than that of the later copies, and on that account receives its testimony whensoever he can make out a plausible case. A single example will illustrate his meaning, unless I have quite failed to apprehend it. In one of the twelve texts we have discussed above (p. 402)—Luke ix. 34—he has adopted in his revised text the imperfect form ἐπεσκίαζεν on the slight evidence of BL*a* (for he was not then aware that א has the same reading), chiefly because ἐπεσκίασεν, which is found in ACD and the mass of copies, is in his judgment derived from Matth. xvii. 5; and that on the ground that "in even the earliest MSS. there has been constant tampering with the text of one Gospel to conform it to that of another" (*ibid.* p. 91). I do not wish to controvert, I have tried to give fair scope to such canons of internal evidence as are here laid down (see Chap. VI. throughout): the only dispute that can well arise is on the limits of their application, and the extent of the influence which is due to them. One thing, however, is plain, that this second reason assigned for maintaining the earlier against the later documents is not "a fact" in the same sense as the first was, capable of being established or refuted by the induction of an adequate number of fairly selected proofs, but must always remain to a great extent a matter for the exercise of individual taste and feeling, whose elementary principles are incapable of strict demonstration, and whose conclusions must in

consequence be very doubtful and precarious. But the true answer to all objections founded on the character of the later manuscripts goes more directly to the point at issue. We do not place the more modern witnesses in one scale, the older in the other, and then decide *numero non pondere* which shall prevail: we advocate the use of the cursive copies principally, and indeed almost exclusively, where the ancient codices are at variance; and if, in practice, this shall be found to amount to a perpetual appeal to the younger witnesses, it is because in nineteen cases out of twenty, the elder *will* not agree. Nor even then should we deem it safe, except perhaps in very exceptional instances, to adopt as true a reading of the cursives, for which but slender ancient authority or none can be produced. There is a risk (we freely grant it) that in the long course of ages, and through the influence of frequent transcription, differences should be reconciled, rugged constructions made smooth, superficial (if not real) contradictions explained away: there are beyond question not a few readings pervading the more recent manuscripts which owe their origin to this source, and which the consentient testimony of antiquity condemns beyond appeal. But limiting the employment of later evidence, or at any rate its determining influence, to the decision between several readings, each of them extant in ancient records, we cannot devise any just cause for the neglect it has received at the hands of modern editors. Does any one suppose that the mass of our cursive documents are only corrupt copies, or copies of copies, drawn from existing uncials? Let the assertion be made and maintained, if it can with any show of reason; but if not, let us frankly accept the sole alternative, that they are representatives of other old copies which have long since perished, "respectable ancestors" (as one has quaintly put the matter) "who live only in their descendants" (Long, *Ciceronis Verrin. Orat. Praef.* p. vi). And to this conclusion we are irresistibly led by a close study of the cursive manuscripts themselves. No one who has paid adequate attention to them can fail to be struck with the *individual character* impressed upon nearly all: it is rare indeed that we find cause to suppose that one even of the latest codices is a mere transcript of any now surviving; we repeatedly find, in those which on the whole recede but little from the *textus receptus*, isolated readings for which no other authority can now be alleged than Cod. B or some such monument of remote antiquity. That the testimony of the cursives ought to be scrutinized, and suspected, and (*when unconfirmed by other witnesses*) as a rule set wholly aside, may be conceded even by those who have laboured the most diligently to collate and vindicate them; but we do trust that Lachmann and Tregelles will be the last, among the editors of the N. T., who will think they can be disposed of by the simple and compendious process of excluding them (the former entirely, the other hardly less so) from the roll of critical authorities. If his most recent labours are to be regarded as the model of his future efforts (*see* p. 399), Dean Alford seems bound, in mere consistency, to illustrate his next edition of the Gospels with a further accession of various readings from the best cursive codices; and the influence which such a practice must needs have on the character of the text will plainly appear from comparing Tischendorf's N. T. of 1859, in whose critical commentary the more recent codices have their due place, with that of 1849, where they appear but rarely, and never seem to influence his decisions. The total sum of variations in the text of these two books being 1292, in no less than 595[1] of these places he has returned in 1859 to the Elzevir readings which he had before deserted, but to which fresh materials and greater experience had brought him back.

18. It is hoped that the general issue of the foregoing discussion may now be embodied in these three practical rules:

(1) That the true readings of the Greek New Testament cannot safely be derived from any one set of authorities, whether manuscripts, versions, or Fathers, but ought to be the result of a patient comparison and careful estimate of the evidence supplied by them all.

(2) That where there is a real agreement between all the documents prior to the tenth century, the testimony of later manuscripts, though not to be rejected unheard, must be re-

[1] Of the rest, no less than 430 places relate to modes of spelling (see Chap. VIII.), for which Tischendorf is now more willing than before to accept the oldest manuscripts as his guides.

garded with great suspicion, and, unless upheld by strong internal evidence, can hardly be adopted.

(3) That in the far more numerous cases where the most ancient documents are at variance with each other, the later or cursive copies are of much importance, as the surviving representatives of other codices, very probably as early, perhaps even earlier, than any now extant.

It is suggested that on such terms the respective claims of the uncial and cursive, the earlier and more recent codices (and those claims are not in reality conflicting) may be fitly and with good reason adjusted.

19. Since we have not been sparing in our animadversions on that species of *Comparative Criticism*, which, setting out from a foregone determination to find an ancient, if not a genuine, text only in a certain limited number of documents of every class, shuts out from view the greater portion of the facts that oppose the theory it maintains; it is all the more incumbent on us to say that from another kind of Comparative Criticism, patiently cultivated, without prejudice or exclusive notions, we look for whatever light is yet to be shed on the history and condition of the sacred records. No employment will prove more profitable to the student than his private and independent research into the relation our documents stand in with regard to each other, their affinities, their mutual agreement or diversity. The publication of Cod. א in full (*see* p. 28) will soon open a wide field to our investigations, which many aspirants will doubtless hasten to occupy and cultivate to the general profit: a single illustration of the nature and results of the process shall now suffice. Those who would seek the primitive text of Scripture rather in the readings of Cod. B, the most widely removed from that commonly received, than in Cod. A[1], which (at least in the Gospels) most nearly

[1] Since the description of Cod. A (pp. 79—84) was printed off, an 8° edition of the *Codex Alexandrinus* in common type has appeared in a form to match the Leipsic reprint of Cod. B (see p. 92), but in this instance under the care of a responsible editor, "B. H. Cowper." Like its predecessor, the reprint of Cod. A is burdened with modern breathings and accents: the paragraphs of his codex are departed from, when Mr Cowper judges them inconvenient, and its hiatus are absurdly supplied from Kuster's Mill (1710). These defects, however, may easily

approaches it, are perpetually urging the approximation to the character of the former of those considerable fragments which yet survive, and date from the fifth or sixth century. Tregelles, for instance, describing Cod. R (*see* p. 114), on which he bestowed such honest, and (for his own fame) such unavailing toil, speaks thus on a matter he might be presumed to have thoroughly examined. "The text of these fragments is ancient; agreeing generally with some of the other copies of the oldest class. The discovery of all such fragments is of importance as affording a *confirmation* of those results which criticism of the text would previously have indicated" (Tregelles' *Horne*, p. 184): a confirmation of his system certainly not to be disparaged or explained away, but entitled, so far as it goes, to much attention. Yet after all how stand the facts of the case, when Cod. R is submitted to the test of Comparative Criticism? I have analysed the readings of all the 25 fragments (505 verses), as they stand in the notes to Tregelles' own Greek Testament, and I respectfully commend to that editor's consideration the summary of a result for which his language had in no wise prepared me. Out of the 1008 various readings cited from R, expressly or by implication, that venerable palimpsest stands alone among the manuscripts on Tregelles' list 46 times; with ABCD (but C is sadly mutilated) 23 times; with ABC 51 times; with ABD 57 times; with AB 97 times; with others against AB 131 times (52 of them with the Received text); with B against A 204 times (55 of them with the Received text); but with Cod. A against Cod. B no less than 399 times, in 366 of which it agrees with the *textus receptus*[1]. Thus the true character of this "ancient text"

be endured if, as he assures us, the editor has revised Woide's great work, by a careful re-examination of the original, and this statement I found no cause to doubt on the slight comparison between them I have yet been able to make. The *Prolegomena* too are useful and painstaking, but since Mr Cowper is evidently a novice in these studies, they are calculated to afford the learned on the continent a low opinion of English scholarship. I cordially assent to the editor's approval of the reverential care with which this precious book is treated by the officers of the British Museum: so frail have some of its leaves become, and so liable is the ink to peel or fly off in a kind of impalpable dust, that "however gently the manuscript is handled, it must be deteriorated; and should therefore only be consulted for some really practical purpose" (p. xix). For his opinion respecting its reading in 1 Tim. iii. 16, see Chap. IX.

[1] On applying this mode of calculation to the first hundred verses of St Luke contained in Codd. PQ (p. 113), of the sixth and fifth centuries respectively, we

is no longer doubtful; the process by which it is arrived at, if somewhat tedious, is rather more trustworthy than the shrewdest conjecture; and we have one warning the more, furnished too by no mean critic, that *ἀταλαίπωρος τοῖς πολλοῖς* (and not *τοῖς πολλοῖς* only) *ἡ ζήτησις τῆς ἀληθείας, καὶ ἐπὶ τὰ ἑτοῖμα μᾶλλον τρέπονται.*

find that out of 216 readings recorded for P, 182 for Q, P stands alone 14 times, Q not once: P agrees with others against AB 21 times, Q 19: P agrees with AB united 50 times, Q also 50: P is with B against A 29 times, Q 38: but (in this respect resembling Cod. R) P accords with A against B in 102 places, Q in 75. Codd. AZ have but 23 verses in common; but judged from them Z resembles B much more than A.

CHAPTER VIII.

CONSIDERATIONS DERIVED FROM THE PECULIAR CHARACTER AND GRAMMATICAL FORM OF THE DIALECT OF THE GREEK TESTAMENT.

1. IT will not be expected of us to enter in this place upon the wide subject of the origin, genius, and peculiarities, whether in respect to grammar or orthography, of that dialect of the Greek in which the N. T. was written, except so far as it bears directly upon the criticism of the sacred volume. Questions, however, are perpetually arising, when we come to examine the oldest manuscripts of Scripture, which cannot be resolved unless we bear in mind the leading particulars wherein the diction of the Evangelists and Apostles differs not only from that of pure classical models, but also of their own contemporaries who composed in the Greek language, or used it as their ordinary tongue.

2. The Greek style of the N. T., then, is the result of blending two independent elements, the debased vernacular speech of the age, and that strange modification of the Alexandrian dialect which first appeared in the Septuagint version of the Old Testament, and which, from their habitual use of that version, had become familiar to the Jews in all nations under heaven; and was the more readily adopted by those whose native language was Aramaean, from its profuse employment of Hebrew idioms and forms of expression. It is to this latter, the Greek of the Septuagint, of the Apocalypse, and of the foreign Jews, that the name of *Hellenistic* (Acts vi. 1) strictly applies. St Paul, who was born in a pure Greek city (Juvenal, III. 114—118); perhaps even St Luke, whose *original* writings[1]

[1] viz. Luke i. 1—4, some portion of the Gospel and most of the Acts: excluding such cases as St Stephen's speech, Act. vii, and the parts of his Gospel

savour strongly of Demosthenes and Polybius, cannot be said to have *affected* the Hellenic, which they must have heard and spoken from their cradles. Without denying that the Septuagint translation and (by reason of their long sojourning in Palestine) even Syriac phraseology would powerfully influence the style of these inspired penmen, it is not chiefly from these sources that their writings must be illustrated, but rather from the kind of Greek current during their lifetime in Hellenic cities and colonies.

3. Hence may be seen the exceeding practical difficulty of fixing the orthography, or even the grammatical forms prevailing in the Greek Testament, a difficulty arising not only from the fluctuation of manuscript authorities, but even more from the varying circumstances of the respective authors. To St John, for example, Greek must have been an alien tongue; the very construction of his sentences and the subtle current of his thoughts amidst all his simplicity of mere diction, render it evident (even could we forget the style of his Apocalypse) that he *thought* in Aramaean: divergencies from the common Greek type might be looked for in him and those Apostles whose situation resembled his, which it is very unlikely would be adopted by Paul of Tarsus. Bearing these facts always in mind (for the style of the New Testament is too apt to be treated as an uniform whole), we will proceed to discuss briefly, yet as distinctly as may be, a few out of the many perplexities of this description to which the study of the original codices at once introduces us.

4. One of the most striking of them regards what is called *ν ἐφελκυστικόν*, the "*ν* attached", which has been held to be an arbitrary and secondary adjunct. This letter, however, which is "of most frequent occurrence at the end of words, is itself of such a weak and fleeting consistency, that it often becomes inaudible, and is omitted in writing" (Donaldson, *Greek Grammar*, p. 53, 2nd edit.). Hence, though, through the difficulty of pronunciation, it became usual to neglect it before a consonant, it always comprised *a real portion of the word to which it was annexed*, and the great Attic poets are full of verses which

which resemble in style, and were derived from the same sources as, those of SS. Matthew and Mark.

cannot be scanned in its absence[1]: on the other hand, the cases are just as frequent where its insertion before a consonant would be fatal to the metre. In these instances the laws of prosody infallibly point out the true reading, and lead us up to a general rule, that the weak or moveable ν is more often dropped before a consonant than otherwise. This conclusion is confirmed by the evidence of surviving classical manuscripts, although but few of these are older than the tenth century, and would naturally be conformed, in such minute points, to the fashion of that period. Codices of the Greek Testament and of the Septuagint, however, which date from the fourth century downwards, present to us this remarkable phenomenon, that they exhibit the final ν before a consonant full as often as they reject it, and speaking generally, the most ancient (e.g. Evan. א[2] ABCD) are the most constant in retaining it, though it is met with frequently in many cursive copies, and occasionally in almost all. Hence arises a difficulty, on the part of modern editors, in dealing with this troublesome letter. Lachmann professes to follow the balance of evidence (such evidence as he received) in each separate case, and while he usually inserted, sometimes omitted it where he had no cause for such inconsistency except the purely accidental variation of his manuscripts; Tischendorf admits it almost always (*Proleg. N. T.* p. liii. 7th edition), Tregelles (I think) invariably. Whether it be employed or not, the practice should at any rate be uniform, and it is hard to assign any reason for using it which would not apply to classical writers, whose manuscripts would no doubt contain it as often as those of the N. T., were they as remote in date[3]. The same facts are true, and the same remarks equally apply to the representing or withdrawing of the weak ς in *οὕτως* before a consonant.

5. In the mode of spelling proper names of places and persons peculiar to Judaea, the general practice of some older codices is to represent harsher forms than those met with in later docu-

[1] e.g. Æschylus, *Persæ*, 411: κόρυμβ', ἐπ' ἄλλην δ' ἄλλος ἴθυνεν δόρυ, or Sophocles, *Antigone*, 219: τὸ μὴ 'πιχωρεῖν τοῖς ἀπιστοῦσῖν τάδε.

[2] So far as we can see at present, Cod. א seldom has the ν with nouns, not always with verbs.

[3] The terminations which admit this moveable ν (including -ει of the pluperfect) are enumerated by Donaldson (*Gr. Gram.* p. 53). Tischendorf however (*Proleg. N. T.* p. liv) demurs to εἴκοσιν, even before a vowel.

ments. Thus in Mark i. 21 *καφαρναούμ* is found in ℵBDΔ. 33. 69, Origen (*twice*), the Latin, Memphitic and Gothic (*but not the Syriac:* ܟܦܪܢܚܘܡ) versions, and, from the facility of its becoming softened by copyists, this may be preferred to *καπερναοὺμ* of AC and the great numerical majority: yet we see PL with C in Matth. iv. 13, where Z sides with BD. In other instances the practice varies, even in the same manuscript, or in different parts of the N. T. Tischendorf, for example, decides that we ought always to read *ναζαρὲθ* in St Matthew, *ναζαρὲτ* in St John (*Proleg. N. T.* p. lv, note): yet the Peshito in all twelve places that the name occurs, and the Curetonian in the four wherein it is extant (Matth. ii. 23; iv. 13; xxi. 11; Luke ii. 51) have the aspirate (ܢܨܪܬ), and being written in a kindred dialect, claim all the more consideration. Everywhere the manuscripts vary considerably: thus in Mark i. 9 *ναζαρὲτ* is found in ℵBLΓΔ. 33, 69, and most cursives (17 of Scrivener's), Origen, the Philoxenian Syriac and Old Latin *a.b.f:* Ναζαρὰτ in AP: but *ναζαρὲθ* in D (not its Latin version, *d*) EFHKMUV. 1, and at least 16 other cursives (but not Cod. 69 by the first hand, as Tregelles states), the Vulgate, *c*, the Memphitic and Gothic as well as the elder Syriac. In Matth. iv. 13 Cod. B has *Ναζαρα* by the first hand with Z. 33 (so Ξ in Luke iv. 16); CPΔ *Ναζαραθ*, which is found in Δ nine times, in A twice: so that regarding the orthography of this word (which is inconstant also in the Received text, *see* p. 310) no reasonable certainty is to be attained. For *Μαθθαιος*, again (the variation from the common form *Ματθαῖος* adopted by Lachmann, Tischendorf, and Tregelles), the authority is but slender, nor is the internal probability great: Codd. ℵBΔ read the former in the title and headings to the first Gospel, while in the five places where it occurs in the text B (*primâ manu*) D have it always, ℵ three times (but *μαθθεος* Matth. x. 3, *ματθαιον* Mark iii. 18), the Thebaic and Gothic each twice: the Peshito and title of the Curetonian too (all that is extant) have ܡܬܝ. For Ἰωάνης the proof is yet weaker, for here Cod. B alone, and not quite consistently (e. g. Acts iii. 4, &c.) reads Ιωανης, Cod. ℵ Ιωαννης, while Cod. D fluctuates between the two.

6. Far more important than these are such variations in orthography as bear upon the dialect of the N. T. Its affinity to

the Septuagint is admitted on all hands, the degree of that affinity must depend on the influence we grant to certain very old manuscripts of the former, which abound in Alexandrian forms, for the most part absent in the great mass of codices. Such are the verbal terminations *-αμεν*, *-ατε*, *-αν* in the plural of the second aorist indicative, *-οσαν* for *-ον* in the plural imperfect or second aorist, *-ουσαν* for *-ουν*, *-αν* for *-ασι* of the perfect, *-άτω* for *-έτω*, *-ατο* for *-ετο*, *-άμενος* for *-όμενος*: in nouns the principal changes are *-αν* for *-α* in the accusative of the third declension, and (more rarely) the converse *-α* for *-αν* in the first[1]. We have conceded to these forms the name of Alexandrian, because it is probable that they actually derived their origin from that city, whose dialectic peculiarities the Septuagint had propagated among all Jews that spoke Greek; although some of them, if not the greater part, have been clearly traced to other regions; as for example *-αν* for *-ασι* to Western Asia Minor also and to Cilicia (Scholz, *Commentatio*, p. 9, notes w, x), occurring too in the Pseudo-Homeric *Batrachomyomachia* (ἐπεὶ κακὰ πολλά μ' ἔοργαν, v. 179). Now when we come to examine our manuscripts closely, we find the forms we have enumerated not quite banished from the most recent, but appearing far more frequent in such copies as ABC (*especially* D) LZ than in those of lower date: so far as it is yet known, Cod. ℵ seems to contain fewer than some others. It has been usual to ascribe such anomalous (or, at all events, unclassical) inflexions to the circumstance that the first-rate codices were written in Egypt; but an assumption which might be plausible in the case of two or three is improbable as regards them all (*see* pp. 84, 93, 96); it will not apply at all to those Greek-Latin manuscripts which must have been made in the West, or to the cursives in which such forms are sparsely met with, but which were certainly not copied from *surviving* uncials[2]. Thus

[1] These last might be supposed to have originated from the omission or insertion of the faint line for ν over the preceding letter, which (especially at the end of a line) we stated in p. 43 to be found, even in the oldest manuscripts. Sometimes the anomalous form is much supported by junior as well as by ancient codices: e.g. *θυγατέραν*, Luke xiii. 16 KXΓ*Λ 209, 69, and ten others of Scrivener's.

[2] Tregelles presses yet another argument: "If Alexandrian forms had been introduced into the N. T. by Egyptian copyists, how comes it that the classical MSS. written in that country are free from them?" (*Account of Printed Text*,

we seem led to the conclusion that the older documents retained these irregularities, because they were found in *their* prototypes, the copies first taken from the sacred originals: that some of them were in all likelihood the production of the skilful scribes of Alexandria, though their exhibiting these forms does not prove the fact, or even render it very probable: and that the sacred penmen, some more than others, but all to some extent, were influenced by their recollections and habitual use of the Septuagint version. Our practical inference from the whole discussion will be, *not* that Alexandrian inflexions should be invariably or even usually received into the text, as some recent editors have been inclined to do, but that they should be judged separately in every case on their merits and the support adduced in their behalf; and be held entitled to no other indulgence than that a lower degree of evidence will suffice for them than when the sense is affected, inasmuch as idiosyncrasies in spelling are of all others the most liable to be gradually and progressively modernised even by faithful and pains-taking transcribers.

7. The same remarks will obviously apply to those other dialectic forms, which, having been once peculiar to some one race of the great Greek family, had in the Apostles' time spread themselves throughout the Greek colonies of Asia and Africa, and become incorporated into the common speech, if they did not enter into the cultivated literary style, of the whole nation. Such are the reputed Dorisms ὀδυνᾶσαι Luke xvi. 25, καυχᾶσαι Rom. ii. 17, 1 Cor. iv. 7, of the Received text, with no *real* variation in any known manuscript: all such examples must stand or fall on their own proper grounds of *external* evidence, the internal, so far as it ought to go, being clearly in their favour. Like to them are the Ionisms μαχαίρῃ Luke xxii. 49 (B*DLT *only*); συνειδυίης Act. v. 2 (AB*E *only:* συνιδυης ℵ); σπείρης *ibid.* xxvii. 1, of the common text, where the only authorities for the more familiar σπείρας seem to be Chrysostom, the cursives 36. 39, and Scrivener's begho. To this class belong such changes of conjugation as κατεγέλουν Mark v. 40 in

p. 178). But what classical MSS. does he know of, written while Egypt was yet Greek or Christian, and now extant for our inspection? I can only think of Cureton's Homer and Babington's papyri.

Kc[scr]. 238. 447; or *vice versâ*, as ἀγανακτῶντες Cod. 69, in Mark xiv. 4.

8. One caution seems called for in this matter, at least if we may judge from the practice of certain critics of high and merited fame. The sacred penmen may have adopted orthographical forms from the dialect of the Septuagint, or the debased diction of common life, but they did not, and *could* not, write what was merely inaccurate or barbarous. Hence repudiate, in St Paul especially, expressions like Tischendorf's ἐφ' ἐλπίδι Rom. viii. 20, as simply incredible on any evidence. He may allege for it Codd. ℵB*D*FG, of which the last three are bilingual codices, the scribes of FG showing marvellous ignorance of Greek (*see* pp. 134, 137). That Codd. ℵB should countenance such a *monstrum* only enables us to accumulate one example the more of the fallibility of the very best documents (*see* p. 377, and Chap. IX, notes on 1 Cor. xiii. 3; Philipp. ii. 1; 1 Pet. i. 23); and to put in all seriousness the enquiry of Kuenen in some like instance: "Quot annorum Codex te impellet ut hoc credas?......ecquis est, cui *fides veterum membranarum* in tali re non admodum ridicula et inepta videatur?" (*N. T. Vatic.* Praef. p. xx). In the same way we utterly disregard the manuscripts which confound οὐχ with οὐκ, μέλλει with μέλει, sense with nonsense.

The reader has, we trust, been furnished with the leading principles on which it is conceived that dialectic peculiarities should be treated in revising the text of the N. T. It would have been out of place to have entered into a more detailed account of variations which will readily be met with (and must be carefully studied) in any good Grammar of the Greek New Testament.

CHAPTER IX.

APPLICATION OF THE FOREGOING MATERIALS AND PRINCIPLES TO THE CRITICISM OF SELECT PASSAGES OF THE NEW TESTAMENT.

IN applying to the revision of the sacred text the diplomatic materials and critical principles it has been the purpose of the preceding pages to describe; we have selected the few passages we have room to examine, chiefly in consideration of their actual importance, occasionally also with the design of illustrating by pertinent examples the canons of internal evidence and the laws of Comparative Criticism. It will be convenient to discuss these passages in the order they occupy in the volume of the New Testament: that which stands first affords a conspicuous instance of undue and misplaced *subjectivity* on the part of Tischendorf and Tregelles.

---

(1). MATTH. i. 18. Τοῦ δὲ Ἰησοῦ Χριστοῦ... is altered by these editors into Τοῦ δὲ Χριστοῦ, Ἰησοῦ being omitted. Michaelis had objected to the term τὸν Ἰησοῦν Χριστόν, Act. viii. 37 (see the verse examined below), on the ground that "In the time of the Apostles the word Christ was never used as the Proper Name of a Person, but as an epithet expressive of the ministry of Jesus;" and although Bp. Middleton has abundantly proved his statement incorrect (*Doctrine of the Greek Article*, note on Mark ix. 41), and Ἰησοῦς Χριστός, especially in some one of the oblique cases after prepositions, is very common, yet the precise form ὁ Ἰησοῦς Χριστὸς occurs only in these places and in 1 John iv. 3; Apoc. xii. 17, where again the reading is unsettled. Hence, apparently, the determination to change the common text in St Matthew, on evidence however slight. Now

Ἰησοῦ is omitted *in no Greek manuscript whatever*[1]. The Latin version of Cod. D (*d*) indeed rejects it, the parallel Greek being lost; but since *d* sometimes agrees with other Latin copies against its own Greek, it cannot be deemed quite certain that the Greek rejected it also. Cod. B reads τοῦ δὲ Χριστοῦ Ἰησοῦ, in support of which Lachmann cites Origen, III. 965 *d* in the Latin, but on very precarious grounds, as Tregelles (*Account of Printed Text*, p. 189, note †) candidly admits. Tischendorf quotes Cod. 74 (after Wetstein), the Persic (of the Polyglott and in manuscript), and Maximus *Dial. de Trinitate* for τοῦ δὲ ἰησοῦ. The real testimony in favour of τοῦ δὲ Χριστοῦ consists of the Old Latin copies *a. b. c. d. f. ff*[1], the Curetonian Syriac (I know not why Cureton should add "the Peshito"), the Latin Vulgate, the Frankish and Anglo-Saxon, Wheelocke's Persic, and Irenaeus in three places, "who (after having previously cited the words '*Christi autem generatio sic erat*') continues 'Ceterum potuerat dicere Matthaeus, *Jesu vero generatio sic erat;* sed praevidens Spiritus Sanctus depravatores, et praemuniens contra fraudulentiam eorum, per Matthaeum ait: *Christi autem generatio sic erat*' (C. H. Lib. III. 16. 2). This is given in proof that Jesus and Christ are one and the same person, and that Jesus cannot be said to be the receptacle that afterwards received Christ; for *the Christ was born*" (*Account of Printed Text*, p. 188). To this most meagre list of authorities Scholz adds, "Pseudo-Theophil. in Evang.," manuscripts of Theophylact, Augustine, and one or two of little account: but even in Irenaeus (Harvey, Vol. II. p. 48) τοῦ δὲ $\overline{\iota\upsilon}$ $\overline{\chi\upsilon}$ (*tacitè*) stands over against the Latin "Christi."

We do not deny the importance of Irenaeus' express testimony, had it been supported by something more trustworthy than the Old Latin versions and their constant associate, the Curetonian Syriac. On the other hand, all uncial and cursive codices (ℵCEKLMPSUVZΔ: ADFG &c. being defective here), the Peshito and Philoxenian Syriac, the Thebaic, Memphitic, Armenian, and Æthiopic versions, Origen (in the Greek) and Eusebius, comprise a body of proof, not to be shaken by subjective notions or even by Western evidence from the second century downwards.

[1] I know not why Tischendorf cites Cod. 71 (g^{scr}) for the omission of Ἰησοῦ. Neither Traheron nor I note that variation.

(2). MATTH. vi. 13: ὅτι σου ἐστιν ἡ βασιλεία καὶ ἡ δύναμις καὶ ἡ δόξα εἰς τοὺς αἰῶνας. ἀμήν (*see* p. 8). It is right to say that I can no longer regard this doxology as *certainly* an integral part of St Matthew's Gospel: but I am just as little convinced of its spuriousness. It is wanting in the oldest uncials extant, ℵBDZ, and since ACP (whose general character would lead us to look for support to the Received text in such a case) are unfortunately deficient here, the burden of the defence is thrown on the later uncials EGKLMSUVΔ, whereof L is conspicuous for usually siding with B. Of the cursives only *five* are known to omit the clause, 1. 17 (*habet* ἀμήν). 118. 130. 209, but h^scr (and as it it would seem some others) has it obelized in the margin, while the scholia in certain other copies indicate that it is doubtful: even 33 contains it, 69 being defective: 157. 225 add to δόξα, τοῦ πατρὸς καὶ τοῦ υἱοῦ καὶ τοῦ ἁγίου πνεύματος. Versions have much influence on such a question, it is therefore important to notice that it is found in all the four Syriac (Cureton's omitting καὶ ἡ δύναμις, and some editions of the Peshito ἀμήν, which is in *at least* one manuscript), the Thebaic (omitting καὶ ἡ δόξα), the Æthiopic, Armenian, Gothic, Slavonic, Georgian, Erpenius' Arabic, the Persic of the Polyglott from Pococke's manuscript, the margin of some Memphitic codices, the Old Latin *k* (quoniam est tibi virtus in saecula saeculorum) *f*. g^1 (?). The doxology is not found in most Memphitic and Arabic manuscripts or editions, in Wheelocke's Persic, in the Old Latin *a*. *b*. *c*. ff^1. *h*. *l*., in the Vulgate or its satellites the Anglo-Saxon and Frankish (the Clementine Vulg. and Sax. add *amen*). Its absence from the Latin avowedly caused the editors of the Complutensian N. T. to pass it over (*see* p. 349 note), though it was found in their Greek copies: the earliest Latin Fathers naturally did not cite what the Latin codices for the most part do not contain. Among the Greeks it is met with in Isidore of Pelusium (412), and in the Pseudo-Apostolic Constitutions, probably of the fourth century: soon afterwards Chrysostom (*Hom. in Matth.* xix. Vol. I. p. 283, Field) comments upon it without showing the least consciousness that its authenticity was disputed. The silence of earlier writers, as Origen and Cyril of Jerusalem, especially when expounding the Lord's Prayer, may be partly accounted for on the supposition that the doxology was regarded not so much a portion of the prayer itself, as a hymn of praise annexed to it; yet this fact is so far unfavourable to its genuineness, and would be fatal unless we knew the precariousness of any argument derived from such silence. The Fathers are constantly overlooking the most obvious citations from Scripture, even where we should expect them most, although, as we learn from other passages in their writings, they were perfectly familiar with them. Internal evidence is not unevenly balanced. It is probable that the doxology was interpolated from the Liturgies, and the variation of reading renders this all the more likely; it is just as probable that it was cast out of St Matthew's Gospel to bring it into harmony with St Luke's (xi. 4): I cannot concede to Scholz and Alford that it is "in interruption of the context," for then the whole of v. 13 would have to be cancelled (a remedy which no one proposes), and not merely this concluding part of it.

It is vain to dissemble the pressure of the adverse case, though it ought not to be looked upon as conclusive. The Syriac and Thebaic versions bring up the existence of the doxology to the second century; Isidore, Chrysostom and perhaps others[1] attest for it in the fourth; then come the Latin codices *f. k*, the Gothic, the Armenian, the Æthiopic, and lastly the whole flood-tide of Greek manuscripts from the eighth century downwards, including even L. 33. Perhaps it is not very wise "*quaerere quae habere non possumus*," yet those who are persuaded, from the well-ascertained affinities subsisting between them, that ACP, or at least two out of the three, would have preserved a reading sanctioned by the Peshito, by Cod. *f*, by Chrysostom, and nearly all the later documents, may be excused for regarding the indictment against the last clause of the Lord's Prayer as hitherto *unproven*.

(3). MATTH. xix. 17 (*see* p. 16). For *Τί με λέγεις ἀγαθόν; οὐδεὶς ἀγαθός, εἰ μὴ εἷς, ὁ Θεός*, Griesbach, Lachmann, Tis-

[1] Why should Gregory Nyssen (371) be classed among the opponents of the clause, whereas Griesbach honestly states, "suam expositionem his quidem verbis concludit: *χάριτι χριστοῦ, ὅτι αὐτοῦ ἡ δύναμις καὶ ἡ δόξα ἅμα τῷ πατρὶ καὶ τῷ ἁγίῳ πνεύματι, νῦν καὶ ἀεὶ καὶ εἰς τοὺς αἰῶνας τῶν αἰώνων, ἀμήν*"? He adds indeed, "sed pro parte sacri textûs neutiquam haec habuisse videtur;" and justly: they were rather a *loose paraphrase* of the sentence before him. Euthymius Zigabenus, who calls the doxology *τὸ παρὰ τῶν θείων φωστήρων καὶ τῆς ἐκκλησίας καθηγητῶν προστεθὲν ἀκροτελεύτιον ἐπιφώνημα*, lived in the twelfth century, and must be estimated accordingly.

chendorf, Tregelles and Alford read Τί με ἐρωτᾷς περὶ τοῦ ἀγαθοῦ; εἷς ἐστὶν ὁ ἀγαθός. The self-same words as in the Received text occur in the parallel places Mark x. 18, Luke xviii. 19 with no variation worth speaking of; a fact which (so far as it goes) certainly lends support to the supposition that St Matthew's autograph contained the other reading: *see* p. 11 (9). Add to this that any change made from St Matthew, *supposing the common reading to be true*, must have been wilfully introduced by one who was offended at the doctrine of the Divine Son's inferiority to the Father which it seemed to assert or imply. Internal evidence, therefore, would be in favour of the alteration approved by Lachmann, Tischendorf, and the rest; and in discussing external authority, their opponents are much hampered by the accident that not more than three first-class uncials can be cited in this place, A being defective and ℵ as yet unknown, though one is disposed to think, *partly from its general character*, partly from Tischendorf's silence in the *Notitia Cod. Sinaitici*, that it does not uphold his view of the question. Under these circumstances we might have been excused from noticing this passage until the evidence of ℵ shall be ascertained, but that it seemed dishonest to suppress a case on which Tregelles (*Account of Printed Text*, pp. 133—8) has laid great stress, and which, when the drift of the internal evidence is duly allowed for, tells more in his favour than any other he has yet alleged, or is likely to meet with elsewhere.

The alternative reading Τί με ἐρωτᾷς περὶ τοῦ ἀγαθοῦ κ.τ.λ. occurs in BD (omitting τοῦ and ὁ) L. 1 (omitting ὁ). 22. In 251 both readings are given, the received one first, in v. 17, the other interpolated after ποίας v. 18, prefaced by ὁ δὲ ἰησοῦς εἶπεν αὐτῷ. Excepting these six all other extant codices reject it, CEFGHKMSUVΔ (omitting λέγεις), even 33. 69. The versions are more seriously divided. The Peshito Syriac, the Philoxenian text, the Thebaic (*Oxford* fragments), the Old Latin *f*, the Arabic, &c. make for the common reading; Cureton's and the Jerusalem Syriac, the Old Latin *a. b. c. e. ff*$^{1.2}$. *l*, the Vulgate (the Anglo-Saxon and Frankish, of course), Memphitic and Armenian for that of Lachmann, &c. Several present a mixed form: τί με ἐρωτᾷς περὶ τοῦ ἀγαθοῦ; οὐδεὶς ἀγαθὸς εἰ μὴ εἷς: viz. the margin of the Philoxenian, the Æthiopic, and *g*^{1}. *h. m* of the Old Latin. A few (Cureton's Syriac, *b. c. ff*^{2}. *g*^{1}.

h. l. m, and the Vulgate) add ὁ θεός, as in the common text; but this is unimportant.

Tregelles presses us hard with the testimony of Origen in favour of the reading he adopts: *ὁ μὲν οὖν Ματθαῖος, ὡς περὶ ἀγαθοῦ ἔργου ἐρωτηθέντος τοῦ σωτῆρος ἐν τῷ, Τί ἀγαθὸν ποιήσω; ἀνέγραψεν. Ὁ δὲ Μάρκος καὶ Λουκᾶς φασι τὸν σωτῆρα εἰρηκέναι, Τί με λέγεις ἀγαθόν; οὐδεὶς ἀγαθός, εἰ μὴ εἷς, ὁ Θεός* (Tom. III. p. 664 *d*). "The reading which is *opposed* to the common text," he writes, "has the express testimony of Origen in its favour" (p. 134); "might I not well ask for some *proof* that the other reading existed, in the time of Origen, in copies of St Matthew's Gospel?" (p. 137). I may say in answer, that the testimony of Origen applies indeed to the former part of the variation which Tregelles maintains (*τί με ἐρωτᾷς περὶ τοῦ ἀγαθοῦ*), but not at all to the latter (*εἷς ἐστιν ὁ ἀγαθός*), and that the Peshito Syriac version of the second, as also the Thebaic of the third century, uphold the common text, without any variation in the manuscripts of the former, that we know of[1]. Or if he asks for the evidence of Fathers to counterbalance that of a Father, we have Justin Martyr: *προσελθόντος αὐτῷ τινος καὶ εἰπόντος* (words which shew, as Tischendorf observes, that St Matthew's is the only Gospel that can be referred to) *Διδάσκαλε ἀγαθέ, ἀπεκρίνατο λέγων, Οὐδεὶς ἀγαθὸς εἰ μὴ μόνος ὁ Θεὸς ὁ ποιήσας τὰ πάντα*, citing loosely, as usual, but not ambiguously. Or if *half* the variation will satisfy, as it did for Origen, Tregelles' own note refers us to Irenaeus 92 for *τί με λέγεις ἀγαθόν; εἷς ἐστὶν ἀγαθός*, and to Eusebius for the other half in the form quoted above from the Æthiopic, &c. Moreover, since he cites the last five words of the subjoined extract *as belonging to St Matthew*, Tregelles entitles us to employ for our purpose the whole passage *Marcosiorum ap. Iren.* 92, which we might not otherwise have ventured to do: *καὶ τῷ εἰπόντι αὐτῷ Διδάσκαλε ἀγαθέ, τὸν ἀληθῶς ἀγαθὸν θεὸν ὡμολογηκέναι, εἰπόντα Τί με λέγεις ἀγαθόν; εἷς ἐστιν ἀγαθός, ὁ πατὴρ ἐν τοῖς οὐρανοῖς.* Jerome and Augustine (for the first clause only: *de Consensu Evan.* II. 63) are with

[1] "Yes," says Tregelles, "the Peshito Syriac, *as it has come down to us*" (p. 136). We might as well disparage the opposing testimony of Origen by rejoining, "Origen, in all *extant* manuscripts and editions." I know no other cause for suspecting the Peshito than that its readings do not suit Dr Tregelles, and if this fact be enough to convict it of corruption, I am quite unable to vindicate it.

the Latin Vulgate, Hilary with the common Greek text, as are also Optatus (fl. 370), Ambrose, Chrysostom, and the main body of later Fathers. Thus the great mass of manuscripts, headed by C, is well supported by versions, and even better by ecclesiastical writers; yet, in virtue of the weight of internal evidence, we would not hold out against the reading of BDL, &c., if Cod. ℵ shall be found to agree with them.

(4). MATTH. xx. 28. The extensive interpolation which follows this verse in some very ancient documents has been given above, p. 8, in the form represented in the Curetonian Syriac version. It bears the internal marks of evident spuriousness, the first sentence consisting of a rhetorical antithesis as unsuitable as can be imagined to the majestic simplicity of our Lord's usual tone, while the sentiment of the rest is manifestly borrowed from Luke xiv. 8—10, although there is little or no resemblance in the words. The only extant Greek for the passage is in Cod. D: *υμεις δε ζητειτε εκ μεικρου αυξησαι και εκ μειζονος ελαττον ειναι· εισερχομενοι δε καὶ παρακληθεντες δειπνησαι μη ανακλεινεσθαι εις τους εξεχοντας τοπους μη ποτε ενδοξοτερος σου επελθη και προσελθων ο δειπνοκλητωρ ειπη σοι ετι κατω χωρει και καταισχυνθηση· εαν δε αναπεσης εις τον ηττονα τοπον και επελθη σου ηττων ερει σοι ο δειπνοκλητωρ συναγε ετι ανω· και εσται σοι τουτο χρησιμον.* The codices of the Old Latin version (*a. b. c. e. ff*$^{1.2}$. *h. n.* and *em.* of the Vulgate) mostly support the same addition, though with many variations: *d*, as usual, agrees with none (*see* p. 266); *g*^{2} has not the first sentence, while *g*^{1}. *m* have nothing else. Besides the Curetonian Syriac the margin of the Philoxenian contains it, in a shape much like *d*, noting that the paragraph is "found in Greek copies in this place, but in ancient copies only in St Luke, *κεφ*. 53" [ch. xiv. 8, &c.]: Cureton has also seen it in one manuscript of the Peshito (Brit. Mus. 14,456), but there too in the margin. Marshall states that it is contained in four codices of the Anglo-Saxon version (*see* p. 280), which proves its wide reception in the West. Of the Fathers, Hilary recognises it, as apparently do Juvencus and Pope Leo the Great (440—461). It was rejected by Jerome, being entirely absent from all Vulgate codices but *and. em.*, nor is it in the Old Latin *f. l.* No other Greek codex, or version, or ecclesiastical writer has any knowledge of the passage: while the whole wording of the Greek of Cod. D, especially such words as δειπνοκλήτωρ, ἐξέχοντας, ἥττων, χρήσιμος is so foreign to the style of St Matthew's Gospel, that it seems rather to have been rendered from the Latin[1], although in the midst of so much variation it is hard to say from what copy. Cureton too testifies that the Syriac of the version named from him must have been made quite independently of that in the margins of the Philoxenian and Peshito.

No one that I know of has ventured to regard this paragraph as genuine, however perplexing it may be to decide at what period or even in what language it originated. The wide divergencies between the witnesses must always dismiss it from serious consideration. Its chief critical use must be to shew that the united testimony of the Old Latin, of the Curetonian Syriac, and Cod. D are quite insufficient in themselves to prove any more than that the reading they exhibit is ancient: as ancient probably as the second century.

(5). MATTH. xxi. 28—31. This passage, so transparently clear in the common text, stands thus in the edition of Tregelles: (28) Τί δὲ ὑμῖν δοκεῖ; ἄνθρωπος εἶχεν τέκνα δύο, καὶ προσελθὼν τῷ πρώτῳ εἶπεν, Τέκνον, ὕπαγε σήμερον ἐργάζου ἐν τῷ ἀμπελῶνι. (29) ὁ δὲ ἀποκριθεὶς εἶπεν, Οὐ θέλω· ὕστερον δὲ μεταμεληθεὶς ἀπῆλθεν. (30) προσελθὼν δὲ τῷ δευτέρῳ εἶπεν ὡσαύτως. ὁ δὲ ἀποκριθεὶς εἶπεν, Ἐγώ, κύριε· καὶ οὐκ ἀπῆλθεν. (31) τίς ἐκ τῶν δύο ἐποίησεν τὸ θέλημα τοῦ πατρός; λέγουσιν, ὁ ὕστερος. This is indeed a brilliant exemplification of Bengel's Canon (*above*, p. 371) "Proclivi scriptioni praestat ardua." Lachmann in 1842 had given the same reading, with a few slight and unimportant exceptions. The question is proposed which of the two sons did their father's will; the reply is ὁ ὕστερος, the one that promised and then failed! Lachmann in 1850 (*N. T.* Vol. II. *Praef.* p. 5)

[1] No passage more favours Bp. Middleton's deliberate conclusion respecting the history of the Codex Bezae: "I believe that no fraud was intended: but only that the critical possessor of the basis filled its margin with glosses and readings chiefly from the Latin, being a Christian of the Western Church; and that the whole collection of Latin passages was translated into Greek, and substituted in the text by some one who had a high opinion of their value, and who was, as Wetstein describes him, "καλλιγραφίας quàm vel Graecae vel Latinae linguae peritior." (*Doctrine of the Greek Article, Appendix* I. p. 485, 3rd edition.)

remarks that had he been sure that πρῶτος (v. 31) was the reading of Cod. C, he should have honoured it, *the only word that makes sense*, with a place in his margin: "Nihilo minus," he naïvely adds, "id quod nunc solum edidi...ὁ ὕστερος veri similius est altero, quod facile aliquis correctori adscribat, illud non item;" and we must fairly confess that no copyist *would* have sought to introduce a plain absurdity into so beautiful and simple a parable. "Quid vero," he goes on to plead, "si id quod veri similius esse dixi ne intellegi quidem potest?" (a pertinent question certainly) "CORRIGETUR, SI MODO NECESSE ERIT:" critical conjecture, as usual, is his panacea (*see* p. 343). Conjecture, however, is justly held inadmissible by Tregelles, whose mode of interpretation is a curiosity in its way. "I believe," he says, "that ὁ ὕστερος refers not to the order in which the two sons have been mentioned, but to the previous expression about the elder son, ὕστερον δὲ μεταμεληθεὶς ἀπῆλθεν, "*afterwards* he repented and went." "Which of the two did his father's will?" ὁ ὕστερος. *He who afterwards* [repented and went]. This answers the charge that the reading of Lachmann is void of sense" (*Account of Printed Text*, p. 107). I entertain deep respect for the character and services of Dr Tregelles, but it is only right to assert at once that what stands in his text is impossible Greek. Even granting that instead of the plain answer "the first," our Lord's adversaries resorted to the harsh and equivocal reply "he who afterwards," they would not have said ὁ ὕστερος, but ὁ ὕστερον, or (the better to point out their reference to ὕστερον in v. 29) ὁ τὸ ὕστερον.

Why then prefer nonsense, for the mere purpose of carrying out Bengel's canon to the extremity? The passage, precisely as it stands in Tregelles' N. T., *is sanctioned by no critical authority whatsoever*. Cod. B indeed has ὕστερος, Cod. 4 δεύτερος, Codd. 13. 69. 124. 238. 262. 346 and perhaps others ἔσχατος, one or other of which is in the Jerusalem Syriac and Memphitic, Æthiopic (two manuscripts) and Armenian versions; but all these authorities transpose the order of the two sons in vv. 29, 30, so that the result is just the same as in the Received text. The suggestion that the clauses were transferred in order to reconcile ὕστερος or ἔσχατος with the context may be met by the counter-statement that ὕστερος was just as likely to be substituted for πρῶτος to suit the inversion of the clauses.

Against such inversion (which we do not pretend to recommend) Origen is an early witness, so that Cod. B and its allies are no doubt wrong: yet as that Father does not notice any difficulty in v. 31, the necessary inference must be that he read πρῶτος. Hippolytus testifies to ἔσχατος in v. 31, but his evidence cannot be used as he gives no indication in what order he took the clauses in vv. 29, 30. The indefensible part of Tregelles' arrangement is that, allowing the answers of the two sons to stand as in our common Bibles, he receives ὕστερος for πρῶτος on evidence that really tells against him. The only true supporters of his general view are Cod. D αἴσχατος (i. e. ἔσχατος), the Old Latin copies *a. b. e. ff*$^{1.2}$. *g*^{1}. *h. l.*, and the best codices of the Vulgate (*am. fuld. for. tol. harl.**) though not the Clementine edition. Hilary perplexes himself by trying to explain the same reading; and Jerome, although he says "Sciendum est in veris exemplaribus non haberi *novissimum* sed *primum*," has an expedient to account for the former[1], which (if *am. fuld.* &c. may be trusted) he did not venture to reject when revising the Old Latin (see p. 261). On no true principles can Cod. D and its Latin allies avail against such a mass of opposing proof, to which Cod. ℵ (πρῶτος) may now be added: even the Curetonian Syriac, which so often favours Cod. D and the Old Latin, is with the textus receptus here.

(6). MATTH. xxvii. 35. After βάλλοντες κλῆρον the Received text, but not the Complutensian edition, has ἵνα πληρωθῇ τὸ ῥηθὲν ὑπὸ τοῦ προφήτου, Διεμερίσαντο τὰ ἱμάτιά μου ἑαυτοῖς καὶ ἐπὶ τὸν ἱματισμόν μου ἔβαλον κλῆρον. Internal evidence may be about equal for the omission of the clause by ὁμοιοτέλευτον of κλῆρον, and for its interpolation from John xix. 24, "with just the phrase τὸ ῥηθὲν ὑπὸ (or ἀπὸ) τοῦ προφήτου assimilated to Matthew's usual form of citation" (*Alford*, ad loc.). External evidence, however, places the spuriousness of the addition beyond doubt. It is first heard of in citations of Eusebius and Athanasius, and is read in the Old Latin codices *a. b. c. g*^{2}. *h.*,

[1] Jerome conceives that the Jews "intelligere quidem veritatem, sed tergiversari, et nolle dicere quod sentiunt;" but of this wilful stubbornness we find no traces in our Lord's rejoinder Ἀμὴν λέγω ὑμῖν ὅτι οἱ τελῶναι κ.τ.λ. Hilary's idea is even more far-fetched: viz. that though the second son disobeyed, it was because he *could* not execute the command. "Non ait noluisse sed non abisse. Res extra culpam infidelitatis est, quia in facti erat difficultate ne fieret."

the Clementine (not the Sixtine) Vulgate and even *am. lux.* (but not *fuld. for. tol*. ing. em.*, nor in *f. ff*$^{1.2}$ *g*^{1}*. l*), the Armenian (whose resemblance to the Vulgate is so suspicious), the Frankish and Anglo-Saxon, and as a matter of course in the Roman edition of the Arabic (*see* p. 282), and the Persic of the Polyglott (*see* p. 281). The clause seems to be found in no manuscript of the Peshito Syriac, and is consequently absent from Widmanstadt's edition and the Antwerp, Paris and London Polyglotts (*see* pp. 232—4). Tremellius first turned the Greek words into Syriac and placed them in the margin of his book, whence they were most unwisely admitted into the text of several later editions (but not Lee's), without the slightest authority. They also appear in the text of the Philoxenian, but the marginal note (*see* p. 242) states that "this passage from the prophet is not in two ["three" *Codd. Assemani*] Greek copies, nor in the ancient Syriac." All other versions and Fathers, and all Greek manuscripts (including ℵ, if we may judge by Tischendorf's silence) reject the clause, except Δ. 1. 17 (*see* p. 144). 61. 69. 118. 124. 262. 300. Evst. 55: Scholz adds "aliis multis" which (judging from my own experience) I must take leave to doubt(*see* p. 67). Besides other slight changes (*αυτοις* Δ, *κλήρους* 69 *secundâ manu*) Codd. Δ. 61. 69. and Eusebius read *διὰ* for *ὑπό*. The present case is one out of many that show an intimate connexion (*see* p. 149) subsisting between 61 and 69.

(7). MARK xvi. 9—20. In Chapter I. we engaged to defend the authenticity of this long and important paragraph, and that "without the slightest misgiving" (p. 7). The authority of Cod. ℵ has since been thrown into the opposite scale, yet we see no cause for altering our judgment, though it may be proper to speak with less confidence. The twelve concluding verses of this Gospel are still found in every Greek manuscript except the two oldest. Cod. B, however, betrays consciousness on the scribe's part that something is left out, inasmuch as after *ἐφοβοῦντο γάρ* v. 8, a whole column is left perfectly blank (*the only blank one in the whole volume*), as well as the rest of the column containing v. 8, which is usual at the end of every book of Scripture (*see* p. 87). It will be interesting to see whether the same peculiarity attaches to Cod. ℵ. The testimony of L, that close companion of B, is very suggestive. Immediately after v. 8

the copyist breaks off, then in the same hand (for all corrections in this manuscript seem *primâ manu:* see p. 109), at the top of the next column we read...*φερετε που και ταυτα...παντα δε τα παρηγγελμενα τοις περι τον πετρον συντομωσ εξηγγιλαν μετα δε ταυτα και αυτος ο ισ, απο ανατολησ και αχρι δυσεωσ εξαπεστιλεν δι αυτων το ιερον και αφθαρτον κηρυγμα—τησ αιωνιου σωτηριασ......εστην δε και ταυτα φερομενα μετα το εφοβουντο γαρ... Αναστασ δε πρωι κ.τ.λ.*, v. 9, *ad fin. capit.* (Tischendorf, *facsimile* in *Monum. sacr. ined.*) : as if vv. 9—12 were just as little to be regarded as the trifling apocryphal supplement which precedes them. Beside these the twelve verses are omitted in none but some old Armenian codices, *k* of the Latin, and an Arabic Lectionary [IX] No. 13, examined by Scholz in the Vatican. The Old Latin codex *k* puts in their room a corrupt and careless version of the subscription in L ending with *σωτηρίας* (*k* adding *amen*) : the same subscription being appended to the end of the Gospel in two Æthiopic manuscripts, and (with *ἀμήν*) in the margin of 274 and the Philoxenian. Of cursive Greek manuscripts 137. 138 and *possibly* more have the passage noted by an asterisk; others contain marginal scholia respecting it, of which the following is the substance. Codd. 20. 300 mark the omission in some copies, adding *ἐν δὲ τοῖς ἀρχαίοις πάντα ἀπαράλειπτα κεῖται*: 22 concludes at *ἐφοβοῦντο γάρ*, then adds in red ink that in some copies the Evangelist ends here, *ἐν πολλοῖς δὲ καὶ ταῦτα φέρεται*, affixing vv. 9—12: in Codd. 1. 206. 209 is the same notice, *ἄλλοις* standing for *πολλοῖς* in 206, with the additional assertion that Eusebius "canonised" no further than v. 8, a statement which is confirmed by the absence of the Ammonian and Eusebian numerals beyond that verse in ALUΓΔ and at least eleven cursives, with *am. fuld. ing.* of the Vulgate. Codd. 23. 34. 39. 41 cite a note of Severus of Antioch [VI] importing that the most accurate copies end with v. 8, while some go on *ἀναστὰς δὲ κ. τ. λ.*, "*but this seems to contain some contradiction* (*ἐναντίωσιν τινα*) *with what precedes.*" Cod. 24 (and 374 to much the same effect) gives weighty testimony in favour of the passage: *παρὰ πλείστοις ἀντιγράφοις οὐ κεῖνται ἐν τῷ παρόντι εὐαγγελίῳ, ὡς νόθα νομίσαντες αὐτὰ εἶναι· ἀλλ' ἡμεῖς ἐξ ἀκριβῶν ἀντιγράφων ἐν πλείστοις εὑρόντες αὐτὰ καὶ κατὰ τὸ παλαιστιναῖον εὐαγγέλιον ὡς ἔχει ἡ ἀλήθεια Μάρκου* (*sic*) *συντεθείκαμεν καὶ τὴν ἐν αὐτῷ ἐπιφερομένην δεσποτικὴν ἀνάστασιν.* There can be little question that the writer of 24 [XI] copied his scholion from the older manuscript which lay before him, and that the elder scribe had ascertained the authenticity of the disputed verses by consulting the famous Palestine codices which had belonged to Origen and Pamphilus (*see* pp. 47, 388), or possibly the Jerusalem copies mentioned in Codd. Evan. Λ. 164. 262, &c. (*see* pp. 125 note, 168). Scholia similar to one or other of the preceding occur in 36—38. 40. 108. 129. 143. 181. 186. 195. 199. 210. 221. 222. *All* other codices, e.g. ACD (which is defective from v. 15, *primâ manu*) EF^{w}GH (begins v. 14) KMSUVXΓΔ. 33. 69, the Peshito, Jerusalem and Curetonian Syriac (which by a singular happiness contains vv. 17—20, though no other part of St Mark), the Philoxenian *text*, the Sahidic (only v. 20 is preserved), Memphitic, Æthiopic, Gothic (to v. 12), Vulgate, all extant Old Latin except *k* (though *a primâ manu* and *b* are defective), the printed Armenian, its later manuscripts, and all the lesser versions (Arabic, &c.) agree in maintaining the paragraph. It is cited by Irenaeus (both in Greek and Latin) and perhaps by Justin Martyr as early as the second century, by Hippolytus (see Tregelles, *Account of Printed Text*, p. 252), and apparently by Celsus in the third, by Cyril of Jerusalem, Ambrose, Augustine, &c. in the fourth.

The earliest objector to *vv.* 9—12 we know of was Eusebius (*Quaest. ad Marin.*), who tells us that they were not ἐν ἅπασι τοῖς ἀντιγράφοις, but after ἐφοβοῦντο γάρ that τὰ ἑξῆς are found σπανίως ἔν τισιν, but not in τὰ ἀκριβῆ: language which Jerome (*see* p. 390) *twice* echoes and almost exaggerates by saying "in raris fertur Evangeliis, omnibus Graeciae libris paene hoc capitulum fine non habentibus." A second cause with Eusebius for rejecting them (the same as Severus pleaded above) is μάλιστα εἴπερ ἔχοιεν ἀντιλογίαν τῇ τῶν λοιπῶν εὐαγγελιστῶν μαρτυρίᾳ. Gregory Nyssen (?) and Victor of Antioch deem the verses spurious; Euthymius mentions an opinion that they were an addition, προσθήκην.

With regard to the argument against these twelve verses arising from their alleged difference in style from the rest of the Gospel, I must say that the same process might be applied—and has been applied—to prove that St Paul was not the writer of the Pastoral Epistles (to say nothing of that to the Hebrews), St John of the Apocalypse, Isaiah and Zechariah of portions of those prophecies that bear their names. Every one used to literary composition may detect, if he will, such minute variations as have been dwelt upon[1], either in his own writings or in those of the authors he is most familiar with.

Persons who, like Eusebius, devoted themselves to the pious task of constructing harmonies of the Gospels, would soon perceive the difficulty of accommodating the events recorded in vv. 9—20 with the narratives of the other Evangelists. Alford regards this inconsistency (more apparent than real, we believe) as "a valuable testimony to the antiquity of the fragment" (*N. T. ad loc.*): we would go further, and claim for the harder reading the benefit of any critical doubt as to its genuineness (Canon I. p. 371). The difficulty was both felt and avowed by Eusebius and after him by Severus of Antioch: whatever Jerome and the rest may have done, these two assigned the ἀντιλογία, the ἐναντίωσις they thought they perceived, as a reason (not the first, nor perhaps the chief, but as *a* reason) for supposing that the Gospel ended with ἐφοβοῦντο γάρ. Yet in the balance of probabilities, can anything be more unlikely than that St Mark broke off so abruptly as this notion would imply, while no ancient writer has noticed or seemed conscious of any such abruptness? This fact has driven those who reject the concluding verses to the strangest fancies;—that like Thucydides the Evangelist was cut off before his work was completed, or even (I tremble while copying the words, and I would not draw them forth from the obscurity of an unknown book) "*that the last leaf of the original Gospel* was *torn away*."

We emphatically deny that such wild surmises are called for by the state of the evidence in this case. All opposition to the authenticity of the paragraph resolves itself into the allegations of Eusebius and the testimony of אB. Let us accord to these the weight which is their due: but against their verdict we can appeal to the reading of Irenaeus and of *both* the elder Syriac translations in the second century; of nearly all other versions; and of all extant manuscripts excepting two.

[1] The following peculiarities have been noticed in these verses: ἐκεῖνος used absolutely, *vv.* 10, 11, 13; πορεύομαι *vv.* 10, 12, 15; τοῖς μετ' αὐτοῦ γενομένοις *v.* 10; θεάομαι *vv.* 11, 14; ἀπιστέω *vv.* 11, 16; μετὰ ταῦτα *v.* 12: ἕτερος *v.* 12; παρακολουθέω *v.* 17; ἐν τῷ ὀνόματι *v.* 17; κύριος for the Saviour, *vv.* 19, 20; πανταχοῦ, συνεργοῦντος, βεβαιόω, ἐπακολουθέω *v.* 20, all of them as not found elsewhere in St Mark.

(8). LUKE vi. 1. Ἐγένετο δὲ ἐν σαββάτῳ δευτεροπρώτῳ. Here again Codd. ℵB coincide in a reading which cannot be approved, omitting δευτεροπρώτῳ by way of getting rid of a difficulty, as do both in Mark xvi. 9—20 and ℵ in Matth. xxiii. 35. The very obscurity of the expression, which does not occur in the parallel Gospels or elsewhere, attests strongly to its authenticity, if there be any truth at all in canons of internal evidence (*see above*, p. 371)[1]. Besides ℵB, δευτεροπρώτῳ is absent from L. 1. 22. 33. 69 (where it is inserted in the margin by *W. Chark*, and should not be noticed, see p. 151). 118. 157. 209. A few (R Γ 13. 117. 124 *primâ manu*. 235) prefer δευτέρῳ πρώτῳ, which differs from the common reading only by a familiar itacism (p. 10). As this verse commences a Church lesson (that for the 7th day or Sabbath of the 3rd week of the new year, see p. 71), Evangelistaria *leave out*, as usual, *the notes of time;* in Scrivener's H P x y z (and no doubt in other such books) the section thus begins, Ἐπορεύετο ὁ Ἰησοῦς τοῖς σάββασιν: this however is not properly speaking a various reading at all (*see* p. 211). Nor ought we to wonder if versions pass over altogether what their translators could not understand[2]; so that we may easily account for the silence of the Peshito Syriac, Memphitic and Æthiopic, of the Old Latin *b. c. l. q* and *f secundâ manu*, and (if they were worth notice) of both Persic and the Polyglott Arabic, though both the Roman and Erpenius' Arabic have δευτέρῳ, and so too the Æthiopic according to Scholz; *e* "sabbato mane," *f* "sabbato a primo:" the Philoxenian Syriac, which renders the word, notes in the margin its absence from some copies (*see* p. 244). Against this list of authorities, few in number, and doubtful as many of them are, we have to place the Old Latin *a. f. ff.* $g^{1,2}$, all copies of the Vulgate, its ally the Armenian, the Gothic and Philoxenian Syriac translations, the uncial codices ACDEHKMRSUVXΓΔΛ, all cursives except the seven cited above, and the Fathers or Scholiasts who have tried, with what-

1 "If the word be a reality and originally in the text, its meaning, since in that case it must have been borrowed from something in the Jewish calendar, would have been traditionally known from the first." (Green, *Course of Developed Criticism*, p. 56.) But why would it?

2 Just as Bentley (in Mr Ellis' *Bentleii Critica Sacra*, p. 35) speaking of the latter part of 1 Cor. vii. 35, says, "In Lat. Codd. OB TRANSLATIONIS DIFFICULTATEM hoc penitus non invenitur."

ever success, to explain the term: viz. Caesarius, Epiphanius, Chrysostom, Isidore, Ambrose (all very expressly, as may be seen in Tischendorf's note), Clement of Alexandria probably, and later writers. Lachmann and Alford place δευτεροπρώτῳ within brackets, Tregelles rejects it, as does Tischendorf in his earlier editions, but restores it in his last. On reviewing the whole evidence, internal and external, we submit the present as a clear instance in which the two oldest copies conspire in a false and highly improbable reading.

(9). LUKE xxii. 43, 44. *ὤφθη δὲ αὐτῷ ἄγγελος ἀπ' οὐρανοῦ ἐνισχύων αὐτόν. καὶ γενόμενος ἐν ἀγωνίᾳ, ἐκτενέστερον προσηύχετο· ἐγένετο δὲ ὁ ἱδρὼς αὐτοῦ ὡσεὶ θρόμβοι αἵματος καταβαίνοντες ἐπὶ τὴν γῆν.* It is a positive relief to know that any lingering doubt which may have hung over the authenticity of these verses, whose sacred words the devout reader of Scripture could so ill spare, is completely dissipated by their being contained in Cod. ℵ: it is more to be desired than hoped, that the admitted error of Cod. B in this place would make some of its advocates more chary of their confidence in cases where it is less countenanced by other witnesses than in the instance before us[1]. The two verses are omitted in ABRT, 124 (in 13 only *ὤφθη δὲ* is *primâ manu*), *f* of the Old Latin, Wilkins' Memphitic and some Thebaic and Armenian manuscripts: A, however, affixes to the latter part of v. 42 (πλὴν), "to which they cannot belong," (*Tregelles*), the proper Ammonian and Eusebian numerals for vv. 43—4 ($\overset{\sigma\pi\gamma}{\iota}$: *see* p. 53), and thus shows that its scribe was acquainted with the passage[2]: some Armenian codices only leave

[1] Implicit faith in Cod. B seems almost an article of their creed with some Biblical critics. Witness worthy Mr Herman Heinfetter, whose obliging circular letters are very well known—at least by sight—to most English students of Scripture. "I...submit," he writes, "that...seeing that the Vatican Manuscript does not contain, *One Single Passage*, that can be Demonstrated to be Spurious; or that by the Evidence of other Manuscripts, and of the Context, admits of, Just Doubt, as to its authenticity [what of e. g. Matth. xxvii. 49?]; *A Position that no other Manuscript enjoys;* That Man is bound to accept the Testimony of that Manuscript, *alone*, as his present Text of the Sacred Record, wherever he possesses its Teaching" (*Circular*, March 1, 1861). One might call this plan *Comparative Criticism made easy.*

[2] These sections and canons illustrate the criticism of the text in some other places: e. g. Matth. xvi. 2, 3 (Tregelles, *Account of Printed Text*, p. 205); xvii. 21, which latter Eusebius virtually rejects, when he refers the parallel passage Mark ix. 28—29 to his *tenth* canon (*see* p. 52).

out v. 44. In Codd. Γ. 123. 344 Scrivener's do (v *secundâ manu* in v. 43) the verses are obelized, and marked by asterisks in ESVΔ, 24. 36. 161. 166. 274. A scholion in Cod. 34 [XI] speaks of its absence from some copies[1]. In all known Evangelistaria and their cognate Cod. 69* (*see* p. 151) the two verses, omitted in this place, follow Matth. xxvi. 39, as a regular part of the lesson for the Thursday in Holy Week (*see* p. 72): in the same place the margin of C (*tertiâ manu*) contains the passage, C being defective in Luke xxii. from v. 19. Codd. LQ place the Ammonian sections and number the Eusebian canons differently from the rest (but this kind of irregularity often occurs in manuscripts), and the Philoxenian margin in one of Adler's manuscripts (Assem. 2) states that it is not found "*in Evangeliis apud Alexandrinos*, et propterea [non?] posuit eam S. Cyrillus in homilia...:" the fact being that the verses are not found in Cyril's *Homilies on Luke* lately published in Syriac, nor does Athanasius ever allude to them. They are read, however, in Codd. DFGHKLMQUXΛ.1. and all other known cursives, without any marks of suspicion, in the Peshito, Curetonian (omitting ἀπ' οὐρανοῦ), Philoxenian and Jerusalem Syriac, the Æthiopic, Thebaic, Memphitic and Armenian manuscripts and editions, the Old Latin *a. b. c. e. ff. g*[1]. *i*, and the Vulgate. The effect of this great preponderance is enhanced by the early and express testimony of Fathers. Justin Martyr (*Trypho*, 103) cites ἱδρὼς ὡσεὶ θρόμβοι as contained ἐν τοῖς ἀπομνημονεύμασι ἅ φημι ὑπὸ τῶν ἀποστόλων αὐτοῦ καὶ τῶν ἐκείνοις παρακολουθησάντων (*see* Luke i. 3, Alford) συντετάχθαι. Irenaeus (III. 222) declares that ἵδρωσε θρόμβους αἵματος. Hippolytus twice, Dionysius of Alexandria, &c. are cited to the same purport by Tregelles, *N. T. ad loc.* Hilary, on the other hand, declares that the passage is not found "in Graecis et in Latinis codicibus compluribus" (p. 1062 a, Benedictine edition, 1693), a statement which Jerome, who leans much on others in such matters, repeats to the echo (*see* pp. 390, 431). Epiphanius, however, in a passage we have before alluded to (p. 391), charges "the orthodox" with removing ἔκλαυσε in ch. xix. 41, though Irenaeus had used it against the Docetae, φοβηθέντες καὶ

[1] ἰστέον ὅτι τὰ περὶ τῶν θρόμβων τινα τῶν ἀντιγράφων οὐκ ἔχουσιν: adding that the clause is cited by Dionysius the Areopagite [V], Gennadius [V], Epiphanius and other holy Fathers.

μὴ νοήσαντες αὐτοῦ τὸ τέλος καὶ τὸ ἰσχυρότατον, καὶ γενόμενος ἐν ἀγωνίᾳ ἵδρωσε, καὶ ἐγένετο ὁ ἱδρὼς αὐτοῦ ὡς θρόμβοι αἵματος, καὶ ὤφθη ἄγγελος ἐνισχύων αὐτόν: Epiphan. *Ancor.* XXXI.[1] Thus too Arius *apud Epiphanium*, Didymus, Gregory Nazianzen, Chrysostom, Theodoret, and a host of later writers acknowledge these two important verses. Davidson adds that "the Syrians are censured by Photius, the Armenians by Nicon [x], Isaac the Catholic, and others, for expunging the passage" (*Bibl. Critic.* II. p. 438).

Of all recent editors, Lachmann alone has doubted the authenticity of the verses, and enclosed them within brackets: but for the accidental presence of the fragment Cod. Q his hard rule —"*mathematica recensendi ratio*," as Tischendorf terms it— would have forced him to expunge them (*see* p. 341), unless indeed he judged (which is probably true) that Cod. A makes as much in their favour as against them. So far as the language of Epiphanius is concerned, it does not appear that *this* passage was rejected by the orthodox as repugnant to their notions of the Lord's Divine character, and such may not have been at all the origin of the variation. We may just as reasonably trace the removal of the paragraph from its proper place in St Luke to the practice of the Lectionaries, whose principal lessons (such as those of the Holy Week would be) were certainly settled in the Greek Church as early as the fourth century (*see above*, p. 64, *and notes*).

(10). JOHN i. 18. ὁ μονογενὴς υἱός, ὁ ὢν εἰς τὸν κόλπον τοῦ πατρός... This passage exhibits in a few ancient documents of high consideration the remarkable variation θεὸς for υἱὸς, which however, according to the form of writing universal in the oldest codices (*see pp.* 14, 43), would require but the change of a single letter, $\overline{\text{YC}}$ or $\overline{\Theta\text{C}}$. In behalf of $\overline{\Theta\text{C}}$ stand Codd. ℵBC *primâ manu*, and L (all wanting the article before μονογενὴς, and ℵ omitting the ὁ ὢν that follows), 33 alone among cursive

[1] The reader will see that I have understood this passage, with Grotius, as applying to an orthodox tampering with Luke xix. 41, not with xxii. 43—44. As the text of Epiphanius stands I cannot well do otherwise, since Mill's mode of punctuation (*N. T. Proleg.* § 797) cannot be endured, and leaves καὶ τὸ ἰσχυρότατον unaccounted for. Yet I confess that there is no trace of any meddling with ἔκλαυσε by any one, and I know not where Irenaeus cites it.

manuscripts, of the versions the Peshito (not often found in such company), and the *margin* of the Philoxenian (whose affinity with Cod. L is very decided, *see* p. 109), the Memphitic, Æthiopic (Roman edition, *see p.* 278), and a host of Fathers, some expressly (e. g. Clement of Alexandria, Didymus *de Trinitate*, Epiphanius, &c.), others by apparent reference. Their testimonies are elaborately set forth by Tregelles, who strenuously maintains θεὸς as the true reading, and thinks it much that Arius, though "opposed to the dogma taught," upholds *μονογενὴς θεός*. It may be that the term suits that heretic's system better than it does the Catholic doctrine: it certainly does not confute it. For the received reading *υἱὸς* we can allege AC (*tertiâ manu*) EFGHKMSUVXΔΛ (D and the other uncials being defective), every cursive manuscript except 33 (including Tregelles' allies 1. 69), all the Latin versions, the Curetonian, Philoxenian and Jerusalem Syriac, the last on Tregelles' own evidence, the Armenian and Platt's Æthiopic. The array of Fathers is less imposing, but includes Athanasius (often), Chrysostom, and the Latin writers, down from Tertullian. Origen, Eusebius and some others have both readings.

Tregelles, who seldom notices internal probabilities in his critical notes, here pleads that an *ἅπαξ λεγόμενον* like *μονογενὴς θεὸς* might easily be changed by copyists into the more familiar *μονογενὴς υἱὸς* from John iii. 16; 18; 1 John iv. 9, and he would therefore apply Bengel's Canon (I. see p. 371). Alford's remark, however, is very sound, "We should be introducing great harshness into the sentence, and a new and [to us moderns] strange term into Scripture, by adopting θεός: a consequence which ought to have no weight whatever where authority is overpowering, but may fairly be weighed where this is not so. The 'praestat procliviori ardua' finds in this case a legitimate limit" (*N. T.* note on John i. 18).

Those who will resort to "ancient evidence exclusively" for the recension of the text may well be perplexed in dealing with this passage. The oldest manuscripts, versions and writers are hopelessly divided, so that we can well understand how some critics (without a shadow of authority worth notice) have come to suspect both θεὸς and *υἱὸς* to be *accretions* or spurious additions to *μονογενής*. If the principles advocated in Chap. VII. be true, the present is just such a case as calls for the interposition of the more recent uncial and cursive codices; and when we find that they all, with the single exception of Cod. 33, defend the reading *μονογενὴς υἱὸς*, we feel safe in concluding that for once Codd. ℵBC and the Peshito do not approach the autograph of St John so nearly as Cod. A, the Curetonian Syriac and Old Latin versions.

(11). JOHN v. 3, 4. *ἐκδεχομένων τὴν τοῦ ὕδατος κίνησιν. ἄγγελος γὰρ κατὰ καιρὸν κατέβαινεν ἐν τῇ κολυμβήθρᾳ, καὶ ἐτάρασσε τὸ ὕδωρ· ὁ οὖν πρῶτος ἐμβὰς μετὰ τὴν ταραχὴν τοῦ ὕδατος, ὑγιὴς ἐγίνετο, ᾧ δήποτε κατείχετο νοσήματι.* This passage is expunged by Tischendorf, Tregelles and Alford, obelized (=) by Griesbach, but retained by Scholz and Lachmann. The evidence against it is certainly very considerable: Codd. ℵBC*D. 33. 157. 314., but D. 33 contain *ἐκδεχομένων... κίνησιν*, which *alone* A*L. 18. omit. The words from *ἄγγελος γὰρ* to *νοσήματι* are noted with asterisks or obeli (employed without much discrimination) in SΛ. 8. 11?. 14 (*ἄγγελος...ὕδωρ* being left out). 21. 24. 32. 36. 145. 161. 166. 230. 262. 269. 299. 348. 408, Scrivener's dkw and Armenian manuscripts. The Philoxenian margin marks from *ἄγγελος* to *ὕδωρ* with an asterisk, the remainder of the verse with obeli. The whole passage is given, although with that unusual variation in the reading which often indicates grounds for suspicion[1], in EFGHIKMUVΔ and all known cursives not enumerated above: of these Cod. I [VI] is of the greatest weight. Cod. A contains the whole passage, but down to *κίνησιν secundâ manu;* Cod. C also the whole, *tertiâ manu.* Of the versions, Cureton's Syriac, the Thebaic, Schwartze's Memphitic, some Armenian manuscripts, *f. l. q* of the Old Latin, *san., harl.** and two others of the Vulgate (*vid. Griesbach.*) are for omission; the Roman edition of the Æthiopic leaves out what the Philoxenian margin *obelizes*, but the Peshito and Jerusalem Syriac, all Latin copies not aforenamed, Wilkins' Memphitic, and Armenian editions are for retaining the disputed words. Tertullian clearly recognises them ("Piscinam Bethsaidam angelus interveniens commovebat," *de Baptismo*, 5),

[1] To give but a very small part of the variations in v. 4: *δὲ* (*pro γὰρ*) L. *a. b. c. ff.* Vulg. – *γὰρ* Evst. 51. Memph. + *κυρίου* (*post γὰρ*) AKLΔ. 12. 13. 69. Scrivener's acdpw, fifteen others: *at τοῦ θεοῦ* 152. Evst. 53. 54. – *κατὰ καιρὸν a. b. ff. ἐλούετο* (*pro κατέβαινεν*) A (K) w^{scr}. 42. Æthiop. – *ἐν τῇ κολυμβήθρᾳ a. b. ff. ἐταράσσετο τὸ ὕδ.* C^3GHIMUVΛ*. Scrivener's abdefkpqvHx, many others. + In piscinam (*post ἐμβὰς*) *c.* Clementine Vulg. *ἐγένετο* FL. 69, at least 15 others.

as do Cyril, Chrysostom, Ambrose (*twice*), Theophylact and Euthymius. No other ecclesiastical writers allude to the narrative, unique and perplexing as it is.

The first clause (ἐκδεχ......κίνησιν) is probably absent from Cod. ℵ, though Tischendorf only speaks of the verse beginning with ἄγγελος: in that case it can hardly stand, in spite of the versions which support it, as DI are the oldest *manuscript* witnesses in its favour, and it bears much of the appearance of a gloss brought in from the margin (*see* p. 373, note). The succeeding verse is harder to deal with; but for the countenance of the versions and the testimony of Tertullian, Cod. A could never resist the joint authority of ℵBCD, illustrated as they are by the marks of suspicion set in so many later copies. Yet if v. 4 be indeed but an "*insertion to complete that implied in the narrative with reference to the popular belief*" (Alford, *ad loc.*), it is much more in the manner of Cod. D and the Curetonian Syriac, than of Cod. A and the Latin versions; and since these last two are not often found in unison, and together with the Peshito, opposed to the other primary documents, it is not very rash to say that when such a conjunction does occur, it proves that the reading was early, widely diffused, and extensively received. Yet, after all, if the passage as it stands in our common text can be maintained as genuine at all, it must be, we apprehend, on the principle suggested above, Chap. I. § 11. p. 16.

(12). JOHN vii. 53—viii. 11. On no other grounds than those just intimated can this celebrated and important paragraph, the *pericope adulterae* as it is called, be regarded as a portion of St John's Gospel. It is absent from too many excellent copies not to have been wanting in some of the very earliest; while the arguments in its favour, internal even more than external, are so powerful, that we can scarcely be brought to think it an unauthorised appendage to the writings of one, who in another of his inspired books deprecated so solemnly the adding to or taking away from the blessed testimony he was commissioned to bear (Apoc. xxii. 18, 19). If ch. xx. 30, 31 show signs of having been the original end of this Gospel, and ch. xxi. be a later supplement by the Apostle's own hand, which I think with Dean Alford is evidently the case, why should not St John have inserted in this second edition both the amplification in ch. v. 4 and this most edifying and eminently Christian narrative? The appended chapter (xxi.) would thus be added at once to all copies of the Gospels then in circulation, though a portion of them might well overlook the minuter change in ch. v. 4, or from obvious though mistaken motives, might hesitate to receive for general use or public reading the history of the woman taken in adultery.

It must be in this way, if at all, that we can assign to the Evangelist ch. vii. 53—viii. 11: on all intelligent principles of mere criticism the passage must needs be abandoned. It is entirely omitted (viii. 12 following continuously to vii. 52) in the uncial Codd. ℵA[1]BC[1]T (all first class authorities) LXΔ, though LΔ leave a void space (like B in Mark xvi. 9—20) too small to contain the verses, *before* which Δ* began to write viii. 12 after vii. 52.

Add to these the cursives 2^pe. b^scr. 3. 12. 21. 22. 33. 36. 44. 49. 72. 87. 95. 96. 97. 106. 108. 123. 131. 134. 139. 143. 149. 157. 168. 169. 181. 186. 194. 195. 210. 213. 228. 249. 250. 253. 255. 261. 269. 314. 331. 388. 392. 401: it is absent in the first, added by a second hand in a^scr. 9. 15. 179. 232. 284. 353: while ch. viii. 3—11 are wanting in 77. 242. 324 (54 cursive copies). The passage is noted by an asterisk or obelus in EMSΛ,[2] Scrivener's klmn, 4. 8. 14. 18. 24. 34. 35. 109. 125. 141. 148 (*secundâ manu*). 156. 161. 166. 167. 178. 179. 189. 196. 198. 202. 212. 226. 230. 231 (*sec. man.*). 241. 246. 271. 274. 277. 284? 285. 338. 355. 360. 361. 363. 376. 391 (*secund. manu*). 394. 408. 436: vv. 3—11 in 128. 137. 147: with explanatory scholia appended in 164. 215. 262[2] (52 cursives). Scholz, who has taken unusual pains in the examination of this question, enumerates 292 cursives, Scrivener 15 more, which contain the paragraph with no trace of suspicion, as do the uncials DF (*partly defective*) GHKUΓ (with an hiatus after *στήσαντες αὐτὴν* v. 3). Cod. 145 has it only *secundâ manu*, with a note that from ch. viii. 3 *τοῦτο τὸ κεφάλαιον ἐν πολλοῖς ἀντιγράφοις οὐ κεῖται.* Codd. 1. 19. 20. 129. 135. 207. 301. 347. tisch[1] (*see* p. 181). Evst.

[1] Codd. AC are defective in this place, but by measuring the space we have shown (p. 80, note) that A does not contain the twelve verses, and the same method applies to C.

[2] The kindred copies Λ. 262, &c. have the following scholium: *τὰ ὠβελισμένα ἔν τισιν ἀντιγράφοις οὐ κεῖται, οὐδὲ Ἀπολ[λ]ιναρίῳ· ἐν δὲ τοῖς ἀρχαίοις ὅλα κεῖται· μνημονεύουσι τῆς περικοπῆς ταύτης καὶ οἱ ἀπόστολοι, ἐν αἷς ἐξέθεντο διατάξεσιν εἰς*

86 (*see* p. 216) banish the whole *pericope* to the end of the Gospel. Of these, Cod. 1 in a scholium pleads its absence ἐν τοῖς πλείστοις ἀντιγράφοις, and from the Commentaries of Chrysostom, Cyril of Alexandria, and Theodore of Mopsuestia; while 135. 301 confess they found it ἐν ἀρχαίοις ἀντιγράφοις: Cod. 20 is obelized, and has a scholium. In 37. 102. 105. ch. viii. 3—11 alone are put at the end of the Gospel, which is all that 259 supplies, though its omission in the text begins at ch. vii. 53. Cod. 237, on the contrary, omits only from ch. viii. 3, but at the end inserts the whole passage from ch. vii. 53: in tisch[1]. vii. 53—viii. 2 is *primâ manu* with an asterisk, the rest later. Cod. 225 sets ch. vii. 53—viii. 11 after ch. vii. 36; in 115, ch. viii. 12 is inserted between ch. vii. 52 and 53, and repeated again in its proper place. Finally, 13. 69. 124. 346 give the whole passage at the end of Luke xxi, that order being apparently suggested from comparing Luke xxi. 37 with John viii. 1; and ὤρθριζε Luke xxi. 38 with ὄρθρου John viii. 2. In the Lectionaries, as we have had occasion to state before (p. 69, note), this section was never read as a part of the lesson for Pentecost (John vii. 37—viii. 12), but was reserved for the festivals of such saints as Theodora Sept. 18, or Pelagia Oct. 8 (*see* p. 74), and in many Service-books, whose Menology was not very full, it would thus be omitted altogether. Accordingly in that remarkable Lectionary, the Jerusalem Syriac, the lesson for Pentecost ends at ch. viii. 2, the other verses (3—11) being assigned to St Pelagia's day.

Of the other versions the paragraph is entirely omitted in the true Peshito (being inserted in printed books under the circumstances before stated, p. 233), and in the Philoxenian, though it appears in the *Codex* Barsalibi (*see* p. 243 and note), from which White appended it to the end of St John: a Syriac note in this copy states that it does not belong to the Philoxenian, but was translated in A.D. 622 by Maras, Bishop of Amida. Maras, however, lived about A.D. 520, and a fragment of a very different version of the section, bearing his name, is cited by Assemani (*Biblioth. Orient.* II. 53) from the *writings* of Barsalibi himself (*Cod. Clem.-Vat. Syr.* 16). Ridley's text bears much resemblance to that of De Dieu (p. 233), as does a fourth version of ch. vii.

οἰκοδομὴν τῆς ἐκκλησίας. The Apostolos (or πραξαπόστολος, *see* pp. 63, 211) would often contain the Menology, in the course of which alone this passage was wont to be read.

53—viii. 11 found by Adler (*N. T. Version. Syr.* p. 57) in a Paris codex, with the marginal annotation that this "*σύνταξις*" is not in all the copies, but was interpreted into Syriac by the Abbot Mar Paulus. Of the other versions it is not found in the Thebaic, some of Wilkins' and all Schwartze's Memphitic copies, the Gothic, Zohrab's Armenian from six ancient codices (but five very recent ones and Uscan's edition contain it), or in *a. f. l* (text). *q* of the Old Latin. In *b* the whole text from ch. vii. 44 to viii. 12 has been wilfully erased, but the passage is found in *c. e* (we have given them at large, p. 268). *ff*². *g. l* (margin), the Vulgate, (see *am., for.*, p. 268), Æthiopic, Slavonic, Anglo-Saxon, Persic (but in a Vatican codex placed in ch. x), and Arabic.

Of the Fathers, Euthymius [XII], the first among the Greeks to mention the paragraph in its proper place, declares that *παρὰ τοῖς ἀκριβέσιν ἀντιγράφοις ἢ οὐχ εὕρηται ἢ ὠβέλισται· διὸ φαίνονται παρέγγραπτα καὶ προσθήκη.* The Apostolic Constitutions had plainly alluded to it, and Eusebius (*Hist. Eccl.* III. 39, *fin.*) had described from Papias, and as contained in the Gospel of the Hebrews, the story of a woman *ἐπὶ πολλαῖς ἁμαρτίαις διαβληθείσης ἐπὶ τοῦ κυρίου,* but did not at all regard it as Scripture. Codd. KM too are the earliest which raise the number of *τίτλοι* or larger *κεφάλαια* in St John from 18 to 19, by interpolating *κεφ. ι. περὶ τῆς μοιχαλίδος.*

Among the Latins, as being in their old version, the narrative was more generally received for St John's. Jerome testifies that it was found in his time "in multis et Graecis et Latinis codicibus;" Ambrose cites it, and Augustine (*de adult. conjugiis*, Lib. II. c. 7) complains that "nonnulli modicae fidei, vel potius inimici verae fidei," removed it from their codices, "*credo metuentes peccandi impunitatem dari mulieribus suis*" (*see* p. 376 and note 1)[1].

When to all these sources of doubt, and to so many hostile authorities, is added the fact that in no portion of the N. T. do the variations of manuscripts (of D beyond all the rest) and other documents bear any sort of proportion, whether in number or extent, to those in these twelve verses (of which full evidence may be seen in any collection of various readings), we cannot help admitting that if this section be indeed the composition of

[1] "Similiter Nicon ejectam esse vult narrationem ab Armenis, *βλαβερὰν εἶναι τοῖς πολλοῖς τὴν τοιαύτην ἀκρόασιν* dicentibus." Tischendorf. *ad loc.* See too p. 436.

St John, it has been transmitted to us under circumstances widely different from those connected with any other genuine passage of Scripture whatever.

(13). Acts viii. 37. Εἶπε δὲ ὁ Φίλιππος, εἰ πιστεύεις ἐξ ὅλης τῆς καρδίας, ἔξεστιν. Ἀποκριθεὶς δὲ εἶπε, Πιστεύω τὸν υἱὸν τοῦ Θεοῦ εἶναι τὸν Ἰησοῦν Χριστόν[1]. We cannot question the spuriousness of this verse, which seems to have been received from the margin, where the formula Πιστεύω κ. τ. λ. had been placed, extracted from some Church Ordinal. This is just the portion cited by Irenaeus, both in Greek[2] and Latin: so early had the words found a place in the sacred text. Yet it is contained in no manuscripts except E (D, which might perhaps be expected to favour it, being here defective) 4 (*secundâ manu*). 13. 15. 18? 27. 29. 36. 60. 69. 100. 105. 106. Apost. 5. 13 once and in the margin, 14. 25 &c., in e alone out of Scrivener's thirteen: manuscripts of good character, but quite inadequate to prove the authenticity of the verse, even though they did not differ considerably in the actual readings they exhibit, which is always in itself a ground of reasonable suspicion (*see above*, pp. 426, 438, 442). Here again, as in Matth. xxvii. 35, Gutbier and Schaaf (*see* p. 233) interpolated in their Peshito texts the passage as translated into Syriac and placed within brackets by Elias Hutter (p. 232): the Philoxenian also exhibits it, but marked with an asterisk (p. 244). It is found in the Old Latin *m* although in an abridged form, in the Vulgate (both printed and *demid.*, but not in *am.* primâ manu, *fuld.* &c.), and in the satellites of the Vulgate, the Armenian, Polyglott Arabic and Slavonic. Bede, however, who used Cod. E, knew *Latin* copies in which the verse was wanting; yet it was known to Cyprian, Jerome, Augustine, Pacian [IV], &c. among the Latins, to Oecumenius and Theophylact (twice quoted) among the Greeks. Erasmus seems to have inserted the verse by a comparison of the later hand of Cod. 4. with the Vulgate[3]; it is not in the Complutensian edition. This passage

[1] The form τὸν Ἰησοῦν Χριστόν, objected to by Michaelis, is vindicated by Matth. i. 18, the reading of which cannot rightly be impugned. See above, p. 419.

[2] ὡς αὐτὸς ὁ εὐνοῦχος πεισθεὶς καὶ παραυτίκα ἀξιῶν βαπτισθῆναι, ἔλεγε, πιστεύω τὸν υἱὸν τοῦ θεοῦ εἶναι Ἰησοῦν Χριστόν. Harvey, Vol. II. p. 62.

[3] "Non reperi in graeco codice, quanquam arbitror omissum librariorum incuria. Nam et haec in quodam codice graeco asscripta reperi, sed in margine." Erasmus, *N. T.* 1516.

affords us a curious instance of an *addition* well received in the Western Church from the second century downwards (see p. 387) and afterwards making some way among the later Greek codices and writers.

(14). ACTS xv. 34. ἔδοξε δὲ τῷ Σίλᾳ ἐπιμεῖναι αὐτοῦ. This verse is omitted in ABEGH (ℵ unknown), and of the cursives by lo[tl] and six more collated by Scrivener (including 31), and by full fifty others. Erasmus inserted it in his editions from the margin of 4. It is wanting in the Peshito (only that Tremellius and Gutbier between them thrust their own version into the text), the Memphitic, Polyglott Arabic, Slavonic, the best manuscripts of the Latin Vulgate (*am.*, *fuld.*, *demid.*, &c), Chrysostom and Theophylact. In C it runs *εδοξεν δε τω σιλα επιμειναι αυτους*, which is followed by many cursives: some of which, however, have *αὐτοῦ*, two *αὐτοῖς*, Scrivener's aef and four others *αὐτόθι*, with the Complutensian Polyglott. The common text is found in the Thebaic, Tremellius' Syriac, the Philoxenian with an asterisk (*see* p. 244), Erpenius' Arabic, Theophylact and Œcumenius. In D we read *εδοξε. δε τω σειλεα επιμειναι* [*προς secundâ manu*] *αυτους* (sustinere eos *d*) *μονος δε ιουδας επορευθη*, which Lachmann cites in Latin as extant *in this form* only in one Vienna Codex (for which see his *N. T. Proleg.* Vol. I. p. xxix.): thus too the Armenian (not that of Venice) and printed Slavonic. The common Vulgate, Cassiodorus (*see* p. 262), and Hutter's Syriac, add "Jerusalem," so that the Clementine Latin stands thus: "Visum est autem Silae ibi remanere; Judas autem solus abiit Jerusalem." The Æthiopic is rendered "Et perseveravit Paulus manens," to which Platt's copies add "ibi."

No doubt this verse is an unauthorised addition, self-condemned indeed by its numerous variations. One can almost trace its growth, and in the shape presented by the Received text it must have been (as Mill conjectures) a marginal gloss, designed to explain how (notwithstanding the terms of v. 33) Silas was at hand in v. 40, conveniently for St Paul to choose him as a companion in travel.

(15). ACTS xx. 28. τὴν ἐκκλησίαν τοῦ θεοῦ, ἣν περιεποιήσατο διὰ τοῦ ἰδίου αἵματος. This reading of the Received text, though different from that of the majority of copies, is pretty sure to be correct. It is upheld by ℵB (the latter now for certain) 4. 22. 46. 65. 66*(?) 68. 84. 89. 154. 162, to which we can now add 23. 25. 37; so also Apost. 12, and *e silentio*, on which one can lay but little stress, 7. 12. 16. 39. 56. 64. and Scrivener's ce, codices not now in England. "Dei" is read by all known manuscripts and editions of the Vulgate except the Complutensian, which was probably altered to suit the parallel Greek. Lee's edition of the Peshito (see p. 234) has θεοῦ, from three codices (the Travancore, a Vatican Lectionary of Adler [XI], and one at the Bodleian), and so has the Philoxenian *text*. Τοῦ κυρίου (differing but by one letter, see our Plates v. 13; IX. 25) is in AC*DE (and therefore in *de*), a[scr]. 13. 15. 18. 36 (*text*). 40. 69. 73. 81. 95*. 130. 156. 163. 180. Apost. 58, the Philoxenian *margin*, the Thebaic, Memphitic, Armenian, and possibly the Roman Æthiopic (*see* p. 278), though *there* the same word is said to represent both θ̄ῡ and κ̄ῡ. Platt's Æthiopic, all editions of the Peshito except Lee's, and its secondary version, Erpenius' Arabic, have τοῦ χριστοῦ, with Origen once, Theodoret twice, and four copies of Athanasius: the Old Latin *m* "Jesu Christi." Other variations too weakly supported to be worth notice are τοῦ κυρίου θεοῦ 3. 95**, the Polyglott Arabic: τοῦ θεοῦ καὶ κυρίου 47, and the Georgian τοῦ κυρίου τοῦ θεοῦ. The great mass of later manuscripts give τοῦ κυρίου καὶ θεοῦ, viz. C (*tertiâ manu*), GH, Scrivener's bdfghklmo, and more than one hundred other cursives, including probably every one not particularized above. This is the reading of the Complutensian, both in the Greek and Latin, and of some modern critics who would fain take a safe and middle course; but is countenanced by no version except the Slavonic (*see* p. 280), and by no ecclesiastical writer before Theophylact [XI]. It is plainly but a device for reconciling the two principal readings; yet from the non-repetition of the article and from the general turn of the sentence it asserts the divinity of the Saviour as unequivocally as θεοῦ could do alone. Our choice evidently lies between κυρίου and θεοῦ, which are pretty equally supported by manuscripts and versions: Patristic testimony, however, may slightly incline to the latter. Foremost comes that bold expression of Ignatius [A.D. 107] ἀναζωπυρήσαντες ἐν αἵματι θεοῦ (*ad Ephes.* i.), which the old Latin version renders "Christi Dei," and the later interpolator softens into χριστοῦ. It may be true that "he does not adopt it as a quotation" (Davidson *ad loc.*), yet nothing short of Scriptural authority could have given such early vogue to a term so startling as *αἷμα θεοῦ*, which is also employed by Tertullian. The elder Basil, Epiphanius, Cyril of Alexandria (*twice*), Ibas (in the Greek), Ambrose, Caelestine, Fulgentius, Primasius, Cassiodorus, &c., not to mention writers so recent as Œcumenius and Theophylact, expressly support the same word. Manuscripts of Athanasius vary between *θεοῦ, κυρίου*, and *χριστοῦ*, but his evidence would be regarded as hostile to the Received text, inasmuch as he states (as alleged by Wetstein) that *οὐδαμοῦ δὲ αἷμα θεοῦ καθ' ἡμᾶς παραδεδώκασιν αἱ γραφαί· 'Αρειανῶν τὰ τοιαῦτα τολμήματα* (*contra Apollinar.*): only that for *καθ' ἡμᾶς* (*which even Tischendorf cites in his last edition*), the correct reading is *δίχα σαρκὸς* or *διὰ σαρκός*, a citation fatal to any such inference. In Chrysostom too the readings fluctuate, and some (e.g. Tregelles) have questioned whether the Homilies on the Acts, wherein he has *θεοῦ*, are of his composition. In behalf of *κυρίου* are cited the Latin version of Irenaeus, Lucifer of Cagliari, Augustine, Jerome, Ammonius, Eusebius, Didymus, Athanasius (?), Chrysostom, and the Apostolic Constitutions, while the exact expression *sanguis Dei* was censured by Origen and others. It has been urged, however, and not without some show of reason (Nolan, *Integrity of Greek Vulgate*, p. 517, note 135), that the course of Irenaeus' argument proves that *θεοῦ* was used in his lost Greek text. After all, internal evidence—subjective feeling if it must be so called—will decide the critic's choice where authorities are so divided as here. It seems reasonable to say that the whole mass of witnesses for *τοῦ κυρίου καὶ θεοῦ* vouches for the existence of *θεοῦ* in the earliest codices, the common-place *κυρίου* being the rather received from other quarters, as it tends to point more distinctly to the Divine Person indicated in the passage. If this view be accepted, the preponderance in favour of *θεοῦ*, *undoubtedly the harder form* (*see* p. 371), is very marked, and when the consideration suggested above (p. 375) from Dean Alford is added, there will remain little room for hesitation. It has been pleaded on both sides of the question, and appears little relevant to the case of either, that St Paul employs in ten places the expression *ἐκκλησία τοῦ θεοῦ*, but never once *ἐκκλησία τοῦ κυρίου* or *τοῦ χριστοῦ*.

It is hardly worth while to mention that, in the place of *τοῦ ἰδίου αἵματος*, the more emphatic form *τοῦ αἵματος τοῦ ἰδίου* ought to be adopted from A (*see* Plate v. No. 13) BCDE, (א is unknown) Scrivener's acm (c being cited here by Sanderson), with some twenty other cursives; Didymus, &c.; while *τοῦ ἰδίου αἵματος* is in GH, the majority of cursives, Athanasius, Chrysostom, &c.

(16). Rom. v. 1. *Δικαιωθέντες οὖν ἐκ πίστεως εἰρήνην ἔχομεν πρὸς τὸν Θεόν.* Here, as in 2 Cor. iii. 3 (see p. 377) we find the chief uncials support a reading which is manifestly unsuitable to the context, although, since it does not absolutely destroy the sense, it does not (like the other passage) lack defenders. Codd. א (*teste Tischendorf.*) B for *ἔχομεν* have *primâ manu ἔχωμεν*, and though some doubt has been thrown on the primitive reading of B, yet Mai and Tregelles (*Account of Printed Text*, p. 156) are eyewitnesses to the fact. Codd. ACDKL, not less than 26 cursives (three out of Scrivener's eleven), including the remarkable copies 17. 37, also read *ἔχωμεν*, as do *d. e. f. g*, the Vulgate ("habeamus"), the Peshito Syriac probably (ܢܗܘܐ ܠܢ ܫܝܢܐ), Memphitic, Æthiopic and Arabic. Chrysostom too supports this view. The case for *ἔχομεν* is weaker in itself: Codd. אB *secundâ manu*, FG (in spite of the contrary testimony of *f. g*, their respective Latin versions), the majority of the cursive manuscripts, Epiphanius, Cyril, and the Slavonic. The later Syriac seems to combine both readings (ܫܝܢܐ ܢܗܘܐ ܐܝܬ ܠܢ ܠܘܬ ܐܠܗܐ): White translates "habemus," but has no note on the passage. Had the scales been equally poised, no one would hesitate to prefer *ἔχομεν*, for the closer the context is examined the clearer it will appear that *inference* not *exhortation* is the Apostle's purpose: hence those who most regard "ancient evidence" have struggled long before they would admit *ἔχωμεν* into the text. The "Five Clergymen" who recently benefited the English Church by revising its Authorised version of this Epistle, even though they render "*let us have peace with God*," are constrained to say, "An overwhelming weight of authority has necessitated a change, which at the first sight seems to impair the logical force of the Apostle's argument. No consideration, however, of this kind can be allowed to interfere with the faithful exhibition of the true text, as far as it can be ascertained; and no doubt the real Word of God, thus faithfully exhibited, will vindicate its own meaning, and need no help from man's shortsighted preference" (Preface, p. vii). Every one must honour the reverential temper in which these eminent men approached their delicate task; yet, if their sentiments be true, where is the place for internal evidence at all? A more "overwhelming weight" of manuscript authority upholds καρδίαις in 2 Cor. iii. 3: shall we place it in the text "leaving the real Word of God to vindicate its own meaning"? Ought we to assume that the reading found in the few most ancient codices—not, in the case of Rom. v. 1, in the majority of the whole collection—must *of necessity* be the "real Word of God, faithfully exhibited"? I see no cause to reply in the affirmative.

We conclude, therefore, that this is a case for the application of the *paradiplomatical* canon (p. 376): that the itacism ω for ο (*see pp.* 10, 15), so familiar to all collators of Greek manuscripts, crept into some very early copy, from which it was propagated among our most venerable codices, even those from which the earliest versions were made:—that this is one out of a small number of well ascertained cases in which the united testimonies of the best authorities conspire in giving a worse reading than that preserved by later and (for the most part) inferior copies.

(17). 1 Cor. xiii. 3. *ἐὰν παραδῶ τὸ σῶμά μου ἵνα καυθήσωμαι*, "though I give my body to be burned." Here we find the undoubtedly false reading *καυχήσωμαι* in the two chief codices AB (*sic*) and in 17: that of א is not yet known. Jerome (*see* p. 356, note) testifies that in his time "apud Graecos ipsos ipsa exemplaria esse diversa," and preferred *καυχήσωμαι* (though all copies of the Latin have *ut ardeam* or *ut ardeat*), which is said to be countenanced by the Æthiopic and by a manuscript of the Memphitic. This variation, which involves the change of but one letter, "is worth notice, as showing that the best uncial MSS. are not always to be depended upon, and sometimes are blemished with errors" (Wordsworth, *N. T. ad loc.*: see above, pp. 377, 418. It may have obtained the more credit as each of the other principal readings (*καυθήσομαι*, DEFGL. 44. 71. 80. 113[2], Scrivener's b[2]cdfhk and at least 12 others), and *καυθήσωμαι* (CK. 29. 37, and many others, Chrysostom, Theodoret, &c.) are anomalous, the former in respect to mood, the latter to tense. The important cursive 73 has *καυθή-*

σεται with some Latin copies: Codd. 1. 108*. Basil (Cyprian?) adopt καυθῇ: the Syriac (ܢܝܩܕ), and I suppose the Arabic, will suit either of these last. Evidence seems to preponderate on the side of καυθήσομαι, but in the case of these itacisms manuscripts are very fallacious (*see* p. 448). Such a subjunctive future as καυθήσωμαι, however, I should have been disposed to question, had it not passed muster with much better scholars than I am: but to illustrate it, as Tregelles does (*Account of Printed Text*, p. 117, note), from ἵνα δώσῃ Apoc. viii. 3, is to accomplish little, since δώσει is found in AC, Scrivener's beghmn (δωσι d), 13. 37. 40. 48. 68, together with many others, including Andreas (δώσῃ B alone of the uncials, ℵ being unknown), and is justly approved by Lachmann and Tischendorf. It seems most likely that in both places ἵνα, the particle of design, is followed by the *indicative* future, as is clearly the case in Eph. vi. 3. In John xvii. 3 even Tregelles adopts ἵνα γινώσκουσιν[1].

(18). PHILIP. ii. 1. εἴ τις κοινωνία πνεύματος, εἴ τινα σπλάγχνα. For τινα, to the critic's great perplexity, τις is found in ℵABCDEFGKL, that is, in *all* the uncials extant at this place. As regards the cursives nearly the same must be said. Of the 13 collated by Scrivener 7 read τις (acdfgkln), and 5 τι (behmo): Mill enumerates 16 others that give τις, one (40) that has τι:

[1] I beg Dr Tregelles' pardon for having nearly forgotten his third and last example of the *subjunctive future* (*Account of Printed Text*, p. 212, note), for the sake of whose visionary charms he is willing for once to be false even to Cod. B. In John xvii. 2 ἵνα...δώσῃ is read by ACGKMSX. 33, c^{scr}, and (so far as I can find) by no other manuscript whatever. On the other hand δώσει is supported by BEHUYΓΔΛ (ℵ is unknown, D has εχῃ, L δως), and (as it would seem) by every other codex extant. Out of the 23 collated by myself for this chapter, it is found in 22, and the following others have been expressly cited for δώσει: 1. 10. 11. 15. 22. 42. 45. 48. 53. 54. 55. 60. 61 (*Dobbin*). 63. 65. 66. 106. 118. 124. 127. 131. 142. 145. 157. 250. 262. Evst. 3. 22. 24. 36, and at least 50 others, one might say all that have been collated with any degree of minuteness: so too the Complutensian and first edition of Erasmus. The constant confusion of ει and η at the period when the uncials were written abundantly accounts for the reading *of the few*, though AC are among them. In later times such itacisms were far more rare in *careful* transcription, and the mediaeval copyists knew their native language too well to fall into the habit in this passage. In 1 Pet. iii. 1, ἵνα κερδηθήσονται is read by the uncials (ACGK), nearly all cursives, and the Complutensian edition, in the place of -σωνται of B (*Mai*) and the Received text. Dr Tregelles has accomplished much, but he is not likely, even with Lachmann's aid, to reform our Greek grammars.

Griesbach reckons 45 in favour of τις, 8 (including Cod. 4) for τι; to which Scholz adds a few more. One cursive (109) and a manuscript of Theodoret have τε. Basil, Chrysostom (in manuscript) and others read τις, as do the Complutensian, and R. Stephens' first two editions (see p. 299). In fact it may be stated that no manuscript whatever has been cited for τινα, which is not therefore likely to be found in many. In spite of what was said above (pp. 377, 418) with regard to far weaker cases, it is impossible to blame editors for putting τις into the text here before σπλάγχνα: to have acted otherwise (as Tischendorf fairly observes) would have been "*grammatici quam editoris partes agere.*" Yet we may believe the reading to be as false as it is intolerable, and to afford us another proof of the early and (as the cursives shew) the well nigh universal corruption of our copies in some minute particulars. Of course Clement and later Fathers give τινα, indeed it is surprising that any cite otherwise; but *in the absence of definite documentary proof*, this can hardly be regarded as genuine. Probably St Paul wrote τι (the reading of about 15 cursives), which would readily be corrupted into τις, by reason of the σ following (TICΠΛΑΓΧΝΑ, *see* p. 10), and the τις which had just preceded.

(19). Coloss. ii. 2. τοῦ μυστηρίου τοῦ Θεοῦ καὶ πατρὸς καὶ τοῦ χριστοῦ, "of the mystery of God the Father, and of Christ." Here again we are under the disadvantage of discussing a passage of great moment, on which the best authorities are divided, in ignorance of the testimony borne by Cod. ℵ. If this document should support the reading of B (approved by Lachmann, Tregelles and Wordsworth), which it often so closely resembles, we should be inclined with Ellicott to adopt its words, τοῦ μυστηρίου τοῦ θεοῦ χριστοῦ ("ita cod. nihil interponens inter θεοῦ et χριστοῦ," *Mai.* 8° ed.), as "having every appearance of being the original reading, and that from which the many perplexing variations have arisen" (see p. 372, Canon. II). At present it stands in great need of confirmation, as Hilary alone supports it (but καὶ χριστοῦ Cyril), though the Scriptural character of the expression is upheld by the language of ch. i. 27 just preceding, and by the received text in 1 Tim. iii. 16. Some, who feel a difficulty in understanding how χριστοῦ was removed from the text, if it ever had a place there, conceive that the verse should end with *θεοῦ*, all additions, including *χριστοῦ* the simplest, being *accretions* to the genuine passage. These alleged accretions are *τοῦ θεοῦ ὅ ἐστι χριστός*, manifestly an expansion of *χριστοῦ* and derived from i. 27: *τοῦ θεοῦ πατρὸς τοῦ χριστοῦ*: *τοῦ θεοῦ καὶ πατρὸς καὶ τοῦ χριστοῦ*, the final form of the received text. Now of these four readings *τοῦ θεοῦ* the shortest, and according to Griesbach, Scholz, Tischendorf, Alford, and Mr Green, the true one, is found only in a few, though confessedly good, cursives: 37. 71. 80*. 116. (*καὶ θεοῦ* 23), the important second hand of 67, and the Venice edition of the Armenian; witnesses too few and feeble, unless we put our third Canon of internal evidence (p. 373) to a rather violent use. Of the longer readings *ὅ ἐστιν χριστὸς* is favoured by D (though obelized by the second hand, which thus would read only *τοῦ θεοῦ*), *d e* (whose parallel Greek speaks differently), Augustine, but apparently by no cursives. The form best vouched for appears to be that of AC. 4, of the Sahidic and an Arabic codex of Tischendorf, *τοῦ θεοῦ πατρὸς τοῦ χριστοῦ*. To these words "*ihu*" is simply added by *f* (FG*g* are unfortunately lost here) and other manuscripts of the Vulgate (*am. fuld.* &c.), though the Clementine Vulgate has "Dei patris et Christi Jesu," the Complutensian (*see* p. 289) "dei et patris et C. J." With the Clementine Vulgate agree the Memphitic, and (omitting *ἰησοῦ*) the Syriac, Arabic, 47. 73. Chrysostom; while 41. 61 (o^{scr}). 115. 213. $\text{b}^{*\text{scr}}$ (*τοῦ θ. καὶ π. τοῦ χ.*) strengthen the case of AC. The received text is found in (apparently) the great mass of cursives, in D (*tertiâ manu*), EKL, the Philoxenian Syriac (but the *καὶ* after *πατρὸς* marked with the asterisk, p. 244), Theodoret, John Damascene and others. The minor variations *τοῦ θεοῦ ἐν χριστῷ* of Clement and Ambrosiaster, *τοῦ θεοῦ τοῦ ἐν χριστῷ* of 17 uphold D*, as *may* the Æthiopic: we also find "dei Christi Jesu patris et domini" in *tol.*, "dei patris et domini nostri Christi" in *demid.*, but these deserve not attention.

On reviewing the whole mass of conflicting evidence, we may unhesitatingly reject the shortest form *τοῦ θεοῦ*, some of whose maintainers do not usually found their text on cursive manuscripts exclusively. We would gladly adopt *τοῦ θεοῦ χριστοῦ*, so powerfully do internal considerations plead in its favour, were it but a little better supported: the important doctrine which it declares, Scriptural and Catholic as it is, will naturally make us only the more cautious in receiving it unreservedly. At present, perhaps, τοῦ θεοῦ πατρὸς τοῦ χριστοῦ may be looked upon as the most strongly attested, but in the presence of so many opposing probabilities, a very small weight might suffice to turn the critical scale.

(20). 1 TIM. iii. 16. Θεὸς ἐφανερώθη ἐν σαρκί. This text has been the *crux criticorum*. All extant Greek manuscripts (D *tertiâ manu*, KL, some 200 cursives) read Θεὸς with the common text, except ℵ* A*? C*? FG 17. 73. 181, which have ὃς, D* which (after the Latin versions) has ὃ: Cod. B is here defective; the Leicester codex, 37, gives ὁ θς̄ (*see* Plate XII. No. 35, l. 1), as if to combine two of the variations. In the abridged form of writing usual in all manuscripts, even the oldest (*see* pp. 14, 43), the difference between OC and ΘC̄ consists only in the presence or absence of two horizontal strokes; hence it is more to be regretted than wondered at that the true reading of each of the uncial authorities for the former is more or less open to question. Respecting Cod. ℵ, indeed, we have as yet no other means of information than the statement of Tischendorf, a most consummate judge in such matters: "*corrector aliquis, qui omnium ultimus textum attigit, saeculi ferè duodecimi,* [*pro* ος *primae manûs*] *reposuit* θεος, *sed hoc tam cautè ut antiquissimam scripturam intactam relinqueret*" (*Notitia Cod. Sinait.* p. 20), which seems unequivocal enough. Nor is there any real doubt respecting the kindred codices FG. From the photographed title-page of the published *Cod. Augiensis* (F) l. 9, and Matthaei's *facsimile* of G (*N. T.* Vol. I. p. 4) it will be seen that while there is not the least trace of the horizontal line within the circle of omicron, the line above the circle in *both* (OC̄) is not horizontal, but rises a little towards the right: such a line not unfrequently in F, oftener in G, is used (as here) to indicate the rough breathing: it sometimes stands even for the *lenis* (e. g. ῑδιον 1 Cor. vi. 18; vii. 4; 37; ῑσσα Phil. ii. 6). Those who never saw Cod. C, must depend on Tischendorf's Excursus (*Cod. Ephraemi*, pp. 39—42) and his *facsimile*, imitated in Plate IX, No. 24. His decision is that the primitive reading was OC, but he was *the first to discern a cross line within* O (*facsimile* l. 3, 8th letter); which, however, from the colour ("*subnigra*") he judges to belong to the second or third hand, rising upwards (a tendency rather exaggerated than otherwise in *our* plate); while the coarse line above, and the musical notes (denoting a word of two syllables) below, are plainly of the third hand. This verdict, especially delivered by such a man, we cannot gainsay, and merely point to the fact that the cross line in Θ, the ninth letter further on, which is certainly *primâ manu*, also ascends towards the right. Cod. A, on the contrary, I have examined at least twenty times within as many years, and yet am not able to assent to the conclusion of Mr Cowper (*see* p. 409, note) when he says "we hope that no one will think it possible, either with or without a lens, to ascertain the truth of the matter by any inspection of the Codex" (*Cod. Alex.* Introd. p. xviii.) On the contrary, seeing (as every one must) with my own eyes, I have always felt convinced with Berriman and the earlier collators that Cod. A read $\overline{\Theta C}$, and so far as I am shaken in my conviction at all, it is less by the adverse opinion even of Dean Ellicott[1], than by the newly-discovered fact (for there

[1] The true reading of the Codex Alexandrinus in 1 Tim. iii. 16 has long been an interesting puzzle with Biblical students. The manuscript, and especially the leaf containing this verse (fol. 145), now very thin and falling into holes, must have been in a widely different condition from the present when it first came to England. At that period Young, Huish (*see p.* 83), and the rest who collated or referred to it, believed that $\overline{\Theta C}$ was written by the first hand. Mill (*N. T. ad loc.*) declares that he had first supposed the primitive reading to be $\overline{OC}$, seeing clearly that the line *over* the letters had not been entirely made, but only thickened, by a later hand, probably the same that traced the coarse, rude, recent, horizontal diameter now running through the circle. On looking more closely, however, he detected "ductus quosdam et vestigia satis certa...praesertim ad partem sinistram, qua peripheriam literae pertingit," evidently belonging to an earlier diameter, which the thicker and later one had almost defaced. This old line was afterwards seen by Dr John Berriman and four other persons with him, when he was preparing his Lady Moyer's Lecture for 1737—8 (*Critical Dissertation on* 1 Tim. iii. 16, p. 156). Wetstein admitted the existence of such a transverse line, but referred it to the tongue or *sagitta* of Є on the reverse of the leaf, an explanation rejected by Woide, but admitted by Tregelles, who states in opposition to Woide that "Part of the Є on the other side of the leaf *does* intersect the O, as we have seen again and again, and which others with us have seen also" (*Horne*, IV. p. 156). This last assertion may be received as quite true, and yet not relevant to the point at issue. In an Excursus appended to 1 Timothy in his edition of *The Pastoral Epistles* (p. 100, 1856), Dean Ellicott declares, as the result of "minute personal inspection," that the original reading was "indisputably" OC. The leaf being held up to the light, the point of an instrument was brought by one of the Librarians of the British Museum "so near to the extremity of the sagitta of the Є as to make a point of

seems no reason to demur to it), that OC—which is adopted by Griesbach, Lachmann, Tischendorf, Davidson, Tregelles, Alford, Ellicott, Wordsworth—was read in ℵ as early as the fourth century.

The secondary witnesses, versions and Fathers, also powerfully incline this way, and they deserve peculiar attention in a case like the present. The Peshito (ܕ) and Philoxenian (text and ܐܠܗܐ in margin) Syriac have a relative (whether ὃς or ὅ); so have the Armenian, the Roman Æthiopic and Erpenius' Arabic. The Gothic, Thebaic, Memphitic, and Platt's Æthiopic favour ὃς: all Latin versions (even *f. g.* whose Greek is OC) read "quod," while θεὸς appears only in the Slavonic (which usually resembles KL and the later copies) and the Polyglott Arabic. Of ecclesi-

shade visible to the observer on the other side:" so that "when the point of the instrument was drawn over the sagitta of the Є, the point of shade was seen *to exactly trace out the suspected diameter of the* O." This might seem indeed a very satisfactory experiment, and would no doubt have been the more so, but for one not trifling drawback. So very delicate is the operation, that out of *two* such experiments which have recently been tried, the result of the one was what the Dean describes, that of the other being to make the sagitta of Є cut the O indeed, as Tregelles mentions, but cut it too high to have been reasonably mistaken by a careful observer for the diameter of Θ. This last state of things corresponds precisely with my own experience. On holding the leaf up to the light one singularly bright hour, February 7, 1861, and gazing at it, with and without a lens, with eyes which have something of the power and too many of the *defects* of a microscope, I saw clearly the tongue of the Є through the attenuated vellum, crossing the circle about two-thirds up (much above the thick modern line), the knob at its extremity falling without the circle. On laying down the leaf, I saw immediately after (but not at the same moment) the slight shadow of the real ancient diameter, only just above the recent one. Even had this last faint line not been seen, Mr Cowper would be right in saying that "The mere absence or invisibility of the cross line of the theta would not of itself be demonstrative, because it has disappeared in a number of cases about which no question ever has been or ever will be raised" (*Cod. Alexand.* Introd. p. xviii).

But one word more. A learned man once suggested to me that the *upper* horizontal line, made by a recent hand, was too thin to cover as it now seems to do all vestiges of such older lines of abridgement as that over ΘC on the same page (ch. iv. 3); furnished, as these lines are, with thick knobs at both ends. Our reply would be (1) that in Mill's time (*vid. supra*) the whole or part of the original upper line (now quite obliterated) was visible to that critic, and (2) that though in the particular instance of ch. iv. 3, and many others, the horizontal line has a bold knob at both ends, in a yet greater number of places the knob is but at one end, or very small, sometimes indeed evanescent, so that to be quite undistinguishable from a portion of a simple straight line, or even to degenerate into two or more points (e.g. ΘΫ, iv. 4), which might easily be covered by the recent line now set above ΘC or OC.

astical writers the best witness for the Received text is Ignatius, Θεοῦ ἀνθρωπίνως φανερουμένου (*Ephes.* 19), both in the Greek and old Latin, although the Syriac abbreviator seems to have τοῦ υἱοῦ: the later interpolator expanded the clause thus: θεοῦ ὡς ἀνθρώπου φαινομένου, καὶ ἀνθρώπου ὡς θεοῦ ἐνεργοῦντος. Hippolytus (*Adv. Noet.* 17) makes a "free reference" to it in the words Οὗτος προελθὼν εἰς κόσμον θεὸς ἐν σώματι ἐφανέρωθη: the testimony of Dionysius of Alexandria (265) can no longer be upheld (Tregelles, *Horne*, IV. p. 339), that of Chrysostom to the same effect is very precarious, since his manuscripts fluctuate, and Cramer's Catena on 1 Tim. p. 31 is adverse; but that of later writers, Theodoret, John Damascene, Theophylact, Oecumenius (as might be looked for) is clear and express. The chief Latins, Hilary, Jerome, Augustine, &c. exhibit either *qui* or *quod:* Cyril of Alexandria (for so we must conclude both from manuscripts and his context)[1], Epiphanius (*twice*), Theodore of Mopsuestia (in Latin), and others of less weight, or whose language is less direct, are cited in critical editions of the N. T. in support of a relative; add to which that θεὸς is not quoted by Fathers (e.g. "Cyprian, p. 35," *Bentleii Crit. Sacra*, p. 67) in many places where it might fairly be looked for; though this argument must not be pushed too far. The idle tale, propagated by Liberatus the Deacon of Carthage, and from him repeated by Hincmar and Victor, that Macedonius Patriarch of Constantinople (A.D. 506) was expelled by the Emperor Anastasius for corrupting Ο or ΟϹ into ΘϹ, although lightly credited by Dr Tregelles (*Account of Printed Text*, p. 229), is sufficiently refuted by Bp. Pearson (*On the Creed*, Art. II. p. 128, 3rd edition).

On a review of the whole mass of external proof, bearing in mind too that ΟϹ (from which ὃ of D* is an evident corruption) is grammatically much the *harder* reading after μυστήριον (p. 371), and that it might easily pass into ΘϹ, we must consider it highly probable (indeed, if we were sure of the testimony of the first-rate uncials, we might regard it as certain) that the second of our rules of Comparative Criticism must here be applied (*see* p. 408), and θεὸς of the more recent many yield place to ὃς of the ancient few.

[1] *Bentleii, Critica Sacra*, p. 67, "Σχόλια Photii MSS. (*Bib. Pub. Cant.*) ad loc. ὁ ἐν ἁγίοις Κύριλλος ἐν τῷ ιβ κεφαλαίῳ τῶν σχολίων φησίν. ὃς ἐφανερώθη ἐν σαρκί." Photius also quoted Gregory Thaumaturgus (or Apollinaris) for θεός.

(21). 1 PET. i. 23. Here we have a remarkable example to illustrate what we saw in the cases of Rom. viii. 20 (p. 418); 2 Cor. iii. 3 (p. 377); Phil. ii. 1 (p. 449), that the chief uncials sometimes conspire in readings which are unquestionably false, and can hardly have arisen independently of each other. For *σπορᾶς φθαρτῆς* Codd. ℵAC have *φθορᾶς φθαρτῆς*, the scribe's eye wandering in writing *σπορᾶς* to the beginning of the next word. When Mill records the variation for Cod. A, he adds (as well he might), "dormitante scribâ:" that the same gross error should be found in three out of the four oldest codices, *and in no other*, is very suggestive and not a little perplexing.

(22). 1 PET. iii. 15. *κύριον δὲ τὸν θεὸν ἁγιάσατε ἐν ταῖς καρδίαις ὑμῶν.* For *θεὸν* we find *χριστὸν* (a change of considerable doctrinal importance) in ABC, Scrivener's ac (two of the best he met with), 7. 8 (Stephens' *ιά*), 13. 33 (*margin*). 69. 137. Apost. 1 ($\overline{ιν}$ $\overline{χν}$ *ἡμῶν*) with its Arabic translation. Thus too read both Syriac versions, the Thebaic, Memphitic, Armenian, Erpenius' Arabic, Vulgate, Clement of Alexandria, Fulgentius and Bede. Jerome has "Jesum Christum:" the Æthiopic and one other (Auctor de Promiss., 4th century) omit both words: we do not yet know the evidence of ℵ. Against this very strong case we can only set up for the common text the more recent uncials GK (only six contain this Epistle), the mass of later cursives (ten out of Scrivener's twelve), the Polyglott Arabic, Slavonic, Theophylact and Oecumenius, authorities of the ninth century and downwards. It is a real pleasure to me in this instance to express my cordial agreement with Tregelles, when he says, "Thus the reading *χριστὸν* may be relied on *confidently*" (*Account of Printed Text*, p. 235). I would further allege this text as one out of many proofs that the great uncials seldom or never conspire in exhibiting a really valuable departure from the later codices, unless supported by some of the best of the cursives themselves (*see above*, pp. 404, 407).

(23). 1 JOHN ii. 23. The English reader will have observed that the latter clause of this verse, "*but he that acknowledgeth the Son hath the Father also*," is printed in italics in our Authorised version, this being the only instance in which variety of reading is thus denoted by the translators, who derived both the words and this method of indicating their doubtful authenticity from the "Great Bible" of 1539. The corresponding Greek *ὁ ὁμολογῶν τὸν υἱὸν καὶ τὸν πατέρα ἔχει* (which seems to have been lost from some copies by *ὁμοιοτέλευτον*, *see* p. 9), was first inserted in Beza's Greek Testament of 1582[1], and is approved by all modern editors (Griesbach, Scholz, Lachmann, Tischendorf, &c.), and though still absent from the *textus receptus*, is pretty surely genuine. This is just such a point as versions are best capable of attesting. The "Great Bible" had no doubt taken the clause from the Latin Vulgate, in whose printed editions and best manuscripts it is found (e. g. in *am. fuld. demid. tol.* but not in *harl.*), as also in both Syriac, both Egyptian, the Armenian, Æthiopic and (were it worth anything) Erpenius' (not the Polyglott) Arabic version. Of manuscripts the great uncials ABC contain the clause, the later GK omit it. Of the cursives only two of Scrivener's (a j) have it, and another (b) *secundâ manu:* from nine or ten of them it is absent: but of the other cursives it is present in at least thirty, whereof 3. 5. 13. 66** (*marg.*). 68. 69. 98 are valuable. It is also acknowledged by Clement, Origen (thrice), Athanasius, both Cyrils, Theophylact and the Western Fathers. Euthalius and one or two others have *ὁμολογεῖ* for the final *ἔχει*: the Old Latin *m*, Cyprian and Hilary repeat *τὸν υἱὸν καὶ* before *τὸν πατέρα ἔχει*. The critical skill of Beza must not be estimated very highly (*see* p. 302), yet in this instance he might well have been imitated by the Elzevir editors.

(24). 1 JOHN v. 7, 8. *Ὅτι τρεῖς εἰσιν οἱ μαρτυροῦντες [ἐν τῷ οὐρανῷ, ὁ Πατήρ, ὁ Λόγος, καὶ τὸ Ἅγιον Πνεῦμα· καὶ οὗτοι οἱ τρεῖς ἕν εἰσι. καὶ τρεῖς εἰσιν οἱ μαρτυροῦντες ἐν τῇ γῇ], τὸ πνεῦμα, καὶ τὸ ὕδωρ, καὶ τὸ αἷμα· καὶ οἱ τρεῖς εἰς τὸ ἕν εἰσιν.*

The authenticity of the words within brackets will, perhaps, no longer be maintained by any one whose judgment ought to have weight; but this result has been arrived at after a long and memorable controversy, which helped to keep alive, especially in England, some interest in Biblical studies, and led to investi-

1 "Restitui in Græcis hoc membrum ex quatuor manuscr. codicum, veteris Latini et Syri interpretis auctoritate. sic etiam assueto Johanne istis oppositionibus contrariorum uti quam saepissimè." Beza, *N. T.* 1582.

gations into collateral points of the highest importance, such as the sources of the Received text, the manuscripts employed by R. Stephens (*see* pp. 299—301), the origin and value of the Velesian readings (*see* p. 156), &c. A critical *résumé* of the whole discussion might be profitably undertaken by some competent scholar; we can at present touch only upon the chief heads of this great debate[1].

The two verses appear in the early editions (adopting again the notation employed above, p. 301), with the following notable variations from the common text: v. 7 – *ἐν τῷ οὐρανῷ usque ad τῇ γῇ* v. 8, Er. 1, 2. – *ὁ prim. et secund.* Er. 3 [*non* C. Er. 4, 5]. + *και* (*post πατήρ*) C. – *τὸ* Er. 3. *τὸ καὶ ἅγιον πνεῦμα* St. 1. *πνεῦμα ἅγιον* Er. 3, 4, 5. – *οὗτοι* C. + *εις το* (*ante εν*) C. v. 8. *επί της γης* C. – *τὸ ter* Er. 3, 4, 5 [*habent* C. Er 1, 2]. – *καὶ οἱ τρεῖς ad fin. vers.* C. They are found, including the clause from *ἐν τῷ οὐρανῷ* to *ἐν τῇ γῇ*, in no more than three Greek manuscripts of very late date, one of them (Cod. Ravianus, Evan. 110), being a mere *worthless* copy from printed books; and in the margin of a fourth, in a hand as late as the sixteenth century. The real witnesses are the Codex Montfortianus, Evan. 61, Act. 34, whose history was described p. 149; Cod. Vat.-Ottob. 298 (Act. 162, *see* p. 196 and note), and for the margin a Naples manuscript (Act. 173, p. 197). On comparing these slight and scanty authorities with the Received text we find that they present the following variations:—v. 7. *ἀπὸ τοῦ οὐρανοῦ* (*pro ἐν τῷ οὐρανῷ*) 162. – *ὁ prim. et secund.* 34. 162. – *τὸ* 34. 162. *π͞ν͞α ἅγιον* 34. 162. – *οὗτοι* 162. + *εἰς τὸ* (*ante ἓν*) 162. v. 8. *εισι* 173 *marg.* *ἐπὶ τῆς γῆς* 162. – *τὸ ter* 34. – *καὶ* (post *π͞ν͞α*) 34. 162. – *καὶ οἱ τρεῖς ad fin. vers.* 34. 162. *fin.* *εισι* 173. No printed edition, therefore, is found to agree with either 34 or 162 (173, whose margin is so very recent, only differs from the common text by dropping *ν ἐφελκυστικὸν*),

[1] Horne (*Introduction*, Vol. II. Pt. II. ch. III. Sect. 4), and after his example Tregelles (*Horne*, IV. pp. 384—8) give a curious list of more than fifty volumes, pamphlets, or critical notices on this question. The following are the most worthy of perusal: *Letters to Edward Gibbon, Esq.* by G. Travis, Archdeacon of Chester, 1785, 2nd edit.: *Letters to Mr Archdeacon Travis*, &c. by Richard Porson, 1790: *Letters to Mr Archdeacon Travis*, &c. by Herbert Marsh [afterwards Bp. of Peterborough] 1795: *A Vindication of the Literary Character of Professor Porson*, by Crito Cantabrigiensis [Thomas Turton, now Bp. of Ely] 1827: *Two Letters on some parts of the Controversy concerning* 1 John v. 7, by Nicholas Wiseman, 1835; for which *see* p. 255.

though on the whole 162 best suits the Complutensian : but the omission of the article in v. 7, while it stands in v. 8 in 162, proves that the disputed clause was interpolated (probably from its parallel Latin) by one who was very ill acquainted with Greek.

The controverted words are not met with in any of the extant uncials (ℵABGK) or in any cursives beside those named above[1]: the cursives that omit them are found by the careful calculation of the Rev. A. W. Grafton, Dean Alford's Secretary (*N. T. ad loc.*), to amount to 188 in all, besides some sixty Lectionaries. The aspect of things is not materially altered when we consult the versions. The disputed clause is not in any manuscript of the Peshito, nor in the best editions (e.g. Lee's : but *see* p. 233) : the Philoxenian, Thebaic, Memphitic, Æthiopic, Arabic do not contain it in any shape: scarcely any Armenian codex has it (*see* p. 277), and only a few *recent* Slavonic copies, the margin of a Moscow edition of 1663 being the first to represent it. The Latin versions, therefore, alone lend it any support, and even these are much divided. The chief and oldest authority in its favour is Wiseman's Speculum *m* (*see* p. 258) of the earlier translation; it is found in the printed Latin Vulgate, and in most of its manuscripts, but not in the best, such as *am.*, *fuld.* (*see* p. 264); nor in Alcuin's reputed copies at Rome (*primâ manu*) and London (*see* p. 262), the book of Armagh (p. 266, note 1), and full fifty others. In one of the most ancient which contain it, *cav.* (*see* p. 265), v. 8 precedes v. 7 (as appears also in *m.*, *tol.*, *demid.*, and a codex [VIII.] cited by Lachmann), while in the margin is written "*audiat hoc Arius et caeteri*," as if its authenticity was unquestioned. In general there is very considerable variety of reading (always a suspicious circumstance, *see* p. 443), and often the doubtful words stand only in the margin: the last clause of v. 8 (*et hi tres unum sunt*) especially is frequently left out when the "Heavenly witnesses" are retained. It is to

[1] It is really surprising how loosely persons who cannot help being scholars, at least in some degree, will talk about codices containing this clause. Dr Edward Tatham, Rector of Lincoln College, Oxford (1792—1834), writing in 1827, speaks of a manuscript in his College Library which exhibited it, but is now missing, as having been once seen by him and Dr Parsons, Bishop of Peterborough (*Crito Cantabrigiensis*, p. 334, note). Yet there can be no question that he meant Act. 33, which does not give the verse, but has long been known to have some connexion with the Codex Montfortianus, which does (*see* p. 189).

defend *this* omission by the opinion of Thomas Aquinas, not to account for the reception of the doubtful words, that the Complutensian editors wrote their long note, reprinted above, p. 363. We conclude, therefore, that the passage from ἐν τῷ οὐρανῷ to ἐν τῇ γῇ had no place in ancient Greek manuscripts, but came into some of the Latin at least as early as the sixth century.

The Patristic testimony in its favour, though quite insufficient to establish the genuineness of the clause, is entitled to more consideration. Of the Greek Fathers no one has cited it, even when it might be supposed to be most required by his argument, or though he quotes consecutively the verses going immediately before and after it. The same must be said of the great Latins, Hilary, Lucifer, Ambrose, Jerome[1] and Augustine, with others of less note. On the other hand the *African* writers, Vigilius of Thapsus, at the end of the fifth century, and Fulgentius of Ruspae (? fl. 520) in two places, expressly appeal to the "three Heavenly Witnesses" as a genuine portion of St John's Epistle; nor is there much reason to doubt the testimony of Victor Vitensis, who records that the passage was insisted on in a confession of faith drawn up by Eugenius Bishop of Carthage at the end of the fifth century, and presented to the Arian Hunneric, king of the Vandals. From that time the clause became well known in other regions of the West, and was in time generally accepted throughout the Latin Church.

But a stand has been made by the maintainers of this passage on the evidence of two African Fathers of a very different stamp from those hitherto named, Tertullian and Cyprian. If it could be proved that these writers cited or alluded to the passage, it would result—*not by any means that it is authentic*—but that like Act. viii. 37 (*see* pp. 387, 444) and a few other like interpolations, it was known and received in some places, as early as the second or third century. Now as regards the language of Tertullian (which will be found in Tischendorf's and the other critical editions of the N. T.: *advers. Prax.* 25; *de Pudic.* 21), it must be admitted that Bp. Kaye's view is the most reasonable, that "far from containing an allusion to

[1] The "Prologus Galeatus in VII Epistolas *Canonicas*," in which the author complains of the omission of v. 7, "ab infidelibus translatoribus," is certainly not Jerome's, and begins to appear in codices of about the ninth century.

1 Jo. v. 7, it furnishes most decisive proof that he knew nothing of the verse" (*Writings of Tertullian*, p. 550, 2nd edition); but I cannot thus dispose of his junior Cyprian (d. 258). I must say with Tischendorf (who, however, manages to explain away his testimony) "*gravissimus* est Cyprianus *de eccles. unitate* 5." His words run, "Dicit dominus, *Ego et pater unum sumus* (Joh. x. 30), et iterum de Patre, et Filio, et Spiritu Sancto scriptum est, *Et tres unum sunt.*" And yet further in his Epistle to Jubaianus (73) on heretical baptism: "Si baptizari quis apud haereticos potuit, utique et remissam peccatorum consequi potuit,—si peccatorum remissam consecutus est, et sanctificatus est, et templum Dei factus est, quaero cujus Dei? Si Creatoris, non potuit, qui in eum non credidit; si Christi, nec hujus fieri potuit templum, qui negat Deum Christum; si Spiritus Sancti, cum tres unum sunt, quomodo Spiritus Sanctus placatus esse ei potest, qui aut Patris aut Filii inimicus est?" If these two passages be taken together (the first is much the stronger[1]), it is surely safer and more candid to admit that Cyprian read v. 7 in his copies, than to resort to the explanation of Facundus [VI], that the holy Bishop was merely putting on v. 8 a spiritual meaning; although we must acknowledge that it was in this way v. 7 obtained a place, first in the margin, then in the text of the Latin copies, and though we have clear examples of the like mystical interpretation in Eucherius (fl. 440) and Augustine (*contra Maximin.* 22), who only knew of v. 8.

Stunica, the chief Complutensian editor, by declaring, in controversy with Erasmus, with reference to this very passage, "Sciendum est, Graecorum codices esse corruptos, nostros [i. e. Latinos] verò ipsam veritatem continere," virtually admits that v. 7 was translated in that edition from the Latin, not derived from Greek sources. The versions (for such we must call them) in Cod. 34. 162 had no doubt the same origin, but were somewhat worse rendered: the margin of 173 seems to be taken from a printed book. Erasmus, after excluding the passage

[1] The writer of a manuscript note in the British Museum copy of Travis' *Letters to Gibbon*, 1785, p. 49, very well observes on the second citation from Cyprian: "That three are one might be taken from the eighth verse, as that was certainly understood of Father, Son, and Holy Ghost, *especially when Baptism was the subject in hand*" [Matth. xxviii. 19].

from his first two editions, inserted it in his third under circumstances we have before mentioned (pp. 149, 297); and notwithstanding the discrepancy of reading in v. 8, there can be little or no doubt of the identity of his "Codex Britannicus" with Montfort's. We have detailed (p. 458) the steps by which the text was brought into its present shape, wherein it long remained, unchallenged by all save a few such bold spirits as Bentley, defended even by Mill, implicitly trusted in by those who had no knowledge of Biblical criticism. It was questioned in fair argument by Wetstein, assailed by Gibbon in 1781 with his usual weapons, sarcasm and insinuation (*Decline and Fall*, Chap. XXXVII). Archdeacon Travis, who came to the rescue, a person "of some talent and attainments" (*Crito Cantab.* p. 335, note), burdened as he was with a weak cause and undue confidence in its goodness, would have been at any rate—*impar congressus Achilli*—no match at all for the exact learning, the acumen, the wit, the overbearing scorn of Porson[1]. The *Letters* of that prince of scholars, and the contemporaneous researches of Herbert Marsh, have completely decided the contest: Bp. Burgess alone, while yet among us [d. 1837], clung obstinately to a few scattered outposts after the main field of battle had been lost beyond recovery.

On the whole, therefore, we need not hesitate to declare our conviction that the disputed words were not written by St John: that they were originally brought into Latin copies in Africa from the margin, where they had been placed as a pious and orthodox gloss on v. 8: that from the Latin they crept into two

[1] I side with Porson against Travis on every important point at issue between them, and yet I must say that if the former lost a legacy (as has been reported) by publishing his "*Letters*," he was entitled to but slender sympathy. The prejudices of good men (especially when a passage is concerned which they have long held to be a genuine portion of Scripture, clearly teaching pure and right doctrine) should be dealt with gently: not that the truth should be dissembled or withheld, but when told it ought to be in a spirit of tenderness and love. Now take one example out of fifty of the tone and temper of Porson. The question was a very subordinate one in the controversy, the evidence borne by the Acts of the Lateran Council, A.D. 1215. "Though this," rejoins Porson, "proves nothing in favour of the verse, it proves two other points. That the clergy then exercised dominion over the rights of mankind, and that able tithe-lawyers often make sorry critics. *Which I desire some certain gentlemen of my acquaintance to lay up in their hearts as a very seasonable innuendo*" (*Letters*, p. 361). As if it were a disgrace for an Archdeacon to know a little about the laws which affect his clergy.

or three late Greek codices, and thence into the printed Greek text, a place to which they had no rightful claim. We will close this slight review with the terse and measured judgment of Griesbach on the subject: "Si tam pauci, dubii, suspecti, recentes testes, et argumenta tam levia, sufficerent ad demonstrandam lectionis cujusdam γνησιότητα, licet obstent tam multa tamque gravia, et testimonia et argumenta: nullum prorsus superesset in re criticâ veri falsique criterium, et *textus Novi Testamenti universus planè incertus esset atque dubius*" (*N. T. ad locum*, Vol. II. p. 709).

(25). Apoc. xiii. 10. Εἴ τις αἰχμαλωσίαν συνάγει, εἰς αἰχμαλωσίαν ὑπάγει. This reading of the received text is perfectly clear; indeed, when compared with what is found in the best manuscripts, it is too simple to be true (Canon I. p. 371). From a communication made by Tischendorf to Mr Kelly (*Revelation of John*, Introd. p. xv.) we know that Cod. ℵ agrees in substance with BC: ει (η C) τις εις αιχμαλωσιαν υπαγει (ὑπάγῃ B *Mai*), the reading of those excellent cursives 28. 38. 95, and a manuscript of Andreas: εις is further omitted in 14 (*sic*). 32. 47. the Memphitic (?), Arabic (Polyglott), and a Slavonic manuscript. The sense of this reading, if admissible at all, is very harsh and elliptical: that of the only remaining uncial A, though apparently unsupported except by a Slavonic manuscript and the best copies of the Vulgate, looks more probable: εἴ τις εἰς αἰχμαλωσίαν, εἰς αἰχμαλωσίαν ὑπάγει: "if any one *is* for captivity, into captivity he goeth" (*Tregelles*, *Kelly*, who compares Jerem. xv. 2, LXX): the second εἰς αἰχμαλωσίαν being omitted by homoeoteleuton (*see* p. 9) in the abovementioned codices. Tregelles, Lachmann, Tischendorf and Kelly follow Cod. A, and it would seem rightly.

All other variations were devised for the purpose of supplying the ellipsis left in the uncials. For συνάγει of the common text (now that it is known not to be found in C) no Greek authority is expressly cited except the *recent* margin of 94 (b^{scr}). The favourite form of the cursives is that printed in the Complutensian Polyglott: εἴ τις ἔχει αἰχμαλωσίαν, ὑπάγει, after 2. 8. 13. 29. 30. 31. 37. 40. 41. 42. 48. 49. 50. 90. 93. 94*. 96. 97. 98, perhaps some six others, a Slavonic manuscript, Andreas in the edition of 1596. The Vulgate, the Pseudo-Peshito Syriac (*see* p. 233), and Primasius in substance, read "Qui in captivitatem duxerit, in captivitatem vadet," but *am. fuld.* (not *demid.*) and the best codices omit "duxerit" and have "vadit" (Syr. ܡܘܒܠ...ܐܙܠ), *which brings the clause into accordance with Cod. A.* The Greek corresponding with the *printed* Vulgate is *εἴ τις εἰς* (33 omits *εἰς*) *αἰχμαλωσίαν* (*ἐς* 87) *ἀπάγει* (*ἐπάγει* 87), *εἰς αἰχμαλωσίαν ὑπάγει*, 33, 35, 87. Other modes of expression (e.g. *εἴ τις αἰχμαλωτίζει εἰς αἰχμαλωσίαν ὑπάγει*, 7: *εἴ τις αἰχμαλωτιεῖ, αἰχμαλωτισθήσεται*, 18: *εἴ τις αἰχμαλώτης εἶ, εἰς αἰχ. ὑπ.* 36, &c.) resemble those already given in their attempt to enlarge and soften what was originally abrupt and perhaps obscure.

God grant that if these studies shall have made any of us better instructed in the letter of His Holy Word; we may find grace to grow, in like measure, in that knowledge which tendeth to salvation, through faith in His mercy by Christ Jesus.

INDICES.

INDEX I.

Index of about 1170 *separate Greek Manuscripts of the New Testament described in Chapter* II, *Sections* II, III, IV, *arranged according to the countries wherein they are now deposited.*

Denmark 3 MSS.; England 250; France 238; Germany 90; Holland 6; Ireland 3; Italy 320; Russia 73; Scotland 7; Spain 19; Sweden 1; Switzerland 14; Turkey 104? Unknown 42?

N.B. *Evan.* means a manuscript of the Gospels; *Act.* of the Acts and Catholic Epistles; *Paul.* of St Paul's Epistles; *Apoc.* of the Apocalypse; *Evst.* a Lectionary of the Gospels; *Apost.* a Lectionary of the Epistles. When a manuscript contains more than one portion of the N.T., the fact is always stated at the place in the present volume, to which the reader is referred in this Index.

PAGE

DENMARK (Copenhagen) 3.

Havniensis 1 ....Evan. 234 166
2 ....Evan. 235 166
3 ....Evst. 44.........214

ENGLAND 250 MSS.

(British and Foreign Bible Soc. London) ....Evan. Ξ. 126

(Cambridge) 19 MSS.

University Library.

Dd. 8. 23...............Evst. 146 218
Dd. 8. 49...............Evst. 4 212
Dd. 9. 69...............Evan. 60 149
Dd. 11. 90 ....Act. 21 188
Ff. 1. 30 ....Paul. 27 201
Hh. 6. 12 ....Evan.............181
Kk. 5. 35 ....Evan. 62 150
Kk. 6. 4 ....Act. 9 187
Ll. 2. 13 ....Evan. 70 152
Mm. 6. 9...............Evan. 440......176
Nn. 2. 36...............Evan. 443......176
Nn. 2. 41 (Cod. Bezae) Evan. D....96–103

Gonville and Caius College.

Codex 403 ....Evan. 59 148

Christ's College.

F. i. 8 ....Evst. z^{scr}. 221
F. i. 13 ....Act. 24 188

Trinity College.

B. x. 16 ....Evan. w^{scr}. ...180
B. x. 17 ....Evan. i^{scr}.......179
B. xvii. 1 (Cod. Augiens.) Paul. F...133–5

Emmanuel College.

I. 4. 35 ....Act. 53 191

(Lambeth) 24 MSS. PAGE

Cod. 528..............Evan. 71......152
1175..............Evan. a^scr. ...178
1176..............Evan. b^scr. ...178
1177..............Evan. c^scr. ...178
1178..............Evan. d^scr. ...178
1179..............Evan. e^scr. ...179
1180..............Evan. v^scr. ...180
1181? (or 1255) Act. e^scr. 199
1182..............Act. a^scr. 198
1183..............Act. b^scr. 198
1184..............Act. c^scr. 198
1185..............Act. d^scr. 199
1186..............Paul. e^scr. ...206
1187, 1188, 1189 Evst. 223
1190, 1191 ......Apost. 225
1192..............Evan. f^scr. ...179
1193..............Evst. 223
1194, 1195, 1196 Apost. 225
1350..............Evan. t^scr. ...180

(Leicester) ....Evan. 69......151

(Middle-Hill, Worcestershire) 4 MSS.

1461 ....Act. 178 197
7681 ....Act. 199
13975 ....Evan. 181
Unknown..............Evst. 221

(Museum Brit. London) 75 MSS.

Codex Alexandrinus Cod. A. ...79–84
Arundel 524...........Evan. h^scr. ...179
536...........Evst. 221
547...........Evst. x^scr. ...220
Burney 18 ....Evan. n^scr. ...179
19 ....Evan. o^scr. ...179
20 ....Evan. p^scr. ...179
21 ....Evan. r^scr. ...180
22 ....Evst. y^scr. ...220
23 ....Evan. s^scr. ...180
48 ....Act. j^scr. 199
Cotton, Vesp. B. xviii. Apost. 2 223
Titus C. xv....Evan. N....110–1
Harleian 1810.........Evan. 113 ...157
5537.........Act. 25.........188
5538.........Evan. 187
5540.........Evan. 114 ...157
5552.........Paul. 66 202
5557.........Act. 26.........189
5559.........Evan. 115 ...157
5567.........Evan. 116 ...158

PAGE

Harleian 5588.........Act. 59.........191
5598.........Evst. 150......218
5613...... { Paul. M. ......138 / Act. 60 ......191 }
5620.........Act. 27.........189
5647.........Evan. 72......152
5650.........Evst. 25, 25^b..213
5678.........Apoc. 31......208
5684.........Evan. G. 106
5731.........Evan. 117 ...158
5736.........Evan. 445 ...176
5776.........Evan. 65......150
5777.........Evan. 446 ...176
5778.........Act. 28.........189
5784.........Evan. 447 ...177
5785.........Evst. 151......218
5787.........Evst. 152......219
5790.........Evan. 448 ...177
5796.........Evan. 444 ...176
King's Library, IBI. Act. 20 188

Additional Manuscripts.

4949 ....Evan. 44 147
(1) 4950, 4951.........Evan. 449......177
5107 ....Evan. 439 ...176
(1) 5111, 5112.........Evan. 438 ...176
(1) 5115, 5116...Act. 22, Paul. 75...188
5117 ....Evan. 109 ...156
5153 ....Evst.............223
7141 ....Evan. 186
7142 ....Paul. 207
11300 ....Evan. k^scr. ...179
11836 ....Evan. 186
11837 ....Evan. 201 ...163
(2) 11838, 11839......Evan. 186
(2) 11840, 11841......Evst.............223
14744 ....Evan. 202...164, 186
(4) 15581, 16183, 16184, 16943 Evan. 186
17136 ....Evan. N^b. ...111
17211 ....Evan. R.......114
17469 ....Evan. (Apoc. j^scr.)...186
17470 ....Evan. 187
17741 ....Evan. 186
(2) 17982, 18211 ......Evan. 187
18212 ....Evst. 223
19387 ....Evan. 187
19388 ......Paul. &c...*Addenda*, p. viii.
19389 ....Evan. 187
(2) 19460, 19993 ......Evst. 223
20003 ....Act. lo^ti 198

PAGE

(Oxford) 103 MSS. *Bodleian.*

Auct. T. Infra I. 1 ...Evan. Λ. 124
II. 2 ...Evan. Γ. 121
Barocc. 3 ....Act. 23.........188
29 ....Evan. 46 147
31 ....Evan. 45 147
48 ....Apoc. 28 208
59 ....Evan. 184
119 ....Evst. 221
202 ....Evst. 5.........212
Canonici 33 ....Evan. 184
34 ...Evan. (Apoc. k^{scr}.) 184
36 ....Evan. 184
(2) 85, 92 ....Evst. 221
110 ....Act. 199
112 ....Evan. 184
119 ....Evst. 221
122 ....Evan. 184
126 ....Evst. 221
E. D. Clarke 4 ......Act. 56.........191
5 ......Evan. 98 155
6 ......Evan. 107 ...155
7 ......Evan. 111 ...156
8 ......Evst. 157......219
9 ......Act. 58.........191
10 ......Evan. 112 ...156
(4) 45, 46, 47, 48 ......Evst. 221
Cromwell 11............Evst. 30 213
(2) 15, 16............Evan. 184
27............Evst.............221
Laud 3 ....Evan. 52 148
31 ....Evan. 51 147
32 ....Evst. 18 212
33 ....Evan. 50 147
34 ....Evst. 20 212
35 ....Act. E.......128–9
36 .... *vid.* p. 212, *note*
Miscellan. 1 ....Evan. 48 147
5.........Evan. O^b......112
8.........Evan. 96 154
9.........Evan. 47 147
10.........Evst. 19 212
11.........Evst. 28 213
12.........Evst. 29 213
13.........Evan. 118......158
17.........Evan. 184
74.........Act. 30.........189
76.........Evan. 67 151
118.........Act. 199
119.........Evst.............221

PAGE

Miscellan. 136.........Evan. 105......155
140.........Evst.............221
141.........Evan. 185
Roe 1 ....Evan. 49 147
16 ....Paul. 47 201
Selden 1 ....Evst. 26 213
2 ....Evst. 27 213
5 ....Evan. 55 148
47 ....Evst. 22 213
49 ....Evst. 21 213
53 ....Evan. 53 148
54 ....Evan. 54 148
New College 58.........Act. 36.........189
59 ....Act. 37.........189
68.........Evan. 58 148
Lincoln College 15 ...Evst. 3.........212
16 ...Evan. 95 154
17 ...Evan. 68 151
18 ...Evan. 56 148
82 ...Act. 33.........189
Magdalen Coll. 7......Paul. 42 201
9......Evan. 57 148
Christ Church, Wake
12 ....(Apoc. 26, &c.) 182
(7) 13, 14, 15, 16, 17, 18, 19...Evst....222
20 ....Evan. 74 152
(2) 21, 22 ....Evan. 182
23 ....Evst.............222
(2) 24, 25 ....Evan. 182
26 ....Evan. 73 152
(6) 27, 28, 29, 30, 31, 32 Evan. 183
33 ....Apost. 58......225
34 .... Evan., Act. 190...183, 198
36 ....Evan. 183
37 ....Act. 192 198
38 ....Act. 191 198
(2) 39, 40 ....Evan. 183

(Parham Park, Sussex) 17 MSS.

Vellum 1 ....Evst. P_2^{scr}. ...220
(8) 6, 7, 8, 9, 10, 11, 12, 13...Evan....182
(3) 14, 15, 16 ....Act. 199
17 ....Apoc. 95 210
18 ....Evst. P^{scr}. ...220
(2) 19, 20 ....Evst.............223
Paper 2...................Apoc. 96 210

(Sion College, London) 4 MSS.

Fragment of the Gospels..............187
Ari. I. 1, Ari. I. 2, Ari. I. 4....Evst....222

PAGE

Winchelsea, Earl of...Evan. 106......155
Wordsworth, Canon..Evan. 1scr.......179

FRANCE, 238 MSS.

Arras....................N.T............181
Besançon ....Evst.............223
Carpentras ......Evst. carpev....181, 220

(Paris) *Royal or Imperial Library.*

Reg. (RI *Tischendorf.*) 9 Cod. C. 94–96
14......Evan. 33 145
19......Apoc. 58 209
32 a ...Evst. 84 216
33 a ...Evst. 85 216
47......Evan. 18 144
48......Evan. M. 109–110
49......Evan. 8.........143
50......Evan. 13 144
50 a ...Evst. 58 215
51......Evan. 260 ...168
52......Evan. 261 ...168
53......Evan. 262 ...168
54......Evan. 16 144
55......Evan. 17 144
56......Act. 51.........190
57......Act. 114 194
58......Act. 115 194
59......Act. 116 194
60......Act. 62.........191
61......Evan. 263 ...168
62......Evan. L. ...108–9
63......Evan. K....107–8
64......Evan. 15 144
65......Evan. 264 ...168
66......Evan. 265 ...168
67......Evan. 266 ...168
68......Evan. 21 144
69......Evan. 267 ...168
70......Evan. 14 144
71......Evan. 7 143
72......Evan. 22 144
73......Evan. 268 ...168
74......Evan. 269 ...168
75......Evan. 270 ...168

PAGE

Reg. 75 a ...Evan. 271 ...168
76......Evan. 272 ...168
77......Evan. 23 145
78......Evan. 26 145
79......Evan. 273 ...168
79 a ...Evan. 274 ...168
80......Evan. 275 ...168
81......Evan. 276 ...168
81 a ...Evan. 277 ...168
82......Evan. 278 ...168
83......Evan. 9.........143
84......Evan. 4.........143
85......Evan. 119......158
86......Evan. 279......168
87......Evan. 280 ...169
88......Evan. 281 ...169
89......Evan. 29 145
90......Evan. 282 ...169
91......Evan. 10 143
92......Evan. 283 ...169
93......Evan. 284 ...169
94......Evan. 31 145
95......Evan. 285 ...169
96......Evan. 286 ...169
98......Evan. 287 ...169
99......Evan. 288 ...169
99 a ...Apoc. 59 209
100......Evan. 30 145
100 a[1]...Evan. 289 ...169
also 100 a[1]...Evst. 59 215
101......Act. 118 194
102......Act. 7 187
102 a ...Act. 119 194
103......Act. 11 187
103 a ...Act. 120 194
104......Act. 121 194
104 a ...Apost. 11......223
105......Act. 122 194
106......Evan. 5 143
106 a ...Act. 123 195
107......Paul. D. 130–132
108......Paul. 145......204
108 a ...Evan. 290 ...169
109......Paul. 146......204

[1] Codd. 100 a, 194 a, 303, 315, 377 are in Scholz's lists both of the Gospels and Evangelistaria, though he does not state, as he ought, that the same copy contains both. Codd. 100 A, 194 A, 377 are undoubtedly the same volumes in both lists, as it is probable that Cod. 303 is also, though in the Gospels he calls it 4°, in the Evst. folio. In the case of Cod. 315 there is perhaps some error, since Scholz puts it in his list for the Gospels as new, though it was known long ago as Evst. 14. Codd. 380, 381 also seem to contain both Evan. and Evst.

PAGE

Reg. 110......Paul. 147......204
111......Paul. 148......204
112......Evan. 6 143
113......Evan. 291 ...169
114......Evan. 292 ...169
115......Evan. 27 145
115 a ...Evst. 96 216
116......Evan. 32 145
117......Evan. 293 ...169
118......Evan. 294 ...169
118 a ...Evan. 323 ...170
120......Evan. 295 ...169
(1) 121, 122......Evan. 11 143
123......Evan. 296 ...169
124......Act. 124 195
125......Act. 125 195
126......Paul. 151......204
136 a ...Paul. 152......204
140 a ...Evan. 297 ...169
175 a ...Evan. 298 ...169
177......Evan. 299 ...169
178......Evan. 24 145
182......Evst. 61 215
185 a ...Evan. 120 ...158
186......Evan. 300 ...169
187......Evan. 301 ...169
188......Evan. 20 144
189......Evan. 19 144
191......Evan. 25 145
193......Evan. 302 ...169
194......Evan. 304 ...170
194 a[1]...Evan. 303 ...169
also 194 a[1]...Evst. 62 215
195......Evan. 305 ...170
196......Evan. 103 ...155
197......Evan. 306 ...170
199......Evan. 307 ...170
200......Evan. 308 ...170
201......Evan. 309 ...170
202......Evan. 310 ...170
203 (*not* 303)...Evan. 311 ...170
206......Evan. 312 ...170
208......Evan. 313 ...170
209......Evan. 314 ...170
210......Evan. 315 ...170
211......Evan. 316 ...170
212......Evan. 317 ...170
213......Evan. 318 ...170
216......Act. 126 195
217......Act. 127 195

PAGE

Reg. 218......Act. 128 195
219......Act. 12.........188
220......Act. 129 195
221......Act. 130 195
222......Paul. 157......204
223......Act. 131 195
224......Paul. 159......204
225......Paul. 160......204
226......Paul. 161......204
227......Paul. 162......204
230......Evan. 12 144
231......Evan. 319 ...170
232......Evan. 320 ...170
237......Act. 10.........187
238......Paul. 163......204
(1) 239, 240......Apoc. 62 209
241......Apoc. 63 209
276......Evst. 82 216
277......Evst. 63 215
278......Evst. 1.........212
279......Evst. 17 212
280......Evst. 2.........212
281......Evst. 64 215
282......Evst. 65 215
283......Evst. 66 215
284......Evst. 67 215
285......Evst. 68 215
286......Evst. 69 215
287......Evst. 10 212
288......Evst. 70 215
289......Evst. 71 215
290......Evst. 72, 72b 215
291......Evst. 73 215
292......Evst. 74 215
293......Evst. 75 215
294......Evst. 83 216
295......Evst. 76 215
296......Evst. 77 215
297......Evst. 16 212
298......Evst. 78 215
299......Evst. 79 215
300......Evst. 80 215
301......Evst. 7.........212
302......Evst. 15 212
303......Evan. 321 ...170
also 303[1].....Evst. 101......216
304......Apost. 22......224
305......Evst. 81 216
306......Apost. 23......224
307......Evst. 9.........212

PAGE
Reg. 308......Apost. 24......224
309......Evst. 11 212
310......Evst. 12 212
311......Evst. 86 216
312......Evst. 8.........212
313......Evst. 87 216
314......Evst. 88 216
314 contains also Evan. W^{a}...117–8
315......Evan. 322 ...170
also 315^{1}.....Evst. 14 212
316......Evst. 89 216
317......Evst. 90 216
318......Evst. 91 216
319......Apost. 25......224
320......Apost. 26......224
321......Apost. 27......224
324......Evst. 92 216
326......Evst. 93 216
330......Evst. 94 216
373......Apost. 30......224
374......Evst. 95 216
375......Evst. 60 215
376......Evan. 324 ...170
377......Evan. 325 ...170
377^{1} also contains Evst. 98...216
378......Evan. 326 ...171
379......Evan. 28 145
380...Evan. 327, p. 171 and Evst. 99 216
381...Evan. 328, p. 171 and Evst. 100 216
382......Apost. 33......224
383......Apost. 34......224
491......Apoc. 61 209
849......Paul. 164......204
Coislin 1 ....Evan. F^{a}...105–6
19 ....Evan. 329 ...171
20 ....Evan. 36 146
21 ....Evan. 37 146
22 ....Evan. 40 146
23 ....Evan. 39 146
24 ....Evan. 41 146
25 ....Act. 15.........188
26 ....Act. 16.........188
27 ....Paul. 20 200
28 ....Paul. 23 201
31 ....Evst. 13 212
195 ....Evan. 34 146
196 ....Evan. 330 ...171
197 ....Evan. 331 ...171
199 ....Evan. 35 146
200 ....Evan. 38 146

PAGE
Coislin 202 ....Paul. H. ...137–8
202, 2 ....Act. 18.........188
204 ....Paul. 59 201
205 ....Act. 17.........188
Arsenal of Paris 4 ...Evan. 43 147
St Geneviève 4. A. 34 Evan. 121. 158, 181
4. A. 35 Paul. 247......206
Royal Institute of Paris...Evan. ...181
Poictiers ....N. T. 181
Strasburg? Boecler...Paul. 248, &c. 199
from Molsheim...Evan. 431 ...175

GERMANY 90 MSS.

(Berlin) Cod. Ravianus...Evan. 110...156
Cod. Diezii.........Evan. 400 ...174
Cod. Knobelsdorf Evan. 433 ...175
(Dresden) Cod. Boerner...Paul. G. 135–7
Matthaei k ....Evan. 241 ...167
z ....Evan. 252 ...167
17 ....Evan. 258 ...167
Dresden 252............Act. 107 194
is perhaps the same as Apoc. 32 ...208
(Frankfort-on-Oder)...Act. 42 190
(Giessen) ....Evan. 97 154
(Gottingen) ....Evan. 89 154
Gottin. 2 ....Apost. 5 223
(Hamburg) Cod. Wolf. Evan. H....106–7
Cod. Uff. 2 or 1 Paul. M. or 53 ....138, 201
Cod. Uff. 1 or 2 ....Act. 45.........190
(Leipsic) Cod. Matth. 18...Evan. 99...155
Cod. Matth. s..........Paul. 76 202
Cod. Tischendorf. i....Evan. Θ 124
Cod. Tischendorf. iv...Evan. $tisch^{1}$...181
Cod. Tischendorf. v....Evst. $tisch^{ev}$...220
6. F. ....Apost. $tisch^{6.f}$ 225
(Munich) Univ. Libr. Evan. X. ...118–9
23............Apoc. 81 209
35........... Paul. 129......204
36............Evan. 423 ...175
37............Evan. 425 ...175
83............Evan. 424 ...175
99............Evan. 432 ...175
110............Paul. 127......203
208............Evan. 429 ...175
210............Evan. 422 ...175
211............Act. 179 197
229............Evst. 34 213
248............Apoc. 79 209
326............Evst. 154......219
375............Act. 46.........190

PAGE

Univ. Libr. 381.........Evan. 428 ...175
383............Evst. 24 213
412............Paul. 54 201
437.. ....Evan. 430 ...175
455............Paul. 126......203
465............Evan. 427 ...175
473............Evan. 426 ...175
504............Paul. 125......203
518............Evan. 83 153
544............Apoc. 80 209
568............Evan. 84 153
569............Evan. 85 153
(Nüremberg) ....Evst. 31 213
(Pesth) Cod. Eubeswald...Evan. 100 155
Cod. Jancovich ......Evan. 78......153
(Posen) Lycaei Aug. Evan. 86......153
(Saxe-Gotha) Matthaei...Evst. 32...213
(Trèves) Cod. Cuzan. Evan. 87 154
Cod. S. Simeon ......Evst. 179......219
(Tübingen) Evst. R. or tubing^{ev}. 114,220

(Vienna) Imperial Library.

Lambec. 1............Evan. 218 ...165
2............Evan. N. 110
15............Evst. 45 214
28............Evan. 76 152
29............Evan. 77 152
30............Evan. 123 ...158
31............Evan. 124 ...158
32............Evan. 219 ...165
33............Evan. 220 ...165
34............Act. 66.........191
35............Act. 63.........191
36............Act. 64.........191
37............Act. 67.........192
38............Evan. 221 ...165
39............Evan. 222 ...165
40............Evan. 223 ...165
41............Evst. 155......219
42............Evan. 434 ...175
46............Paul. 214......206
248............Apoc. 35 208
Forlos. 5, Kollar. 4......Evan. 108...156
Forlos. 15, Kollar. 5 ...Evan. 3 ...143
Forlos. 16, Kollar. 6 ...Evan. 125...158
Forlos. 19, Kollar. 10...Paul. 71 ...202
Forlos. 23, Kollar. 7 ...Evst. 46 ...214
Forlos. 29, Kollar. 26...Apoc. 36 ...208
Forlos. 30, Kollar. 8 ...Evan. 224...165
Forlos. 31, Kollar. 9 ...Evan. 225...165

PAGE

(Wolfenbüttel) ....Evan. O^a ...112
Codex Carolinus A, B...Evan. P, Q. 113-4
xvi. 7...............Act. 69......192
xvi. 16 ....Evan. 126...158
Gud. gr. 104. 2...Act. 97......193

HOLLAND 6 MSS.

(Leyden) 74? ....Evan. 79 ...153
77 ....Act. 38......189
Meermann. 116............Evan. 122...158
Gronovii 131 ....Evan. 435...176
Scaligeri 243...............Evst. 6 212
(Utrecht) ....Evan. F. 104-5

IRELAND 3 MSS. (Trin. Coll. Dublin).

Cod. Barrett......... Evan. Z....119-121
Cod. Ussher, A. 1. 8 ...Evan. 63...150
[N.B. Evan. 64 is lost]...150
Cod. Montfort. G. 97 ...Evan. 61 ...149

ITALY 320 MSS.

(Bologna) Can. Reg.
640.........Evan. 204 ...164

(Florence) 47 or 48 MSS.

Laurent. iv. 1.........Act. 84 192
iv. 5.........Act. 85 192
iv. 20.........Act. 86 193
iv. 29.........Act. 87 193
iv. 30.........Act. 147 ...196
iv. 31.........Act. 88 193
iv. 32.........Act. 89 193
vi. 2.........Evst. 113 ...217
vi. 5.........Act. 143 ...195
vi. 7.........Evst. 114 ...217
vi. 11.........Evan. 182...162
vi. 13.........Evan. 363...172
vi. 14.........Evan. 183...162
vi. 15.........Evan. 184...163
vi. 16.........Evan. 185...163
vi. 18.........Evan. 186...163
vi. 21.........Evst. 115...217
vi. 23.........Evan. 187...163
vi. 24.........Evan. 364...172
vi. 25.........Evan. 188...163
vi. 27.........Evan. 189...163
vi. 28.........Evan. 190...163
vi. 29.........Evan. 191 ...163

PAGE

Laurent. vi. 30.........Evan. 192...163
vi. 31.........Evst. 116...217
vi. 32.........Evan. 193...163
vi. 33.........Evan. 194...163
vi. 34.........Evan. 195...163
vi. 36.........Evan. 365...172
vii. 9.........Apoc. 77...209
viii. 12.........Evan. 196...163
viii. 14.........Evan. 197...163
x. 4.........Paul. 100...202
x. 6.........Paul. 101...202
x. 7.........Paul. 102...203
x. 19.........Paul. 103...203
176.........Act. 149...196
244.........Evst. 117...217
256.........Evan. 198...163
2574.........Act. 148...196
2607.........Evan. 366...172
2708.........Evan. 367...172
2742.........Evst. 112...217
Cista.........Evst. 118...217
Richard. 84.........Evan. 368...172
90.........Evan. 369...172
Richard. K. i. n. 11...Evan. 370...172
St Mark's?[1] Apost. 4...223

(Messina) 1............Evan. 420...175
2............Act. 175......197

(Milan) 23 MSS.
Ambros. 6.........Paul. 171...205
13.........Evan. 343...171
15.........Paul. 172...205
16.........Evan. 344...171
17.........Evan. 345...171
23.........Evan. 346...171
35.........Evan. 347...171
56.........Evan. 348...171
61.........Evan. 349...171
62.........Evst. 102...216
B. 62.........Evan. 350...171
63.........Apost. 46...224
67.........Evst. 103...216
70.........Evan. 351...171
72.........Evst. 104...217
81.........Evst. 105...217
91.........Evst. 106...217

PAGE

Ambros. B. 93.........Evan. 352...172
M. 93.........Evan. 353...172
97.........Act. 137...195
102.........Act. 138...195
104.........Act. 139...195
125.........Paul. 175...205

(Modena) 6 MSS. 9...Evan. 358...172
14...Paul. 177...205
27...Evst. 111...217
196...Act. H.......129
242...Evan. 359...172
243...Act. 142...195

(Naples) 9 MSS.
1 B. 12.........Act. 83......192
1 B. 14.........Evst. 138...218
1 C. 24.........Evan. 401...174
1 C. 26.........Act. 174......197
1 C. 28.........Evan. 402...174
1 C. 29.........Evan. 403...174
2 C. 15...Evan. W^b or R...114
Scotti.........Evan. 404...174
No mark.........Act. 173......197

(Palermo) Bibl. Reg....Paul. 217...206

(Parma) De Rossi 1...Evan. 360...172
2...Evan. 361...172

(Rome) 159 MSS. *Vatican* (109)
Cod. Vatic. 165.........Paul. 58...201
349.........Evan. 127...159
351.........Evst. 35...213
354.........Evan. S....115
356.........Evan. 128...159
358.........Evan. 129...159
359.........Evan. 130...159
360.........Evan. 131...159
361.........Evan. 132...159
363.........Evan. 133...159
364.........Evan. 134...159
365.........Evan. 135...159
366.........Act. 72......192
367.........Act. 73......192
579.........Apoc. 38......208
665.........Evan. 136...159

[1] This manuscript, as Codd. 201—3 of the Gospels (*see* p. 163), was cited by Lamy (but only for 1 John v. 7) and, like them, has probably disappeared; as also Cod. Evan. 370.

PAGE
Cod. Vatic. 756.........Evan. 137...159
757.........Evan. 138...159
758.........Evan. 139...159
760.........Act. 74......192
761.........Paul. 81......202
762.........Paul. 82......202
765.........Paul. 83......202
766.........Paul. 84......202
1067.........Evst. 36......213
1136.........Paul. 85......202
1155.........Evst. 119...217
1156[1]......Evst. 120...217
1157.........Evst. 121...217
1158.........Evan. 140...159
1159.........Evan. 371...172
1160.........Evan. 141...159
1161.........Evan. 372...172
1168.........Evst. 122...217
1209.........Cod. B. and Apoc. 91...84–94, 210
1210.........Evan. 142...160
1229.........Evan. 143...160
1254.........Evan. 144...160
1423.........Evan. 373...172
1430.........Act. 155......196
1445.........Evan. 374...173
1522.........Evst. 123...217
1528.........Apost. 38...224
1533.........Evan. 375...173
1539.........Evan. 376...173
1548.........Evan. 145...160
1618.........Evan. 377...173
1649.........Paul. 189...205
1650.........Act. 156......196
1658.........Evan. 378...173
1714.........Act. 157......196
1743.........Apoc. 67......209
1761.........Act. 158......196
1769.........Evan. 379...173
1904.........Apoc. 68...209
1968.........Act. 159......196
1983.........Evan. 173...162
1988.........Evst. 124...217
2002.........Evan. 174...162
2017.........Evst. 125...217
2041.........Evst. 126...217
2062.........Act. 160......196

PAGE
Cod. Vatic. 2063.........Evst. 127...217
2066.........Apoc. B...140–1
2070.........Evan. 382...173
2080.........Evan. 175...162
2113.........Evan. 176...162
2133.........Evst. 128...217
2139.........Evan. 380...173
ol. lat. 3785.........Evan. N. ...110
olim Basil. 163.........Evan. 177...162
Alexand. Vat. 12.........Evst. 129...217
28.........Evan. 154...160
29.........Act. 78......192
68 (*not* 69)..Apoc. 41...208
79.........Evan. 155...160
179.........Act. 40......190
189.........Evan. 156...160
Vat. Ottobon. 2.........Evst. 130...217
31.........Paul. 195...205
61.........Paul. 196...205
66.........Evan. 386...173
175.........Evst. 131...217
176.........Paul. 197...205
204.........Evan. 387...173
212.........Evan. 388...173
258.........Act. 161......196
297.........Evan. 389...173
298.........Act. 162......196
325.........Act. 163......197
326.........Evst. 132...217
356.........Paul. 202...205
381.........Evan. 390...173
416.........Evst. 133...218
417.........Act. 165......197
432.........Evan. 391...173
Palatino-Vat. 5.........Evan. 146...160
20.........Evan. 381...173
89.........Evan. 147...160
136.........Evan. 148...160
171.........Evan. 149...160
189.........Evan. 150...160
220.........Evan. 151...160
227.........Evan. 152...160
229.........Evan. 153...160
Pio-Vat. 50.........Act. 80......192
53.........Evan. 158...161
Urbino-Vat. 2.........Evan. 157...160
3.........Act. 79......192

[1] So Scholz's index, and I suppose correctly, but in his Catalogue of Evangelistaria he numbers it 1256.

PAGE

Angelica Convent
A. 1. 5.........Evan. 178...162
A. 2. 15.........Act. G=L...129
A. 4. 11.........Evan. 179...162

Barberini 8.........Evan. 159 161
9.........Evan. 160 161
10.........Evan. 161 161
11.........Evan. 162 161
12.........Evan. 163 161
13.........Evan. 164 161
14.........Evan. 165 161
15.........Evst. 134 218
16.........Evst. 135, 136......218
18.........Apost. 40 224
23.........Apoc. 43 208
29.........Paul. 213 206
115.........Evan. 166 161
208.........Evan. 167 161
211.........Evan. 168 161
225...Evan. Y and 392...119, 173
377.........Act. 81 192
No mark.. Apost. 41 224

Borgia (now *Propaganda*)
1.........Evan. T. 116
250.........Evan. 180......162
287.........Evst. 37 214

Casanatensis
A. R. V. 33......Evan. 395...173

Collegii Romani
(3) Evan. 383, 384, 385......173
(2) Act. 171, 172...............197

Corsini 838...............Apoc. 73 ...209

Ghigian. R. iv. 6.........Evan. 396...173
R. iv. 8.........Apoc. 72 ...209
R. v. 29 ......Act. 169 ...197
R. v. 32 ......Paul. 207...205
viii. 55 ......Paul. 208...205

Malatestian. xxvii. 4 ...Evst. 144...218
xxix. 2......Evst. 145 ...218

Vallicell. B. 86 ....Act. 166 ...197
B. 133 ......Evan. 169...161
C. 4 ....Evan. 397...173
C. 46 ....Apost. 42...224
C. 61 ....Evan. 170...161
C. 73 ....Evan. 171...161
D. 20 ....Apoc. 21 ...207
(missing) D. 41 (*or* 4. 1) Evst. 156 ...219
D. 63 ....Evst. 137...218

PAGE

Vallicell. E. 22 ....Evan. 393...173
F. 13 ....Act. 168 ...197
F. 17 ....Evan. 394...173

(Syracuse) ....Evan. 421...175

(Turin) 19 MSS.
Psalter............Evan. O^d ...112
iv. b. 4............Evan. 333...171
xx. b. iv. 20......Evan. 332...171
43. b. v. 23 ......Evan. 334...171
44. b. v. 24 ......Evan. 335...171
52. b. v. 32 ......Evan. 337...171
92. c. iv. 6 ......Evan. 398...173
101. c. iv. 17......Evan. 336...171
109. c. iv. 29......Evan. 399...173
149. b. ii. 3 ......Evan. 342...171
284. c. i. 39 ......Paul. 165...204
285. c. i. 40 ......Act. 133 ...195
302. c. ii. 5 ......Evan. 339...171
(*now* 19) 315. c. ii. 17...Act. 134 ...195
325. c. ii. 38......Paul. 168 ...205
(*now* 1) 328. c. ii. 31 ...Act. 136 ...195
335. b. i. 3 ......Evan. 338...171
344. b. i. 13 ......Evan. 340...171
350. b. i. 21 ......Evan. 341...171

(Venice) 46 or 48 MSS.
St Mark 5...............Evan. 205...164
6...............Evan. 206...164
8...............Evan. 207...164
9...............Evan. 208...164
10...............Evan. 209...164
11...............Act. 96......193
12...............Evst. 139 ...218
27...............Evan. 210...164
28...............Evan. 357...172
29...............Evan. 354...172
33...............Paul. 110 ...203
34...............Paul. 111 ...203
35...............Paul. 112 ...203
539...............Evan. 211...164
540...............Evan. 212...164
541...............Evan. 355...172
542...............Evan. 213...164
543...............Evan. 214...164
544...............Evan. 215...164
545...............Evan. 356...172
546...............Act. 140 ...195
548...............Evst. 107 ...217

PAGE
St Mark 549..............Evst. 108...217
550..............Evst. 109...217
551..............Evst. 110...217
626..............Evst. 140...218
Nanian. 1..............Evan. U. ...117
2..............Evst. 141...218
3 (I. x.)......Evan. 405...174
4 (i. 11)......Evan. 406...174
5 (i. 12)......Evan. 407...174
7 (i. 14)......Evan. 408...174
8 (i. 15)......Evan. 409...174
10 (i. 17)......Evan. 410...174
11..............Evan. 411...174
12 (i. 19)......Evan. 412...174
13 (i. 20)......Evan. 413...174
14 (i. 21)......Evan. 414...174
15 (i. 22)......Evan. 415...174
16..............Evst. 142...218
17 (i. 24)......Evan. 416...174
18 (i. 25)......Evan. 417...174
21..............Evan. 418...174
St Mark's, Canonici......Evan. 216...164
i. 3........Evan. 217...164
Palimpsest..............Evst. ven^ev...220

The following seem missing:
St Michael's, Venice
49........Evst. 143...218
241........Evan. 419...174
(Verona) Psalter...Evan. O^c ...112

RUSSIA 73 MSS.

(Moscow).
S. Syn. 4......Apost. 13..........223
5......Act. 99..........193
42......Evan. 237..........166
43......Evst. 47..........214
44......Evst. 48..........214
45......Evan. 259..........167
47......Evan. 239..........166
48......Evan. 238..........166
49......Evan. 240..........166
61......Paul. N^c..........140
67......Apoc. 49..........208
94......Evan. 249..........167
98......Act. K and 102[1]... 130, 193
99......Paul. 123..........203
120......Evan. O and 257...112, 167

PAGE
S. Syn. 139......Evan. 255..........167
193......Act. 103..........193
206......Apoc. 50..........208
250......Paul. 124..........203
261......Evan. 246..........167
264......Evan. 248..........167
265......Evan. 245..........167
266......Evst. 52..........214
267......Evst. 53..........214
268......Evst. 54..........214
291......Apost. 14..........224
292......Paul. 119..........203
328......Act. 106..........194
333......Act. 101..........193
334......Act. 100..........193
373......Evan. 247..........167
380......Evan. 242..........167
Cista......Evan. V and 250...117, 167
Typ. S. Syn. 1...Evan. 244..........167
3...Evan. 256..........167
9...Evst. 51 and 56...214–5
11...Evst. 49..........214
12...Evst. 50..........214
13...Evan. 243..........167
31...Apost. 15..........224
47...Evst. 55..........214
University 25........Apoc. 65...209
Tabul. Imp.........Evan. 251...167
Matth. a........Act. 98......193
Matth. r (Syn. ?)...Apoc. 50² or 90...208
Cod. Pogodini, 472...Evan. 4^pe...178
(Odessa)..................Evst. 10^pe...178

(St Petersburg)
Codex Sinaiticus.........N. T. ℵ ...76–9
Cod. Sangerm. ....Paul. E...132–3
Tischendorf. II. ....Evan. I......107
olim Coislin. ....Evan. 437...176
(7) Four fragments of the Gospels, one of the Acts, one of St Paul, and one copy of the Gospels, described 127
Petropol. iv. 13........Evst. 1^pe ...178
vi. 470......Evan. 2^pe ...178
vii. 179......Evst. 3^pe ...178
viii. 80......Apost. 3^pe...178
ix. 1........Evan. 5^pe ...178
ix. 3. 471...Evan. 7^pe ...178

[1] See p. 225, *note*.

PAGE

Petropol. x. 180 ......Evst. 6pe ...178
xi. 1.2.330...Evan. 8pe ...178
xi. 3. 181 ...Evst. 9pe ...178
Q. v. 1. 15......Evan. 11pe...178
Notitia Cod. Sin. Evan. tisch.[2] 181
Evan. tisch.[3] 181
ibid.........Evst. Petrop.ev. ...220
Evst. Petrop.ev.2...220
Double palimpsest..Apost. Petrop...225

SCOTLAND 7 MSS.[1]

(Glasgow) *Hunter. Mus.*
B. B. *or* 1633 ...Apost. 44...224
C. C. *or* 1634......Apost. 45...224
Q. 122..............Evan. 181
Q. 123..............Evan. 181
Q. 1. (*or* 3) 35, 36...Evst. 223
S. 8. 141 ....Evan. 181
(Edinburgh) *Univ. Libr*....Evan.......181

SPAIN 19 MSS.

(Escurial) i................Evst. 40 ...214
Υ. ii. 8......Evan. 233...166
Φ. iii. 5 ...Evan. 230...165
Φ. iii. 6 ...Evan. 231...166
Φ. iii. 7 ...Evan. 232...166
X. iii. 12 ...Evst. 41 ...214
X. iii. 13 ...Evst. 42 ...214
X. iii. 15 ...Evan. 227...165
X. iii. 16 ...Evst. 43 ...214
X. iv. 12 ...Evan. 228...165
X. iv. 17 ...Evan. 226...165
X. iv. 21 ...Evan. 229...165
Six codices of Act. &c. ...199, 206, 210
(Toledo) ......Evan. 181

SWEDEN (Upsal) one MS.

Sparwenfeld 42 ....Act. 68......192

SWITZERLAND 14 MSS.

(Basle) B. ii. 5.........Act. &c. 199
B. vi. 17 ......Paul. 7.........200
B. vi. 21 (*now* K. iv. 35)
Evan. E. and Apoc. 15...103–4, 207
B. vi. 25 ......Evan. 2......143

PAGE

B. vi. 27 (*now* K. iii. 3)...Evan. 1......142
B. vi. 29 ......Act. &c. ...199
B. ix. 38? ......Act. 2 187
B. x. 20.........Act. 4 187
(S. Gall) ....Evan. Δ...122–4
17.........Evan. Oe ...112
Evan. Wc ...118
(Geneva) 19...............Evan. 75 ...152
20...............Act. 29 189
(Zurich) Zwingle ......Paul. 56 ...201

TURKEY (*Oriental Monasteries*) 104? MSS.

(Cairo) Patriarch of Alexandria's Library, 5 copies of Gospels 185
3 copies of the Acts and Epistles ...200
One copy of a Lectionary? 222
One copy of the Gospels and Psalter, at *Μετοικία* of St Catherine's, Sinai 185

(Chalké) Seven codices in Lamy's list (?) and eight in Dr Millingen's 181

(Constantinople) Patriarch of Jerusalem's Library: at least six codices of Gospels &c. ......180, note
Also a palimpsest Evst. 222

(Jerusalem) *Great Greek Monastery of the Holy Sepulchre.*

Scholz Codd. 1–7 ...Evan. 450–6...177
Coxe's 14 codices of Gospels 185
Codd. 8, 9 (Scholz)...Act. 183, 184...198
Cod. 10 (Scholz)......Evst. 158 219
College of Holy Cross: No. 3..Evan...185
S. Melanae ....Evst. 159...219
(Larnaka) Bp. of Citium...Evan.......186
(Milo) ....Evan. 186
Evst. 222
(Patmos) *S. John's Convent.*
(3) Scholz......Evan. 467, 468, 469...177

[1] We copy the numbers and descriptions of the Glasgow manuscripts from Haenel and Scholz, but there are probably less than six separate codices.

PAGE

Two others seen by Coxe 185
Two of Act. numbered 182 by Scholz..197
Coxe No. 24 ....Paul. 206
(7) Scholz Evst. 172–178 219
(S. Saba) 2..............Evan. 457...177
3..............Evan. 458...177
7..............Evan. 459...177
8..............Evan. 460...177
9..............Evan. 461...177
10..............Evan. 462...177
11..............Evan. 463...177
12..............Evan. 464...177
19..............Evan. 465...177
20..............Evan. 466...177

Coxe saw ten *more* copies of the Gospels, besides three in the Tower Library 185

Scholz 1..................Act. 185 ...198
15..................Act. 188 ...198
4..................Evst. 160...219
5..................Evst. 161...219
6..................Evst. 162...219
13..................Evst. 163...219
14..................Evst. 164...219
17..................Evst. 165...219
21..................Evst. 166...219
22..................Evst. 167...219
23..................Evst. 168...219
24..................Evst. 169...219
25..................Evst. 170...219
No mark...............Evst. 171...219
16..................Apost. 49...225
18..................Apost. 50...225
26..................Apost. 51...225
No mark...............Apost. 54...225
Compare Coxe's list of Lectionaries...222

(Sinai) St Catherine's ?
Evst. Λ^{ev}.........124

PAGE

Manuscripts whose present location is unknown (42 ?)
Evan. O or Evst. Bandur^{ev} ...112, 220
Evan. T^{s} 116
Evan. 42 146
Evan. 64 150
Evan. 66 151
Evan. 80, 81, 82 153
Evan. 88, 90, 91, 92, 93, 94 154
Evan. 101 (*not* 102), 104...............155
Evan. 199, 200...........................163
Evan. 203 164
Evan. 253, 254...........................167
Evan. 362 (370 ?).........................172
Evan. 419 ? 174
Evan. 436 or Evst. 153 176
Evan. q^{scr}..................................180
(2) Lowes late Askew ...Evan.......181
Askew 619 ....Evan....182, note
Act. 8 187
Act. 39 189
Act. 44 190
Act. 50 190
Act. 52 190
Act. 55, i.e. Evan. 90 191
Paul. 13 200
Paul. 15 200
Paul. 60 201
Apoc. 1 207
Apoc. 3 207
Apoc. 5 207
Evst. 23 213
Evst. 33 213
Evst. 38 }
Evst. 39 } 214
Evst. 143 ? 218
Evst. 153 or Evan. 436............219
Evst. 156 219
Apost. 3 (Batteley) 223
Apost. 4 ? 223

INDEX II.

General Index of the principal persons and subjects referred to in this volume.

N.B. For Greek manuscripts of the N. T. consult Index I. Where *passim* is annexed to a reference, only a portion of the passages are cited in which that person's name or subject occurs. n indicates *note.*

PAGE

Abbreviations in manuscripts...14, 29, 38, 43, 44, 135, 294, 436, 452
Accents employed in manuscripts...39—42, 86, 290
Accretions 373, 451
Acts and Cath. Epist., divisions of...53, 54, 58
Acus employed by scribes.........24, 102
Adamantius (Origen) 384, 390, 392
Adams, Sir *Th*...........................281
Adler, J. G. C. ...234, 238, 240 n, 244, 245, 247, 330, 331, 442
Æschylus ....4, 414 n. 1
Æthiopic version.........277, 316, 395 n.
Affre, D. Archp. 345
African form of Old Latin version...... 132, 255, 259
Aganon, Bp...........................122 n.
Agen 176, 208
Alcala de Henares 289, 291
Alcuin's Latin manuscripts ...262, 459
Aldus N. T. &c. 159, 288, 298
Alexandrian forms......13, 79, 84, 99, 109, 111, 374, 412—418
Alford, B. H. ....116, 196 n, 208
Alford, H. Dean...116, 126, 236, 298 n, 372, 375, 378, 399, 400, 403, 405, 406, 408, 437, 439, 446, 451
Alter, F. K.............152, 164, 257, 279
—— his N. T. ....329—330
Ambrose, Archp. ....50 n. 2
Ambrosian. Cod. Lat. 258

PAGE

Amelotte 147
Amiatinus, Cod. Lat. (*am.*) ...264, 342
Ammonian sections......50—53, 58, 142, 297, 434 *passim*
Ammonius of Alexandria 50
Analogy of God's Providence prepares us for various readings...............1—3
Ἀναστασιμὰ εὐαγγέλια 72, 213
Andreas, Archp., his Chapters &c....54, 56, 207—9
Andrew, St., Avignon, Cod. Lat. (*and.*) 265
Angelus Vergecius ......38 n. 2, 195, 204
Anglo-Saxon versions 280
Antonio Ae. of Lebrixa 289
Apocalypse, ancient divisions of...54, 58
Apocryphal supplements to N. T.......8, 425, 430
Apostolical Constitutions...421, 442, 446
Apostolos (and ἀποστολοευαγγέλια)...63, 211, 214, 441 n.
Apostrophus used in manuscripts...43, 95
Aquinas, Thomas ....363 n, 459
Arabic versions.........225, 281—2, 460
Arethas, Archp. on Apocalypse 56, 209, 210
Argenteus, Cod. Gothicus 274
Aristophanes of Byzantium 40
Arius, heretic 436, 437
Armagh, book of............266 n. 1, 459
Armenian version ....276—277
Article, Greek, fluctuating use of......14

PAGE

Ascetic temper traced in manuscripts... 376 and n. 1
Askew, Anthony...176 n. 1, 181 and n, 213
Asper, value of...176 n. 2
Assemani, J. S. ...243, 247, 441
Assemani, S. E. ...245
Asterisks ...244, 248, 435, 438, 440
Athanasius, Patriarch ...49, 83, 446
Athos, Mount...79, 166, 186, 327, *passim*
Augia Dives ...133
Augustine, Bp....41 n, 64 nn. 2 and 3, 252, 259 and n, 261 and n, 266 n. 3, 386, 424, 442
Autographs of the N. T. ...2, 379—381
Aymont, J. ...131

B and Υ confounded ...37 n. 3
Baber, H. H....40, 81 n, 84
Babington, Churchill, papyri...20, 417 n.
Banduri, Anselmo ...112, 220
Barbarous readings inadmissible ...418
Barberini, readings &c. 88, 119, 157, 314
Barnabas ...28, 77
Barrow, Is. his posthumous works ...4
Barrett, Jo....119, 149, 210
Barsalabi, Dion. Bp. 243 and n, 246, 441
Bartolocci, collation of Cod. B...88, 341
Basil, Bp. ...89 n.
Basilides, heretic ...381
Basmuric fragments of N. T. ...273
Battier, Jo. ...104, 187
Beaumont and Fletcher's works ...4
Bede, the Venerable ...128, 443
Bengel, J. A. ...60 n, 117 n, 329, 333
—— his N. T. and collations, 322—324
—— his Canon ...371—2, 437
Bentleii Critica Sacra (Ellis, A. A.)... 320 n. 2, 433 n. 2, 455 and n.
Bentley, Richard...7, 88, 106, 133, 158, 179, 207, 220, 253 n. 1, 264, 266, 324, 344, 462
—— his projected N. T....319—321
Bentley, Thomas...89
Bernard, Edw....315
Bernstein, G. H. ...242
Berriman, J. ...453 and n.
Bessarion, Jo. Cardinal...85, 164
Beza, Theod....17, 60, 96, 97, 98 and n, 103, 457 and n.
—— his N. T. reviewed ...302—3

PAGE

Bezae, Cod. Lat. (*d*)...256
Bible, the Great (in English) ...456—7
Bible, Hebrew, first printed...288
—— *Latin*, first printed ...262, 288
Bingham, J....53 n. 1, 64 n. 2, 138 n. 1, 241 n. 1, 387
Birch, Andr....86, 89, 115, 117, 157, 159, 164—5, 213 *passim*
—— his N. T. and collations...330—332
Blanchini, Jos. ...133 n, 140, 162, 207, 214, 219, 253 and n. 2, 256, 262, 264, 265 *passim*
Bloomfield, S. T....85 n. 2, 186, 187, 200, 207, 210, 223, 225, 405 n, *Addenda*, p. viii.
Bobbienses, Codd. Lat. (*k. s.*)...257, 258
Bode, C. A. ...279, 281
Bodleian, Cod. Lat. (*bodl.*)...265
Boerner, C. F. ...135 n. 2, 153
Boetticher, P. Memphitic vers. ...272
Bombasius, Paul ...88
Book of Common Prayer...11, 63
Boreel, John ...104
Bowring, Sir *J.*...292 n. 1
Bowyer, W. ...326, 370 n.
Breathings in manuscripts ...39—42, 86
Brixianus, Cod. Lat. (*f*)...257
Burgess, Th. Bp. ...196 n, 462
B[urgon], J. W. ...85 n. 1, 93 n. 2
Burney, Ch. his manuscripts ...179, 180
Butler, S. Bp. ...163
Buttmann, Phil. ...264, 340, 342

Calosirius ...271
Cambridge Texts, Greek Testament...17
Camps, Francis des ...110
Canons of internal evidence ...371—376
Canons of Comparative Criticism ...408—9, 455
Capernaum, its orthography ...415
Capitals in manuscripts...44, 78, 86, 96
Carlyle, J. D. ...178, 180 n, 199
Caro, Hugo de S. Cardinal ...58, 153 n.
Carolinus, Cod. Gothicus ...275
Carpianus, Epistle to ...50—52, 142, 290, 297
Carshunic characters ...245, 282
Caryophilus, J. M. Bp. 157, 192, 202 n. 1
Casaubon, Is. ...381 n. 1
Cassiodorus ...262

PAGE

Castiglione, C. O. Count, Gothic palimpsest 275
Catherine, St, on Sinai......76, 174, 218
Cava, Naples, Cod. Lat. (*cav.*) 265
Chaldee forms in Jerus. Syriac...245 nn.
Chapters, larger (κεφάλαια) ......48—50, 142, 297
——— *Latin* or *modern* 58, 59
Chark, Wm. ....67 n, 149, 151, 433
Christian VII. of Denmark 330
Christina, Q. of Sweden 160, 217, 266, 275
Chronicon Paschale ....381 n. 1
Chrysostom, Patriarch ...44, 64 nn. 1, 2, 278 n, 328, 349 n, 421
Cicero, M. T. ....29 n. 3
Clarendon, Lord, his History............4
Clarke, E. D. ....185 n. 2, 275
Claromontanus, Cod. Lat. (*h*).........257
Classes, six, of manuscripts 65
Clement of Alexandria...49, 384 and n. 1, 386 n.
——— of Rome...80, 83, 98, 402, 404 n.
Clementine Vulgate...263, 267, 268, 320, 428, 438 n.
Colbert, Cod. Lat. (*c*) 256
Coleridge, S. T......................380 n. 2
Colinaeus, S. his N. T. 298
Collins, A..................................316
Columns in manuscripts ......25 and n. 2
Comparative Criticism ....395 and n.
——————— exemplified ...401—404, 409—411
Complete copies of N. T. ...61 and n. 1.
Complutensian Polyglott......16, 87, 147, 190, 262, 284, 299, 443, 445
——————— N. T. reviewed...288—294
——————— collation of 349—368
Conflict of internal evidence 377
Confusion of uncial letters ...9, 376 n. 2
——— of vowels and diphthongs...10
Conjectural emendation inadmissible... 369 and n, 376 n. 2, 427
Continuous writing.........10, 14, 42, 44
Coptic language, &c. ....270, 395 n.
Corbeienses, Codd. Lat. (*ff*1, *ff*2)......257
Correctorium, Bibl. Lat. ....153 and n, 201, 262, 265
Correctors (διορθωταί) ......46—7 and n, 383 n, 385 n, 391

PAGE

Corruptions of text in second century... 385—7
Cosmas Indicopleustes 56, 230
Cotton fr. of Genesis ...29 n. 1, 30—35
Cotton paper (*bombycina*) 21
Covell, Jo. 151, 176, 189, 218
Cowper, B. H..........409 n, 453, 454 n.
Coxe, H. O.......155, 177 and nn, 180 n, 185 and nn, 199, 200, 206, 210, 222, 225
Craik, H. ....269 n.
Cramer, J. A. 188, 455
Critical revision a source of various readings 15
Crito Cantabrigiensis (*Turton, T.* Bp.)... 458 n, 459 n, 462
Curcellaeus, S. N. T. ....313 and n.
Cureton, W. Canon ...39, 115, 236, 425, 426
Curetonian Syriac version ...8 n, 236—241, 400
Cursive letters ....26, 36—38
Cursive manuscripts, list of ...142—225
Curzon, Hon. *R.* 182, 210, 220
Cuza, Nich. de, Cardinal...154, 159, 191
Cyprian...255, 342, 382 n, 387, 460—1
Cyril and *Methodius,* Apostles of the Slavonians 280
Cyril of Alexandria, Bp ......455 and n.

Damasus, Pope 252, 260, 261
Darmarius, Andr. ....381 n.
Dated manuscripts...26, 36 and nn. 2, 3, 37 n. 2, 38 n. 1, 115, 397 n.
Davidson, S. cited......23, 64 n. 1, 103, 241, 378, 436, 445
De Dieu, L. Apocal. &c. 233, 442
Demidovian. Cod. Lat. (*demid.*) ...265, 328
Demosthenes ....385 n, 413
Dermout, J. his collations, 176, 189, 212
Des Adrets 98
Designed alterations alleged in text... 16, 375, 381, 423
Dialectic forms 13, 417
Diocletian's persecution 271, 387
Dionysius, Bp. of Corinth 381
Divisions in N. T. ....47—60
——— in the Vatican manuscript... 47—48, 58

PAGE

Dobbin, Orlando...90 n. 3, 93, 148, 149, 150, 189, 313
Dobrowsky, J. 265, 280
Donaldson, J. W. ...38, 321 n. 2, 413—414 and n. 3
Dorisms in N. T. 417
Dorotheus, Bp. of Tyre ...193, 197, 297
Ducas, Demetrius............289, 290 n. 2
Ducat of Rhodes ....203 n.

Ebionite Gospel 386
Ecclesiastical writers, dated list of, 286—7
Eclogadion defined 65, 108
——— list throughout the year ... 68—74
Editions, primitive, of books of N. T.... 16, 439
——— early printed and later critical 288—348
Egyptian versions of N. T. ...270—274
Eichhorn, J. F. ....255, 391—2
Ellicott, C. J., Dean ...229, 376, 394 n, 450, 453 and n., *Addenda* pp. vii, viii
Elzevir editions of N. T.......17, 303—4
Emendation and *recension* distinguished, 343, 370
Emmeram, St, Cod. Lat. (*em.*) 265
Engelbreth, W. F. (Basmuric)...164, 273
Ephraem Syrus...94, 197, 230, 238, 239
Epiphanius, Bp., 44, 45 n. 1, 62 n. 2, 386, 391 and n, 435—6 and n.
Erasmus, Desid. ......88, 104, 143, 187, 200, 201, 202, 207, 293, 443 and n. 3, 444, 461.
——— his N. T. reviewed...294—298
Erlangen, Cod. Lat. (*erl.*) 265
Ernesti, J. A. 253, 327, 380
Erpenius, T., Arabic vers. ...282 and n.
Evangelistaria 11, 63, 211
Euclid, dated in Bodleian ...36 and n. 3
Eumenes, King of Pergamus............20
Eusebius, Pamphili, Bp......25 n. 1, 50, 51 n. 1, 229, 230, 254, 270, 348, 381 and n. 1, 382 n, 383 and n, 387, 388, 431, 442
Eusebian canons ...50—53, 82, 83, 142, 297, *passim*
——— their critical use ...434 and n. 2
Euthalius, Bp..........45, 54, 55, 57, 290
Euthalius, his Chapters ...53, 58, 293, 297, *passim*
Euthymius Zigabenus...422 n, 431, 442
Extent of various readings.........17, 314

Faber, John 154
Families of manuscripts ......323 and n, 333—336, 338—340
Fathers, their silence of little weight, 422
Fell, Jo., Bp. 271, 276, 284, 315
—— his N. T. 1675 ....313—315
Ferdinand of Valladolid 289
"*Five* Clergymen," the, cited 447
Fleck, F. F. 94, 164, 257, 264
Floriacensis, Cod. Lat. (*flor.*).........265
Ford, Henry 89, 116, 210, 272
Foreign matter in manuscripts.........56
Form of mânuscripts 24
Forojuliensis, Cod. Lat. (*for.*) ......265, 381 n. 1
Fossatensis, Cod. Lat. (*fos.*) 265
Frankish version 280
Friderico-Augustanus, Cod. 20, 27, 30—35, 39, 42, 43, 44, 47 and n, 76, 86 n.
Frisingensis, Cod. Lat. (*r*) 259
Froben, J.............................295, 297
Fuldensis, Cod. Lat. (*fuld.*) ...264, 342

Gabelentz, H. C. de, Ulfilas............276
Gachon, J. 190, 315
Gall, St ....112, 122, *passim*
Gatien, St, Cod. Lat. (*gat.*) 265
Gelasius, Pope ....392 and n.
Georgian version 279
Gerhard à Mästricht, N. T....152, 313 n, 319, 377 n. 3
Germain, St, des Prez, 132, 137, 176, 257
Gibbon, Edw. ...274 and n, 458 n, 462
Giorgi, A. A. 116, 272, 273
Godeschalk, heretic 122
Goeze on Complut. Bible......293 and n.
Goldhagen, Herm., N. T. 175
Gospels, ancient divisions of...47—53, 58
Gothic version of N. T....274—6, 395 n.
Grafton, A. W.............................459
Grammatical forms, peculiar ...294, 416
Green, T. S. ....373, 433 n. 1, 451
Greenfield, W., Peshito N. T. 234
Gregory Bar-Hebraeus ......231, 246—7

PAGE

Gregory Nyssen ....422 n.
Gregory I. Pope 262
Griesbach, J. J....39, 49, 66, 139 and n, 166, 208, 213, 285, 301, 327, 329, 330, 373, 374, 375 and n, 377, 393 n, 463 *passim*
——— his N. T. and collations...332—336
Guelferbytani, Codd. Lat. (*gue.*) 258, 265
Guizot, F. P. G. 345
Gutbier, Giles, Peshito N. T. ...233, 443
Gutierrez, José ....291, 292 n. 1

Haenel, G. 181, 199, 206
Haitho, King of Armenia 277
Harkel, Thomas of ...231, 242, 244, 248
Harleian, Codd. Lat. 1772, 1775 (*harl.*) 265
Harley, R., Earl of Oxford...........131
Harmonies of the Gospel History, 11, 50
Hearne, T. 129, 166
Hebrew idioms softened.................13
Hebrew (or *Jewish*) Gospel 125, 442
Heinfetter, Hermann ....434 n. 1
Hellenistic dialect 412, 413
Hentenius, Jo. (Louvain Lat. Bible) ... 263, 312
Herculanean papyri ...20, 26, 29, 30—35, 38, 41, 42, 44, 86
Heringa, Professor 105
Hermas 28, 77
Hermonymus, G., of Sparta ... 144, 152
Herodotus....................21, 22 n, 374
Hesychius of Egypt......389, 392 and n.
Hieronymus or *Jerome*...23 and n, 25 n. 3, 228 n, 252, 260 and n, 261 and n. 1, 266, 356 n, 357 n. 2, 377, 380 n. 1, 388, 389, 390 and n. 1, 391, 392, 428 and n, 431, 442, 448, 460 n.
Hilary cited.........342, 390, 428 and n.
Hippolytus...............................454
Homer and his manuscripts...4, 30—35, 39, 40, 90 n. 2, 115, 416, 417 n.
Homœoteleuton 9, 78, 374
Hook, W. F., Dean....................128
Hope for Biblical criticism in England, 348
Horne, T. H., Introduction ......62 n. 1, 275, 347, 458 n.

PAGE

Hug, J. L.......86 n, 89, 93, 271 n, 338
—— his system of recensions ...391—3
Huish, Alex. ....83, 453 n.
Hutter, Elias, Peshito N. T....232, 443
Hyperides, papyrus fragments of......... 30—35, 36, 41, 42, 44

Iberian version..........................279
Ignatius............379 and n. 2, 445, 455
Ihre, Jo., Gothic N. T. 276
Indiction ....37 n, 183 n.
Ingoldstadt, Cod. Lat. (*ing.*) 265
Ink, ancient, its composition 23
—— red ....24, 138 and n. 2
Internal evidence considered...369—378
Interpolations, various readings arising from 7, 386
Ionisms in N. T. 417
Iota, ascript and subscript, 38, 39, 139 and n, 294, 296, 297
Irenæus ...314 n. 1, 342, 379 n. 1, 382—3 and n, 385, 399 n, 404 n, 420, 424 *bis*, 435, 443 and n. 2
Irici, J. A. 256
Irish monks at St Gall...124, 136 and n. 2, 258
Irregular constructions softened 12
Itacisms......10, 79, 376, 448, 449 and n.
Italics of English version 456

Jacobi, St, Cod. Lat. (*jac.*)............265
Jacobson, W., Canon.........81 n, 152 n.
James, St, collation of his Epistle in the early editions ....301—2
James, T., Bellum Papale 263
Jerusalem copies of N. T.......47, 125 n, 161, 431
Jerusalem Syriac version ...245—6, 441
Jewish sacred books...............314 n. 1
John, Bp. of Seville, Arabic version ... 281, 282
Junius, Fr. 276, 313
Justin Martyr ......386 n, 424, 431, 435
Juvenal 412
Juynboll, T. W. J. 282
Ἰωάννης, orthography of..............415

Karkaphensian Syriac version ...246—8
Kaye, J., Bp. ......380 n. 2, 386 n, 460
Kelly, W......................207, 210, 463

PAGE

Kipling, T., Dean, 98, 99, *Addenda* p. vii
Knappe, G. C., N. T. ....370 n.
Knittel, F. A. 113, 192, 258, 275
Kuenen, A. and *Cobet, C. G.*, Vat. N.T. 376 n. 2, 385 n, 418, *Addenda* p. viii
Kuster, L. .... 83, 94, 110, 409 n.
——— his manuscripts 318

Lachmann, C..........17, 259 and n, 264, 286, 370, 378, 436
——— his N. T. and system reviewed 340—344
Lamy, John......163, 172, 181, 199, 206
Land, P. N., on Curetonian Syriac, 240 n.
Lanfranc, Archp. 262
Laodicea, Council of 80, 83
Laodiceans, Epistle to 137, 232
Lascar, A. J. 94
Latinising, charges of......128, 293, 326
Laud, W., Archp.........................129
Laurence, R., Archp. ....335 and n.
Laurentian Library at Florence......162
Le Barbier.................................186
Le Fevre, Guy, Peshito N. T. 232
Leaning uncial letters.........36 and n. 1
Lectionaries of N.T....11, 60, 62—65, 142, 211, 373, 433, 435, 436
——— of Old Testament...64, 73, 212 n.
Lee, Edw., Archp. 297
Lee, Sam., Peshito N. T.......234, 282 n, 429, 445, 459
Leo X, Pope ......289, 291 and nn, 295
Linen Paper (*charta*) 21
Lipsienses, Codd. Latt. (*lips.* 4, 5, 6)...265
Lloyd, C., Bp. (N. T. Oxon.) 51, 57
Loebe, T., Ulfilas 276
Loftus, Dudley 279
Long, G....................................407
Lotze, J. A. 326
Lucar, Cyril, Patriar. ....79, 282 n.
Lucas, F., Brugensis ...88, 153 n, 263, 265, 312
Lucian of Antioch ......389, 392 and n.
Lucifer of Cagliari 342
Luxoviensis, Cod. Lat. (*lux.*) 265
Lye, Ed., Gothic N.T...................276

Mace, D. or *W.*, his N. T. 321

PAGE

Macedonius, Patriarch..................455
Madden, Sir *F.* ....20, 40, 391 n.
Magee, W., Archp. 374
Mai, Angelo, Cardinal ...40, 86, 90—92, 140, 258, 275, 377 n. 2, 447
Majoris Monasterii, Cod. Lat. (*mm.*), 265
Mangey, Th. 183, 213
Marcion, heretic.....................381—2
Marcosii, apud Iren. 424
Marianae, Cod. Lat. (*mar.*)............265
Marsh, Herbert, Bp...99, 150, 156, 187, 293, 300 n. 1, 301, 458 n, 462
Marshall, Th....271, 276, 280, 314, 425
Martianay, T. 257, 258, 265
Martin, St, Tours, Cod. Lat. (*mt.*), 265
Massmann, H. F., Ulfilas 275
Materials for writing ....20—23
Ματθαῖος, orthography of 415
Matthaei, Ch. F....63, 117, 130, 132, 136, 166, 193, 213, 214, 265, 286, 332, 452
—— his N. T. and collations, 327—329
Medicean manuscripts at Paris,...94 and n. 2, 147, 195, 204
Meermann's manuscripts ... 158 and n, 197, 219
Memphitic version of N. T. ......271—2
Menology defined 65, 142
—— list of throughout the year, 74—5
Michaelis, J. D.,...66, 156, 293, 327, 329, 419, 443 n. 1
Mico, Abbate 88, 210
Middleton, T. F., Bp....14, 295 n. 1, 327, 419, 426 n.
Miesrob, Armenian 276
Mill, J.... 49, 53, 57, 66, 104, 191, 223, 230, 254, 262, 271, 276, 280, 282, 284, 292, 298, 299, 300, 304, 313, 319, 436 n, 444, 462, *passim.*
——— his N. T. ....315—318
——— list of his manuscripts 317
Millingen, Dr. 181
Mingarelli, J. A., Thebaic fragments, 272
Miracles sparingly resorted to ......1—2
Missy, Caesar de, 147, 180, 181, 223, 224
Mittarelli, J. B. 174, 218
Mixed uncial and cursive letters...112 n.
Moldenhawer, D. G.......165, 213, 214, 292 n. 1, 330, 331, 332, 335
Monacensis, Cod. Lat. (*q*) 258

PAGE

Montfaucon, Bernard de......19, 40, 54, 63, 105, 112, 138, 146, 154 n, 162, 176, 182, 200, 212, 216, 388
Moore, John, Bp. ....149 and n, 180
Moses, Chorenensis 276
Moveable type, supposed cases of, 111, 275
Muhammedan sacred books ... 314 n. 1
Münter, F., Egyptian fragments, 272, 273
Muralt, Edw. de...67, 90, 178, 206, 222, 225

N, *abridged form of* ...43, 111, 416 n. 1
N ἐφελκυστικὸν or *attached* ...293, 413 *passim*
Nathan, Rabbi 60
Nazareth, its orthography 415
Nicholas, Sir *H.* ....291 n. 1
Nitrian desert, manuscripts from 115
Nolan, Fred.............266 n. 2, 388, 446
Notation of manuscripts of N. T., 65—7, 317
Notitia, Cod. Sinaitici (Tischendorf) ... 28, 76, 77, 121, 125, 127, 181, 220, 346, 401, 423, 452
Number of extant manuscripts of N.T... 4, 225, *Addenda* p. viii
Number of various readings estimated... 3, 7

Obeli...............244, 248, 435, 438, 440
Obsolete style of Old Latin version ...256
Oecolampadius 296
Oecumenii, ὑποθέσεις to N.T., 57, 191, 201
Old Latin version, its history and character ....252—260
Omissions, various readings arising from, 7
Order of words, variations in 9
Order of books in N.T. ...48, 61—2, 77, 80, 131 n, 247, 290
Order of Gospels 62, 256, 275
Order of St Paul's Epistles...48, 62 and n. 2, 77, 80, 90 n, 201
Origen......109, 266, 285, 335, 342, 348, 377, 384—5, 390, 392, 393, 402 n. 1, 424
——— Hexapla 244, 388
Orthodox readings not improbable...375 and n.
Orthography of manuscripts of N.T., 294
Owen, Jo. .... 314 and n. 2

PAGE

Pachomius.................................271
Palatine Elector's Library ....160 n.
Palatinus, Cod. Lat. (*e*) 256
Palimpsest described 22
——— double 112
——— Syriac fragment............246
Pamphilus, martyr, 47 and n, 54, 188, 192, 266, 388, 390, 431
Paper, cotton and linen..................21
Pappelbaum, G. G. 156
Papyrus, manufacture of............21—2
Paradiplomatic evidence ...376—7, 448
Particles omitted or interchanged......13
Pauline Epistles, ancient divisions of... 53, 58
Paulus 208, 257
Pearson, John, Bp. 455
Pelagia, St ...74 and n. 3, 216, 246, 441
Pericopae of Church-lessons 11
——— of Bengel 60
Persic versions of N. T. 281
Perugian. Cod. Lat. (*per.*) 265
Peshito Syriac version, its history and character ....229—236, 424 n.
——— its chief manuscripts 235
Peter of Alexandria, Bp. ......381 n. 1
Petermann, J. H., Georgian version...279
Phileleutherus Lipsiensis 7, 319
Philodemus περὶ κακιῶν 26, 29
Philoxenian Syriac version ...109, 227, 233, 241—244, 435, 441, 447 *passim*
Philoxenus or *Xenaias*, Bp. ...241, 242
Pickering, W. 180
Pierius 266, 390
Pierson 281
Pindar 44
Pinophi dicta 134, 137
Piques, L.......................271, 276, 277
Plantin Peshito N. T.............232, 233
Plato, dated manuscript of in the Bodleian, 36 and n. 3, 110, 118, 185 n. 2
Platt, T. P., Æthiopic N. T..........279
Plinius, C. S., Nat. Hist................22
Pococke, Edw. 233, 242, 281
Polybius...................................413
Polyglott, Antwerp (Plantin) ...232, 265
——— Bagster's ....234, 282 n.
——— Complutensian (see *Complutensian*)
——— London (see *Walton*)

PAGE

Polyglott, Paris....................232, 282
Porson, R................458 n, 462 and n.
Porter, J. Scott...........246, 338 and n.
Praxapostolos.......................63, 211
Primasius......................259, 342, 463
Printing, invention of 3, 21, 262
Psalms of Solomon, &c..................80
Punctuation of manuscripts, &c. 42—3, 86, 95, 294, 391 n.
Purple and gold manuscripts 23

Quotations from Old Test. in New......12
Quotations from Fathers, their use and defects ....283—6, 314, 316, 404

Rabanus Maurus, Archp. 134, 137
Ragusio, John de, Cardinal 103
Rapheleng, F., N. T., Greek and Syr.... 191, 232
Raymundi, J. Bapt.....................282
Received Text in its various forms collated ....304—311
Reed used for writing....................24
Regii, Codd. Lat. Paris (*reg.*) 265
Reiche, J. G....194, 195, 204, 209, 405 n.
ῥήματα or ῥήσεις ....54, 57 and n, 58
Rettig, H. C. M. 122, 136
Reuchlin, J...................143, 144, 207
Rhedigerianus, Cod. Lat. (*l*) 257
Rheims, Slavonic Evangelistarium...280
Rhodiensis, Cod. 190, 291
Rhythm, cause of various readings...377
Ridley, Gloucester.................243, 441
Rieu, Charles............................277
Rink, C. F. 164, 203, 213
Rolled manuscripts or scrolls...........25
Rosen, Professor ....235 n.
Rosetta stone, account of......27, 30—35
Rowe, Sir *T.* 79, 147
Rozan de, Abbate.......................265
Rulotta, Abbate ....89, 320 n. 2
Russell, A. T.............................153

Sabatier, P...............253 and n. 2, 257
Sahidic or *Thebaic* version of N. T....272
Sanctes Pagninus..........................59
Sanftl, P. C...............................265
Sangallenses, Codd. Lat. (δ. *n. o. p. san.*) 258, 265
Sangermanenses, Codd. Lat. (g^1, g^2)...257

PAGE

Schaaf, Ch. and *Leusden, J.*, Peshito N. T...............................233, 443
Scheibel, J. E. 257
Schmeller, J. A...........................280
Scholz, J. M. A....57, 66, 67, 108, 168, 177, 194, 203, 209, 215, 224, 301, 416
——— his N. T. and collations, 336—340
Schulz, D. ....83, 257, 336 n, 344
Schwartze, M. G., Memphitic N. T....272
Scott, C. B. 313
Scrivener, F. H., his collations...17, 67, 134, 178, 198, 206, 210, 218, 220—1, 234, 340 n. 1, 395 n. 1, 400
Semler, J. S..........133 n, 323, 326, 333
Septuagint version...27, 29 n. 1, 31—32, 47 n, 412—416
Sepulveda, J. G...........................87
Servius Tullius, his classes 334
Shakespeare's dramas 4
Shape of uncial letters used to determine their date ....30—35
Sharp, J., Archp. 315
Silvestre, M. J. B., Paléographie Universelle...19, 23, 36 n. 2, 40, 86, 105, 213, 217
Sinaiticus, Codex, its internal character, 389
Sionita, Gabriel, Peshito N. T....232—3, 282
Sixtus V, Pope, his Latin Bible, 263, 429
Slavonic version 280
Slips of the pen, a source of various readings 15
Sophocles.......................... 414, n. 1
Specimens of five Syriac versions of N. T. ....248—251
———— of Latin versions ...267—269
Speculum, Cod. Lat. (*m*)...............258
Spelling, variations in manuscripts ...13
Steininger, B. M.........................219
Stephens, Henry 60, 300, 301, 302
Stephens, Robert ...17, 57, 60, 97, 187, 190 n, 207, 263
——— his N. T. reviewed ...299—302
——— manuscripts used by him ......97 n. 2, 299—301, 458
Stichometry in manuscripts...44—46, 54, 57—59, 77, 78, 86, 99, 108, 117, 123, 128, 130, 138, 155, 208, *Addenda* p. vii

PAGE

Stiernhielm, G., Gothic N. T. 276
Stops, their power varies with their position 42, 104
Storr, G. C. 243, 282
Strabo ......385 n.
Stunica, J. Lopez de...190, 289, 296, 461
Style of different writers of N. T. varies, 2, 413
Style, change of, no decisive proof of spuriousness 431
Stylus used for writing 24
Subjectivity 370, 378, 419, 446
Subjunctive future......449 and n.
Subscriptions to books of N. T. 54
—— to manuscripts...47 and n, 125 and n, 138, 168
Suicer, J. C. ......44, 65 n, 72, 83, 114
Suidas ......49 n.
Sulci or *Sulca*......53 n. 1, 138 n. 1
Sylburg, F. 209, 313
Synaxarion defined......65 and n, 142
—— list of, throughout the year ......68—74
Synonymous words interchanged 12
Syrian Christians, sects of 230, 241
Syriac language 229, 412, 413

Table of ancient and modern divisions of N. T. 58
Tatham, Edw. ......459 n.
Tatian......11, 48, 50
Taurinensis, Cod. Lat. (*taur.*) 265
Taylor, Isaac ......16 and n. 2
Terence ......385 n.
Terrot, C. H., Bp. 59
Tertullian ......49, 380, 404 n, 438, 460
Textual criticism and its results ... 4—6
Thebaic (see *Sahidic*)
Thecla, St 79, 80, 82
Theocritus 44
Theodora, St ......74 and n. 2, 216, 441
Theodore of Tarsus, Archp......128
Theodore the calligrapher ...37 n. 2, 166
Theodoret, prologues to Epistles......290
Theophrastus cited......22 n.
Thorpe, Benj., Anglo-Saxon Gospels, 280
Thucydides 411,432
Tischendorf, Aen. F. C., 17, 90 n. 1, 181, 220, 225, 256, 281, 304, 320 n. 1, 338, 343, 372, 414 and n. 3, 415, 442 n, 450, 452 *passim*
Tischendorf, his N.T. and critical labours ......344—346, 408
Τίτλοι ......48—50, 58, 142, 402 n. 2
Toletanus, Cod. Lat. (*tol.*) 264
Traditores...... 387
Traheron, Philip......152, 420 n.
Travis, G., Archd., 301, 458 n, 462 and n.
Tregelles, S. P....16 n. 1, 17, 37 n. 1, 90 and n. 3, 126, 145, 246, 368 n. 1, 378, 384 n. 1, 393 n, 416 n. 2, 423, 426, 437, 447, 449 and n, 453 n, 455, 456 *passim*
—— his N.T. and critical labours...346—348
—— his scheme of Comparative Criticism ......396—404
Tremellius, Im., Peshito N.T...232, 233, 302, 429
Trent, Council of 262
Trevirensis, Cod. Lat. (*trevir.*)......265
Trinity College, Cambridge, Cod. Lat. (*trin.*) 265
Trost, Martin, Peshito N.T 232
Twycross, John 150
Tychsen, O. G. 330, 331
Typicum defined 114

Uffenbach, Z. C. 139, 155, 190, 201
Ulphilas or *Ulfilas*, Bp...... 274
Uncial letters 9, 25
Uncial manuscripts, list of, 76—141, 211
Uppström, And., Gothic N.T......276
Uscan, Bp., Armenian Bible 277
Ussher, James, Archp....98, 131, 149, 150, 233, 312

Valentinus, heretic...... 381
Valla, Laurentius 153, 190, 207
Variations, when a ground for suspicion, 426, 438, 442, 443, 459
Various readings defined 3
—— different classes of them ...7—16
Vaticanus, Cod. Lat. (*vat.*)......266
Velesian readings......156, 312, 458
Vellum, manufacture of 20
Vercellensis, Cod. Lat. (*a*)...... 256
Vercellone, C.......91, 92, 291 and n. 2
Vermilion paint (κιννάβαρις) 51, 140

PAGE

Veronensis, Cod. Lat. (*b*)...............256
Verses, modern in N.T 58, 59
Versions of N.T., their use and defects... 226—9
—— their date and relative value...227
Villiers, G., Duke of Buckingham...282 n.
Vindobonensis, Cod. Lat. (*i*)............257
Virgil 44
Vulgate, Latin version, its history, &c.... 260—269
Wake, Wm., Archp....152 n, 182, 198, 221, 225, 320
Walker, John ......183, 184 n, 320, 321
Walton, Brian, Bp....66, 98, 131, 156, 230 n, 233, 254, 262, 263 n, 265, 278, 279, 281, 282
—— his N. T. and collations...312—313
Wechelian readings 312
Werner of Nimeguen..................... 88
Westcott, B. F. ......155, *Addenda* p. vii
Wetstein, Caspar.............183, 188, 208
Wetstein, J. J....66, 79, 83, 88, 95 and n, 98 n, 105, 156, 157, 243, 292, 298 n, 301, 303, 319, 372 and n, 462
—— his N. T. and collations...324—327
Wheelocke, Abr. 281
Whitby, Dan. 316

PAGE

White, Joseph ......243 and n, 441, 447
Widmanstadt, Albert, Peshito N. T.... 231, 234, 429
Wilkins, D., Memphitic N. T....271, 273 n, 330
Winchelsea, Earl of (1661) 155, 212
Wiseman, Nich., Cardinal...90, 196 n, 234, 247, 255, 258, 458 n.
Woide, C. G....81 n, 83, 128, 272, 326, 410 n, 453 n.
Wolff, Joseph.............................234
Wolff, J. C. 106, 139
Wordsworth, Christ., Canon ...15, 95 n, 179, 372, 373 n, 376, 448, 450

Ximenes, Fr. de Cisneros, Cardinal...288, 289, 294, 296

Year, ecclesiastical, of Greeks 73
Young, Patrick...............83, 98, 453 n

Zacagni, L. A., 86, 88, 138 n. 1, 190, 218
Zahn, J. C., Gothic N .T. 276
Zoega, G., Cat. Codd. Copt....116, 271 n, 272, 273
Zohrab, Armenian Bible 277

INDEX III.

Of Texts of the New Testament illustrated or referred to in this volume.

PAGE

Matthew i. 8 ....237 n. 2, 239
18........... 387, 399 n, 419
ii. 23 415
iii. 17..........................386 n.
iv. 13 415
18 11
v. 22 ....8, 377, 390
vi. 1 12
13................8, 349, 421
vii. 2 12
14 14
28 12
viii. 1 228
5......................11, 228
28 15
ix. 13 11
17 11
29 12
36 12
x. 3 415
23 9
25 (xii. 24, 27) 293
xi. 16 10
xiii. 15 10
40 12
xiv. 22 11
xv. 5 ....10, 13
8..........................12
xvi. 2, 3 ....434 n. 2
xvii. 5 406
21 ....434 n. 2
xviii. 28 ....67 n.
xix. 17 ....16, 422
19 385
xx. 28.................8, 387, 425

PAGE

Matthew xxi. 11 415
23 13
28—31.........372, 390, 426
xxii. 37 12
xxiii. 14—16 9
35...15, 221 n, 374, 388, 433
xxiv. 15 11
36 390
38 372
xxv. 16 12
xxvi. 39 ....10, 435
xxvii. 4....................12, 335 n.
9 15
28 343
35 ....11, 428
49 ....434 n. 1
60 14
xxviii. 19 ....461 n.
Mark i. 2 15
9 415
21 415
ii. 17 11
26 14
iii. 3 10
18 415
v. 14 9
40 417
vii. 2 12
12 13
ix. 28, 29 ....434 n. 2
x. 18 423
30 11
xiii. 14 11
32 16
xiv. 4 418

PAGE

Mark xiv. 35 10
65 10
xv. 28 11
xvi. 9—20 ....7, 390, 429
Luke i. 1—4..........412 n.
3 435
64..........292
ii. 22 ....16, 152, 303
51..........415
iii. 22..........386 and n.
iv. 16..........415
18 12
v. 32 11
35 13
38 11
vi. 1 433
vii. 31 11
viii. 30..........401
37..........401
38..........401
ix. 13..........401
19..........401
23..........390, 401
26..........402
34..........402, 406
49 10
x. 1 *ter*..........402
22 11
25..........402
xi. 4 422
36..........9
xii. 54 14
xiii. 16..........416 n. 1
xiv. 8—10 425
xvi. 20..........9
25..........417
xvii. 36..........9
xviii. 19..........423
xix. 41..........435, 436 n.
xxii. 37 12
43, 44..........8, 390, 434
49..........417
xxiv. 32..........240
John i. 18 ....16, 436
28 ....15, 399 n.
44 11
iii. 16, 18 437
v. 3, 4 ....8, 438
35 10
vii. 8..........15

PAGE

John vii. 39..........372
vii. 53—viii. 11...7, 80 n., 390, 439
xvii. 2 ....449 n.
3 449
xix. 14 15
24 ....11, 428
John xx. 30, 31 ; xxi. 439
Acts iii. 4 415
6..........10
v. 2 417
vi. 1 412
vii. 20 ....376 n. 2
37 12
vii. ....412 n.
viii. 37...8, 373, 387, 399 n., 443
ix. 5, 6..........12, 297, 373
12..........9
x. 35.......... 376 n. 2
xiii. 33..........399 n.
xiv. 8 13
xv. 20, 29 .... 370 n.
34 444
xvi. 3 12
7 16
24..........12
xvii. 25, 26 14
xx. 28 ....16, 375, 444
xxvi. 14, 15..........12, 297, 373
xxvii. 1..........417
9 ....370 n.
16..........88
Rom. ii. 17 417
v. 1 ....15, 447
viii. 1..........8
20 418
xii. 11..........14
13 .... 376 n. 1
xiii. 9 12
xiv. 17 ....376 n. 1
1 Cor. iv. 7..........417
vii. 5..........376 n. 1
35 ....433 n. 2
x. 22..........46
xi. 29 8
xiii. 3 ....10, 356 n, 448
xv. 31 ....357 n. 1
49..........15
51..........15, 357 n. 2
2 Cor. iii. 3..........377, 448
10..........10

PAGE

2 Cor. viii. 4 12
xii. 1 11
xiii. 2 12
Gal. iii. 1 ....8, 390
Ephes. i. 1 ....89 n.
v. 30 375
vi. 3 449
Phil. i. 30 10
ii. 1 449
Col. i. 27 ....450—1
ii. 2 .... 373, 450
1 Thess. ii. 15 382
1 Tim. ii. 6 15
iii. 16 .... 14, 375, 452
2 Tim. iv. 5 11
13 21
15 12
Heb. ii. 7 12
xi. 23 ....376 n. 2
xii. 20 12
James iii. 12 373
1 Pet. i. 3; 12 11

PAGE

2 Pet. i. 23 455
ii. 3 11
21 *bis* 11
iii. 1 ....10, 449 n.
1 Pet. iii. 15 456
18; 21 11
20 10
v. 10 11
1 John ii. 23 ....9, 456
iv. 3 419
9 437
v. 7, 8...8, 293, 363 n, 387, 457
2 John 12 21
3 John 13 24
Jude 4 ....16, 375
Apoc. ii. 20 13
iii. 16 9
xii. 17 419
xiii. 10 463
18 ....382—3
xxii. 16—21 ....296 n.
18, 19 ....314, 439

THE END.

CAMBRIDGE: PRINTED BY C. J. CLAY, M.A. AT THE UNIVERSITY PRESS.

(1)

Α Β Γ Δ Ε Ι Η Θ Ι Κ Λ Μ Ν Ξ Ο Π Ρ Σ Τ Υ Φ
Χ Ψ Ω.

(2)

Α Β Γ Δ Ε Ζ Η Θ Ι Κ Λ Μ Ν Ξ Ο Π Ρ C Τ Υ Φ Χ Ψ Ω.

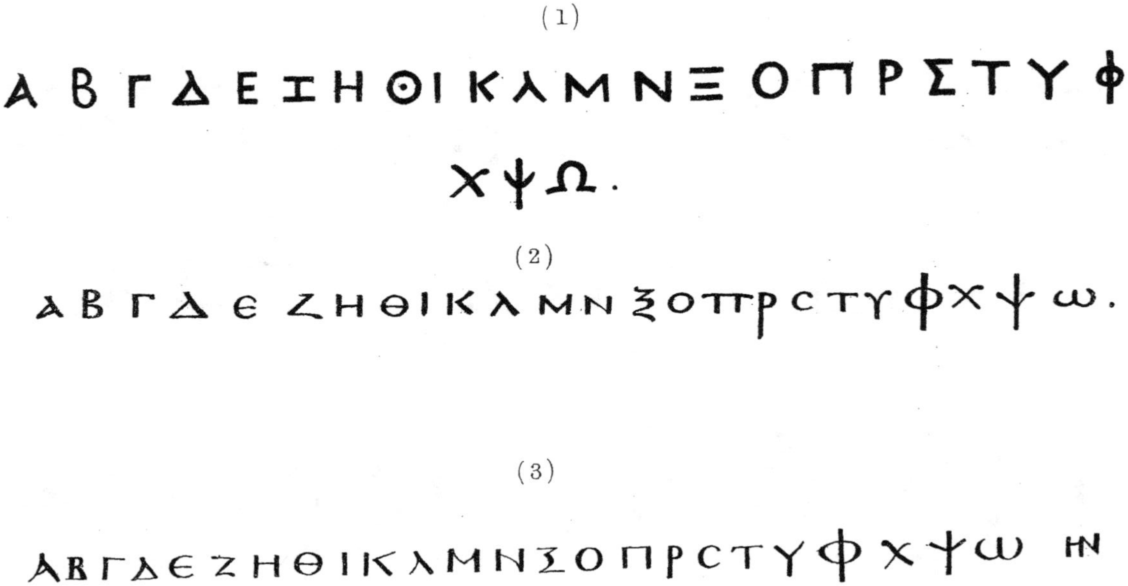

(3)

Α Β Γ Δ Ε Ζ Η Θ Ι Κ Λ Μ Ν Ξ Ο Π Ρ C Τ Υ Φ Χ Ψ Ω ΗΝ

(4)

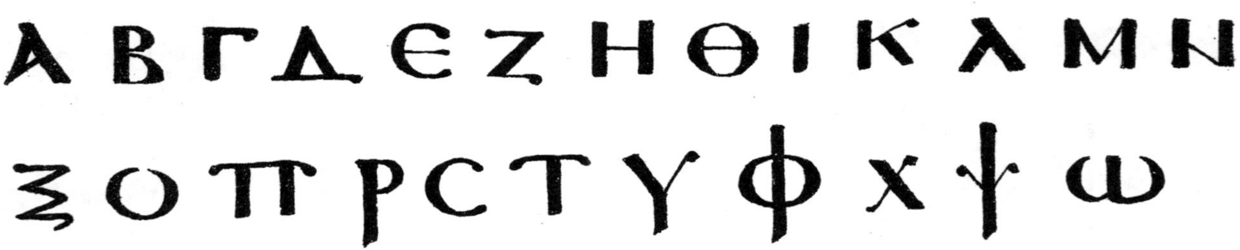

Α Β Γ Δ Є Ζ Η Θ Ι Κ Λ Μ Ν

Ξ Ο Π Ρ C Τ Υ Φ Χ Ψ Ω

(5)

Α Β Γ Δ Є Ζ Η Θ Ι Κ Λ Μ

Ν Ξ Ο Π Ρ C Τ Υ Φ Χ Ψ Ω

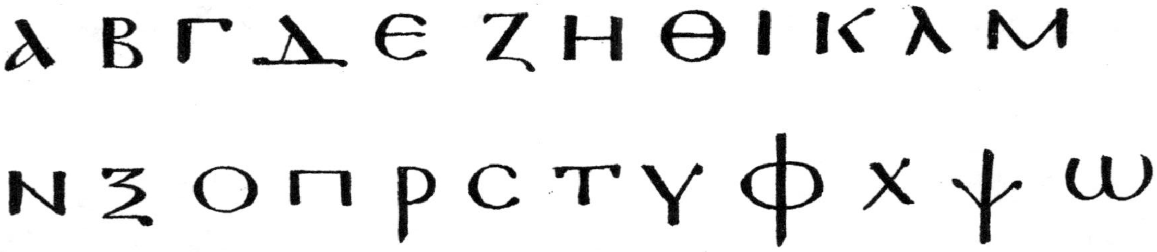

(6)

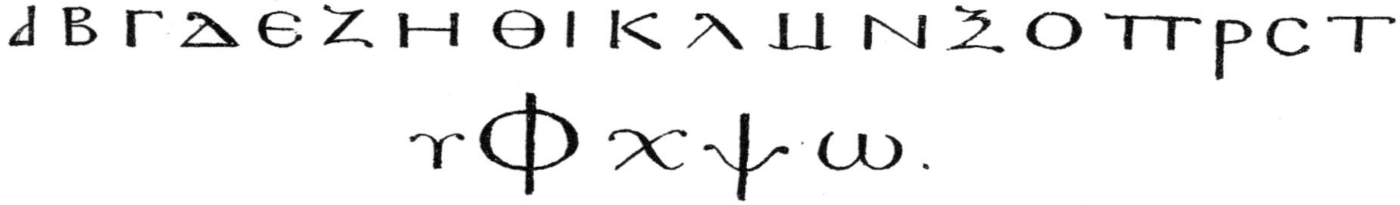

ΑΒΓΔΕΖΗΘΙΚΛΜΝΞΟΠΡϹΤ

υΦχψω.

(7)

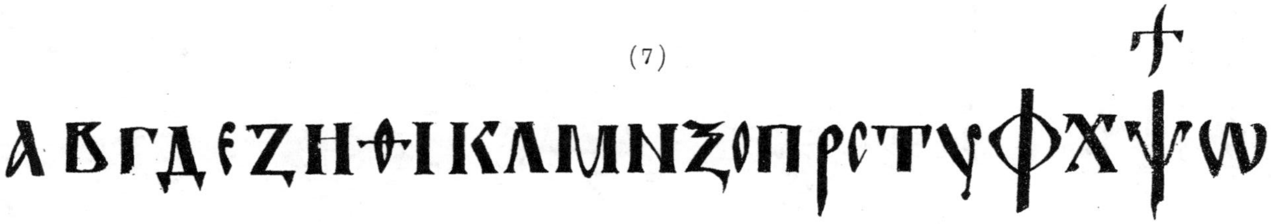

ΑΒΓΔΕΖΗΘΙΚΛΜΝΞΟΠΡϹΤΥΦΧΨΩ

(8.c)

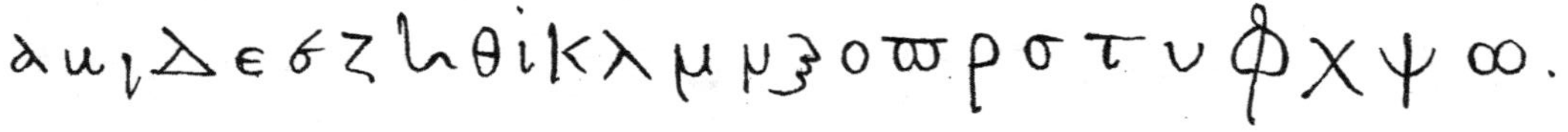

αβγδεϛζηθικλμνξοπρστυφχψω.

(9)

ΧΥΝ ΠΑCΙΝΑΤΩΝΤΙΟ
ΛΙΠΩΝΑΛΙΚΩC ΔΕΟ
ΜΑΙΥΛΛΩΝΚΑΙΕΤΩΙ
ΚΑΙΑΝΤΙΒΟΛΩΙΚΕ
ΛΕΥCΑΙΚΑΙΜΕΚΑΛΕCΑΙ
ΤΟΥCCΥΝΕΡΓΟΥΝΤΑC

(10)

ΟΝΤΩCΠΟΛΥΜΑΘΕCΤΑΤΟΝΠΡ
ΑΓΟΡΕΥΟΜΕΝΟΝΟΙΕΤΑΙΠΑΝΤΑ
ΔΥΝΑCΘΑΙΓΙΝΩCΚΕΙΝΚΑΙΠΟΙ
ΕΙΝΟΥΧΟΙΟΝΕΑΥΤΟΝ ΟCΕΝΙΟΙC
ΟΥΔΕΝΤΙΦΩΡΑΤΑΙ ΚΑΤΕΧΩΝ
ΚΑΙΟΥCΥΝΟΡΩΝΟΤΙΠΟΛΛΑΔΕΙ
ΤΑΙΤΡΙΒΗCΑΝΚΑΙΑΠΟΤΗCΑΥ
ΤΗCΓΙΝΗΤΑΙΜΕΘΟΔΟΥ ΚΑΘΑ
ΠΕΡΤΑΤΗCΠΟΙΗΤΙΚΗCΜΕΡΗ ΚΑΙ
ΔΙΟΤΙΠΕΡΙΤΟΥCΠΟΛΥΜΑΘΕΙC

(11.a)

CΕΑΥΤΟΝ ΚΑΘΩC ΑΡ
ΧΗCΚΑΙΑΦΗΜΕΡΩ
ΩΝΕΤΑΞΑΚΡΙΤΑC
ΕΠΙΤΟΝΛΑΟΝΜΟΥ
ΙCΛΚΑΙΕΤΑΠΙΝΩ
CΑΑΠΑΝΤΑCΤΟΥC
ΕΧΘΡΟΥCCΟΥΚΑΙ
ΑΥΞΗCΩCΕΚΑΙΟΙ

(11.b)

ΤΗΩΡΑΥΠΕCΤΡΕ
ΨΑΝΕΙCΙΕΡΟΥCΑ
ΛΗΜΚΑΙΕΥΡΟΝΗ
ΘΡΟΙCΜΕΝΟΥCΤΟΥC
ΕΝΔΕΚΑΚΑΙΤΟΥC
CΥΝΑΥΤΟΙCΛΕΓΟ

(12)

ΕΝΑΡΧΗΕΠΟΙΗΣΕΝΟΘΣΤΟΝΟΥ
ΡΑΝΟΝΚΑΙΤΗΝΓΗΝ ΗΔΕΓΗΗΝΑΟ
ΡΑΤΟΣΚΑΙΑΚΑΤΑΣΚΕΥΑΣΤΟΣ·
ΚΑΙΣΚΟΤΟΣΕΠΑΝΩΤΗΣΑΒΥΣΣΟΥ·

(13)

ΠΡΟΣΕΧΕΤΕΕΑΥΤΟΙΣΚΑΙΠΑΝΤΙΤΩ
ΠΟΙΜΝΙΩ·ΕΝΩΥΜΑΣΤΟΠΝΑΤΟ
ΑΓΙΟΝΕΘΕΤΟΕΠΙΣΚΟΠΟΥΣ·
ΠΟΙΜΑΙΝΕΙΝΤΗΝΕΚΚΛΗΣΙΑΝ
ΤΟΥΚΥΗΝΠΕΡΙΕΠΟΙΗΣΑΤΟΔΙΑ
ΤΟΥΑΙΜΑΤΟΣΤΟΥΙΔΙΟΥ·

(14)

ΡΛΘ Γ ΤΟΥΛΟΓΟΥΟΥ
ΕΓΩΕΙΠΟΝΥ
ΜΙΝ·ΟΥΚΕΣΤΙΝ
ΔΟΥΛΟΣΜΙΖΩ
ΤΟΥΚΥΑΥΤΟΥ

(15)

προ καταμίου· ἀμὴν ἀμὴν λέγω σοι·
ὅτι τοῦ ἠσμένου τύρος, ἐν Βαομμν ... ἐν
αυτον· καὶ πάριε πάτης ὁ ποιὴς θυ
λῷ· ὁ ταμεῦ γηράσησ, ἐκ τυμείο

(16)

ΑΥΤΩΟΙΦΑΡΙCΑΙ
ΟΙ·C·ΥΠΕΡΙCΕΑΥΤΟΥ
ΜΑΡΤΥΡΕΙC·Η·ΜΑΡ
ΤΥΡΙΑCΟΥ·ΟΥΚΕC
ΤΙΝΑΛΗΘΗCΑΠΕ

(17)

ΖΑΖΟΝΤΟΝΘΝ
ΚΑΙΕΠΛΗCΘΗ
CΑΝΦΟΒΟΥΛΕ
ΓΟΝΤΕCΟΤΙ

(18)

ΑΝΟΙΓΩCΙΝΟΙΟΦΘΑΛ
ΜΟΙ ΗΜΩΝ
CΠΛΑΓΧΝΙCΘΕΙC ΔΕ Ο ΙC̄
ΗΨΑΤΟ ΤΩΝ ΟΜΜΑΤΩ̄
ΑΥΤΩΝ ΚΑΙ ΕΥΘΕΩC

(19)

ΜῊ ΑἸCΧΡΟΚΕΡΔΗ͂
ἈΛΛᾺ ΦΙΛΌΞΕΝΟΝ
ΦΙΛΑΓΑΘΟΝ CΏΦΡΟΝΑ
ΔΊΚΑΙΟΝ ὍCΙΟΝ
ἘΓΚΡΑΤΗ͂
ἈΝΤΕΧΌΜΕΝΟΝ

non turpilucrum
sed hospitalem
benignum sobrium
iustum sanctum
continentem
adpectentem

Plate VIII.

(20)

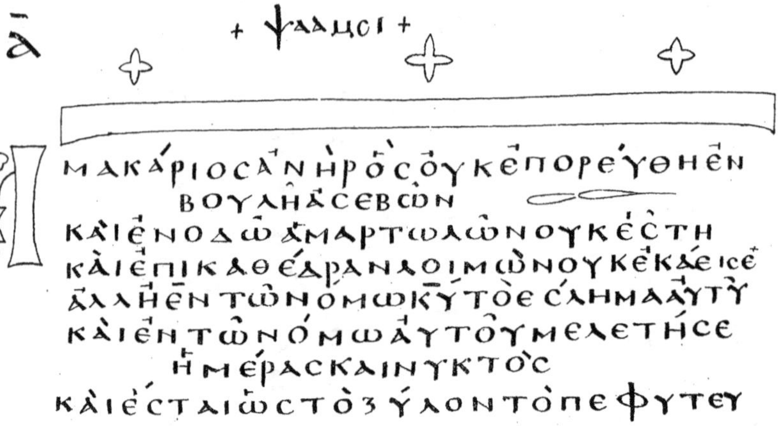

Α

+ ΨΑΛΜΟΙ +

ΜΑΚΑΡΙΟϹΑΝΗΡΟϹΟΥΚΕΠΟΡΕΥΘΗΕΝ
ΒΟΥΛΗΑϹΕΒΩΝ
ΚΑΙΕΝΟΔΩΑΜΑΡΤΩΛΩΝΟΥΚΕϹΤΗ
ΚΑΙΕΠΙΚΑΘΕΔΡΑΝΛΟΙΜΩΝΟΥΚΕΚΑΘΙϹΕ
ΑΛΛΗΕΝΤΩΝΟΜΩΚΥΤΟΘΕΛΗΜΑΑΥΤΟΥ
ΚΑΙΕΝΤΩΝΟΜΩΑΥΤΟΥΜΕΛΕΤΗϹΕΙ
ΗΜΕΡΑϹΚΑΙΝΥΚΤΟϹ
ΚΑΙΕϹΤΑΙΩϹΤΟΞΥΛΟΝΤΟΠΕΦΥΤΕΥ

(21)

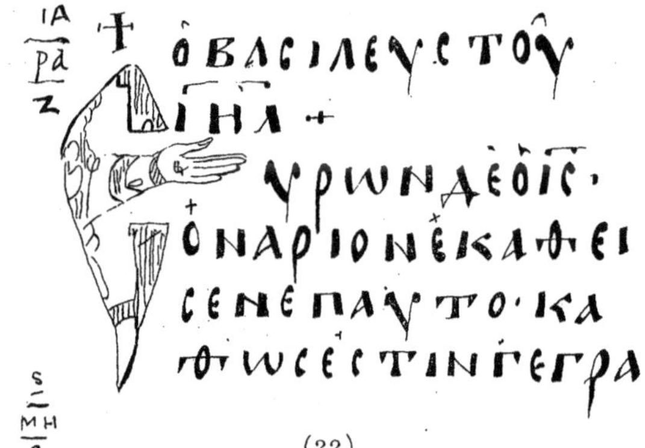

ΙΑ
ΡΑ
Ζ

+ ΟΒΑϹΙΛΕΥϹΤΟΥ
ΙΗΛ +
ΥΡΩΝΔΕΟΙϹ·
ΟΝΑΡΙΟΝΕΚΑΘΕΙ
ϹΕΝΕΠΑΥΤΟ·ΚΑ
ΘΩϹΕϹΤΙΝΓΕΓΡΑ

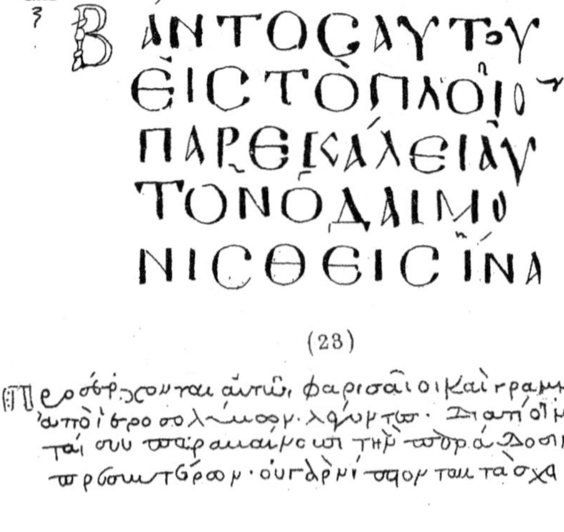

ϛ
ΜΗ
ϛ Β ϛ
ζ

(22)

ΒΑΝΤΟϹΑΥΤΟΥ
ΕΙϹΤΟΠΛΟΙΟΝ
ΠΑΡΕΚΑΛΕΙΑΥ
ΤΟΝΟΔΑΙΜΟ
ΝΙϹΘΕΙϹΙΝΑ

(23)

Προσέρχονται αὐτῷ φαρισαῖοι καὶ γραμματεῖς οἱ
ἀπὸ ἱεροσολύμων λέγοντες· διατί οἱ μαθη
ταί σου παραβαίνουσι τὴν παράδοσιν τῶν
πρεσβυτέρων· οὐ γὰρ νίπτονται τὰς χεῖρας

(24)

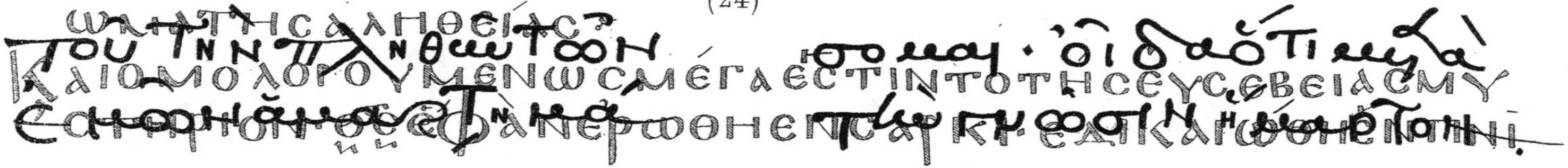

ωλ ΤΗΣ ΑΛΗΘΕΙΑΣ

ΤΟΥ ΙΝΝ ΠΛ Ν ΘΕΩ ΤΟΟΝ σωμαι · οἶδα ὅτι μεγάλ

ΚΑΙ ΟΜΟΛΟΓΟΥΜΕΝΩΣ ΜΕΓΑ ΕΣΤΙΝ ΤΟ ΤΗΣ ΕΥΣΕΒΕΙΑΣ ΜΥ

ΕΦΑΝΕΡΩΘΗ ΕΝ ΣΑΡΚΙ ΕΔΙΚΑΙΩΘΗ ΕΝ ΠΝΙ

(25)

REGERE
ECCLESIAM
DOMINI

B Θ Φ

ΠΟΙΜΕΝΕΙΝ
ΤΗΝΕΚΚΛΗΣΙΑΝ
ΤΟΥΚΥ

Δ Ξ Ψ

(37)

/Τοªκατά[b] ματθαίομ[c]άγιομ[d]ευαγγέλιομ. Cap̄. I.	[d]Euangeliumªscd̄m[b] Mattheū. Cap̄.j.
ίβλος [b]γενεσεως [c]ιησού [d]χρισ=	Liber [b]gn̄atiōis [c]iesu[d]chri
τού [c]υιού [f]Δαυίδ[g] υιού [h]αβραάμ.	sti [e]filij [f]dauid[g]filij [h]abraā.
[i]αβραάμ [k]εγέμμησε/Τομ [l] ισαάκ. [m]ι=	[i]Abraā [k]genuit [l]ysaac. [m]J
σαάκ [n]Δε[o]εγέμμησε/Τομ[p]ιακώβ. [q]ια=	saac[n]āt[o] genuit [p]iacob.[q]Ja
κώβ [r]Δε [s] εγεμμησε/ Τομ [t]ιουΔαμ,	cob [r]aūt [s] genuit [t]iudam:
[u]και/Τους[x]αΔελφούς[y]αυτού.[z]ιούΔας[a]Δε[b] εγεμ=	[u]et [x] fratres[y]eius.[z] Judas [a]autem [b]genuit
μησε/Τομ[c]φαρές[d] και/Τομ[e]ζαρά[f] εκ/Της[g]θάμαρ.	[c] phares [d]et [e]zaram [f]de [g]thamar. ∞∞∞

(26)

ϛξα Δ ΚΑΙ ΕΖΗΤΟΥΝ ΟΙ ΑΡΧΙΕΡΕΙΣ ΚΑΙ ΟΙ
ΓΡΑΜΜΑΤΕΙΣ, ΤΟ ΠΩΣ ΑΝΕΛΩ
ΣΙΝ ΑΥΤΟΝ, ΕΦΟΒΟΥΝΤΟ ΓΑΡ
ϛξβ ΤΟΝ ΛΑΟΝ· ΕΙΣΗΛΘΕΝ ΔΕ ΣΑ

(27)

ϙϛ ΚΑΙ ΠΡΟΣΕΦΕΡΟΝ
ΑΥΤΩ ΠΑΙΔΙΑ
ΙΝΑ ΑΨΗΤΑΙ ΑΥ
ΤΩΝ· ΟΙ ΔΕ ΜΑΘΗ
ΤΑΙ ΕΠΕΤΙΜΩΝ

(28)

ΒΛΗΘΗ· ΕΙΣ ΓΕΕΝ
ΝΑΝ· ΤΕ ΤΗΣ Λ
ΔΡ ΕΡΡΗΘΗ ΔΕ· ΟΤΙ ΟΣ
ΑΝ ΑΠΟΛΥΣΗ ΤΗΝ
ΓΥΝΑΙΚΑ ΑΥΤΟΥ·

(29)

ΓΕΙΝ ΤΗΝ ΠΑΡΑΒΟΛΗΝ ΤΑΥΤΗΝ· ΑΝΟΣ ΕΦΥΤΕΥ
ΣΕΝ ΑΜΠΕΛΩΝΑ· ΚΑΙ ΕΞΕΔΟΤΟ ΑΥΤΟΝ ΓΕΩΡΓΟΙΣ·

(8.b)

ΠΟϛ ΣΑΝΤΕΣ· ΚΑΙ ΤΙΣ
ΔΥΝΑΤΑΙ ΣΩΘΗΝΑΙ·
Ο Δ. ΙΣ. ΕΙΠΕΝ·

ΤΟΥΤΩ· ΚΑΙ ΕΝ
ΤΩ ΑΙΩΝΙ ΤΩ ΕΡ
ΧΟΜΕΝΩ ΖΩΗΝ

(30)

ΤΟΥϹΑΚΟΛΟΥΘΟΥΝΤΑϹ ΛΕΓΕΙ ΑΥΤΟΙϹ ΤΙ ΖΗ
ΤΕΙΤΕ ΟΙ ΔΕ ΕΙΠΟΝ ΑΥΤΩ ΡΑΒΒΕΙ Ο ΛΕΓΕ
ΤΑΙ ΕΡΜΗΝΕΥΟΜΕΝΟΝ ΔΙΔΑϹΚΑΛΕ ΠΟΥ ΜΕ
ΝΕΙϹ ΛΕΓΕΙ ΑΥΤΟΙϹ ΕΡΧΕϹΘΕ ΚΑΙ ΙΔΕΤΕ ΗΛ

(31)

ΙΑ
Α

ΕΓΩ ΜΕΝ ΒΑΠΤΙΖΩ
ΥΜΑϹ ΕΝ ΥΔΑΤΙ ΕΙϹ
ΜΕΤΑΝΟΙΑΝ Ο ΔΕ Ο
ΠΙϹΩ ΜΟΥ ΕΡΧΟΜΕ

(31.b)

31 c

(38)

παρακλησεως ο παρακαλων
ημας επι παση τη θλιψει εις το
δυνασθαι ημας παρακαλειν
τους εν παση θλιψει δια της πα
ρακλησεως ης παρακαλουμε
θα αυτοι υπο του θυ οτι καθως

(8.a)

(34)

ΓΟΝΤΟϹ ἘΓΕΝΕΤΟ ΝΕ
ΦΕΛΗ ΚΑῚ ἘΠΕϹΚΙΑϹΕΝ
ΑΥΤΟΥϹ ἘΦΟΒΗΘΗϹΑΝ

Α Ζ Φ Ξ Ρ Ω

(36)

[illegible] ορθ
[illegible] τὴν κληρονομ[illegible]
τὸ δαιμόνιον ὃ ἐξε
ληλυθὼς :—

[illegible]

(33)

Τ ΙΟΙϹ ΗΜΦΙΕϹΜΕΝΟΝ· ἸΔΟΥ ΟἹ
ἘΝ ἹΜΑΤΙϹΜῼ ἘΝΔΟΞῼ ΚΑΙ ΤΡΥ
ΦΗ ὙΠΑΡΧΟΝΤΕϹ ἘΝ ΤΟΙϹ ΒΑϹΙΛΕΙ
ΟΙϹ ΕἸϹΙΝ· ἈΛΛΑ ΤΙ ἘΞΕΛΗΛΥΘΑ

(35)

BY THE REV. F. H. SCRIVENER, M.A.

A full and exact Collation of about Twenty Greek Manuscripts of the Holy Gospels (hitherto unexamined), deposited in the British Museum, the Archiepiscopal Library at Lambeth, &c., with a Critical Introduction. 8vo. 6*s*.

JOHN W. PARKER AND SON, LONDON.

Novum Testamentum Græcum,

Textus Stephanici, 1550. Accedunt variæ Lectiones editionum Bezæ, Elzeviri, Lachmanni, Tischendorfii, et Tregellesii. 16mo. cloth, 4*s*. 6*d*.

"One of the latest additions to the admirably printed pocket series of 'Cambridge Greek and Latin Texts' is a very compact and convenient edition of the Greek New Testament, edited by the Rev. F. H. SCRIVENER, A.M. Those portions of the text of which various readings are given at the foot of each page are printed in a thicker character of type, so as to be readily perceived."—*English Churchman.*

An Exact Transcript of the Codex Augiensis,

a Græco-Latin Manuscript in Uncial Letters of S. Paul's Epistles, preserved in the Library of Trinity College, Cambridge. To which is added a full Collation of Fifty Manuscripts containing various portions of the Greek New Testament deposited in English Libraries: with a full Critical Introduction. Royal 8vo. 26*s*.

Contributions to the Criticism of the Greek Testament.

Being the Introduction to a Transcript of the Codex Augiensis. Royal 8vo. 5*s*.

DEIGHTON, BELL & CO., CAMBRIDGE.

CLASSICAL, THEOLOGICAL, AND MISCELLANEOUS BOOKS,

PUBLISHED BY MESSRS.

DEIGHTON, BELL, AND CO.

(AGENTS TO THE UNIVERSITY)

CAMBRIDGE.

CLASSICAL.

Cambridge Greek and Latin Texts. Carefully
reprinted from the best Editions:

This Series is intended to supply for the use of schools and students cheap and accurate editions of the Classics, which shall be superior in mechanical execution to the small German editions now current in this country, and more convenient in form. The Texts of the *Bibliotheca Classica* and Grammar-school Classics, so far as they have been published, will be adopted. These editions have taken their place among scholars as valuable contributions to the classical literature of this country, and are admitted to be good examples of the judicious and practical nature of English scholarship; and as the editors have formed their texts from a careful examination of the best editions extant, it is believed that no texts better for general use can be found. The volumes will be well printed at the Cambridge University Press, in 16mo. size, and will be issued at short intervals, neatly bound in cloth.

NOVUM TESTAMENTUM GRÆCUM, TEXTUS STEPHANICI, 1550. Accedunt variæ lectiones editionum Bezæ, Elzeviri, Lachmanni, Tischendorfii, et Tregellesii. Curante F. H. SCRIVENER, A.M. 4*s.* 6*d.*

An Edition on Writing Paper, for Notes, 4to. half-bound. 12*s.*

ÆSCHYLUS, ex novissima recensione F. A. PALEY, A.M. 3*s.*

CÆSAR DE BELLO GALLICO, ex recensione G. LONG, A.M. 2*s.*

CICERO DE SENECTUTE et DE AMICITIA, recensuit G. LONG, A.M. 1*s.* 6*d.*

EURIPIDES, ex recensione F. A. PALEY, A.M. 3 Vols. Vol. I. 3*s.* 6*d.* Vol. II. 3*s.* 6*d.* Vol. III. 3*s.* 6*d.*

HERODOTUS, recensuit J. W. BLAKESLEY, S.T.B. 2 vols. 7*s.*

HORATIUS, ex recensione A. J. MACLEANE, A.M. 2*s.* 6*d.*

LUCRETIUS, recognovit H. A. J. MUNRO, M.A. 2*s.* 6*d.*

THUCYDIDES, recensuit J. G. DONALDSON, S.T.P. 2 vols. 7*s.*

VERGILIUS, ex recensione J. CONINGTON, A.M. 3*s.* 6*d.*

XENOPHONTIS EXPEDITIO CYRI, recensuit J. F. MACMICHAEL, A.B. [*In the Press.*

Others in Preparation.

Passages in Prose and Verse from English
Authors for Translation into Greek and Latin; together with selected Passages from Greek and Latin Authors for Translation into English: forming a regular course of Exercises in Classical Composition. By H. ALFORD, M.A., late Fellow of Trinity College, Cambridge. 8vo. 6*s.*

Gems of Latin Poetry. With Translations by
various Authors, to which are added Notes and Illustrations. By A. AMOS, Esq., late Downing Professor of the Laws of England. 8vo. 12*s.*

Arundines Cami. Sive Musarum Cantabrigien-
sium Lusus Canori. Collegit atque ed. H. DRURY, A.M. *A New and cheaper Edition (the Fifth), revised and corrected.* Crown 8vo. 7*s.* 6*d.*

Demosthenes de Falsa Legatione. *Second Edition,*
carefully revised. By R. SHILLETO, M.A. 8vo. 8*s.* 6*d.*

Demosthenes, Select Private Orations of. After
the Text of DINDORF, with the various Readings of REISKE and BEKKER. With English Notes. For the use of Schools. By C. T. PENROSE, A.M. *Second Edition.* 12mo. 4*s.*

A Complete Latin Grammar. *Second Edition.*
Very much enlarged, and adapted for the use of University Students. By J. W. DONALDSON, D.D. 8vo. 14*s.*

The enlarged Edition of the Latin Grammar has been prepared with the same object as the corresponding work on the Greek Language. It is, however, especially designed to serve as a convenient handbook for those students who wish to acquire the habit of writing Latin; and with this view it is furnished with an Antibarbarus, with a full discussion of the most important synonyms, and with a variety of information not generally contained in works of this description.

A Complete Greek Grammar. *Second Edition.*
Very much enlarged and adapted for the use of University Students. By J. W. DONALDSON, D.D. 8vo. 16*s.*

This enlarged Edition has been prepared with the intention of placing within the reach of Students at the Universities, and in the highest classes at Schools, a Manual of Instruction and Reference, which, without exceeding the limits of the most popular Works of the kind, would exhibit a more exact and philosophical arrangement of the materials than any similar book; would connect itself more immediately with the researches of comparative Philologers; and would contain the sort of information which the Author's long experience as a Teacher and Examiner has indicated to him as most likely to meet the actual wants of those who are engaged in the critical study of the best Greek authors.

Without being formally based on any German Work, it has been written with constant reference to the latest and most esteemed of Greek Grammars used on the Continent.

Varronianus. A Critical and Historical Intro-
duction to the Philological Study of the Latin Language. *Third Edition, considerably enlarged.* By J. W. DONALDSON, D.D. 8vo. 16*s.*

Independently of the original matter which will be found in almost every page, it is believed that this book presents a collection of known facts respecting the old languages of Italy which will be found in no single work, whether British or foreign, and which must be gleaned from a considerable number of rare and expensive publications; and while the lists of Oscan and Etruscan glosses, and the reprint of fragments and inscriptions, may render the treatise an indispensable addition to the dictionary, and a convenient manual for the professed student of Latin, it is hoped that the classical traveller in Italy will find the information amassed and arranged in these pages, sufficient to spare him the trouble of carrying with him a voluminous library of reference in regard to the subjects of which it treats.

The Theatre of the Greeks. A Treatise on the History and Exhibition of the Greek Drama: with various Supplements. By J. W. DONALDSON, D.D. *Seventh Edition*, revised, enlarged, and in part remodelled; with numerous illustrations from the best ancient authorities. 8vo. 14*s.*

Classical Scholarship and Classical Learning con-sidered with especial reference to Competitive Tests and University Teaching. A Practical Essay on Liberal Education. By J. W. DONALDSON, D.D. Crown 8vo. 5*s.*

A Treatise on Hannibal's Passage of the Alps, in which his Route is traced over the Little Mont Cenis. By R. ELLIS, B.D., Fellow of St. John's College, Cambridge. With Maps. 8vo. 7*s.* 6*d.*

Euripides. Fabulæ Quatuor. Scilicet, Hippo-lytus Coronifer, Alcestis, Iphigenia in Aulide, Iphigenia in Tauris. Ad fidem Manuscriptorum ac veterum Editionum emendavit et Annotationibus instruxit J. H. MONK, S.T.P. *Editio nova.* 8vo. 12*s.*

Separately—HIPPOLYTUS. 8vo. cloth, 5*s.* ALCESTIS. 8vo. sewed, 4*s.* 6*d.*

Euripides. Tragœdiæ Priores Quatuor, ad fidem Manuscriptorum emendatæ et brevibus Notis instructæ. Edidit R. PORSON, A.M., &c. recensuit suasque notulas subjecit J. SCHOLEFIELD, A.M. *Editio tertia.* 8vo. 10*s.* 6*d.*

Foliorum Silvula. Part I. Being Select Passages for Translation into Latin Elegiac and Heroic Verse. Arranged and Edited by H. A. HOLDEN, M.A., Head Master of Queen Elizabeth's School, Ipswich, late Fellow of Trinity College, Cambridge. *Second Edition.* Post 8vo. 6*s.*

Foliorum Silvula. Part II. Being Select Passages for Translation into Latin Lyric and Greek Verse. By H. A. HOLDEN, M.A. *Second Edition.* Post 8vo. 7*s.* 6*d.*

Foliorum Centuriæ. Selections for Translation into Latin and Greek Prose, chiefly from the University and College Examination Papers. By H. A. HOLDEN, M.A. *Second Edition.* Post 8vo. 8*s.*

Hyperides, The Funeral Oration of, over Leosthe-nes and his Comrades in the Lamian War. The Fragments of the Greek Text edited with Notes and an Introduction, and an engraved Facsimile of the whole Papyrus. By C. BABINGTON, B.D. *Second Edition, corrected.* 8vo. 3*s.* 6*d.*

Imperial 4to. *Edition, with 7 tinted plates, in imitation of the Papyrus.* 15*s.*

Hyperides, The Oration of, against Demosthenes

respecting the Treasure of Harpalus. The Fragments of the Greek Text, now first edited from the Facsimile of the MS. discovered at Egyptian Thebes in 1847; together with other Fragments of the same Oration cited in Ancient Writers. With a Preliminary Dissertation and Notes, and a Facsimile of a portion of the MS. By C. BABINGTON, B.D. 4to. 6*s.* 6*d.*

Progressive Exercises in Greek Tragic Senarii,

followed by a Selection from the Greek Verses of Shrewsbury School, and prefaced by a short Account of the Iambic Metre and Style of Greek Tragedy. For the use of Schools and Private Students. Edited by B. H. KENNEDY, D.D., Head Master of Shrewsbury School. *Second Edition, altered and revised.* 8vo. 8*s.*

Dissertations on the Eumenides of Æschylus,

from the German of C. O. MÜLLER. With Critical Remarks and an Appendix. Translated from the German. *Second Edition.* 8vo. 6*s.* 6*d.*

Platonis Protagoras. The Protagoras of Plato.

The Greek Text revised, with an Analysis and English Notes. By W. WAYTE, M.A., Fellow of King's College, Cambridge, and Assistant Master at Eton. 8vo. 5*s.* 6*d.*

M. A. Plautus. Aulularia. Ad fidem Codicum

qui in Bibliotheca Musei Britannici exstant aliorumque nonnullorum recensuit, Notisque et Glossario locuplete instruxit J. HILDYARD, A.M. *Editio Altera.* 8vo. 7*s.* 6*d.*

M. A. Plautus. Menæchmei. Ad fidem Codicum

qui in Bibliotheca Musei Britannici exstant aliorumque nonnullorum recensuit, Notisque et Glossario locuplete instruxit J. HILDYARD, A.M. *Editio Altera.* 7*s.* 6*d.*

Sex Aurelii Propertii Carmina. The Elegies of

Propertius. With English Notes and a Preface on the State of Latin Scholarship. By F. A. PALEY, Editor of Æschylus, &c. With copious Indices. 10*s.* 6*d.*

Sophocles, The Œdipus Coloneus of, with Notes,

intended principally to explain and defend the Text of the Manuscripts as opposed to conjectural emendation. By the Rev. C. E. PALMER, M.A. 9*s.*

Cornelii Taciti Opera, ad Codices antiquissimos

exacta et emendata, Commentario critico et exegetico illustrata. 4 vols. 8vo. Edidit F. RITTER, Prof. Bonnensis. 1*l.* 8*s.*

THEOLOGICAL.

GREEK TESTAMENT.

The Greek Testament: with a Critically revised Text; a Digest of various Readings; Marginal References to Verbal and Idiomatic Usage; Prolegomena; and a Critical and Exegetical Commentary. For the Use of Theological Students and Ministers. By HENRY ALFORD, D.D., Dean of Canterbury. 8vo.

Vol. I. FOURTH EDITION, containing the Four Gospels. 1*l.* 8*s.*

Vol. II. FOURTH EDITION, containing the Acts of the Apostles, the Epistles to the Romans and Corinthians. 1*l.* 4*s.*

Vol. III. SECOND EDITION, containing the Epistles to the Galatians, Ephesians, Philippians, Colossians, Thessalonians,—to Timotheus, Titus and Philemon. 18*s.*

Vol. IV. Part I. SECOND EDITION. The Epistle to the Hebrews: The Catholic Epistles of St. James and St. Peter. 18*s.*

Vol. IV. Part II. The Epistles of St. John and St. Jude, and the Revelation. 14*s.*

Novum Testamentum Græcum, Textus Stephanici, 1500. Accedunt variæ lectiones editionum Bezæ, Elzeviri, Lachmanni, Tischendorfii, et Tregellesii. Curante F. H. SCRIVENER, A.M. 16mo. 4*s.* 6*d.*

An Edition on Writing-paper, for Notes. 4to. *half-bound.* 12*s.*

Bentleii Critica Sacra. Notes on the Greek and Latin Text of the New Testament, extracted from the Bentley MSS. in Trinity College Library. With the Abbé Rulotta's Collation of the Vatican MS., a specimen of Bentley's intended Edition, and an account of all his Collations. Edited, with the permission of the Master and Seniors, by the Rev. A. A. ELLIS, M.A., late Fellow and Junior Dean of Trinity College, Cambridge. *Nearly Ready.*

A Plain Introduction to the Criticism of the New Testament. With numerous facsimiles. For the use of Biblical Students. By F. H. SCRIVENER, A.M. *Ready.*

Hints for some Improvements in the Authorized Version of the New Testament. By the late J. SCHOLEFIELD, M.A., Regius Professor of Greek in the University. *Fourth Edition.* Fcap. 8vo. 4*s.*

Notes on the Proposed Amendment of the Author-ized Version of the Holy Scriptures. By W. SELWYN, B.D. 8vo. 1*s.*

A Companion to the New Testament. Designed for the use of Theological Students and the Upper Forms in Schools. By A. C. BARRETT, M.A. Fcp. 8vo. 5*s.*

A General Introduction to the Apostolic Epistles, with a Table of St. Paul's Travels, and an Essay on the State after Death. *Second Edition, enlarged.* To which are added a Few Words on the Athanasian Creed, on Justification by Faith, and on the Ninth and Seventeenth Articles of the Church of England. By A BISHOP'S CHAPLAIN. 8vo. 8*s.* 6*d.*

Annotations on the Acts of the Apostles. De-signed principally for the use of Candidates for the Ordinary B.A. Degree, Students for Holy Orders, &c., with College and Senate-House Examination Papers. By the Rev. T. R. MASKEW. *Second Edition,* enlarged. 12mo. 5*s.*

Butler's Three Sermons on Human Nature, and Dissertation on Virtue. Edited by W. WHEWELL, D.D. With a Preface and a Syllabus of the Work. *Third Edition.* Fcp. 8vo. 3*s.* 6*d.*

Butler's Six Sermons on Moral Subjects. A Sequel to the "Three Sermons on Human Nature." Edited by W. WHEWELL, D.D., with a Preface and Syllabus of the Work. Fcp. 8vo. 3*s.* 6*d.*

A Translation of the Epistles of Clement of Rome, Polycarp, and Ignatius; and of the Apologies of Justin Martyr and Tertullian; with an Introduction and Brief Notes illustrative of the Ecclesiastical History of the First Two Centuries. By T. CHEVALLIER, B.D. *Second Edition.* 8vo. 12*s.*

Pearsoni Præfatio Parænetica ad Vetus Testa-mentum Græcum ex Versione Septuaginta Interpretum; juxta exemplar Vaticanum Romæ Editum. Cantabrigiæ, 1665. Cum Notulis EDVARDI CHURTON, A.M., Eccl. Ebor. Archidiac. et Canonici. 8vo. 1*s.*

On Sacrifice, Atonement, Vicarious Oblation, and Example of Christ, and the Punishment of Sin. Five Sermons, preached before the University of Cambridge, March 1856. By B. M. COWIE, B.D., St. John's College. 8vo. 5*s.*

Three Plain Sermons, preached in the Chapel of Trinity College, Cambridge, in the course of the year 1859. By the Rev. E. W. BLORE, Fellow of Trinity College. 8vo. 1*s.* 6*d.*

Five Sermons preached before the University of Cambridge. By the late J. J. BLUNT, B.D., Lady Margaret Professor of Divinity. 8vo. 5*s.* 6*d.*

CONTENTS:—1. The Nature of Sin.—2. The Church of the Apostles.—3. On Uniformity of Ritual.—4. The Value of Time.—5. Reflections on the General Fast-Day (March 1847).

Five Sermons preached before the University of Cambridge. The first Four in November, 1851, the Fifth on Thursday, March 8th, 1849, being the Hundred and Fiftieth Anniversary of the Society for Promoting Christian Knowledge. By the late Rev. J. J. BLUNT, B.D.

CONTENTS: 1. Tests of the Truth of Revelation.—2. On Unfaithfulness to the Reformation.—3. On the Union of Church and State.—4. An Apology for the Prayer-Book.—5. Means and Method of National Reform.

Two Introductory Lectures on the Study of the Early Fathers, delivered in the University of Cambridge. By the late J. J. BLUNT, B.D. *Second Edition.* With a brief Memoir of the Author, and a Table of Lectures delivered during his Professorship. 8vo. 4*s.* 6*d.*

Examination Questions and Answers on Butler's Analogy. By the Rev. Sir G. W. CRAUFURD, M.A., King's Coll. 18mo. 1*s.* 6*d.*

The Church of England on the Fourth Com-mandment. 2. The Word of God on a Seventh-Day Sabbath. By the Rev. F. EXTON. 8vo. 2*s.*

The Example of Christ and the Service of Christ, Considered in Three Sermons preached before the University of Cambridge, in February, 1861. To which are appended A Few Remarks upon the Present State of Religious Feeling. By FRANCIS FRANCE, B.D., Archdeacon of Ely, and Fellow of St. John's College. Crown 8vo. 2*s.* 6*d.*

On The Imitation of Christ. A New Translation. By the Very Rev. the DEAN OF ELY. 18mo. 3*s.* 6*d.*

A Commentary on the Gospel of S. Matthew. By the Very Rev. HARVEY GOODWIN, D.D., Dean of Ely. Crown 8vo. 12*s.*

A Commentary on the Gospel of S. Mark. By H. GOODWIN, D.D. Crown 8vo. 7*s.* 6*d.*

Intended for the English Reader, and adapted for either domestic or private use.

The Doctrines and Difficulties of the Christian Religion contemplated from the Standing-point afforded by the Catholic Doctrine of the Being of our Lord Jesus Christ. Being the Hulsean Lectures for the year 1855. By H. GOODWIN, D.D. 8vo. 9*s.*

'The Glory of the Only Begotten of the Father seen in the Manhood of Christ.' Being the Hulsean Lectures for the Year 1856. By H. GOODWIN, D.D. 8vo. 7*s.* 6*d.*

Four Sermons preached before the University of Cambridge in the Season of Advent, 1858. By H. GOODWIN, D.D. 12mo. 3*s.* 6*d.*

Four Sermons preached before the University of Cambridge in the month of November 1853. By H. GOODWIN, D.D. 12mo. 4*s.*

CONTENTS :—1. The Young Man cleansing his way.—2. The Young Man in Religious Difficulties.—3. The Young Man as a Churchman.—4. The Young Man called by Christ.

Christ in the Wilderness. Four Sermons preached before the University of Cambridge in the month of February 1855. By H. GOODWIN, D.D. 12mo. 4*s.*

Parish Sermons. 1st Series. By H. GOODWIN, D.D. *Third Edition.* 12mo. 6*s.*

———— 2nd Series. By H. GOODWIN, D.D. *Third Edition.* 12mo. 6*s.*

———— 3rd Series. By H. GOODWIN, D.D. *Second Edition.* 12mo. 7*s.*

———— 4th Series. By H. GOODWIN, D.D. 12mo. 7*s.*

Short Sermons at the Celebration of the Lord's Supper. By H. GOODWIN, D.D. *New Edition.* 12mo. 4*s.*

Lectures upon the Church Catechism. By H. GOODWIN, D.D. 12mo. 4*s.*

A Guide to the Parish Church. By H. GOODWIN, D.D. *Second Edition.* 18mo. 3*s.* 6*d.*

*** A cheaper Edition for distribution. Price 1*s.* sewed, 1*s.* 6*d.* cloth.

Confirmation Day. Being a Book of Instruction for Young Persons how they ought to spend that solemn day, on which they renew the Vows of their Baptism, and are confirmed by the Bishop with prayer and the laying on of hands. By H. GOODWIN, D.D. *Second Edition.* 2*d.*, or 25 for 3*s.* 6*d.*

Plain Thoughts concerning the meaning of Holy Baptism. By H. GOODWIN, D.D. *Second Edition.* 2*d.*, or 25 for 3*s.* 6*d.*

The Worthy Communicant; or, 'Who may come to the Supper of the Lord?' By H. GOODWIN, D.D. *Second Edition.* 2*d.*, or 25 for 3*s.* 6*d.*

A History of the Articles of Religion. To which is added a series of Documents from A.D. 1536 to A.D. 1615. Together with illustrations from contemporary sources. By CHARLES HARDWICK, B.D., late Archdeacon of Ely. *Second Edition, corrected and enlarged.* 8vo. 12*s.*

⁂ A considerable amount of fresh matter has been incorporated, especially in the two Chapters which relate to the construction and revision of our present code of Articles.

Sermons for Young Men on the Grace of Christ. Preached before the University of Cambridge during the month of February 1853. By W. W. HARVEY, B.D., late Fellow of King's College. 8vo. 4*s.*

Sermons on some of the Principal Doctrines and Evidences of the Christian Religion. By W. W. HARVEY, B.D. Foolscap 8vo. 5*s.*

The History and Theology of the "Three Creeds." By W. W. HARVEY, B.D. 2 vols. Post 8vo. 14*s.*

Ecclesiæ Anglicanæ Vindex Catholicus, sive Articulorum Ecclesiæ Anglicanæ cum Scriptis SS. Patrum nova collatio. Cura G. W. HARVEY, B.D., Collegii Regalis Socii. 3 vols. 8vo. Reduced to 16*s.*

Prælectio in Prov. viii. 22, 23. Quam munus Lectoris Regii in Literis Hebraicis petendo habuit G. WIGAN HARVEY, A.M., III Id. Octob. 1848. 4to. sewed. 3*s.*

Apostolic Missions. Five Sermons preached before the University of Cambridge in May 1852. By W. B. HOPKINS, M.A., late Fellow of St. Catharine's College. 8vo. 5*s.*

Psalter (The), or Psalms of David in English Verse. With Preface and Notes. By a Member of the University of Cambridge. Dedicated by permission to the Lord Bishop of Ely, and the Reverend the Professors of Divinity in that University. 5*s.*

An Historical and Explanatory Treatise on the Book of Common Prayer. By W. G. HUMPHRY, B.D., late Fellow of Trinity College, Cambridge. *Second Edition, enlarged and revised.* Post 8vo. 7*s.* 6*d.*

Liturgiæ Britannicæ, or the several Editions of the Book of Common Prayer of the Church of England, from its compilation to the last revision, together with the Liturgy set forth for the use of the Church of Scotland, arranged to shew their respective variations. By W. KEELING, B.D., late Fellow of St. John's College. *Second Edition.* 8vo. 12*s.*

The Seven Words Spoken Against the Lord Jesus: or, an Investigation of the Motives which led His Contemporaries to reject Him. Being the Hulsean Lectures for the Year 1860. By JOHN LAMB, M.A., Senior Fellow of Gonville and Caius College, and Minister of S. Edward's, Cambridge. 8vo. 5*s.* 6*d.*

Twelve Sermons preached on Various Occasions at the Church of St. Mary, Greenwich. By R. MAIN, M.A. Radcliffe Observer at Oxford. 12mo. 5*s.*

Lectures on the Catechism. Delivered in the Parish Church of Brasted, in the Diocese of Canterbury. By the late W. H. MILL, D.D., Regius Professor of Hebrew, Cambridge. Edited by his Son-in-Law, the Rev. B. WEBB, M.A. Fcp. 8vo. 6*s.* 6*d.*

Sermons preached in Lent 1845, and on several former occasions, before the University of Cambridge. By W. H. MILL, D.D. 8vo. 12*s.*

Four Sermons preached before the University on the Fifth of November, and the three Sundays preceding Advent, in the year 1848. By W. H. MILL, D.D. 8vo. 5*s.* 6*d.*

An Analysis of the Exposition of the Creed, written by the Right Reverend Father in God, J. PEARSON, D.D., late Lord Bishop of Chester. Compiled, with some additional matter occasionally interspersed, for the use of Students of Bishop's College, Calcutta. By W. H. MILL, D.D. *Third Edition, revised and corrected.* 8vo. 5*s.*

Observations on the attempted application of Pantheistic Principles to the Theory and Historic Criticism of the Gospels. By W. H. MILL, D.D., late Regius Professor of Hebrew in the University of Cambridge. *Second Edition, with the Author's latest notes and additions.* Edited by B. WEBB, M.A. 8vo. [*Ready.*

Bishop Pearson's Five Lectures on the Acts of the Apostles and Annals of St. Paul. Edited in English, with Notes, by J. R. CROWFOOT, B.D. Crown 8vo. 4*s.*

The Essential Coherence of the Old and New Testaments. By T. T. PEROWNE, M.A., Fellow of Corpus Christi College, Cambridge. Crown 8vo. 6*s.*

A Manual of Prayer for Students. Consisting mostly of Selections from various Authors. In 3 parts. By R. G. PETER, M.A., late Fellow of Jesus College. 18mo. 1*s.* 6*d.*

Phraseological and Explanatory Notes on the Hebrew Text of the Book of GENESIS. By T. PRESTON, M.A., Fellow of Trinity College. Crown 8vo. 9*s.* 6*d.*

The Influence of Christianity on the Language of Modern Europe. The Essays which obtained the Hulsean Prize for the year 1855. By W. J. REES, St. John's College, and W. AYERST, Caius College. 8vo. 4*s.*

A Plain Introduction to the Criticism of the New Testament. For the use of Biblical Students. By F. H. SCRIVENER, M.A., Trinity College, Cambridge. 8vo.

Sermons preached in the English Church at Heidelberg in the years 1858-59. By S. H. SAXBY, M.A. Fcp. 8vo. 6*s.*

An Exact Transcript of the CODEX AUGIENSIS, a Græco-Latin Manuscript in Uncial Letters of S. Paul's Epistles, preserved in the Library of Trinity College, Cambridge. To which is added a full Collation of Fifty Manuscripts containing various portions of the Greek New Testament deposited in English Libraries: with a full Critical Introduction. By F. H. SCRIVENER, M.A. Royal 8vo. 26*s.*

Contributions to the Criticism of the Greek Testament. Being the Introduction to a Transcript of the Codex Augiensis. By F. H. SCRIVENER, M.A. Royal 8vo. 5*s.*

Horae Hebraicae. Critical and Expository Observations on the Prophecy of Messiah in Isaiah, Chapter IX. and on other Passages of Holy Scripture. By W. SELWYN, B.D., Lady Margaret's Reader in Theology. Revised Edition, with Continuation. 8*s.*
THE CONTINUATION, separately. 3*s.*

Excerpta ex Reliquiis Versionum, Aquilæ, Symmachi Theodotionis, a Montefalconia aliisque collectis. GENESIS. Edidit G. SELWYN, S.T.B. 8vo. 1*s.*

Notæ Criticæ in Versionem Septuagintaviralem. EXODUS, Cap. I.—XXIV. Curante G. SELWYN, S.T.B. 8vo. 3*s.* 6*d.*

Notæ Criticæ in Versionem Septuagintaviralem. Liber NUMERORUM. Curante G. SELWYN, S.T.B. 8vo. 4*s.* 6*d.*

Notæ Criticæ in Versionem Septuagintaviralem. Liber DEUTERONOMII. Curante G. SELWYN, S.T.B. 8vo. 4*s.* 6*d.*

Origenis Contra Celsum. Liber I. Curante G. SELWYN, S.T.B. 8vo. 3*s.* 6*d.*

Testimonia Patrum in Veteres Interpretes, Septuaginta, Aquilam, Symmachum, Theodotionem, a Montefalconio aliisque collecta paucis Additis. Edidit G. SELWYN, S.T.B. 8vo. 6*d.*

The Will Divine and Human. By T. SOLLY, B.D., late of Caius College, Cambridge. 8vo. 10*s.* 6*d.*

Tertulliani Liber Apologeticus. The Apology of Tertullian. With English Notes and a Preface, intended as an Introduction to the Study of Patristical and Ecclesiastical Latinity. By H. A. WOODHAM, LL.D. *Second Edition.* 8vo. 8*s.* 6*d.*

Three Sermons on the Lord's Supper. With Questions and References. By a Country Curate. Crown 8vo. 1*s.* 6*d.*

Parish Sermons, according to the order of the Christian Year. By the late C. A. WEST, B.A. Edited by J. R. WEST, M.A. 12mo. 6*s.*

Sermons preached in the Chapel of Trinity

College, Cambridge. By W. WHEWELL, D.D., Master of the College. 8vo. 10*s.* 6*d.*

Rational Godliness. After the Mind of Christ

and the Written Voices of the Church. By R. WILLIAMS, D.D., Professor of Hebrew at Lampeter. Crown 8vo. 10*s.* 6*d.*

Paraméswara-jnyána-goshthi. A Dialogue of the

Knowledge of the Supreme Lord, in which are compared the Claims of Christianity and Hinduism, and various questions of Indian Religion and Literature fairly discussed. By R. WILLIAMS, D.D. 8vo. 12*s.*

A Discourse preached before the University of

Cambridge on Commencement Sunday, 1857. With some review of Bishop Ollivant's Charge. By R. WILLIAMS, D.D. 8vo. 2*s.* 6*d.*

An earnestly respectful Letter to the Lord Bishop

of St. David's, on the Difficulty of Bringing Theological Questions to an Issue; with Special Reference to his Lordship's Charge of 1857, and his Forthcoming Charge of 1860. By R. WILLIAMS, D.D. 8vo. 2*s.*

A Critical Appendix to the Lord Bishop of St. David's Reply. 1*s.*

A Charge addressed to the Clergy of the Arch-

deaconry of Ely, on Thursday, June 13, 1861. By FRANCIS FRANCE, B.D. Archdeacon of Ely, and Fellow of St. John's College, Cambridge. (Published by request of the Clergy.) 8vo. 1*s.*

The Historical and Descriptive Geography of the

Holy Land, with an Alphabetical List of Places, and Maps. By G. WILLIAMS, B.D., Fellow of King's College, Cambridge. [*Preparing.*

MISCELLANEOUS.

Athenae Cantabrigienses. By C. H. COOPER,

F.S.A. and THOMPSON COOPER, F.S.A.

This work, in illustration of the biography of notable and eminent men who have been members of the University of Cambridge, comprehends, notices of: 1. Authors. 2. Cardinals, archbishops, bishops, abbats, heads of religious houses and other Church dignitaries. 3. Statesmen. diplomatists, military and naval commanders. 4. Judges and eminent practitioners of the civil or common law. 5. Sufferers for religious and political opinions. 6. Persons distinguished for success in tuition. 7. Eminent physicians and medical practitioners. 8. Artists, musicians, and heralds. 9. Heads of Colleges, professors, and principal officers of the university. 10. Benefactors to the university and colleges or to the public at large.

Volume I. 1500—1585. 8vo. *cloth.* 18*s.* Volume II. 1586—1609. 18*s.* Volume III. *Preparing.*

Cairo to Sinai and Sinai to Cairo; being an

Account of a Journey in the Desert of Arabia, November and December, 1860. By W. J. BEAMONT, M.A., Fellow of Trinity College, Cambridge. With Maps and Illustrations. Fcp. 8vo. 5*s.*

A Concise Grammar of the Arabic Language.

By W. J. BEAMONT, M.A. Revised by SHEIKH ALI NADY EL BARRANY, one of the Sheikhs of the El Azhar Mosque in Cairo. 12mo. 7*s.*

Cambridge University Calendar. (*Continued*

annually.) 12mo. 6*s.* 6*d.*

Printed by Jonathan Palmer, Cambridge.

Wheatly *on the Common Prayer, edited by* G. E. CORRIE, D.D. Master of Jesus College, Examining Chaplain to the Lord Bishop of Ely. 12*s.* 6*d.*

Sancti Irenæi *Episcopi Lugdunensis Libros quinque* adversus Hæreses textu Græco in locis nonnullis locupletato, versione Latina cum Codicibus Claromontano ac Arundeliano denuo collata, præmissa de placitis Gnosticorum prolusione, fragmenta necnon Græce, Syriace, Armeniace, commentatione perpetua et indicibus variis edidit W. WIGAN HARVEY, S.T.B. Collegii Regalis olim socius. 2 Vols. Demy Octavo. 36*s.*

*The Gospel according to Saint Matthew in Anglo-*Saxon and Northumbrian Versions, synoptically arranged: with Collations of the best Manuscripts. By J. M. KEMBLE, M.A. and Archdeacon HARDWICK, late Christian Advocate. 10*s.*

Cambridge Greek and English Testament, in Parallel Columns on the same page. Edited by J. SCHOLEFIELD, M.A. late Regius Professor of Greek in the University. A new Edition printed on Demy 4to. *Writing Paper*, with large margin for MS. notes. 12*s.*

Cambridge Greek and English Testament, in Parallel Columns on the same page. Edited by J. SCHOLEFIELD, M.A. late Regius Professor of Greek in the University. Fourth Edition. Small Octavo. 7*s.* 6*d.*

Cambridge Greek Testament. Ex editione Stephani tertia, 1550. Small Octavo. 3*s.* 6*d.*

A Catalogue of the Manuscripts preserved in the Library of the University of Cambridge. Vol. I. Demy Octavo. 30*s.* Vol. II. 20*s.* Vol. III. 25*s.*

Vol. IV. *In the Press.*

*Catalogus Bibliothecæ Burckhardtianæ, cum Appen-*dice librorum aliorum Orientalium in Bibliotheca Academiæ Cantabrigiensis asservatorum. Jussu Syndicorum Preli Academici confecit T. PRESTON, A.M. Collegii SS. Trinitatis Socius. Demy 4to. 5*s.*

M. T. Ciceronis *de Officiis Libri tres, with Marginal* Analysis, an English Commentary, and copious Indices, by H. A. HOLDEN, M.A. Head Master of Ipswich School, late Fellow and Assistant Tutor of Trinity College, Cambridge. Post 8vo. 9*s.* 6*d.*

M. T. Ciceronis *Oratio pro Tito Annio Milone*, with a Translation of Asconius' Introduction, Marginal Analysis, and English Notes, by J. S. PURTON, M.A. President and Tutor of St Catharine's College. Post Octavo. 3*s.* 6*d.*

M. Minucii Felicis *Octavius. The text newly revised* from the Original MS. with an English Commentary, Analysis, Introduction, and Copious Indices. Edited by H. A. HOLDEN, M.A. Head Master of Ipswich School, late Fellow and Assistant Tutor of Trinity College, Cambridge. Crown Octavo. 9*s.* 6*d.*

Cæsar Morgan's *Investigation of the Trinity of Plato*, and of Philo Judæus, and of the effects which an attachment to their writings had upon the principles and reasonings of the Fathers of the Christian Church. A new Edition, revised by H. A. HOLDEN, M.A. Head Master of Ipswich School, late Fellow and Assistant Tutor of Trinity College, Cambridge. Crown Octavo. 4*s.*

Theophili *Episcopi Antiochensis Libri Tres ad Autolycum.* Edidit, Prolegomenis Versione Notulis Indicibus instruxit GULIELMUS GILSON HUMPHRY, S.T.B. Collegii Sanctiss. Trin. apud Cantabrigienses quondam Socius. Post Octavo. 6*s.*

De Obligatione Conscientiæ Prælectiones Decem Oxonii in Schola Theologica habitæ a ROBERTO SANDERSON, SS. Theologiæ ibidem Professore Regio. With English Notes, including an abridged Translation, by W. WHEWELL, D.D. Master of Trinity College. Octavo. 9*s.*

Grotius *de Jure Belli et Pacis, with the notes of* Barbeyrac and others; accompanied by an abridged Translation of the Text, by W. WHEWELL, D.D. Master of Trinity College. Three Volumes, Octavo, 42*s.* The translation separate, 14*s.*

The Homilies, with Various Readings, and the Quotations from the Fathers given at length in the Original Languages. Edited by G. E. CORRIE, D.D. Master of Jesus College, Examining Chaplain to the Lord Bishop of Ely. Octavo. 10*s.* 6*d.*

Archbishop Usher's *Answer to a Jesuit, with other* Tracts on Popery. Edited by J. SCHOLEFIELD, M.A. late Regius Professor of Greek in the University. Octavo. 13*s.* 6*d.*

Wilson's *Illustration of the Method of explaining the* New Testament, by the early opinions of Jews and Christians concerning Christ. Edited by T. TURTON, D.D. Lord Bishop of Ely. Octavo. 8*s.*

Lectures on Divinity delivered in the University of Cambridge. By John Hey, D.D. Third Edition, by T. TURTON, D.D. Lord Bishop of Ely. 2 vols. 8vo. 30*s.*

Theophylacti *in Evangelium S. Matthœi Commentarius.* Edited by W. G. HUMPHRY, B.D. Prebendary of St Paul's, and Vicar of St Martin's-in-the-Fields, London, late Fellow of Trinity College. Octavo. 14*s.*

Tertullianus *de Corona Militis, de Spectaculis, de* Idololatria, with Analysis and English Notes, by GEORGE CURREY, B.D. Preacher at the Charter House, late Fellow and Tutor of St John's College. Crown Octavo. 7*s.* 6*d.*

Astronomical Observations, for the Years 1849, 1850, and 1851, made at the Observatory of Cambridge, by the Rev. JAMES CHALLIS, M.A. Plumian Professor of Astronomy and Experimental Philosophy in the University of Cambridge, and late Fellow of Trinity College. Royal 4to. *Ready.* 25*s.*

Astronomical Observations, for the Years 1846, 1847, and 1848, made at the Observatory of Cambridge, by the Rev. JAMES CHALLIS, M.A. Plumian Professor of Astronomy and Experimental Philosophy in the University of Cambridge, and late Fellow of Trinity College. Royal 4to, 420 pages, 25*s.*

⁂ The Publishers are directed to offer a limited number of Copies of the Cambridge Observations of former years at the following reduced prices:—

For the years		For the years	
1828 and 29	at 4*s.* each year	1839	at 11*s.* 6*d.*
1830, 31, 32, 33, 34, and 35	5*s.* each year	1840 and 1841	17*s.* 6*d.*
1836	8*s.* 6*d.*	1842	17*s.*
1837	10*s.* 6*d.*	1843	15*s.*
1838	14*s.*	1844 and 1845	8*s.*

Cambridge: DEIGHTON, BELL AND CO.
London: GEORGE COX, CAMBRIDGE WAREHOUSE, 32 PATERNOSTER ROW.

www.ingramcontent.com/pod-product-compliance
Lightning Source LLC
LaVergne TN
LVHW021304110826
845150LV00003B/471
* 9 7 8 1 4 2 5 5 6 0 5 9 1 *